FLORIDA

ALGEBRA 1

Analyze • Connect • Explore

Edward B. Burger

Juli K. Dixon

Timothy D. Kanold

Matthew R. Larson

Steven J. Leinwand

Martha E. Sandoval-Martinez

Edward B. Burger, Ph.D., is the president of Southwestern University, a former Francis Christopher Oakley Third Century Professor of Mathematics at Williams College, and a former vice provost at Baylor University. He has authored or coauthored more than sixty-five articles, books, and video series; delivered over five hundred addresses and workshops throughout the world; and made more than fifty radio and television appearances. He is a Fellow of the American Mathematical Society as well as having earned many national honors, including the Robert Foster Cherry Award for Great Teaching in 2010. In 2012, Microsoft Education named him a "Global Hero in Education."

Juli K. Dixon, Ph.D., is a Professor of Mathematics Education at the University of Central Florida. She has taught mathematics in urban schools at the elementary, middle, secondary, and post-secondary levels. She is an active researcher and speaker with numerous publications and conference presentations. Key areas of focus are deepening teachers' content knowledge and communicating and justifying mathematical ideas. She is a past chair of the NCTM Student Explorations in Mathematics Editorial Panel and member of the Board of Directors for the Association of Mathematics Teacher Educators.

Timothy D. Kanold, Ph.D., is an award-winning international educator, author, and consultant. He is a former superintendent and director of mathematics and science at Adlai E. Stevenson High School District 125 in Lincolnshire, Illinois. He is a past president of the National Council of Supervisors of Mathematics (NCSM) and the Council for the Presidential Awardees of Mathematics (CPAM). He has served on several writing and leadership commissions for NCTM during the past decade. He presents motivational professional development seminars with a focus on developing professional learning communities (PLC's) to improve the teaching, assessing, and learning of students. He has recently authored nationally recognized articles, books, and textbooks for mathematics education and school leadership, including *What Every Principal Needs to Know about the Teaching and Learning of Mathematics*.

Matthew R. Larson, Ph.D., is the K-12 mathematics curriculum specialist for the Lincoln Public Schools and served on the Board of Directors for the National Council of Teachers of Mathematics from 2010 to 2013. He is a past chair of NCTM's Research Committee and was a member of NCTM's Task Force on Linking Research and Practice. He is the author of several books on implementing the Common Core Standards for Mathematics. He has taught mathematics at the secondary and college levels and held an appointment as an honorary visiting associate professor at Teachers College, Columbia University.

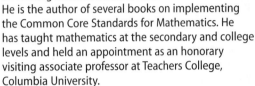

Steven J. Leinwand is a Principal Research Analyst at the American Institutes for Research (AIR) in Washington, D.C., and has over 30 years in leadership positions in mathematics education. He is past president of the National Council of Supervisors of Mathematics and served on the NCTM Board of Directors. He is the author of numerous articles, books, and textbooks and has made countless presentations with topics including student achievement, reasoning, effective assessment, and successful implementation of standards.

Martha E. Sandoval-Martinez is a mathematics instructor at El Camino College in Torrance, California. She was previously a Math Specialist at the University of California at Davis and former instructor at Santa Ana College, Marymount College, and California State University, Long Beach. In her current and former positions, she has worked extensively to improve fundamental pre-algebra and algebra skills in students who have historically struggled with mathematics.

Florida Reviewers

UNIT 1A — Numbers and Expressions

MODULE 1

Relationships Between Quantities

FL

MODULE 2

Exponents and Real Numbers

FL

UNIT 1B Equations and Functions

MODULE 4 Equations and Inequalities in One Variable

MODULE 5 Equations in Two Variables and Functions

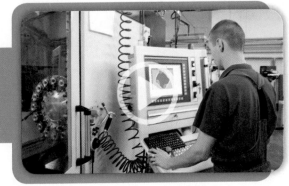

UNIT 2A — Linear Relationships

MODULE 6 — Linear Functions

FL

MODULE 7 · Building Linear Functions

MODULE 8 · Modeling with Linear Functions

UNIT 2B Exponential Relationships

MODULE 10 Exponential Functions and Equations

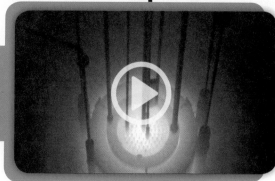

FL

MODULE 11 Modeling with Exponential Functions

FL

UNIT 3 Statistics and Data

MODULE 12 Descriptive Statistics

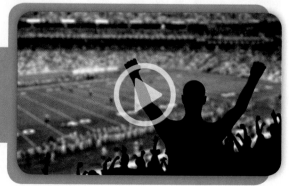

MODULE 13 Data Displays

UNIT 4 Polynomial Expressions and Equations

MODULE 14 Polynomials and Operations

MODULE 15 Factoring Polynomials

Real-World Video. 559
Are You Ready?. 560
Reading Start-Up 561
Unpacking the Standards. . 562

UNIT 5 Functions and Modeling

MODULE 17 Quadratic Functions

FL

MODULE 18 Piecewise and Absolute Value Functions

FL

MODULE 19 **Square Root and Cube Root Functions**

FL

APPENDIX

FL

Florida Standards for Algebra 1

Correlations for *HMH Algebra 1: Analyze, Connect, Explore*

NUMBER AND QUANTITY

Standard	Descriptor	Citations
Domain: NUMBER AND QUANTITY: THE REAL NUMBER SYSTEM		
Cluster 1: Extend the properties of exponents to rational exponents.		
MAFS.912.N-RN.1.1	Explain how the definition of the meaning of rational exponents follows from extending the properties of integer exponents to those values, allowing for a notation for radicals in terms of rational exponents.	**Develop Conceptual Understanding:** SE: 27, 28, 29–33, 45 **Fluency:** SE: 34–36, 46, 76 **Application:** SE: 34–36, 46, 563
MAFS.912.N-RN.1.2	Rewrite expressions involving radicals and rational exponents using the properties of exponents.	**Develop Conceptual Understanding:** SE: 27, 28, 29–33, 45 **Fluency:** SE: 34–36, 46, 76 **Application:** SE: 34–36, 46
Cluster 2: Use properties of rational and irrational numbers.		
MAFS.912.N-RN.2.3	Explain why the sum or product of two rational numbers is rational; that the sum of a rational number and an irrational number is irrational; and that the product of a nonzero rational number and an irrational number is irrational.	**Develop Conceptual Understanding:** SE: 27, 37–41 **Fluency:** SE: 42–44, 45, 76, 77 **Application:** SE: 42–44
Domain: NUMBER AND QUANTITY: QUANTITIES		
Cluster 1: Reason quantitatively and use units to solve problems.		
MAFS.912.N-Q.1.1	Use units as a way to understand problems and to guide the solution of multi-step problems; choose and interpret units consistently in formulas; choose and interpret the scale and the origin in graphs and data displays.	**Develop Conceptual Understanding:** SE: 6, 15–19, 51–54, 65–68, 187–189 **Fluency:** SE: 20–22, 23, 24, 55–56, 69–72, 190–192 **Application:** SE: 20–22, 24, 55–56, 69–72, 190–192
MAFS.912.N-Q.1.2	Define appropriate quantities for the purpose of descriptive modeling.	**Develop Conceptual Understanding:** SE: 65–68, 89–93, 255–259 **Fluency:** SE: 69–72, 73, 94–96, 113, 114, 260–262 **Application:** SE: 69–72, 94–96, 260–262

Standard	Descriptor	Citations
MAFS.912.N-Q.1.3	Choose a level of accuracy appropriate to limitations on measurement when reporting quantities.	**Develop Conceptual Understanding:** SE: 7–10 **Fluency:** SE: 11–14, 23, 46, 79–80, 81, 114, 148, 329 **Application:** SE: 11–14, 24, 75, 79–80, 384, 401

ALGEBRA

Standard	Descriptor	Citations
Domain: ALGEBRA: SEEING STRUCTURE IN EXPRESSIONS		
Cluster 1: Interpret the structure of expressions.		

MAFS.912.A-SSE.1.1	Interpret expressions that represent a quantity in terms of its context.
	  a. Interpret parts of an expression, such as terms, factors, and coefficients.
	  b. Interpret complicated expressions by viewing one or more of their parts as a single entity.
		Develop Conceptual Understanding: SE: 51–53, 57–60, 65–68, 587–590, 595–598
		Fluency: SE: 54–56, 61–64, 69–72, 591–594, 599–602
		Application: SE: 54–56, 61–64, 69–72, 591–594, 599–602

MAFS.912.A-SSE.1.2	Use the structure of an expression to identify ways to rewrite it.	**Develop Conceptual Understanding:** SE: 57–60, 65–68, 509–513, 523–528, 533–536, 541–544, 549–553 **Fluency:** SE: 61–64, 69–72, 514–516, 529–532, 537–540, 545–548, 554–556 **Application:** SE: 61–64, 69–72, 514–516, 529–532, 537–540, 545–548, 554–556
Cluster 2: Write expressions in equivalent forms to solve problems.		

MAFS.912.A-SSE.2.3	Choose and produce an equivalent form of an expression to reveal and explain properties of the quantity represented by the expression.
	  a. Factor a quadratic expression to reveal the zeros of the function it defines.
	  b. Complete the square in a quadratic expression to reveal the maximum or minimum value of the function it defines.
	  c. Use the properties of exponents to transform expressions for exponential functions.
		Develop Conceptual Understanding: SE: 337–340, 345–349, 353–357, 523–528, 533–536, 541–544, 549–553, 571–574, 579–582, 587–590
		Fluency: SE: 341–344, 350–352, 358–360, 529–532, 537–540, 545–548, 554–556, 575–578, 583–586, 591–594
		Application: SE: 341–344, 350–352, 358–360, 529–532, 537–540, 545–548, 554–556, 575–578, 583–586, 591–594

Standard	Descriptor	Citations

Domain: ALGEBRA: ARITHMETIC WITH POLYNOMIALS AND RATIONAL EXPRESSIONS

Cluster 1: Perform arithmetic operations on polynomials.

Standard	Descriptor	Citations
MAFS.912.A-APR.1.1	Understand that polynomials form a system analogous to the integers, namely, they are closed under the operations of addition, subtraction, and multiplication; add, subtract, and multiply polynomials.	**Develop Conceptual Understanding:** SE: 485–488, 493–497, 501–505, 509–513 **Fluency:** SE: 489–492, 498–500, 506–508, 514–516 **Application:** SE: 489–492, 498–500, 506–508, 514–516

Cluster 2: Understand the relationship between zeros and factors of polynomials.

Standard	Descriptor	Citations
MAFS.912.A-APR.2.3	Identify zeros of polynomials when suitable factorizations are available, and use the zeros to construct a rough graph of the function defined by the polynomial.	**Develop Conceptual Understanding:** SE: 533–536, 663, 671 **Fluency:** SE: 537–540, 666, 667–668, 674, 675, 688 **Application:** SE: 537–540, 667–668, 676

Domain: ALGEBRA: CREATING EQUATIONS

Cluster 1: Create equations that describe numbers or relationships.

Standard	Descriptor	Citations
MAFS.912.A-CED.1.1	Create equations and inequalities in one variable and use them to solve problems. Include equations arising from linear and quadratic functions, and simple rational, absolute [value], and exponential functions.	**Develop Conceptual Understanding:** SE: 89–93, 97–103, 367–370, 563–566, 571–574, 579–582, 669–673, 765–769 **Fluency:** SE: 94–96, 104–106, 371–374, 567–570, 575–578, 583–586, 674–676, 770–772 **Application:** SE: 94–96, 104–106, 371–374, 567–570, 575–578, 583–586, 674–676, 770–772
MAFS.912.A-CED.1.2	Create equations in two or more variables to represent relationships between quantities; graph equations on coordinate axes with labels and scales.	**Develop Conceptual Understanding:** SE: 179–183, 201–204, 219–222, 337–340, 367–370, 381–383, 635–640, 643–647, 651–655, 669–673, 693–697 **Fluency:** SE: 184–186, 204–206, 223–226, 341–344, 371–374, 384–386, 641–642, 648–650, 656–658, 674–676, 698–700 **Application:** SE: 184–186, 204–206, 223–226, 341–344, 371–374, 384–386, 641–642, 648–650, 656–658, 674–676, 698–700

Standard	Descriptor	Citations
MAFS.912.A-CED.1.3	Represent constraints by equations or inequalities, and by systems of equations and/or inequalities, and interpret solutions as viable or nonviable options in a modeling context.	**Develop Conceptual Understanding:** SE: 89–93, 97–103, 277–280, 285–289, 293–299, 303–307, 311–315 **Fluency:** SE: 94–96, 104–106, 281–284, 290–292, 300–302, 308–310, 316–318 **Application:** SE: 94–96, 104–106, 281–284, 290–292, 300–302, 308–310, 316–318
MAFS.912.A-CED.1.4	Rearrange formulas to highlight a quantity of interest, using the same reasoning as in solving equations.	**Develop Conceptual Understanding:** SE: 15–18, 107–109, 603 **Fluency:** SE: 19–22, 110–112, 603 **Application:** SE: 19–22, 110–112, 170, 603

Domain: ALGEBRA: REASONING WITH EQUATIONS AND INEQUALITIES

Cluster 1: Understand solving equations as a process of reasoning and explain the reasoning.

MAFS.912.A-REI.1.1	Explain each step in solving a simple equation as following from the equality of numbers asserted at the previous step, starting from the assumption that the original equation has a solution. Construct a viable argument to justify a solution method.	**Develop Conceptual Understanding:** SE: 89–93, 97–103, 107–109 **Fluency:** SE: 94–96, 104–106, 110–112 **Application:** SE: 14, 56, 94–96, 104–106, 110–112

Cluster 2: Solve equations and inequalities in one variable.

MAFS.912.A-REI.2.3	Solve linear equations and inequalities in one variable, including equations with coefficients represented by letters.	**Develop Conceptual Understanding:** SE: 89–93, 97–103, 277–280, 293–299 **Fluency:** SE: 94–96, 103–106, 110–112, 113, 114, 281–284, 300–302 **Application:** SE: 94–96, 103–106, 110–112, 281–284, 300–302
MAFS.912.A-REI.2.4	Solve quadratic equations in one variable. **a.** Use the method of completing the square to transform any quadratic equation in x into an equation of the form $(x - p)^2 = q$ that has the same solutions. Derive the quadratic formula from this form. **b.** Solve quadratic equations by inspection (e.g., for $x^2 = 49$), taking square roots, completing the square, the quadratic formula and factoring, as appropriate to the initial form of the equation. Recognize when the quadratic formula gives complex solutions and write them as $a \pm bi$ for real numbers a and b.	**Develop Conceptual Understanding:** SE: 563–566, 571–574, 579–582, 587–590, 595–598, 603–607, 611–614, 669–673 **Fluency:** SE: 567–570, 575–578, 583–586, 591–594, 599–602, 608–610, 615–618, 674–676 **Application:** SE: 567–570, 575–578, 583–586, 591–594, 599–602, 608–610, 615–618, 674–676

Standard	Descriptor	Citations
Cluster 3: Solve systems of equations.		
MAFS.912.A-REI.3.5	Prove that, given a system of two equations in two variables, replacing one equation by the sum of that equation and a multiple of the other produces a system with the same solutions.	**Develop Conceptual Understanding:** SE: 293–299, 303–307 **Fluency:** SE: 300–302, 308–310, 319, 326 **Application:** SE: 300–302, 308–310
MAFS.912.A-REI.3.6	Solve systems of linear equations exactly and approximately (e.g., with graphs), focusing on pairs of linear equations in two variables.	**Develop Conceptual Understanding:** SE: 277–280, 285–289, 293–299, 303–307 **Fluency:** SE: 281–284, 290–292, 300–302, 308–310, 319, 320, 325–326 **Application:** SE: 281–284, 290–292, 300–302, 308–310
Cluster 4: Represent and solve equations and inequalities graphically.		
MAFS.912.A-REI.4.10	Understand that the graph of an equation in two variables is the set of all its solutions plotted in the coordinate plane, often forming a curve (which could be a line).	**Develop Conceptual Understanding:** SE: 119–121, 277–280, 285–289, 293–299, 303–305 **Fluency:** SE: 122–124, 281–284, 290–292, 300–302, 319, 320 **Application:** SE: 122–124, 281–284, 290–292, 300–302
MAFS.912.A-REI.4.11	Explain why the x-coordinates of the points where the graphs of the equations $y = f(x)$ and $y = g(x)$ intersect are the solutions of the equation $f(x) = g(x)$; find the solutions approximately, e.g., using technology to graph the functions, make tables of values, or find successive approximations. Include cases where $f(x)$ and/or $g(x)$ are linear, polynomial, rational, absolute value, exponential, and logarithmic functions.	**Develop Conceptual Understanding:** SE: 125–129, 277–280, 669–673, 701–705 **Fluency:** SE: 130–132, 144, 145, 148, 281–284, 322, 674–676, 706–708 **Application:** SE: 130–132, 281–284, 674–676, 706–708
MAFS.912.A-REI.4.12	Graph the solutions to a linear inequality in two variables as a halfplane (excluding the boundary in the case of a strict inequality), and graph the solution set to a system of linear inequalities in two variables as the intersection of the corresponding half-planes.	**Develop Conceptual Understanding:** SE: 233–237, 311–315 **Fluency:** SE: 147, 238–240, 241, 242, 316–318, 319, 320 **Application:** SE: 238–240, 316–318

FUNCTIONS

Standard	Descriptor	Citations
Domain: FUNCTIONS: INTERPRETING FUNCTIONS		
Cluster 1: Understand the concept of a function and use function notation.		
MAFS.912.F-IF.1.1	Understand that a function from one set (called the domain) to another set (called the range) assigns to each element of the domain exactly one element of the range. If *f* is a function and *x* is an element of its domain, then $f(x)$ denotes the output of *f* corresponding to the input *x*. The graph of *f* is the graph of the equation $y = f(x)$.	Develop Conceptual Understanding: SE: 125–129, 141, 148, 182, 187–189 Fluency: SE: 130–132, 142, 144, 145, 190–192 Application: SE: 130–132, 146, 190–192
MAFS.912.F-IF.1.2	Use function notation, evaluate functions for inputs in their domains, and interpret statements that use function notation in terms of a context.	Develop Conceptual Understanding: SE: 125–129, 187–189, 227–229, 635–639, 643–647, 651–655, 693–697 Fluency: SE: 130–132, 190–192, 230–232, 640–642, 648–650, 656–658, 698–700 Application: SE: 130–132, 190–192, 230–232, 640–642, 648–650, 656–658, 698–700
MAFS.912.F-IF.1.3	Recognize that sequences are functions, sometimes defined recursively, whose domain is a subset of the integers.	Develop Conceptual Understanding: SE: 133–136, 213–215, 353–357, 358–360 Fluency: SE: 137–140, 141, 142, 145, 148, 216–218 Application: SE: 137–140, 145
Cluster 2: Interpret functions that arise in applications in terms of the context.		
MAFS.912.F-IF.2.4	For a function that models a relationship between two quantities, interpret key features of graphs and tables in terms of the quantities, and sketch graphs showing key features given a verbal description of the relationship.	Develop Conceptual Understanding: SE: 163–167, 171–175, 179–183, 193–197, 345–349, 611–614, 635–639, 643–647, 651–655, 659–665, 693–697, 701–705 Fluency: SE: 168–170, 176–178, 184–186, 198–200, 350–352, 615–618, 640–642, 648–650, 656–658, 666–668, 698–700, 706–708 Application: SE: 168–170, 176–178, 184–186, 198–200, 350–352, 615–618, 640–642, 648–650, 656–658, 666–668, 698–700, 706–708

Standard	Descriptor	Citations
MAFS.912.F-IF.2.5	Relate the domain of a function to its graph and, where applicable, to the quantitative relationship it describes.	**Develop Conceptual Understanding:** SE: 125–129, 155–159, 187–189, 337–340, 345–349, 635–639, 693–697 **Fluency:** SE: 130–132, 160–162, 190–192, 341–344, 350–352, 640–642, 698–700 **Application:** SE: 130–132, 160–162, 190–192, 341–344, 350–352, 640–642, 698–700
MAFS.912.F-IF.2.6	Calculate and interpret the average rate of change of a function (presented symbolically or as a table) over a specified interval. Estimate the rate of change from a graph.	**Develop Conceptual Understanding:** SE: 154, 171–175, 182–184, 201–203, 677–682 **Fluency:** SE: 176–178, 185–186, 204–206, 683–686 **Application:** SE: 176–178, 185–186, 204–206, 683–686
Cluster 3: Analyze functions using different representations.		

MAFS.912.F-IF.3.7	Graph functions expressed symbolically and show key features of the graph, by hand in simple cases and using technology for more complicated cases.
	  a. Graph linear and quadratic functions and show intercepts, maxima, and minima.
	  b. Graph square root, cube root, and piecewise-defined functions, including step functions and absolute value functions.
	  c. Graph polynomial functions, identifying zeros when suitable factorizations are available, and showing end behavior.
	  e. Graph exponential and logarithmic functions, showing intercepts and end behavior, and trigonometric functions, showing period, midline, and amplitude, and using phase shift.
		Develop Conceptual Understanding: SE: 155–159, 163–167, 171–175, 179–183, 337–340, 345–349, 635–639, 643–647, 651–655, 693–697, 701–705, 709–713, 723–727, 739–743
		Fluency: SE: 160–162, 168–170, 176–178, 184–186, 341–344, 350–352, 640–642, 648–650, 656–658, 698–700, 706–708, 714–716, 728–730, 744–746
		Application: SE: 160–162, 168–170, 176–178, 184–186, 341–344, 350–352, 640–642, 648–650, 656–658, 698–700, 706–708, 714–716, 728–730, 744–746

MAFS.912.F-IF.3.8	Write a function defined by an expression in different but equivalent forms to reveal and explain different properties of the function.
	  a. Use the process of factoring and completing the square in a quadratic function to show zeros, extreme values, and symmetry of the graph, and interpret these in terms of a context.
	  b. Use the properties of exponents to interpret expressions for exponential functions.
		Develop Conceptual Understanding: SE: 345–349, 353–357, 571–574, 579–582, 587–590, 659–665
		Fluency: SE: 350–352, 358–360, 575–578, 583–586, 591–594, 666–668
		Application: SE: 350–352, 358–360, 575–578, 583–586, 591–594, 666–668

Standard	Descriptor	Citations
MAFS.912.F-IF.3.9	Compare properties of two functions each represented in a different way (algebraically, graphically, numerically in tables, or by verbal descriptions).	**Develop Conceptual Understanding:** SE: 187–189, 693–697, 701–705, 723–727, 731–735, 739–743, 747–751 **Fluency:** SE: 190–192, 698–700, 706–708, 728–730, 736–738, 744–746, 752–754 **Application:** SE: 190–192, 698–700, 706–708, 728–730, 736–738, 744–746, 752–754

Domain: FUNCTIONS: BUILDING FUNCTIONS

Cluster 1: Build a function that models a relationship between two quantities.

MAFS.912.F-BF.1.1	Write a function that describes a relationship between two quantities.
	  a. Determine an explicit expression, a recursive process, or steps for calculation from a context.
	  b. Combine standard function types using arithmetic operations.
	  c. Compose functions.
		Develop Conceptual Understanding: SE: 133–136, 201–203, 213–215, 219–222, 353–357, 367–370, 635–639, 643–647, 651–655, 693–697
		Fluency: SE: 137–140, 204–206, 216–218, 223–226, 358–360, 367–370, 640–642, 648–650, 656–658, 698–700
		Application: SE: 137–140, 204–206, 216–218, 223–226, 358–360, 367–370, 640–642, 648–650, 656–658, 698–700

Cluster 2: Build new functions from existing functions.

MAFS.912.F-BF.2.3	Identify the effect on the graph of replacing $f(x)$ by $f(x) + k$, $k \cdot f(x)$, $f(kx)$, and $f(x + k)$ for specific values of k (both positive and negative); find the value of k given the graphs. Experiment with cases and illustrate an explanation of the effects on the graph using technology.	**Develop Conceptual Understanding:** SE: 193–197, 361–363, 635–639, 643–647, 651–655, 693–697, 701–705, 709–713, 731–735, 747–751 **Fluency:** SE: 198–200, 364–366, 640–642, 648–650, 656–658, 698–700, 706–708, 714–716, 736–738, 752–754 **Application:** SE: 198–200, 364–366, 640–642, 648–650, 656–658, 698–700, 706–708, 714–716, 736–738, 752–754

Standard	Descriptor	Citations
Domain: FUNCTIONS: LINEAR AND EXPONENTIAL MODELS		
Cluster 1: Construct and compare linear and exponential models and solve problems.		

MAFS.912.F-LE.1.1	Distinguish between situations that can be modeled with linear functions and with exponential functions.
	  a. Prove that linear functions grow by equal differences over equal intervals, and that exponential functions grow by equal factors over equal intervals.
	  b. Recognize situations in which one quantity changes at a constant rate per unit interval relative to another.
	  c. Recognize situations in which a quantity grows or decays by a constant percent rate per unit interval relative to another.
		Develop Conceptual Understanding: SE: 171–175, 179–183, 213–215, 345–349, 353–357, 387–391, 677–682
		Fluency: SE: 176–178, 184–186, 216–218, 350–352, 358–360, 392–394, 683–686
		Application: SE: 176–178, 184–186, 216–218, 350–352, 358–360, 392–394, 683–686

MAFS.912.F-LE.1.2	Construct linear and exponential functions, including arithmetic and geometric sequences, given a graph, a description of a relationship, or two input-output pairs (include reading these from a table).	**Develop Conceptual Understanding:** SE: 201–203, 213–215, 219–222, 337–340, 345–349, 353–357, 367–370 **Fluency:** SE: 204–206, 216–218, 223–226, 341–344, 350–352, 358–360, 371–374 **Application:** SE: 204–206, 216–218, 223–226, 341–344, 350–352, 358–360, 371–374
MAFS.912.F-LE.1.3	Observe using graphs and tables that a quantity increasing exponentially eventually exceeds a quantity increasing linearly, quadratically, or (more generally) as a polynomial function.	**Develop Conceptual Understanding:** SE: 387–391, 677–682 **Fluency:** SE: 392–394, 404, 683–686, 687 **Application:** SE: 392–394, 395, 401, 683–686
Cluster 2: Interpret expressions for functions in terms of the situation they model.		
MAFS.912.F-LE.2.5	Interpret the parameters in a linear or exponential function in terms of a context.	**Develop Conceptual Understanding:** SE: 187–189, 193–197, 219–222, 255–259, 345–349, 381–383 **Fluency:** SE: 190–192, 198–200, 223–226, 260–262, 350–352, 384–386 **Application:** SE: 190–192, 198–200, 223–226, 260–262, 350–352, 384–386

STATISTICS AND PROBABILITY

Standard	Descriptor	Citations
Domain: STATISTICS AND PROBABILITY: INTERPRETING CATEGORICAL AND QUANTITATIVE DATA		
Cluster 1: Summarize, represent, and interpret data on a single count or measurement variable.		
MAFS.912.S-ID.1.1	Represent data with plots on the real number line (dot plots, histograms, and box plots).	**Develop Conceptual Understanding:** SE: 439–442, 447–450, 451–457, 461–465 **Fluency:** SE: 443–446, 451–454, 458–460, 466–468 **Application:** SE: 443–446, 451–454, 458–460, 466–468
MAFS.912.S-ID.1.2	Use statistics appropriate to the shape of the data distribution to compare center (median, mean) and spread (interquartile range, standard deviation) of two or more different data sets.	**Develop Conceptual Understanding:** SE: 431–435, 439–442, 455–457, 461–465 **Fluency:** SE: 436–438, 443–446, 458–460, 466–468, 469, 470, 473–476, 477–478 **Application:** SE: 436–438, 443–446, 450, 458–460, 466–468, 473–476
MAFS.912.S-ID.1.3	Interpret differences in shape, center, and spread in the context of the data sets, accounting for possible effects of extreme data points (outliers).	**Develop Conceptual Understanding:** SE: 431–435, 439–442, 455–457, 461–465 **Fluency:** SE: 436–438, 444–446, 458–460, 466–468 **Application:** SE: 436–438, 444–446, 458–460, 466–468
Cluster 2: Summarize, represent, and interpret data on two categorical and quantitative variables.		
MAFS.912.S-ID.2.5	Summarize categorical data for two categories in two-way frequency tables. Interpret relative frequencies in the context of the data (including joint, marginal, and conditional relative frequencies). Recognize possible associations and trends in the data.	**Develop Conceptual Understanding:** SE: 411–413, 417–421, 463–464 **Fluency:** SE: 414–416, 422–424, 425, 426, 471–472 **Application:** SE: 414–416, 422–424

MAFS.912.S-ID.2.6	Represent data on two quantitative variables on a scatter plot, and describe how the variables are related.
	   a. Fit a function to the data; use functions fitted to data to solve problems in the context of the data.
	   b. Informally assess the fit of a function by plotting and analyzing residuals.
	   c. Fit a linear function for a scatter plot that suggests a linear association.
		Develop Conceptual Understanding: SE: 247–251, 255–259, 263–267, 381–383
		 Fluency: SE: 252–254, 260–262, 268–270, 384–386, 396, 398
		 Application: SE: 252–254, 260–262, 268–270, 384–386

Standard	Descriptor	Citations
Cluster 3: Interpret linear models.		
MAFS.912.S-ID.3.7	Interpret the slope (rate of change) and the intercept (constant term) of a linear model in the context of the data.	**Develop Conceptual Understanding:** SE: 182, 183, 255–259, 263–267 **Fluency:** SE: 260–262, 268–270, 271 **Application:** SE: 185, 260–262, 268–270
MAFS.912.S-ID.3.8	Compute (using technology) and interpret the correlation coefficient of a linear fit.	**Develop Conceptual Understanding:** SE: 247–251, 255–259, 263–267 **Fluency:** SE: 252–254, 260–262, 268–270 **Application:** SE: 252–254, 260–262, 268–270
MAFS.912.S-ID.3.9	Distinguish between correlation and causation.	**Develop Conceptual Understanding:** SE: 245, 247–251 **Fluency:** SE: 252–254, 272 **Application:** SE: 252–254

Standard	Descriptor	Citations
MP Mathematical Practices Standards		*The mathematical practices standards are integrated throughout the book. See, for example, the citations below.*
MAFS.K12.MP.1.1	**Make sense of problems and persevere in solving them.** Mathematically proficient students start by explaining to themselves the meaning of a problem and looking for entry points to its solution. They analyze givens, constraints, relationships, and goals. They make conjectures about the form and meaning of the solution and plan a solution pathway rather than simply jumping into a solution attempt. They consider analogous problems, and try special cases and simpler forms of the original problem in order to gain insight into its solution. They monitor and evaluate their progress and change course if necessary. Older students might, depending on the context of the problem, transform algebraic expressions or change the viewing window on their graphing calculator to get the information they need. Mathematically proficient students can explain correspondences between equations, verbal descriptions, tables, and graphs or draw diagrams of important features and relationships, graph data, and search for regularity or trends. Younger students might rely on using concrete objects or pictures to help conceptualize and solve a problem. Mathematically proficient students check their answers to problems using a different method, and they continually ask themselves, "Does this make sense?" They can understand the approaches of others to solving complex problems and identify correspondences between different approaches.	SE: 21, 35, 55, 56, 63, 64, 71, 72, 95, 105, 112, 124, 138, 139, 162, 170, 178, 185, 224, 225, 226, 282, 291, 292, 317, 373, 374, 386, 393, 437, 453, 467, 468, 490, 491, 492, 499, 500, 507, 508, 515, 516, 531, 532, 539, 540, 546, 547, 548, 555, 556, 569, 577, 585, 594, 610, 617, 618, 641, 649, 657, 658, 675, 676, 700, 707, 729, 737
MAFS.K12.MP.2.1	**Reason abstractly and quantitatively.** Mathematically proficient students make sense of quantities and their relationships in problem situations. They bring two complementary abilities to bear on problems involving quantitative relationships: the ability to decontextualize—to abstract a given situation and represent it symbolically and manipulate the representing symbols as if they have a life of their own, without necessarily attending to their referents—and the ability to contextualize, to pause as needed during the manipulation process in order to probe into the referents for the symbols involved. Quantitative reasoning entails habits of creating a coherent representation of the problem at hand; considering the units involved; attending to the meaning of quantities, not just how to compute them; and knowing and flexibly using different properties of operations and objects.	SE: 13, 22, 35, 44, 55, 56, 95, 96, 105, 109, 111, 124, 131, 140, 162, 170, 178, 186, 191, 200, 206, 218, 221, 225, 232, 240, 251, 254, 259, 262, 265, 270, 282, 284, 292, 300, 309, 318, 343, 352, 360, 366, 370, 373, 383, 386, 390, 394, 413, 416, 421, 423, 438, 443, 445, 454, 460, 468, 487, 492, 500, 505, 508, 510, 515, 532, 539, 541, 546, 548, 556, 565, 570, 578, 586, 588, 593, 596, 602, 603, 605, 609, 618, 642, 650, 654, 658, 660, 664, 668, 676, 686, 699, 701, 708, 716, 729, 738, 745, 748, 754

Standard	Descriptor	Citations
MAFS.K12.MP.3.1	**Construct viable arguments and critique the reasoning of others.** Mathematically proficient students understand and use stated assumptions, definitions, and previously established results in constructing arguments. They make conjectures and build a logical progression of statements to explore the truth of their conjectures. They are able to analyze situations by breaking them into cases, and can recognize and use counterexamples. They justify their conclusions, communicate them to others, and respond to the arguments of others. They reason inductively about data, making plausible arguments that take into account the context from which the data arose. Mathematically proficient students are also able to compare the effectiveness of two plausible arguments, distinguish correct logic or reasoning from that which is flawed, and—if there is a flaw in an argument—explain what it is. Elementary students can construct arguments using concrete referents such as objects, drawings, diagrams, and actions. Such arguments can make sense and be correct, even though they are not generalized or made formal until later grades. Later, students learn to determine domains to which an argument applies. Students at all grades can listen or read the arguments of others, decide whether they make sense, and ask useful questions to clarify or improve the arguments.	SE: 12, 14, 20, 21, 36, 40, 54, 94, 104, 106, 110, 111, 130, 136, 137, 160, 162, 168, 170, 176, 184, 186, 190, 192, 198, 204, 206, 216, 220, 226, 228, 230, 232, 237, 238, 248, 252, 254, 260, 262, 264, 265, 280, 281, 290, 291, 292, 296, 300, 301, 302, 308, 310, 316, 318, 341, 344, 350, 352, 358, 360, 364, 368, 371, 373, 384, 386, 388, 389, 392, 414, 422, 424, 436, 444, 452, 458, 466, 489, 498, 499, 506, 528, 530, 532, 538, 539, 540, 544, 545, 548, 554, 568, 570, 576, 578, 584, 592, 597, 600, 602, 608, 610, 674, 616, 618, 640, 648, 652, 656, 666, 668, 683, 698, 706, 714, 728, 733, 736, 738, 744, 748, 749, 752
MAFS.K12.MP.4.1	**Model with mathematics.** Mathematically proficient students can apply the mathematics they know to solve problems arising in everyday life, society, and the workplace. In early grades, this might be as simple as writing an addition equation to describe a situation. In middle grades, a student might apply proportional reasoning to plan a school event or analyze a problem in the community. By high school, a student might use geometry to solve a design problem or use a function to describe how one quantity of interest depends on another. Mathematically proficient students who can apply what they know are comfortable making assumptions and approximations to simplify a complicated situation, realizing that these may need revision later. They are able to identify important quantities in a practical situation and map their relationships using such tools as diagrams, two-way tables, graphs, flowcharts and formulas. They can analyze those relationships mathematically to draw conclusions. They routinely interpret their mathematical results in the context of the situation and reflect on whether the results make sense, possibly improving the model if it has not served its purpose.	SE: 8, 14, 15, 22, 53, 66, 67, 93, 106, 111, 112, 121, 123, 126–127, 128, 131, 132, 136, 158, 161, 162, 166, 174, 175, 181–182, 185, 189, 191, 192, 199, 200, 202, 203, 205, 206, 215, 228, 239, 240, 255, 284, 287, 291, 297, 299, 301, 302, 304, 307, 309, 310, 318, 340, 342, 344, 347, 349, 351, 356, 357, 359, 365, 366, 369, 372, 373, 385, 412, 488, 490, 491, 501, 505, 507, 508, 509, 516, 525, 533, 539, 546, 549, 552, 566, 569, 570, 577, 578, 585, 586, 590, 646, 593, 594, 601, 602, 609, 610, 614, 638, 646, 647, 653, 655, 657, 663, 665, 667, 673, 684, 685, 700, 727, 730, 737, 742, 745

Standard	Descriptor	Citations
MAFS.K12.MP.5.1	**Use appropriate tools strategically.** Mathematically proficient students consider the available tools when solving a mathematical problem. These tools might include pencil and paper, concrete models, a ruler, a protractor, a calculator, a spreadsheet, a computer algebra system, a statistical package, or dynamic geometry software. Proficient students are sufficiently familiar with tools appropriate for their grade or course to make sound decisions about when each of these tools might be helpful, recognizing both the insight to be gained and their limitations. For example, mathematically proficient high school students analyze graphs of functions and solutions generated using a graphing calculator. They detect possible errors by strategically using estimation and other mathematical knowledge. When making mathematical models, they know that technology can enable them to visualize the results of varying assumptions, explore consequences, and compare predictions with data. Mathematically proficient students at various grade levels are able to identify relevant external mathematical resources, such as digital content located on a website, and use them to pose or solve problems. They are able to use technological tools to explore and deepen their understanding of concepts.	SE: 10, 13, 14, 169, 178, 193, 194, 257, 266, 267, 268, 270, 271, 272, 280, 289, 315, 345, 347, 361, 362, 366, 373, 381, 383, 384, 385, 388, 389, 391, 396, 400, 402, 435, 441, 445, 453, 459, 461, 501, 509, 533, 534, 537, 549, 586, 594, 613, 614, 617, 644, 648, 655, 657, 659, 662, 672, 673, 677, 678, 686, 709, 710, 714, 726, 729, 738, 745, 746, 751
MAFS.K12.MP.6.1	**Attend to precision.** Mathematically proficient students try to communicate precisely to others. They try to use clear definitions in discussion with others and in their own reasoning. They state the meaning of the symbols they choose, including using the equal sign consistently and appropriately. They are careful about specifying units of measure, and labeling axes to clarify the correspondence with quantities in a problem. They calculate accurately and efficiently, express numerical answers with a degree of precision appropriate for the problem context. In the elementary grades, students give carefully formulated explanations to each other. By the time they reach high school they have learned to examine claims and make explicit use of definitions.	SE: 10, 13, 14, 21, 159, 163, 192, 206, 218, 239, 253, 256, 258, 261, 262, 269, 280, 318, 352, 354, 355, 360, 366, 368, 370, 382, 393–394, 438, 454, 464, 468, 500, 512, 514, 532, 540, 547, 564, 570, 572, 580, 582, 587, 588, 589, 591, 594, 610, 635, 650, 660, 661, 716, 729, 740, 743, 746, 754

Standard	Descriptor	Citations
MAFS.K12.MP.7.1	**Look for and make use of structure.** Mathematically proficient students look closely to discern a pattern or structure. Young students, for example, might notice that three and seven more is the same amount as seven and three more, or they may sort a collection of shapes according to how many sides the shapes have. Later, students will see 7×8 equals the well remembered $7 \times 5 + 7 \times 3$, in preparation for learning about the distributive property. In the expression $x^2 + 9x + 14$, older students can see the 14 as 2×7 and the 9 as $2 + 7$. They recognize the significance of an existing line in a geometric figure and can use the strategy of drawing an auxiliary line for solving problems. They also can step back for an overview and shift perspective. They can see complicated things, such as some algebraic expressions, as single objects or as being composed of several objects. For example, they can see $5 - 3(x - y)^2$ as 5 minus a positive number times a square and use that to realize that its value cannot be more than 5 for any real numbers x and y.	SE: 40, 44, 63, 106, 111, 121, 165, 169, 185, 186, 189, 192, 204, 205, 232, 262, 269, 270, 284, 292, 296, 270, 284, 292, 296, 301, 303, 311, 313, 344, 351, 365, 372, 373, 386, 389, 393, 415, 416, 423, 424, 446, 531, 539, 546, 547, 569, 570, 577, 586, 602, 618, 641, 642, 644, 649, 650, 652, 667, 668, 675, 684, 703, 713, 725, 733, 734
MAFS.K12.MP.8.1	**Look for and express regularity in repeated reasoning.** Mathematically proficient students notice if calculations are repeated, and look both for general methods and for shortcuts. Upper elementary students might notice when dividing 25 by 11 that they are repeating the same calculations over and over again, and conclude they have a repeating decimal. By paying attention to the calculation of slope as they repeatedly check whether points are on the line through $(1, 2)$ with slope 3, middle school students might abstract the equation $\frac{(y-2)}{(x-1)} = 3$. Noticing the regularity in the way terms cancel when expanding $(x - 1)(x + 1)$, $(x - 1)(x^2 + x + 1)$, and $(x - 1)(x^3 + x^2 + x + 1)$ might lead them to the general formula for the sum of a geometric series. As they work to solve a problem, mathematically proficient students maintain oversight of the process, while attending to the details. They continually evaluate the reasonableness of their intermediate results.	SE: 32, 35, 63, 91, 102, 120, 133, 138, 155, 159, 161, 171, 177, 187, 193, 194, 213, 214, 217, 224, 236, 265, 308, 343, 359, 360, 361, 362, 367, 383, 388, 391, 393, 488, 493, 495, 501, 503, 504, 512, 513, 515, 555, 580, 581, 587, 635, 643, 651, 659, 669, 671, 672, 679, 682, 697, 699, 700, 707, 708, 711, 715, 732, 738, 753, 754

Florida English Language Arts Standards

HMH Florida Algebra 1: Analyze, Connect, Explore supports English language learners at all proficiency levels. The *HMH Florida Algebra 1: Analyze, Connect, Explore Student Edition* provides integrated resources to assist all levels of learners, as shown in the correlation tables provided below.

In addition, students at various levels may benefit from additional program support:

Beginning—Students at a Beginning level are supported by *Spanish Student Edition, Spanish Assessment Resources*, Success for Every Learner and Leveled Practice A worksheets in *Differentiated Instruction, Math On the Spot* videos with Spanish closed captioning, and the Multilingual Glossary.

Intermediate—Students at the Intermediate level may use any of the resources above and may also use Reading Strategies in *Differentiated Instruction*.

Advanced and Advanced High—Students at these levels will be successful as the *Student Edition* promotes vocabulary development through visual and context clues. The Multilingual Glossary may also be helpful.

English Language Arts Standard	Student Edition Citations
LAFS.910.RST.1.3 Follow precisely a complex multistep procedure when carrying out experiments, taking measurements, or performing technical tasks, attending to special cases or exceptions defined in the text.	Develop Conceptual Understanding: SE: 8, 15, 29, 52 Fluency: SE: 57, 175, 292 Application: SE: 15, 57, 96, 170, 175, 240, 292, 302
LAFS.910.RST.2.4 Determine the meaning of symbols, key terms, and other domain-specific words and phrases as they are used in a specific scientific or technical context relevant to grades 9–10 texts and topics.	Develop Conceptual Understanding: SE: 5, 6, 27, 28, 49, 50, 87, 88, 117, 118, 153, 154 Fluency: SE: 71 Application: SE: 71–72
LAFS.910.RST.3.7 Translate quantitative or technical information expressed in words in a text into visual form (e.g., a table or chart) and translate information expressed visually or mathematically (e.g., in an equation) into words.	Develop Conceptual Understanding: SE: 27, 49, 51, 117, 165–166 Fluency: SE: 36, 65–66, 103, Application: SE: 54, 65–66, 68, 155–156, 213

English Language Arts Standard	Student Edition Citations
LAFS.910.SL.1.1 Initiate and participate effectively in a range of collaborative discussions (one-on-one, in groups, and teacher-led) with diverse partners on grades 9–10 topics, texts, and issues, building on others' ideas and expressing their own clearly and persuasively. a. Come to discussions prepared, having read and researched material under study; explicitly draw on that preparation by referring to evidence from texts and other research on the topic or issue to stimulate a thoughtful, well-reasoned exchange of ideas. b. Work with peers to set rules for collegial discussions and decision-making (e.g., informal consensus, taking votes on key issues, presentation of alternate views), clear goals and deadlines, and individual roles as needed. c. Propel conversations by posing and responding to questions that relate the current discussion to broader themes or larger ideas; actively incorporate others into the discussion; and clarify, verify, or challenge ideas and conclusions. d. Respond thoughtfully to diverse perspectives, summarize points of agreement and disagreement, and, when warranted, qualify or justify their own views and understanding and make new connections in light of the evidence and reasoning presented.	Application: SE: 7, 12, 17, 20, 29, 34, 37, 42, 94, 104
LAFS.910.SL.1.2 Integrate multiple sources of information presented in diverse media or formats (e.g., visually, quantitatively, orally) evaluating the credibility and accuracy of each source.	Application: SE: 3, 25, 36, 47, 85, 115, 123, 151, 155, 170
LAFS.910.SL.1.3 Evaluate a speaker's point of view, reasoning, and use of evidence and rhetoric, identifying any fallacious reasoning or exaggerated or distorted evidence.	Application: SE: 14, 22, 40, 44, 56, 64, 106, 124, 200, 228
LAFS.910.SL.2.4 Present information, findings, and supporting evidence clearly, concisely, and logically such that listeners can follow the line of reasoning and the organization, development, substance, and style are appropriate to purpose, audience, and task.	Application: SE: 12, 17, 20, 32, 34, 37, 42, 51, 94, 104, 108, 157

English Language Arts Standard	Student Edition Citations

LAFS.910.WHST.1.1 Write arguments focused on *discipline-specific content*.
   a. Introduce precise claim(s), distinguish the claim(s) from alternate or opposing claims, and create an organization that establishes clear relationships among the claim(s), counterclaims, reasons, and evidence.
   b. Develop claim(s) and counterclaims fairly, supplying data and evidence for each while pointing out the strengths and limitations of both claim(s) and counterclaims in a discipline-appropriate form and in a manner that anticipates the audience's knowledge level and concerns.
   c. Use words, phrases, and clauses to link the major sections of the text, create cohesion, and clarify the relationships between claim(s) and reasons, between reasons and evidence, and between claim(s) and counterclaims.
   d. Establish and maintain a formal style and objective tone while attending to the norms and conventions of the discipline in which they are writing.
   e. Provide a concluding statement or section that follows from or supports the argument presented.
	Application: SE: 11, 14, 29, 30, 41, 44, 52, 63, 96, 98, 106, 112, 124, 167, 186, 192, 462, 547, 676

LAFS.910.WHST.2.4 Produce clear and coherent writing in which the development, organization, and style are appropriate to task, purpose, and audience.	Application: SE: 5, 14, 22, 27, 36, 44, 49, 56, 64, 72, 87, 117, 153, 211, 245, 275, 335, 378, 409, 429, 483, 521, 561, 633
LAFS.910.WHST.3.9 Draw evidence from informational texts to support analysis, reflection, and research.	Application: SE: 7, 8, 11, 14, 15, 22, 29, 36, 37, 44, 56, 64, 72, 98, 103, 129, 227, 234

Succeeding with
HMH Algebra 1: Analyze, Connect, Explore

Actively participate in your learning with your write-in Student Edition. Explore concepts, take notes, answer questions, and complete your homework right in your textbook!

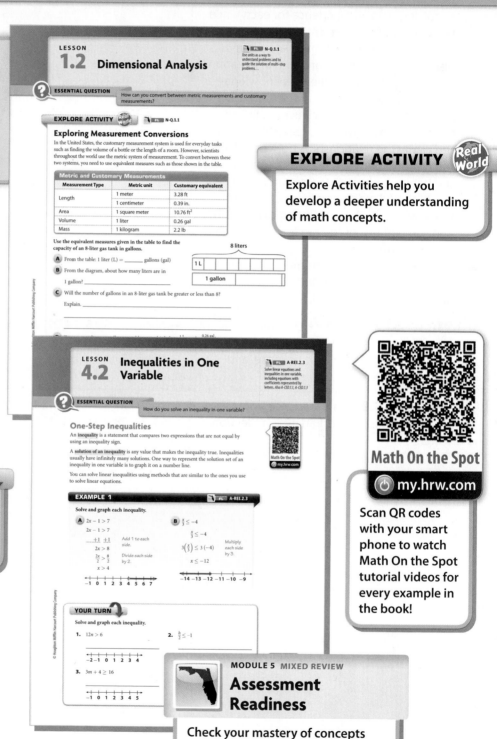

EXPLORE ACTIVITY *Real World*

Explore Activities help you develop a deeper understanding of math concepts.

YOUR TURN

Your Turn exercises check your understanding of new concepts.

Math On the Spot
my.hrw.com

Scan QR codes with your smart phone to watch Math On the Spot tutorial videos for every example in the book!

Assessment Readiness

Check your mastery of concepts through review and practice for high-stakes tests.

GO DIGITAL
my.hrw.com

Enhance Your Learning!

my.hrw.com

The Interactive Student Edition provides additional videos, activities, tools, and learning aids to support you as you study!

Practice skills and complete your homework online with the **Personal Math Trainer**. Your Personal Math Trainer provides a variety of learning aids, including videos, guided examples, and step-by-step solutions, that develop and improve your understanding of math concepts.

Personal Math Trainer

Online Assessment and Intervention

my.hrw.com

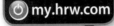

Math On the Spot

my.hrw.com

Math On the Spot video tutorials provide step-by-step instruction of the math concepts covered in each example.

Animated Math activities let you interactively explore and practice key math concepts and skills.

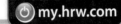

Animated Math

my.hrw.com

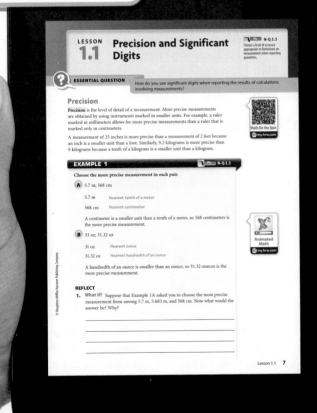

LESSON **1.1** **Precision and Significant Digits**

N-Q.1.3 Choose a level of accuracy appropriate to limitations on measurement when reporting quantities.

ESSENTIAL QUESTION How do you use significant digits when reporting the results of calculations involving measurements?

Precision

Precision is the level of detail of a measurement. More precise measurements are obtained by using instruments marked in smaller units. For example, a ruler marked in millimeters allows for more precise measurements than a ruler that is marked only in centimeters.

A measurement of 25 inches is more precise than a measurement of 2 feet because an inch is a smaller unit than a foot. Similarly, 9.2 kilograms is more precise than 9 kilograms because a tenth of a kilogram is a smaller unit than a kilogram.

EXAMPLE 1 N-Q.1.3

Choose the more precise measurement in each pair.

A 5.7 m; 568 cm

5.7 m — Nearest tenth of a meter

568 cm — Nearest centimeter

A centimeter is a smaller unit than a tenth of a meter, so 568 centimeters is the more precise measurement.

B 31 oz; 31.32 oz

31 oz — Nearest ounce

31.32 oz — Nearest hundredth of an ounce

A hundredth of an ounce is smaller than an ounce, so 31.32 ounces is the more precise measurement.

REFLECT

1. **What if?** Suppose that Example 1A asked you to choose the most precise measurement from among 5.7 m, 5.683 m, and 568 cm. Now what would the answer be? Why?

Lesson 1.1 **7**

© Houghton Mifflin Harcourt Publishing Company

FL21

Standards for Mathematical Practice

The topics described in the Standards for Mathematical Content will vary from year to year. However, the *way* in which you learn, study, and think about mathematics will not. The Standards for Mathematical Practice describe skills that you will use in all of your math courses. These pages show some features of your book that will help you gain these skills and use them to master this year's topics.

MP.1.1 Make sense of problems and persevere in solving them.

Mathematically proficient students start by explaining to themselves the meaning of a problem… They analyze givens, constraints, relationships, and goals. They make conjectures about the form… of the solution and plan a solution pathway…

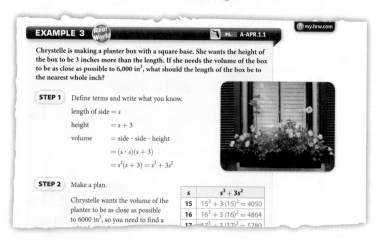

Problem-solving examples and exercises lead students through problem solving steps.

MP.2.1 Reason abstractly and quantitatively.

Mathematically proficient students… bring two complementary abilities to bear on problems…: the ability to decontextualize— to abstract a given situation and represent it symbolically… and the ability to contextualize, to pause… in order to probe into the referents for the symbols involved.

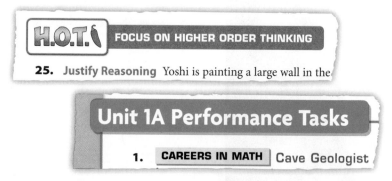

Focus on Higher Order Thinking exercises in every lesson and **Performance Tasks** in every unit require you to use logical reasoning, represent situations symbolically, use mathematical models to solve problems, and state your answers in terms of a problem context.

MP.3.1 Construct viable arguments and critique the reasoning of others.

Mathematically proficient students... justify their conclusions, [and]... distinguish correct... reasoning from that which is flawed.

REFLECT

1. **Make a Conjecture** How can you write the square root or the cube number *n* as the number *n* with an exponent?

 **ESSENTIAL QUESTION CHECK-IN**

Essential Question Check-in and **Reflect** in every lesson ask you to evaluate statements, explain relationships, apply mathematical principles, make conjectures, construct arguments, and justify your reasoning.

MP.4.1 Model with mathematics.

Mathematically proficient students can apply... mathematics... to... problems... in everyday life, society, and the workplace.

EXAMPLE 2 Real World

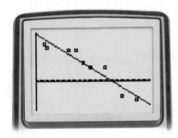 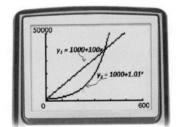

Real-world examples and **mathematical modeling** apply mathematics to other disciplines and real-world contexts such as science and business.

MP.5.1 Use appropriate tools strategically.

Mathematically proficient students consider the available tools when solving a... problem... [and] are... able to use technological tools to explore and deepen their understanding...

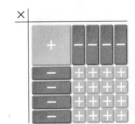  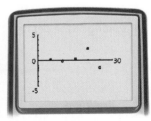

Exploration Activities in lessons use concrete and technological tools, such as manipulatives or graphing calculators, to explore mathematical concepts.

MP.6.1 Attend to precision.

Mathematically proficient students… communicate precisely… with others and in their own reasoning… [They] give carefully formulated explanations…

Key Vocabulary

accuracy *(exactitud)*
The closeness of a given measurement to the actual measurement.

Precision refers not only to the correctness of calculations but also to the proper use of mathematical language and symbols. **Communicate Mathematical Ideas** exercises and **Key Vocabulary** highlighted for each module and unit help you learn and use the language of math to communicate mathematics precisely.

MP.7.1 Look for and make use of structure.

Mathematically proficient students… look closely to discern a pattern or structure… They can also step back for an overview and shift perspectives.

$$(x + y)(x + z) = x^2 + xz + xy + yz$$

Product = a — Product = c

$$\left(\boxed{}\, x + \boxed{} \right)\left(\boxed{}\, x + \boxed{} \right) = ax^2 + bx + c$$

Sum of outer and inner products = b

Throughout the lessons, you will observe regularity in mathematical structures in order to make generalizations and make connections between related problems. For example, you can see the same structure used when learning to multiply binomials and factor trinomials.

MP.8.1 Look for and express regularity in repeated reasoning.

Mathematically proficient students… look both for general methods and for shortcuts… [and] maintain oversight of the process, while attending to the details.

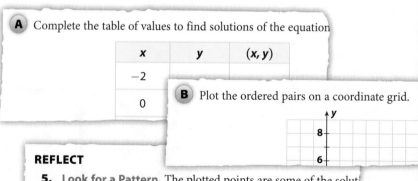

A Complete the table of values to find solutions of the equation

x	y	(x, y)
−2		
0		

B Plot the ordered pairs on a coordinate grid.

REFLECT

5. **Look for a Pattern** The plotted points are some of the soluti equation. What appears to be true about them?

Examples in your book group similar types of problems together to allow you to look for patterns and make generalizations.

REVIEW OF GRADE 8 PART 1

Review Test

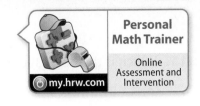

Personal
Math Trainer

Online
Assessment and
Intervention

my.hrw.com

Selected Response

1. Which is equivalent to $(3^{-4})^6$?

(A) 3^2

(C) $\dfrac{1}{3^{24}}$

(B) -12^6

(D) $\dfrac{1}{3^{10}}$

2. Simplify $-8\sqrt{-15+31}$.

(A) -44.5

(C) 8

(B) -32

(D) 31

3. A passenger plane travels at about 7.62×10^2 feet per second. The plane takes 1.23×10^4 seconds to reach its destination. About how far must the plane travel to reach its destination?

(A) 9.37×10^6 feet

(C) 8.85×10^8 feet

(B) 9.37×10^8 feet

(D) 8.85×10^6 feet

4. Which describes the linear function in the table?

x	$f(x)$
-5	25
-3	13
2	-17
3	-23

(A) $f(x) = \frac{1}{6}x + 5$

(C) $f(x) = -6x + 5$

(B) $f(x) = \frac{1}{6}x - 5$

(D) $f(x) = -6x - 5$

5. A remote-control airplane descends at a rate of 3 feet per second. After 6 seconds the plane is 89 feet above the ground. Which equation models this situation, and what is the height of the plane after 12 seconds?

(A) $y - 89 = -3(x - 6)$; 71 feet

(B) $y - 3 = 89(x - 6)$; 537 feet

(C) $y - 89 = -6(x - 3)$; 35 feet

(D) $y - 6 = -3(x - 89)$; 237 feet

6. Which of the following is *not* a congruence transformation?

(A) a dilation with scale factor 1

(B) a reflection across the *y*-axis

(C) a translation 5 units down

(D) a dilation with scale factor 2

7. In the gift shop of the History of Flight museum, Elisa bought a kit to make a model of a jet airplane. The actual plane is 20 feet long with a wingspan of 16 feet. The finished model will be 15 inches long. What will be the wingspan of the model?

(A) 6 inches

(C) 18.8 inches

(B) 12 inches

(D) 21.3 inches

8. What is the value of n?

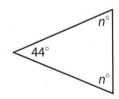

(A) $n = 11.7°$

(C) $n = 68°$

(B) $n = 18°$

(D) $n = 118°$

9. Melanie is making a piece of jewelry that is in the shape of a right triangle. The two shorter sides of the piece of jewelry are 12 mm and 9 mm. Find the perimeter of the piece of jewelry.

(A) 36 mm

(C) 32 mm

(B) 34 mm

(D) 30 mm

10. What is the distance, to the nearest tenth, from $S(4, -1)$ to $W(-2, 3)$?

(A) -2.0 units

(C) 2.6 units

(B) 0.0 units

(D) 7.2 units

11. Which is the best estimate of $\sqrt{285}$?

Ⓐ 12.83 Ⓒ 20.88

Ⓑ 16.88 Ⓓ 20.93

12. Harry and Selma start driving from the same location. Harry drives 42 miles north while Selma drives 144 miles east. How far apart are Harry and Selma when they stop?

Ⓐ 20,736 miles

Ⓑ 22,500 miles

Ⓒ 1,764 miles

Ⓓ 150 miles

Mini-Tasks

13. In Hannah's science report, she says that the average distance between the Sun and Earth is about 9.3×10^7 miles. Show how to write this number in standard notation.

_____

14. A summer theater pass costs $24.75. Every time the pass is used, $2.75 is deducted from the balance. Write an equation to represent this situation.

_____

15. Describe a possible situation that could be modeled by the graph.

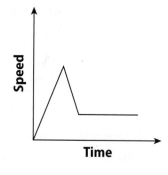

_____

_____

_____

16. Dilate the figure by a scale factor of 1.5 with the origin as the center of dilation. Graph the new figure below with the original figure.

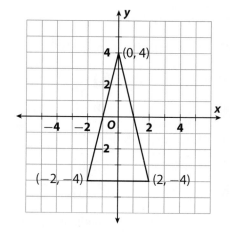

17. Does the following graph display a function? Explain.

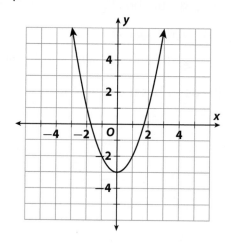

_____

_____

_____

REVIEW OF GRADE 8 PART 2

Review Test

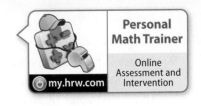

Personal
Math Trainer

Online
Assessment and
Intervention

my.hrw.com

Selected Response

1. What is the equation of the line shown in the graph?

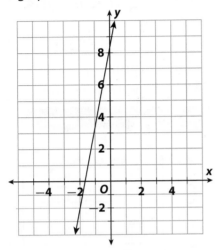

(A) $y = -5x + 8$ (C) $y = -6x + 8$

(B) $y = 6x + 8$ (D) $y = 5x + 8$

2. What is the solution of $-4c + 10 + 8c = 86$?

(A) $c = -8$ (C) $c = 24$

(B) $c = 19$ (D) $c = 76$

3. Which of the following equations has exactly one solution?

(A) $c + 2 = c + 2$ (C) $c + 2 = c - 2$

(B) $c = -c + 2$ (D) $c - c = 2$

4. Which ordered pair is a solution of the system of equations?

$$\begin{cases} y = 3x + 1 \\ y = 5x - 3 \end{cases}$$

(A) $(2, 3)$ (C) $(1, 2)$

(B) $(0, 1)$ (D) $(2, 7)$

5. A bicyclist heads east at 18 km/h. After she has traveled 19.2 kilometers, another cyclist sets out from the same starting point in the same direction going 30 km/h. How long will it take the second cyclist to catch up to the first cyclist?

(A) 2.6 hours (C) 1.6 hours

(B) 2.1 hours (D) 1.1 hours

6. Which of these functions is *not* a linear function?

(A) $f(x) = 3 - \frac{x}{3}$

(B) $f(x) = 3^x + 4$

(C) $f(x) = 3^3 - 3x$

(D) $f(x) = 3(4 - x) + 3$

7. Which function has the greatest rate of change?

(A) $y = 11x - 8$

(B) A fitness club charges a $200 membership fee plus monthly fees of $25.

(C) $y = -8x$

(D) $\{(-1, -2), (1, 2), (3, 6), (5, 10), (7, 14)\}$

8. You buy hats for $12 and sell them for $8 each. What does the graph of the profits look like?

(A) a curve that goes up

(B) a line that goes down

(C) a curve that goes down

(D) a line that goes up

9. An artist is creating a large conical sculpture for a park. The cone has a height of 19 feet and a diameter of 28 feet. What is the volume of the sculpture to the nearest hundredth?

Ⓐ 278.41 ft³   Ⓒ 3,897.79 ft³

Ⓑ 1,241.33 ft³   Ⓓ 11,693.36 ft³

10. A cylindrical barrel has a radius of 4.2 meters and a height of 3 meters. Tripling which dimension(s) will triple the volume of the barrel?

Ⓐ height

Ⓑ radius

Ⓒ both height and radius

Ⓓ neither height nor radius

11. Which equation best models the data in the scatter plot?

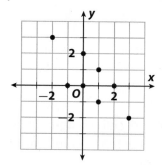

Ⓐ $y = -x + 1$ Ⓒ $y = x + 1$

Ⓑ $y = -x - 1$ Ⓓ $y = x - 1$

Mini-Tasks

12. Write a function that converts x days to y hours.

_____

13. Solve $h - 8 = 3h + 3$.

_____

14. Solve the system using any method.

$$\begin{cases} 2x - 5y = -22 \\ x + 3y = 11 \end{cases}$$

_____

15. Rewrite the equation $2y + 3x = 4$ in slope-intercept form. Then find the slope and y-intercept.

_____

_____

16. Find the slope of the line that passes through the points $(-3, 6)$ and $(4, 2)$.

_____

17. Describe the correlation in the scatter plot and explain what it means in the given situation.

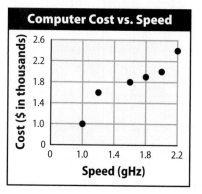

_____

_____

18. Use the graph to identify the slope and y-intercept. Then explain what each means in the context of the problem.

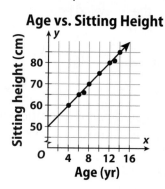

_____

_____

_____

_____

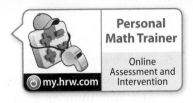
Selected Response

1. A movie theater charges $8.50 for a ticket. To help the local animal shelter, the theater agrees to reduce the price of each ticket by $0.50 for every can of pet food a customer donates. Which equation gives the ticket cost y for a customer who contributes x cans?

   Ⓐ $y = 8.5 - 0.50x$

   Ⓑ $y = 9x - 0.5$

   Ⓒ $y = 8.5 + 0.50x$

   Ⓓ $y = -9x - 0.5$

2. The population of a Midwestern suburb is growing exponentially. The chart shows its population for four consecutive years. Which rule gives the population P_n after n years? Use $n = 1$ to represent Year 1.

Year	Year 1	Year 2	Year 3	Year 4
Population	6500	7800	9360	11,232

   Ⓐ $P_1 = 7800, P_n = 2.3P_{n-1}$

   Ⓑ $P_1 = 6500, P_n = 1.2P_{n-1}$

   Ⓒ $P_1 = 6500, P_n = 2.3P_{n-1}$

   Ⓓ $P_1 = 7800, P_n = 1.2P_{n-1}$

3. Ticket sales for the first 5 nights of a new play form the sequence 400, 399, 396, 387, 360, ... If this pattern continues, what rule gives the number of tickets sold on the nth night?

   Ⓐ $a_n = a_{n-1} - 3^{(n-1)}$

   Ⓑ $a_n = a_n - 3^{(n-1)}$

   Ⓒ $a_n = a_n - 3^n$

   Ⓓ $a_n = a_{n-1} - 3^n$

4. Which is the graph of $\begin{cases} y < -3x + 2 \\ y \geq 4x - 1 \end{cases}$?

Ⓐ

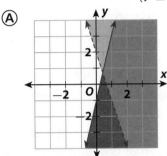

Ⓑ

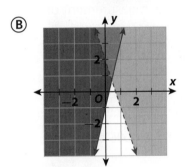

Ⓒ

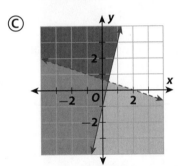

Ⓓ

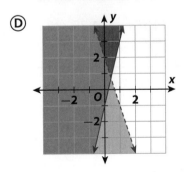

5. Which represents a price that increases at a constant rate per ounce for ordered pairs in the form (ounces, price)?

  Ⓐ (8, 0.50), (12, 1.00), (24, 1.50), (32, 2.00)

  Ⓑ (8, 0.60), (12, 0.90), (24, 1.80), (32, 2.40)

  Ⓒ (8, 0.80), (12, 1.20), (24, 1.60), (32, 2.00)

  Ⓓ (8, 0.40), (12, 0.80), (24, 1.60), (32, 3.20)

6. A micrometer used in a factory measures thickness to one hundredth of a millimeter. This micrometer is used to measure the diameter of a ball bearing that is about 1.7 cm across. What is a reasonable value and error for the measurement of the bearing's diameter?

  Ⓐ 2.25 cm $\pm$ 0.05 cm

  Ⓑ 1.715 cm $\pm$ 0.005 cm

  Ⓒ 2.354 cm $\pm$ 0.005 cm

  Ⓓ 1.6713 cm $\pm$ 0.0005 cm

Mini-Tasks

7. How many terms are in the algebraic expression $2x - 9xy + 17y$?

_____

8. Solve $y = \frac{5}{8}b + 10$ for b.

_____

9. Solve $-0.25 + 1.75x < -1.75 + 2.25x$.

_____

10. Solve $\begin{cases} -7x + 5y = -5 \\ -9x + 5y = 5 \end{cases}$ by elimination. Express your answer as an ordered pair.

_____

11. Write an exponential function to model a population of 390 animals that decreases at an annual rate of 11%. Then estimate the value of the function after 5 years (to the nearest whole number).

_____

12. Kristi rides her bike to school and has an odometer that measures the distance traveled so far. She subtracts this distance from the distance to the school and records the distance that remains. What are the intercepts of the function represented by the table? What do the intercepts represent?

Time traveled (min)	Distance remaining (ft)
0	5,000
2	3,750
4	2,500
6	1,250
8	0

_____

_____

_____

_____

_____

ALGEBRA 1 PART 2

Benchmark Test

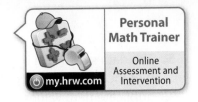

Personal
Math Trainer

Online
Assessment and
Intervention

my.hrw.com

Selected Response

1. Aaron won $500 in an essay contest. He invests the money in an interest-earning account. The table shows how much money he has in the account. Find an appropriate model for the amount that Aaron will have in the account after t years. Then, use the model to predict approximately when Aaron will have $1000 in the account.

Aaron's Account	
Year	Value
1	$520.00
2	$540.80
3	$562.43
4	$584.93
5	$608.33

Ⓐ $V(t) = 500(1.04)^t$; about 18 years

Ⓑ $V(t) = 500(1.04t)$; about 20 years

Ⓒ $V(t) = 500(1.04t)$; about 10 years

Ⓓ $V(t) = 400(1.06)^t$; about 9 years

2. How could you translate the graph of $y = -x^2$ to produce the graph of $y = -x^2 - 4$?

Ⓐ Translate the graph of $y = -x^2$ down 4 units.

Ⓑ Translate the graph of $y = -x^2$ up 4 units.

Ⓒ Translate the graph of $y = -x^2$ left 4 units.

Ⓓ Translate the graph of $y = -x^2$ right 4 units.

3. Which shows a box-and-whisker plot of the data 7, 9, 11, 12, 13, 15, 12, 17, 18, 12, 9, 7, 12, 15, 18, 10?

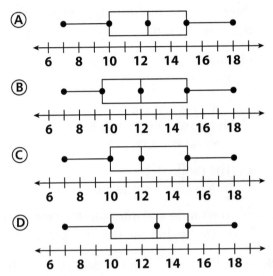

4. Explain whether $p + 4r^2$ will be positive or negative if p is positive. Is this always true?

Ⓐ $p + 4r^2$ will always be positive because the value of p can never be less than 4.

Ⓑ $p + 4r^2$ will always be positive because the value of p depends on the value of $4r^2$.

Ⓒ $p + 4r^2$ will always be positive because the value of p is always greater than the value of $4r^2$.

Ⓓ $p + 4r^2$ will always be positive because p and $4r^2$ are each always positive.

5. The data set shown by the box-and-whisker plot includes a single outlier and no duplicate data values.

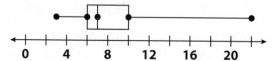

Which statement describes the effect on the range and interquartile range of the data set when the outlier is removed?

Ⓐ The interquartile range increases, but the range decreases.

Ⓑ The range and interquartile range both decrease, but the interquartile range decreases more.

Ⓒ The range decreases, but the interquartile range increases.

Ⓓ The range and interquartile range both decrease, but the range decreases more.

6. Look for a pattern in the data set. Which kind of model best describes the data?

Population Growth of Bacteria	
Time (hours)	Number of bacteria
0	2,000
1	5,000
2	12,500
3	31,250
4	78,125

Ⓐ cubic

Ⓑ exponential

Ⓒ quadratic

Ⓓ linear

7. Subtract. Simplify your answer.

$$\frac{x^2 + x + 6}{5x^3 + 8x^2 + 3x} - \frac{-4x^2 + 6}{5x^3 + 8x^2 + 3x}$$

Ⓐ $\dfrac{1}{x + 3}$

Ⓒ $\dfrac{-3x^2 + x + 12}{5x^3 + 8x^2 + 3x}$

Ⓑ $\dfrac{5x + 1}{5x^2 + 8x + 3}$

Ⓓ $\dfrac{5x^2 + x}{5x^3 + 8x^2 + 3x}$

Mini-Tasks

8. What is the coefficient of x in the expression $(5a)x - 17x^2 + 14a$?

_____

9. Consider the following box plots.

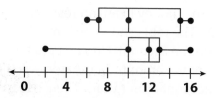

Which data set has the greater median? Which has the greater interquartile range?

_____

_____

_____

10. The PGA tour is for male professional golfers; the LPGA tour is for female professional golfers. Earnings for the top 50 golfers on each tour in 2010 are modeled by the functions in the table and the graph. Compare earnings as a function of rank for the PGA and the LPGA.

PGA Earnings, 2010

Rank	Earnings ($1000s)
1	4.95
10	3.53
20	2.87
30	2.41
40	1.88
50	1.61

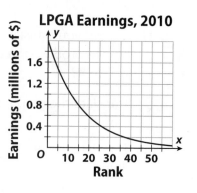

_____

_____

_____

_____

Numbers and Expressions

MODULE **1**

Relationships Between Quantities

FL N-Q.1.1, N-Q.1.3

MODULE **2**

Exponents and Real Numbers

FL N-RN.1.1, N-RN.1.2, N-RN.2.3

MODULE **3**

Expressions

FL N-Q.1.1, N-Q.1.2, A-SSE.1.1, A-SSE.1.1a, A-SSE.1.1b, A-SSE.1.2

CAREERS IN MATH

Cave Geologist A cave geologist uses math from algebra and geometry up through higher-level math to study caves, find resources in them, or organize their excavation. He or she uses math for statistical analysis of the data he or she gathers.

If you're interested in a career in cave geology, you should study these mathematical subjects:
- Algebra
- Geometry
- Statistics
- Calculus

Research other careers that require the use of geometry and statistics.

Unit 1A Performance Task

At the end of the unit, check out how **cave geologists** use math.

Vocabulary Preview

Use the puzzle to preview key vocabulary from this unit. Unscramble the circled letters to answer the riddle at the bottom of the page.

Across

4. expressions that represent the same quantity are said to be this (Lesson 3.2)

5. a word that describes terms that have the same variable raised to the same exponent (Lesson 3.2)

7. a mathematical phrase that contains operations, numbers, and/or variables (Lesson 3.1)

Down

1. how a set of numbers under an operation is described when the result of that operation is an element of the same set (Lesson 2.2)

2. number multiplied by a variable (Lesson 3.1)

3. the quantity under a radical symbol (Lesson 2.1)

6. nth root indicated in a radical expression (Lesson 2.1)

Q: What did the cucumber say to the vinegar?

A: We are in a ___ ___ ___ ___ ___ ___!

Relationships Between Quantities

MODULE 1

LESSON 1.1
Precision and Significant Digits
 FL N-Q.1.3

LESSON 1.2
Dimensional Analysis
 FL N-Q.1.1

ESSENTIAL QUESTION

How do you calculate when the numbers are measurements?

Real-World Video

In order to function properly and safely, electronics must be manufactured to a high degree of accuracy. Material tolerances and component alignment must be precisely matched in order to not interfere with each other.

 my.hrw.com

Are YOU Ready?

Complete these exercises to review skills you will need for this module.

Rounding and Estimation

EXAMPLE   Round 25.35 to the nearest whole number.

25.35   Locate the digit to the right of the whole number.

25   Because it is not 5 or greater, do not round up the whole number.

Round to the place value in parentheses.

1. 3.24 (tenths) _____

2. 0.51 (ones) _____

3. 35.8 (tens) _____

Compare and Order Real Numbers

EXAMPLE   Compare 2.11 to 2.02.

2.11   Align the numbers at the decimal point.

2.02   Compare each place value from left to right.

$2.11 > 2.02$ Because $1 > 0$

Compare. Write $<$, $>$, or $=$.

4. 3.01 ◯ 4

5. 80.2 ◯ 8.03

6. 9.001 ◯ 9.010

7. 1.11 ◯ 1.01

8. 3.2 ◯ 3.2

9. 0.154 ◯ 0.145

Measure with Customary and Metric Units

EXAMPLE   Measure the line segment in inches and in centimeters.

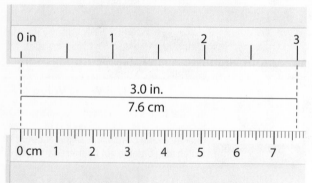

Measure from end to end, starting at 0.

Remember that metric rulers are divided into tens, but customary rulers are not.

3.0 in.

7.6 cm

Measure each item to the unit in parentheses.

10. the length of your foot (inches) _____

11. the width of your index finger (millimeters) _____

12. the height of your desk chair (feet) _____

Reading Start-Up

Visualize Vocabulary

Use the review words to complete the bubble map. You may put more than one word in each bubble.

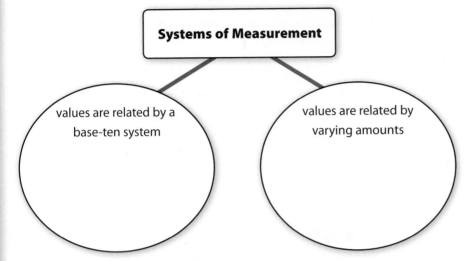

Systems of Measurement

values are related by a base-ten system

values are related by varying amounts

Vocabulary

Review Words
- customary system of measurement *(sistema usual de medidas)*
- decimal system *(sistema decimal)*
- metric system of measurement *(sistema métrico)*

Preview Words
- conversion factor
- dimensional analysis
- precision
- significant digits

Understand Vocabulary

Complete the sentences using the preview words. You may refer to the module, the glossary, or a dictionary.

1. The level of detail of a measurement, determined by the unit of measure, is _____.

2. _____ are the digits used to express the precision of a measurement.

3. _____ is a method of determining the proper units in an algebraic solution.

4. The ratio of two equal quantities in different units is a _____.

Active Reading

Layered Book Before beginning the module, create a Layered Book for taking notes as you read a chapter. Use two flaps for each lesson from this module. As you study each lesson, write important ideas such as vocabulary, properties, and formulas under the appropriate flap.

Unpacking the Standards

Understanding the standards and the vocabulary terms in the standards will help you know exactly what you are expected to learn in this module.

 **N-Q.1.3**

Choose a level of accuracy appropriate to limitations on measurement when reporting quantities.

What It Means to You

You will learn to use precision and significant digits when calculating with measurements.

UNPACKING EXAMPLE N-Q.1.3

Which is the more precise measurement: 5.7 m or 568 cm?
Which measurement uses more significant digits: 5.7 m or 568 cm?

	Precision	Significant Digits
5.7 m	5.7 m = **570** cm is measured to nearest *ten* centimeters.	**5.7** has 2 significant digits.
568 cm	**568** cm is measured to the nearest centimeter.	**568** has 3 significant digits.

568 cm is more precise because it is measured to a smaller unit.
568 cm has more significant digits.

 **N-Q.1.1**

Use units as a way to understand problems and to guide the solution of multi-step problems…

Key Vocabulary

unit analysis/ dimensional analysis (*análisis dimensional*)
A practice of converting measurements and checking among computed measurements.

What It Means to You

You will learn to convert between measurements and calculated quantities.

UNPACKING EXAMPLE N-Q.1.1

Li's car gets 40 miles per gallon of gas. At this rate, she can go 420 miles on a full tank. She has driven 245 miles on the current tank. How many gallons of gas are left in the tank?

STEP 1   Find the number of miles remaining.

$$420 \text{ mi} - 245 \text{ mi} = 175 \text{ mi}$$

STEP 2   Find the number of gallons.

$$x = 175 \text{ mi} \cdot \frac{\text{gal}}{40 \text{ mi}} = \frac{175 \text{ mi}}{40 \text{ mi}} \text{ gal} = 4.375 \text{ gal}$$

According to these measurements there are 4.375 gallons left in the tank.

Visit **my.hrw.com** to see all **Florida Math Standards** unpacked.

⏻ my.hrw.com

Precision and Significant Digits

FL N-Q.1.3
Choose a level of accuracy appropriate to limitations on measurement when reporting quantities.

? ESSENTIAL QUESTION How do you use significant digits when reporting the results of calculations involving measurements?

Precision

Precision is the level of detail of a measurement. More precise measurements are obtained by using instruments marked in smaller units. For example, a ruler marked in millimeters allows for more precise measurements than a ruler that is marked only in centimeters.

A measurement of 25 inches is more precise than a measurement of 2 feet because an inch is a smaller unit than a foot. Similarly, 9.2 kilograms is more precise than 9 kilograms because a tenth of a kilogram is a smaller unit than a kilogram.

Math On the Spot
my.hrw.com

EXAMPLE 1
FL N-Q.1.3

Choose the more precise measurement in each pair.

A 5.7 m; 568 cm

5.7 m	*Nearest tenth of a meter*
568 cm	*Nearest centimeter*

A centimeter is a smaller unit than a tenth of a meter, so 568 centimeters is the more precise measurement.

B 31 oz; 31.32 oz

31 oz	*Nearest ounce*
31.32 oz	*Nearest hundredth of an ounce*

A hundredth of an ounce is smaller than an ounce, so 31.32 ounces is the more precise measurement.

Animated Math
my.hrw.com

REFLECT

1. **What if?** Suppose that Example 1A asked you to choose the most precise measurement from among 5.7 m, 5.683 m, and 568 cm. Now what would the answer be? Why?

_____

_____

_____

_____

YOUR TURN

Choose the more precise measurement in each pair.

2. 2 lb; 31 oz _____

3. 4 in.; 0 ft _____

4. 6.77 m; 676.5 cm _____

5. 1 mi; 5,280 ft _____

EXPLORE ACTIVITY 🏴 **FL** **N-Q.1.3**

Exploring Effects of Precision on Calculations

A Measure the width of a book cover to the nearest centimeter.

Width of book cover: _____ cm

Measure the length of the book cover to the nearest tenth of a centimeter.

Length of book cover: _____ cm

B Determine the minimum and maximum possible values for the actual width and length of the book cover.

Example: When you measure to the nearest centimeter and get a measurement of 3 cm, the actual measurement is greater than or equal to 2.5 cm and less than 3.5 cm.

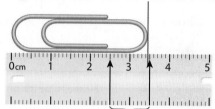

When measuring to the nearest centimeter, lengths in this range are rounded to 3 cm.

Minimum width: _____   Maximum width: _____

Minimum length: _____   Maximum length: _____

C Calculate the minimum and maximum possible areas of the book cover. Round your answers to the nearest square centimeter.

Minimum area = minimum width × minimum length

= (_____) × (_____) ≈ (_____)

Maximum area = maximum width × maximum length

= (_____) × (_____) ≈ (_____)

REFLECT

6. Analyze Relationships How would the precision of the calculated area change if the length and width measurements were more precise?

_____

_____

Significant Digits

In the preceding Explore Activity, there was a wide range of possible values for the area of the book cover. This raises the question of how a calculated measurement, like an area, should be reported. Keeping track of **significant digits** is one way to resolve this dilemma. Significant digits are the digits in a measurement that carry meaning about the precision of the measurement.

Math On the Spot

my.hrw.com

Identifying Significant Digits

Rule	Examples
All nonzero digits are significant.	37.85 has 4 significant digits. 622 has 3 significant digits.
Zeros between two other significant digits are significant.	806 has 3 significant digits. 0.9007 has 4 significant digits.
Zeros at the end of a number to the right of a decimal point are significant.	1.4000 has 5 significant digits. 0.270 has 3 significant digits.
Zeros to the left of the first nonzero digit in a number are *not* significant.	0.0070 has 2 significant digits. 0.01048 has 4 significant digits.
Zeros at the end of a number without a decimal point are assumed *not* to be significant.	404,500 has 4 significant digits. 12,000,000 has 2 significant digits.

Math Talk

Mathematical Practices

A student claimed that 0.045 m and 0.0045 m have the same number of significant digits. Do you agree or disagree? Why?

EXAMPLE 2

FL N-Q.1.3

Determine the number of significant digits in the measurement 840.090 m.

STEP 1 Find all nonzero digits. These are significant digits.

840.090   *8, 4, and 9 are nonzero digits.*

STEP 2 Find zeros after the last nonzero digit and to the right of the decimal point. These are significant digits.

840.090   *The zero after the 9 in the hundredths place is significant.*

STEP 3 Find zeros between the significant digits found in the previous steps. These are significant digits.

840.090   *There are 2 zeros between the significant digits 4 and 9.*

STEP 4 Count all the significant digits you have found.

840.090   *All the digits in this number are significant.*

So, 840.090 m has 6 significant digits.

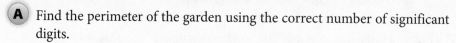

YOUR TURN

Determine the number of significant digits in each measurement.

7. 36,000 ft _____   **8.** 0.01 kg _____   **9.** 15.0 L _____

Operations with Significant Digits

When you perform calculations with measurements of differing precision, the number of significant digits in the solution may differ from the number of significant digits in the original measurements. Use the rules in this table to determine how many significant digits to include in the result of a calculation.

Rules for Significant Digits in Calculations	
Operation	**Rule**
Addition or Subtraction	The sum or difference must be rounded to the same place value as the last significant digit of the least precise measurement.
Multiplication or Division	The product or quotient must have no more significant digits than the least precise measurement.

EXAMPLE 3

 FL N-Q.1.3

A rectangular garden plot measures 16 feet by 23.6 feet.

A Find the perimeter of the garden using the correct number of significant digits.

$$\begin{aligned} \text{Perimeter} &= \text{sum of side lengths} \\ &= 16 \text{ ft} + 16 \text{ ft} + 23.6 \text{ ft} + 23.6 \text{ ft} \\ &= 79.2 \text{ ft} \end{aligned}$$

The least precise measurement is 16 ft. Its last significant digit is in the ones place. So round the sum to the ones place: 79 ft.

The perimeter is 79 feet.

B Find the area of the garden using the correct number of significant digits.

$$\begin{aligned} \text{Area} &= \text{width} \cdot \text{length} \\ &= 16 \text{ ft} \cdot 23.6 \text{ ft} \\ &= 377.6 \text{ ft}^2 \end{aligned}$$

The least precise measurement, 16 ft, has 2 significant digits, so round to a number containing 2 significant digits: 380 ft^2.

The area is 380 ft^2.

REFLECT

10. Justify Reasoning Why must the area have no more than 2 significant digits?

_____

_____

_____

_____

11. Critical Thinking Can the perimeter of a rectangular garden have more significant digits than the measures of its length or width have? Explain.

_____

_____

_____

YOUR TURN

12. Find the perimeter and area of a sandbox that has a width of 4.5 ft and a length of 3.45 ft. Write your answers using the correct number of significant

digits. _____

13. In chemistry class, Julio measured the mass and volume of an unknown substance in order to calculate its density. It had a mass of 23.92 g and a volume of 2.1 mL. Find the density of the substance in g/mL, using the

correct number of significant digits. _____

Guided Practice

Choose the more precise measurement in each pair. Then state the minimum and maximum possible values for the more precise measurement. (Example 1 and Explore Activity)

1. 18 cm; 177 mm

_____

_____

2. 3 yd; 10 ft

_____

_____

3. 71 cm; 0.7 m

_____

_____

4. 1.5 ft; 19 in.

_____

_____

Determine the number of significant digits in each measurement. (Example 2)

5. 12,080 ft _____

6. 0.8 mL _____

7. 1.0065 km _____

A rectangular window has a length of 81.4 cm and a width of 38 cm. Use the correct number of significant digits to write each indicated measure. (Example 3)

8. Find the perimeter.

81.4 cm + 81.4 cm + 38 cm + 38 cm

The unrounded perimeter is _____ cm.

The least precise measurement is _____ cm

Its last significant digit is in the _____ place.

Perimeter rounded to the _____ place:

_____ cm

9. Find the area.

81.4 cm × 38 cm

The unrounded area is _____ cm².

The least precise measurement is _____ cm

It has _____ significant digits.

Area rounded to _____ significant

digits: _____ cm²

10. A model car rolls down a 125.3 centimeter ramp, and continues to roll along the floor for 4.71 meters before it comes to a stop. The car's entire trip takes 2.4 seconds. Find the total distance traveled and the average speed of the car. Use the correct number of significant digits. (Example 3)

STEP 1 Total distance = [____] cm + [____] m

= [____] m + [____] m = [____] m

The least precise measurement is _____ m.

So round the total distance to the _____ place: _____ m.

STEP 2 Speed = $\dfrac{\text{unrounded total distance}}{\text{time}}$ = $\dfrac{[\quad]\text{ m}}{[\quad]\text{ s}}$ = [____] ... m/s

The measurement with the fewest significant digits is _____ s,

with _____ significant digits. So rounding the speed to _____

significant digits is _____ m/s.

The car's average speed is _____.

ESSENTIAL QUESTION CHECK-IN

11. How are significant digits related to calculations using measurements?

_____

_____

1.1 Independent Practice

FL N-Q.1.3

Personal Math Trainer

Online Assessment and Intervention

my.hrw.com

Write each measurement with the indicated number of significant digits.

12. 454.12 kg; 3 significant digits _____

13. 8.45 lb; 2 significant digits _____

14. 9.1 in.; 1 significant digit _____

Order each list of units from most precise to least precise.

15. centimeter, millimeter, decameter, meter, kilometer

_____

_____

16. feet, inches, miles, yards

_____

_____

17. pints, quarts, cups, gallons

_____

_____

18. **Analyze Relationships** How is the precision used in measuring the length and width of a rectangle related to the precision of the resulting area measurement?

_____

_____

_____

_____

Express each calculator result using the rules for significant digits.

19.

40.23+17.0
            57.23

_____

20.

40.23*17.0
           683.91

_____

21.

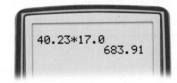

40.23/17.0
       2.366470588

_____

22.

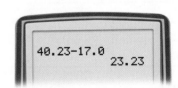

40.23-17.0
           23.23

_____

23. Write this sum to the correct number of significant digits:
34.01 m + 1940 m + 4.6 m ≈

_____

24. Measure the length and width of the pictured book to the nearest tenth of a centimeter. Then use the correct number of significant digits to write the perimeter and area of the book.

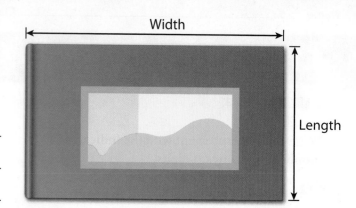

Width

Length

_____

_____

_____

 FOCUS ON HIGHER ORDER THINKING

Work Area

25. Justify Reasoning Yoshi is painting a large wall in the park. He measures the wall and finds that the dimensions are 4 m by 20 m. Yoshi has a can of paint that will cover an area of 81 m². Should he buy more paint? Explain?

_____

_____

_____

_____

_____

26. Make a Conjecture If two measurements have the same number of decimal places and the same number of significant digits, is it ever possible for the result of an operation performed using these measurements to have a different number of decimal places or significant digits than the original measurements? Explain.

_____

_____

_____

27. Explain the Error A student found that the side lengths of a square rug were 1.30 m. The student was asked to report the area using the correct number of significant digits. He wrote the area as 1.7 m². Explain the student's error.

_____

_____

28. Communicate Mathematical Ideas Consider the calculation 4.3 m ÷ 16 s = 0.26875 m/s. Why is it important to use significant digits to round the answer?

_____

_____

_____

LESSON
1.2 Dimensional Analysis

FL N-Q.1.1

Use units as a way to understand problems and to guide the solution of multi-step problems...

? ESSENTIAL QUESTION

How can you convert between metric measurements and customary measurements?

EXPLORE ACTIVITY  FL N-Q.1.1

Exploring Measurement Conversions

In the United States, the customary measurement system is used for everyday tasks such as finding the volume of a bottle or the length of a room. However, scientists throughout the world use the metric system of measurement. To convert between these two systems, you need to use equivalent measures such as those shown in the table.

Metric and Customary Measurements		
Measurement Type	**Metric unit**	**Customary equivalent**
Length	1 meter	3.28 ft
	1 centimeter	0.39 in.
Area	1 square meter	10.76 ft^2
Volume	1 liter	0.26 gal
Mass	1 kilogram	2.2 lb

Use the equivalent measures given in the table to find the capacity of an 8-liter gas tank in gallons.

A From the table: 1 liter (L) = _____ gallons (gal)

B From the diagram, about how many liters are in

1 gallon? _____

8 liters

1 L							

1 gallon	

C Will the number of gallons in an 8-liter gas tank be greater or less than 8?

Explain. _____

_____

_____

D To convert 8 liters to gallons, would you multiply by $\frac{1\ L}{0.26\ gal}$ or by $\frac{0.26\ gal}{1\ L}$?

_____

8 L = _____ gal

REFLECT

1. Analyze Relationships How would you convert from 8 gallons to liters?

_____

Math On the Spot

my.hrw.com

Converting Measurements

Dimensional analysis is a way of using units to help solve problems involving measurements. You can use dimensional analysis to convert units by setting up ratios of two equivalent measurements, such as $\frac{12 \text{ in.}}{1 \text{ ft}}$. These ratios are called **conversion factors**.

EXAMPLE 1

My Notes

The body of a large adult male contains about 12 pints of blood. Use dimensional analysis to convert this quantity to liters. There are about 2.1 pints in a liter.

Identify the given unit and the unit you need to find. Use that information to set up your conversion factor. The given unit should be in the denominator of the conversion factor, so that it will cancel out when multiplied by the given measurement.

$$x \text{ liters} \approx 12 \text{ pt} \cdot \boxed{\text{conversion factor}}$$

$$\approx \frac{12 \text{ pt}}{1} \cdot \frac{1 \text{ liter}}{2.1 \text{ pt}}$$

The pints in the denominator cancel with pints in the numerator.

$$\approx \frac{12 \text{ liters}}{2.1}$$

$$\approx 5.7 \text{ liters}$$

The given quantity has 2 significant digits, so round the converted quantity to 2 significant digits.

The body of a large adult male contains approximately 5.7 liters of blood.

REFLECT

2. **Explain the Error** Elena wanted to convert 30 inches to centimeters. She multiplied 30 by $\frac{1 \text{ in}}{2.5 \text{ cm}}$ and got an answer of 12. What was her error?

_____

_____

_____

_____

_____

Personal Math Trainer

Online Assessment and Intervention

my.hrw.com

YOUR TURN

Use dimensional analysis to convert each measurement.

3. 3 feet ≈ _____ meters

4. 4 inches ≈ _____ yards

5. 12 kg ≈ _____ lb

6. 4 inches ≈ _____ centimeters

Converting Rates

Sometimes you will need to convert not just one measurement, but a ratio of measurements.

When working with a rate such as 50 miles per hour, you might need to know the rate in different units, such as meters per second. This requires two conversion factors: one to convert miles into meters, and one to convert hours into seconds.

Math On the Spot
my.hrw.com

EXAMPLE 2  FL N-Q.1.1

A cyclist travels 105 kilometers in 4.2 hours. Use dimensional analysis to convert the cyclist's speed to miles per minute. Write your answer with the correct number of significant digits. Use 1 mi = 1.61 km.

STEP 1 Identify the rate given and the rate you need to find. Use that information to set up your conversion factors.

$$x \ \frac{\text{miles}}{\text{minute}} \approx \frac{105 \text{ km}}{4.2 \text{ hr}} \cdot \boxed{\textbf{conversion factor}} \cdot \boxed{\textbf{conversion factor}}$$

$$\approx \frac{105 \text{ k\!m}}{4.2 \text{ h\!r}} \cdot \frac{1 \text{ mi}}{1.61 \text{ k\!m}} \cdot \frac{1 \text{ h\!r}}{60 \text{ min}} \qquad \textit{Set up conversion factors so that both km and hr units cancel.}$$

$$\approx \frac{105 \text{ mi}}{4.2 \cdot 1.61 \cdot 60 \text{ min}}$$

$$\approx 0.2588 \text{ mi/min}$$

STEP 2 Determine the number of significant digits in each value: the distance, the time, and both conversion factors:

- 105 km has 3 significant figures.
- 4.2 hours has 2 significant figures.
- 1 mi/1.61 km has 3 significant figures.
- 1 hr/60 min is an exact conversion factor. Significant figures do not apply here, or to any conversion within a measurement system.

The value with the fewest significant digits is the time, 4.2 hr, with 2 significant digits. So the result should be rounded to 2 significant digits.

The cyclist travels approximately 0.26 miles per minute.

REFLECT

7. **Communicate Mathematical Ideas** Tell which of the following conversion factors are exact, and which are approximate: 1000 grams per kilogram, 0.26 gallon per liter, 12 inches per foot. Explain.

_____

_____

_____

_____

YOUR TURN

Use dimensional analysis to make each conversion.

8. A box of books weighs 4.10 kilograms for every meter of its height. Convert this ratio into pounds per foot.

_____

9. A go-kart travels 21 miles per hour. Convert this speed into feet per minute.

_____

10. A tortoise walks 52.0 feet per hour. Convert this speed into inches per minute.

_____

11. A pitcher throws a baseball 90 miles per hour. Convert this speed into feet per second.

_____

Converting Areas

Dimensional analysis can also be used for converting areas. When converting areas, the conversion factor must be squared because area is expressed in square units.

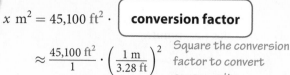

EXAMPLE 3　　　　　　　　FL　N-Q.1.1

The area of a practice field is 45,100 ft². How large is the field in square meters? Write your answer with the correct number of significant digits. Use 1 m = 3.28 ft.

Identify the given unit and the unit you need to find. Use that information to set up your conversion factor.

45,100 ft²

Math Talk

Mathematical Practices

When would you multiply by the cube of a conversion factor?

$$x \text{ m}^2 = 45{,}100 \text{ ft}^2 \cdot \boxed{\textbf{conversion factor}}$$

$$\approx \frac{45{,}100 \text{ ft}^2}{1} \cdot \left(\frac{1 \text{ m}}{3.28 \text{ ft}}\right)^2 \quad \begin{array}{l}\textit{Square the conversion}\\\textit{factor to convert}\\\textit{square units.}\end{array}$$

$$\approx \frac{45{,}100 \text{ ft}^2}{1} \cdot \frac{1 \text{ m}^2}{10.7584 \text{ ft}^2} \quad \begin{array}{l}\textit{The ft}^2 \textit{ in the numerator}\\\textit{cancel the ft}^2 \textit{ in the}\\\textit{denominator.}\end{array}$$

$$\approx \frac{45{,}100 \text{ m}^2}{10.7584}$$

$$\approx 4192.073 \text{ m}^2$$

Because the given measure and the conversion factor both have 3 significant digits, the product should also be rounded to 3 significant digits. The area of the practice field is 4190 square meters.

Personal
Math Trainer

Online Assessment
and Intervention

(⏻) my.hrw.com

YOUR TURN

Use dimensional analysis to make each conversion. Use the equivalent
measures indicated.

12. The surface area of a swimming pool is 373 square feet. What is its surface
area in square meters? (1 m = 3.28 ft) _____

13. A birthday card has an area of 29.1 square inches. What is its area in square
centimeters? (1 in. = 2.54 cm) _____

14. Tom's backyard has an area of 9 square yards. What is its area in square
inches? (1 yd = 36 in.) _____

Guided Practice

Use the diagrams to determine whether you need to multiply or divide by the
indicated value to convert each measurement. (Explore Activity)

1. To convert 5 meters to feet, you need to _____ 5 meters by
3.28 feet per meter.

5 meters ≈ _____ feet

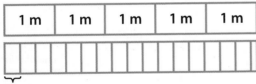

2. To convert 11 liters to gallons, you need to _____ 11 liters by
3.8 liters per gallon.

11 liters ≈ _____ gallons

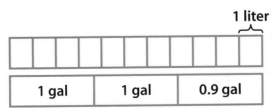

Set up the conversion factor needed for each conversion. Use the table
of equivalent measures on p. 15. (Example 1)

3. meters into feet

4. gallons into liters

5. lb into kg

_____   _____   _____

6. A dripping faucet is wasting 0.5 mL of water every second. How many liters of water does it waste per week? Write your answer with the correct number of significant digits. (Example 2)

STEP 1 Identify equivalent measures. 1 L = _____ mL

1 wk = _____ days   1 day = _____ hr

1 hr = _____ min   1 min = _____ s

STEP 2 Set up conversion factors, cancel units, and calculate.

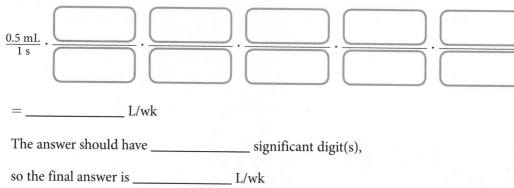

$\dfrac{0.5 \text{ mL}}{1 \text{ s}} \cdot \dfrac{\boxed{}}{\boxed{}} \cdot \dfrac{\boxed{}}{\boxed{}} \cdot \dfrac{\boxed{}}{\boxed{}} \cdot \dfrac{\boxed{}}{\boxed{}} \cdot \dfrac{\boxed{}}{\boxed{}}$

= _____ L/wk

The answer should have _____ significant digit(s),

so the final answer is _____ L/wk

7. If an area can be washed at a rate of 3100 cm^2/minute, how many square inches can be washed per hour? Use the table of equivalent measures on page 15. Write your answer with the correct number of significant digits. (Examples 2 and 3)

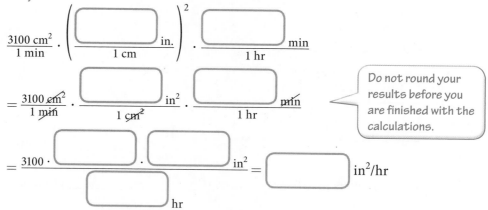

Do not round your results before you are finished with the calculations.

Because the given measure and conversion factor both have _____

significant digits, the equivalent rate is _____ square inches per hour.

ESSENTIAL QUESTION CHECK-IN

8. How is dimensional analysis useful in calculations that involve measurements?

_____

_____

_____

1.2 Independent Practice

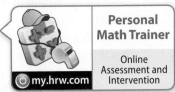

Personal
Math Trainer

Online
Assessment and
Intervention

⏻ my.hrw.com

FL   N-Q.1.1

For Exercises 9–14, choose the conversion factor you need to multiply by to carry out each conversion.

A. $\dfrac{3.28 \text{ ft}}{1 \text{ m}}$ **B.** $\dfrac{0.39 \text{ in.}}{1 \text{ cm}}$ **C.** $\dfrac{2.2 \text{ lb}}{1 \text{ kg}}$

D. $\dfrac{1 \text{ cm}}{0.39 \text{ in.}}$ **E.** $\dfrac{1 \text{ kg}}{2.2 \text{ lb}}$ **F.** $\dfrac{1 \text{ m}}{3.28 \text{ ft}}$

9. feet to meters _____

10. meters to feet _____

11. inches to centimeters _____

12. centimeters to inches _____

13. kg to lb _____

14. lb to kg _____

Use dimensional analysis to make each conversion. Write your answer with the correct number of significant digits. Use the equivalent measures indicated.

15. A bedroom is 5.2 meters wide. Find its width in feet. (1 m ≈ 3.28 ft)

_____

16. A bag of rice has a mass of 3.18 pounds. Find its mass in kilograms. (1 kg ≈ 2.2 lb)

_____

17. A giraffe can run about 14 meters per second. Find its speed in miles per hour. (1 mi = 5280 ft; 1 m ≈ 3.28 ft)

_____

18. The cover of a photo album has an area of 97.5 square inches. Find its area in square centimeters. (1 cm ≈ 0.39 in.)

_____

19. A carpet costs $15 per square foot. (When calculating the price, any fraction of a square foot is counted as a whole square foot.) If the area you want to carpet is 19.7 square meters, how much will it cost to buy the carpet? (1 m ≈ 3.28 ft)

_____

20. Measure the length and width of the outer rectangle to the nearest tenth of a centimeter. Using the correct number of significant digits, write the perimeter in inches and the area in square inches.

Length to nearest tenth of cm:

_____

Width to nearest tenth of cm:

_____

Perimeter in inches:

_____

Area in square inches:

_____

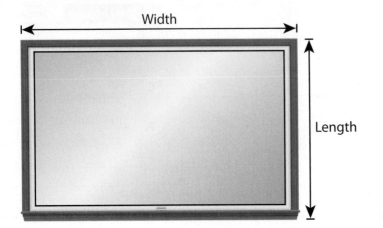

Width

Length

 **FOCUS ON HIGHER ORDER THINKING**

Work Area

21. Represent Real-World Problems Write a real-world scenario in which 12 fluid ounces would need to be converted into liters. Make the conversion, and write the converted measure with the correct number of significant digits. Use 1 fl oz = 0.0296 L.

_____

_____

_____

_____

22. Analyze Relationships When a measurement in inches is converted to centimeters, will the number of centimeters be greater than or less than the number of inches? Explain.

_____

_____

23. Explain the Error A student measured the area of a bulletin board as 2.1 m². To find its area in square feet, he multiplied 2.1 by 3.28, getting an answer of about 6.9 ft². Explain the student's error. What is the correct area in square feet?

_____

_____

_____

_____

Ready to Go On?

1.1 Precision and Significant Digits

Write each measurement with the indicated number of significant digits.

1. 982.1 m^2 (3) _____

2. 1.5244 kg (2) _____

Give the result of each operation with the correct number of significant digits.

3. $170.1 \text{ lb} + 3.44 \text{ lb}$ _____

4. $1.1 \text{ cm} \times 4.28 \text{ cm}$ _____

5. A circle has a radius of 3.07 inches. Using the correct number of significant digits, find the circumference and area of the circle.

_____

1.2 Dimensional Analysis

6. Use dimensional analysis to convert 8 milliliters to fluid ounces.

Use $1 \text{ mL} \approx 0.034 \text{ fl oz}$. _____

Use the table of equivalent measures to answer each question.

7. A designer found the area of a wall to be 3.0 square yards. What is the area of the wall

   in square meters? _____

Measurement type	Metric unit	Customary equivalent
Length	1 m	1.09 yards
Volume	1 L	2.11 pints
Mass	1 kg	2.20 lb

8. Will a stand that can hold up to 40 pounds support a 21-kilogram television? Explain.

_____

9. Scientist A dissolved 1.0 kilogram of salt in 3.0 liters of water. Scientist B dissolved 2.0 pounds of salt in 7.0 pints of water. Which scientist made a more concentrated salt solution? Explain.

_____

_____

? ESSENTIAL QUESTION

10. How are significant digits used in calculations with measurements?

_____

_____

_____

Personal Math Trainer

Online Assessment and Intervention

my.hrw.com

Selected Response

1. Which is the most precise measurement?

   (A) grams

   (B) kilograms

   (C) centigrams

   (D) milligrams

2. Which of the following has 3 significant digits?

   (A) 0.00608

   (B) 0.314

   (C) 94.1

   (D) All of the above

3. Which of the following is the correct conversion factor to multiply by when converting from yards into meters?

   (A) $\dfrac{1.09 \text{ yard}}{1 \text{ meter}}$

   (B) $\dfrac{1 \text{ meter}}{1.09 \text{ yard}}$

   (C) 1 meter

   (D) 1.09 yard

4. What is the cost of 4 pounds of butter if 2 kilograms cost $3.20? Use 1 kg = 2.20 lb.

   (A) $3.20

   (B) $6.40

   (C) $2.91

   (D) $1.45

5. If an area is measured to be 9.1 square meters, what is the area in square yards? Use 1 m = 1.09 yd.

   (A) 8.3 yd²

   (B) 9.9 yd²

   (C) 11 yd²

   (D) 7.7 yd²

6. Which of these values gives the area of a 35.1 cm by 2.6 cm rectangle to the correct number of significant digits?

   (A) 91 cm²

   (B) 91.26 cm²

   (C) 91.3 cm²

   (D) 91.0 cm²

7. Water depth is measured in a unit called *fathoms*. 1 fathom equals exactly 6 feet. The Mariana Trench is 6033.5 fathoms deep. What is its depth in meters? Use 1 m = 3.28 ft.

   (A) 1,840 m

   (B) 19,800 m

   (C) 11,000 m

   (D) 3,290 m

8. A cheetah can run about 68 miles per hour. How fast can it run in meters per minute? Use 1 mi = 1609 m.

   (A) 11,000 m/min

   (B) 2.5 m/min

   (C) 30 m/min

   (D) 1,800 m/min

Mini-Tasks

9. Arrange the following mass measurements in order from least to greatest: 21.3 lb, 2064 g, 16.7 kg, 452 oz. Explain.

   _____

   _____

   _____

   _____

Exponents and Real Numbers

LESSON 2.1
Radicals and Rational Exponents
FL N-RN.1.1, N-RN.1.2

LESSON 2.2
Real Numbers
FL N-RN.2.3

? **ESSENTIAL QUESTION**

What sets of numbers are included in the real numbers?

Real-World Video

Wildlife managers must estimate the sizes of wildlife populations and maintain records on the changes in population. Population increase or decrease is often estimated by using real numbers with exponents.

⏻ my.hrw.com

Getty Images

GO DIGITAL

my.hrw.com

my.hrw.com

Go digital with your write-in student edition, accessible on any device.

Math On the Spot

Scan with your smart phone to jump directly to the online edition, video tutor, and more.

Animated Math

Interactively explore key concepts to see how math works.

Personal Math Trainer

Get immediate feedback and help as you work through practice sets.

Are YOU Ready?

Complete these exercises to review skills you will need for this module.

Personal Math Trainer

Online Assessment and Intervention

my.hrw.com

Exponents

EXAMPLE   Write $(-5)^3$ as a multiplication of factors.
$(-5)(-5)(-5)$ *Write the base −5 times itself 3 times.*

EXAMPLE   Write $21 \cdot 21 \cdot 21 \cdot 21 \cdot 21 \cdot 21$ using a base and an exponent.
21^6 *The base is 21 and the exponent is the number of factors 6.*

Write each expression as a multiplication of factors.

1. 4^2

2. $(-6)^4$

3. 12^1

Write each expression using a base and an exponent.

4. $7 \cdot 7 \cdot 7 \cdot 7 \cdot 7$

5. $33 \cdot 33 \cdot 33 \cdot 33$

6. $(-2) \cdot (-2)$

Evaluate Powers

EXAMPLE   Evaluate $(-3)^4 - 6^2$.
$(-3)(-3)(-3)(-3) - 6 \cdot 6$ *Write as a multiplication of factors.*
$81 - 36$ *Simplify.*
45

Evaluate each expression.

7. $5^1 + (-9)^2$

8. $3^2 \cdot 2^3$

9. $(25)^0 - 5^3$

Squares and Square Roots

EXAMPLE   Find $\sqrt{49}$.
7 *Because $7 \cdot 7 = 49$, 7 is the square root of 49.*

Find each square root.

10. $\sqrt{16}$

11. $\sqrt{81}$

12. $\sqrt{10,000}$

Reading Start-Up

Vocabulary

Review Words

exponent *(exponente)*

rational numbers *(números racionales)*

irrational numbers *(números irracionales)*

Preview Words

radical expression

radicand

index

real numbers

closed

Visualize Vocabulary

Fill in the missing information in the chart below.

Word	Definition	Example
exponent		$3^4 = 3 \cdot 3 \cdot 3 \cdot 3 = 81$ 4 is the exponent.
rational numbers	A number that can be written in the form b/a, where a and b are integers and $b \neq 0$	
	A real number that cannot be expressed as the ratio of two integers	$\pi, \sqrt{2}, e$

Understand Vocabulary

To become familiar with some of the vocabulary terms in the module, complete the following sentences using appropriate preview words. You may refer to the module, the glossary, or a dictionary.

1. The _____ consist of the rational numbers and the irrational numbers.

2. The _____ of a radical expression indicates which root to take of the

   _____ .

Active Reading

Key-Term Fold Before beginning the module, create a Key-Term Fold Note to help you organize what you learn. Write a vocabulary term on each tab of the key-term fold. Under each tab, write the definition of the term and an example of the term.

Unpacking the Standards

Understanding the standards and the vocabulary terms in the standards will help you know exactly what you are expected to learn in this module.

 FL N-RN.1.1

...the meaning of rational expressions follows from extending the properties of integer exponents to those values, allowing for a notation for radicals in terms of rational exponents.

Key Vocabulary

radical *(radical)*
An indicated root of a quantity.

What It Means to You

You can rewrite expressions containing radicals as expressions with rational exponents and vice versa.

UNPACKING EXAMPLE N-RN.1.1

Rewrite $32^{\frac{1}{5}}$ as a radical and simplify.

Raising to the $\frac{1}{5}$ power is the same as taking the 5th root.

$$32^{\frac{1}{5}} = \sqrt[5]{32}$$

$$= \sqrt[5]{2^5}$$

$$= 2$$

 FL N-RN.1.2

Rewrite expressions involving radicals and rational exponents using the properties of exponents.

Key Vocabulary

exponent *(exponente)*
The number that indicates how many times the base in a power is used as a factor.

What It Means to You

You can use the properties of exponents to rewrite and simplify radical expressions and expressions containing rational exponents.

UNPACKING EXAMPLE N-RN.1.2

Simplify $8^{\frac{5}{3}}$.

$$8^{\frac{5}{3}} = 8^{\frac{1}{3} \cdot 5}$$

$$= \left(8^{\frac{1}{3}}\right)^5$$

$$= \left(\sqrt[3]{8}\right)^5$$

$$= \left(\sqrt[3]{2^3}\right)^5$$

$$= 2^5 = 32$$

Visit **my.hrw.com** to see all **Florida Math Standards** unpacked.

my.hrw.com

Radicals and Rational Exponents

FL N-RN.1.1

Explain how the definition of the meaning of rational exponents follows from extending the properties of integer exponents to those values, allowing for a notation for radicals in terms of rational exponents. *Also N-RN.1.2*

ESSENTIAL QUESTION

How are radicals and rational exponents related?

EXPLORE ACTIVITY  FL N-RN.1.1

Defining Rational Exponents

The **radical symbol** $\sqrt{}$ is used to indicate roots.
An expression that contains the radical symbol is a **radical expression**.

Index $\rightarrow \sqrt[3]{125} \leftarrow$ Radicand

Recall the Power of a Power Property of Exponents: $(a^m)^n = a^{mn}$.

Complete the steps below to explore the relationship between radical expressions and rational exponents.

$$\sqrt{4} = 4^k$$

A $\left(\boxed{}\right)^2 = \left(\boxed{}\right)^2$ *Square both sides of the equation.*

B $4^1 = 4^{2k}$ _____ Property

C $\boxed{} = \boxed{}$ *If $b^m = b^n$, then $m = n$.*

D $\boxed{} = k$ *Solve for k.*

E   Substitute your value for k in the original equation: $\sqrt{4} = 4^{\boxed{}}$

$$\sqrt[3]{8} = 8^k$$

F $\left(\boxed{}\right)^3 = \left(\boxed{}\right)^3$ *Cube both sides of the equation.*

G $8^1 = 8^{3k}$ _____ Property

H $\boxed{} = \boxed{}$ *If $b^m = b^n$, then $m = n$.*

I $\boxed{} = k$ *Solve for k.*

J   Substitute your value for k in the original equation: $\sqrt[3]{8} = 8^{\boxed{}}$

REFLECT

1. **Make a Conjecture** How can you write the square root or the cube root of a number n as the number n with an exponent?

_____

Math On the Spot

my.hrw.com

Simplifying Expressions with Rational Exponents

Definition of $b^{\frac{1}{n}}$	
General Rule	**Examples**
A number raised to the power of $\frac{1}{n}$ is equal to the nth root of that number: $$b^{\frac{1}{n}} = \sqrt[n]{b},$$ where $b \geq 0$ and n is an integer > 1.	$b^{\frac{1}{2}} = \sqrt{b}$ $\quad 25^{\frac{1}{2}} = \sqrt{25} = 5$ $b^{\frac{1}{3}} = \sqrt[3]{b}$ $\quad 64^{\frac{1}{3}} = \sqrt[3]{64} = 4$ $b^{\frac{1}{4}} = \sqrt[4]{b}$ $\quad 81^{\frac{1}{4}} = \sqrt[4]{81} = 3$

You can use the definition of $b^{\frac{1}{n}}$ to simplify expressions with rational exponents.

EXAMPLE 1

 FL   N-RN.1.1, N-RN.1.2

Simplify each expression.

A $64^{\frac{1}{3}}$

$$64^{\frac{1}{3}} = \sqrt[3]{64} \qquad \text{Use the definition of } b^{\frac{1}{n}}.$$
$$= \sqrt[3]{4^3} \qquad \text{Rewrite the radicand as a cube.}$$
$$= 4$$

B $32^{\frac{1}{5}} - 81^{\frac{1}{2}}$

$$32^{\frac{1}{5}} - 81^{\frac{1}{2}} = \sqrt[5]{32} - \sqrt{81} \qquad \text{Use the definition of } b^{\frac{1}{n}}.$$
$$= \sqrt[5]{2^5} - \sqrt{9^2} \qquad \text{Rewrite both radicands as powers.}$$
$$= 2 - 9$$
$$= -7$$

REFLECT

2. Justify Reasoning Is $b^{\frac{1}{n}}$ where $b > 0$ and n is a positive integer always a positive integer? Justify your answer with reasoning or a counterexample.

_____

YOUR TURN

Simplify each expression.

3. $16^{\frac{1}{4}}$

_____

4. $125^{\frac{1}{3}}$

_____

5. $49^{\frac{1}{2}} + 27^{\frac{1}{3}}$

_____

6. $1000^{\frac{1}{3}} - 64^{\frac{1}{6}}$

_____

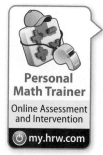

Personal Math Trainer

Online Assessment and Intervention

my.hrw.com

Using Properties with Rational Exponents

You can use properties of exponents to simplify expressions containing rational exponents. Recall the following properties of exponents.

Math On the Spot
⊙ my.hrw.com

Properties of Exponents		
Property		**Numerical example**
Product of Powers Property	$a^m \cdot a^n = a^{m+n}$	$2^2 \cdot 2^3 = 2^5 = 32$
Quotient of Powers Property	$\dfrac{a^m}{a^n} = a^{m-n}, a \neq 0$	$\dfrac{2^5}{2^3} = 2^2 = 4$
Power of a Product Property	$(a \cdot b)^n = a^n \cdot b^n$	$(2 \cdot 3)^2 = 2^2 \cdot 3^2 = 36$
Power of a Quotient Property	$\left(\dfrac{a}{b}\right)^n = \dfrac{a^n}{b^n}, b \neq 0$	$\left(\dfrac{1}{2}\right)^2 = \dfrac{1^2}{2^2} = \dfrac{1}{4}$
Power of a Power Property	$\left(a^m\right)^n = a^{mn}$	$(2^2)^2 = 2^{2 \cdot 2} = 2^4 = 16$
Negative Exponent Property	$a^{-n} = \dfrac{1}{a^n}, a \neq 0$	$2^{-2} = \dfrac{1}{2^2} = \dfrac{1}{4}$

Simplifying expressions with rational exponents will often require you to use properties of exponents.

EXAMPLE 2

 FL N-RN.1.1, N-RN.1.2

Simplify each expression.

 $125^{\frac{2}{3}}$

$$125^{\frac{2}{3}} = 125^{\frac{1}{3} \cdot 2} \qquad \text{Write the exponent as a product}$$

$$= \left(125^{\frac{1}{3}}\right)^2 \qquad \text{Power of a Power Property}$$

$$= \left(\sqrt[3]{125}\right)^2 \qquad \text{Definition of } b^{\frac{1}{n}}$$

$$= \left(\sqrt[3]{5^3}\right)^2 \qquad 5^3 = 125$$

$$= (5)^2$$

$$= 25$$

 $81^{\frac{3}{4}}$

$$81^{\frac{3}{4}} = 81^{\frac{1}{4} \cdot 3} \qquad \text{Write the exponent as a product}$$

$$= \left(81^{\frac{1}{4}}\right)^3 \qquad \text{Power of a Power Property}$$

$$= \left(\sqrt[4]{81}\right)^3 \qquad \text{Definition of } b^{\frac{1}{n}}$$

$$= \left(\sqrt[4]{3^4}\right)^3 \qquad 3^4 = 81$$

$$= (3)^3$$

$$= 27$$

C $64^{\frac{3}{2}} = 64^{\frac{1}{2} \cdot 3}$ Write the exponent as a product

$\qquad = \left(64^{\frac{1}{2}} \right)^3$ Power of a Power Property

$\qquad = \left(\sqrt{64} \right)^3$ Definition of $b^{\frac{1}{n}}$

$\qquad = \left(\sqrt{8^2} \right)^3$ $8^2 = 64$

$\qquad = 8^3$

$\qquad = 512$

REFLECT

7. Communicate Mathematical Ideas Explain how you simplify any expression of the form $a^{\frac{m}{n}}$.

_____

_____

_____

_____

8. Example 2A showed how to simplify $125^{\frac{2}{3}}$. Is it possible to simplify $125^{\frac{3}{2}}$ using similar steps? Explain.

_____

_____

Personal Math Trainer

Online Assessment and Intervention

⏻ my.hrw.com

YOUR TURN

Simplify each expression.

9. $8^{\frac{4}{3}}$

10. $25^{\frac{3}{2}}$

_____   _____

11. $1^{\frac{3}{5}}$

12. $1000^{\frac{4}{3}}$

_____   _____

Math On the Spot

⏻ my.hrw.com

Rational Exponents in Real-World Contexts

You can use rational exponents to describe relationships in real-world contexts, such as the relationship between an animal's required caloric intake and its mass.

EXAMPLE 3 **FL** N-RN.1.1, N-RN.1.2

The approximate number of Calories C that an animal needs each day is given by $C = 72m^{\frac{3}{4}}$, where m is the animal's mass in kilograms. Find the number of Calories that each animal needs daily.

A a Siberian tiger with a mass of 256 kilograms

$C = 72m^{\frac{3}{4}}$

$= 72(256)^{\frac{3}{4}}$ Substitute 256 for m.

$= 72(256)^{\frac{1}{4} \cdot 3}$ $\frac{3}{4} = \frac{1}{4} \cdot 3$

$= 72\left(256^{\frac{1}{4}}\right)^3$ Power of a Power Property

$= 72 \cdot \left(\sqrt[4]{256}\right)^3$ Definition of $b^{\frac{1}{n}}$

$= 72 \cdot \left(\sqrt[4]{4^4}\right)^3$ $4^4 = 256$

$= 72 \cdot (4)^3$

$= 72 \cdot 64$

$= 4608$

The tiger needs 4608 Calories per day.

B an Asian elephant with a mass of 4096 kilograms

$C = 72m^{\frac{3}{4}}$

$= 72(4096)^{\frac{3}{4}}$ Substitute 4096 for m.

$= 72(4096)^{\frac{1}{4} \cdot 3}$ $\frac{3}{4} = \frac{1}{4} \cdot 3$

$= 72\left(4096^{\frac{1}{4}}\right)^3$ Power of a Power Property

$= 72\left(\sqrt[4]{4096}\right)^3$ Definition of $b^{\frac{1}{n}}$

$= 72\left(\sqrt[4]{8^4}\right)^3$ $8^4 = 4096$

$= 72(8)^3$

$= 72 \cdot 512$

$= 36{,}864$

The elephant needs 36,864 Calories per day.

YOUR TURN

13. Use $C = 72m^{\frac{3}{4}}$ to find the number of Calories that an Australian shepherd dog with a mass of 16 kilograms needs each day.

_____

Personal Math Trainer

Online Assessment and Intervention

my.hrw.com

Guided Practice

Simplify each expression. (Example 1)

1. $100^{\frac{1}{2}}$

2. $1000^{\frac{1}{3}}$

3. $32^{\frac{1}{5}}$

4. $25^{\frac{1}{2}} + 81^{\frac{1}{4}}$

5. $216^{\frac{1}{3}} - 27^{\frac{1}{3}}$

6. $81^{\frac{1}{2}} - 64^{\frac{1}{6}}$

Simplify each expression. (Example 2)

7. $1000^{\frac{2}{3}}$

8. $27^{\frac{4}{3}}$

9. $64^{\frac{5}{6}}$

10. $64^{\frac{2}{3}}$

11. $32^{\frac{3}{5}}$

12. $128^{\frac{4}{7}}$

13. Near Earth's surface, the time t required for an object to fall a distance d is given by $t = \frac{1}{4}d^{\frac{1}{2}}$, where t is measured in seconds and d is measured in feet. Find the time it will take an object to fall 100 feet. (Example 3)

14. The relationship between the radius, r, of a sphere and its volume, V, is $r = \left(\frac{3V}{4\pi}\right)^{\frac{1}{3}}$. What is the radius of a sphere that has a volume of 36π cubic units? (Example 3)

15. The relationship between the radius, r, of a sphere and its surface area, A, is $r = \left(\frac{A}{4\pi}\right)^{\frac{1}{2}}$. What is the radius of a sphere that has a surface area of 64π square units? (Example 3)

ESSENTIAL QUESTION CHECK-IN

16. What does the denominator of a rational exponent represent?

2.1 Independent Practice

FL N-RN.1.1, N-RN.1.2

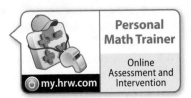

Personal
Math Trainer

Online
Assessment and
Intervention

my.hrw.com

Simplify each expression.

17. $25^{\frac{1}{2}} \cdot 81^{\frac{1}{4}}$ _____

18. $343^{\frac{1}{3}} \cdot 27^{\frac{1}{3}}$ _____

19. $125^{\frac{2}{3}} \div 25^{\frac{1}{2}}$ _____

20. $10{,}000^{\frac{1}{2}} \div 1000^{\frac{2}{3}}$ _____

21. $64^{\frac{2}{3}} - 81^{\frac{3}{4}} + 9^{\frac{3}{2}}$ _____

Use the equation $t = \frac{1}{4} d^{\frac{1}{2}}$, where t is the time in seconds and d is the distance in feet, to find the time it takes for an object to fall each distance.

22. 144 feet _____

23. 36 feet _____

24. 16 feet _____

25. 1 foot _____

26. Use the equation $t = \frac{1}{4} d^{\frac{1}{2}}$ to determine the height from which an object fell if it took 4 seconds to reach the ground.

_____

If a right triangle has legs of length a and b and hypotenuse of length c, then $c = (a^2 + b^2)^{\frac{1}{2}}$. Determine the length of the hypotenuse for a right triangle with the given leg lengths.

27. $a = 5$ in., $b = 12$ in.

_____

28. $a = 6$ cm, $b = 8$ cm

_____

29. $a = 12$ mi, $b = 9$ mi

_____

Write the name of the property that is demonstrated by each equation.

30. $\left(25^2\right)^{\frac{1}{2}} = 25$

_____

31. $3^7 = 3^3 \cdot 3^4$

_____

32. $3^{-2} = \frac{1}{9}$

_____

33. $\left(\frac{2}{3}\right)^3 = \frac{8}{27}$

_____

34. $2^2 \cdot 3^2 = (2 \cdot 3)^2$

_____

35. $\frac{3^7}{3^5} = 3^2$

_____

For each property, give an example that demonstrates the property. Do not use an example that has been shown in this lesson.

36. Power of a Power

_____

37. Power of a Product

_____

38. Negative Exponent

_____

39. Quotient of Powers

_____

40. Power of a Quotient

_____

41. **Communicate Mathematical Ideas** Use the Commutative Property of Multiplication and the properties of rational exponents to rewrite $2.5^{\frac{m}{n}}$ as two equivalent radical expressions. Explain what these two expressions mean about different ways to evaluate $2.5^{\frac{m}{n}}$.

_____

_____

_____

_____

_____

42. **Multiple Representations** Show that a^6 can be written as a perfect square and as a perfect cube.

_____

_____

_____

43. **Critical Thinking** Use the Commutative Property of Multiplication and the Associative Property of Multiplication to show the Power of a Product Property $(a \cdot b)^n = a^n \cdot b^n$ is true.

_____

_____

_____

_____

_____

44. **Critique Reasoning** Jay said that by the Quotient of Powers property, $\frac{0^5}{0^2} = 0^{5-2} = 0^3 = 0$. Is this correct? Explain.

_____

_____

_____

_____

Real Numbers

FL N-RN.2.3

Explain why the sum or product of two rational numbers is rational; that the sum of a rational number and an irrational number is irrational; and that the product of a nonzero rational number and an irrational number is irrational.

ESSENTIAL QUESTION

What are the subsets and properties of real numbers?

EXPLORE ACTIVITY 1   FL N-RN.2.3

Understanding Real Numbers

Recall that a rational number can be expressed in the form $\frac{p}{q}$, where p and q are integers and $q \neq 0$. The decimal form of a rational number either terminates or repeats. For instance, $\frac{3}{4} = 0.75$ and $-\frac{5}{6} = -0.8333\ldots$.

An irrational number cannot be written as the quotient of two integers, and its decimal form is nonrepeating and nonterminating. Examples of irrational numbers include square roots of non-perfect squares and cube roots of non-perfect cubes. For instance, the decimal form of $\sqrt{3}$ is $1.7320508\ldots$, which neither repeats nor terminates.

Real numbers consist of all rational and irrational numbers.

The Venn diagram shows subsets of the set of real numbers. Each of the subsets includes one example of a real number belonging to that subset.

Classify each number by writing it in the most specific area of the diagram.

$-5, 0, -\sqrt{10}, -\frac{8}{17}, 8, -12, \sqrt[3]{2}$

A -5

B 0

C $-\sqrt{10}$

D $-\frac{8}{17}$

E 8

F -12

G $\sqrt[3]{2}$

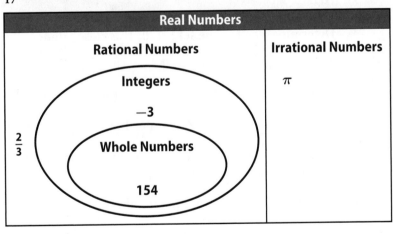

Animated Math

my.hrw.com

REFLECT

1. **Communicate Mathematical Ideas** How does the diagram show that all whole numbers are integers and that all integers are rational numbers?

_____

_____

_____

_____

Properties of Real Numbers

All real numbers have the following properties with respect to addition and multiplication.

Properties of Real Numbers	
Commutative Property of Addition	$a + b = b + a$
Associative Property of Addition	$(a + b) + c = a + (b + c)$
Additive Identity	The additive identity is 0, because $a + 0 = a$.
Additive Inverse	The additive inverse of a is $-a$, because $a + (-a) = 0$.
Commutative Property of Multiplication	$a \cdot b = b \cdot a$
Associative Property of Multiplication	$(a \cdot b) \cdot c = a \cdot (b \cdot c)$
Multiplicative Identity	The multiplicative identity is 1, because $1(a) = a$.
Multiplicative Inverse	The multiplicative inverse of a for $a \neq 0$ is $\frac{1}{a}$, because $a\left(\frac{1}{a}\right) = 1$.
Distributive Property	$a(b + c) = ab + ac$

A set of numbers is **closed** under an operation if the result of the operation on any two numbers in the set is also a number in that set.

EXAMPLE 1

 **FL** N-RN.2.3

A **Determine whether the set {−1, 0, 1} is closed under addition.**

Add each pair of elements in the set. Check whether each sum is in the set.

$-1 + (-1) = -2$ [✗] $\qquad$ $-1 + 0 = -1$ ✔ $\qquad$ $-1 + 1 = 0$ ✔

$0 + 0 = 0$ ✔ $\qquad$ $0 + 1 = 1$ ✔ $\qquad$ $1 + 1 = 2$ [✗]

The sums −2 and 2 are not in the original set, so the set {−1, 0, 1} is not closed under addition.

B **Show that the set of irrational numbers is not closed under addition.**

Find two irrational numbers whose sum is not an irrational number.

$\sqrt{3} + (-\sqrt{3}) = 0$ *0 is not irrational.*

The set of irrational numbers is not closed under addition.

REFLECT

2. Give an example that shows the set of integers is not closed under division.

_____

My Notes

3. Give an example that shows the set of irrational numbers is not closed under multiplication. _____

4. **Communicate Mathematical Ideas** Under which operations is the set of whole numbers closed? Not closed? Explain.

_____

_____

_____

_____

5. Is the set $\{-2, 0, 2\}$ closed under addition? Explain.

_____

_____

6. Give an example that shows the set of irrational numbers is not closed under division. _____

Personal Math Trainer

Online Assessment and Intervention

⊙ my.hrw.com

EXPLORE ACTIVITY 2

FL N-RN.2.3

Proving that Sets are Closed

The set of integers is closed under addition and multiplication. Complete Steps 1–5 to prove that the set of rational numbers is closed under addition. Begin with the definition of rational numbers a and b.

STEP 1   Let a and b be _____ numbers.

Then $a = \frac{p}{q}$ and $b = \frac{r}{s}$, where p, q, r, and s are integers and q and s are not 0. $a + b = \frac{p}{q} + \frac{r}{s}$

STEP 2   Find a common denominator. $= \frac{p}{q}\left(\frac{s}{s}\right) + \frac{r}{s}\left(\frac{q}{q}\right)$

STEP 3   Multiply. $= \dfrac{\boxed{}}{\boxed{}} + \dfrac{\boxed{}}{\boxed{}}$

STEP 4   Add the numerators. $= \dfrac{\boxed{}}{\boxed{}}$

STEP 5 Conclusion: Because the numerator $pq + qr$ and the denominator qs

are both _____, $\frac{ps + qr}{qs}$ is a rational number.

Summary: For each set of numbers in rows **A**–**D**, enter "Yes" if the set of numbers is closed under the operation. Enter "No" if the set of numbers is not closed under the operation.

Closure of Number Sets				
Set	**Addition**	**Subtraction**	**Multiplication**	**Division**
A Real numbers				
B Irrational numbers				
C Rational numbers				
D Integers				

REFLECT

7. Critique Reasoning In Step 5, how do you know that $ps + qr$ and qs are integers?

_____

_____

8. Critique Reasoning How does $a + b = \frac{ps + qr}{qs}$ prove that the set of rational numbers is closed under addition?

_____

_____

_____

_____

9. Draw Conclusions Given that the set of rational numbers is closed under addition, how can you prove that the set of rational numbers is closed under subtraction?

_____

_____

_____

_____

Complete Steps 1–8 to prove that the sum of an irrational number and a rational number is irrational.

STEP 1 Let a be an irrational number and let b be a rational number.

Then $b = \frac{r}{s}$, where r and s are _____ and $s \neq 0$.

> This proof is called a "proof by contradiction." This is when an assumption is made at the beginning, and if the logical outcome is false, then the assumption must be false.

STEP 2 The sum $a + b$ must be either rational or irrational.

Assume that the sum $a + b$ is rational.

Then $a + b = \boxed{}$, where p and q are _____ and $q \neq 0$.

$$a + b = \frac{p}{q}$$

STEP 3 Subtract b from each side. $a + b - \boxed{} = \frac{p}{q} - \boxed{}$

STEP 4 Substitute $\frac{r}{s}$ for b. $a = \boxed{}$

STEP 5 Find a common denominator. $a = \frac{p}{q}\left(\frac{s}{s}\right) - \frac{r}{s}\left(\frac{q}{q}\right)$

STEP 6 Multiply. $a = \dfrac{\boxed{}}{\boxed{}} - \dfrac{\boxed{}}{\boxed{}}$

STEP 7 Subtract. $a = \dfrac{\boxed{}}{\boxed{}}$

STEP 8 Because $ps - qr$ and qs are integers with $qs \neq 0$, $\frac{ps - qr}{qs}$ is a rational number. But in Step 1, a is given as an irrational number. This means

that the assumption that _____ was incorrect. So the sum of an irrational number and a rational

number must be _____.

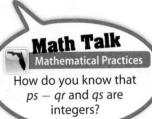

Math Talk
Mathematical Practices

How do you know that $ps - qr$ and qs are integers?

REFLECT

10. Justify Reasoning Use the results of Explore Activity 3 to justify that the difference of an irrational number and a rational number is irrational.

_____

_____

_____

Guided Practice

Tell whether each set is closed under the given operation. (Example 1)

1. {0, 1}; multiplication _____

2. {0, 1}; addition _____

3. even integers; addition _____

4. Prove that the set of rational numbers is closed under multiplication. (Explore Activity 2)

Let a and b be rational numbers.

Then $a = \frac{p}{q}$ and $b = \frac{r}{s}$, where p, q, r, and s are integers and q and s are not 0.

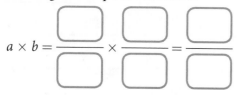

Because pr and qs are integers, $\dfrac{\Box}{\Box}$ is a

rational number. So the set of rational numbers is closed under multiplication.

5. Prove that the product of an irrational number and a nonzero rational number is irrational. (Explore Activity 3)

Let a be an irrational number and let b be a nonzero rational number.

Then $b = \frac{r}{s}$, where r and s are integers and

r and s are not _____. The product $a \times b$ must be either rational or irrational. Assume

that _____

Then $a \times b = \dfrac{\Box}{\Box}$, where p and q are

integers and q is not 0.

$$a \times b \cdot \frac{1}{b} = \frac{\Box}{\Box} \cdot \frac{1}{b} \ (b \neq 0)$$

$$a = \frac{\Box}{\Box} \div \Box \quad (b \neq 0)$$

$$a = \frac{\Box}{\Box} \div \frac{\Box}{\Box} \quad (s \neq 0)$$

$$a = \frac{\Box}{\Box} \times \frac{\Box}{\Box} \quad (r \neq 0)$$

$$a = \frac{\Box}{\Box}$$

The final statement shows that a is a _____ number. But a is given as an irrational number.

Therefore the assumption _____

_____ is incorrect. So the product of an irrational number and a nonzero

rational number is _____.

? ESSENTIAL QUESTION CHECK-IN

6. How do you show that a set of numbers is not closed under a given operation?

_____

2.2 Independent Practice

 N-RN.2.3

Write two numbers that fit each description. If there is no such number, write *none*.

7. negative integer

_____

8. negative rational number that is not an integer

_____

9. irrational integer

_____

10. negative irrational number

_____

Using *whole*, *integer*, *rational*, and *irrational*, name all the subsets of the real numbers to which each number belongs.

11. 15

_____

12. $\frac{\pi}{2}$

_____

13. $-\frac{\sqrt[3]{8}}{2}$

_____

14. $\frac{\sqrt{36}}{\sqrt{9}}$

_____

15. $\frac{0}{\sqrt{7}}$

_____

Tell whether the set is closed under the operation. If it is not closed, justify your answer using an example.

16. negative integers; subtraction

_____

17. negative integers; addition

_____

18. rational numbers; division

_____

19. {−2, 0, 2}; multiplication

_____

20. negative integers; multiplication

_____

21. negative rational numbers; multiplication

_____

22. positive irrational numbers; addition

_____

23. positive irrational numbers; multiplication

_____

24. {0, 1, 10}; multiplication

_____

25. even integers; subtraction

_____

26. Make a Conjecture Consider any subset of the real numbers that consists only of negative numbers. What can you conclude about whether the set is closed under multiplication? Explain.

_____

_____

_____

_____

27. Communicate Mathematical Ideas Explain why any real number must be either a rational number or an irrational number.

_____

_____

_____

_____

_____

_____

28. Explain the Error Drew wanted to determine whether the set of rational numbers is closed under division. He concluded that the set is not closed because $\frac{3}{4} \div \frac{1}{4} = 3$, and 3 is an integer. Explain Drew's error.

_____

_____

29. Draw Conclusions Consider a set of numbers that is closed under addition and subtraction. What number must be in such a set? Explain.

_____

_____

_____

30. Draw Conclusions Consider a set of numbers that is closed under multiplication and division. What number must be in such a set? Explain.

_____

_____

_____

Ready to Go On?

Personal
Math Trainer

my.hrw.com

Online
Assessment and
Intervention

2.1 Radicals and Rational Exponents

Simplify each expression.

1. $36^{\frac{1}{2}} - 81^{\frac{1}{4}}$ _____

2. $64^{\frac{2}{3}} \div 32^{\frac{2}{5}}$ _____

3. $1^{\frac{5}{3}} \div 16^{\frac{3}{2}}$ _____

4. $125^{\frac{2}{3}} - 64^{\frac{1}{2}} - 8^{\frac{2}{3}}$ _____

Write the name of the property that is demonstrated by each equation.

5. $4^3 \cdot 5^3 = 20^3$

6. $4^3 \cdot 4^5 = 4^8$

_____

_____

7. Use the equation $t = \frac{1}{2}a^{\frac{3}{2}}$ to find the value of t when $a = 16$.

_____

2.2 Real Numbers

Using *whole*, *integer*, *rational*, and *irrational*, name all the subsets of the
real numbers to which each number belongs.

8. $\sqrt{5}$ _____

9. $\sqrt{9}$ _____

_____

_____

10. -6 _____

11. $\sqrt[3]{\frac{1}{8}}$ _____

_____

_____

Tell whether the set is closed under the operation. If it is not closed,
justify your answer using an example.

12. irrational numbers; addition

13. rational numbers; multiplication

_____

_____

? ESSENTIAL QUESTION

14. What sets of numbers are included in the real numbers?

_____

_____

_____

_____

Assessment Readiness

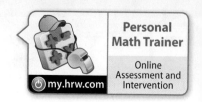

Personal Math Trainer

Online Assessment and Intervention

my.hrw.com

Selected Response

1. Which is equal to 3?

   Ⓐ $9^{\frac{1}{3}}$ Ⓒ $\sqrt{27}$

   Ⓑ $81^{\frac{1}{4}}$ Ⓓ $27^{\frac{1}{2}}$

2. Which of the statements is true?

   Ⓐ The sum of two rational numbers can be irrational.

   Ⓑ The sum of two irrational numbers can be rational.

   Ⓒ The product of two rational numbers can be irrational.

   Ⓓ The quotient of two rational numbers can be irrational.

3. How many significant digits are there in 0.07010?

   Ⓐ 2

   Ⓑ 3

   Ⓒ 4

   Ⓓ 5

4. A common speed at which adults roll bowling balls is 15 mi/h. 15 mi/h is equivalent to how many feet per second?

   Ⓐ 0.045

   Ⓑ 15

   Ⓒ 22

   Ⓓ 1320

5. How many significant digits are there in the sum of 45.10 and 102.203?

   Ⓐ 3

   Ⓑ 4

   Ⓒ 5

   Ⓓ 6

6. How many significant digits are there in the product of 45.10 and 101?

   Ⓐ 7

   Ⓑ 5

   Ⓒ 4

   Ⓓ 3

7. The approximate number of Calories C an animal needs each day is given by $C = 72m^{\frac{3}{4}}$, where m is the animal's mass in kilograms. How many Calories does an 81 kilogram adult male need each day?

   Ⓐ 216 Calories

   Ⓑ 1944 Calories

   Ⓒ 4374 Calories

   Ⓓ 5832 Calories

8. Under which operation is the set of integers **not** closed?

   Ⓐ addition

   Ⓑ subtraction

   Ⓒ multiplication

   Ⓓ division

Mini-Tasks

9. Near Earth's surface, the time t required for an object to fall a distance d is given by $t = \frac{1}{4}d^{\frac{1}{2}}$, where t is measured in seconds and d is measured in feet.

   a. How long would it take for an object to fall 256 feet?

   _____

   b. If it takes 2.5 seconds for an object to fall to the ground, from what height did the object fall?

   _____

Expressions

? ESSENTIAL QUESTION

How can you use algebraic expressions to solve problems?

Real-World Video

In a grocery store receipt, some items are taxed and some items are not taxed. You can write an expression that shows a simplified method for calculating the total grocery bill.

my.hrw.com

GO DIGITAL
my.hrw.com

my.hrw.com

Go digital with your write-in student edition, accessible on any device.

Math On the Spot

Scan with your smart phone to jump directly to the online edition, video tutor, and more.

Animated Math

Interactively explore key concepts to see how math works.

Personal Math Trainer

Get immediate feedback and help as you work through practice sets.

Are YOU Ready?

Complete these exercises to review skills you will need for this module.

Order of Operations

> **EXAMPLE** Simplify $6 + 2(5 - 8)^2 + 7$
>
> $$6 + 2(5 - 8)^2 + 7 = 6 + 2(-3)^2 + 7 \quad \text{Parentheses}$$
> $$= 6 + 2(9) + 7 \quad \text{Powers}$$
> $$= 6 + 18 + 7 \quad \text{Multiplication and division}$$
> $$= 31 \quad \text{Addition and subtraction}$$

Simplify each expression.

1. $7^2 + 3(8) \div 3$

2. $(4 - 9)(13 - 16) + 5$

3. $11^2 - 4(2^3 - 8) + 5$

_____

4. $(5 + 3)^2 \div 16 + 2$

5. $6 + (-9 - 12 + 7)5$

6. $(6 + 2)(28 - 3^3)^5$

_____

Combine Like Terms

> **EXAMPLE** $x - 1 - 2x + 9$
>
> $x - 2x - 1 + 9$ Reorder terms with same variable factors.
> $(1 - 2)x + (-1 + 9)$ Add or subtract the coefficients of the like terms.
> $-1x + 8$, or $-x + 8$

Simplify each expression.

7. $9y - 2x - 4y + 11x - 3x$

8. $-2x^2 - 12x + 5 - x + 8x^2 - 1$

_____

9. $4a^2 - 9b^2 + a^2 - 1 + 2b^2 + 5$

10. $\frac{1}{2}m^2 - 9n^2 - m^2 - 12 + n$

_____

Connect Words and Algebra

> **EXAMPLE**   12 decreased by a number
>   ↓   ↓   ↓   Represent the unknown number with a variable.
>   12   − x Decreased by means subtraction.

Write an algebraic expression for each word phrase.

11. the quantity 9 more than a number _____

12. the difference between 3 times a number and 21 _____

13. the product of 4 and the sum of 7 and a number _____

Reading Start-Up

Vocabulary

Review Words
- Associative Property
  (*Propiedad asociativa*)
- Commutative Property
  (*Propiedad conmutativa*)
- constant (*constante*)
- Distributive Property
  (*Propiedad distributiva*)
- variable (*variable*)

Preview Words
- algebraic expression
- coefficient
- equivalent expressions
- expression
- like terms
- numerical expressions
- order of operations
- simplify
- term

Visualize Vocabulary

Use the review words to complete the diagram. Write an example for each oval.

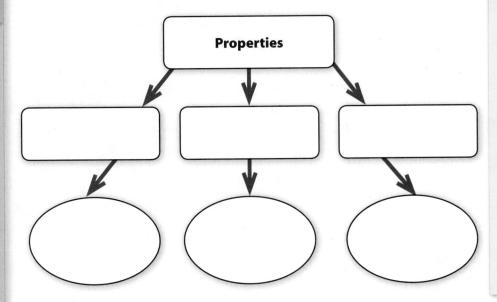

Understand Vocabulary

To become familiar with some of the vocabulary terms in the module, consider the following. You may refer to the module, the glossary, or a dictionary.

1. The word *express* is used when you want to demonstrate that an idea is solid and real. What do you think an **algebraic expression** might be?

   _____

   _____

Active Reading

Trifold Before beginning the module, create a Trifold Note to help you organize what you learn. Write vocabulary terms with definitions on the left and right folds and take notes in the center fold.

MODULE 3
Unpacking the Standards

Understanding the standards and the vocabulary terms in the standards will help you know exactly what you are expected to learn in this module.

 FL A-SSE.1.1

Interpret expressions that represent a quantity in terms of its context.

Key Vocabulary

expression (expresión)
A mathematical statement written in terms of numbers, variables, and operations.

What It Means to You

You can translate a real-world situation in words into an expression that represents specific quantities.

EXAMPLE

Fleetwood Delivery charges $6.50 per pound to deliver a small package plus a $12 pick-up fee.

The charge in dollars for delivering a small package weighing p pounds is

$$6.5p + 12$$

Rates:

Under 10 pounds:	$6.50 per pound
10–30 pounds:	$4.50 per pound
Over 30 pounds:	$6.50 per pound
Pick-up fee:	$12

Quantity: cost of delivery

Quantity: pick-up fee

 **FL N-Q.1.1**

Use units as a way to understand problems and to guide the solution of multi-step problems; choose and interpret units consistently in formulas; choose and interpret the scale and the origin in graphs and data displays

Key Vocabulary

unit (unidad)
a quantity used as a standard relative to which other quantities of the same type are measured, such as a pound or a centimeter

What It Means to You

Units can help you confirm that you are on the right track when solving a problem. If your units work out right, your answer is probably right.

UNPACKING EXAMPLE N-Q.1.1

Rina wants to express the time for her 195-second video in minutes rather than seconds. Should she multiply by 60 or divide? Using units guides her to the correct answer.

$$195 \text{ seconds} \cdot \frac{1 \text{ minute}}{60 \text{ seconds}} = 3.25 \text{ minutes}$$

Visit **my.hrw.com** to see all **Florida Math Standards** unpacked.

my.hrw.com

FL **A-SSE.1.1**

Interpret expressions that
represent a quantity in terms
of its context. *Also N-Q.1.1,
A-SSE.1.1a, A-SSE.1.1b*

ESSENTIAL QUESTION

How do you evaluate and interpret algebraic expressions?

EXPLORE ACTIVITY FL **A-SSE.1.1**

Interpreting Expressions

An **expression** is a mathematical phrase that contains operations, numbers, and/or variables. A **numerical expression** contains only numbers and operations, while an **algebraic expression** contains at least one variable.

A An algebraic expression can have both variables and numbers. In the expressions $5b$, $7k$, and $2q$, the blue numbers are called **coefficients**. Write a definition of *coefficient* in your own words.

_____

_____

B The expression $6c$ has one term. The expression $8a + 5$ has two terms. The expression $4 - 5x + t$ has three terms. Write a definition of *term* in your own words.

_____

_____

C Compare your definitions in **A** and **B** to those of other students, and discuss any differences between them. If necessary, make changes to your definitions.

_____

REFLECT

1. Identify the terms and coefficients in the expression $4p + 5 - 3g$.

_____

2. **Communicate Mathematical Ideas** Explain and illustrate the difference between a term and a coefficient.

_____

_____

3. What is the coefficient of n in the expression $n - 9$? Explain your reasoning.

_____

_____

Evaluating Algebraic Expressions

To evaluate an algebraic expression, substitute the value(s) of the variable(s) into the expression and simplify using the order of operations.

Recall that **order of operations** is a rule for simplifying an expression.

Order of Operations	
Parentheses (simplify inside parentheses)	$7 - 5(9 - 6) + 4^2 = 7 - 5 \cdot 3 + 4^2$
Exponents (simplify powers)	$= 7 - 5 \cdot 3 + 16$
Multiplication and Division (left to right)	$= 7 - 15 + 16$
Addition and Subtraction (left to right)	$= 8$

EXAMPLE 1 FL A-SSE.1.1

Evaluate the algebraic expression $n(5n - 13)^3$ for $n = 3$.

$$n(5n - 13)^3 = 3(5 \cdot 3 - 13)^3 \qquad \text{Substitute 3 for } n.$$
$$= 3(15 - 13)^3 \qquad \text{Multiply within parentheses.}$$
$$= 3(2)^3 \qquad \text{Subtract within parentheses.}$$
$$= 3(8) \qquad \text{Simplify exponents.}$$
$$= 24 \qquad \text{Multiply.}$$

REFLECT

4. Justify Reasoning Compare multiplying 5 by 3 within parentheses to multiplying 3 by 8 in the last step. Explain why some multiplication is done first and some multiplication is done later.

_____

_____

_____

YOUR TURN

Evaluate each expression for $x = 4$ and $y = 7$.

5. $7x + 3y - 12$ _____

6. $2x(3y - 4x)^2$ _____

Evaluating Real-World Expressions

When evaluating expressions that represent real-world situations, pay attention to units of measurement.

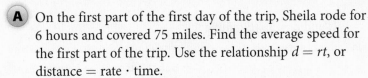

EXAMPLE 2 (Real World) FL N-Q.1.1

Sheila is riding in a multi-day bike trip. Each day she rides a different distance in a different period of time. On the first day Sheila rides 100 miles.

A On the first part of the first day of the trip, Sheila rode for 6 hours and covered 75 miles. Find the average speed for the first part of the trip. Use the relationship $d = rt$, or distance = rate · time.

$r = \dfrac{d}{t}$ *(Rate is the same as speed.)* Solve $d = rt$ for r.

$= \dfrac{75 \text{ miles}}{6 \text{ hours}}$ Substitute 75 miles for d and 6 hours for t.

$= 12.5$ miles per hour

B On the second day of the trip, Sheila rode for 7 hours at the same average speed as the first part of the first day. Find the total distance Sheila rides in two days.

Total distance = Day 1 distance + Day 2 distance
$= 100$ miles   + Day 2 distance

STEP 1 Find the distance for Day 2.
$d = rt$

$= 12.5 \dfrac{\text{miles}}{\text{hour}} \cdot 7 \text{ hour}$

$= 87.5$ miles

STEP 2 Find the total distance.

Total distance $= 100$ mi + Day 2 distance

$= 100$ miles $+ 87.5$ miles

$= 187.5$ miles

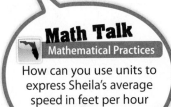

Math Talk
Mathematical Practices

How can you use units to express Sheila's average speed in feet per hour rather than miles per hour?

YOUR TURN

7. For the second part of the trip on the first day, Sheila rode for an additional 1.5 hours. Find the average speed for the second part of the trip. Use the relationship $d = rt$, or distance = rate · time.

_____

Personal Math Trainer

Online Assessment and Intervention

⊙ my.hrw.com

Identify the terms and coefficients of each expression. (Explore Activity)

1. $7 + 8p - 2r^3$

terms: _____

coefficients: _____

2. $g^2 - 14h + 10$

terms: _____

coefficients: _____

3. Evaluate $(4x + y)^2 - 3z$ for $x = 2$, $y = -1$, and $z = 5$. (Example 1)

$(4x + y)^2 - 3z = (4 \cdot \boxed{} + \boxed{})^2 - 3\boxed{}$ Substitute values for variables.

$= (\boxed{})^2 - \boxed{}$ Simplify within parentheses.

$= (\boxed{}) - \boxed{}$ Simplify powers.

$= \boxed{}$ Subtract.

4. As a lifeguard, Sara earns a base pay of $60 per day. If her day involves swim instruction, Sara also earns an additional $9t$ dollars, where t represents the number of hours she gives instruction and $9 is her hourly pay rate. The total amount that Sara earns in a day can be expressed as $60 + 9t$. (Example 2)

a. What does $9t$ represent in this context?

_____

b. What are the terms and the coefficients in the expression $60 + 9t$?

Terms: _____ Coefficients: _____

c. Rewrite the expression for 5 hours of swim instruction.

_____

d. How much will Sara earn in all? _____

? ESSENTIAL QUESTION CHECK-IN

5. How do you evaluate and interpret algebraic expressions?

_____

_____

_____

3.1 Independent Practice

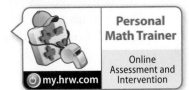

FL A-SSE.1.1, A-SSE.1.1a, A-SSE.1.1b, N-Q.1.1

Personal Math Trainer

Online Assessment and Intervention

my.hrw.com

Evaluate each expression for $a = 2$, $b = 3$, and $c = -2$.

6. $7a - 5b + 4$ _____

7. $b^2(c + 4)$ _____

8. $8 - 2b$ _____

9. $a^2 + 2b^2 - c^2$ _____

10. $(a - c)(c + 5)$ _____

11. $12 - 2(a - b)^2$ _____

12. $a + (b - c)^2$ _____

13. $(a + b) - ab$ _____

14. $5a^2 + bc^2$ _____

15. For each of the indicated values given for x and y, determine which expression has a greater value: $(x + y)^2$ or $(x - y)^2$.

    a. $x = 5, y = -3$

    _____

    _____

    b. $x = -5, y = -3$

    _____

    _____

16. **Analyze Relationships** Jared sells square frames of various sizes made of wood. To find the area of a frame, Jared uses the formula $A = s^2 - (s - 2w)^2$, where s is the length of a side of the frame and w is the width of the frame.

    a. What does each term in the formula represent?

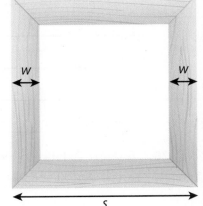

    _____

    _____

    _____

    _____

    b. Find the area of a frame that measures 20 inches on each side and has a width of 3 inches. _____

    c. Jared charges 18 cents per square inch for his frames. How much will he charge for a frame that measures 16 inches on each side and has a width of 2 inches?

    _____

17. At a rate of 25 miles per hour, it takes Henry 15 minutes to drive from the library to his house. Show how to find the distance that Henry traveled. Include units in your calculation.

_____

_____

Work Area

18. **Explain the Error** Joan works on commission for a furniture store. She gets a base pay of $80 a day plus 5 percent of the value of any merchandise she sells that exceeds a total of $400. Joan wrote the expression $400 + 0.05(t - 80)$, where t represents her sales total in dollars, to compute the total amount of money that she will make. For sales of $475 Joan calculated that she will make $419.75. Explain Joan's error.

_____

_____

_____

19. **Justify Reasoning** Nita finds that the expression $(a + 1)^2$ is sometimes, but not always, greater in value than $(a + 1)^3$ when she evaluates both expressions for the same value of a. How do you explain this finding?

_____

_____

_____

_____

_____

_____

20. **Analyze Relationships** Find the values of x and y that make the expression $5 + 4x(x - y) - x$ equal to zero. Explain how you got your answer.

_____

_____

_____

_____

_____

_____

ESSENTIAL QUESTION

How do you simplify algebraic expressions?

EXPLORE ACTIVITY

FL   A-SSE.1.1

Expressions

Equivalent expressions are algebraic expressions that simplify to the same value for any value(s) substituted for the variables that they contain. For example, the expressions $2x + y$ and $y + 2x$ are equivalent for any values of x and y.

Follow the steps below to determine which of the following expressions appear to be equivalent expressions.

$3(n - 4)$	$3(n - 2)$	$3n + 4$
$3n - 12$	$3n - 6$	$4 + 3n$

A Substitute 5 for n in each expression, and evaluate.

$3(n - 4)$	$3(n - 2)$	$3n + 4$
$= 3(\boxed{} - 4)$	$= 3(\boxed{} - 2)$	$= 3 \cdot \boxed{} + 4$
$= \boxed{}$	$= \boxed{}$	$= \boxed{}$
$3n - 12$	$3n - 6$	$4 + 3n$
$= 3 \cdot \boxed{} - 12$	$= 3 \cdot \boxed{} - 6$	$= 4 + 3 \cdot \boxed{}$
$= \boxed{}$	$= \boxed{}$	$= \boxed{}$

B Which expressions appear to be equivalent?

_____

_____

_____

_____

REFLECT

1. **Communicating Mathematical Ideas** Which of the pairs of expressions in the Explore Activity can be shown to be equivalent using the commutative property? Explain.

_____

_____

_____

2. **Communicating Mathematical Ideas** Which property could you use to show that the expressions $3(n - 4)$ and $3n - 12$ in the Explore Activity are equivalent? Explain.

_____

_____

_____

Math On the Spot

⏻ my.hrw.com

Combining Like Terms

Like terms are terms with the same variables raised to the same power. If there is no variable associated with a number, then it is called a *constant*. Constants are also like terms. Look at the chart below for examples of like terms and unlike terms.

Like terms	Unlike terms
$2x, 3x, x$	x, y, z
$1, 5, 100, 7$	$1x, 5, 100y$
$3y, 19y, y$	$7a, 5b, 7$
$5z, z, 12z$	$4c, 100, 3x$

EXAMPLE 1  FL   A-SSE.1.1a

My Notes

Combine like terms in each expression.

A $3x + 2x = x(3 + 2)$ Distributive Property

           $= x(5)$

           $= 5x$ Commutative Property

B $7x - 4x = x(7 - 4)$ Distributive Property

           $= x(3)$

           $= 3x$ Commutative Property

C $4x - x + 2x = x(4 - 1 + 2)$ Distributive Property

                $= x(5)$

                $= 5x$ Commutative Property

REFLECT

3. **Communicating Mathematical Ideas** Examine A, B, and C in Example 1. Describe how you combine like terms.

_____

_____

YOUR TURN

Combine like terms in each expression.

4. $7x + 3x$ _____

5. $17y + 8y$ _____

6. $13r - r$ _____

7. $9z - 8z + 2z$ _____

Simplifying Algebraic Expressions

To **simplify** an algebraic expression, you can use the properties of real numbers to combine like terms and eliminate grouping symbols.

EXAMPLE 2 FL A-SSE.1.1a

Simplify each expression.

A $3a + 5b^2 + 2a + 4b^2$.

$3a + 5b^2 + 2a + 4b^2$ Identify like terms.

$= 3a + 2a + 5b^2 + 4b^2$ Commutative Property of Addition

$= 5a + 9b^2$ Combine like terms.

B $4x - (3x + 1) - 2$

$= 4x - 3x - 1 - 2$ Distributive Property

$= 4x - 3$ Combine like terms.

Math Talk
Mathematical Practices

Are $2a$ and a^2 like terms? Explain.

YOUR TURN

Simplify each expression.

8. $7x + 18y^2 - 9y^2 - 5x$

9. $6n^3 + 3n^2 - 4n^3$

_____

_____

10. $4y^4 - (3y^2 + 3y^4) + y^2$

11. $-m^3 - (2n^2 - m^3) + 6n^2$

_____

_____

Simplifying Real-World Expressions

You can use algebraic expressions to represent real-world situations.

EXAMPLE 3

 FL A-SSE.1.1b

Write and simplify an expression to answer each question.

A Carlos buys p packages of hot dogs at $3.50 per package and p packages of hot dog buns at $2.50 per package. What is the cost for hot dogs and hot dog buns?

$3.5p + 2.5p$ *Cost of p hot dogs plus cost of p hot dog buns.*

$= 6p$ *Combine like terms.*

B Andrea buys 2 fewer containers of coleslaw than packages of hot dogs. Coleslaw costs $1.50 per container. What is the cost for coleslaw?

$1.50(p - 2)$ *Cost of coleslaw.*

$= 1.50p - 3$ *Use the Distributive Property.*

C What is the total cost for hot dogs and hot dog buns from part A and coleslaw from part B?

$6p + 1.50p - 3$ *Cost of all items.*

$= 7.50p - 3$ *Combine like terms.*

My Notes

REFLECT

12. The coefficients from the original expression $3.5p + 2.5p$ in part A represent what unit?

_____

13. What does each term represent?

_____

_____

_____

_____

14. Show two ways of finding the total cost of 7 packs of hot dogs and buns.

_____

_____

_____

YOUR TURN

Personal Math Trainer

Online Assessment and Intervention

my.hrw.com

Write and simplify an expression to answer each question.

15. Rory buys t play tickets at $14.50 per ticket and t choir concert tickets at $5.50 per ticket. What is the cost for play tickets and choir concert tickets?

_____

16. Use your expression from Exercise 15 to find the total cost of 8 play tickets and 8 choir concert tickets.

_____

17. Carly buys 3 more band concert tickets than choir concert tickets. Band concert tickets cost $3.50 per ticket. What is the cost for the choir concert and band concert tickets?

_____

Guided Practice

1. Which expressions are equivalent for all values of k? (Explore Activity)

$3(k - 3)$	$9k - 9$	$3k + 3$
$3 + 3k$	$9(k - 1)$	$3k - 9$

_____

_____

_____

Combine like terms. (Example 1)

2. $8x - x =$ _____

3. $6b + (2b + 4c) =$ _____

4. $-5r - 3r =$ _____

5. $2g + 8g - 3g =$ _____

6. $11x + 4x =$ _____

7. $6z - 2z =$ _____

8. $5m - 3n + 2m - m$ _____

9. $4x + 3y - x$ _____

10. $-2z^2 + 4z + 2z^2$ _____

11. $6r^3 + 2r^3 - r^2$ _____

12. $6 - 3h^2 + 6h^2 + 2$ _____

13. $4a + 2b^2 + b^2 - a$ _____

Simplify. (Example 2)

14. $4(m - 7) + 15$

$= \underline{\hspace{2cm}} + 15$

$= \underline{\hspace{2cm}}$

15. $10g - 2(4h) + 7g$

$= 10g + \underline{\hspace{2cm}}$

$= \underline{\hspace{2cm}}$

16. $4(m - 2) + 3m$

$= \underline{\hspace{2cm}} + 3m$

$= \underline{\hspace{2cm}}$

17. $4x + 3(5x) + 4y - x$

$= 4x \underline{\hspace{2cm}} 4y - x$

$= \underline{\hspace{2cm}}$

18. $12 - 3(4 - t) + 4t$

$= 12 \underline{\hspace{2cm}} + 4t$

$= \underline{\hspace{2cm}}$

19. $3g + 3(2 - g) + 4(g + 1)$

$= 3g \underline{\hspace{3cm}}$

$= \underline{\hspace{4cm}}$

20. In basketball, Carmela's team scored seven 1-point free throws and four times as many 2-point baskets as 3-point baskets. The expression that represents the total number of points that the team scored is $3b + 7 + 2(4b)$ where b stands for the number of 3-point baskets that the team scored. Simplify the expression. (Example 3)

$3b + 7 + 2(4b)$

$= 3b + \boxed{} + \boxed{}$ Commutative Property.

$= 3b + \boxed{} + 7$ Simplify.

$= \boxed{}$ Combine like terms.

21. A rectangle has a width w and a length that is two more than its width. What is the perimeter of the rectangle? Write and simplify an expression. (Example 3)

_____

ESSENTIAL QUESTION CHECK-IN

22. How do you simplify algebraic expressions?

_____

_____

_____

_____

3.2 Independent Practice

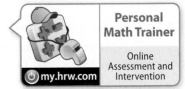

Personal Math Trainer

Online Assessment and Intervention

my.hrw.com

FL A-SSE.1.1, A-SSE.1.1a, A-SSE.1.2

Identify each property being illustrated.

23. $6(5x + 2) = 30x + 12$

_____

24. $a(9 - 7) = (9 - 7)a$

_____

25. $9 + (3b + 8) = (3b + 8) + 9$

_____

26. $k + 5k + 8 = (1 + 5)k + 8$

_____

Simplify each expression.

27. $a - 4 + 7a + 11$ _____

28. $11k - (k + 3) + 2$ _____

29. $6(n - 8) - 4n$ _____

30. $-2(2x - 5) + 5x + 6$ _____

31. $8b + 3(2b + c) - 3$ _____

32. $x - 5(y + 2) + (3y - x)$ _____

33. **Draw Conclusions** Marina burns calories at a rate of 15 calories per minute when running and 6 calories per minute when walking. Suppose she exercises for 60 minutes by running for r minutes and walking for the remaining time. The expression $15r + 6(60 - r)$ represents the calories burned during the 60-minute session.

a. What does $15r$ represent? Use unit analysis to explain.

_____

_____

b. What does $60 - r$ represent? What are the units associated with $6(60 - r)$?

_____

_____

c. Simplify $15r + 6(60 - r)$. What are the units associated with the entire expression?

_____

d. Evaluate $15r + 6(60 - r)$ for $r = 20$, 30, and 40. What conclusion can you draw?

_____

_____

_____

Simplify each expression and identify the units.

34. You purchase n cartons of tennis balls at $25 per carton from an online retailer that charges 8% tax and $17 in shipping costs. The expression $25n + 0.08(25n) + 17$ can be used to represent the total cost.

_____

35. Six friends all order the same lunch at a restaurant. Each lunch costs c dollars plus 5% tax and 20% tip. The friends use a $10 gift certificate. The total cost of the lunch is $6c + (0.05 + 0.20)(6c) - 10$.

_____

36. **Explain the Error** A student says that the perimeter of a rectangle with side lengths $(2x - 1)$ inches and $3x$ inches can be written as $(10x - 1)$ inches, because $2(2x - 1) + 2(3x) = 10x - 1$. Explain why this statement is incorrect.

_____

_____

H.O.T.   **FOCUS ON HIGHER ORDER THINKING**

Work Area

37. **Represent Real-World Problems** Miguel is baking cookies for the bake sale using a recipe that requires flour, sugar, and butter in a ratio of 5 to 2 to 1 by volume in cups. Suppose Miguel uses c cups of butter. His mother tells him to use one cup less of sugar than the recipe requires. Then the expression $5c + (2c - 1) + c$ represents the total number of cups of ingredients that Miguel uses. How many cups of butter would he use to have a total of 27 cups of ingredients? Explain how you got your answer.

_____

_____

_____

_____

38. **Analyze Relationships** The gas tank of Michelle's car holds g gallons, and the car does 30 miles per gallon. With 3 gallons of gas left in the tank, Michelle added a bottle of MilePlus, an additive that boosts mileage by 10 percent. Overall, the number of miles she drove on the tank is given by the expression $30(g - 3) + [(30 + 0.1(30)]3$. How many extra miles did Michelle drive as a result of adding MilePlus? Explain.

_____

_____

_____

39. **Explain the Error** A rectangle with sides of length $n + 2$ and n is compared to a square with sides of length $n + 1$. Steve says that the two shapes are equal in area. Explain Steve's mistake.

_____

LESSON
3.3 Writing Expressions

FL N-Q.1.1

Use units as a way to understand problems and to guide the solution of multi-step problems... *Also A-SSE.1.1, A-SSE.1.1a, A-SSE.1.1b, A-SSE.1.2, N-Q.1.2*

ESSENTIAL QUESTION

How do you write algebraic expressions to model quantities?

EXPLORE ACTIVITY 1    **FL** A-SSE.1.1b

Writing Algebraic Expressions

Expressions can be written with constants and variables, or they may be described in words. When given an expression in words, it is important to be able to translate the words into algebraic terms.

There are several key words that indicate that a particular operation is being used.

Key Words for Operations			
Addition	**Subtraction**	**Multiplication**	**Division**
• added to • plus • sum • more than	• subtracted from • minus • difference • less than • take away • taken from	• times • multiplied by • product of • groups of	• divided by • divided into • quotient of • ratio of

How can you write the verbal phrase "the quotient of 5 and the quantity 3 more than a number" as an algebraic expression?

A Which words in the expression identify an operation done to two quantities?

_____

_____

B Complete the expression for the quotient by filling in an operation symbol.

Quantity 1 ◯ Quantity 2

C What key words does Quantity 2 have that identify an operation? Write Quantity 2 as an algebraic expression with an operation.

_____

D Write values for Quantity 1 and Quantity 2 in the boxes. Place parentheses around Quantity 2. Fill in an operation sign.

REFLECT

1. **Communicating Mathematics** Why did Quantity 2 require parentheses? Explain.

   _____

   _____

   _____

2. **Justify Reasoning** Use a value for n to explain why the expressions $5 \div (n + 3)$ and $5 \div n + 3$ are not the same.

   _____

   _____

   _____

   _____

3. **What If?** What is another verbal phrase with an algebraic expression equivalent to the expression in the Explore Activity?

   _____

Math On the Spot
my.hrw.com

Modeling with Algebraic Expressions

You can create a verbal model to help translate a verbal expression into an algebraic expression.

EXAMPLE 1   FL N-Q.1.2

Write an algebraic expression to model the following phrase: "the price of lunch plus a 15% tip for the lunch."

STEP 1   Use the phrase to write a verbal model.

Price of lunch	+	15% of price of lunch
Quantity	**Operation**	**Quantity**

STEP 2   Use a variable such as p for the price of lunch.

$$p \qquad\qquad + \qquad\qquad 0.15p$$

The algebraic expression is $p + 0.15p$.

REFLECT

4. Communicating Mathematics What does the expression represent? Include the units in your answer.

_____

_____

_____

5. Use a property to write an expression that is equivalent to the expression you wrote in Example 1. Identify the property and simplify the expression, if possible.

_____

_____

6. Justify Reasoning What could the expression $\frac{p + 0.15p}{2}$ represent? Explain.

_____

_____

_____

7. What If? Suppose the tip was increased to 20% and then the price p of lunch is divided among 5 friends. What expression could represent this situation?

_____

YOUR TURN

Write an algebraic expression to model each phrase.

8. "The base price of a car plus 7.5% tax" represents the total cost of the car.

Simplify your expression. _____

9. "The base salary of $500 per week plus a commission of 10.5% of sales"

represents the total salary for the week. _____

10. "The original cost c less a discount of 20%" represents the sale price of the

sweater. Simplify your expression. _____

11. "The wholesale price p plus a markup of 33%, plus $50" represents the final

price of the necklace. Simplify your expression. _____

Personal Math Trainer

Online Assessment and Intervention

⏻ my.hrw.com

Math On the Spot

my.hrw.com

Using Unit Analysis to Guide Modeling

You can create a model to help translate a verbal expression into an algebraic expression.

EXPLORE ACTIVITY 2  **FL** N-Q.1.1

Last month, Lizzie volunteered 20 hours at her town library. In the weeks to come, she plans to volunteer 5 hours per week at the library. Write an algebraic expression to represent the total number of hours she will have volunteered *w* weeks from now.

A Use unit analysis to write a model.

$$\boxed{} \bigcirc \frac{\boxed{}}{\boxed{}} \bigcirc \boxed{}$$

B Express the unit model as a verbal model.

_____

_____

C Write an algebraic model for the total number of hours volunteered after *w* weeks have passed.

_____

D The expression _____ represents the total number of _____ Lizzie will volunteer after *w* weeks have passed.

Math Talk

Mathematical Practices

How would your expression change if Lizzie decided to volunteer 7 hours a week rather than 5?

REFLECT

12. Explain why you chose the units you chose in Step A above.

_____

_____

_____

_____

13. How many hours will Lizzie have volunteered by the end of 10 weeks? Explain how you solved this problem.

_____

_____

_____

_____

Solve each problem.

14. Suppose Lizzie plans to volunteer 3 hours a week at the shelter in addition to her library work. Rewrite the expression from the example to reflect this new fact.

_____

15. Marco rode 120 miles on the first day of his cross-country bicycle trip. He planned to ride an additional 100 miles each day. Write an algebraic expression to represent the total number of miles he will ride after d days have passed.

_____

16. Mario has saved $200 towards the cost of a $1000 computer. In the weeks to come, he plans to save an additional $30 per week.

  a. Write an algebraic expression to represent the total amount he still needs to save after w weeks have passed.

  _____

  b. How much more does he need to save after 8 weeks?

  _____

17. Irene has 50,000 airline miles in her account. She is planning to redeem the miles on a trip that costs 100,000 miles. In the months to come, she expects to accumulate an additional 2000 miles per month in her account.

  a. Write an algebraic expression to represent the total number of miles she still needs to accumulate after m months.

  _____

  b. How long will it take her to reach her goal of 100,000 miles?

  _____

Guided Practice

Write and simplify an algebraic expression to represent each scenario.

1. Alex purchased a phone card for $30. He has used t minutes of access time at 10 cents per minute. To write an algebraic expression to represent how many dollars Alex has left on his card, fill in the boxes. (Explore Activity 1)

Write your expression. _____

2. It costs $20 per hour to play pool and $3 for cue stick rental. Write a verbal model and an algebraic expression to represent the cost for n hours of playing pool and identify the units for the expression. (Example 1)

_____

3. Karla purchased a gym membership for $175. She also pays $5 per hour when using the gym. Write an algebraic expression to represent the total cost for h hours of gym usage, and identify the units for the expression. (Example 1)

_____

4. To convert dog years to human years, count 21 human years for the first two dog years and then 4 human years per dog year for each dog year thereafter. Write an expression that represents the human age of a dog that is y dog years old, where y is greater than 2. (Explore Activity 2)

_____

5. Kelsey has saved $35 towards the cost of a $390 video game system. In the weeks to come, she plans to save an additional $10 per week. (Explore Activity 2)

    a. Use unit analysis to represent the amount she has saved after w weeks and identify the units for the expression.

    _____

    b. Write an algebraic expression for the amount Kelsey has saved after w weeks.

    _____

    c. Write an algebraic expression to represent the total amount she still needs to save after w weeks have passed.

    _____

ESSENTIAL QUESTION CHECK-IN

6. How do you write algebraic expressions to model quantities?

_____

_____

_____

_____

_____

3.3 Independent Practice

FL A-SSE.1.1, A-SSE.1.1a, A-SSE.1.1b, A-SSE.1.2, N-Q.1.1, N-Q.1.2

Personal
Math Trainer

Online
Assessment and
Intervention

my.hrw.com

7. Two more than 4 times the sum of yesterday's high temperature in degrees Fahrenheit and 7 is equal to the current temperature in degrees Fahrenheit.

    a. Write an expression for the current temperature using t as yesterday's high temperature in your expression.

    _____

    b. Simplify the expression.

    _____

    c. If yesterday's high temperature was 3 °F, what is the current temperature?

    _____

8. Jared earns 0.25 vacation day for every week that he works in a calendar year. He also gets 10 paid holidays per year.

    a. Use unit analysis to represent the amount of paid time off Jared gets in a year after working for w weeks, and identify the units for the expression.

    _____

    b. Write an algebraic expression to represent the amount of paid time off Jared gets in a year after working for w weeks, and identify the units for the expression.

    _____

    c. Identify the units of each term, variable, and coefficient in the expression.

    _____

9. Tracie buys tickets to a concert for herself and two friends. There is an 8% tax on the cost of the tickets and an additional $10 booking fee for a single order of any size.

    a. Write an algebraic expression to represent the cost per person. Simplify the expression, if possible.

    _____

    b. Define what the variable represents and identify the units for the expression.

    _____

10. Explain the Error George claims that at 42 years of age he is 3 years less than 3 times as old as Pam will be one year from now. Pam is 15 right now. What is wrong with George's claim? Write an expression to explain your answer.

    _____

 **FOCUS ON HIGHER ORDER THINKING**

11. Critical Thinking Physicists measure velocity (speed) in units of distance per unit time. Acceleration is measured as the *change* in velocity per unit time, or velocity divided by time. Suppose you have measured velocity in meters per second. What units would acceleration have, using seconds as your time units? Explain how you got your answer.

_____

_____

_____

12. Make a Prediction Hannah invests money in a fund that promises to provide 10 percent interest each year. Write an expression to show how much money Hannah has in the fund after 1 year, with p representing the principal amount she invests. Simplify the expression. Suppose Hannah invests $1000 in the fund and leaves it there for 3 years. How much money will she then have? Explain.

_____

_____

_____

13. Justify Reasoning A right triangle has sides of length n, $n + 1$, and $n + 2$. Monica uses the basic formula, area $= \frac{1}{2}$ base $\cdot$ height, to compute the area of the triangle and comes up with an area of $\frac{n^2 + 3n + 2}{2}$. Sunil uses the same formula and comes up with an area of $\frac{n^2 + n}{2}$. Which area is correct? Explain.

_____

_____

_____

_____

_____

14. Represent Real-World Problems Suppose a sports event paid $1,000,000 for an insurance policy if the event was cancelled due to bad weather. The policy stated that for each inch of snow above the average snowfall of 39 inches, the policy would pay $75,000, up to a maximum of $1,500,000. Write an algebraic expression in terms of s, the number of inches of snowfall, that represents how much the policy pays. Estimate how many inches of snow would have to fall before the event receives a payout equal to the cost of the policy. How many inches of snow would have to fall before the policy reaches the maximum payout?

_____

Ready to Go On?

Personal
Math Trainer

my.hrw.com

Online
Assessment and
Intervention

3.1 Evaluating Expressions

Evaluate each expression for $r = 5$, $s = -3$, and $t = 7$.

1. $7 - 3s - 3t$

_____

2. $9r - 5s + 4$

_____

3. $8 + s^2 (t + 4 - 3r)$

_____

4. $(r - t)(2t + 5)$

_____

5. $r^3 - 10s^2 + t^2$

_____

6. $23 + 2(r + s)^3$

_____

7. $3(r + s)^4 - rs^2$

_____

8. $12r + (s - t)^2$

_____

9. $5r^3 + st^2$

_____

3.2 Simplifying Expressions

Simplify each expression.

10. $5(n - 8) - 4n$

_____

11. $3b + 2(7b + c) - 3$

_____

12. $-4(3x - 5) + 9x + 4$

_____

13. $7(m - n) - 4(-4m)$

_____

14. $x + 6(y + 3) - (3y - x)$

_____

15. $d - e(3d + 8)$

_____

3.3 Writing Expressions

Write an expression. Simplify if possible.

16. Cruz has d $10-bills and 3 fewer $20-bills than he has $10-bills.
Write an algebraic expression to represent how much money Cruz has
in dollars. Simplify the expression, if possible.

_____

? ESSENTIAL QUESTION

17. How can you use algebraic expressions to solve problems?

_____

_____

_____

_____

Selected Response

1. What are the coefficients in the expression $z + 4z^2 + 7a + 11$?

(A) 4, 7, 11   (C) 1, 4, 7

(B) 1, 11   (D) 4, 7

2. Starting on page 40, Savannah reads her book at a pace of 15 pages an hour for t hours. The expression $40 + 15t$ represents Savannah's page number in her book. If she reads for 1.6 hours, what page is Savannah on?

(A) 64   (C) 40

(B) 24   (D) 55

3. Which property is illustrated by the equation $7(x + 4) = (x + 4) \cdot 7$?

(A) Commutive Property of Addition

(B) Commutive Property of Multiplication

(C) Distributive Property

(D) Associative Property of Addition

4. Which expression is equivalent to $6a - 4(2a - 6)$?

(A) $2a - 24$ (C) $14a - 24$

(B) $14a - 6$ (D) $24 - 2a$

5. In which number set does $5^{\frac{1}{2}}$ belong?

(A) Whole numbers   (C) Rational numbers

(B) Integers   (D) Irrational numbers

6. Which set is **not** closed under multiplication?

(A) {0}   (C) {−1, 0, 1}

(B) {0, 1}   (D) {−1, 0, 2}

7. You make a profit on s shirts at \$12 per shirt less a 10% discount according to the expression $12s - 0.1(12s)$. What are the units of the coefficient 12?

(A) $\frac{\text{dollars}}{\text{shirt}}$ (C) shirts

(B) dollars   (D) $\frac{\text{shirts}}{\text{dollar}}$

8. Ana pays 15% tax on her gross income of I minus the \$12,000 deductions that are subtracted from her gross. Which expression represents Ana's tax bill in simplified form?

(A) $0.15(I + 12{,}000)$ (C) $0.15(I - 12{,}000)$

(B) $0.15I - 12{,}000$ (D) $0.15I + 0.5(12{,}000)$

Mini-Tasks

9. Gia starts with a square with sides x and progressively adds 1 to make a series of squares.

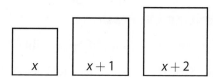

a. What is the perimeter of each square?

_____

b. What pattern do you see in the perimeter?

_____

_____

c. What is the area of each square? Write each area in two different forms if possible.

_____

_____

Relationships between Quantities

Key Vocabulary
precision *(precisión)*
significant digits *(dígitos significativos)*
dimensional analysis *(análisis dimensional)*
conversion factors *(factor de conversión)*

? ESSENTIAL QUESTION

How do you calculate when the numbers are measurements?

EXAMPLE 1

A cyclist travels 100 kilometers in 4 hours. Use dimensional analysis to convert the cyclist's speed to miles per minute.

Use the conversion factor $\frac{1\text{ mile}}{1.61\text{ km}}$ to convert kilometers to miles, and use $\frac{1\text{ hour}}{60\text{ min}}$ to convert hours to minutes.

$$\frac{100\text{ km}}{4\text{ h}} \cdot \frac{1\text{ mi}}{1.61\text{ km}} \cdot \frac{1\text{ h}}{60\text{ min}} \approx 0.3\frac{\text{mile}}{\text{minute}}$$

EXAMPLE 2

Sharon is building a wooden crate in the shape of a rectangular prism with dimensions 12 meters by 10.2 meters by 15.5 meters. Find the volume of the crate. Write your answer using the correct number of significant digits.

$$A = l \times w \times h$$
$$= 12 \times 10.2 \times 15.5$$
$$= 1897.2$$

The least precise measurement is 12 meters, which has 2 significant digits. Round the volume to a number that has 2 significant digits: 1900 m^3.

EXERCISES

1. Shaniqua's bedroom is 12.6 feet long and 8 feet wide. She wants to put a 1 foot high wallpaper border around the room and cover the floor with carpet. How many feet of wallpaper does she need, and how many square feet of carpet? Show your answer with the correct number of significant digits. (Lesson 1.1)

_____

2. Rachel's biscuits require 0.75 cup of milk for 1 batch. Use dimensional analysis to convert this amount into liters. Use the conversion factors $\frac{1\text{ cup}}{0.5\text{ pint}}$ to convert cups to pints, $\frac{1\text{ pint}}{0.5\text{ quart}}$ to convert pints to quarts, and $\frac{1\text{ quart}}{0.94\text{ liter}}$ to convert quarts to liters. Use the correct number of significant digits to give your answer. (Lessons 1.1, 1.2)

_____

Exponents and Real Numbers

Key Vocabulary
radical expression *(expresión radical)*
radicand *(radicando)*
index *(índice)*
real numbers *(número real)*
closed *(cerrado)*

? **ESSENTIAL QUESTION**

What sets of numbers are included in the real numbers?

EXAMPLE 1

Simplify each expression.

A $64^{\frac{1}{3}}$

$64^{\frac{1}{3}} = \sqrt[3]{64} = \sqrt[3]{4^3}$ *Use the definition of $b^{\frac{1}{n}}$.*

$= 4$

B $32^{\frac{1}{5}} - 81^{\frac{1}{2}}$

$32^{\frac{1}{5}} - 81^{\frac{1}{2}} = \sqrt[5]{32} - \sqrt{81}$ *Use the definition of $b^{\frac{1}{n}}$.*

$= \sqrt[5]{2^5} - \sqrt{9^2}$

$= 2 - 9$

$= -7$

C $256^{\frac{3}{4}}$

$256^{\frac{3}{4}} = 256^{\frac{1}{4} \times 3}$

$= \left(256^{\frac{1}{4}}\right)^3 = \left(\sqrt[4]{256}\right)^3$ *Use the definition of $b^{\frac{1}{n}}$.*

$= \left(\sqrt[4]{4^4}\right)^3 = (4)^3$

$= 64$

EXAMPLE 2

A **Is the set $\{-1, 0, 1\}$ closed under addition?**

Add each pair of elements in the set. Check whether each sum is in the set.

$-1 + (-1) = -2$ ✗ $-1 + 0 = -1$ ✔ $-1 + 1 = 0$ ✔

$0 + 0 = 0$ ✔ $0 + 1 = 1$ ✔ $1 + 1 = 2$ ✗

The set $\{-1, 0, 1\}$ is not closed under addition.

B **Show that the set of irrational numbers is not closed under addition.**

Find two irrational numbers whose sum is not an irrational number.

$$\sqrt{3} + (-\sqrt{3}) = 0 \qquad \textit{0 is not irrational.}$$

The set of irrational numbers is not closed under addition.

EXERCISES

Simplify. (Lesson 2.1)

3. $8^{\frac{2}{3}} + 100^{\frac{1}{2}}$ _____

4. $1^{\frac{9}{5}}$ _____

5. Tou is a director working on a play, and he needs to know the area of a circular stage with a radius of 7 feet. Use the formula $A = 3.14r^2$ to find the area. (Lesson 2.1)

_____

Using *whole*, *integer*, *rational*, **and** *irrational*, **name all the subsets of the real numbers to which each number belongs.** (Lessons 2.1, 2.2)

6. $(-2)^4$ _____

7. $(27)^{\frac{1}{4}}$ _____

8. $-\dfrac{\sqrt[3]{125}}{5}$ _____

9. $\left(\dfrac{1}{4}\right)^2$ _____

Tell whether the set is closed under the operation. If it is not closed, give an example that shows that the set is not closed under the operation. (Lesson 2.2)

10. positive irrational numbers; division _____

11. negative rational numbers; multiplication _____

12. negative integers; addition _____

13. positive integers; subtraction _____

MODULE 3

Expressions

? ESSENTIAL QUESTION

How can you use algebraic expressions to solve problems?

EXAMPLE 1

Evaluate the algebraic expression $n(5n - 13)^3$ for $n = 3$.

$$n(5n - 13)^3 = [3] \cdot (5 \cdot [3] - 13)^3$$

$$= [3] \cdot (15 - 13)^3$$

$$= [3] \cdot (2)^3$$

$$= [3] \cdot 8$$

$$= 24$$

EXAMPLE 2

Simplify $3a + 5b^2 + 2a + 4b^2$.

$3a + 5b^2 + 2a + 4b^2$

$= 3a + 2a + 5b^2 + 4b^2$ Commutative Property of Addition

$= a(3 + 2) + b^2(5 + 4)$ Distributive Property

$= a(5) + b^2(9)$ Combine like terms

$= 5a + 9b^2$ Commutative Property of Multiplication

EXAMPLE 3

"The price for a dozen eggs plus 8% tax, divided by 12" represents the cost of one egg. Write and simplify an algebraic expression to model the phrase.

Use the verbal model to identify each quantity and the operations.

Price of a Dozen Eggs	+	8% of Price of a Dozen Eggs	÷	12 Eggs per Dozen
Quantity	Operation	Quantity	Operation	Quantity

Let d represent the price of a dozen eggs.

d	+	$0.08d$	÷	12 Eggs per Dozen

$$= \frac{(d + 0.08d)}{12}$$

$$= \frac{1.08d}{12}$$

EXERCISES

Evaluate each expression for $x = 2$ and $y = 4$. (Lesson 3.1)

14. $\dfrac{2x^2 + 3x}{y}$

_____

15. $(xy)^2 - x + y$

_____

16. $(9x - 3y)^2$

_____

17. $3x(3y - 5x)$

_____

Simplify. (Lesson 3.2)

18. $2(x + y - 3) - x$

_____

19. $2 + (6 - x) + 2x$

_____

20. $15g - 3(5h) + 5g$

_____

21. $6(m - 3) + 17$

_____

Write an algebraic expression for each situation, then evaluate the expression for the given values. (Lessons 3.1 and 3.3)

22. Samuel earns $10 per hour plus $1 per suitcase he sells. Find his earnings when he works 8 hours and sells 20 suitcases.

_____

23. Claire and Li are evenly sharing the cost of 7 yards of red fabric and 3 yards of blue fabric. Find the amount each pays when red fabric is $6.50 per yard and blue fabric is $8.00 per yard

_____

24. Jason is buying 2 hats and 3 scarves for each of his 4 children. Find the amount Jason spends when hats cost $8.50 and scarves cost $5.50.

_____

Unit 1A Performance Tasks

1. **CAREERS IN MATH** **Cave Geologist** Maria is studying a cave. She finds a granite boulder that is roughly spherical.

   a. Maria determines that the mass of the boulder is about 21.5 kilograms. Using the fact that the density of granite is about 2.7 g/cm^3, find the approximate volume of the boulder. Show your work, and give your answer to the correct number of significant digits.

   _____

   _____

   _____

   b. Maria wants to find the approximate radius of the boulder. The expression $1.33V^{\frac{1}{3}}$ gives the radius of a sphere with volume V. Use the expression to the estimate the boulder's radius. Show your work, and give your answer to two significant digits.

   _____

   _____

   c. As a check on her results, Maria measures the circumference of the boulder and finds that it is about 126 cm. Explain how this measurement helps Maria.

   _____

   _____

   _____

2. Reynaldo, Brianna, and Carter are preparing for a bicycle race. During their last practice, Reynaldo traveled at a speed of 9.78 meters per second, Brianna traveled at a speed of 18.75 miles per hour, and Carter traveled at a speed of 0.54 kilometers per minute. Use 1 mile = 1.61 kilometers.

   a. Who had the greatest speed during their last practice? Explain.

   _____

   _____

   _____

   _____

   _____

   b. How much faster than Carter was Reynaldo? Give your answer in meters per second. Use the correct number of significant digits.

   _____

   _____

   _____

   c. How much faster than Brianna was Carter? Give your answer in miles per hour. Use the correct number of significant digits.

   _____

   _____

   _____

   _____

   d. How much faster than Brianna was Reynaldo? Give your answer in meters per second. Use the correct number of significant digits.

   _____

   _____

   _____

   _____

   e. The race Reynaldo, Brianna, and Carter are training for is 50 miles. Estimate how many hours it will take each to complete the race.

   _____

   _____

Selected Response

1. Which represents the most precise measurement?

Ⓐ 3 cm

Ⓑ 3.12 km

Ⓒ 3.1 m

Ⓓ 3.2 cm

2. The width of a table is 2.2 ft. The length of the table is 4 ft. Which represents the area of the tabletop with the correct number of significant digits?

Ⓐ 8.8 ft²

Ⓑ 8 ft²

Ⓒ 9 ft²

Ⓓ 12.4 ft²

3. Which is the correct conversion factor for converting centimeters to inches?

Ⓐ $\frac{3.28 \text{ feet}}{1 \text{ meter}}$

Ⓑ $\frac{1 \text{ centimeter}}{0.39 \text{ inches}}$

Ⓒ $\frac{1 \text{ meter}}{3.28 \text{ feet}}$

Ⓓ $\frac{0.39 \text{ inches}}{1 \text{ centimeter}}$

4. Near Earth's surface, the time, t, required for an object to fall a distance, d, is given by $t = \frac{1}{4} d^{\frac{1}{2}}$, where t is measured in seconds, and d is measured in feet. Find the time it will take an object to fall 625 feet.

Ⓐ 12.5 s

Ⓑ 97,656.25 s

Ⓒ 156.25 s

Ⓓ 6.25 s

5. Which property is demonstrated by $16^{-2} = \frac{1}{16^2}$?

Ⓐ negative exponent

Ⓑ power of a quotient

Ⓒ product of powers

Ⓓ quotient of powers

Hot Tip! **Try to solve the problem a second time using a different method to make sure your answer is correct.**

6. Simplify: $25^{\frac{1}{2}} + 16^{\frac{3}{4}}$

Ⓐ 41

Ⓑ 21

Ⓒ 7

Ⓓ 13

7. Which property allows one to simplify $2(x + 2)$ to $2x + 4$?

Ⓐ Commutative Property

Ⓑ Associative Property

Ⓒ Distributive Property

Ⓓ Replicative Property

8. Which of the following is NOT a set to which 3.5 belongs?

Ⓐ Positive Numbers

Ⓑ Real Numbers

Ⓒ Integers

Ⓓ Rational Numbers

Look for key words and context clues to help you translate the problem into an expression.

9. Elizabeth and her friend purchase identical team shirts to wear to a football game. There is a 7% sales tax. If c represents the cost of the two shirts without tax, which algebraic expression represents the tax for one shirt?

(A) $\frac{c}{2}$

(B) $\frac{0.07c}{2}$

(C) $\frac{1.07c}{2}$

(D) $1.07c$

10. Evaluate $x^2 + 3x - 18$ for $x = 3$.

(A) -6

(B) 0

(C) 6

(D) 9

11. When Kathryn makes rice, she adds a cup of water for every half a cup of rice and then adds an extra quarter cup of water. If Kathryn is making half a cup of rice per person eating, and is feeding 5 people, including herself, how many cups of water does she need?

(A) 2.75 cups

(B) 5 cups

(C) 2.5 cups

(D) 5.25 cups

12. Simplify: $2a + 3\left(\frac{5a + 30b}{15}\right)$

(A) $3a + 6b$

(B) $3a + 2b$

(C) $17a + 6b$

(D) $17a + 2b$

13. Malia is booking train tickets for her family. Tickets cost $75 per adult, $50 per senior or per person between the ages of 12 and 18, and $25 per child under the age of 12. There is also a $10 booking fee for any trip. If Malia is 16 years old and is traveling with her senior-citizen grandmother, her mother, and her infant brother, how much will their trip cost?

(A) $235

(B) $210

(C) $200

(D) $175

Mini-Tasks

14. Frieda's construction shop charges $200 per room painted and $150 per room carpeted, but gives half off the carpeting for each room that is painted and carpeted. Write an expression showing the cost to have x rooms painted, half of which are also carpeted, while z rooms are just carpeted.

_____

15. Sally claims that "six more than twice the sum of x and y" means $6 + 2 + (x + y)$. Explain why she is incorrect.

_____

_____

16. Logan is buying ribbon to put around a set of circular tables for prom, so he needs to know the circumference of the tables. Logan knows the formula for the circumference of a circle is $C = 2\pi r$ and he knows that he has four centerpiece tables and five large tables to decorate.

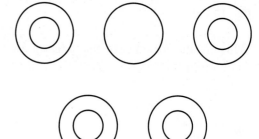

a. If the centerpiece tables have radius $\frac{(16^{\frac{3}{4}}a - 3a)}{5}$ and the big tables have radius $\frac{(27^{\frac{2}{3}}a + 9^{\frac{1}{2}}a)}{4}$, what are the circumferences of the little tables and the big tables in terms of π? Simplify your answers as much as possible.

_____

b. If ribbon costs $1.75 a foot, and $a = \left(\frac{7}{4\pi}\right)$ ft, then how much mooney will Logan need for ribbon?

_____

Equations and Functions

CAREERS IN MATH

Astronomer An astronomer uses equations and functions to calculate models of star and planet movements and to calculate the speed of heavenly bodies. Using a telescope and a computer, an astronomer creates equations to accurately measure things light-years away.

If you're interested in astronomy, you should study mathematical subjects such as:
- Algebra
- Geometry
- Trigonometry
- Calculus

Unit 1B Performance Task

At the end of the unit, check out how **astronomers** use math.

Vocabulary Preview

Use the puzzle to preview key vocabulary from this unit. Unscramble the circled letters within the found words to answer the riddle at the bottom of the page.

1. **TINQAUEO**

2. **IFNOTCUN NNOOATTI**

3. **ONIDMA**

4. **UNTLSOIO**

5. **DTIITENY**

6. **NEARG**

7. **QSNEEEUC**

1. A comparison of two statements that are equal (Lesson 4.2)

2. $y = f(x)$ (2 words) (Lesson 5.2)

3. The x-values of a function (Lesson 5.2)

4. For a two variable equation, an ordered pair that makes the equation true (Lesson 5.1)

5. An equation that is always true, no matter what the value of the variable might be (Lesson 4.2)

6. The y-values of a function (Lesson 5.2)

7. An ordered list of items (Lesson 5.3)

Q: What kind of plates do you use in space?

A: _ _ _ _ _ _ _ _ _ _ _ _ _ _ _ _ _!

Equations and Inequalities in One Variable

? ESSENTIAL QUESTION

How can you solve an equation or inequality in one variable?

Real-World Video

In some sports, such as boxing and wrestling, the athletes and their competitions are categorized by weight. The weight divisions are defined by specific upper and lower weight limits, which can be efficiently described using inequalities.

my.hrw.com

GO DIGITAL

my.hrw.com

my.hrw.com

Go digital with your write-in student edition, accessible on any device.

Math On the Spot

Scan with your smart phone to jump directly to the online edition, video tutor, and more.

Animated Math

Interactively explore key concepts to see how math works.

Personal Math Trainer

Get immediate feedback and help as you work through practice sets.

Are YOU Ready?

Complete these exercises to review skills you will need for this module.

Personal Math Trainer

Online Assessment and Intervention

my.hrw.com

Order of Operations

EXAMPLE Simplify: $17 + 3(7 - 5) + 3^2$

$= 17 + 3(2) + 3^2$ Parentheses

$= 17 + 3(2) + 9$ Exponents

$= 17 + 6 + 9$ Multiplication and division

$= 32$ Addition and subtraction

Simplify.

1. $15 - 3^2 + 2(7 \cdot 3)$

2. $5^2 + 4^2 + 3(2 - 10)$

3. $(10^2 - 9^2) + 5 \cdot 7 + 3$

_____

_____

_____

4. $10 \div 5 \, (2 \cdot 4) - 5^2$

5. $17 - 5 \cdot 2 \div 5 - 1^2$

6. $18 \div 3 \div 3 \cdot 5^2$

_____

_____

_____

One-Step Equations

EXAMPLE Solve:

$y - 5.5 = 11$

$y = 11 + 5.5$ Isolate the variable by adding 5.5 to both sides

$y = 16.5$ of the equation.

Solve each equation.

7. $5x = 100$

8. $-25 = x + 100$

9. $\frac{z}{3} = 17$

_____

_____

_____

One-Step Inequalities

EXAMPLE Solve:

$x + 5 < 14$

$x < 14 - 5$ Isolate the variable by subtracting 5 from

$x < 9$ both sides of the equation.

Solve each inequality.

10. $x - 22 < 17$

11. $f - 110 \geq 25$

12. $\frac{z}{12} < 11$

_____

_____

_____

Reading Start-Up

Vocabulary

Review Words

one-step equation
(*ecuación de un paso*)

one-step inequality
(*desigualdad de un paso*)

Preview Words

equivalent equations

formula

identity

literal equation

solution of an equation

solution of inequality

Visualize Vocabulary

Use the review words to complete the case diagram. Write an example for each oval.

```
        One-Step
  Mathematical Statement
     ↙            ↘
  [        ]    [        ]
     ↓            ↓
  (  oval  )   (  oval  )
```

Understand Vocabulary

To become familiar with some of the vocabulary terms in the module, consider the following. You may refer to the module, the glossary, or a dictionary.

1. One definition of identity is "exact sameness." An equation consists of two expressions. If an equation is an *identity*, what do you think is true about the expressions?

   _____

2. The word *literal* means "of letters." How might a literal equation be different from an equation like $3 + 5 = 8$?

   _____

Active Reading

Two-Panel Flip Chart Before beginning the module, create a Two-Panel Flip Chart to help you organize what you learn about equations and inequalities. Organize the characteristics of the two topics side by side for easy comparison.

Unpacking the Standards

Understanding the standards and the vocabulary terms in the standards will help you know exactly what you are expected to learn in this module.

 FL A-CED.1.1

Create equations … in one variable and use them to solve problems.

Key Vocabulary

equation *(ecuación)*
A mathematical statement that two expressions are equivalent.

variable *(variable)*
a symbol used to represent a quantity that can change

What It Means For You

You can write an equation to represent a real-world problem and then use algebra to solve the equation and find the answer.

EXAMPLE

Michael is saving money to buy a trumpet. The trumpet costs $670. He has $350 saved, and each week he adds $20 to his savings. How long will it take him to save enough money to buy the trumpet?

$$\text{cost of trumpet} = \text{current savings} + \text{additional savings}$$

$$670 = 350 + 20w$$

$$320 = 20w$$

$$16 = w$$

It will take Michael 16 weeks to save enough money.

 FL A-CED.1.3

Represent constraints by … inequalities … in a modeling context.

Key Vocabulary

inequality *(desiguladad)*
A mathematical sentence that shows the relationship between quantities that are not equivalent.

solution of an inequality in one variable *(solucion de una desiguladad en una variable)*
A value or values for the variable that make the inequality true.

What It Means for You

You can use inequalities to represent limits on values so that the solutions make sense in a real-world context.

EXAMPLE

Anyone riding the rollercoaster at a park must be at least 40 inches tall.

Let h represent a person's height.

Height is at least 40 inches

$$h \qquad \geq \qquad 40$$

Visit **my.hrw.com** to see all **Florida Math Standards** unpacked.

my.hrw.com

FL A-REI.2.3
Solve linear equations ... in
one variable ... *Also A-CED.1.1,
A-CED.1.3, N-Q.1.2*

ESSENTIAL QUESTION

How do you solve an equation in one variable?

Solving Two-Step and Multi-Step Equations

Recall that an equation shows that two quantities are equal. Often an equation contains a variable. A solution of an equation is a value for the variable that makes the equation true.

$$x + 2 = 5 \leftarrow \text{equation}$$

$$x = 3 \leftarrow \text{solution because } 3 + 2 = 5 \checkmark$$

Math On the Spot
my.hrw.com

To solve an equation, perform inverse operations to isolate the variable on one side of the equation. The properties of equality can be used to justify the steps taken in solving an equation.

Properties of Equality

Property	Algebra	Numerical example
Addition Property of Equality	If $a = b$, then $a + c = b + c$	$12 = 7 + 5$, so $12 + 3 = 7 + 5 + 3$
Subtraction Property of Equality	If $a = b$, then $a - c = b - c$	$12 = 7 + 5$, so $12 - 3 = 7 + 5 - 3$
Multiplication Property of Equality	If $a = b$, then $ac = bc$	$12 = 7 + 5$, so $12 \cdot 3 = (7 + 5)3$
Division Property of Equality	If $a = b$ and $c \neq 0$, then $\frac{a}{c} = \frac{b}{c}$	$12 = 7 + 5$, so $\frac{12}{3} = \frac{7+5}{3}$

You can use the properties of equality to solve two-step and multi-step equations.

EXAMPLE 1
FL A-REI.2.3

Solve each equation.

A $18 = 2 - 4x$

$$
\begin{array}{ll}
\begin{aligned}
18 &= 2 - 4x \\
\underline{-2} & \underline{-2} \\
16 &= -4x
\end{aligned} & \text{Subtraction Property of Equality} \\[2em]
\begin{aligned}
\frac{16}{-4} &= \frac{-4x}{-4} \\[1em]
-4 &= x
\end{aligned} & \text{Division Property of Equality}
\end{array}
$$

Math Talk
Mathematical Practices

How do you check your solution?

B $\frac{1}{2}z - 12 = 36$

$$\frac{1}{2}z - 12 = 36$$
$$\underline{\qquad +12 \quad +12}$$ Addition Property of Equality
$$\frac{1}{2}z = 48$$
$$2 \cdot \frac{1}{2}z = 2 \cdot 48$$ Multiplication Property of Equality
$$z = 96$$

C $\frac{3}{4} = 6w + 1$

$$\frac{3}{4} = 6w + 1$$
$$\frac{3}{4} - 1 = 6w + 1 - 1$$ Subtraction Property of Equality
$$-\frac{1}{4} = 6w$$
$$-\frac{1}{4}\left(\frac{1}{6}\right) = 6w\left(\frac{1}{6}\right)$$ Multiplication Property of Equality
$$-\frac{1}{24} = w$$

D $8 - (y + 3) = 11$

$$8 - (y + 3) = 11$$
$$8 - y - 3 = 11$$ Distribute the negative sign.
$$5 - y = 11$$ Combine like terms.
$$5 - y = 11$$
$$\underline{-5 \qquad -5}$$ Subtraction Property of Equality
$$-y = 6$$
$$\frac{-y}{-1} = \frac{6}{-1}$$ Division Property of Equality
$$y = -6$$

Math Talk

Mathematical Practices

Is there a different property you could use to express y without a negative sign?

YOUR TURN

Solve each equation.

1. $6k - 9 = -15$

_____

2. $17 = -5m + 32$

_____

3. $23 = 16 - (2z - 4)$

_____

4. $8 = \frac{1}{2}(-m - 1)$

_____

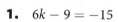

Solving Equations with Variables on Both Sides

In some equations, the variable appears on both sides. You can use the properties of equality to collect the variable terms so that they are all on one side of the equation.

Math On the Spot
my.hrw.com

EXAMPLE 2   FL   A-REI.2.3

Solve each equation.

A $8n - 7 = 2n + 5$

$$
\begin{array}{rl}
8n - 7 = 2n + 5 & \\
\underline{-2n \qquad -2n} & \text{Subtraction Property of Equality} \\
6n - 7 = \quad 5 & \\
\underline{+7 \qquad +7} & \text{Addition Property of Equality} \\
6n = \quad 12 & \\
\end{array}
$$

$$\frac{6n}{6} = \frac{12}{6} \qquad \text{Division Property of Equality}$$

$$n = 2$$

Check: $8n - 7 = 2n + 5$ Substitute 2 for n in the original equation.
$$8(2) - 7 = 2(2) + 5$$
$$9 = 9 \checkmark$$

B $-4(3x - 1) = 10 - 4x$

$$
\begin{array}{rl}
-4(3x - 1) = 10 - 4x & \\
-12x + 4 = 10 - 4x & \text{Distributive Property} \\
\underline{+12x \qquad\quad +12x} & \text{Addition Property of Equality} \\
4 = 10 + 8x & \\
\underline{-10 \quad -10} & \text{Subtraction Property of Equality} \\
-6 = \quad 8x & \\
\end{array}
$$

$$\frac{-6}{8} = \frac{8x}{8} \qquad \text{Division Property of Equality}$$

$$-\frac{3}{4} = x \qquad \text{Simplify.}$$

> Equations are often easier to solve when the variable has a positive coefficient. Keep this in mind when deciding on which side to "collect" variable terms.

YOUR TURN

Solve each equation.

5. $13b = b + 27$

6. $6n + 21 = -3 - 2n$

7. $2p - 9 = 3(2p - 5)$

8. $t - 3 + 4t = 3(3t - 9)$

Personal Math Trainer

Online Assessment and Intervention

my.hrw.com

Math On the Spot

my.hrw.com

Infinitely Many Solutions or No Solutions

An **identity** is an equation that is always true, no matter what value is substituted for the variable. The solutions of an identity are all real numbers. Some equations are always false. Such equations have no solutions.

EXAMPLE 3

FL   A-REI.2.3

Solve each equation.

A $4d - 5(d - 1) = 3 - d + 2$

$$4d - 5(d - 1) = 3 - d + 2$$

$$4d - 5d + 5 = 3 - d + 2 \qquad \text{Distributive Property}$$

$$-d + 5 = 5 - d \qquad \text{Combine like terms}$$

$$\underline{+d} \qquad \underline{+d} \qquad \text{Addition Property of Equality}$$

$$5 = 5 \checkmark \qquad \text{True statement}$$

The equation $4d - 5(d - 1) = 3 - d + 2$ is an identity. All values of d will make the equation true. All real numbers are solutions.

B $3q + 6 - 5q = 8 - 2q + 1$

$$3q + 6 - 5q = 8 - 2q + 1$$

$$-2q + 6 = 9 - 2q \qquad \text{Combine like terms.}$$

$$\underline{+2q} \qquad \underline{+2q} \qquad \text{Addition Property of Equality}$$

$$6 = 9 \text{ ✗} \qquad \text{False statement}$$

> The solution set is an empty set — it contains no elements. The empty set can be written as ϕ or { }.

The equation $3q + 6 - 5q = 8 - 2q + 1$ is always false. There is no value of q that will make the equation true. There are no solutions.

Personal
Math Trainer

Online Assessment
and Intervention

my.hrw.com

YOUR TURN

Solve each equation.

9. $3h + 6(h - 1) = 9h - 6$

10. $4n - 3 - 5n = 6 - n + 4$

Writing and Solving Real-World Equations

You can write and solve an equation to model a real-world situation. Check that the solution to the equation makes sense in the context of the situation.

EXAMPLE 4   **FL** **A-CED.1.3**

Leon paid $26.50 for a shirt with a sales tax of 6% included, but he doesn't remember the price without tax. What was the price of the shirt?

STEP 1 Write a verbal model for the situation.

price of shirt + (6% of price of shirt) = total paid

STEP 2 Choose a variable for the unknown quantity. Include units. Write an equation to model the situation.

Let p represent the price of the shirt in dollars.

$$p + 0.06p = 26.50$$

STEP 3 Solve the equation.

$$p + 0.06p = 26.50$$

$$1.06p = 26.50 \qquad \text{Combine like terms.}$$

$$\frac{1.06p}{1.06} = \frac{26.50}{1.06} \qquad \text{Division Property of Equality}$$

$$p = 25$$

So the price of the shirt is $25.

STEP 4 Check that the answer makes sense in the context of the problem.

6% of $25 is $1.50, so the sales tax on the shirt is $1.50.

$25.00 + $1.50 = $26.50

So the answer does make sense.

> **Math Talk**
> **Mathematical Practices**
> Would a negative solution make sense in this situation? Explain.

YOUR TURN

11. Maria bought a blouse on sale for 20% off. The sale price was $28.76. What was the original price? Write an equation to model the situation and solve it.

_____

Personal Math Trainer

Online Assessment and Intervention

⏱ my.hrw.com

Guided Practice

Identify the steps you would take to solve each equation. Then solve. (Example 1)

1. $18x + 17 = -19$

2. $7y + 6 + 4y - 13 = 26$

_____

_____

_____

_____

_____

_____

_____

_____

Solve each equation. (Examples 1 and 2)

3. $13 = 4x - 9$

4. $55 - 6(3b - 1) = -11$

5. $2.5k + 5 - 1.5k = 14$

_____

_____

_____

6. $12n + 9 = 6 - 3n$

7. $6z = 4\left(\frac{1}{2}z - 8\right)$

8. $2r - 6 + 5r = 3 - r + 7$

_____

_____

_____

Solve each equation. Determine whether the equation has infinitely many solutions or no solution. Explain. (Example 3)

9. $7t - 13 - 2t = 9 + 5t$

10. $4(2x - 3) = x - 12 + 7x$

11. $6 - 2r + 1 = 3r - 5(r - 2)$

_____

_____

_____

_____

_____

_____

Write an equation to model each problem and solve it. (Example 4)

12. **Represent Real-World Problems** At 12 noon in Anchorage, Alaska, Janice noticed that the temperature outside was $12\,°\text{F}$. The temperature dropped at a steady rate of $2\,°\text{F}$ per hour. At what time was the temperature $-4\,°\text{F}$?

_____

13. Zelly works 20 hours a week at a food market for $7.50 an hour. She takes home $6.75 an hour after deductions. What is her rate for deductions?

_____

? ESSENTIAL QUESTION CHECK-IN

14. How do you use the properties of equality to solve an equation in one variable?

_____

_____

4.1 Independent Practice

Personal
Math Trainer

Online
Assessment and
Intervention

my.hrw.com

FL A-REI.2.3

Solve each equation.

15. $6y - (2y - 5) = 29$

16. $5x - 9 = 7x + 6 - 2x$

17. $8(3m + 5) = 2m - 4$

18. $15q - 3(4q - 6) =$
$3q + 9 - 9q$

19. $6z + 10 = 4z + 19$

20. $8b + 12 - b =$
$8 + 7b + 4$

21. $5a - (8 - a) = 4a - 10$

22. $7n - 2 = 6n - 2n$

23. $8d - \frac{1}{3}(6 - 9d) = 42$

Write and solve an equation to solve each problem.

24. Mari and Jen each work 20 hours a week at different jobs. Mari earns twice as much as Jen. Together they earn $480. How much does each girl earn in a week?

25. David's bowling score is 5 less than 3 times Aaron's score. The sum of their scores is 215. Find the score of each student.

26. **Multi-Step** One month, Jon worked 3 hours less than Chaya, and Angelica worked 4 hours more than Chaya. Together they worked 196 hours. Find the number of hours each person worked.

27. The teacher separated her class of twenty-eight students into two groups. One group has 4 more than twice as many students as the other group. How many students are in each group?

28. An equilateral triangle and a square have the same perimeter. Each side of the square measures 6 cm. What is the length of each side of the triangle?

29. Gaetano spent $37.80, including tax, on a pair of jeans. How much did the jeans cost if there was an 8% sales tax?

30. The temperature at 4 a.m. was $-13\,°$F. The temperature was rising at a steady rate of $5\,°$F an hour. At what time will the temperature be $12\,°$F ?

31. Brian is fencing a rectangular area in the backyard for his dog. He has 25 ft of fence. He does not need fencing on the side that runs along the garage. This side is 9 ft long. What are the dimensions of the kennel?

Lesson 4.1 **95**

 **FOCUS ON HIGHER ORDER THINKING**

32. Justify Reasoning Suppose you want to solve the equation $2a + b = 2a$, where a and b are nonzero real numbers. Describe the solution to this equation. Justify your description.

_____

_____

_____

33. Persevere in Problem Solving A rectangular garden is fenced on all sides with 160 feet of fencing. The garden is 6 feet longer than it is wide. What is the area of the garden?

a. What information do you need to find the area? How can you find the information?

_____

_____

_____

_____

b. Describe how to find the area of the garden. Include the steps you used.

_____

_____

_____

_____

_____

_____

_____

_____

_____

_____

_____

_____

LESSON 4.2 Inequalities in One Variable

FL A-REI.2.3

Solve linear equations and inequalities in one variable, including equations with coefficients represented by letters. *Also A-CED.1.1, A-CED.1.3*

ESSENTIAL QUESTION

How do you solve an inequality in one variable?

One-Step Inequalities

An **inequality** is a statement that compares two expressions that are not equal by using an inequality sign.

A **solution of an inequality** is any value that makes the inequality true. Inequalities usually have infinitely many solutions. One way to represent the solution set of an inequality in one variable is to graph it on a number line.

You can solve linear inequalities using methods that are similar to the ones you use to solve linear equations.

Math On the Spot
my.hrw.com

EXAMPLE 1 FL A-REI.2.3

Solve and graph each inequality.

A $2x - 1 > 7$

$$2x - 1 > 7$$

$$\underline{\quad +1 \quad +1\quad}$$ Add 1 to each side.

$$2x > 8$$

$$\frac{2x}{2} > \frac{8}{2}$$ Divide each side by 2.

$$x > 4$$

B $\frac{x}{3} \leq -4$

$$\frac{x}{3} \leq -4$$

$$3\left(\frac{x}{3}\right) \leq 3\,(-4)$$ Multiply each side by 3.

$$x \leq -12$$

YOUR TURN

Solve and graph each inequality.

1. $12n > 6$

_____

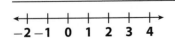

2. $\frac{h}{2} \leq -1$

_____

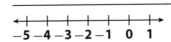

3. $3m + 4 \geq 16$

_____

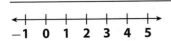

4. $2(s - 1) < 4$

_____

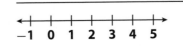

Personal Math Trainer

Online Assessment and Intervention

my.hrw.com

 **FL** A-REI.2.3

Multiplying and Dividing by a Negative Number

What happens when you multiply each side of an inequality by the same number?

A Multiply both sides of $2 > -1$ by 2. Does it result in a true inequality?

Explain. _____

B Multiply both sides of $2 > -1$ by -2. Does it result in a true inequality?

Explain. _____

C Multiply both sides of $2 > -1$ by -2 AND reverse the inequality symbol from $>$ to $<$. Does it result in a true inequality? Explain.

_____

_____

REFLECT

5. Make a Conjecture Does multiplying both sides of an inequality by a negative number result in an equivalent inequality? Explain.

_____

_____

Math On the Spot
⏻ my.hrw.com

Solving Multi-Step Inequalities

You can use the properties in the box below to help you solve inequalities.

Properties of Inequality		
Property	$a > b$	$a < b$
Addition Property of Inequality	For all numbers a, b, and c, if $a > b$, then $a + c > b + c$.	For all numbers a, b, and c, if $a < b$, then $a + c < b + c$.
Subtraction Property of Inequality	For all numbers a, b, and c, if $a > b$, then $a - c > b - c$.	For all numbers a, b, and c, if $a < b$, then $a - c < b - c$.
Multiplication Property of Inequality	For all numbers a, b, and c, if c is positive and $a > b$, then $ac > bc$.	For all numbers a, b, and c, if c is positive and $a < b$, then $ac < bc$.
	For all numbers a, b, and c, if c is negative and $a > b$, then $ac < bc$.	For all numbers a, b, and c, if c is negative and $a < b$, then $ac > bc$.
Division Property of Inequality	For all numbers a, b, and c, if c is positive and $a > b$, then $\frac{a}{c} > \frac{b}{c}$.	For all numbers a, b, and c, if c is positive and $a < b$, then $\frac{a}{c} < \frac{b}{c}$.
	For all numbers a, b, and c, if c is negative and $a > b$, then $\frac{a}{c} < \frac{b}{c}$.	For all numbers a, b, and c, if c is negative and $a < b$, then $\frac{a}{c} > \frac{b}{c}$.

EXAMPLE 2 FL A-REI.2.3

Solve and graph each inequality.

A $240 + 3d \leq 600$

$$240 + 3d \leq 600$$
$$\underline{-240 \qquad -240} \qquad \text{Subtraction Property of Inequality}$$
$$3d \leq 360$$

$$\frac{3d}{3} \leq \frac{360}{3} \qquad \text{Division Property of Inequality}$$

$$d \leq 120$$

B $12 - 5k > 72$

$$12 - 5k > 72$$
$$\underline{-12 \qquad -12} \qquad \text{Subtraction Property of Inequality}$$
$$-5k > 60$$

$$\frac{-5k}{-5} < \frac{60}{-5} \qquad \begin{array}{l}\text{Division Property of Inequality}\\ \text{Reverse the inequality symbol.}\end{array}$$

$$k < -12$$

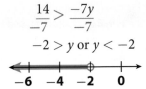

C $6^2 - 1 < -7(y - 3)$

$$6^2 - 1 < -7(y - 3)$$
$$35 < -7y + 21 \qquad \begin{array}{l}\text{Simplify.}\\ \text{Subtraction Property of Inequality}\end{array}$$
$$\underline{-21 \qquad \quad -21}$$
$$14 < -7y$$

$$\frac{14}{-7} > \frac{-7y}{-7} \qquad \begin{array}{l}\text{Division Property of Inequality}\\ \text{Reverse the inequality symbol.}\end{array}$$

$$-2 > y \text{ or } y < -2$$

When you read an inequality containing a variable, begin with the variable. $-2 > y$ is read, "y is less than -2." You can write $y < -2$.

My Notes

D $-\frac{2}{3}x > -\frac{1}{2}$

$$-\frac{2}{3}x > -\frac{1}{2}$$

$$\left(-\frac{3}{2}\right)-\frac{2}{3}x < \left(-\frac{3}{2}\right)-\frac{1}{2}$$ Multiplication Property of Inequality
Reverse the inequality symbol.

$$x < \frac{3}{4}$$

YOUR TURN

Solve and graph each inequality.

6. $-7t \geq 4.9$

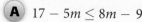

7. $-\frac{5}{6}y < -\frac{3}{4}$

8. $-3(x-4) < 18$

9. $5y + 2(3-4y) < 330$

Solving Inequalities with Variables on Both Sides

Solving inequalities with variables on both sides is similar to solving equations with variables on both sides. Use inverse operations and the properties of inequality to "collect" the variable terms on one side.

EXAMPLE 3 FL   A-REI.2.3

Solve and graph each inequality.

A $17 - 5m \leq 8m - 9$

$$17 - 5m \leq 8m - 9$$

$$\underline{+5m\ +5m}$$ Addition Property of Inequality

$$17\ \ \ \ \ \ \leq 13m - 9$$

$$\underline{+9 \ \ \ \ \ \ \ \ \ \ +9}$$ Addition Property of Inequality

$$26\ \ \ \ \ \ \leq 13m$$

$$\frac{26}{13} \leq \frac{13m}{13}$$ Division Property of Inequality

$$2 \leq m \text{ or } m \geq 2$$

B $24 - 6y - 5y \leq -9$

$$24 - 6y - 5y \leq -9$$

$24 - 11y \leq -9$ Combine the like terms

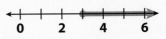

$-24 \qquad\qquad -24$ Subtraction Property of Inequality

$-11y \leq -33$

$\dfrac{-11y}{-11} \geq \dfrac{-33}{-11}$ Division Property of Inequality
Reverse the inequality symbol.

$y \geq 3$

C $6(z - 5) > -5(7 - 2z)$

$$6(z - 5) > -5(7 - 2z)$$

$6z - 30 > -35 + 10z$ Distributive Property

$-6z \qquad\qquad -6z$ Subtraction Property

$-30 > -35 + 4z$

$+35 \qquad +35$ Addition Property of Inequality

$5 > \qquad 4z$

$\dfrac{5}{4} > \dfrac{4z}{4}$ Division Property of Inequality

$1.25 > z$ or $z < 1.25$

YOUR TURN

Solve and graph each inequality.

10. $10 - k > 5 + \dfrac{2k}{3}$ _____

11. $\dfrac{3}{5}(a + 3) \geq 0.4(2 + a)$ _____

Personal Math Trainer

Online Assessment and Intervention

my.hrw.com

Infinitely Many Solutions or No Solutions

Some inequalities are always true and some inequalities are always false, no matter what value is substituted for the variable.

My Notes

EXAMPLE 4

 FL   A-REI.2.3

Solve and graph each inequality.

A $2x - 7 + x < 3x + 10$

$$2x - 7 + x < 3x + 10$$
$$3x - 7 < 3x + 10 \qquad \text{Combine the like terms.}$$
$$\underline{-3x \qquad -3x} \qquad \text{Subtraction Property of Inequality}$$
$$-7 < 10 \checkmark \qquad \text{True statement}$$

Since this is a true statement, any real number substituted for the variable in the original inequality will make the inequality true and is therefore a solution. Its graph is shown.

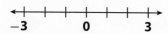

B $5(x + 4) \geq 8x + 25 - 3x$

$$5(x + 4) \geq 8x + 25 - 3x$$
$$5x + 20 \geq 5x + 25 \qquad \text{Combine the like terms.}$$
$$\underline{-5x \qquad -5x} \qquad \text{Subtraction Property of Inequality}$$
$$20 \geq 25 \; \textbf{✗} \qquad \text{False statement}$$

There is no real number that when substituted for the variable will make the statement true. The inequality has no solution. Its graph is shown.

YOUR TURN

Solve and graph each inequality.

12. $3d + 6 < 5d - 2(d + 3)$

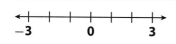

13. $18p - 15 + 6p \geq -10 + 24p - 5$

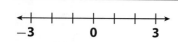

Writing and Solving Real-World Inequalities

You can use inequalities to solve some real-world problems. Words like "at most" and "at least" imply that there is more than one solution to the problem.

EXAMPLE 5 FL A-CED.1.3

Kristin decides to spend at most $50 for a birthday dinner at a restaurant, including a 15% tip. What is the most that the meal can cost before tip?

STEP 1 Write a verbal model for the situation.

cost before tip + 15% of cost before tip ≤ $50

STEP 2 Choose a variable for the unknown quantity. Include units. Write an inequality to model the situation.

Let x represent the cost of the dinner in dollars before the tip.

$x + 0.15x \leq 50$

STEP 3 Solve and graph the inequality.

$x + 0.15x \leq 50$

$1.15x \leq 50$

$\dfrac{1.15x}{1.15} \leq \dfrac{50}{1.15}$

$x \leq 43.478260\ldots$

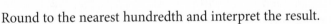

Round to the nearest hundredth and interpret the result.

The most that the meal can cost before the tip is $43.48. You also know that the cost of the meal must be more than $0.

REFLECT

14. Why are there no negative numbers in the solution set?

_____

_____

YOUR TURN

15. Ammon and Nakia volunteer at an animal shelter. Nakia worked 3 more hours than Ammon. They each worked a whole number of hours. Together they worked more than 27 hours. What is the least number of hours each worked?

_____

Complete the steps to solve and graph each inequality (Examples 1 and 2)

1. $4 \le -9y + y$

$$4 \le \boxed{}$$

$$\frac{4}{\boxed{}} \ge \frac{-8y}{\boxed{}}$$

$$\boxed{} \ge y$$

2. $7 - 4x < -1$

$$\boxed{} \quad \boxed{}$$

$$7 \qquad < -1 \quad \boxed{}$$

$$\boxed{} \quad \boxed{}$$

$$\frac{8}{\boxed{}} < \frac{4x}{\boxed{}}$$

$$\boxed{}$$

Solve and graph each inequality. (Examples 2, 3, and 4)

3. $3 - 9d < 30$

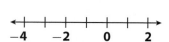

4. $k + 3 - 2k > 50$

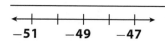

5. $4m \le 6m - 4$

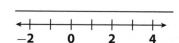

6. $\frac{1}{5}(30 + a) < 5$

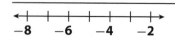

7. $3(x - 4) > 5(x + 2) - 2x$

8. $9y + 4 \ge -2(1 - 3y)$

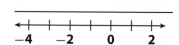

Solve each problem. (Example 5)

9. Mari has a part time job. She earns $7 an hour. She makes at most $143.50 a week. What is the greatest number of hours that she works? _____

10. Alexis received an 85, 89, and 92 on three tests. How many points does she need to score on her next test in order to have an average of at least 90? _____

? ESSENTIAL QUESTION CHECK-IN

11. How do you solve an inequality in one variable?

_____

_____

4.2 Independent Practice

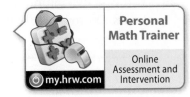

Personal Math Trainer

Online Assessment and Intervention

my.hrw.com

 **FL** A-REI.2.3

Solve and graph each inequality.

12. $-20x \geq -400$ _____

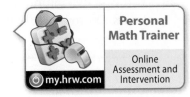
$$-30 \quad -10 \quad 10 \quad 30$$

13. $0 < -10k + 5k$ _____

$$-4 \quad -2 \quad 0 \quad 2$$

14. $6 - 5d > 21$ _____

$$-6 \quad -4 \quad -2 \quad 0$$

15. $3(10 + 2m) \leq 96$ _____

$$6 \quad 8 \quad 10 \quad 12$$

16. $5a - 6 \geq 3a$ _____

$$0 \quad 2 \quad 4 \quad 6$$

17. $5q \geq 8q - \frac{3}{2}$ _____

$$-4 \quad -2 \quad 0 \quad 2$$

18. $2b - 15 > 5b$ _____

$$-8 \quad -6 \quad -4 \quad -2$$

19. $7 - 6x < 2x + 89$ _____

$$-12 \quad -10 \quad -8 \quad -6$$

For Exercises 20–22, determine whether each inequality is sometimes, always, or never true for any value of the variable.

20. $w + 6 \leq w - 6$

_____

21. $12s \geq 10s$

_____

22. $3k - 4 < 2k + 1$

_____

23. After selling a dozen copies of the daily newspaper, a newsstand had fewer than 75 copies left. How many copies did the newsstand have at the beginning of the day?

_____

24. Ken wants to rent a car for a week and to pay no more than $130. How far can he drive if the car rental costs $94 a week plus $0.40 a mile?

_____

25. Lana's car averages 25 miles per gallon. What is the greatest number of gallons of gasoline that she will need if she travels no more than 450 miles?

_____

26. The length of a rectangle is 4 cm longer than the width, and the perimeter is at least 48 cm. What are the smallest possible dimensions of the rectangle?

_____

27. David charges $15 plus $5.50 per hour to mow lawns. Ari charges $12 plus $6.25 per hour to mow lawns. In what situations is Ari's charge greater than or equal to David's charge?

_____

28. Critique Reasoning David said he charges less than Ari if the job takes 4 hours. Do you agree with David's statement? Explain.

_____

_____

_____

29. Draw Conclusions Find a value of b such that the number line shows all the solutions of $bx + 4 \leq -12$. Explain.

```
  ←─┼──┼──┼──┼──┼──┼──┼─→
  −12  −10   −8    −6
```

_____

_____

_____

30. Explain the Error Is the stepped-out solution correct? Explain.

$$17 - 5y < 8y - 9$$
$$-13y < -26$$
$$y < 2$$

_____

_____

_____

31. Communicate Mathematical Ideas Give an example of an inequality that could be solved by using the Multiplication Property of Inequality where both sides of an inequality are multiplied by a negative number. Show the steps of the solution.

_____

32. Justify Reasoning Given the inequality $3(x - 4) > bx$, for what value of b are there no solutions? Use properties of inequality to justify your solution.

_____

_____

_____

_____

Solving for a Variable

FL **A-CED.1.4**

Rearrange formulas to highlight a quantity of interest, using the same reasoning as in solving equations. *Also A-REI.2.3*

ESSENTIAL QUESTION

How do you solve formulas and literal equations for a variable?

Solving a Formula for a Variable

A **formula** is an equation that describes a relationship among quantities. You can "rearrange" a formula using inverse operations and properties of equality to isolate any variable in that formula. This is called solving for a variable. The result of solving a formula for a variable is not a number but a variable expression.

Math On the Spot

⏻ my.hrw.com

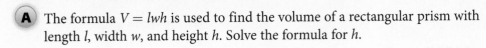

EXAMPLE 1

FL **A-CED.1.4**

Solve the formula for the indicated variable.

A The formula $V = lwh$ is used to find the volume of a rectangular prism with length l, width w, and height h. Solve the formula for h.

$$V = lwh$$

$$\frac{V}{lw} = \frac{lwh}{lw} \qquad \text{Division Property of Equality}$$

$$\frac{V}{lw} = h$$

B The formula $E = \frac{1}{2}kx^2$ is used to find the potential energy E of a spring with spring constant k that has been stretched by length x. Solve the formula for k.

$$E = \frac{1}{2}kx^2$$

$$(2)(E) = (2)(\tfrac{1}{2}kx^2) \qquad \text{Multiplication Property of Equality}$$

$$2E = kx^2$$

$$\frac{2E}{x^2} = \frac{kx^2}{x^2} \qquad \text{Division Property of Equality}$$

$$\frac{2E}{x^2} = k$$

YOUR TURN

Solve each formula for the indicated variable.

1. The formula for the perimeter P of a triangle with sides of length a, b, and c is

   $P = a + b + c$. Solve the formula for b. _____

2. The formula for the volume of a cylinder of radius r and height h is $V = \pi r^2 h$.

   Solve the formula for h. _____

Personal Math Trainer

Online Assessment and Intervention

⏻ my.hrw.com

Modeling with Formulas

Sometimes you are given a formula solved for one variable, but the formula would be more convenient to use if it were solved for one of the other variables. You can solve for a variable in a formula so that it is more convenient for you to use.

My Notes

 **EXAMPLE 2** Real World   FL   A-CED.1.4

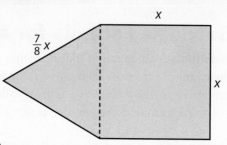

A flower garden is made up of a square and an isosceles triangle with dimensions as shown. Use the formula for perimeter to write a formula for the side length of the square in terms of the perimeter.

STEP 1   Write and simplify a formula for the perimeter of the garden.

$$P = x + x + x + \frac{7}{8}x + \frac{7}{8}x$$

$$P = 3x + \frac{14}{8}x \qquad \text{Combine like terms.}$$

$$P = 4\frac{3}{4}x \qquad \text{Combine like terms.}$$

STEP 2   Solve the formula for x.

$$P = 4\frac{3}{4}x$$

$$P = \frac{19}{4}x$$

$$\left(\frac{4}{19}\right)P = \left(\frac{4}{19}\right)\frac{19}{4}x \qquad \text{Multiplication Property of Equality}$$

$$\frac{4}{19}P = x$$

So the formula for the length of a side of the square is $x = \frac{4}{19}P$.

REFLECT

3. **Communicate Mathematical Ideas** How could you use the formula you derived to find the side lengths of the garden with perimeter 133 feet?

_____

_____

Personal Math Trainer

Online Assessment and Intervention

my.hrw.com

 **YOUR TURN**

Solve each formula for the indicated variable.

4. Formula for density, $D = \frac{m}{V}$, for V

5. Formula for the lateral surface area of a cylinder, $S = 2\pi rh$, for r

_____   _____

Solving a Literal Equation for a Variable

A **literal equation** is an equation with two or more variables. A formula is a type of literal equation. To solve a literal equation for a variable, use inverse operations and properties of equality.

Math On the Spot
my.hrw.com

EXAMPLE 3
FL A-REI.2.3

Solve each literal equation for the indicated variable.

Math Talk
Mathematical Practices

Why are both sides of the equation divided by a?

A $a(x + b) = c$, where $a \neq 0$, for x

$$\frac{a(x + b)}{a} = \frac{c}{a}$$ Division Property of Equality

$$x + b = \frac{c}{a}$$ Simplify.

$$x + b - b = \frac{c}{a} - b$$ Subtraction Property of Equality

$$x = \frac{c}{a} - b$$ Simplify.

B $A = \frac{1}{2}h(b_1 + b_2)$, where $h \neq 0$, for b_1

$$A = \frac{1}{2}h(b_1 + b_2)$$

$$2A = h(b_1 + b_2)$$ Multiplication Property of Equality

$$\frac{2A}{h} = \frac{h(b_1 + b_2)}{h}$$ Division Property of Equality

$$\frac{2A}{h} = b_1 + b_2$$ Simplify.

$$\frac{2A}{h} - b_2 = b_1 + b_2 - b_2$$ Subtraction Property of Equality

$$\frac{2A}{h} - b_2 = b_1$$ Simplify.

$$b_1 = \frac{2A}{h} - b_2$$

REFLECT

6. Justify Reasoning Another way to solve $a(x + b) = c$ is to start by using the Distributive Property. Show and justify the solution steps using this method. _____

_____

_____

YOUR TURN

Solve each literal equation for the indicated variable.

7. $2(k + m) = 5$, for m _____

8. $ax - b = c$, for x _____

9. $2x + 10 = 5y - 4$, for y

10. $s = 3(w - s)$, for s

_____   _____

Personal Math Trainer

Online Assessment and Intervention

my.hrw.com

Solve the formula for the indicated variable. (Example 1)

1. Formula for distance traveled, $d = rt$, for t

2. Formula for the flow of current in an electrical circuit, $V = IH$, for I

3. Formula for the surface area of a cylinder, $SA = 2\pi r^2 + 2\pi rh$, for h

4. Formula for the area of a trapezoid, $A = \frac{1}{2}(a + b)h$, for h

5. Formula for the average of 3 numbers, $A = \frac{a + b + c}{3}$, for c

6. Formula for Celsius temperature, $C = \frac{5}{9}(F - 32)$, for F

7. The formula $T = p + sp$ can be used to calculate the total cost of an item with price p and sales tax rate s, expressed as a decimal. Describe a situation in which you would want to solve the formula for s. Then solve the formula for s. (Example 2)

Solve each equation for the indicated variable. (Example 3)

8. $bx = c$, for x

9. $kn + mp = q$, for p

10. $a = b + rb$, for r

11. $A = P + Prt$, for t

12. $\frac{y - b}{m} = x$, for y

13. $\frac{m}{n} = \frac{p}{q}$, for p

? ESSENTIAL QUESTION CHECK-IN

14. How do you solve formulas and literal equations for a variable?

4.3 Independent Practice

 **FL** A-CED.1.4

Solve the formula for the indicated variable.

15. Formula for the volume of a cylinder,
$V = \pi r^2 h$, for h

_____

16. Formula for the area of a polygon,
$A = \frac{1}{2} aP$, for a

_____

17. Formula for the sum of the measures of the
interior angles of a polygon, $S = 180(n - 2)$,
for n

_____

18. The Pythagorean theorem, $a^2 + b^2 = c^2$,
for c

_____

19. Formula for the volume of a square pyramid,
$V = \frac{1}{3} \ell wh$, for w

_____

20. Formula for surface area of a cone,
$S = \pi r^2 + \pi r \ell$, for ℓ

_____

21. Formula for Fahrenheit temperature,
$F = 32 + \frac{9}{5}C$, for C

_____

22. Formula for the volume of a sphere,
$V = \frac{4}{3} \pi r^3$, for r

_____

Solve each equation for the variable in blue.

23. $km = \frac{m}{2} + p$ _____

24. $\frac{2}{3} c = d$ _____

25. $rs - t = us + v$ _____

26. $\frac{2}{5}(z + 1) = y$ _____

27. $g\left(h + \frac{2}{3}\right) = 1$ _____

28. $a(n - 3) + 8 = bn$ _____

29. Ken purchased a plot of land shaped like the
figure shown. How can he find the length of
the side labeled x if he knows the area A of
this lot?

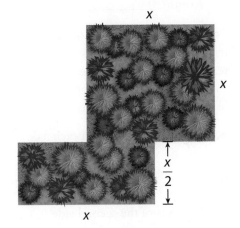

_____

_____

30. An electrician sent Bonnie an invoice in the
amount of a dollars for the six hours of work
done on Saturday. The electrician charges a
weekend fee f in addition to an hourly rate r.
Write a formula Bonnie can use to find r,
the rate the electrician charges per hour, in
terms of a and f. If the invoice amount is
$450 and the weekend fee is $75, what is the
hourly rate?

_____

31. The formula for the surface area of a cylinder is $S = 2\pi r^2 + 2\pi rh$. The surface area of a cylinder is 112π square inches and the radius is 4 inches. What is the height of the cylinder?

_____

Work Area

32. Marion's dinner at a restaurant came to $32.40. This included an 8% tax. Marion wants to leave a 15% tip on the cost of the dinner alone. How much should she leave as a tip?

_____

33. **Multi-Step** A rectangle has a perimeter of 48 cm and a width of 6 cm. Use the formula $P = 2l + 2w$ to find the length.

   a. Write the formula in terms of l. _____

   b. Substitute the values you are given into the rearranged formula. What is the

     length? _____

34. **Persevere in Problem Solving** One side of a triangle is twice as long as the second side. The remaining side is 4 cm greater than the second side. The perimeter of the triangle is 24 cm. Find the length of each side of the triangle.

   a. Draw a picture. Label each side in terms of the second side.

   b. Write a formula for the perimeter of the triangle

     in terms of the second side. _____

   c. Use the formula to find the length of each side of the triangle.

_____

35. **Communicate Mathematical Ideas** Liam receives a basic salary of $600 a week plus 7% of his sales as a commission.

   a. Write a formula for the amount Liam can expect to earn each week.

_____

   b. Last week Liam earned $740. How much were his sales last week?

_____

36. **Make a Conjecture** Write a formula for the area of a square in terms of the perimeter.

_____

Ready to Go On?

4.1 Equations in One Variable

Solve the following equations for x.

1. $3x - 2 = 8 - 2x$

2. $7 - 8x = 1 - 5x$

3. $15 + \dfrac{(5-x)}{x} = 30$

_____

_____

_____

4.2 Inequalities in One Variable

Solve and graph each inequality.

4. $7x - 20 \leq 3x$

_____

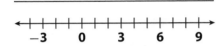

5. $2x + 20 \geq 14$

_____

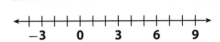

6. $x - 10 \geq 2(x - 4)$

_____

7. $3x - (x + 2) > x - 14$

_____

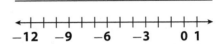

4.3 Solving for a Variable

Solve the formula for the indicated variable.

8. The volume of a cone $V = \frac{1}{3}\pi r^2 h$, for h _____

9. Surface area of cylinder $S = 2\pi r^2 + 2\pi rh$, for h _____

10. Damien has enough red paint to cover an area, of 36 square meters. The surface area of the playground tunnel he must paint has a radius, r, of 3 meters. The formula for surface area is $S = 2\pi rl$ where l is the length.

Solve the formula for l and find the length of the tunnel Damien can paint.

_____

? ESSENTIAL QUESTION

11. How can you solve an equation or inequality in one variable?

_____

_____

_____

Selected Response

1. Which value of x gives the solution of $\frac{14}{x} + 21 = 7$?

Ⓐ $x = 7$ Ⓒ $x = -1$

Ⓑ $x = -2$ Ⓓ $x = -21$

2. Which value of x gives the solution of $\frac{1}{2}(6 + 4x) = x + 2(x + 4)$?

Ⓐ $x = 2$ Ⓒ $x = -6$

Ⓑ $x = -5$ Ⓓ $x = -4$

3. Which graph shows the solution of $2(2x + 1) \geq 30$?

Ⓐ

Ⓑ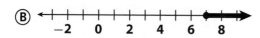

Ⓒ

Ⓓ

4. Which is the solution of $\frac{x}{-5} - 1 < 11$?

Ⓐ $x < \frac{12}{5}$ Ⓒ $x < -60$

Ⓑ $x > -\frac{12}{5}$ Ⓓ $x > -60$

5. Which is $6(a - b) + 4b$ simplified?

Ⓐ $6a - 2b$ Ⓒ $6a + 2b$

Ⓑ $6a - 10b$ Ⓓ $6a + 10b$

6. How many significant digits are in 21.50?

Ⓐ 2   Ⓒ 4

Ⓑ 3   Ⓓ 5

7. If you solve the formula $A = \frac{bh}{2}$ for h, which formula do you get?

Ⓐ $h = \frac{2b}{A}$ Ⓒ $hb = \frac{2}{A}$

Ⓑ $h = \frac{2b}{A}$ Ⓓ $h = \frac{2A}{b}$

8. For the formula $C = 2\pi r$, which equation is the solution for the variable r?

Ⓐ $r = \frac{C}{2\pi}$ Ⓒ $r = \frac{2\pi}{C}$

Ⓑ $r = \frac{1}{2\pi C}$ Ⓓ $r = 2\pi C$

Mini-Tasks

9. Lamar is mowing a lawn shaped like the figure. The perimeter, P, is 32 feet.

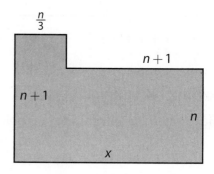

a. Write a formula for the perimeter of the lawn.

_____

_____

_____

_____

b. Solve your perimeter formula for n. What is the value of n if x represents 10 feet?

_____

_____

Equations in Two Variables and Functions

? ESSENTIAL QUESTION

What is a function and how can a function be represented?

Real-World Video

A function can be thought of as like an industrial machine:only accepting of certain predefined inputs, performing a series of operations on what it's been fed, and delivering an output dependent on the initial input.

⏻ my.hrw.com

GO DIGITAL
my.hrw.com

my.hrw.com

Go digital with your write-in student edition, accessible on any device.

Math On the Spot

Scan with your smart phone to jump directly to the online edition, video tutor, and more.

Animated Math

Interactively explore key concepts to see how math works.

Personal Math Trainer

Get immediate feedback and help as you work through practice sets.

Are YOU Ready?

Complete these exercises to review skills you will need for this module.

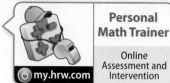
Ordered Pairs

EXAMPLE (−3, 1)

Start at (0, 0).
Move 3 units to the left.   *The x-coordinate is −3.*
Move 1 unit up.   *The y-coordinate is 1.*

Graph each point on the coordinate plane.

1. (−2, 4)

2. (0, −5)

3. (1, −3)

4. (4, 2)

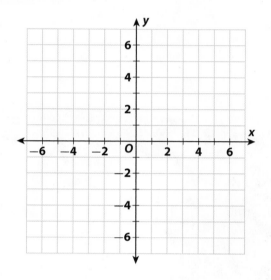

Evaluate Expressions

EXAMPLE Evaluate $4x$ for $x = 3$

$4x = 4(3)$ *Substitute 3 for x.*

$\quad = 12$ *Simplify.*

Evaluate each expression for $x = -2, -1, 0, 1,$ and 2.

5. $-2x - 1$

6. $x - 1$

7. $x^2 - 1$

_____

8. $3(x + 2)$

9. $15 - 5x$

10. $2x^2 - 5x + 2$

_____

11. $\frac{1}{2}x + \frac{3}{2}$

12. $0.05x - 0.1$

13. $(x + 1)^3 - x$

_____

Reading Start-Up

Vocabulary

Review Words

coefficient (*coeficiente*)

constant (*constante*)

equation in one variable (*ecuación en una variable*)

solution of an equation in one variable (*solución de una ecuación en una variable*)

variable (*variable*)

Preview Words

equation in two variables

solution of an equation in two variables

function

domain

range

function notation

sequence

term

explicit rule

recursive rule

Visualize Vocabulary

Complete the graphic using each review word.

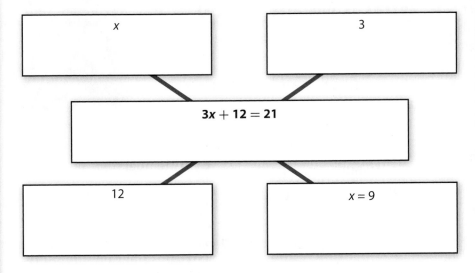

Understand Vocabulary

To become familiar with some of the vocabulary in the module, answer each question. You may refer to the module or the glossary.

1. You've learned what a solution of an equation in one variable is. What do you think the **solution of an equation in two variables** is?

   _____

2. Have you heard the term **sequence** before? What do you think it may mean mathematically?

   _____

Active Reading

Key-Term Fold Before beginning the module, create a Key-Term Fold Note to help you organize what you learn. Write a vocabulary term on each tab of the key-term fold. Under each tab, write the definition of the term and an example of the term.

MODULE 5
Unpacking the Standards

Understanding the standards and the vocabulary terms in the standards will help you know exactly what you are expected to learn in this module.

 FL A-REI.4.10

Understand that the graph of an equation in two variables is the set of all its solutions plotted in the coordinate plane, often forming a curve (which could be a line).

Key Vocabulary

solution of an equation in two variables *(solución de una ecuación en dos variables)* An ordered pair of values for the variables making the equation true.

What It Means to You

You can represent mathematical relationships with words, equations, tables, and graphs.

UNPACKING EXAMPLE A-REI.4.10

Membership costs $150 plus $75 per month.

$$y = 75x + 150$$

Months	Cost ($)
0	150
1	225
2	300
3	375
4	450

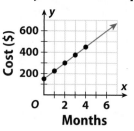

Gym Membership

FL F-IF.1.1

Understand that a function from one set (called the domain) to another set (called the range) assigns to each element of the domain exactly one element of the range…

Key Vocabulary

domain *(dominio)*
The set of all possible input values of a function.

range *(recorrido o rango)*
The set of all possible output values of a function.

Visit **my.hrw.com** to see all **Florida Math Standards** unpacked.

my.hrw.com

What It Means to You

A function model guarantees that for any input value, you will get a unique output value.

UNPACKING EXAMPLE F-IF.1.1

Categorize each of the following as a function or not a function.

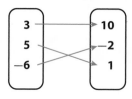

A function: each input number in the left box is matched with exactly one output number in the right box.

{(0, 3), (2, −1), (0, 0)}

Not a function: the input 0 is matched to two outputs (3 and 0).

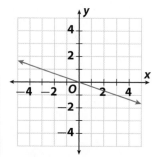

A function: each input (x-value) is matched with exactly one output (y-value).

Equations in Two Variables

FL A-REI.4.10

Understand that the graph of an equation in two variables is the set of all its solutions plotted in the coordinate plane, often forming a curve (which could be a line).

ESSENTIAL QUESTION

What is the relationship between the solutions of an equation in two variables and its graph?

Solutions of Equations in Two Variables

Most equations in one variable have one solution. **Equations in two variables** usually have infinitely many solutions.

A **solution of an equation in two variables** x and y is any ordered pair (x, y) that makes the equation true. To determine whether an ordered pair (x, y) is a solution of an equation, substitute the values of x and y into the equation.

Math On the Spot

⊙ my.hrw.com

EXAMPLE 1

FL A-REI.4.10

Tell whether each ordered pair is a solution of the given equation.

A $3x + 5y = 15$; $(8, 1)$

$3(8) + 5(1) \overset{?}{=} 15$ Substitute.
$24 + 5 \overset{?}{=} 15$ Simplify.
$29 \neq 15$

$(8, 1)$ is NOT a solution of $3x + 5y = 15$.

B $3x + 5y = 15$; $(0, 3)$

$3(0) + 5(3) \overset{?}{=} 15$ Substitute.
$0 + 15 \overset{?}{=} 15$ Simplify.
$15 = 15$

$(0, 3)$ is a solution of $3x + 5y = 15$.

C $x^2 - y = 23$; $(-5, 2)$

> Remember that squaring a negative number results in a positive number: $(-5)^2$ means $(-5)(-5)$, which is positive 25.

$(-5)^2 - 2 \overset{?}{=} 23$ Substitute.
$25 - 2 \overset{?}{=} 23$ Simplify.
$23 = 23$

$(-5, 2)$ is a solution of $x^2 - y = 23$.

D $x^2 - y = 23$; $(5, 2)$

$(5)^2 - 2 \overset{?}{=} 23$ Substitute.
$25 - 2 \overset{?}{=} 23$ Simplify.
$23 = 23$

$(5, 2)$ is a solution of $x^2 - y = 23$.

Math Talk
Mathematical Practices

What do you know about the point $(0, 3)$ and its relationship to the graph of $3x + 5y = 15$?

YOUR TURN

Tell whether each ordered pair is a solution of the given equation.

1. $x - 2y = 3$; $(5, 2)$ _____

2. $x - 2y = 3$; $(9, 3)$ _____

3. $2(x + 1)^2 + 3y = 15$; $(0, 5)$ _____

4. $2(x + 1)^2 + 3y = 15$; $(1, -1)$ _____

EXPLORE ACTIVITY

 FL A-REI.4.10

Exploring the Graph of an Equation

A Complete the table of values to find solutions of the equation $x + y = 5$.

x	y	(x, y)
-2		
0		
1		
3		
5		
7		

B Plot the ordered pairs on a coordinate grid.

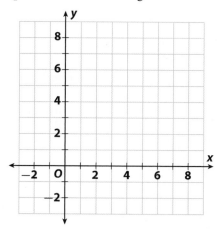

REFLECT

5. Look for a Pattern The plotted points are some of the solutions of the equation. What appears to be true about them?

_____

_____

Graphing a Two-Variable Equation

An equation and its graph can model a real-world situation. By reasoning about the quantities in the situation, you can determine the real-world meaning of each ordered pair.

EXAMPLE 2

The equation $y = 25{,}000x$ describes the average number of species y that become extinct in x years. Graph the equation.

STEP 1 Create a table of values for the equation $y = 25{,}000x$. Choose several nonnegative values of x to find the corresponding values of y.

> The x represents years, so the values must be nonnegative.

x	$y = 25{,}000x$	(x, y)
0	$y = 25{,}000(0)$	$(0, 0)$
2	$y = 25{,}000(2)$	$(2, 50{,}000)$
4	$y = 25{,}000(4)$	$(4, 100{,}000)$
6	$y = 25{,}000(6)$	$(6, 150{,}000)$

STEP 2 Plot the ordered pairs on a graph. Draw the line that passes through the points and contains all the solutions to the equation.

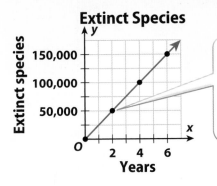

> The x-value (2) represents 2 years. The y-value (50,000) represents the number of species that have become extinct in that amount of time.

My Notes

YOUR TURN

6. Mark wants to have a laser tag party. The cost of the party, y, can be modeled by the equation $y = 20x + 15$, where x is the number of guests. Complete the table and graph the equation.

x	$y = 20x + 15$	(x, y)
3	$y = 20(3) + 15$	$(3, 75)$
5	$y = 20(\ \ ) + 15$	$(\quad\quad)$
7	$y =$	$(\quad\quad)$
8	$y =$	$(\quad\quad)$

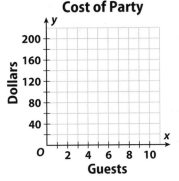

Personal Math Trainer

Online Assessment and Intervention

my.hrw.com

Tell whether each ordered pair is a solution to $6x - 3y = 24$. (Example 1)

1. (5, 1)

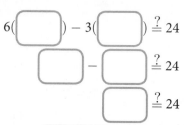

$6\left(\boxed{} \right) - 3\left(\boxed{} \right) \stackrel{?}{=} 24$

$\boxed{} - \boxed{} \stackrel{?}{=} 24$

$\boxed{} \stackrel{?}{=} 24$

(5, 1) | **is / is not** | a solution.

2. (0, −8)

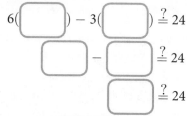

$6\left(\boxed{} \right) - 3\left(\boxed{} \right) \stackrel{?}{=} 24$

$\boxed{} - \boxed{} \stackrel{?}{=} 24$

$\boxed{} \stackrel{?}{=} 24$

(0, −8) | **is / is not** | a solution.

Tell whether the ordered pair is a solution to the equation. (Example 1)

3. $2x + y^2 = 10$; (3, 2)

4. $\frac{1}{2}x - 4y = 4$; $\left(10, \frac{1}{2}\right)$

5. $x^2 + y^2 = 2$; (0, 1)

_____   _____   _____

6. Complete the table of values and graph the ordered pairs to find solutions of the equation $4x - 6 = y$. (Explore Activity and Example 2)

x	$4x - 6 = y$	(x, y)
	$4(\quad) - 6 = y$	
	$4(\quad) - 6 = y$	
	$4(\quad) - 6 = y$	
	$4(\quad) - 6 = y$	
	$4(\quad) - 6 = y$	

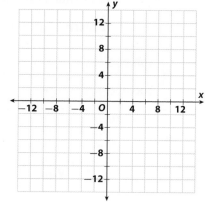

7. Kelly is saving money to buy a concert ticket. Her savings y for x days can be represented by the equation $y = x + 10$. Graph the equation. (Example 2)

Savings

8. How does a graph show solutions to a linear equation?

_____

_____

5.1 Independent Practice

FL A-REI.4.10

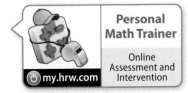

Tell whether each ordered pair is a solution to the equation. Justify your answers.

9. $-5x + 2y = 4$; $(4, 8)$

_____

_____

10. $2x - 7y = 1$; $(11, 3)$

_____

_____

11. $\frac{1}{3}x - 2y = 7$; $(9, -2)$

_____

_____

12. a. Complete the table for the equation $-2x + y = 3$. Then draw the graph.

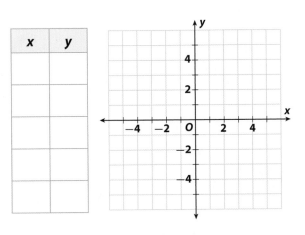

b. Using the graph, locate another solution to the equation. Explain how you can check to see if you are correct.

_____

_____

_____

13. Multiple Representations Trish can run the 200-meter dash in 25 seconds. The equation $8x + y = 200$ gives the distance y that Trish has left to run x seconds after the start of the race. The graph of this equation is shown.

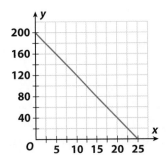

a. Identify three points on the graph and write their coordinates below.

_____

_____

b. Choose one of the ordered pairs and explain what the values mean.

_____

_____

_____

c. Select one ordered pair. Show that the ordered pair is a solution to $8x + y = 200$.

_____

_____

d. Select a point not on the line. Show that the ordered pair represented by this point is not a solution of the equation $8x + y = 200$.

_____

_____

14. Alex is making a rectangular wall hanging from fabric scraps. He has 36 inches of trim to go around the outside border, and he wants to use all of the trim. Let x represent the width of the wall hanging and let y represent the length. The solutions to the equation $2x + 2y = 36$ give the possible dimensions of Alex's wall hanging. Complete the table and graph the equation.

x	y	(x, y)
2		
4		
6		
8		
10		

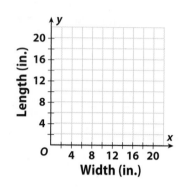

15. **Represent Real-World Problems** A family swimming pool holds 60 m³ of water. It loses 0.18 m³ of water to evaporation each day. This situation can be represented by the equation $y + 0.18x = 60$. Find an ordered pair solution to the equation and explain its real-world meaning.

_____

_____

H.O.T. | **FOCUS ON HIGHER ORDER THINKING**

Work Area

16. **Justify Reasoning** Jackie wants to earn $250 this summer by babysitting and dog walking. She earns $20 each time she babysits and $15 each time she walks dogs. This situation can be represented by the equation $20x + 15y = 250$. Use the equation to determine whether or not Jackie will earn $250 if she babysits 8 times and walks dogs 6 times. Justify your answer.

_____

_____

17. **Critique Reasoning** Max is asked to find 15 solutions for a linear equation. How could Max use a graph to help him find these solutions?

_____

_____

_____

18. **Explain the Error** Chanasia thinks that $(3, 2)$ is a solution of the equation $5y + 10x = 35$ because $5(3) + 10(2) = 35$. Explain her error.

_____

_____

FL **F-IF.1.1**

Understand that a function from one set (called the domain) to another set (called the range) assigns to each element of the domain exactly one element of the range. If *f* is a function ..., the graph of *f* is the graph of the equation $y = f(x)$. *Also F-IF.1.2, F-IF.2.5, A-REI.4.11*

ESSENTIAL QUESTION

How do you represent functions?

Understanding Functions

A **function** is a set of ordered pairs in which each *x*-value is paired with exactly one *y*-value. The *x*-values are the **domain** of the function and the *y*-values are the **range** of the function. Functions can be expressed as tables, graphs, and mapping diagrams.

Math On the Spot
my.hrw.com

EXAMPLE 1

FL **F-IF.1.1, F-IF.1.2, F-IF.2.5, A-REI.4.11**

A trivia contest awards $30 for first place, $20 for second place, $10 for third place, and $5 for fourth place. This function can be written as ordered pairs: $\{(1, 30), (2, 20), (3, 10), (4, 5)\}$. Express this function as a table, a graph, and a mapping diagram.

FUND RAISING

Table	**Ranking / Prize in dollars** 1 — 30 2 — 20 3 — 10 4 — 5	Write each *x*-value under "Ranking" and the corresponding *y*-value next to it, under "Prize, in Dollars".
Graph	**Trivia Prizes** (graph plotting points (1,30), (2,20), (3,10), (4,5); Dollars on y-axis, Ranking on x-axis)	Plot each ordered pair on the graph.
Mapping diagram	**Ranking → Prize, in Dollars** 1 → 30 2 → 20 3 → 10 4 → 5	Write each *x*-value under "Ranking" and every *y*-value under "Prize, in Dollars". Use arrows to connect each *x*-value to the corresponding *y*-value.

REFLECT

1. The domain of the function in Example 1 is {1, 2, 3, 4}. What is the range?

_____

YOUR TURN

2. Suppose each prize for the trivia contest was doubled. Complete the table, graph, and mapping diagram to show the new prize system.

Ranking	Prize, in Dollars
	60
	40
3	
4	

Trivia Prizes

Representing Functions with Equations

Another way to represent a function is with an equation in two variables, like $y = 2x + 8$. The x-value is the input for the function, and after performing one or more operations to the x-value, the output is the y-value.

Since not every equation in two variables is a function, we use function notation to describe functions. To write an equation in two variables using function notation, replace y with $f(x)$, which is read "f of x". In function notation, the equation $y = 2x + 8$ is written as $f(x) = 2x + 8$.

EXAMPLE 2 *Real World*  **FL** A-REI.4.10

The number of dollars Julio earns for working x hours can be represented by the function $f(x) = 9x$. Graph this function.

STEP 1 Make a table of values. Choose values for x, and substitute them into the function to find the corresponding y-values.

x	f(x) = 9x	(x, y)
0	$f(0) = 9(0)$ $= 0$	(0, 0)
1	$f(1) = 9(1)$ $= 9$	(1, 9)
2	$f(2) = 9(2)$ $= 18$	(2, 18)
3	$f(3) = 9(3)$ $= 27$	(3, 27)

Remember that $y = f(x)$.

STEP 2 Graph the function by plotting the ordered pairs.

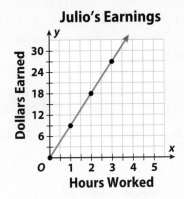

Julio's Earnings

REFLECT

3. **Explain the Error** Julio looks at the graph in Example 2 and concludes that the domain for the function is {0, 1, 2, 3}. Explain his error.

_____

_____

_____

YOUR TURN

4. The cost for x gallons of heating oil can be represented by the function $f(x) = 4x + 6$. Graph this function.

x	f(x) = 4x + 6	(x, y)
0	f(0) =	
2	f(2) =	
3	f(3) =	
5	f(5) =	

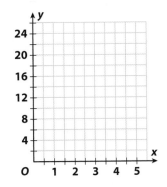

Equality of Functions

When dealing with two different functions, you can use letters other than f to name the function, like the two functions $f(x) = 3x + 2$ and $g(x) = -x + 10$. The function $g(x)$ is read "g of x". You can find values that satisfy both functions by using properties of equality or by graphing.

EXAMPLE 3

FL A-REI.4.11

Given the functions $f(x) = 3x + 2$ and $g(x) = -x + 10$, find the value of x for which $f(x) = g(x)$.

Method 1   Set the functions equal to each other. Then solve the equation.

> Solving this equation will give you the value of x when the y-values are <u>equal</u> to each other.

Math Talk
Mathematical Practices

In this example, can there be more than one value of x such that $f(x) = g(x)$?

$$3x + 2 = -x + 10$$

$$\underline{\begin{array}{l} +x \qquad\quad +x \\ 4x + 2 = \qquad 10 \end{array}}$$ Add x to both sides.

$$4x + 2 = 10$$

$$\underline{\begin{array}{l} \quad -2 \quad -2 \\ 4x \quad = 8 \end{array}}$$ Subtract 2 from both sides.

$$4x = 8$$

$$\frac{4x}{4} = \frac{8}{4}$$ Divide both sides by 4.

$$x = 2$$

So $f(x) = g(x)$ when $x = 2$.

Method 2   Create tables to find a set of ordered pairs for each function. Then graph each function and identify where the lines intersect.

x	f(x) = 3x + 2	(x, y)
0	f(0) = 2	(0, 2)
1	f(1) = 5	(1, 5)
2	f(2) = 8	(2, 8)
3	f(3) = 11	(3, 11)

x	g(x) = −x + 10	(x, y)
0	g(0) = 10	(0, 10)
3	g(3) = 7	(3, 7)
6	g(6) = 4	(6, 4)
9	g(9) = 1	(9, 1)

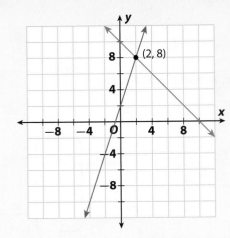

$f(x) = 3x + 2$

$g(x) = -x + 10$

The x-coordinate at the point of intersection is 2, so $f(x) = g(x)$ when $x = 2$.

REFLECT

5. In Example 3, $f(x) = g(x)$ when $x = 2$. Describe two ways to find the y-coordinate when $f(x) = g(x)$.

_____

_____

_____

6. **Analyze Relationships** What does the y-coordinate of the point of intersection represent?

_____

_____

7. **What If?** Given two functions m and n, is it possible for there to be no value of x that makes $m(x) = n(x)$? Can all real numbers make $m(x) = n(x)$? Explain.

_____

_____

_____

YOUR TURN

8. Given the functions $f(x) = 4x - 2$ and $g(x) = 2x + 4$, find the value of x for which $f(x) = g(x)$.

_____

9. Given the functions $a(x) = 6x + 2$ and $b(x) = 3x - 1$, find the value of x for which $a(x) = b(x)$.

_____

Personal Math Trainer

Online Assessment and Intervention

my.hrw.com

Express the function $\{(0, -1), (1, 1), (3, 5)\}$ as a table, a graph, and a mapping diagram. (Example 1)

1.

Domain	Range

2.

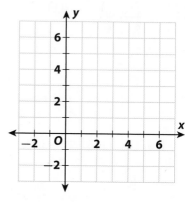

3. Domain   Range

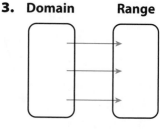

4. Complete the table for the function $f(x) = 2x - 4$. Then draw the graph. (Example 2)

x	$f(x) = 2x - 4$	(x, y)
−2	$f(-2) = 2(-2) - 4 = $ ____	$(-2, -8)$
0	$f(0) = 2(___) - 4 = $ ____	$(0, \_\_\_)$
2	$f(2) = 2(___) - 4 = $ ____	$(\_\_\_, \_\_\_)$
4	$f(4) = 2(___) - 4 = $ ____	$(\_\_\_, \_\_\_)$

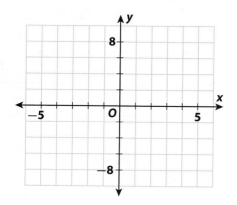

Given the functions $f(x) = -2x + 4$ and $g(x) = 2x - 8$, find the value of x for which $f(x) = g(x)$. (Example 3)

5. Set the functions equal to each other.

Step 1:

$-2x + 4 = 2x - 8$

$+2x$ ⬜

_____

$4 = 4x - 8$

Step 2:

$4 = 4x - 8$

$+8 = \quad + 8$

_____

$12 = $ ⬜

Step 3:

$\dfrac{12}{⬜} = \dfrac{4x}{⬜}$

⬜ $= x$

The x-coordinate at the point of intersection is ___.

So $f(x) = g(x)$ when $x = $ ___.

6. Graph the functions.

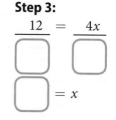

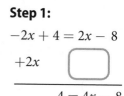

7. How do you represent functions? _____

_____

5.2 Independent Practice

Personal
Math Trainer

Online
Assessment and
Intervention

my.hrw.com

 FL F-IF.1.1, F-IF.1.2, F-IF.2.5, A-REI.4.11

Tell whether each pairing of numbers describes a function. If so, identify the domain and the range. If not, explain why.

8. Each whole number from 0 to 9 is paired with its opposite.

_____

_____

_____

9. $(36, 6)$, $(49, 7)$, $(64, 8)$, $(36, -6)$, $(49, -7)$,

$(64, -8)$ _____

_____

10. Each even number from 2 to 10 is paired with half the number.

_____

_____

11. Multiple Representations Neal has a $5 gift card for music downloads. Each song costs $1 to download. The amount of money left on the card, in dollars, can be represented by the function $f(x) = 5 - x$, where x is the number of downloaded songs.

a. Use the function to complete the table.

x	0				5
f(x)					

b. Graph the function.

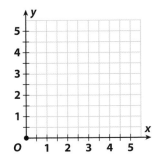

c. Identify the domain and range of the function.

_____

_____

d. Explain the Error Neal decided to connect the points on his graph. Explain Neal's error.

_____

_____

_____

_____

12. Sam is trying to lose weight, and George is trying to gain weight. Sam's weight in pounds can be represented by the function $f(x) = 240 - 2x$, where x is the number of weeks since Sam started losing weight. George's weight in pounds can be represented by the function $g(x) = 180 + 4x$, where x is the number of weeks since George starting gaining weight.

a. What is the x-value when $f(x) = g(x)$?

_____

b. When $f(x) = g(x)$, what does the x-value represent?

_____

_____

_____

c. When Sam and George weigh the same, what will their weight be?

_____

13. Represent Real-World Problems Jasmine has $15 dollars and saves $2.50 every month. Radha has $0 and saves $3.50 every month. Jasmine's savings after x months can be represented by the function $f(x) = 2.5x + 15$. Radha's savings after x months can be represented by the function $g(x) = 3.5x$.

   a. After how many months will they both have the same amount in savings? Find the values of x for which $f(x) = g(x)$.

   _____

   b. Explain how to check your work.

   _____

   c. Explain what the graph of the pair of functions would look like.

   _____

   _____

H.O.T. FOCUS ON HIGHER ORDER THINKING

14. Critical Thinking Can a linear function be continuous but *not* have a domain and range of all real numbers? Justify your answer.

_____

_____

15. Justify Reasoning Fred's weekly earnings for mowing lawns can be represented by the function $f(x) = 45x - 40$, and George's weekly earnings for delivering papers can be represented by the function $g(x) = 85x - 110$. Fred says that after 3 weeks they will have earned the same amount. Determine whether Fred is correct. Explain.

_____

_____

_____

16. Communicate Mathematical Ideas The whole numbers from 10 to 12 are paired with their factors. Explain why this pairing of numbers does *not* describe a function.

_____

_____

_____

FL   F-IF.1.3
Recognize that sequences are functions, sometimes defined recursively, whose domain is a subset of the integers. *Also F-BF.1.1, F-BF.1.1a , F-BF.1.2*

ESSENTIAL QUESTION

How are sequences and functions related?

EXPLORE ACTIVITY    FL   F-IF.1.3

Understanding Sequences

A go-cart racing track charges $7 for a go-cart license and $2 per lap. If you list the charges for 1 lap, 2 laps, 3 laps, and so on, in order, the list forms a sequence of numbers:

9, 11, 13, 15, …

A **sequence** is a list of numbers in a specific order. Each element in a sequence is called a **term**. In a sequence, each term has a position number. In the sequence 9, 11, 13, 15, …, the second term is 11, so its position number is 2.

A The total cost of riding a go-cart for different numbers of laps is shown below. Complete the table.

Position number, n	1	2		4		6		8	Domain
Term of the sequence, $f(n)$	9	11	13		17				Range

B Using function notation for this sequence, $f(2) = 11$ indicates that the second term is 11. Use the table to complete the following statements:

$f(1) =$ _____, $f(4) =$ _____

$f(8) =$ _____, $f($ _____$) = 13$

REFLECT

1. Explain how to find the missing values in the table in the Explore Activity.

_____

_____

2. Describe the domain of the function in the Explore Activity.

_____

_____

3. The go-cart racing track records the number of gallons of gas they have at the beginning of each day. The numbers form the following sequence: 25, 21, 17... Predict the next term in the sequence. Justify your answer.

_____

Math On the Spot

⏻ my.hrw.com

Using an Explicit Rule to Generate a Sequence

An **explicit rule** for a sequence defines the *n*th term as a function of *n*. Explicit rules can be used to find any specific term in a sequence without finding any of the previous terms.

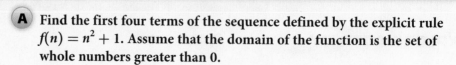

EXAMPLE 1

FL F-IF.1.3

A Find the first four terms of the sequence defined by the explicit rule $f(n) = n^2 + 1$. Assume that the domain of the function is the set of whole numbers greater than 0.

Make a table and substitute values for *n*.

n	$f(n) = n^2 + 1$	$f(n)$
1	$f(1) = (1)^2 + 1 = 1 + 1 = 2$	2
2	$f(2) = (2)^2 + 1 = 4 + 1 = 5$	5
3	$f(3) = (3)^2 + 1 = 9 + 1 = 10$	10
4	$f(4) = (4)^2 + 1 = 16 + 1 = 17$	17

My Notes

The first four terms are 2, 5, 10, 17.

B Find the 20th term of the sequence defined by the explicit rule $f(n) = n^2 + 1$. Assume that the domain of the function is the set of whole numbers greater than 0.

$$f(20) = (20)^2 + 1 \quad \text{Substitute 20 for } n.$$

$$= 400 + 1 \quad \text{This means that } n \text{ has a value of 20.}$$

$$= 401$$

The 20th term in the sequence is 401.

REFLECT

4. Explain how to find the 6th term of the sequence defined by the explicit rule $f(n) = 3n - 2$. Assume that the domain of the function is the set of whole numbers greater than 0.

_____

_____

5. The number 121 is a term of the sequence defined by the explicit rule $f(n) = 3n - 2$. Assume that the domain of the function is the set of whole numbers greater than 0. Which term in the sequence is 121? Justify your answer.

_____

_____

134 Unit 1B

YOUR TURN

6. Write the first 4 terms of the sequence defined by the rule $f(n) = 3n + 1$. Assume that the domain of the function is the set of whole numbers greater than 0.

n	$f(n) = 3n + 1$	$f(n)$
1	$f(1) = 3(1) + 1$	
2		
3		
4		

The first four terms of the sequence are _____

7. What is the 15th term of the sequence defined by the explicit rule $f(n) = n^2 + n$? Assume that the domain of the function is the set of whole numbers greater than 0. _____

8. What is the 8th term of the sequence defined by the explicit rule $f(n) = 2n^2 + 6$? Assume that the domain of the function is the set of whole numbers greater than 0. _____

Using a Recursive Rule to Generate a Sequence

A **recursive rule** for a sequence defines the nth term by relating it to one or more previous terms. Unlike an explicit rule, a recursive rule cannot be used to find a specific term directly. To find a specific term's value, you need to know the value of one or more of the previous terms. The following is an example of a recursive rule:

$f(1) = 4$

$f(n) = f(n - 1) + 10$ for each whole number n greater than 1.

This rule means that after the first term of the sequence, every term $f(n)$ is the sum of the previous term $f(n - 1)$ and 10. The function table below shows the first 4 terms of the sequence.

n		$f(n)$
1	1st term	4
2	1st term + 10	$4 + 10 = 14$
3	2nd term + 10	$14 + 10 = 24$
4	3rd term + 10	$24 + 10 = 34$

EXAMPLE 2

Write the first 4 terms of the sequence defined by the recursive rule below.

$$f(1) = 3$$

$$f(n) = f(n-1) + 2 \text{ for each whole number } n \text{ greater than } 1.$$

STEP 1 Identify the domain of the function and the first term of the sequence. Describe the recursive rule.

The domain of the function is the set of whole numbers greater than 0.

The first term of the sequence is 3, and the recursive rule is adding 2 to each term to find the next term.

STEP 2 Create a table to find the first 4 terms in the sequence. Use 2, 3, and 4 as values for n.

n	$f(n) = f(n-1) + 2$	$f(n)$
1	1st term	3
2	$f(2) = f(2-1) + 2$ $= f(1) + 2$ $= 3 + 2$	5
3	$f(3) = f(3-1) + 2$ $= f(2) + 2$ $= 5 + 2$	7
4	$f(4) = f(4-1) + 2$ $= f(3) + 2$ $= 7 + 2$	9

The first four terms of the sequence are 3, 5, 7, 9.

My Notes

Math Talk
Mathematical Practices

Describe how to find the 12th term of the sequence.

REFLECT

9. Suppose you want to find the 50th term of a sequence. Would you rather use a recursive rule or an explicit rule? Explain your reasoning.

_____

_____

_____

Personal Math Trainer

Online Assessment and Intervention

⊙ my.hrw.com

YOUR TURN

10. Write the first 8 terms of the sequence with $f(1) = 37$ and $f(n) = f(n-1) - 3$ for each whole number greater than 1.

_____

Guided Practice

Use the table to complete the statements. (Explore Activity)

1. $f(4) =$ _____

2. $f(7) =$ _____

n	1	2	3	4	...	7
$f(n)$	5	8	11	?	...	?

Write the first four terms of each sequence. Assume that the domain of the function is the set of whole numbers greater than 0. (Example 1)

3. $f(n) = (n-1)^2$

n	$f(n) = (n-1)^2$	$f(n)$
1	$(1-1)^2$	0
2	$(2-1)^2$	
3	$(\_\_ - 1)^2$	
4	$(\_\_ - 1)^2$	

4. $f(n) = 2n - 2$

n	$f(n) = 2n-2$	$f(n)$
1	$2(\_\_) - 2$	
2		
3		
4		

5. $f(n) = \frac{1}{2}n + 3$

n	$f(n)$
1	
2	
3	
4	

Use the explicit rule to find the 25th term of each sequence. Assume that the domain of each function is the set of whole numbers greater than 0. (Example 1)

6. $f(n) = \frac{1}{2}n + 3$

$f(25) = \frac{1}{2} \boxed{} + 3 = \boxed{}$

7. $f(n) = \frac{n-3}{11}$

$f(25) = \frac{\boxed{} - 3}{11} = \boxed{}$

8. Complete the table to find the first 4 terms of the sequence with $f(1) = 2$ and $f(n) = f(n-1) + 6$ for each whole number greater than 1. (Example 2)

The first 4 terms of the sequence are

_____

n	$f(n) = f(n-1) + 6$	$f(n)$
1	1st term	2
2	$f(2-1) + 6 = f(1) + 6$ $+ 6 =$	
3		
4		

ESSENTIAL QUESTION CHECK-IN

9. Why is a sequence a function?

_____

_____

_____

5.3 Independent Practice

FL A-IF.1.3

Write the first four terms of each sequence. Assume that the domain of each function is the set of whole numbers greater than 0.

10. $f(n) = \sqrt{n-1}$

_____

11. $f(n) = 2n(n+1)$

_____

12. $f(1) = 16$ and $f(n) = \frac{1}{2} \cdot f(n-1)$ for each whole number greater than 1

_____

13. $f(1) = 1$ and $f(n) = 2 \cdot f(n-1) + 1$ for each whole number greater than 1

_____

14. $f(n) = 1.5n + 6$

_____

15. $f(1) = 6.2$ and $f(n) = 20 - 2 \cdot f(n-1)$ for each whole number greater than 1

_____

Write the 12th term of each sequence.

16. $f(n) = \frac{5}{n}$

_____

17. $f(1) = 181$ and $f(n) = f(n-1) - 17$ for each whole number greater than 1

_____

18. $f(1) = 3.5$ and $f(n) = f(n-1) + 1.5$ for each whole number greater than 1

_____

19. $f(1) = 1$ and $f(n) = 2 \cdot f(n-1)$ for each whole number greater than 1

_____

20. Represent Real-World Problems A movie rental club charges $4.95 for membership and $18.95 for each month of subscription.

a. Complete the table to represent the fees paid over the first three months.

n	$f(n) = 18.95n + 4.95$

b. What would $f(0) = 4.95$ represent?

_____

c. What would the cost be for a year's

membership? _____

d. If the first month were free, what would be the total cost of a yearly membership?

_____

e. Determine an explicit rule for the total fees paid to the movie rental club if the first month were free.

_____

21. Jessica had $150 in her savings account on the first Sunday of November. Beginning that week, she saved $35 each week.

a. Write a recursive rule that describes how much money Jessica had in her savings account at the end of n weeks.

_____

_____

b. How much money will Jessika have in her savings account at the end of

6 weeks? _____

22. Copper Creek Pizza is having a special. If you order a large pizza for the regular price of $17, you can order any number of additional large pizzas for $8.50 each.

a. Complete the table to show the cost of ordering up to 4 large pizzas.

Number of Large Pizzas	1	2	3	4
Total Cost				

b. Write an explicit and a recursive rule for the cost of placing an order for n large pizzas. _____

_____

c. What is the cost of placing an order for 20 large pizzas? _____

d. Five people each make an order for 3 large pizzas. How much money would they have saved if they placed one order for 15 pizzas? Explain.

_____

_____

_____

23. The explicit rule for a sequence is $f(n) = 1.25(n - 1) + 6.25$. Determine the recursive rule for the same sequence.

_____

24. The recursive rule for a sequence is $f(1) = 8\frac{1}{2}$, $f(n) = f(n - 1) - \frac{1}{2}$. Determine the explicit rule for the same sequence.

_____

25. The 5th term in a sequence is 25, and each term is 3 less than the previous term. Write an explicit rule and a recursive rule to describe the sequence.

_____

_____

26. An amusement park charges $12 for one round of mini-golf and a reduced fee for each additional round played. Tom paid $47 for 6 rounds of mini-golf.

a. What is the price per round for additional rounds of mini-golf?

_____

b. Write an explicit and a recursive rule for the cost of playing n rounds of mini-golf. _____

_____

c. What is the cost of playing 9 rounds of mini-golf? _____

27. **Represent Real-World Problems** Carrie borrowed money interest-free to pay for a car repair. She is repaying the loan in equal monthly payments. The table shows the loan balance at the end of each month, after she makes the payment.

Monthly payment number	n	1	2	3	4
Loan balance ($)	$f(n)$	840	720	600	480

a. After 6 months, how much money will Carrie have left to repay on her loan? _____

b. How many months will it take Carrie to pay off the loan?

_____

28. Kendall is stacking boxes that are 7.5 inches tall.

a. Explain how to find the height (in inches) of the stack of boxes after Kendall adds the nth box.

_____

b. A sequence is defined by the rule $f(n)$ = the height (in inches) of n boxes.

What is the fourth term of the sequence? _____

 **FOCUS ON HIGHER ORDER THINKING**

Work Area

29. **Analyze Relationships** Determine an explicit rule and a recursive rule to describe the following sequence.

2, 4, 6, 8, ...

_____

_____

30. **Explain the Error** Shane is trying to find the 5th term of a sequence where $f(1) = 4$ and $f(n) = 2 \cdot f(n - 1) + 1$ for each whole number greater than 1. He reasons that he can find the 5th term by calculating $(4 \times 2 \times 2 \times 2 \times 2) + 1$. Explain Shane's error.

_____

_____

_____

_____

31. Write a recursive rule for a sequence where every term is the same.

_____

_____

Ready to Go On?

5.1 Equations in Two Variables

Complete the table of values to find solutions of the equation
$-x + y = 5$. Then graph the ordered pairs.

1.

x	y
−2	
−1	
0	
1	
2	

2.

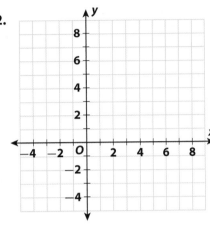

5.2 Representing Functions

3. Marco owed his father $150 and began paying him back $20 at the end of
each week, beginning November 1. Joni owed her father $130 and began
paying him back $15 at the end of each week, beginning on the same
day. What Marco owed his father in dollars at the end of n weeks can be
represented by $f(n) = 150 - 20n$. What Joni owed her father in dollars at the
end of n weeks can be represented by $g(n) = 130 - 15n$.

Find the value of n for which $f(n) = g(n)$. What does that value mean in this
situation?

_____

_____

5.3 Sequences

4. Write the first 4 terms of the sequence defined
by the rule $f(n) = 2n^2 + 1$.

n	1	2	3	4
f(n)				

? ESSENTIAL QUESTION

5. What is a function and how can it be represented?

_____

_____

_____

Assessment Readiness

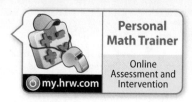
Selected Response

1. Which ordered pair is a solution to $5x + y = 3$?

   Ⓐ $(6, 27)$　　Ⓒ $(-4, 15)$

   Ⓑ $(2, 7)$　　Ⓓ $(-3, 18)$

2. Which graph represents $f(x) = -2x + 4$?

   Ⓐ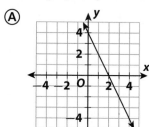

   Ⓑ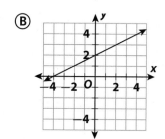

   Ⓒ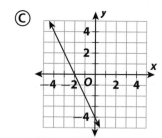

   Ⓓ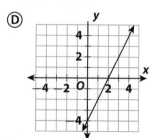

3. Which is an equivalent expression to $y(5) + x(5) - b^2(5)$?

   Ⓐ $5xy - b^2$　　Ⓒ $5(y + x - b^2)$

   Ⓑ $5(y + x)b^2$　　Ⓓ $5(yx - b^2)$

4. Which is the most precise measurement?

   Ⓐ 26 in.　　Ⓒ 26.615 in.

   Ⓑ 26.6 in.　　Ⓓ 26.62 in.

5. Given the functions $f(x) = -x + 23$ and $g(x) = 2x - 7$, find the value of x for which $f(x) = g(x)$.

   Ⓐ 5　　Ⓒ 16

   Ⓑ 10　　Ⓓ 30

6. Which are the first 4 terms of the sequence defined by the function $f(n) = n^3 + 1$? Assume that the domain of the function is the set of whole numbers greater than 0.

   Ⓐ 0, 1, 2, 9　　Ⓒ 2, 9, 28, 65

   Ⓑ 1, 2, 9, 28　　Ⓓ 4, 7, 10, 13

7. Which are the first 4 terms of the sequence defined by the function with $f(1) = 5$ and $f(n) = f(n - 1) + 4$ for each whole number n greater than 1.

   Ⓐ 4, 5, 6, 7　　Ⓒ 5, 9, 10, 11

   Ⓑ 5, 9, 13, 17　　Ⓓ 9, 12, 15, 18

Mini-Tasks

8. Julie opens an account with $350 and deposits $75 at the end of each month. Her account balance at the end of each month can be represented by the function $f(n) = 75n + 350$.

   a. How many months will it take for Julie to have $1175?

   _____

   b. What is a recursive rule that describes this situation?

   _____

   _____

   _____

Study Guide Review

Equations and Inequalities in One Variable

Key Vocabulary
equation *(ecuación)*
identity *(identidad)*
inequality *(desigualdad)*
solution of an inequality
    *(solución de una
    desigualdad)*
formula *(fórmula)*
literal equation *(ecuación
    literal)*

? ESSENTIAL QUESTION

How can you solve an equation or inequality in one variable?

EXAMPLE 1

Francine opens a savings account with $150. At the end of every week, she adds $35 to her account. After how many weeks will Francine have $360 in her saving account?

Let w represent the number of weeks Francine has been saving.

$$150 + 35w = 360$$
$$\underline{-150 \qquad\qquad -150}$$
$$35w = 210$$

$$\frac{35w}{35} = \frac{210}{35}$$

$$w = 6$$

EXAMPLE 2

A test car has a velocity of 280 miles per hour minus five times the gear setting. The track has a speed limit of 150 miles per hour. What are the gear settings that can be used for the car in this trial?

Let x equal the gear setting.

$$280 - 5x \leq 150$$
$$\underline{-280 \qquad\qquad -280}$$
$$-5x \leq -130$$

$$\frac{-5x}{-5} \geq \frac{-130}{-5}$$

$$x \geq 26$$

EXERCISES

1. Megan has $25 to buy groceries. She has $15 worth of groceries in her cart, and would like to buy some melons that cost $1.25 each. Write an equation that describes the situation, and determine how many melons Megan can afford. (Lesson 4.1)

_____

2. Is 20 a solution for $2x - 5 > 30$? Explain your answer. (Lesson 4.2)

_____

Equations in Two Variables and Functions

Key Vocabulary

equation in two variables *(ecuación en dos variables)*

solution of an equation in two variables *(solución de una ecuación en dos variables)*

function *(función)*

domain *(dominio)*

range *(rango)*

function notation *(notación de función)*

sequence *(sucesión)*

term *(término)*

? ESSENTIAL QUESTION

What is a function and how can a function be represented?

EXAMPLE 1

Graph the equation $y = 2x + 4$.

Make a table.

x	y
−4	−4
−3	−2
−2	0
−1	2
0	4
1	6

Graph the ordered pairs.

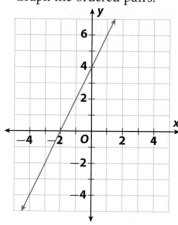

EXAMPLE 2

The functions $f(x)$ and $g(x)$ are defined by the explicit rules $f(x) = 5x + 1$ and $g(x) = 49 - 3x$. Find the value of x for which $f(x) = g(x)$.

Set the functions equal to each other, then solve.

$$f(x) = g(x)$$
$$5x + 1 = 49 - 3x$$
$$\underline{+3x \qquad\qquad +3x}$$
$$8x + 1 = 49$$

$$8x + 1 = 49$$
$$\underline{\quad -1 \quad -1}$$
$$8x \quad\; = 48$$

$$\frac{8x}{8} = \frac{48}{8}$$

$$x = 6$$

EXAMPLE 3

Find the first 5 terms of the sequence defined by the explicit rule
$f(n) = 8n + 6$. Assume that the domain of each function is the set of whole
numbers greater than 0.

Use the explicit rule and substitute the values 1 through 5 for n.

$f(1) = 8(1) + 6 = 14$

$f(2) = 8(2) + 6 = 22$

$f(3) = 8(3) + 6 = 30$

$f(4) = 8(4) + 6 = 38$

$f(5) = 8(5) + 6 = 46$

The first five terms are 14, 22, 30, 38, 46.

EXERCISES

3. Does $y = 6x + 5$ represent a function? Explain your answer.
   (Lesson 5.2)

   _____

   _____

4. Given the functions $f(x) = 7x - 2$ and $g(x) = 3x + 6$, find the value of x
   for which $f(x) = g(x)$. (Lesson 5.2)

   _____

   _____

Consider the function $y = 2x + 8$. Determine if each ordered pair is a
solution. (Lesson 5.1)

5. (1, 10) _____   6. (3, 16) _____

7. (4, 16) _____   8. (5, 20) _____

9. Write the first four terms of the sequence. The domain of the function
   is the set of consecutive integers starting with 1. (Lesson 5.3)

   $f(n) = 3n(n + 3)$

   _____

1. **CAREERS IN MATH** **Astronomer** Astronomers must sometimes predict the speed of an object. An astronomer discovers an object moving at 2,000 kilometers per minute. The object was spotted at 2,500,000 kilometers from Earth. Assuming constant speed, how long will it take for the object to reach the Moon's orbit, which is 160,000 kilometers away from Earth? Write and solve an equation.

   _____

   _____

2. Georgia owns a bakery. She pays her employees $10 per hour plus a base pay of $150 per week. This week, Michael worked 15 hours, Sarah worked 20 hours, Carol 25 hours, and Scott 40 hours. Write an equation representing an employee's pay. What did each employee earn this week, and how much does Georgia owe in total?

   _____

   _____

3. The magnification range of a new telescope is given by $y = 42x - 12.5$, where y is the distance between the focusing screen and the ocular piece in millimeters, and x is the adjustment setting. Complete the table below, then graph the function.

x	−3	−2	−1	0	1	2	3
y							

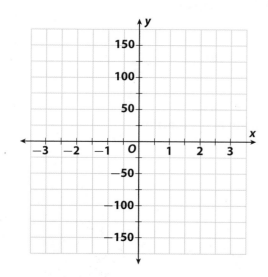

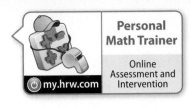
Selected Response

1. Which ordered pair is **not** a solution to $4x + 3y = 24$?

   (A) $(0, 8)$ (C) $(8, 3)$

   (B) $(3, 4)$ (D) $(6, 0)$

2. Which statement about $y = 5x + 2$ is **not** true?

   (A) The equation represents a function.

   (B) This equation is linear.

   (C) $(0, 2)$ is a valid solution.

   (D) $(5, 8)$ is a valid solution.

3. Which ordered pair is a solution to $-5x + 3y > 12$?

   (A) $(3, 9)$ (C) $(3, -6)$

   (B) $(-2, -5)$ (D) $(2, 8)$

4. A new car costs $15,000. Gasoline costs $4 a gallon. Which function shows the cost of the car and x gallons of gasoline?

   (A) $f(x) = 4x - 15{,}000$

   (B) $f(x) = 4x + 15{,}000$

   (C) $f(x) = 4x$

   (D) $f(x) = 15{,}000$

5. Which inequality best represents the graph?

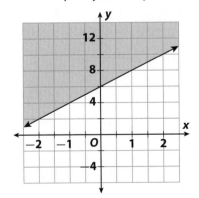

   (A) $y \geq 2x + 6$ (C) $y \leq 2x + 6$

   (B) $y > 4x - 5$ (D) $y < 4x - 5$

6. The fare for a cab is $3.50 per trip plus $1.25 per mile. Which describes the cab fare in dollars as a function of x miles traveled?

   (A) $f(x) = 3.5x + 1.25$

   (B) $f(x) = 3.5x + 0.125$

   (C) $f(x) = 1.25x + 3.5$

   (D) $f(x) = 1.25x + 0.35$

Read each question carefully before looking at the answer choices or beginning your calculations.

7. Consider the rule $y = 2x + 12$ with a domain of $\{0, 2, 4, 6, 8\}$. What is not a member of the set of the rule's range?

   (A) 12   (C) 24

   (B) 14   (D) 28

8. Which is the solution for $0 = 9x + 81$?

   (A) -9 (C) 0

   (B) 9   (D) x

9. Which of the following is a solution of the equation $2x + 3y = -6$?

   (A) $(0, 0)$

   (B) $(0, 2)$

   (C) $(0, -2)$

   (D) $(1, -1)$

10. What is $10 > -2x + 4$ simplified?

   (A) $-3 > x$

   (B) $-3 < x$

   (C) $3 > x$

   (D) $3 < x$

11. Determine the most precise measurement.

    Ⓐ 12 ft   Ⓒ 125 in.

    Ⓑ 12.5 ft   Ⓓ 12.5 yd

12. How many significant digits are there in the measurement 160.0 km?

    Ⓐ 1   Ⓒ 2

    Ⓑ 3   Ⓓ 4

13. Tony has 55 ft^2 of fabric. How many square meters of fabric does Tony have? Round to the nearest tenth.

    Ⓐ 5.1 m^2 Ⓒ 6.2 m^2

    Ⓑ 7.2 m^2 Ⓓ 10.8 m^2

14. A sequence is described by the explicit rule $f(n) = 100 - 9n$. Find the first 4 terms of the sequence.

    Ⓐ 100, 91, 82, 73

    Ⓑ 91, 82, 73, 64

    Ⓒ 109, 118, 127, 136

    Ⓓ 91, 83, 74, 65

15. Given the functions $f(x) = 30 - 8x$ and $g(x) = 27 - 7x$, find the value of x for which $f(x) = g(x)$.

    Ⓐ $x = 3$ Ⓒ $x = 12$

    Ⓑ $x = 5$ Ⓓ $x = 15$

16. Evaluate and simplify the expression $15x^{\frac{5}{6}}$ when $x = 64$.

    Ⓐ 480   Ⓒ 860

    Ⓑ 800   Ⓓ 960

17. Which number is irrational?

    Ⓐ $\sqrt{324}$ Ⓒ $\sqrt{900}$

    Ⓑ $\sqrt{625}$ Ⓓ $\sqrt{1,000}$

Mini-Tasks

18. The water level of a river is 34 feet, and it is dropping at a rate of 0.5 foot per day.

    a. Write an equation that represents the water level, w, after d days.

    _____

    _____

    b. Graph the equation that would represent the water level if it were dropping 2 feet per day.

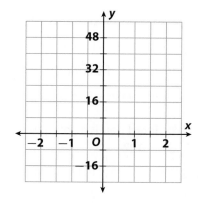

    c. What is the domain of this function? Explain.

    _____

    _____

    _____

19. The speed limit is 65 miles per hour. Your car has an idle speed of 10 miles per hour and a maximum speed of 15 additional miles per hour per gear.

    a. Write an inequality that represents how many gears can be engaged while obeying the speed limit.

    _____

    _____

    b. What would the inequality be if the speed limit were raised to 80?

    _____

    _____

Linear Relationships

CAREERS IN MATH

Environmental Scientist An environmental scientist uses math to make models to analyze data and understand the effects of human activity on nature.

If you're interested in a career as an environmental scientist, you should study these subjects of math:

- Algebra
- Calculus
- Statistics

Research other careers that involve modeling data with mathematical functions.

Unit 2A Performance Task

At the end of the unit, check out how an **environmental scientist** uses math.

Vocabulary Preview

Use the word search to preview vocabulary from this unit. Unscramble the circled letters within the found words to answer the riddle at the bottom of the page.

1. The x-coordinate of the point where a line intersects the x-axis (Lesson 6.2)
2. $m = \frac{(y_2 - y_1)}{(x_2 - x_1)}$, where (x_1, y_1) and (x_2, y_2) are two points on a line (Lesson 6.3)
3. A measure of the strength and direction of the relationship between two variables or data sets (Lesson 8.1)
4. The difference between consecutive terms is constant in this type of sequence (Lesson 7.1)
5. A method of solving systems of equations in which one variable is eliminated (Lesson 9.3)
6. The function that results from exchanging the input and output values of a one-to-one function (Lesson 7.3)
7. A method of solving systems by solving an equation for one variable and substituting the result into the other equation (Lesson 9.2)

Q: Who was the roundest knight at the round table?

A: _

Linear Functions

? ESSENTIAL QUESTION

How do equations, graphs, tables, and word descriptions related to linear functions?

Real-World Video

Cyclists adjust their gears to climb up a steep grade or through rocky terrain. Check out how gear ratios, rates of speed, and slope ratios can be used to solve problems involving speed, distance, and time when mountain biking.

my.hrw.com

GO DIGITAL
my.hrw.com

my.hrw.com

Go digital with your write-in student edition, accessible on any device.

Math On the Spot

Scan with your smart phone to jump directly to the online edition, video tutor, and more.

Animated Math

Interactively explore key concepts to see how math works.

Personal Math Trainer

Get immediate feedback and help as you work through practice sets.

Are YOU Ready?

Complete these exercises to review skills you will need for this chapter.

Personal Math Trainer

Online Assessment and Intervention

⏻ my.hrw.com

Solve Multi-Step Equations

EXAMPLE Solve $3x + 4 = 28$.

$$3x + 4 - 4 = 28 - 4 \qquad \text{Subtract 4 from both sides.}$$
$$3x = 24$$
$$3x \cdot \frac{1}{3} = 24 \cdot \frac{1}{3} \qquad \text{Multiply both sides by } \frac{1}{3}.$$
$$x = 8$$

Solve each equation.

1. $2x + 7 = 19$ **2.** $0.4y + 8 = -1$ **3.** $0 = 3z - 6$

_____   _____   _____

Ordered Pairs

EXAMPLE Graph $(2, 4)$ on the coordinate plane.

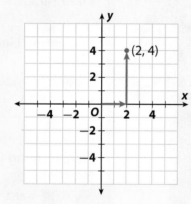

$(2, 4) \rightarrow (x, y)$
The x-coordinate or horizontal coordinate is 2.
Move *right* 2 units.
The y-coordinate or vertical coordinate is 4.
Move *up* 4 units.
Negative coordinates indicate movement to the *left* and *down*.

Graph each point on the coordinate plane provided.

4. $(-1, 3)$
5. $(4, -2)$
6. $(0, 1)$
7. $(-2, -3)$

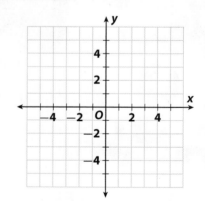

Reading Start-Up

Visualize Vocabulary

Use the Review Words to complete the chart.

Representation	Uses
	To show two expressions are equivalent
	To represent a relationship that has exactly one output for each input
	To visually represent a function on a coordinate plane
	To locate a single point on a coordinate plane

Understand Vocabulary

Complete the sentences using the preview words.

1. An equation written as $Ax + By = C$, where A, B, and C are real numbers is said to be in the

   _____

2. An equation written as $y = mx + b$, where m is the slope and b is the y-intercept is said to be in the

   _____

3. The _____ is the y-coordinate of the point where the graph of a line crosses the y-axis.

4. The _____ is the x-coordinate of the point where the graph of a line crosses the x-axis.

Active Reading

Key-Term Fold Before beginning the module, create a Key-Term Fold for taking notes as you read the module. Each tab can contain a key term on one side and its definition on the other. As you study each lesson, write important vocabulary and definitions under the appropriate tab.

Vocabulary

Review Words

✓ equation *(ecuación)*

✓ function *(función)*

✓ graph of a function *(gráfica de una función)*

line *(línea)*

✓ ordered pair *(par ordenado)*

Preview Words

family of functions

linear function

linear equation

parent function

parameter

rate of change

rise

run

slope

slope formula

slope-intercept form

standard form of a linear equation

x-intercept

y-intercept

 **FL** **F-IF.2.4**

For a function that models a relationship between two quantities, interpret key features of graphs and tables in terms of the quantities, and sketch graphs showing key features given a verbal description of the relationship.

Key Vocabulary

slope *(pendiente)*
   The slope of a line is the ratio of rise to run for any two points on the line.

What It Means to You

Learning to interpret a graph enables a deep visual understanding of all sorts of relationships.

UNPACKING EXAMPLE F-IF.2.4

A group of friends walked to the town market, did some shopping there, then returned home.

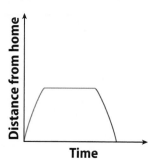

FL **F-IF.2.6**

Calculate and interpret the average rate of change of a function (presented symbolically or as a table) over a specified interval. Estimate the rate of change from a graph.

Key Vocabulary

rate of change *(tasa de cambio)*
   A ratio that compares the amount of change in a dependent variable to the amount of change in an independent variable.

What It Means to You

Average rate of change measures the change in the dependent variable over the change in the independent variable. This helps you understand how quickly the values in a function change.

UNPACKING EXAMPLE F-IF.2.6

Average rate of change $= \frac{180 - 60}{3 - 1} = 60$ mi/h

Time (hours)	1	2	3	4
Distance (miles)	60	120	180	240

Visit **my.hrw.com** to see all **Florida Math Standards** unpacked.

my.hrw.com

Linear Functions

FL **F-IF.3.7**

Graph functions expressed symbolically... *Also F-IF.3.7a, F-IF.2.5*

? ESSENTIAL QUESTION

How can you use graphs and equations to identify linear functions?

EXPLORE ACTIVITY FL **F-IF.2.5, F-IF.3.7, F-IF.3.7a**

Exploring Linear Functions

You get a job planning birthday parties. You are paid a flat fee of $80 and then $15 for each hour you work. The function defined by $f(x) = 15x + 80$ represents your earnings in dollars when you work x hours. Assume you get paid for fractions of hours.

A Complete the table to represent the total wages for 0–4 hours worked.

Number of hours, x	Earnings in dollars, $f(x)$
0	
1	
2	
3	
4	

B Graph the function from Part A.

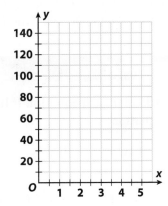

C How do you know that this is a function?

_____

REFLECT

1. Multiple Representations Identify the reasonable domain and range for the function $f(x) = 15x + 80$.

Domain: _____

Range: _____

2. Look for a Pattern Describe the pattern formed by the points in the graph that are from the table.

_____

_____

Identifying Linear Functions

A **linear function** is a function whose graph forms a line that is not vertical.

The graph at the right is the graph of a linear function.

Both the domain and the range of the function are the set of all real numbers

If a function is linear, then it can be represented by a *linear equation*. A **linear equation** is any equation that can be written in the *standard form* below.

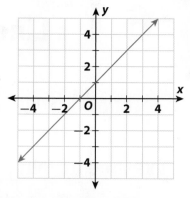

Standard Form of a Linear Equation

$Ax + By = C$ where A, B, and C are real numbers and A and B are not both 0.

Notice that when a linear equation is written in standard form the following are true.

- x and y both have exponents of 1.
- x and y are not multiplied together.
- x and y do not appear in denominators, exponents, or radicands.

EXAMPLE 1

FL   F-IF.3.7, F-IF.3.7a

Tell whether each equation is linear. If so, graph the function represented by the equation.

A $-12x + y = -4$

The equation is linear because it is in the standard form of a linear equation: $A = -12$, $B = 1$, and $C = -4$.

To graph the function, first solve the equation for y.

$$-12x + y = -4$$

$$\underline{+12x \qquad\qquad +12x}$$ Subtraction Property of Equality

$$y = -4 + 12x$$

Make a table and plot the points. Then connect the points.

x	−2	0	2	4
y	−28	−4	20	44

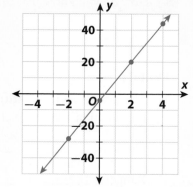

B $y = 12x^2 - 4$

The exponent on x in this equation is not 1, so the function is not linear.

C $xy - 4 = 12$

$$xy - 4 = 12$$

Since x and y are multiplied together, this function is not linear.

My Notes

REFLECT

3. Communicate Mathematical Ideas Use the bulleted list above Example 1 to write at least two more equations that are not linear. Explain why they are not linear.

_____

_____

_____

4. Make a Conjecture Why do you think the graph of a linear function has to be a non-vertical line?

_____

_____

_____

_____

_____

YOUR TURN

Tell whether each equation is linear. If so, graph the function represented by the equation.

5. $y - 3 = 2x$

_____

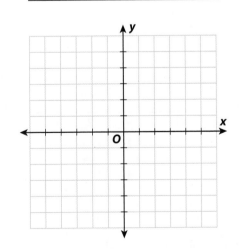

6. $y = \frac{2}{x}$

_____

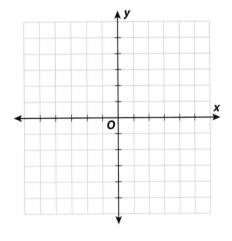

Personal Math Trainer

Online Assessment and Intervention

⏻ my.hrw.com

Horizontal and Vertical Lines

As stated earlier in this lesson, a linear equation is in standard form if it is in the form $Ax + Bx = C$, where A, B, and C are real numbers and A and B are not both 0. Notice that in this definition, A and B cannot both be 0, but one or the other can be 0.

EXAMPLE 2

FL F-IF.3.7, F-IF.3.7a

Graph each line.

A $y = 8$

$0x + 1y = 8$ This is a linear equation in standard form $A = 0, B = 1, C = 8$.

x	y
0	8
1	8
2	8
3	8
4	8

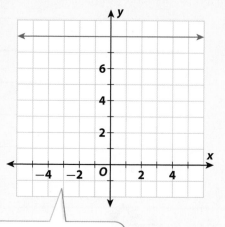

Notice that all ordered pairs have a y-coordinate of 8.

B $x = -1$

$1x + 0y = -1$ This is a linear equation in standard form $A = 1, B = 0, C = -1$.

x	y
−1	0
−1	1
−1	2
−1	3
−1	4

 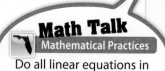

Math Talk

Mathematical Practices

Do all linear equations in two variables represent linear functions?

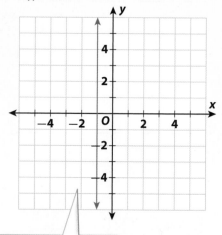

Notice that all ordered pairs have an x-coordinate of −1.

REFLECT

7. **Communicate Mathematical Ideas** When the equation of the graph of a horizontal line is written in standard form, the coefficient of x must be 0. Explain why.

_____

_____

_____

YOUR TURN

Tell whether the equation represents a horizontal line, vertical line, or neither. Graph the equation.

8. $y = 2x$ _____

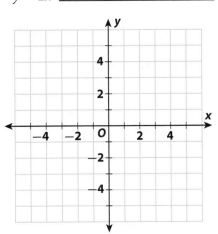

9. $y = -4$ _____

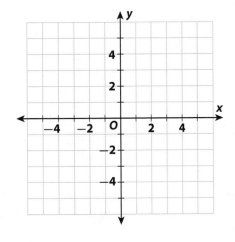

10. $3y = -4$ _____

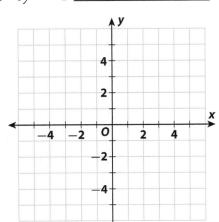

11. $x + 3 = 0$ _____

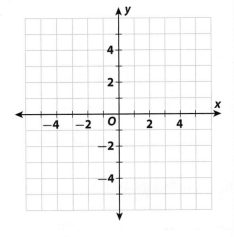

Personal Math Trainer

Online Assessment and Intervention

⏻ my.hrw.com

Write a linear equation in the form $Ax + By = C$ for the given values of A, B, and C. Then simplify the equation. Tell whether the equation represents a horizontal line, vertical line, or neither. (Examples 1 and 2)

1. $A = 0, B = 3, C = 1$

2. $A = 5, B = 0.1, C = 4$

3. $A = -\frac{1}{2}, B = 0, C = 14$

_____

_____

_____

_____

_____

_____

Create a table of values for the function $y = 3x - 4$. Then graph the function, making sure to label the axes to show the scale. (Example 1)

4. $y = 3x - 4$

x	y
0	
1	
2	

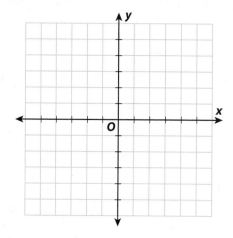

5. Andrea receives a $40 gift card to use at a town pool. It costs her $8 per visit to swim. A function relating the value of the gift card, v, to the number of visits, n, is $v(n) = 40 - 8n$. (Explore Activity)

a. Identify a reasonable domain of the function. Explain why you chose that domain.

_____

_____

b. Given that domain, what is the range of the function.

_____

ESSENTIAL QUESTION CHECK-IN

6. How can you use the equation of a linear function to predict what the graph will look like?

_____

_____

Name _____ Class _____ Date _____

6.1 Independent Practice

FL **F-IF.3.7, F-IF.3.7a**

Personal
Math Trainer

Online
Assessment and
Intervention

my.hrw.com

7. Two friends work at the same company. Friend A gets paid $50,000 for the year, no matter how many hours she works. Friend B gets paid $20 an hour. Write an equation for each person that shows the relationship between the annual salary y and the number of hours x that friend works. Fill in each table of values and graph each function.

a. Function for Friend A

_____

x	y
0	
1,000	
2,000	

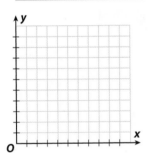

b. Function for Friend B

_____

x	y
0	
1,000	
2,000	

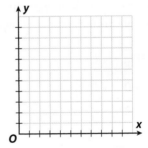

Tell whether each of the following equations represents a linear function.

8. $y = x^2 + 3$ _____

9. $3x = 4$ _____

10. $y = 1$ _____

11. $0.3x + y = 2$ _____

12. $x^2 \left(\frac{1}{y}\right) = 3$ _____

13. $y = x$ _____

14. Select a linear equation from Questions 8–13 and create a graph from it.

_____

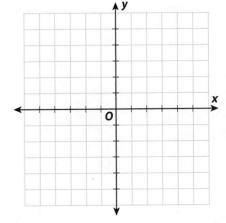

Lesson 6.1   **161**

15. **Represent Real-World Problems** Write a real-world problem that could represent a function that has a range that includes negative numbers.

_____

_____

_____

_____

_____

16. **Communicate Mathematical Ideas** Recall that the standard form of a linear equation is $Ax + By = C$ where A, B, and C are real numbers and A and B are not both 0. Why do you think that A and B cannot both be zero?

_____

_____

17. **Explain the Error** A student was using a table of values to create a graph of a function. The table and graph are shown below. Explain the student's error.

x	y
0	0
1	3
−1	−3

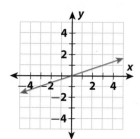

_____

_____

_____

18. **Communicate Mathematical Ideas** Consider the following graphs. They are for the same line. How is this possible?

_____

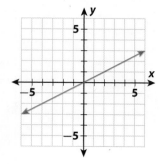   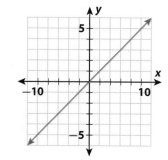

LESSON
6.2 Using Intercepts

FL **F-IF.3.7a**

Graph linear and quadratic functions and show intercepts, maxima, and minima. *Also F-IF.2.4, F-IF.3.7*

? ESSENTIAL QUESTION

How can you find and use intercepts to model real-world linear relationships?

EXPLORE ACTIVITY

FL **F-IF.2.4, F-IF.3.7, F-IF.3.7a**

Identifying Intercepts

A diver explored the ocean floor at 120 feet below the surface. The diver then ascended at a constant rate over a period of 4 minutes until he reached the surface.

In the coordinate grid below, the horizontal axis represents the time in minutes from when the diver started ascending and the vertical axis represents the diver's elevation in feet.

A What point represents the diver's elevation at the beginning

of the ascent? Graph this point. _____

B What point represents the diver's elevation at the end of the

ascent? Graph this point. _____

C Connect the points with a line segment. The graph now shows the diver's elevation below sea level during the 4-minute ascent.

Look at points $(4, 0)$ and $(0, -120)$. Notice that these are points where the graph intersects the axes. These points are known as *intercepts*.

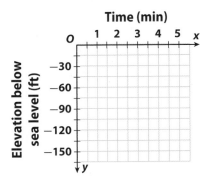

REFLECT

1. **Communicate Mathematical Ideas** The diver begins his ascent at the depth represented by the point where a graph intersects the y-axis of the graph. Will the point where a graph intersects the y-axis always be the lowest point of a linear graph? Explain.

_____

_____

_____

_____

_____

© Thewada 1976/Shutterstock

Lesson 6.2 **163**

Math On the Spot

my.hrw.com

Finding Intercepts of Linear Equations

In the previous Explore Activity, the graph intersected the axes at $(0, -120)$ and $(4, 0)$.

The **y-intercept** is the y-coordinate of the point where the graph intersects the y-axis. The x-coordinate of this point is always 0. This was point $(0, -120)$ in the Explore Activity.

The **x-intercept** is the x-coordinate of the point where the graph intersects the x-axis. The y-coordinate of this point is always 0. This was point $(4, 0)$ in the Explore Activity.

EXAMPLE 1 FL F-IF.3.7, F-IF.3.7a

Find the x- and y-intercepts.

My Notes

A

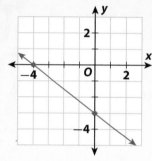

The graph crosses the x-axis at $(-4, 0)$.

The x-intercept is -4.

The graph crosses the y-axis at $(0, -3)$.

The y-intercept is -3.

B $3x - 2y = 12$

To find the x-intercept, replace y with 0 and solve for x.

$$3x - 2y = 12$$
$$3x - 2(0) = 12$$
$$3x - 0 = 12$$
$$3x = 12$$
$$\frac{3x}{3} = \frac{12}{3}$$
$$x = 4$$

The x-intercept is 4.

To find the y-intercept, replace x with 0 and solve for y.

$$3x - 2y = 12$$
$$3(0) - 2y = 12$$
$$0 - 2y = 12$$
$$-2y = 12$$
$$\frac{-2y}{-2} = \frac{12}{-2}$$
$$y = -6$$

The y-intercept is -6.

YOUR TURN

Find the x- and y-intercepts.

2.

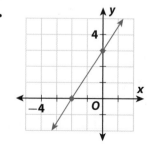

3. $-3x + 5y = 30$

_____

Personal Math Trainer

Online Assessment and Intervention

my.hrw.com

_____

Interpreting Intercepts of Linear Equations

EXAMPLE 2 **FL** F-IF.4, F-IF.3.7, F.IF.3.7a

The Sandia Peak Tramway in Albuquerque, New Mexico, travels a distance of about 4500 meters to the top of Sandia Peak. Its speed is 300 meters per minute. The function $f(x) = 4500 - 300x$ gives the tram's distance in meters from the top of the peak after x minutes.

Graph this function and find the intercepts. What does each intercept represent?

x	$f(x) = 4500 - 300x$
0	4500
2	3900
5	3000

Neither time nor distance can be negative, so choose several nonnegative values for x. Use the function to generate ordered pairs.

Sandia Peak Tramway

Distance from peak (m) vs. Time (min)

y-intercept: 4500

In the real world, the y-intercept represents the distance from the top at the start (time $= 0$).

x-intercept: 15

In the real world, the x-intercept represents the time it takes for the tram to reach the top (distance from peak $= 0$).

Math On the Spot
my.hrw.com

Math Talk
Mathematical Practices

A student says that the graph shows the path of the tram. Why is the student incorrect?

YOUR TURN

4. The temperature in an experiment is reduced at a constant rate over a period of time until the temperature reaches 0°C. The equation $y = 20 - \frac{2}{3}x$ gives the temperature y in degrees Celsius x hours after the beginning of the experiment.

   a. Graph this function and find the x- and y-intercepts.

   _____

   b. What does each intercept represent?

   _____

   _____

   _____

   _____

   _____

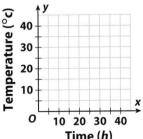

Temperature (°C) vs. Time (h)

Personal Math Trainer

Online Assessment and Intervention

my.hrw.com

Math On the Spot

my.hrw.com

Using Intercepts to Graph Linear Equations

EXAMPLE 3

 FL   F-IF.3.7, F-IF.3.7a

Use intercepts to graph the line described by each equation.

A $2x - 4y = 8$

STEP 1   Find the intercepts.

x-intercept:	y-intercept:
$2x - 4y = 8$	$2x - 4y = 8$
$2x - 4(0) = 8$	$2(0) - 4y = 8$
$2x = 8$	$-4y = 8$
$\dfrac{2x}{2} = \dfrac{8}{2}$	$\dfrac{-4y}{-4} = \dfrac{8}{-4}$
$x = 4$	$y = -2$

STEP 2   Graph the line.

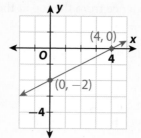

Plot (4, 0) and (0, −2).

Connect the points with a straight line.

B $\frac{2}{3}y = 4 - \frac{1}{2}x$

STEP 1   Write the equation in standard form.

$\frac{1}{2}x + \frac{2}{3}y = 4 - \frac{1}{2}x + \frac{1}{2}x$ Add $\frac{1}{2}x$ to both sides so both variables are on the same side.

$\frac{1}{2}x + \frac{2}{3}y = 4$

STEP 2   Find the intercepts.

x-intercept:	y-intercept:
$\frac{1}{2}x + \frac{2}{3}y = 4$	$\frac{1}{2}x + \frac{2}{3}y = 4$
$\frac{1}{2}x + \frac{2}{3}(0) = 4$	$\frac{1}{2}(0) + \frac{2}{3}y = 4$
$\frac{1}{2}x = 4$	$\frac{2}{3}y = 4$
$2\left(\frac{1}{2}x\right) = 2(4)$	$\frac{3}{2}\left(\frac{2}{3}y\right) = \frac{3}{2}(4)$
$x = 8$	$y = 6$

My Notes

STEP 3 Graph the line.

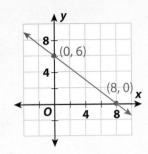

Plot (8, 0) and (0, 6).

Connect the points with a straight line.

REFLECT

5. **Draw Conclusions** Find the intercepts for a linear equation of the form $Ax = C$, where A and C are real numbers and A is not 0.

_____

_____

_____

_____

YOUR TURN

Use intercepts to graph the line described by each equation.

6. $-3x + 4y = -12$

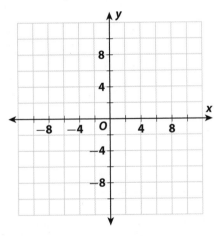

7. $y = \frac{1}{3}x - 2$

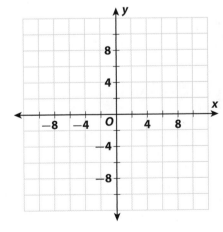

8. A function has x-intercept 4 and y-intercept 2. Name two other points on the graph of this function.

_____

Personal Math Trainer

Online Assessment and Intervention

my.hrw.com

Find the x- and y-intercepts. (Example 1)

1.

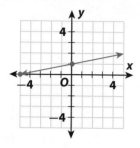

_____

2.

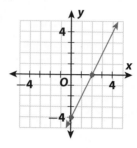

_____

3.

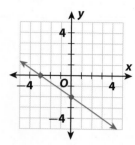

_____

4. $2x - 4y = 4$

_____

5. $-2y = 3x - 6$

_____

6. $4y + 5x = 2y - 3x + 16$

_____

Use intercepts to graph the line described by each equation. (Example 3)

7. $4x - 5y = 20$

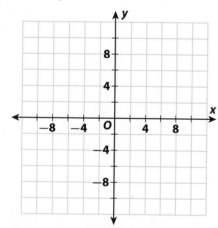

8. $y = \frac{1}{2}x - 4$

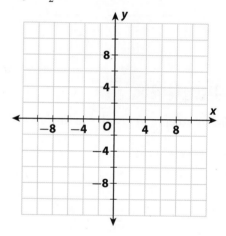

? ESSENTIAL QUESTION CHECK-IN

9. How are intercepts often interpreted in the real world? Consider the examples from this lesson.

_____

_____

_____

_____

6.2 Independent Practice

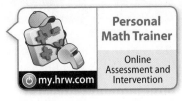

Personal
Math Trainer

Online
Assessment and
Intervention

my.hrw.com

FL **F-IF.3.7, F-IF.3.7a**

10. To thaw a specimen stored at −25 °C, the temperature of a refrigeration tank is raised 5 °C every hour. The temperature in the tank after x hours can be described by the function

$f(x) = -25 + 5x$.

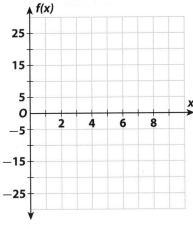

    a. Graph the function and find its intercepts.

    _____

    b. What does each intercept represent?

    _____

    _____

    _____

    _____

11. A fishing lake was stocked with 300 bass. Each year, the population decreases by 25. The population of bass in the lake after x years is represented by the function $f(x) = 300 - 25x$.

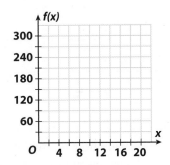

    a. Graph the function and find its intercepts.

    _____

    b. What does each intercept represent?

    _____

    _____

    _____

    _____

12. A bamboo plant is growing 1 foot per day. When first measured, it is 4 feet tall.

    a. Write an equation to describe the height, y, in feet, of the bamboo plant

    x days after you measure it. _____

    b. What is the y-intercept? What does the y-intercept represent?

    _____

    _____

13. **Represent Real-World Problems** Write a real-world problem that could be modeled by a linear function whose x-intercept is 5 and y-intercept is 60.

_____

_____

_____

_____

14. **Draw Conclusions** For any linear equation $Ax + By = C$, what are the intercepts in terms of A, B, and C?

_____

15. **Multi-Step** Kirsten is driving to a city that is 400 miles away. When Kirsten left home, she had 15 gallons of gas in her car. Assume that her car gets 25 miles per gallon of gas. Define a function f so that $f(x)$ is the amount of gas left in her car after she has driven x miles from home. What are the intercepts for that function? What do they represent?

_____

_____

_____

_____

16. **Multiple Representations** Find the intercepts of $3x + 40y = 1200$ Explain how to use the intercepts to determine appropriate scales for the graph and then create a graph.

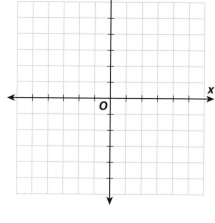

_____

_____

_____

_____

_____

_____

_____

_____

Using Slope

FL **F-IF.2.6**

Calculate and interpret the average rate of change of a function (presented symbolically or as a table) over a specified interval. Estimate the rate of change from a graph. *Also F-IF.2.4, F-IF.3.7, F-LE.1.1b*

? ESSENTIAL QUESTION

How can you describe rate of change in real-world linear relationships?

EXPLORE ACTIVITY 1   FL **F-IF.2.4, F-IF.2.6**

Finding Rates of Change

For a function defined in terms of x and y, the **rate of change** over a part of the domain of the function is a ratio that compares the change in y to the change in x in that part of the domain.

$$\text{rate of change} = \frac{\text{change in } y}{\text{change in } x}$$

A In 2004, the cost of sending a 1-ounce letter was 37 cents. In 2008, the cost was 42 cents. Find the rate of change in cost for this time period.

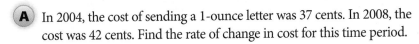

$$\text{rate of change} = \frac{\text{change in } y}{\text{change in } x} = \frac{\boxed{} - \boxed{}}{2008 - 2004} = \frac{\boxed{}}{\boxed{}} = \boxed{}$$

The rate of change was $\boxed{}$ cents per year.

B Find the rate of change for each time period.

Year (x)	1988	1990	1991	2004	2008
Cost in cents (y)	25	25	29	37	42

$$1988 \text{ to } 1990 = \frac{\boxed{} - \boxed{}}{1990 - 1988} = \boxed{} \text{ cents per year}$$

$$1990 \text{ to } 1991 = \frac{\boxed{} - \boxed{}}{1991 - 1990} = \boxed{} \text{ cents per year}$$

> Round to the nearest hundredth of a cent.

$$1991 \text{ to } 2004 = \frac{\boxed{} - \boxed{}}{2004 - 1991} = \boxed{} = \boxed{} \text{ cents per year}$$

$$2004 \text{ to } 2008 = \frac{\boxed{} - \boxed{}}{2008 - 2004} = \boxed{} = \boxed{} \text{ cents per year}$$

REFLECT

1. **Interpret the Answer** The rate of change for 2004 to 2008 was 1.25 cents per year. Does this mean the actual change in cost each year was 1.25 cents? Explain.

_____

_____

_____

Finding Slope of a Line

In the previous Explore Activity, the rate of change was not constant. It varied from 0 to 4 cents per year. However, for linear functions, the rate of change is constant.

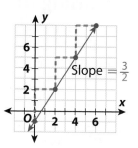

The rate of change for a linear function can be calculated using the rise and run of the graph of the function. The **rise** is the difference in the *y*-values of two points on a line. The **run** is the difference in the *x*-values of two points on a line.

The **slope** of a line is the ratio of rise to run for any two points on the line.

$$\text{slope} = \frac{\text{rise}}{\text{run}} = \frac{\text{change in } y}{\text{change in } x}$$

EXAMPLE 1   FL   F-IF.2.6

Find the slope of each line.

A

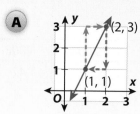

Use (2, 3) as the starting point. Subtract *y*-values to find the change in *y* or rise. Then subtract *x*-values to find the change in *x* or run.

slope $= \frac{1-3}{1-2} = \frac{-2}{-1} = 2$.

It doesn't matter at which point you start as long as you are consistent. If you start at (1, 1), then

slope $= \frac{3-1}{2-1} = \frac{2}{1} = 2$

B

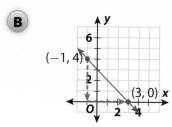

Use (−1, 4) as the starting point. Subtract *y*-values to find the change in *y* or rise. Then subtract *x*-values to find the change in *x* or run.

slope $= \frac{0-4}{3-(-1)} = \frac{-4}{4} = -1$

YOUR TURN

2. Find the slope of the line in the graph.

_____

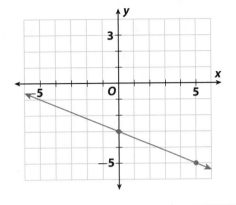

EXPLORE ACTIVITY 2

FL F-IF.2.6

Classifying Slopes

As shown in the previous examples, slope can be positive or negative. What about the slope of horizontal and vertical lines?

Find the slope of each line.

Ⓐ

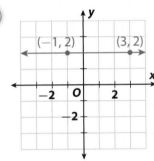

slope $= \dfrac{\text{rise}}{\text{run}} = \dfrac{\boxed{}}{\boxed{}} = \dfrac{\boxed{}}{\boxed{}} = \boxed{}$

Ⓑ

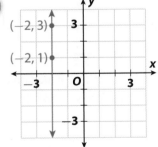

slope $= \dfrac{\text{rise}}{\text{run}} = \dfrac{\boxed{}}{\boxed{}} = \dfrac{\boxed{}}{0}$

Since you cannot divide by 0, the slope is undefined.

Positive Slope	Negative Slope	Zero Slope	Undefined Slope

Line rises from left to right.	Line falls from left to right.	Horizontal line	Vertical line

REFLECT

3. **Communicate Mathematical Ideas** Explain why the slope of a vertical line is undefined.

_____

_____

_____

Math On the Spot

⏻ my.hrw.com

Using the Slope Formula

The **slope formula** for the slope of a line is the ratio of the difference in y-values to the difference in x-values between any two different points on the line.

This means if (x_1, y_1) and (x_2, y_2) are any two points on a line, the slope is $m = \frac{y_2 - y_1}{x_2 - x_1}$.

EXAMPLE 2

FL · F-IF.2.6

Find the slope of the line passing through the points (5, 3) and (–1, 15). Describe the slope as positive, negative, zero, or undefined.

Animated Math

⏻ my.hrw.com

STEP 1 Find the rise or difference in y-values.

$$y_2 - y_1 = 15 - 3 = 12$$

STEP 2 Find the run or difference in x-values.

$$x_2 - x_1 = -1 - 5 = -6$$

STEP 3 Find the slope.

$$\text{slope} = \frac{\text{rise}}{\text{run}} = \frac{12}{-6} = -2$$

STEP 4 Describe the slope.

The slope is negative. The line falls from left to right.

Personal Math Trainer

Online Assessment and Intervention

⏻ my.hrw.com

YOUR TURN

4. Find the slope of the line passing through the points (9, 1) and (–1, –4). Describe the slope as positive, negative, zero, or undefined.

_____

Interpreting Slope

EXAMPLE 3 🏴 **FL** F-IF.2.4, F-IF.2.6, F-IF.3.7, F-LE.1.1b

The graph shows the relationship between a person's age and his or her estimated maximum heart rate.

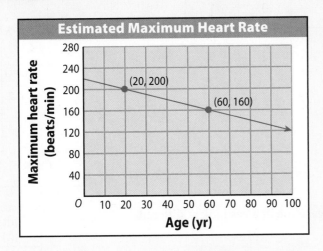

My Notes

A Find the slope.

Use the two points that are labeled on the graph.

$$\text{slope} = \frac{\text{rise}}{\text{run}} = \frac{160 - 200}{60 - 20} = \frac{-40}{40} = -1$$

B Interpret the slope.

The slope of −1 means that for every year a person's age increases, his or her maximum heart rate decreases by 1 beat per minute.

REFLECT

5. Multi-Step Tara and Jade are hiking up a hill together. Each has a different stride. The run for Tara's stride is 32 inches, and the rise is 8 inches. The run for Jade's stride is 36 inches. What is the rise of Jade's stride? What is the slope and what does it mean in this problem?

_____

_____

Math Talk
Mathematical Practices

Why is it important to know both the formula and the description of what slope is?

YOUR TURN

6. In an experiment, a car began traveling at a constant speed at 1:00 PM. Over a period of 5 hours, the car traveled a total 160 miles A graph shows the relationship between the length of time that the car had been traveling since 1:00 PM and the number of miles that it had traveled. What is the slope of the line? What does the slope mean?

_____

_____

Personal Math Trainer

Online Assessment and Intervention

🔘 my.hrw.com

Given the linear relationship, find the slope. (Examples 1 and 2)

1. Line passing through the points $(2, -1)$ and $(0, 5)$

_____

2.

x	y
0	1
1	3
2	5

_____

3.

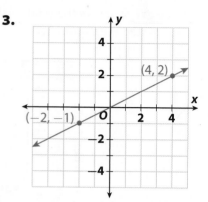

_____

4. The table shows the volume of gasoline in a gas tank at different times. (Examples 1 and 3)

Time (h)	Volume (gal)
0	12
1	9
3	5

a. Find the rate of change for each time interval.

_____

b. What does the difference in the rates of change mean in this situation?

_____

_____

_____

Tell whether the slope is positive, negative, zero, or undefined. (Explore Activity 2)

5.

_____

6.

_____

7.

_____

8.

_____

? ESSENTIAL QUESTION CHECK-IN

9. Give examples of rates of change in at least two real-world situations.

_____

_____

_____

6.3 Independent Practice

Personal Math Trainer

Online Assessment and Intervention

🔴 my.hrw.com

FL   F-IF.2.4, F-IF.2.6, F-IF.3.7, F-LE.1.1b

10. At a particular college, a full-time student must take at least 12 credit hours per semester and may take at most 18 credit hours per semester. Tuition costs $200 per credit hour.

Credit Hours	Cost ($)
12	
13	
14	
15	
16	
17	
18	

a. Complete the table by using the information above.

b. What number is added to the cost in each row to get the cost in the next row?

_____

c. What does your answer to part b represent?

_____

_____

d. Graph the ordered pairs from the table.

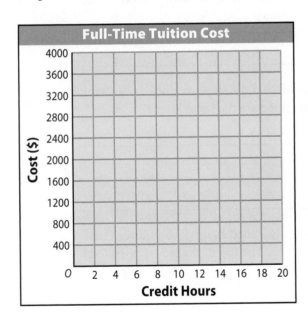

e. Describe how the points in the graph are related.

_____

_____

11. **Multi-Step** The graph shows the number of files scanned by a computer virus detection program over time. Use estimation to find the rate of change between points A and B?

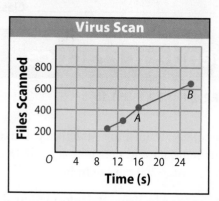

Virus Scan

(y-axis: Files Scanned, marked at 200, 400, 600, 800)
(x-axis: Time (s), marked at 4, 8, 12, 16, 20, 24)

_____

_____

H.O.T.

FOCUS ON HIGHER ORDER THINKING

Work Area

12. **Explain the Error** A student is asked to find the slope of a line containing the points (4, 1) and (−1, 11). He finds the slope the following way:
slope $= \frac{\text{rise}}{\text{run}} = \frac{4-(-1)}{1-11} = \frac{5}{-10} = -\frac{1}{2}$. Explain the error.

_____

_____

_____

13. **Critical Thinking** In this lesson, you learned that the slope of a line is constant. Does this mean that all lines with the same slope are the same line? Explain.

_____

_____

_____

14. **Represent Real-World Problems** A ladder is leaned against a building. The bottom of the ladder is 9 feet from the building. The top of the ladder is 16 feet above the ground.

   a. What is the slope of the ladder? _____

   b. What does the slope of the ladder mean in the real world?

   _____

   _____

   c. If the ladder were set closer to the building, would it be harder or easier to climb? Explain in terms of the slope of the ladder.

   _____

   _____

Slope-Intercept Form

FL   F-IF.2.4

For a function that models a relationship..., interpret key features of graphs and tables..., and sketch graphs showing key features given a verbal description of the relationship. *Also A-CED.1.2, F-IF.3.7, F-IF.3.7a, F-LE.1.1b*

ESSENTIAL QUESTION   How can you use the slope-intercept form of a linear equation to model real-world linear relationships?

Using Slopes and Intercepts

If you know the equation that describes a line, you can find its slope by using any two ordered pairs of numbers that are solutions of the equation. It is often easiest to use the ordered pairs that contain the intercepts.

Math On the Spot
my.hrw.com

EXAMPLE 1   FL   F-LE.1.1b

Find the slope of the line described by $6x - 5y = 30$.

STEP 1   Find the x-intercept.

Substitute 0 for y in the equation and solve for x.

$6x - 5y = 30$

$6x - 5(0) = 30$ Substitute.

$6x - 0 = 30$ Simplify.

$6x = 30$

$x = 5$ Divide both sides by 6.

STEP 2   Find the y-intercept.

Substitute 0 for x in the equation and solve for y.

$6x - 5y = 30$

$6(0) - 5y = 30$ Substitute.

$0 - 5y = 30$ Simplify.

$-5y = 30$

$y = -6$ Divide both sides by -5.

STEP 3   The line contains (5, 0) and (0, −6). Use the slope formula.

$$m = \frac{\text{change in } y\text{-coordinates}}{\text{change in } x\text{-coordinates}}$$

$$= \frac{-6 - 0}{0 - 5}$$

$$= \frac{-6}{-5}$$

$$= \frac{6}{5}$$

The slope of the line is $\frac{6}{5}$.

Math Talk
Mathematical Practices

How can you check if the slope you calculated is correct?

Personal Math Trainer
Online Assessment and Intervention

⊕ my.hrw.com

YOUR TURN

1. Find the slope of the line described by $3x + 4y = 12$. _____

Exploring the Slope Formula

If you know the slope of a line and the y-intercept, you can write an equation that describes the line.

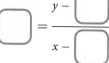

EXPLORE ACTIVITY   **FL** A-CED.1.2

My Notes

Write an equation for the line that has slope 2 and y-intercept 3.

STEP 1 The line has a slope of ▢ and a y-intercept of ▢.
Since ▢ is the y-intercept, (▢, ▢) is a point on the line.
Substitute these values into the slope formula. Since you don't know the coordinates of any other point on the line, use a generic ordered pair (x, y).

$$m = \frac{\text{change in } y\text{-coordinates}}{\text{change in } x\text{-coordinates}} \qquad ▢ = \frac{y - ▢}{x - ▢}$$

STEP 2 Solve for y.

$$▢ = \frac{y - ▢}{x - ▢}$$

$$▢ = \frac{y - ▢}{▢}$$

$$▢ = y - ▢$$

$$▢ + ▢ = y$$

In this equation, the coefficient of x is equal to the _____,

and the constant is equal to the _____.

If a line has slope m and the y-intercept is b, then the line is described by the equation $y = mx + b$. This equation is called the **slope-intercept form** of a linear equation. A linear equation can be written in slope-intercept form by solving for y and simplifying.

2. Why can it be helpful to solve a linear equation for *y*?

_____

_____

Graphing a Linear Function
Using the Slope and *y*-intercept

You can graph the linear function $f(x) = mx + b$ using only the slope *m* and *y*-intercept *b*. First, locate the point $(0, b)$ on the *y*-axis. Next, use the rise and run of the slope to locate another point on the line. Draw a line through the two points.

Math On the Spot
⏻ my.hrw.com

EXAMPLE 2   FL   F-IF.3.7a

Graph the function $f(x) = -\frac{2}{3}x + 4$ and determine its domain and range.

STEP 1 The *y*-intercept is 4. Plot the point $(0, 4)$.

STEP 2 The slope is $-\frac{2}{3}$. If you use −2 as the rise, then the run is 3.

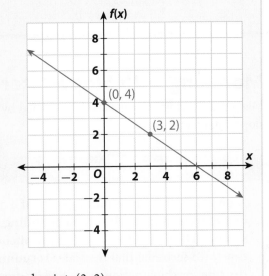

Use the slope to move from the *y*-intercept to a second point. Begin by moving down 2 units, because the rise is negative. Then move right 3 units because the run is positive. Plot the second point, $(3, 2)$.

STEP 3 Draw a line through the two points.

STEP 4 The domain is the set of real numbers.

The range is the set of real numbers.

REFLECT

3. Multiple Representations How does the graph of the linear function show that the domain is the set of real numbers and the range is the set of real numbers?

_____

_____

_____

YOUR TURN

Graph each function.

4. $f(x) = -\frac{1}{2}x + 3$

5. $f(x) = 2x - 1$

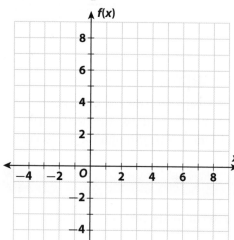

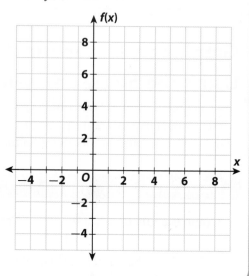

Modeling with Slope-Intercept Form

Many real-world situations can be modeled by a linear equation in slope-intercept form.

 EXAMPLE 3 Real World   FL   F-IF.2.4

A pitcher with a maximum capacity of 4 cups contains 1 cup of apple juice concentrate. A faucet is turned on, filling the pitcher at a rate of 0.25 cup per second. The amount of liquid in the pitcher, $A(t)$, (in cups), is a function of the time t (in seconds) that the water is running. Graph the function $A(t)$, write the rule for the function, and state its domain and range.

STEP 1 The y-intercept is 1 because there is 1 cup in the pitcher at time 0. Plot the point that corresponds to the y-intercept, (0, 1).

STEP 2 The slope is the rate of change: 0.25 cup per second, or 1 cup in 4 seconds. So the rise is 1 and the run is 4.

STEP 3 Use the rise and run to move from the first point to a second point on the line by moving up 1 unit and right 4 units. Plot the second point, (4, 2).

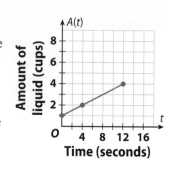

STEP 4 Connect the points and extend the line segment to the maximum value of the function, where $A(t) = 4$ cups.

STEP 5   Use $m = \frac{1}{4}$ and $b = 1$ to write the rule for the function: $A(t) = \frac{1}{4}t + 1$.

STEP 6   The domain is the set of all real numbers t such that $0 \leq t \leq 12$.

The range is the set of all real numbers $A(t)$ such that $1 \leq A(t) \leq 4$.

REFLECT

6. **Critical Thinking** Why are the domain and range restricted in Example 3, rather than each being the set of all real numbers?

_____

_____

_____

_____

_____

YOUR TURN

7. A pump is set to dispense chlorine from a full 5-gallon container into a swimming pool to sanitize the water. The pump will dispense the chlorine at a rate of 0.5 gallon per minute and will shut off when the container is empty. The amount of chlorine in the container, $A(t)$, (in gallons), is a function of the time t (in minutes) that the pump is running. Graph the function $A(t)$, write the rule for the function, and state its domain and range.

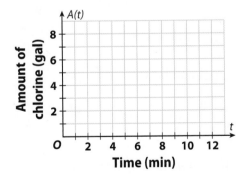

$A(t) =$ _____

Domain: _____

Range: _____

_____

Find the slope of the line described by each equation. (Example 1)

1. $5x - 2y = 10$

$m = $ _____

2. $3y = 4$

$m = $ _____

3. $x - 3y = 6$

$m = $ _____

4. $4x + 2y = 12$

$m = $ _____

5. Graph the function $f(x) = -2x + 3$ and determine its domain and range. (Example 2)

STEP 1 The y-intercept is ☐.

Plot the point (☐, ☐).

STEP 2 The slope is ☐.

Use ☐ as the rise; then the run is ☐.

Use the slope to move from the y-intercept to

a second point. Begin by moving _____

unit(s). Then move _____ unit(s).

Plot the second point, (☐, ☐).

STEP 3 Draw a line through the two points.

STEP 4 The domain is the set of _____ numbers.

The range is the set of _____ numbers.

ESSENTIAL QUESTION CHECK-IN

6. How is the rate of change in a real-world linear relationship related to the slope-intercept form of the equation that represents the relationship?

_____

_____

_____

_____

_____

6.4 Independent Practice

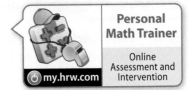

FL   F-IF.2.4

Find the slope of the line described by each equation.

7. $5x + 3y = 0$

8. $3y = 6$

9. $6x - 12y = 36$

$m =$ _____

$m =$ _____

$m =$ _____

10. When graphing a linear function in slope-intercept form, why do you have to plot the y-intercept first? Why can't you use the slope first?

_____

_____

_____

Graph each linear function.

11. $f(x) = \frac{1}{4}x - 3$

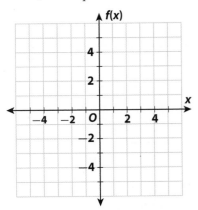

12. $f(x) = -5x + 1$

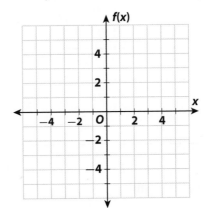

13. $f(x) = -1$

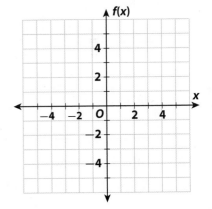

14. A company rents moving vans for a charge of $30 plus $0.50 per mile. The company only allows its vans to be used for "in-town" moves, with total mileage limited to 100 miles. The total rental cost, $C(m)$, (in dollars) is a function of the distance m (in miles) that the van is driven. State a rule for the function, graph the function, and state its domain and range.

$C(m) =$ _____

Domain: _____

_____

Range: _____

_____

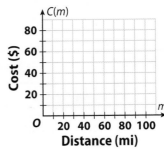

H.O.T. FOCUS ON HIGHER ORDER THINKING

Work Area

15. Draw Conclusions The standard form of a linear equation is $Ax + By = C$. Rewrite this equation in slope-intercept form. What is the slope? What is the y-intercept?

____

16. What If? What if the person filling the pitcher in Example 3 gets distracted by a phone call and does not get to turn the faucet off as soon as the pitcher is full? How does this affect the domain and range of the function? How does it affect the graph?

____

____

____

____

____

17. Find the Error Alyssa correctly determines that the graph of a linear equation intersects the x-axis at (6, 0) and intersects the y-axis at (0, 2). She calculates the slope and then writes the slope-intercept equation for the line as $y = -\frac{1}{3}x + 6$. What error did Alyssa make? What is the correct slope-intercept equation for this line?

____

____

____

____

18. Justify Reasoning Is it possible to write the equation of every line in slope-intercept form? Explain your reasoning.

____

____

____

____

____

____

____

____

LESSON
6.5

FL F-IF.3.9
Compare properties of two
functions each represented in a
different way . . .
Also F-IF.1.1, F-IF.1.2, F-IF.2.5,
F-LE.2.5, N-Q.1.1

Comparing Linear Functions

ESSENTIAL QUESTION

How can you compare linear functions that are represented in different ways?

EXPLORE ACTIVITY   FL F-IF.3.9

Comparing Linear Relationships

Comparing linear relationships sometimes involves comparing relationships that
are expressed in different ways.

Joe's Plumbing and Mark's Plumbing have different ways of charging their
customers. The function defined by $J(t) = 40t$ represents the total amount in
dollars that Joe's Plumbing charges for t hours of work. Mark's Plumbing
Service charges $40 per hour plus a $25 trip charge.

A Define a function $M(t)$ that represents the total amount Mark's Plumbing
Service charges for t hours of work and then complete the charts below.

$M(t) = 40t + 25$ represents the total amount in dollars that Mark's Plumbing
Service charges for t hours of work.

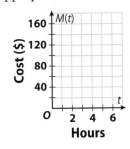

Cost for Joe's Plumbing		
t	$J(t) = 40t$	$(t, J(t))$
0	0	$(0, 0)$
1		
2		
3		

Cost for Mark's Plumbing Service		
t	$M(t) = 40t + 25$	$(t, M(t))$
0	0	$(0, 25)$
1		
2		
3		

B What domain values for the functions $J(t)$ and for $M(t)$ are reasonable in this
context? Explain.

_____

_____

C Graph the two cost functions for all appropriate domain values.

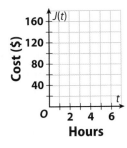

D Compare the graphs. How are they alike? How are they different?

_____

_____

REFLECT

1. Describe the range for $J(t)$ and $M(t)$.

_____

_____

_____

Math On the Spot

⟳ my.hrw.com

Comparing Linear Functions Given a Table and a Rule

A table and a rule are two ways that a linear relationship may be expressed. Sometimes it may be helpful to convert one representation to the other when comparing two relationships. Other times, making comparisons may be possible without converting either representation.

EXAMPLE 1

FL   F-IF.3.9

The functions $f(x)$ and $g(x)$ are linear functions. The domain of each function is the set of all real numbers x such that $4 \le x \le 7$. The table shows some ordered pairs belonging to $f(x)$. The function $g(x)$ is defined by the rule $g(x) = 2x + 3$. Find the initial value and the range of each function.

x	f(x)
4	8
5	10
6	12
7	14

The initial value is the output that is paired with the least input.

The initial value of $f(x)$ is $f(4) = 8$ *The least input for f(x) is 4.*

The initial value of $g(x)$ is $g(4) = 2(4) + 3 = 11$.   *The least input for g(x) is 4.*

Since $f(x)$ is a linear function, and its domain is the set of all real numbers from 4 to 7, its range will be the set of all real numbers from $f(4)$ to $f(7)$. $f(4) = 8$ and $f(7) = 14$. Therefore, the range of $f(x)$ is the set of all real numbers $f(x)$ such that $8 \le f(x) \le 14$.

Since $g(x)$ is a linear function, and its domain is the set of all real numbers from 4 to 7, its range will be the set of all real numbers from $g(4)$ to $g(7)$. $g(4) = 2(4) + 3 = 11$ and $g(7) = 2(7) + 3 = 17$. Therefore, the range of $g(x)$ is the set of all real numbers $g(x)$ such that $11 \le g(x) \le 17$.

YOUR TURN

2. The rule for the function $f(x)$ in Example 1 is $f(x) = 2x$. How do the slopes and y-intercepts of the graphs of the two functions compare?

_____

_____

_____

Comparing Linear Functions Given a Description and a Graph

Information about a relationship may have to be inferred from the context given in the problem.

EXAMPLE 2 FL F-IF.3.9

Compare the following functions.

- A rainstorm in Atlanta lasted for 2.5 hours, during which time it rained at a steady rate of 0.5 inch per hour. The function $A(t)$ represents the amount of rain that fell in t hours.

- The graph at the right shows the amount of rain that fell during a rainstorm in Knoxville, $K(t)$ (in inches), as a function of time t (in hours).

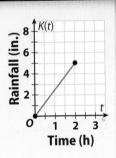

STEP 1 Write a rule for each function.

$A(t) = 0.5t$ for $0 \leq t \leq 2.5$

Since $(0, 0)$ and $(2, 5)$ are the coordinates of points on the line representing $K(t)$, the slope of the line is $\frac{5-0}{2-0} = \frac{5}{2} = 2.5$. The y-intercept is 0, so substituting 2.5 for m and 0 for b in $y = mx + b$ produces $y = 2.5t$, which yields $K(t) = 2.5t$ for $0 \leq t \leq 2$.

STEP 2 Compare the y-intercepts of the graphs of $A(t)$ and $K(t)$.

They are both 0.

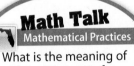

Math Talk

Mathematical Practices

What is the meaning of the y-intercepts for the functions $A(t)$ and $K(t)$?

YOUR TURN

3. How do the slopes of the graphs of the functions $A(t)$ and $K(t)$ compare?

_____

_____

The linear function $f(x)$ is defined by the table below. The linear function $g(x)$ is defined by the graph below. Assume that the domain of $f(x)$ includes all real numbers between the least and greatest values shown in the table. (Examples 1–2)

x	f(x)
0	−2
1	1
2	4
3	7
4	10
5	13

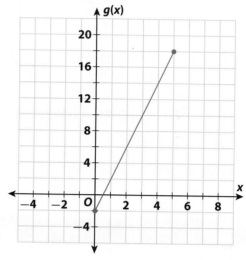

1. Compare the domains, initial values, and ranges of the functions.

   Domain of $f(x)$: _____

   Domain of $g(x)$: _____

   Initial value of $f(x)$: _____

   Initial value of $g(x)$: _____

   Range of $f(x)$: _____

   Range of $g(x)$: _____

2. Calculate how many inches of rain fell per hour during the Knoxville storm in Example 2. How many more inches per hour is this than in the Atlanta storm? (Example 2)

   _____

? ESSENTIAL QUESTION CHECK-IN

3. How can you compare a linear function represented in a table to one represented as a graph?

   _____

   _____

   _____

6.5 Independent Practice

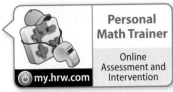

Personal
Math Trainer

Online
Assessment and
Intervention
my.hrw.com

FL **F-IF.3.9**

4. Grace works from 10 to 20 hours per week while attending college. She earns $9.00 per hour. Her roommate Frances also has a job. Her pay for t hours each week is given by the function $f(t) = 10t$, where $5 \leq t \leq 15$.

   a. Find the domain and range of each function.

   _____

   _____

   _____

   _____

   _____

   b. Compare their hourly wages and the amount they each earn per week.

   _____

   _____

5. The linear function $f(x)$ is defined by the table below. The linear function $g(x)$ is defined by the graph below. Assume that the domain of $f(x)$ includes all real numbers between the least and greatest values shown in the table.

x	f(x)
−1	7
0	4
1	1
2	−2

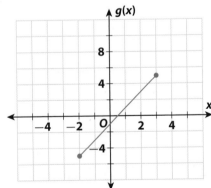

   a. Find the domain and range of each function.

   _____

   _____

   _____

   _____

   b. What is the slope of the line represented by each function? What is the

   y-intercept for each function? _____

   _____

6. Complete the table so that $f(x)$ is a linear function with a slope of 2 and a y-intercept of 5.

x	f(x)
−1	
0	
1	
2	

Work Area

7. Communicate Mathematical Ideas Describe a linear function for which the least value in the range does not occur at the least value of the domain, that is, the least value in the range is not the initial value.

_____

_____

_____

_____

8. Draw Conclusions Two linear functions have the same slope, same x-intercept, and same y-intercept. Must these functions be identical? Explain your reasoning.

_____

_____

_____

_____

_____

_____

9. Justify Reasoning One student says that if everyone always wrote linear functions by defining a function rule, it would be much easier to compare different functions. Another student says that there are reasons to represent functions in different ways. With which student do you agree more? Explain.

_____

_____

_____

_____

Transforming Linear Functions

FL F-BF.2.3

Identify the effect on the graph of replacing $f(x)$ by $f(x) + k$, $k\,f(x)$, $f(kx)$, and $f(x + k)$ for specific values of k (both positive and negative); find the value of k given the graphs. Also F-IF.2.4, F-LE.2.5

ESSENTIAL QUESTION

How are changes to the parameters of a linear function reflected in its graph?

EXPLORE ACTIVITY 1 FL F-BF.2.3

Changing Parameters

Changing the value of m or b in $f(x) = mx + b$ causes a change in the graph of that function.

Investigate what happens to the graph of $f(x) = x + b$ when you change the value of b.

A Use a graphing calculator. Start with the standard viewing window, which you can obtain by pressing **ZOOM** and selecting ZStandard. If the distances between consecutive tick marks on the x-axis and y-axis are not equal, you can make them equal by pressing **ZOOM** again and selecting ZSquare.

What interval on each axis does the viewing window now show? (Press **WINDOW** to find out.)

_____

B Graph the function $f(x) = x$ by pressing **Y=** and entering the function's rule next to $Y_1=$. As shown, the graph of the function is a line that makes a 45° angle with each axis.

What are the slope and y-intercept of the graph of $f(x) = x$?

_____

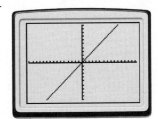

C Graph other functions of the form $f(x) = x + b$ by entering their rules next to $Y_2=$, $Y_3=$, and so on. Be sure to choose both positive and negative values of b. For instance, graph $f(x) = x + 2$ and $f(x) = x - 3$.

What do the graphs have in common? How are they different?

_____

_____

REFLECT

1. A *vertical translation* moves all points on a figure the same distance either up or down. Use the idea of a vertical translation to describe what happens to the graph of $f(x) = x + b$ when you increase the value of b and decrease the value of b.

_____

_____

Investigate what happens to the graph of $f(x) = mx$ when you change the value of m.

A Use a graphing calculator. Press [Y=] and clear out all but the function $f(x) = x$ from the previous Explore Activity. Then graph other functions of the form $f(x) = mx$ by entering their rules next to $Y_2=$, $Y_3=$, and so on. Use only values of m that are greater than 1. For instance, graph $f(x) = 2x$ and $f(x) = 6x$.

What do the graphs have in common? How are they different?

_____

_____

As the value of m increases from 1, does the graph become steeper or less

steep? _____

B Again, press [Y=] and clear out all but the function $f(x) = x$. Then graph other functions of the form $f(x) = mx$ by entering their rules next to $Y_2=$, $Y_3=$, and so on. This time use only values of m that are less than 1 but greater than 0. For instance, graph $f(x) = 0.5x$ and $f(x) = 0.2x$.

As the value of m decreases from 1 to 0, does the graph become steeper or

less steep? _____

C Again, press [Y=] and clear out all but the function $f(x) = x$. Then graph the function $f(x) = -x$ by entering its rule next to $Y_2=$.

What are the slope and y-intercept of the graph of $f(x) = -x$?

_____

How are the graphs of $f(x) = x$ and $f(x) = -x$ geometrically related?

_____

_____

D Again, press [Y=] and clear out all the functions. Graph $f(x) = -x$ by entering its rule next to $Y_1=$. Then graph other functions of the form $f(x) = mx$ where $m < 0$ by entering their rules next to $Y_2=$, $Y_3=$, and so on. Be sure to choose values of m that are less than -1 as well as values of m between -1 and 0.

Describe what happens to the graph of $f(x) = mx$ as the value of m decreases from -1 and as it increases from -1 to 0.

_____

_____

_____

REFLECT

2. A function $f(x)$ is called an *increasing function* when the value of $f(x)$ always increases as the value of x increases. For what values of m is the function $f(x) = mx$ an increasing function? How can you tell from the graph of a linear function that it is an increasing function?

_____

3. A function $f(x)$ is called a *decreasing function* when the value of $f(x)$ always decreases as the value of x increases. For what values of m is the function $f(x) = mx$ a decreasing function? How can you tell from the graph of a linear function that it is a decreasing function?

_____

4. When $m > 0$, increasing the value of m results in an increasing linear function that increases *faster*. What effect does increasing m have on the graph of the function?

_____

5. When $m > 0$, decreasing the value of m toward 0 results in an increasing linear function that increases *slower*. What effect does decreasing m have on the graph of the function?

_____

6. When $m < 0$, decreasing the value of m results in a decreasing linear function that decreases *faster*. What effect does decreasing m have on the graph of the function?

_____

7. When $m < 0$, increasing the value of m toward 0 results in a decreasing linear function that decreases *slower*. What effect does increasing m have on the graph of the function?

_____

8. The *steepness* of a line refers to the absolute value of its slope. The greater the absolute value of the slope, the steeper the line. Complete the table to summarize, in terms of steepness, the effect of changing the value of m on the graph of $f(x) = mx$.

How the Value of m Changes	Effect on the Graph of $f(x) = mx$
Increase m when $m > 0$.	
Decrease m toward 0 when $m > 0$.	
Decrease m when $m < 0$.	
Increase m toward 0 when $m < 0$.	

EXPLORE ACTIVITY 3

 FL F-BF.2.3

A A **family of functions** is a set of functions whose graphs have basic characteristics in common. What do all these variations on the original function $f(x) = x$ have in common?

_____

B The most basic function of a family of functions is called the **parent function**. What is the parent function of the family of functions explored in the first two explore activities?

_____

C A **parameter** is one of the constants in a function or equation that determines which variation of the parent function one is considering. For functions of the form $f(x) = mx + b$, what are the two parameters?

_____

For the family of all linear functions, the parent function is $f(x) = x$, where the parameters are $m = 1$ and $b = 0$. Other examples of families of linear functions are shown below. The example on the left shows a family with the same parameter m and differing parameters b. The example on the right shows a family with the same parameter b and differing parameters m.

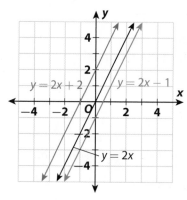
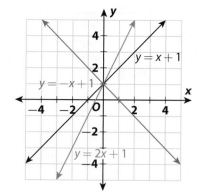

REFLECT

9. Describe the parameter that is left unchanged in the equations of the lines in the graph on the left above.

_____

Math On the Spot
⏻ my.hrw.com

Modeling with Parameter Changes

Real-world scenarios can often be modeled by linear functions. Changes in a particular scenario can be analyzed by making changes in the corresponding parameter of the linear function.

EXAMPLE 1    FL   F-IF.2.4, F-LE.2.5

A gym charges a one-time joining fee of $50 and then a monthly membership fee of $25. The total cost *C* of being a member of the gym is given by the function $C(t) = 25t + 50$, where *t* is the time (in months) since joining the gym. For each situation described below, sketch a graph using the given graph of $C(t) = 25t + 50$ as a reference. Describe the impact of the changes on the domain and range of the function.

A   The gym decreases its one-time joining fee.

Rather than graphing a specific function for this situation, sketch a representative graph of a function related to the function $C(t) = 25t + 50$ with the appropriate parameter changed.

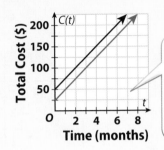

To sketch a graph that represents the new situation, make the y-intercept of the graph lower, but leave the slope the same.

The one-time joining fee is represented by the constant in the equation; the constant represents the *y*-intercept of the graph. There is no change in the domain, but the range now starts at the new (lower) joining fee rather than at 50.

B   The gym increases its monthly membership fee.

Rather than graphing a specific function for this situation, sketch a representative graph of a function related to the function $C(t) = 25t + 50$ with the appropriate parameter changed.

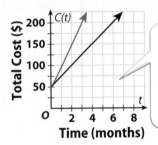

To sketch a graph that represents the new situation, increase the slope of the graph but leave the y-intercept the same.

The monthly membership fee is represented by the coefficient of *t* in the equation; the coefficient of *t* represents the slope of the graph.

There is no change in the domain or the range.

Animated Math

my.hrw.com

Math Talk

Mathematical Practices

Why is the graph of the function only in the first quadrant?

YOUR TURN

10. Once a year the gym offers a special in which the one-time joining fee is waived for new members. What impact does this special offer have on the graph of the original function $C(t) = 25t + 50$?

_____

_____

Personal Math Trainer

Online Assessment and Intervention

my.hrw.com

1. The graph of the function $f(x) = x + 3$ is shown below. Graph two more functions in the same family for which the parameter being changed is the y-intercept. (Example 1)

2. The graph of the function $f(x) = x + 3$ is shown below. Graph two more functions in the same family for which the parameter being changed is the slope. (Example 1)

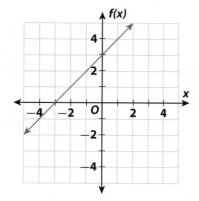

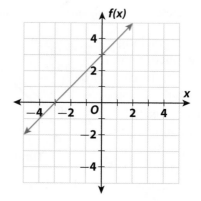

3. For the family of linear functions of the form $f(x) = mx + b$, the parameter

   that causes the steepness of the graph of the line to change is _____.
   (Explore Activities 1 and 2)

4. The graph of the parent linear function $f(x) = x$ is shown in black on the coordinate grid. Write the color of the line that represents this function with the indicated parameter changes. (Explore Activities 1 and 2)

   a. m increased, b unchanged

   _____

   b. m decreased, b unchanged

   _____

   c. m unchanged, b increased

   _____

   d. m unchanged, b decreased

   _____

? ESSENTIAL QUESTION CHECK-IN

5. How do changes in m and b in $y = mx + b$ affect the graph of the equation?

   _____

   _____

6.6 Independent Practice

FL F-BF.2.3

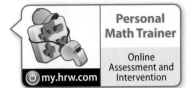

Personal Math Trainer

Online Assessment and Intervention

my.hrw.com

6. A salesperson earns a base monthly salary of $2000 plus a 10% commission on sales. The salesperson's monthly income I (in dollars) is given by the function $I(s) = 0.1s + 2000$, where s is the sales (in dollars) that the salesperson makes. Sketch a graph to illustrate each situation using the graph of $I(s) = 0.1s + 2000$ as a reference.

a. The salesperson's base salary is increased.

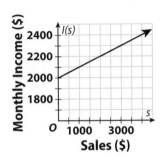

b. The salesperson's commission rate is decreased.

7. Mr. Resnick is driving at a speed of 40 miles per hour to visit relatives who live 100 miles away from his home. His distance d (in miles) from his destination is given by the function $d(t) = 100 - 40t$, where t is the time (in hours) since his trip began. Sketch a graph to illustrate each situation. The graphs shown already represent the function $d(t)$.

a. He increases his speed to get to his destination sooner.

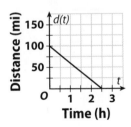

b. He encounters a detour that increases the driving distance.

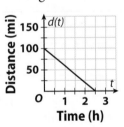

c. Give an example of another linear function within the same family of functions as $d(t) = 100 - 40t$. Explain the meaning of each parameter in your example.

_____

_____

8. Use the graph of $d(t) = 100 - 40t$ in Exercise 7 to identify the domain and range of the function. Then tell whether the domain, the range, neither, or both are affected by the changes described in each part.

_____

_____

9. For each linear function graphed on the coordinate grid, state the value of m and the value of b.

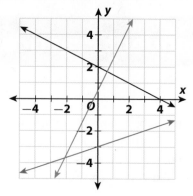

   a. black line: $m =$ _____, $b =$ _____

   b. blue line: $m =$ _____, $b =$ _____

   c. green line: $m =$ _____, $b =$ _____

10. Suppose the gym increases its one-time joining fee and decreases its monthly membership fee in Example 1. Describe how you would alter the graph of $C(t) = 25t + 50$ to illustrate the new cost function.

_____

_____

_____

 **FOCUS ON HIGHER ORDER THINKING**

Work Area

11. Critique Reasoning Geoff says that changing the value of m while leaving b unchanged in $f(x) = mx + b$ has no impact on the intercepts of the graph. Marcus disagrees with this statement. Who is correct? Explain your reasoning.

_____

_____

_____

_____

12. Multiple Representations The graph of $y = x + 3$ is a vertical translation of the graph of $y = x + 1$, 2 units upward. Examine the intercepts of both lines and state another way that the geometric relationship between the two graphs can be described.

_____

_____

13. Critique Reasoning Stephanie says that the graphs of $y = 3x + 2$ and $y = 3x - 2$ are parallel. Isabella says that the graphs are perpendicular.

Who is correct? Explain your reasoning. _____

_____

_____

FL **F-LE.1.2**

Construct linear ... functions ... given a graph, a description of a relationship, or two input-output pairs (include reading these from a table). *Also A-CED.1.2, F-IF.2.6, F-BF.1.1*

ESSENTIAL QUESTION

How can you represent a function symbolically from a graph, verbal description, or table of values?

Using Slope to Write a Linear Function

The information needed to write the equation of a linear function can be provided in different ways, including presented as a graph, given as a description of a relationship, or as input-output pairs. If you know the slope and the y-intercept of a linear function, you can find an equation representing the function.

Math On the Spot
my.hrw.com

EXAMPLE 1   **FL** **F-LE.1.2**

Write an equation for the linear function $f(x)$ whose graph has a slope of 3 and a y-intercept of -1.

A linear function has the form $f(x) = mx + b$ where m is the slope and b is the y-intercept.

$f(x) = mx + b$

$f(x) = 3x + (-1)$ The slope was given as 3, so substitute 3 for m.
The y-intercept was given as -1, so substitute -1 for b.

$f(x) = 3x - 1$

An equation for the function is $f(x) = 3x - 1$.

Math Talk
Mathematical Practices

If you graph the function $f(x)$, how can you use the graph to find more ordered pairs that satisfy the equation $f(x) = 3x - 1$?

REFLECT

1. How can you use the equation $f(x) = 3x - 1$ to find more ordered pairs that are part of the function?

_____

_____

YOUR TURN

Write an equation for the linear function $f(x)$ whose graph has the given slope and y-intercept.

2. slope of 4, y-intercept of -2

_____

3. slope of -3, y-intercept of 5

_____

4. slope of 6, y-intercept of 0

_____

5. slope of 0, y-intercept of 6

_____

Personal Math Trainer

Online Assessment and Intervention

my.hrw.com

Math On the Spot

my.hrw.com

EXAMPLE 2

FL F-LE.1.2

The table shows several ordered pairs for the linear function $f(x)$. Write an equation for $f(x)$.

x	f(x)
−1	5
3	−3
7	−11

STEP 1 Calculate the slope using any two ordered pairs from the table. Choose $(−1, 5)$ as the first point and $(3, −3)$ as the second point.

$$\text{slope} = \frac{\text{rise}}{\text{run}}$$ Definition of slope

$$m = \frac{-3 - 5}{3 - (-1)}$$ Substitute values.

$$= \frac{-8}{4}$$ Simplify numerator and denominator.

$$= -2$$ Simplify fraction.

STEP 2 Find the value of b using the fact that $m = -2$ and $f(-1) = 5$.

$$f(x) = -2x + b$$ Write the function with the known value of m.

$$5 = -2(-1) + b$$ Substitute −1 for x and 5 for $f(x)$.

$$5 = 2 + b$$ Simplify the right side of the equation.

$$3 = b$$ Solve for b.

So, the function is $f(x) = -2x + 3$.

REFLECT

6. How can you check that the equation is correct?

_____

_____

YOUR TURN

Write an equation of the linear function represented by each table of values.

7.

x	f(x)
−1	−4
1	6
3	16

8.

x	f(x)
−1	1
2	−5
4	−9

_____   _____

Personal Math Trainer

Online Assessment and Intervention

my.hrw.com

Writing a Linear Function from a Graph

Writing a linear function from a graph requires the same information and steps as writing a linear function from a table of values. The difference is that the ordered pairs must be determined from the graph. The ordered pairs may or may not be explicitly labeled.

Math On the Spot

⊙ my.hrw.com

EXAMPLE 3 Real World   FL   F-LE.1.2

The graph below shows the increase in pressure (measured in pounds per square inch) as a scuba diver descends from a depth of 10 feet to a depth of 30 feet. Pressure is a linear function of depth. At the water's surface, the pressure on the diver is a result of the pressure of the air in the atmosphere. What is the pressure on the diver at the water's surface?

STEP 1   Interpret the question.

Let $P(d)$ represent the pressure in pounds per square inch on the diver at a depth of d feet. At the water's surface, $d = 0$. If the graph below is extended to meet the vertical axis, the value $P(0)$ would represent the pressure on the diver at the water's surface.

STEP 2   Find the value of m in $P(d) = md + b$. Use the fact that $P(10) = 19.1$ and $P(30) = 28.0$.

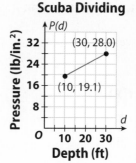

Scuba Dividing

$$\text{slope} = \frac{\text{rise}}{\text{run}}$$ Definition of slope

$$m = \frac{P(30) - P(10)}{30 - 10}$$ Write the slope formula.

$$= \frac{28.0 - 19.1}{30 - 10}$$ Substitute values.

$$= \frac{8.9}{20}$$ Simplify numerator and denominator.

$$= 0.445$$ Write in decimal form.

STEP 3   Now that you know the slope, you can find the value of b in $P(d) = md + b$. Use the value of m from Step 2 as well as the fact that $P(10) = 19.1$.

$$P(d) = 0.445d + b$$ Write the function with the known value of m.

$$19.1 = 0.445(10) + b$$ Substitute 10 for d and 19.1 for P(d).

$$19.1 = 4.45 + b$$ Simplify the right side of the equation.

$$14.7 \approx b$$ Solve for b. Round to the nearest tenth.

An equation for the function is $P(d) = 0.445d + 14.7$.

STEP 4   Find the pressure at the water's surface, where $d = 0$.

$$P(0) = 0.445(0) + 14.7$$

$$= 14.7$$

The pressure on the diver at the water's surface is 14.7 pounds per square inch.

YOUR TURN

9. The graph of the linear function
$f(x)$ is shown. Write an equation
for the function. Then find $f(0)$.

_____

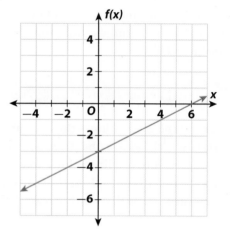

Guided Practice

Write an equation for the linear function $f(x)$ using the given information. (Examples 1–3)

1. slope $-\frac{3}{2}$, y-intercept 1 _____

2.

x	f(x)
−4	5
−2	6
4	9

_____

3.

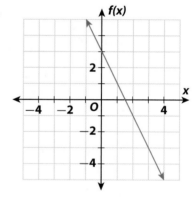

_____

ESSENTIAL QUESTION CHECK-IN

4. What information can you use from the graph of a linear function
to write the function?

_____

_____

_____

6.7 Independent Practice

 **F-LE.1.2**

Personal
Math Trainer

Online
Assessment and
Intervention

my.hrw.com

Write an equation for the linear function $f(x)$ using the given information.

5. The graph of the function has a slope of $-\frac{2}{3}$ and a y-intercept of 5.

_____

6. The graph of the function has a slope of $\frac{7}{4}$ and a y-intercept of 0.

_____

7.

x	$f(x)$
0	−3
2	0
4	3

_____

8.

x	$f(x)$
5	−2
10	−6
15	−10

_____

9.

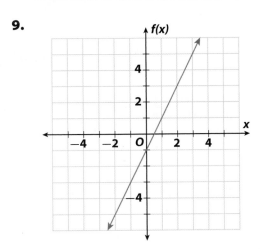

_____

10.

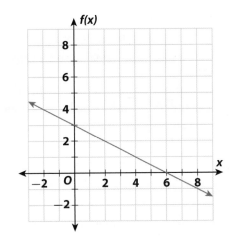

_____

11. Represent Real-World Problems Javier begins to save for a new bicycle that costs $410. He already has $140 and plans to save $25 per week. Let w represent the number of weeks he has been saving and $s(w)$ represent the total amount in dollars that he has saved. How long does he have to save?

a. Write a linear function using the given information. _____

b. Give the slope and the y-intercept of the function.

_____

c. Describe how to use the function to answer the question, and then answer the question.

_____

12. The graph shows the amount of gas remaining in the gas tank of Mrs. Liu's car as she drives at a steady speed for 2 hours. How long can she drive before her car runs out of gas?

Fuel Consumption

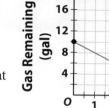

a. Interpret the question by describing what aspect of the graph would answer the question.

_____

_____

b. Write a linear function whose graph includes the segment shown.

_____

c. Describe how to use the function to answer the question, and then answer the question.

_____

_____

H.O.T.   FOCUS ON HIGHER ORDER THINKING

Work Area

13. Counter example Maria says that there is only one equation representing a linear function whose graph has a slope of 2 and y-intercept of -3. Show that there is more than one such equation.

_____

14. Communicate Mathematical Ideas You are given a table of values that represent a function, but you are not told whether the function is linear. How could you use the table to determine whether the function is linear?

_____

_____

_____

15. Explain the Error Andrew was told that a linear function had a slope of 3 and that $(-2, 0)$ was on the graph. He wrote the function as $f(x) = 3x - 2$. What error did Andrew make? Write the function correctly.

_____

_____

_____

Ready to Go On?

Personal
Math Trainer

Online
Assessment and
Intervention

my.hrw.com

6.1 Linear Functions

Tell whether or not each equation represents a linear function.

1. $12x + 3y = 6$ **2.** $-x^2 + 6y = 24$ **3.** $6x - \frac{1}{2}y = 3$

_____   _____   _____

6.2 Using Intercepts

Find the x- and y-intercepts.

4. $5x - 4y = 20$ **5.** $3x + 7y = 42$

_____   _____

6.4 Slope-Intercept Form

Find the slope of the line described by each equation.

6. $2x + 2y = 7$ **7.** $4x - 3y = 0$ **8.** $9 = 3y$

_____   _____   _____

Graph each linear function.

9. $f(x) = 3x - 2$ **10.** $f(x) = \frac{1}{3}x + 2$

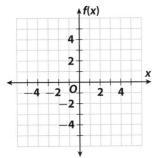   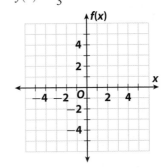

6.7 Writing Linear Functions

11. The graph of the linear function $f(x)$ has a slope of $-\frac{3}{2}$ and a y-intercept

of -1. Write an equation for the function. _____

? ESSENTIAL QUESTION

12. What are some ways that linear functions can be represented? Give an
example of how different representations are related.

_____

_____

_____

Assessment Readiness

Personal Math Trainer

Online Assessment and Intervention

my.hrw.com

Selected Response

1. What is the slope of the line containing the points $(3, 1)$ and $(-1, 3)$?

(A) -2 (C) $\frac{1}{2}$

(B) $-\frac{1}{2}$ (D) 2

2. Which best describes the slope and y-intercept of the graph?

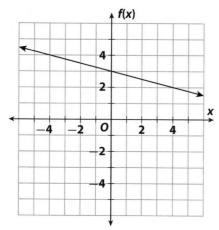

(A) $m = -\frac{1}{4}, b = -3$

(B) $m = -\frac{1}{4}, b = 3$

(C) $m = 3, b = -\frac{1}{4}$

(D) $m = 4, b = -3$

3. What is $5a = \frac{b-1}{2}$ solved for b?

(A) $b = 9a - 1$

(B) $b = 9a + 1$

(C) $b = 10a - 1$

(D) $b = 10a + 1$

4. Which of the following is **not** a function?

(A) $(1, 2), (3, 4), (5, 6), (7, 8)$

(B) $(1, 2), (1, 3), (1, 4), (1, 5)$

(C) $(1, 1), (2, 1), (3, 1), (4, 1)$

(D) $(1, 1), (2, 2), (3, 3), (4, 4)$

5. The ordered pair $(0.5, 3)$ is a solution to which of the following equations?

(A) $y = 2x + 2$ (C) $y = 4x - 1$

(B) $y = 2x + 1$ (D) $y = 2x - 1$

6. Which is a linear function whose graph has a slope of -1 and a y-intercept of 2?

(A) $f(x) = 2x - 1$

(B) $f(x) = x - 2$

(C) $f(x) = -x - 2$

(D) $f(x) = -x + 2$

7. Which equation is the standard form of a line that contains the point $(2, 1)$?

(A) $y = -2x + 5$ (C) $y = 2x + 1$

(B) $2x + y = 5$ (D) $y = x - 1$

Mini-Tasks

8. A landscaper uses a water hose to fill a tank. The water flows at a rate of 5 gallons per minute. The tank holds 400 gallons of water. There are 50 gallons of water in the tank when the landscaper starts filling it.

a. Write the linear function that expresses the amount of water in the tank $A(t)$ in gallons after t minutes.

_____

b. Find the domain and range of the function $A(t)$.

_____

_____

_____

_____

_____

Building Linear Functions

? ESSENTIAL QUESTION

How are mathematical operations related to solving linear equations and inequalities and creating new functions?

my.hrw.com

Real-World Video

Periodic comets have orbital periods of less than 200 years. Halley's comet is the only short-period comet that is visible to the naked eye. It returns every 76 years. You can build functions to represent and model predictable occurrences, such the recurrence of Halley's comet.

GO DIGITAL
my.hrw.com

my.hrw.com

Go digital with your write-in student edition, accessible on any device.

Math On the Spot

Scan with your smart phone to jump directly to the online edition, video tutor, and more.

Animated Math

Interactively explore key concepts to see how math works.

Personal Math Trainer

Get immediate feedback and help as you work through practice sets.

Are YOU Ready?

Complete these exercises to review skills you will need for this module.

Personal Math Trainer

Online Assessment and Intervention

my.hrw.com

Evaluate Expressions

EXAMPLE   Evaluate $3x - 1$ for $x = 2$.
$3(2) - 1$ Substitute 2 for x.
$6 - 1$ Simplify.
5

Evaluate each expression for $x = -3$, 0, and 3.

1. $2x - 3$

2. $\frac{2}{3}x + 1$

3. $-2x + 4$

_____

_____

_____

4. $-x$

5. $x - 5$

6. $\frac{x}{2}$

_____

_____

_____

Solve for a Variable

EXAMPLE   Solve $4x - 2y = 10$ for y.
$$4x - 2y = 10$$
$$-2y = -4x + 10$$ Subtract 4x from both sides.
$$y = 2x - 5$$ Divide both sides by –2.

Solve each equation for y.

7. $y + 2 = 3x$

8. $2x - \frac{3}{4}y = -6$

9. $14 = x + (-2y)$

Solve and Graph Inequalities

EXAMPLE   Solve and graph $x - 9 > -10$.
$$x - 9 > -10$$
$$\underline{+9 > +9}$$ Add 9 to both sides.
$$x \quad > -1$$

Use an open circle for $>$.

Solve and graph each inequality.

10. $1 > x - 3$

11. $-5x \le -15$

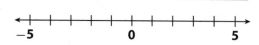

Reading Start-Up

Vocabulary

Review Words

constant function *(función constante)*

function *(función)*

function rule *(fórmula de función)*

inequality *(desigualdad)*

linear function *(función lineal)*

nonlinear function *(función no lineal)*

rate of change *(tasa de cambio)*

Preview Words

arithmetic sequence

boundary line

common difference

function of *x*

half-plane

inverse function

linear inequality

one-to-one function

solution of an inequality

Visualize Vocabulary

Use the Review words to complete the bubble map. You may put more than one word in each bubble. Some words may not be used.

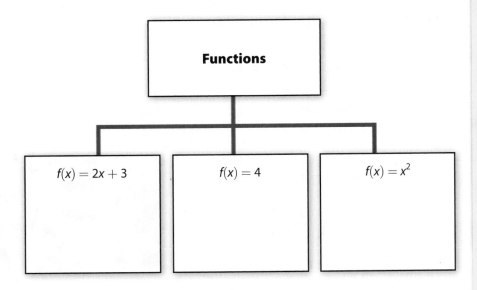

Functions

$f(x) = 2x + 3$

$f(x) = 4$

$f(x) = x^2$

Understand Vocabulary

To become familiar with some of the vocabulary terms in the module, consider the following. You may refer to the module, the glossary, or a dictionary.

1. Functions in which each *y*-value corresponds to only one *x*-value

   are called _____.

2. The term **boundary line** refers to part of the graph of a linear inequality. What part of the graph do you think **boundary line** refers to?

   _____

Active Reading

Four-Corner Fold Before beginning the module, create a four-corner fold to help you organize what you learn. As you study this module, note important ideas, vocabulary, properties, and formulas on the flaps. Use one flap for each lesson in the module. You can use your FoldNote later to study for tests and complete assignments.

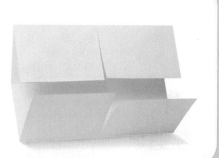

Unpacking the Standards

Understanding the standards and the vocabulary terms in the standards will help you know exactly what you are expected to learn in this module.

 **FL** F-BF.1.1

Write a function that describes a relationship between two quantities.

Key Vocabulary

function *(función)*
A type of relation that pairs each element in the domain with exactly one element in the range.

What It Means to You

You can add, subtract, or multiply with linear functions to model real-world situations.

UNPACKING EXAMPLE F-BF.1.1

A cable company charges $40 per month for basic cable plus an additional $8 per month for each premium cable channel. There is a tax of 9% charged on the total monthly bill.

$C(c)$ = amount charged by the cable company before taxes
$R(c)$ = tax rate
$T(c)$ = the tax charged on the monthly cable bill

$C(c) = 40 + 8c$
$R(c) = 0.09$
$T(c) = C(c) \times R(c) = 3.6 + 0.72c$

FL F-BF.1.4a

Solve an equation ... for a simple function f that has an inverse and write an expression for the inverse.

Key Vocabulary

inverse function *(función inversa)*
The function that results from exchanging the input and output values of a one-to-one function.

What It Means to You

You can find the inverse of a function by using inverse operations to solve for one variable and then switching the variables.

UNPACKING EXAMPLE F-BF.1.4A

To find the inverse of $f(x) = 3x - 12$, replace $f(x)$ with y.

$$y = 3x - 12$$

Then, solve the equation for x.

$$y + 12 = 3x$$
$$\tfrac{1}{3}y + 4 = x$$

Switch x and y in the equation.

$$\tfrac{1}{3}x + 4 = y$$

Replace y with the inverse function notation.

$$f^{-1}(x) = \tfrac{1}{3}x + 4$$

Visit **my.hrw.com** to see all **Florida Math Standards** unpacked.

my.hrw.com

FL F-BF.1.2

Write arithmetic and geometric sequences both recursively and with an explicit formula, use them to model situations, and translate between the two forms. *Also F-LE.1.1a, F-LE.1.1b, F-LE.1.2, F-BF.1.1, F-BF.1.1A, F-IF.1.3*

ESSENTIAL QUESTION

How are rules for arithmetic sequences and linear functions alike, and how are they different?

EXPLORE ACTIVITY FL F-IF.1.3

Exploring Arithmetic Sequences

Avocados cost $1.50 each at the local market. The total cost, in dollars, of a avocados can be found using $C(a) = 1.5a$.

A Complete the table of values for $C(a) = 1.5a$.

Avocados	0	1	2	3
Total Cost ($)				

B List the consecutive elements of the range. _____

C What is the difference between any two consecutive elements of the

range? _____

Math Talk
Mathematical Practices

How is the domain limited for this situation?

Writing Rules for an Arithmetic Sequence

In an **arithmetic sequence**, the difference between consecutive terms is always the same. The constant difference is called the **common difference**, often written as d.

To write rules for an arithmetic sequence, first find the common difference.

Math On the Spot
⏺ my.hrw.com

EXAMPLE 1 Real World FL F-IF.1.3

This table shows the end-of-month balances in a bank account that does not earn interest. Write a recursive rule and an explicit rule for the arithmetic sequence described by the table.

Month	n	1	2	3	4	5
Account Balance ($)	$f(n)$	60	80	100	120	140

Write the recursive rule.

$f(1) = 60$ $f(1)$ is the first term.

$f(n) = 20 + f(n-1)$ for $n \geq 2$ All other terms are the sum of the previous term and the common difference.

Write the explicit rule.

n	$f(n)$	$f(1) + d \cdot x = f(n)$
1	60	$60 + 20(0) = 60$
2	80	$60 + 20(1) = 80$
3	100	$60 + 20(2) = 100$

Remember, d is the difference between two consecutive terms.

Since d is always multiplied by a number equal to $(n - 1)$, we can generalize the results from the table: $f(n) = 60 + 20(n - 1)$.

Personal Math Trainer

Online Assessment and Intervention

⏻ my.hrw.com

YOUR TURN

1. The table shows the number of members in a theater group after n weeks. Write a recursive rule and an explicit rule for the arithmetic sequence.

Week	n	1	2	3	4	5
Members	$f(n)$	35	47	59	71	83

_____

_____

Math On the Spot

⏻ my.hrw.com

General Rules for Arithmetic Sequences

Arithmetic sequences can be described by general rules. You can substitute values into the general rules to find the recursive rule and explicit rule for a given sequence.

General Recursive Rule	General Explicit Rule
Given $f(1)$, $f(n) = f(n - 1) + d$ for $n \geq 2$	$f(n) = f(1) + d(n - 1)$

EXAMPLE 2

 **FL** F-BF.2.3

Write a recursive rule and an explicit rule for the sequence 6, 9, 12, 15, 18...

Write the recursive rule.

Given $f(1)$, $f(n) = f(n - 1) + d$ for $n \geq 2$ Write the general form.

$f(1) = 6$, $f(n) = f(n - 1) + 3$ for $n \geq 2$ Use $f(1) = 6$. Substitute 3 for d.

The recursive rule is $f(1) = 6$, $f(n) = f(n - 1) + 3$ for $n \geq 2$.

Write the explicit rule.

$$f(n) = f(1) + d(n - 1) \qquad \text{Write the general form.}$$
$$f(n) = 6 + 3(n - 1) \qquad \text{Substitute 6 for } f(1) \text{ and 3 for } d.$$

The explicit rule is $f(n) = 6 + 3(n - 1)$.

YOUR TURN

2. Write a recursive rule and an explicit rule for the arithmetic sequence
    20, 25, 30, 35, . . .

    _____

    _____

Relating Arithmetic Sequences and Linear Functions

The explicit rule for an arithmetic sequence can be expressed as a linear function.
You can use the graph of a linear function to help you write an explicit rule.

EXAMPLE 3 Real World

FL   F-BF.1.2, F-LE.1.2

The graph shows how the cost of a whitewater
rafting trip depends on the number of passengers.
Write an explicit rule for the sequence of costs.

Whitewater Rafting

STEP 1 Represent the sequence in a table.

n	1	2	3	4
f(n)	75	100	125	150

STEP 2 Find the common difference.   Find the difference between two
consecutive terms.
$$d = 100 - 75 = 25$$

STEP 3 Write an explicit rule for the sequence.

$$f(n) = f(1) + d(n - 1)$$
$$f(n) = 75 + 25(n - 1)$$

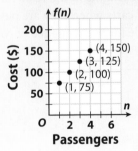

Start with the general rule,
then substitute values to
find the explicit rule.

YOUR TURN

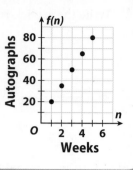

3. Ed collects autographs. The graph shows the number of autographs that Ed has collected. Determine the explicit rule for the sequence.

_____

Autographs / Weeks

Guided Practice

Write a recursive rule and an explicit rule for the sequence. (Example 1)

1.

n	1	2	3	4	5
$f(n)$	6	7	8	9	10

$f(1) = 6,$

$f(n) = f(\boxed{}) + \boxed{}$ for $n \geq 2$

$f(n) = \boxed{} + \boxed{}$

Write a recursive rule and an explicit rule for the sequence. (Example 2)

2. $3, 7, 11, 15, \ldots$

_____

_____

Write an explicit rule for the sequence. (Example 3)

3. The graph shows the lengths of the rows formed by various numbers of grocery carts when they are nested together. Write an explicit rule for the sequence of row lengths.

_____

Nested Grocery Carts

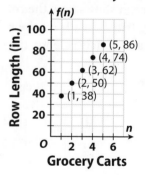

Row Length (in.) / Grocery Carts

(5, 86)
(4, 74)
(3, 62)
(2, 50)
(1, 38)

❓ ESSENTIAL QUESTION CHECK-IN

4. What two values do you need to know in order to write a recursive rule and an explicit rule for an arithmetic sequence?

_____

_____

7.1 Independent Practice

FL F-BF.2.3

Personal Math Trainer

Online Assessment and Intervention

my.hrw.com

5. Write a recursive rule and an explicit rule for each sequence.

n	1	2	3	4	5
f(n)	27	24	21	18	15

_____

_____

_____

6.

n	1	2	3	4	5
f(n)	3	6	9	12	15

_____

_____

_____

7. Write a recursive rule and an explicit rule for the arithmetic sequence 9, 24, 39, 54, . . .

_____

_____

_____

8. Write a recursive rule and an explicit rule for the arithmetic sequence 19, 9, −1, −11, . . .

_____

_____

_____

9. Write a recursive rule and an explicit rule for the arithmetic sequence 1, 2.5, 4, 5.5, . . .

_____

_____

_____

10. The explicit rule for an arithmetic sequence is $f(n) = 6 + 5(n − 1)$. What are the first three terms? _____

11. The explicit rule for an arithmetic sequence is $f(n) = 1 + 3(n − 1)$. What are the fourth and fortieth terms? _____

12. Indicate whether the sequence is arithmetic. If it is, list the common difference. $−21, −18, −15, −12, . . .$

_____

13. The first term of an arithmetic sequence is 4, and the common difference is 10. How can you find the sixth term of the sequence?

_____

_____

_____

_____

_____

14. Carrie borrowed money interest-free to pay for a car repair. The table shows how much money remains for Carrie to pay back after making n monthly payments.

Monthly Payment Number	n	1	2	3	4	5
Loan Balance ($)	f(n)	840	720	600	480	360

a. Explain how you know that the sequence of loan balances is arithmetic.

_____

_____

b. Write recursive and explicit rules for the sequence of loan balances.

_____

_____

c. How many months will it take Carrie to pay off the loan? Explain.

_____

d. How much money did Carrie borrow? Explain.

_____

_____

H.O.T. | FOCUS ON HIGHER ORDER THINKING

Work Area

15. Explain the Error The cost of postage for a 1-ounce letter is $0.45. Each additional ounce costs $0.20. Cindy wrote this explicit rule to describe the sequence of costs: $f(n) = 0.20 + 0.45(n - 1)$. She then determined the cost of postage for a 6-ounce letter to be $2.45. Is she correct? If not, identify her error.

_____

_____

_____

16. Communicate Mathematical Ideas What do the graphs of all arithmetic sequences have in common?

_____

17. Critical Thinking Trevor knows that the 5th term in a sequence is 32, and the 7th term in the same sequence is 48. Explain how he can find the common difference for this sequence.

_____

_____

_____

_____

18. Represent Real-World Problems Describe a situation whose sequence could be represented by the explicit rule $f(n) = 8 + 3(n - 1)$.

_____

_____

_____

_____

FL   F-BF.1.1b

Combine standard function types using arithmetic operations.

Also A-CED.1.2, F-BF.1.1, F-LE.1.2, F-LE.2.5

ESSENTIAL QUESTION

How can you use operations with linear functions to model real-world situations?

Adding and Subtracting Linear Functions

You can add and subtract linear functions just as you would add and subtract two linear expressions. When adding and subtracting functions, be sure to use a different letter to name each function, like $h(x) = f(x) + g(x)$.

Math On the Spot

my.hrw.com

EXAMPLE 1

FL   F-BF.1.1b

Given the linear functions $f(x) = 2x + 9$ and $g(x) = 6x - 1$, find each new function.

A $h(x) = f(x) + g(x)$

$h(x) = (2x + 9) + (6x - 1)$ Substitute for $f(x)$ and $g(x)$.

$h(x) = (2x + 6x) + (9 - 1)$ Combine like terms.

$h(x) = 8x + 8$ Simplify.

B $j(x) = f(x) - g(x)$

$j(x) = (2x + 9) - (6x - 1)$ Substitute for $f(x)$ and $g(x)$.

$j(x) = (2x + 9) - 6x + 1$ Multiply by -1.

$j(x) = (2x - 6x) + (9 + 1)$ Combine like terms.

$j(x) = -4x + 10$ Simplify.

REFLECT

1. **Critical Thinking** James thinks that $f(x) - g(x)$ and $g(x) - f(x)$ are equal when $f(x) = 3x + 6$ and $g(x) = 5x + 2$. Is he correct? Explain.

_____

_____

YOUR TURN

2. Given $f(x) = 3x + 4$ and $g(x) = -x + 2$, find the sum $h(x) = f(x) + g(x)$ and the difference $j(x) = f(x) - g(x)$.

_____

Personal Math Trainer

Online Assessment and Intervention

my.hrw.com

Math On the Spot

⊙ my.hrw.com

Multiplying Linear and Constant Functions

Multiplying a linear function by a constant function is just like multiplying two expressions together. When you multiply a linear function by a constant, the result is also a linear function.

My Notes

EXAMPLE 2

FL   F-BF.1.1b

Given the linear functions $f(x) = 4$ and $g(x) = -3x + 2$, find the linear function $h(x) = f(x) \times g(x)$.

$h(x) = f(x) \times g(x)$

$h(x) = (4)(-3x + 2)$ Substitute for $f(x)$ and $g(x)$.

$h(x) = -12x + 8$ Multiply using the Distributive Property.

REFLECT

3. Critical Thinking Enrique knows that $f(x)$ is a constant function and that $g(x) = 5x + 6$. If $f(x) \times g(x) = 0$, determine $f(x)$.

_____

4. Explain the Error Kelly thinks that the product of $f(x) = 6$ and $g(x) = 4x + 8$ is $24x + 8$. Is she correct? If not, explain her error.

_____

_____

_____

Personal Math Trainer

Online Assessment and Intervention

⊙ my.hrw.com

YOUR TURN

Given the constant function $f(x)$ and the linear function $g(x)$, find the linear function $h(x) = f(x) \times g(x)$.

5. $f(x) = 7, g(x) = 4x - 2$

_____

6. $f(x) = -3, g(x) = 2x - 11$

_____

7. $f(x) = \frac{1}{2}, g(x) = 14x - 8$

_____

Adding Linear Models

Real-world problems can often be solved by writing linear functions to model the situation, then adding the linear functions as you did in Example 1.

Math On the Spot
my.hrw.com

EXAMPLE 3 Real World
FL   F-BF.1.1b

Harriet rides from her house to her job using Friendly Taxi Company, who charges $5 plus $1.35 per mile. After work, Harriet uses the Great Taxi company to go home. They charge $2 plus $1.85 per mile. Find the total amount that Harriet spent on cab rides as a function of x, the distance in miles between her house and her job.

STEP 1   Write $f(x)$, the cost of the Friendly Taxi cab ride, as a function of x.

$$f(x) = 5 + 1.35x$$

STEP 2   Write $g(x)$, the cost of the Great Taxi cab ride, as a function of x.

$$g(x) = 2 + 1.85x$$

STEP 3   Write $t(x)$, the total cost of both cab rides, as a function of x. Find the sum of the costs of each taxi ride.

$$t(x) = f(x) + g(x)$$
$$t(x) = (5 + 1.35x) + (2 + 1.85x) \qquad \text{Substitute for } f(x) \text{ and } g(x).$$
$$t(x) = (1.35x + 1.85x) + (5 + 2) \qquad \text{Combine like terms.}$$
$$t(x) = 3.2x + 7 \qquad \text{Simplify.}$$

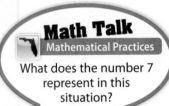

Math Talk
Mathematical Practices

What does the number 7 represent in this situation?

The cost of Harriet's rides can be represented by $t(x) = 3.2x + 7$.

REFLECT

8. **What If?** Describe the change to $t(x)$ if Harriet used Friendly Taxi to travel to and from her job.

_____

YOUR TURN

9. A tennis club is formed for boys and girls. In the first year, 4 boys and 5 girls join the club. Each year after, 2 more boys and 1 more girl join the club. Let t be the number of years since the club was formed. Find a rule for the function $f(t)$, representing the total number of club members.

_____

Personal Math Trainer

Online Assessment and Intervention

my.hrw.com

Multiplying Linear and Constant Models

Some real-world situations are modeled by constant functions. To multiply these functions, use the same steps as in Example 2.

EXAMPLE 4  FL F-BF.1.1b

My Notes

A phone company charges $20 a month for service plus $0.05 per minute for calls. Tax is added to the total charge, and the tax rate is 8%. Find the amount of tax on a monthly bill for t minutes of calls.

STEP 1 Write $f(t)$, the amount charged by the phone company before taxes for service and t minutes of calls.

$$f(t) = 20 + 0.05t$$

STEP 2 Write $g(t)$, the tax rate applied to phone company charges.

$$g(t) = 0.08$$

STEP 3 Write $h(t)$, the tax charged for a monthly bill with t minutes of calls. Find the product of the amount charged by the phone company $f(t)$ and the constant tax rate $g(t)$.

$$h(t) = f(t) \times g(t)$$
$$h(t) = (20 + 0.05t)(0.08) \qquad \text{Substitute for } f(t) \text{ and } g(t).$$
$$h(t) = 1.6 + 0.004t \qquad \text{Multiply using the distributive property.}$$

The amount of tax on a monthly bill for t minutes of calls is $h(t) = 1.6 + 0.004t$.

REFLECT

10. Interpret the Answer Interpret the number 1.6 in the simplified form of $h(t)$ in Example 4.

_____

_____

YOUR TURN

11. Sunshine Coffee Shop has 8 employees working, each of whom buy a large coffee. During the day, they sell x large coffees to customers. Each large coffee costs $1.75. Write a function $c(x)$ that represents the amount of money Sunshine Coffee Shop made selling large coffees.

_____

Given the functions $f(x) = 3x + 9$ and $g(x) = -2x + 5$, find each new function. (Example 1)

1. $h(x) = f(x) + g(x)$

$h(x) = (3x + 9) + (\boxed{})$

$h(x) = (3x + \boxed{}) + $

$(9 + \boxed{})$

$h(x) = \boxed{}$

2. $j(x) = f(x) - g(x)$

$j(x) = (\boxed{}) - (-2x + 5)$

$j(x) = (\boxed{} + 2x)$

$+ (\boxed{} - 5)$

$j(x) = \boxed{}$

Given a constant function $f(x)$ and a linear function $g(x)$, find the function $h(x) = f(x) \times g(x)$. (Example 2)

3. $f(x) = 4, g(x) = 2x + 3$

$h(x) = f(x) \times g(x)$

$h(x) = 4(\boxed{})$

$h(x) = \boxed{}$

4. $f(x) = -2, g(x) = 4x - 1$

$h(x) = f(x) \times g(x)$

$h(x) = \boxed{}(4x - 1)$

$h(x) = \boxed{}$

5. Colton is making cookie gift bags. He has 120 chocolate chip cookies, and puts 3 in each gift bag. He also has 75 sugar cookies, and puts 2 in each gift bag. Write the function $f(x)$ that represents how many cookies Colton has after making x gift bags. (Example 3)

_____

6. Brenda is buying 6 concert tickets online. Each ticket costs $15, plus a service fee of x dollars. Write the function $g(x)$ that shows the total amount that Brenda will pay for the tickets. (Example 4)

_____

? ESSENTIAL QUESTION CHECK-IN

7. How is the sum of linear functions related to the rules of the functions?

_____

_____

_____

7.2 Independent Practice

  F-BF.1.1

Personal Math Trainer

Online Assessment and Intervention

my.hrw.com

Given the functions $f(x)$ and $g(x)$, find the function $h(x) = f(x) + g(x)$.

8. $f(x) = 2x + 9, g(x) = 8x - 3$

_____

9. $f(x) = 17x - 1, g(x) = 5x + 5$

_____

10. $f(x) = -x - 2, g(x) = 4x - 3$

_____

Given the functions $f(x)$ and $g(x)$, find the function $h(x) = f(x) - g(x)$.

11. $f(x) = 4x + 10, g(x) = -2x + 8$

_____

12. $f(x) = 3x - 1, g(x) = 12x + 2$

_____

13. $f(x) = 6x + 7, g(x) = x + 6$

_____

Given the functions $f(x)$ and $g(x)$, find the function $h(x) = f(x) \times g(x)$.

14. $f(x) = 3, g(x) = 7x + 1$

_____

15. $f(x) = -2, g(x) = 4x - 6$

_____

16. $f(x) = \frac{1}{3}, g(x) = 9x - 6$

_____

17. A school is raising money for new desks. They have collected $400 in donations, and are hosting a dinner, which costs $10 to attend. Every person at the dinner buys a $2 raffle ticket, and the winner of the raffle gets $500.

a. Write a rule for the function $R(t)$, the profit the school makes on the raffle.

_____

b. Write a rule for the function $D(t)$, the earnings made from the donations and dinner.

_____

c. Describe how the function $T(t)$, the total amount of money raised by the school for new desks, is related to $R(t)$ and $D(t)$. Then, write a rule for $T(t)$.

_____

18. A birthday party is being planned for 20 people at an arcade. It costs $5 a person to provide food for everyone, and each game costs $1 per play. Assume that each person at the party plays the same number of games, x.

a. Write a rule for the function $C(x)$, the total cost per person.

_____

b. Write a rule for the function $n(x)$, the number of people who attend.

_____

c. Describe how the function $T(x)$, the total cost of the party, can be obtained from the functions $C(x)$ and $n(x)$. Then, write a rule for $T(x)$.

_____

19. Let $f(x) = 3$, $g(x) = -2x + 5$, and $h(x) = x - 4$.

a. Find the function $j(x) = f(x) \times [g(x) + h(x)]$.

_____

_____

b. Find the function $k(x) = [f(x) \times g(x)] + [f(x) \times h(x)]$.

_____

_____

c. Find the function $l(x) = j(x) - k(x)$.

_____

_____

d. Explain how you could find $l(x)$ without finding $j(x)$ or $k(x)$.

_____

_____

_____

_____

20. A police department issues speeding tickets for $50 plus an additional dollar for each mile per hour over the speed limit the driver was going. Half of the money from speeding tickets goes toward buying new equipment for the police officers. Write a rule for the function $E(x)$, the amount of money for new equipment generated by a ticket for driving x miles per hour over the speed limit.

_____

_____

21. Use the information in the table below to answer the following questions.

x	f(x)	g(x)
0	3	−2
2	−1	4
5	−7	13

a. Use the table to write rules for the functions $f(x)$ and $g(x)$.

_____

_____

b. Find the sum $h(x) = f(x) + g(x)$ and the difference $j(x) = f(x) - g(x)$.

_____

_____

c. Compare the functions $h(x)$ and $j(x)$ when $x = 3$.

_____

22. A new computer is valued at $1,000, and its value depreciates by $150 per year. A new printer is valued at $100, and its value depreciates by $5 per year.

a. Write a rule for the combined value of the computer and printer in terms of t, the time in years since the equipment was purchased.

_____

b. When will the computer and the printer have a combined value of $480?

_____

c. When the computer is worth $100, how much will the combined value of the computer and the printer be?

_____

23. Randy and Heloise both open savings accounts. Randy opens his savings account with $7 and deposits $10 every week. Heloise opens her savings account with $82, and withdraws $5 every week.

   a. Write a function $r(x)$ to represent the amount of money Randy has in his savings account after x weeks.

_____

   b. Write a function $h(x)$ to represent the amount of money Heloise has in her savings account after x weeks.

_____

   c. Write a function $b(x)$ to represent the combined total in both savings accounts after x weeks.

_____

   d. When Randy has $47 in his savings account, what is the combined total in both accounts?

_____

   e. When Heloise has $47 in her savings account, what is the combined total in both accounts?

_____

 **FOCUS ON HIGHER ORDER THINKING**

Work Area

24. Justify Reasoning Suppose $B(t)$ is a linear function representing the number of boys who attend a school in year t, and $G(t)$ is a linear function representing the number of girls who attend the same school in year t. What does the function $T(t) = G(t) + B(t)$ represent?

_____

_____

25. Persevere in Problem Solving The function $f(x) = 3x + 3$. Find the function $g(x)$ such that $f(x) + g(x) = 0$ and $f(x) - g(x) = 2 \times f(x)$.

_____

26. Counter examples Kendra says that $f(x) - g(x)$ can never be equal to $g(x) - f(x)$. Give an example of functions $f(x)$ and $g(x)$ that contradicts her statement. Justify your example.

_____

_____

FL F-BF.2.4a

Solve an equation... for a simple function *f* that has an inverse and write an expression for the inverse. *Also F-BF.2.4, F-IF.1.2*

LESSON 7.3 Linear Functions and Their Inverses

? ESSENTIAL QUESTION

How can you find the inverse of a linear function?

EXPLORE ACTIVITY   FL F-BF.2.4a

Using Inverse Operations to Find an Inverse Function

The **inverse of a function** "undoes" every operation performed in the original function. Use inverse operations to find the inverse of the function $f(x) = 2x + 6$.

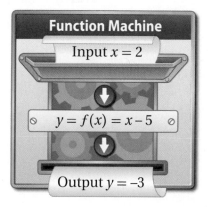

Function Machine

Input $x = 2$

$y = f(x) = x - 5$

Output $y = -3$

A Use the function $f(x) = 2x + 6$ to complete the table.

x	−2	1	3	6
y = 2x + 6				

B To complete the table, you must first _____ each *x*-value by 2, and then _____ 6 to the result.

C Identify the inverse operations. The inverse of multiplying by 2 is _____ . The inverse of adding 6 is _____ .

D To find the inverse function, use the inverse operations in reverse order.

First, _____ 6 from each *x*-value, then _____ the result by 2.

Math Talk
Mathematical Practices

How are the input and output values of a function and its inverse related?

E The inverse of $f(x) = 2x + 6$, denoted by $f^{-1}(x)$, is

$f^{-1}(x) = (x \bigcirc 6) \bigcirc 2$.

F Use the inverse function to complete the table.

x		2	8	12	18
y = (x 6) 2					

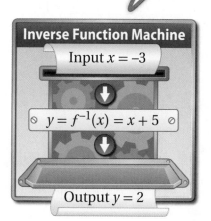

Inverse Function Machine

Input $x = -3$

$y = f^{-1}(x) = x + 5$

Output $y = 2$

REFLECT

1. Analyze Relationships Compare the *x*- and *y*-values in the two completed tables. How are they related?

_____

My Notes

Solving for *x* to Find an Inverse Function

Another method for finding the inverse of a function involves rewriting the original function so that *x* is isolated on one side of the equation.

EXAMPLE 1   FL   F-BF.2.4a

Find the inverse of $f(x) = \frac{1}{2}x + 3$.

STEP 1 Replace $f(x)$ with y in the function.

$$y = \frac{1}{2}x + 3$$

STEP 2 Solve the equation for x.

$$y = \frac{1}{2}x + 3$$

$$y - 3 = \frac{1}{2}x \qquad \text{Subtract 3 from both sides.}$$

$$2(y - 3) = x \qquad \text{Multiply both sides by 2.}$$

$$2y - 6 = x \qquad \text{Distribute to simplify.}$$

STEP 3 Switch x and y in the equation.

$$2x - 6 = y$$

STEP 4 Replace y with the inverse function notation, $f^{-1}(x)$.

$$f^{-1}(x) = 2x - 6$$

REFLECT

2. **Critique Reasoning** Jodie thinks that the inverse of the function $f(x) = 5x + 2$ is $f^{-1}(x) = -5x - 2$, because $(5x + 2) + (-5x - 2) = 0$. Has Jodie found the correct inverse function? Explain.

_____

_____

Personal Math Trainer

Online Assessment and Intervention

⏻ my.hrw.com

YOUR TURN

3. Find the inverse of $f(x) = \frac{1}{3}x - 6$.

_____

Graphing the Inverse of a Linear Function

You graph the inverse of a linear function in the same manner as you graph the function.

EXAMPLE 2

FL   F-BF.2.4a

The function $f(x) = 3x - 12$ is shown on the graph. Find and graph the inverse function $f^{-1}(x)$.

STEP 1 Find the inverse of $f(x) = 3x - 12$.

$y = 3x - 12$	Substitute y for $f(x)$.
$y + 12 = 3x$	Add 12 to both sides.
$\frac{1}{3}(y + 12) = x$	Multiply both sides by $\frac{1}{3}$.
$\frac{1}{3}y + 4 = x$	Simplify.
$\frac{1}{3}x + 4 = y$	Switch x and y.
$f^{-1}(x) = \frac{1}{3}x + 4$	Substitute $f^{-1}(x)$ for y.

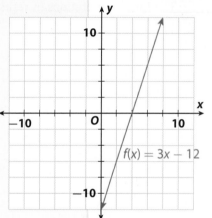

STEP 2 Make a table of ordered pairs for the inverse function.

x	$f^{-1}(x) = \frac{1}{3}x + 4$
-6	$f^{-1}(-6) = \frac{1}{3}(-6) + 4 = 2$
0	$f^{-1}(0) = \frac{1}{3}(0) + 4 = 4$
3	$f^{-1}(3) = \frac{1}{3}(3) + 4 = 5$

STEP 3 Plot the ordered pairs, and connect them with a line.

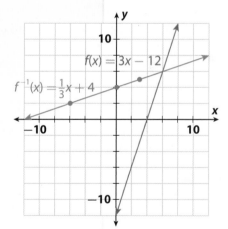

YOUR TURN

4. The graph of $f(x) = \frac{1}{2}x - 1$ is shown. Find the inverse function $f^{-1}(x)$ and graph it.

$f(x) = \frac{1}{2}x - 1$

1. Use inverse operations to find the inverse of $f(x) = \frac{x}{2} - 3$. (Explore Activity)

   To find values for $f(x)$, first you _____ x by 2, then you _____ 3 from the result.

   The inverse operations in reverse order are _____.

   The inverse function $f^{-1}(x) =$ _____.

Find the inverse of each function. (Example 1)

2. $f(x) = x - 1$

   $\boxed{} = x - 1$

   $y + \boxed{} = x$

   $\boxed{} + 1 = \boxed{}$

   $f^{-1}(x) = \boxed{} + \boxed{}$

3. $f(x) = x + 8$

   $\boxed{} = x + 8$

   $y - \boxed{} = x$

   $\boxed{} - 8 = \boxed{}$

   $f^{-1}(x) = \boxed{} - \boxed{}$

Find the inverse of each function and graph $f^{-1}(x)$. (Example 2)

4. _____

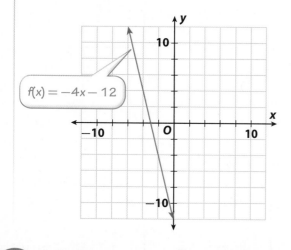

$f(x) = -4x - 12$

5. _____

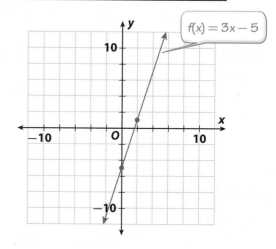

$f(x) = 3x - 5$

ESSENTIAL QUESTION CHECK-IN

6. How can you find the inverse of a linear function?

   _____

   _____

   _____

7.3 Independent Practice

FL F-BF.2.4a

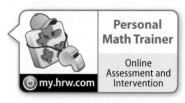

Personal Math Trainer

Online Assessment and Intervention

my.hrw.com

7. Carla is ordering pizzas for delivery. Each pizza costs $8, and there is a $6 delivery charge per order.

  a. Write the function $f(x)$ that Carla can use to determine the amount she will pay for having x pizzas delivered.

  _____

  b. Find the inverse of function $f(x)$.

  _____

  c. What does x represent in the inverse function $f^{-1}(x)$ in Part B?

  _____

  _____

8. Henry is a painter. He uses the function $h(x) = 50x - 20$ to determine the amount he charges for a painting that took him x hours to make.

  a. Find the inverse of function $h(x)$.

  _____

  b. What can the inverse function $h^{-1}(x)$ be used to determine?

  _____

  _____

9. The function $f(x) = \frac{5}{9}(x - 32)$ can be used to determine the temperature in °C when the temperature is x °F. Find the inverse function that can be used to determine the temperature in °F when the temperature is x °C.

  _____

10. Is the function $f(x) = -x$ its own inverse? Justify your answer.

  _____

  _____

  _____

  _____

  _____

  _____

11. The graph shows the function $f(x) = -3x - 6$. Find the inverse function $f^{-1}(x)$ and graph it.

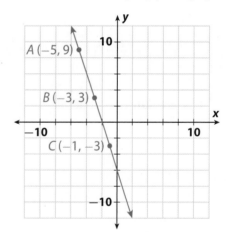

  _____

12. The general form of a linear function is $f(x) = mx + b$, where m and b and constants.

  a. Find $f^{-1}(x)$. _____

  b. Will $f^{-1}(x)$ always be a linear function? Explain.

  _____

  _____

  _____

13. Analyze Relationships The functions $f(x)$ and $g(x)$ intersect at the point $(0, 1)$. Is $g(x)$ the inverse of $f(x)$? Explain.

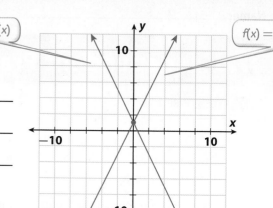

g(x)

f(x) =

_____

_____

_____

14. Keshawn thinks that the graph of a function $f(x)$ and its inverse $f^{-1}(x)$ will always intersect. Give a counterexample to disprove his statement.

_____

15. For the functions $f(x) = 3x + 2$ and $g(x) = -2x - 7$, $h(x) = f(x) + g(x)$, $j(x) = f(x) - g(x)$, and $k(x) = g(x) - f(x)$.

a. Find the inverse of function $h(x)$. _____

b. Find the inverse of function $j(x)$. _____

c. Find the inverse of function $k(x)$. _____

 **FOCUS ON HIGHER ORDER THINKING**

Work Area

16. Draw Conclusions When a function and its inverse intersect, what must be true about the point of intersection?

_____

_____

17. Critique Reasoning If f^{-1} is the inverse of f, then is it reasonable to describe f as an inverse of f^{-1}?

_____

_____

_____

18. Critical Thinking Micah is running a hot dog eating contest. The entrance fee is $20, and the winner will get $500. Micah will keep what is left over after paying the winner. The function $f(x) = 20x - 500$ describes how much money Micah earns if x people enter the contest. What does the inverse function $f^{-1}(x)$ describe?

_____

_____

LESSON 7.4
Linear Inequalities in Two Variables

FL A-REI.4.12

Graph the solutions to a linear inequality in two variables as a halfplane (excluding the boundary in the case of a strict inequality), and graph the solution set to a system of linear inequalities in two variables as the intersection of the corresponding half-planes.

? **ESSENTIAL QUESTION**

How do you graph a linear inequality in two variables?

Graphing a Linear Inequality

A **linear inequality** results when you replace the $=$ sign in a linear equation by $<$, $>$, $\leq$, or $\geq$. For example, $7x + 14 \leq 28y$ is a linear inequality. A **solution of an inequality** is any ordered pair (x, y) that makes the inequality true.

Math On the Spot
⊙ my.hrw.com

EXAMPLE 1

FL A-REI.4.12

Graph the solution set for $2x - 3y \geq 6$.

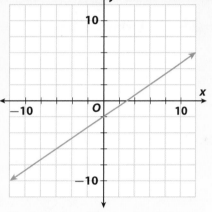

STEP 1 First solve the inequality for y.

$$2x - 3y \geq 6$$

Subtract $2x$ from both sides.

$$-3y \geq 6 - 2x$$

Divide both sides by -3.

$$y \leq \frac{6 - 2x}{-3}$$

Simplify.

$$y \leq -2 + \frac{2}{3}x$$

Write in standard form.

$$y \leq \frac{2}{3}x - 2$$

> Reverse the inequality sign when dividing both sides of an equation by a negative number.

Consider the line where the inequality is replaced by an equal sign: $y = \frac{2}{3}x - 2$. The line is called the **boundary line** of the solution set.

STEP 2 Graph the boundary line. The equation $y \leq \frac{2}{3}x - 2$ uses the inequality $\leq$, so the line will be solid, to show that the points on the line are part of the solution.

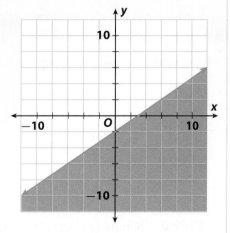

STEP 3 Shade the appropriate part of the graph. The equation $y \leq \frac{2}{3}x - 2$ uses the inequality $\leq$, so shade below the boundary line.

STEP 4 To check your work, choose one point above the boundary line and one point below the boundary line. Substitute both points into the original inequality, and verify that the point below the boundary line makes the inequality true.

Point	Above or Below Line	Inequality	True or False?
$(0, 0)$	Above	$2(0) - 3(0) \geq 6$	False
$(0, -4)$	Below	$2(0) - 3(-4) \geq 6$	True

The point below the line makes the equation true, so the shaded graph is correct.

REFLECT

1. The set of solutions to an inequality is represented on a graph by a shaded region and boundary line. This area is called a **half-plane**. Why is half-plane a good name for this region?

_____

_____

YOUR TURN

2. Graph the solution set for $4x - 8y \geq 32$.

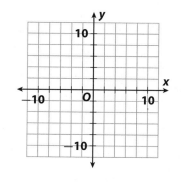

Graphing a Linear Inequality in Two Variables

EXAMPLE 2   FL   F-IF.2.4

Graph the solution set for the inequality $26 + 2y > 14x$.

STEP 1

$26 + 2y > 14x$

$2y > 14x - 26$ Subtract 26 from both sides.

$y > \frac{14x - 26}{2}$ Divide both sides by 2.

$y > 7x - 13$ Simplify.

STEP 2 Graph the boundary line. The equation $y > 7x - 13$ uses the inequality $>$, so use a dashed line to show that points on the line are not part of the solution.

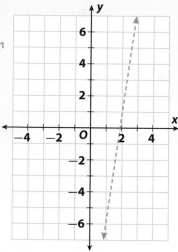

STEP 3 Shade the appropriate part of the graph. The equation $y > 7x - 13$ uses the inequality $>$, so shade above the boundary line.

STEP 4 To check your work, choose one point above the boundary line and one point below the boundary line. Substitute both points into the original inequality, and verify that the point above the boundary line makes the inequality true.

Math Talk
Mathematical Practices

How would the shaded region change if the inequality were $26 + 2y < 14x$?

Point	Above or Below Line	Inequality	True or False?
$(0, 0)$	Above	$26 + 2(0) > 14(0)$	True
$(4, 0)$	Below	$26 + 2(0) > 14(4)$	False

REFLECT

3. For the linear inequality, $6x - 3y < 24$, which of the following is a solution: $(0, -9)$, $(6, 4)$, or $(4, 1)$?

_____

_____

4. Is $(4, 0)$ a solution for the inequality $6x - 3y < 24$? Explain.

_____

_____

YOUR TURN

5. Graph $6x + 3y < -12$.

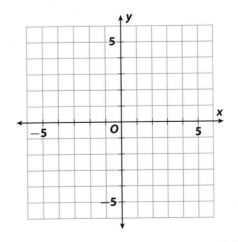

Personal Math Trainer

Online Assessment and Intervention

⟳ hrw.com

Writing and Solving Linear Inequalities

When writing a linear inequality for a situation, make sure to use the appropriate inequality symbol.

EXAMPLE 3    FL A-REI.4.12

Francesca can spend at most $6.75 on healthy snacks for a party. Veggie chips cost $1.00 per package and grapes cost $0.75 per bunch. Find two combinations of veggie chips and grapes that Francesca can buy.

STEP 1 Write a linear inequality to describe the situation.

Let x represent the number of packages of veggie chips and let y represent the number of bunches of grapes.

Write an inequality. Use $\leq$ for "at most."

Total cost of veggie chips	plus	Total cost of grapes	is at most	$6.75
$1.00x$	$+$	$0.75y$	$\leq$	6.75

Solve the inequality for y.

$1.00x + 0.75y \leq 6.75$

$(100)(1.00x + 0.75y) \leq 100(6.75)$ *Multiply both sides of the equation by 100 to eliminate the decimals.*

$100x + 75y \leq 675$

$75y \leq 675 - 100x$ *Subtract 100x from both sides.*

$y \leq \dfrac{675 - 100x}{75}$ *Divide both sides by 75.*

$y \leq 9 - \dfrac{4}{3}x$ *Simplify.*

STEP 2 Graph the boundary line. The inequality $y \leq 9 - \frac{4}{3}x$ uses the symbol $\leq$, so the line will be solid to show that the points on the line are part of the solution.

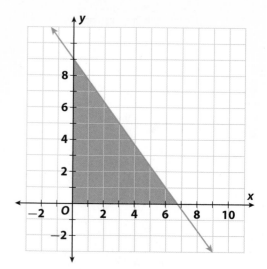

STEP 3 Shade the appropriate part of the graph. The inequality $y \leq 9 - \frac{4}{3}x$ uses the symbol $\leq$, so shade below the boundary line. Since the number of snacks cannot be negative, only shade in Quadrant 1.

STEP 4 Since the line is solid, any point on or underneath the line (in Quadrant 1) will be a solution.

Choose two points, and make sure they make the inequality true.

$1.00(3) + 0.75(5) \leq 6.75$
$1.00(2) + 0.75(3) \leq 6.75$

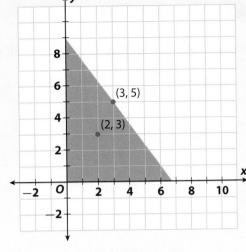

Two different combinations that Francesca could buy for $6.75 or less are 3 packages of veggie chips and 5 bunches of grapes, or 2 packages of veggie chips and 3 bunches of grapes.

REFLECT

6. **What if?** How would the graph of solutions change if grapes were sold at $0.25 per bunch?

_____

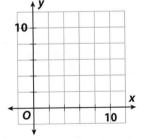

YOUR TURN

7. Lamar has $15.00 that he can spend on food for his cat. Dry cat food costs $4.50 per small bag and wet cat food costs $1.50 per tin can. Write a linear inequality that describes how many bags and cans of cat food Lamar can buy.

_____

_____

8. Graph the solution set of your linear inequality for Lamar.

9. Identify two combinations of dry and wet cat food that Lamar can afford.

_____

_____

_____

Personal Math Trainer

Online Assessment and Intervention

🔵 my.hrw.com

Graph the solution set for each linear equality. (Examples 1 and 2)

1. $4y + 3x - y > -6x + 12$

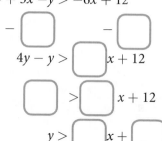

$$4y - y > \boxed{} x + 12$$

$$\boxed{} > \boxed{} x + 12$$

$$y > \boxed{} x + \boxed{}$$

2. $5y + 3 < 2x$

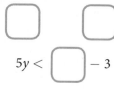

$$5y < \boxed{} - 3$$

$$y < \tfrac{2}{5}x - \tfrac{3}{5}$$

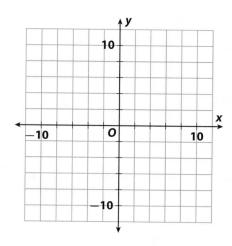

Sam is buying chairs that cost $15 and tables that cost $20.
He wants to spend no more than $140. (Example 3)

3. Write a linear inequality to represent the amount Sam pays for x

chairs and y tables. _____

4. Solve the inequality for y.

_____

5. Graph the inequality.

6. What are two combinations of chairs
and tables that Sam could buy?

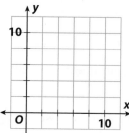

_____

7. How do you graph a linear inequality in two variables?

_____

_____

7.4 Independent Practice

 FL **A-REI.4.10, F-IF.3.7a**

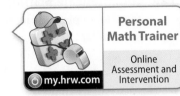

Graph the inequality.

8. $y \le 5$

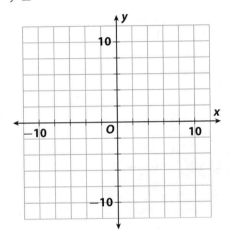

9. $x + 5y < 30$

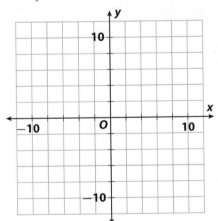

10. $3x - 3y \ge 21$

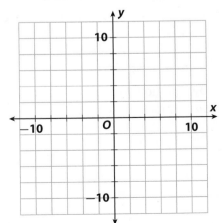

11. Represent Real World Problems Sandra was given a $60.00 gift card to an online music store. She can buy single songs for $1.00 and albums for $12.00.

a. Write the linear inequality that represents how many songs, x, and albums, y, that Sandra can buy with her gift card.

_____

b. Explain the steps you would take to solve the linear inequality for y, the number of albums Sandra buys.

_____

_____

_____

c. Complete the table to verify which points make the inequality true.

Point	Inequality	True or False?
(6, 4)		
(8, 5)		

d. Explain the meaning of the point in the table that makes the inequality true.

_____

_____

e. If you were to shade a graph of this linear inequality, would you shade the point $(-3, 4)$? Explain.

_____

_____

_____

12. Communicate Mathematical Ideas How is graphing a linear inequality on a coordinate plane different from graphing an inequality on a number line? How is it similar?

_____

_____

_____

_____

_____

_____

H.O.T. FOCUS ON HIGHER ORDER THINKING

Work Area

13. Multi-step The fare for a taxi cab is $2.25 per passenger and $0.75 for each mile. A group of friends has $16.00 for cab fare.

a. Write a linear inequality to represent how many miles, y, the group can travel if there are x people in the group.

_____

b. If there are 3 people in the group, how far can they travel by taxi? Explain.

_____

_____

c. If the group wants to travel 10 miles, what is the greatest number of passengers that can travel by taxi? Explain.

_____

_____

_____

14. Analyze Relationships For the graph of $x \geq 5$, the boundary line is the vertical line $x = 5$. Would you shade to the left or right of the boundary? Explain.

_____

_____

15. Critique Reasoning Baxter thinks that the inequality $2x - 3y \geq 6$ should be shaded above the boundary line because it uses the $\geq$ inequality symbol. Is he correct? Explain.

_____

_____

_____

Ready to Go On?

7.1 Arithmetic Sequences

Indicate whether each sequence is arithmetic. If so, write an explicit rule for the sequence.

1. 1, 3, 5, 7, …

_____

2. 3, 6, 9, 14, …

_____

3. 25, 20, 15, 10, …

_____

7.2 Operations with Linear Functions

For $f(x) = 5x - 3$ and $g(x) = 2 - x$, compute the following functions.

4. $h(x) = f(x) + g(x)$

_____

5. $j(x) = f(x) - g(x)$

_____

6. $k(x) = 6 \cdot f(x)$

_____

7.3 Linear Functions and Their Inverses

Find the inverse function for the following linear functions.

7. $f(x) = 4x + 2$

_____

8. $g(x) = \frac{x + 5}{7}$

_____

9. $h(x) = \frac{1}{2}x + \frac{2}{3}$

_____

7.4 Linear Inequalities in Two Variables

Graph the following linear inequalities.

10. $3x + 2y \le 12$

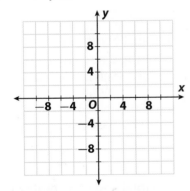

11. $5x - y \ge 10$

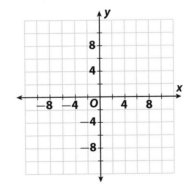

? **ESSENTIAL QUESTION**

12. How is the use of mathematical rules related to solving and graphing linear equations and inequalities?

_____

_____

Selected Response

1. Which arithmetic sequence has a common difference of 4?

Ⓐ 1, 6, 11, 16, ...　Ⓒ 12, 8, 4, 0, ...

Ⓑ 8, 1, −6, −13, ...　Ⓓ 11, 15, 19, 23, ...

2. Which function represents $j(x) = f(x) + g(x)$ for $f(x) = 3x - 1$ and $g(x) = 2 - 3x$?

Ⓐ $j(x) = 6x + 3$　Ⓒ $j(x) = 6x + 1$

Ⓑ $j(x) = 1$　Ⓓ $j(x) = 3$

3. A line passes through points $(5, 8.4)$ and $(8, 6.8)$. What is its slope?

Ⓐ 1.53　Ⓒ 0.53

Ⓑ 1.17　Ⓓ −0.53

4. Which function is the inverse of $f(x) = 2x + 3$?

Ⓐ $f^{-1}(x) = -2x - 3$

Ⓑ $f^{-1}(x) = \left(\frac{1}{2}\right)x + \frac{1}{3}$

Ⓒ $f^{-1}(x) = 3x + 2$

Ⓓ $f^{-1}(x) = \left(\frac{1}{2}\right)x - \frac{3}{2}$

5. Which inequality is represented by the graph?

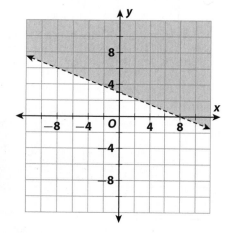

Ⓐ $3x + 8y > 24$　Ⓒ $3x + 8y < 24$

Ⓑ $8x + 3y > 24$　Ⓓ $8x + 3y < 24$

6. Solve $3(x - 2) = 9 - x$. What is the solution?

Ⓐ $x = 1.5$　Ⓒ $x = 5.5$

Ⓑ $x = 3.75$　Ⓓ $x = 7.5$

7. Which is the 7th term in an arithmetic sequence with initial term 5 and common difference of 4?

Ⓐ 29　Ⓒ 34

Ⓑ 33　Ⓓ 39

8. Which function represents $f(x)$ in $h(x) = 3f(x)$, if $h(x) = 15x - 18$?

Ⓐ $f(x) = 15x - 15$　Ⓒ $f(x) = 45x - 54$

Ⓑ $f(x) = 18x - 18$　Ⓓ $f(x) = 5x - 6$

9. Which point is a solution to the linear inequality $4x - 5y \le 10$?

Ⓐ $(5, 6)$　Ⓒ $(12, 7)$

Ⓑ $(3, -2)$　Ⓓ $(-1, -4)$

Mini-Tasks

10. Online, baseballs cost $5 each plus $1 shipping for the entire order, no matter how many baseballs are ordered.

a. What is the total cost to order 1 baseball? 2 baseballs?

_____

b. Can the total cost of an order of baseballs be represented by an arithmetic sequence? If so, what is the common difference?

_____

c. Write an explicit rule to determine the total cost for n baseballs.

_____

Modeling with Linear Functions

ESSENTIAL QUESTION

How can you use statistical methods to find relationships between sets of data?

my.hrw.com

Real-World Video

A fossil is a remnant or trace of an organism of a past geologic age that has been preserved in the earth's crust. Fossils are often dated by using interpolation, a type of calculation that uses an observed pattern to estimate a value between two known values.

GO DIGITAL

my.hrw.com

my.hrw.com

Go digital with your write-in student edition, accessible on any device.

Math On the Spot

Scan with your smart phone to jump directly to the online edition, video tutor, and more.

Animated Math

Interactively explore key concepts to see how math works.

Personal Math Trainer

Get immediate feedback and help as you work through practice sets.

Are YOU Ready?

Complete these exercises to review skills you will need for this module.

Personal Math Trainer

Online Assessment and Intervention

my.hrw.com

Ordered Pairs

EXAMPLE Graph the ordered pairs $A(2, 2)$, $B(-2, 0)$, and $C(-1, -3)$.

The first coordinate refers to position on the x-axis, and the second coordinate refers to position on the y-axis.

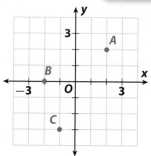

Graph each point on the coordinate plane provided.

1. $A(4, 0)$

2. $B(3, -4)$

3. $C(-1, -2)$

4. $D(-1, 3.5)$

5. $E(0, 5)$

6. $F(4.5, -3)$

7. $G(-2.5, 0.5)$

8. $H(-4, -2.5)$

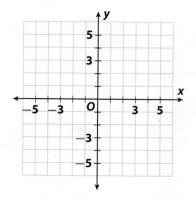

Graph Linear Functions

EXAMPLE Graph $y = -2x + 1$.

Find two points that satisfy the equation. Then connect the points with a straight line.

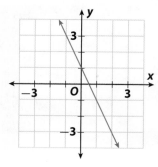

Graph each function.

9. $y = x - 2$

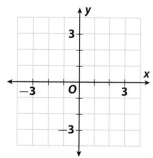

10. $y = -\frac{2}{3}x + 2$

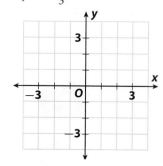

11. $y = \frac{5}{2}x - \frac{1}{2}$

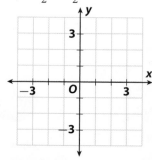

Reading Start-Up

Visualize Vocabulary

Use the review words to complete the sequence diagram. Complete the blanks in each box.

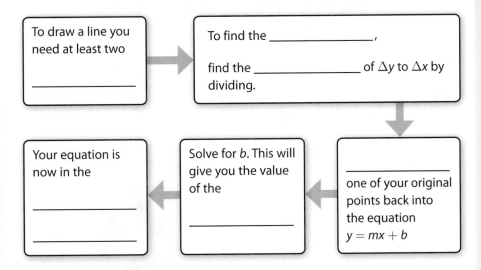

To draw a line you need at least two

_____

→

To find the _____ , find the _____ of Δy to Δx by dividing.

↓

Your equation is now in the

_____

_____

←

Solve for b. This will give you the value of the

_____

←

_____ one of your original points back into the equation $y = mx + b$

Understand Vocabulary

To become familiar with some of the vocabulary terms in the module, consider the following. You may refer to the module, the glossary, or a dictionary.

1. The word *regress* is used when you want to return to a less well-developed state. What do you think an **linear regression** might be?

    _____

2. The word *residual* refers to what is left over. What do you think a **residual plot** might be?

    _____

    _____

Vocabulary

Review Words

✓ point *(punto)*

✓ ratio *(razón)*

✓ slope *(pendiente)*

✓ slope-intercept form *(forma de pendiente-intersección)*

✓ y-intercept *(intersección con el eje y)*

Preview Words

causation

correlation

correlation coefficient

interpolation

linear regression

least squares regression line

line of best fit

residual

residual plot

scatter plot

Active Reading

Three-Panel Flip Chart Before beginning the module, create a three-panel flip chart to help you organize what you learn. Label each flap with one of the lesson titles from this module. As you study each lesson, write important ideas like vocabulary under the appropriate flap.

Unpacking the Standards

Understanding the standards and the vocabulary terms in the standards will help you know exactly what you are expected to learn in this module.

 **FL S-ID.2.6**

Represent data on two quantitative variables on a scatter plot, and describe how the variables are related.

Key Vocabulary

scatter plot *(diagrama de dispersión)*
A graph with points plotted to show a possible relationship between two variables.

What It Means to You

You can graph real-world data in two variables to see how the variables are related.

UNPACKING EXAMPLE S-ID.2.6

Reed took a survey about social media attitudes and age. He used a scatter plot to display his data.

The scatter plot suggests that as participants get older they like social media less.

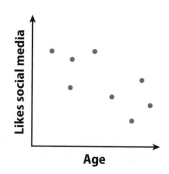

FL S-ID.2.6C

Fit a linear function for a scatter plot that suggests a linear association.

Key Vocabulary

linear function *(función lineal)*
A function whose graph is a straight line.

What It Means to You

In a linear relationship one quantity is directly proportional to another. For example, the greater the altitude, the thinner the air is in the atmosphere.

UNPACKING EXAMPLE S-ID.2.6C

Reed drew a line in his scatter plot, suggesting a linear correlation between age and how much people like social media.

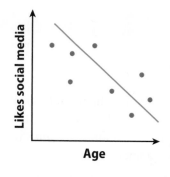

Visit **my.hrw.com** to see all **Florida Math Standards** unpacked.

 my.hrw.com

LESSON
8.1 Correlation

FL S-ID.2.6

Represent data on two quantitative variables on a scatter plot, and describe how the variables are related. *Also S-ID.3.8, S-ID.3.9*

? **ESSENTIAL QUESTION**

How can you describe the relationship between two variables?

EXPLORE ACTIVITY  FL S-ID.2.6

Graphing Bivariate Data

Bivariate data is data that involves two variables. A **scatter plot** graphs bivariate data as a set of points whose coordinates correspond to the two variables. Scatter plots can help you see relationships between two variables. We say there is a **correlation** between two variables if their values are linked, as shown below.

 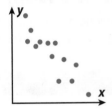 

Positive Correlation	Negative Correlation	No Correlation
As the value of one variable increases, the value of the other variable also increases.	The value of one variable decreases as the other one increases.	There is no relationship between the two variables.

The table below shows the number of species of mammals on the International Union for the Conservation of Nature's "Red List" of endangered species during the years 2004 to 2012.

IUCN Red List, Number of Endangered Mammal Species							
2004	2006	2007	2008	2009	2010	2011	2012
352	348	349	448	449	450	447	446

Source: *IUCN Red List version 2012*

A Make a scatter plot, using the data in the table as the coordinates of points on the graph. Use the calendar year as the x-value and the number of species as the y-value. One point is plotted for you.

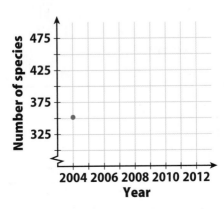

REFLECT

1. **Conjecture** Look at the pattern of points. Is there a positive correlation, negative correlation, or no correlation between the number of endangered mammal species and the year? What is the trend? Is the number of endangered species increasing or decreasing over time?

_____

_____

_____

_____

Math On the Spot
my.hrw.com

Describing Correlations from Scatter Plots

Scatter plots can help to visualize whether the correlation between variables is positive or negative—or if there is no correlation between the variables.

EXAMPLE 1 FL S-ID.2.6

Describe the correlation illustrated by the scatter plot.

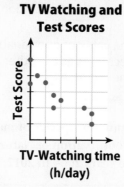

TV Watching and Test Scores

Test Score

TV-Watching time (h/day)

As the number of hours spent watching TV increased, test scores decreased. There is a negative correlation between the two data variables.

My Notes

REFLECT

2. **What if?** What would you expect to be true of a person from this survey who watches very few hours of TV? Is it possible for that person to have low test scores?

_____

_____

_____

_____

YOUR TURN

3. Describe the correlation illustrated by the scatter plot.

_____

_____

_____

_____

Snowboarding Competition

Number of participants (y-axis: 0, 10, 20, 30, 40, 50)

Year (x-axis: 2001, 2003, 2005, 2007)

Correlation Coefficients

One measure of the strength and direction of a correlation is the **correlation coefficient**, denoted by r. The value of r ranges from -1 to 1. Although r can be precisely calculated, in this lesson we examine qualitatively how its value describes a correlation.

A positive r value indicates a positive correlation, and a negative r value indicates a negative correlation. The stronger the correlation, the closer the correlation coefficient will be to -1 or 1. The weaker the correlation, the closer r will be to zero.

	Negative	**Positive**
Strong	Strong negative correlation points lie close to a line with negative slope. r is close to -1.	Strong positive correlation points lie close to a line with positive slope. r is close to 1.
Weak	Weak negative correlation points loosely follow a line with negative slope. r is between 0 and -1.	Weak positive correlation points loosely follow a line with positive slope. r is between 0 and 1.

If there is no correlation between the two variables in a data set, the points in a scatter plot do not lie along a line, and r is close to zero.

EXAMPLE 2 FL S-ID.3.8

The table lists the latitude and average annual temperature for various cities in the Northern Hemisphere. Describe the correlation between latitude and temperature, and estimate the correlation coefficient.

City	Latitude	Avg. Annual Temperature
Bangkok, Thailand	13.7°N	82.6°F
Cairo, Egypt	30.1°N	71.4°F
London, England	51.5°N	51.8°F
Moscow, Russia	55.8°N	39.4°F
New Delhi, India	28.6°N	77.0°F
Tokyo, Japan	35.7°N	58.1°F
Vancouver, Canada	49.2°N	49.6°F

STEP 1 Make a scatter plot.

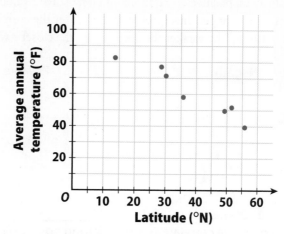

Math Talk

Mathematical Practices

If the point (19.4, 60.8) for Mexico City was added to the scatter plot, how would the correlation coefficient change?

STEP 2 Describe the correlation, and estimate the correlation coefficient. Because the plotted points appear to lie very close to a line with a negative slope, the scatter plot shows a strong negative correlation. So the correlation coefficient is close to −1.

YOUR TURN

4. Examine the scatter plot titled Snowboarding Competition in the previous Your Turn. Is the correlation coefficient for the data closer to 0, 1, or −1? Explain.

_____

_____

Personal Math Trainer

Online Assessment and Intervention

🔵 my.hrw.com

Distinguishing Causation from Correlation

A common error when interpreting paired data is confusing correlation and *causation*. If a correlation exists between two variables, this does not necessarily mean that one variable causes the other. When one variable increases, the other variable may increase (or decrease) as a result of other variables that are not being considered. Such variables are sometimes called *lurking variables*.

Math On the Spot
my.hrw.com

EXAMPLE 3　　　　FL　S-ID.3.9

Read the article. Does it describe a positive or negative correlation? Discuss whether the correlation is a result of causation.

STEP 1 Identify the two variables.

- size of amygdala
- size of social network

STEP 2 Determine the correlation.

A larger amygdala corresponds to a larger social network, so there is a positive correlation.

STEP 3 Discuss whether the correlation is a result of causation.

Causation is possible, but it's unknown which variable causes the other. Having a larger amygdala might cause a person to develop a larger social network, or having a large social network might cause a person's amygdala to grow. And it's possible that neither factor causes the other, but that a lurking third variable causes the amygdala to grow and causes the person to develop a large social network.

Brain's Amygdala Connected To Social Behavior

An almond-shaped part of the brain called the amygdala has long been known to play a role in people's emotional states. Now scientists studying the amygdala have discovered a connection between its size and the size of a person's social network. The scientists used a brain scanner to determine the size of the amygdala in the brains of 58 adults. They also gave each person a survey that measured the size of a person's social network. After analyzing the data, they found that people with larger amygdalas tend to have larger social networks.

YOUR TURN

5. A survey found that students who spent more time doing Algebra homework also spent more time doing Biology homework. Identify the two variables, indicate whether they have a positive or negative correlation, and discuss whether the correlation is a result of causation.

_____

_____

_____

_____

Personal Math Trainer

Online Assessment and Intervention

my.hrw.com

Juan and his parents are visiting a university 205 miles from their home. As they travel, Juan uses the car odometer and his watch to keep track of the distance they travel and the amount of time that passes.

(Explore Activity and Example 1)

Time (min)	0	30	60	90	120	150	180	210
Distance (mi)	0	28	58	87	117	148	178	205

1. Make a scatter plot for this set of data. What does the x value represent? What does the y value represent?

   _____

   _____

2. Describe the correlation. Explain.

   _____

   _____

   _____

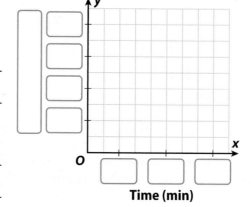

Time (min)

3. Is the correlation coefficient for the data likely to be closest to -1, -0.5, 0, 0.5, or 1? (Example 2) _____

4. Suppose Juan also kept track of the temperature as they drove, and he found that temperature was negatively correlated with distance traveled. Is this correlation due to causation? Explain. (Example 3)

   _____

   _____

   _____

5. How can you describe the relationship between two variables?

   _____

   _____

   _____

   _____

   _____

8.1 Independent Practice

FL   S-ID.3.8, S-ID.2.6, S-ID.3.9

Personal
Math Trainer

Online
Assessment and
Intervention

my.hrw.com

The table lists the heights and weights of the six wide receivers that played for the New Orleans Saints during the 2010 football season.

Wide Receiver	Height (inches)	Weight (pounds)
Arrington	75	192
Colston	76	225
Henderson	71	200
Meachem	74	210
Moore	69	190
Roby	72	189

6. Make a scatter plot.

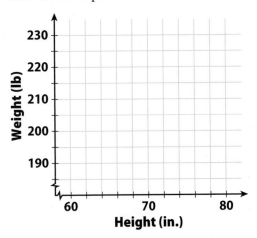

7. Describe the correlation. Is the correlation coefficient likely to be closest to -1, -0.5, 0, 0.5, or 1?.

_____

8. Researchers studying senior citizens discovered that an elderly person's walking speed was correlated to that person's chance of living longer. The fastest walkers were more likely to live another 10 years than were the slowest walkers. Describe the correlation, and discuss whether it is due to causation.

_____

_____

_____

_____

Identify the correlation you would expect to see between each pair of variables. State whether the correlation coefficient is likely to be closer to -1, 0, or 1.

9. The temperature in Houston and the number of cars sold in Boston.

_____

10. The number of members in a family and the size of the family's weekly grocery bill.

_____

11. The number of times you sharpen your pencil and the length of the pencil.

_____

Work Area

12. Justify Reasoning Choose the scatter plot that best represents the relationship between the number of days since a sunflower seed was planted and the height of the plant. Explain.

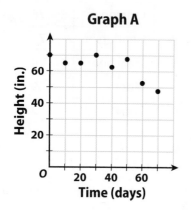

Graph A

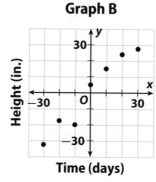

Graph B

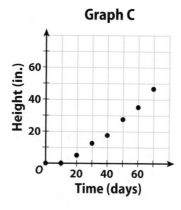

Graph C

_____

_____

_____

_____

_____

13. Make a Prediction The scatter plot shows the average ocelot population in Laguna Atascosa National Wildlife Refuge near Brownsville, Texas. Based on this information, predict the number of ocelots living at the wildlife refuge in 2014 if conditions do not change.

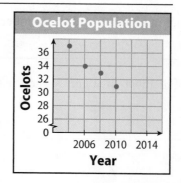

_____

LESSON
8.2 Fitting Lines to Data

FL **S-ID.2.6c**

Fit a linear function for a scatter plot that suggests a linear association. *Also S-ID.2.6, S-ID.2.6a, S-ID.2.6b, N-Q.1.2, F-LE.2.5, and S-ID.3.7*

ESSENTIAL QUESTION

How do you find a linear model for a bivariate data set, and how do you evaluate the quality of fit?

EXPLORE ACTIVITY   FL **S-ID.2.6c**

Finding a Line of Fit for Data

When the two variables in a bivariate data set have a strong positive or negative correlation, you can find a linear model for the data. The process is called fitting a line to the data or finding a **line of fit** for the data.

The table lists the median age of females living in the United States, based on the results of the U.S. Census over the past few decades. Determine whether a linear model is reasonable for the data. If so, find a linear model for the data.

Year	Median age of females
1970	29.2
1980	31.3
1990	34.0
2000	36.5
2010	38.2

A To simplify calculations with the data, let x represent time in years after 1970.

Let y represent the median age of females.

Make a table of paired values of x and y.

x				
y				

B Make a scatter plot of the data.

If the points fall close to a straight line, then a linear model may provide a good description of the data. Do the points appear to form a line?

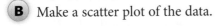

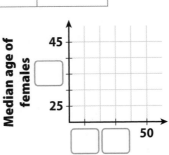

Time (years since 1970)

C Using a ruler, draw a line that passes as close as possible to the plotted points. This is called a line of fit. Your line does not necessarily have to pass through any of the points, but you should try to have about the same number of points above and below the line.

D Find the equation of the line of fit.

We will do the calculation for a line that passes through the points (20, 34) and (50, 40).

STEP 1 Find the slope.

$$m = \frac{40 - 34}{50 - 20}$$

$$m = \boxed{}$$

STEP 2 Find the y-intercept using (20, 34).

$$y = mx + b$$

$$\boxed{} = \boxed{} (\boxed{}) + b$$

$$\boxed{} = \boxed{} + b$$

$$\boxed{} = b$$

So, in terms of the variables x and y, the equation of the line of fit is

_____

REFLECT

1. What does the slope of the line of fit tell you about the data?

_____

_____

_____

2. What does the y-intercept of the line of fit tell you about the data?

_____

_____

_____

3. **Communicate Mathematical Ideas** How does the slope of the line of fit relate to the type of correlation in the data?

_____

_____

_____

Creating a Residual Plot

Some lines will fit a data set better than others. One way to evaluate how well a line fits a data set is to use *residuals*. A **residual** is the signed vertical distance between a data point and a line of fit.

After calculating residuals, you can draw a **residual plot**, which is a graph of points whose *x*-coordinates are the values of the independent variable and whose *y*-coordinates are the corresponding residuals.

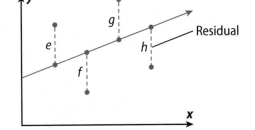

Math On the Spot
my.hrw.com

Looking at the distribution of residuals can help you determine how well a line of fit actually describes the data. The plots below illustrate how the residuals might be distributed for three different data sets and lines of fit.

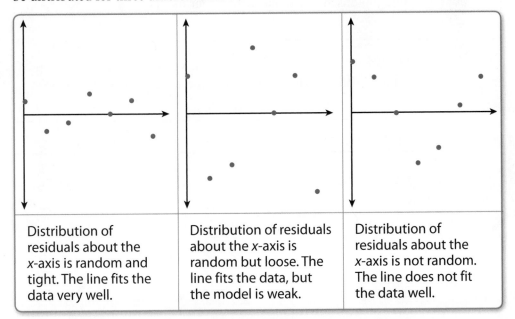

| Distribution of residuals about the *x*-axis is random and tight. The line fits the data very well. | Distribution of residuals about the *x*-axis is random but loose. The line fits the data, but the model is weak. | Distribution of residuals about the *x*-axis is not random. The line does not fit the data well. |

EXAMPLE 1 (Real World)

FL   S-ID.2.6b

Consider the data from the Explore Activity on median ages of females over time. Use residuals to evaluate the quality of fit for the line $y = 0.25x + 29$, where *x* is years since 1970, and *y* is median age.

STEP 1 Calculate the residuals.

x	actual *y*	predicted *y*, based on $y = 0.25x + 29$	residual Subtract predicted from actual to find the residual
0	29.2	29.0	0.2
10	31.3	31.5	−0.2
20	34.0	34.0	0
30	36.5	36.5	0
40	38.2	39.0	−0.8

STEP 2 Plot the residuals.

STEP 3 Evaluate the quality of fit to the data for
the line $y = 0.25x + 29$.

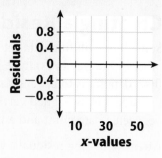

- The residuals are all small, so the
  points on the residual plot are tightly
  distributed around the x-axis.
- Therefore, the line given by $y = 0.25x + 29$ is
  an appropriate model.

REFLECT

4. If you are comparing two lines of fit for the same data set, how does the size
of the residuals indicate which one is the better model?

_____

5. Communicate Mathematical Ideas Suppose you know that a linear model
is a good fit for a data set. How would you expect the residual plot to look?

_____

_____

_____

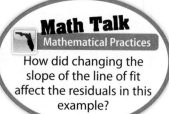

Math Talk

How did changing the
slope of the line of fit
affect the residuals in this
example?

YOUR TURN

6. Consider the data used in the Explore Activity and in Example 1 on median
ages of females over time. Graph the residuals and evaluate the quality of fit
for the line $y = 0.2x + 29.2$.

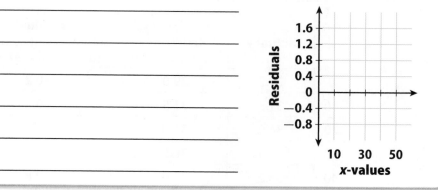

**Personal
Math Trainer**

Online Assessment
and Intervention

⏻ my.hrw.com

Using a Line of Fit to Make Predictions

Finding a linear model for a data set establishes one variable as a linear function of another variable. The domain of the function is determined by the least and greatest values of the *x*-values in the actual data.

A linear model can be used to make predictions. Making a prediction based on a value *within* the model's domain is called **interpolation**. Basing a prediction on a value *outside* the domain is called **extrapolation**.

Math On the Spot

my.hrw.com

EXAMPLE 2  **FL** **S-ID.3.7**

Suppose you used the data table in the Explore Activity to derive the model $y = 0.25x + 29$, where *x* is the number of years since 1970 and *y* is the median age of females in the United States. Use this model to predict the median age of females for the years 1995 and 2015. State whether each prediction is an interpolation or an extrapolation.

My Notes

A Let $x = 25$ because $1995 - 1970 = 25$.

The predicted value of *y* is $0.25(25) + 29 \approx 35.3$ years old.
The *x*-values in the data go from 0 to 40.
The *x*-value 25 is between 0 and 40, so this prediction is an interpolation.

B Let $x = 45$ because $2015 - 1970 = 45$.

The predicted value of *y* is $0.25(45) + 29 \approx 40.3$ years old.
The *x*-values in the data go from 0 to 40.
The *x*-value 45 is greater than 40, so this prediction is an extrapolation.

REFLECT

7. The Census Bureau used interpolation to estimate the median age of females in 1995 and used extrapolation to predict the median age for 2033. They used only the data in the table at the start of this lesson. Which of their predictions is more likely to be accurate? Explain.

_____

_____

_____

_____

YOUR TURN

Use the linear model $y = 0.25x + 29$, where *x* is the number of years since 1970 and *y* is the median age of females, to predict the median age of females in the years below. State whether each prediction is an interpolation or an extrapolation.

8. 1989 _____

9. 2022 _____

_____

_____

Personal Math Trainer

Online Assessment and Intervention

my.hrw.com

The table lists the median age of males based on the results of the U.S. Census.
(Explore Activity)

Year	1970	1980	1990	2000	2010
Median age of males	26.8	28.8	31.6	34.0	35.5

1. Let x represent time in years after 1970 and let y represent median age. Make a table of paired values of x and y.

x	0		20	30	
y		28.8			35.5

2. Draw a scatter plot and line of fit.

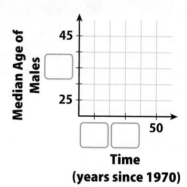

Median Age of Males

45

25

50

Time
(years since 1970)

3. Find an equation of the line of fit. (Explore Activity)

_____

A student fit the line $y = 0.23x + 27$ to the data above. Use this model for Exercises 4–6.

4. Calculate the residuals. (Example 1)

x	y actual	y predicted	Residual
0		27	
	28.8		−0.5
20			
30		33.9	
	35.5		−0.7

5. Predict the median age of males in 1995. (Example 2)

$$y + 0.23 \left(\boxed{} \right) + 27 \approx \boxed{}$$

6. Is the prediction for 1995 an interpolation or extrapolation? (Example 2)

_____

ESSENTIAL QUESTION CHECK-IN

7. How do you find a linear model for bivariate data, and how do you evaluate the quality of fit?

_____

_____

8.2 Independent Practice

FL S-ID.2.6c, S-ID.2.6b, S-ID.3.7

Personal
Math Trainer

Online
Assessment and
my.hrw.com Intervention

The table lists the length (in centimeters) and median weight
(in kilograms) of male and female infants in the United States.

Length (cm)	50	60	70	80	90	100
Median weight (kg) of male infants	3.4	5.9	8.4	10.8	13.0	15.5
Median weight (kg) of female infants	3.4	5.8	8.3	10.6	12.8	15.2

8. Let l represent an infant's length in excess of 50 centimeters (for instance,
for an infant whose length is 60 cm, $l = 10$) and let w represent the median
weight of female infants. Make a table of paired values of l and w.

l						
w						

9. Draw a scatter plot of the data for female infants, and draw a line of fit.

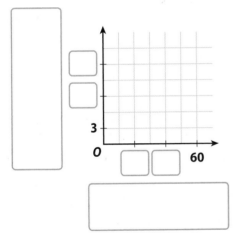

3

O   60

10. **Critical Thinking** Find an equation for the line of fit you drew on the scatter plot.
According to your model, at what rate does the weight change as length increases?

_____

_____

_____

11. Calculate the residuals, and make a residual plot.

l	*w* actual	*w* predicted	Residual
0	3.4		
10	5.8		
20	8.3		
30	10.6		
40	12.8		
50	15.2		

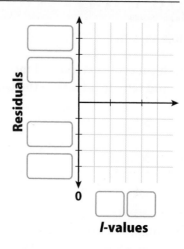

Residuals

0

l-values

12. Evaluate the suitability of a linear fit and the quality of the fit.

FOCUS ON HIGHER ORDER THINKING

Work Area

13. Critique Reasoning Hector found a linear model based on the data for the length and weight of male infants, and he used it to predict the weight of a boy who is 150 centimeters tall. Is his prediction likely to be reliable? Explain.

14. Analyze Relationships Suppose the line of fit in Example 1 with equation $w = 0.25l + 29$ is changed to $w = 0.25l + 28.8$. What effect does this change have on the residuals? On the residual plot?

15. What If? If the median weight of male infants is 0.2 kg above the median weight of female infants at the same length, how would the line of fit on a scatter plot for male infants' length and weight compare to the one for female infants?

LESSON
8.3 Linear Regression

FL S-ID.2.6b

Informally assess the fit of a function by plotting and analyzing residuals. *Also S-ID.2.6, S-ID.2.6a, S-ID.2.6c, S-ID.3.7, S-ID.3.8*

ESSENTIAL QUESTION How can you use the linear regression function on a graphing calculator to find the line of best fit for a bivariate data set?

EXPLORE ACTIVITY  FL S-ID.2.6

Calculating Squared Residuals

In a previous lesson, you fit a line to data for the median age of females over time. Because each person in your class fit a line by eye, any two students are likely to have chosen slightly different lines of fit. Suppose one student came up with the equation $y = 0.25x + 29.0$ while another came up with $y = 0.25x + 28.8$ where in each case, x is the time in years since 1970 and y is the median age of females.

A Complete each table below in order to calculate the squares of the residuals for each line of fit.

		$y = 0.25x + 29.0$		
x	**y (actual)**	**y (predicted)**	**Residual**	**Square of residual**
0	29.2	29.0	0.2	0.04
10	31.3			
20	34.0			
30	36.5			
40	38.2			

		$y = 0.25x + 28.8$		
x	**y (actual)**	**y (predicted)**	**Residual**	**Square of residual**
0	29.2	28.8	0.4	0.16
10	31.3			
20	34.0			
30	36.5			
40	38.2			

B Find the sum of squared residuals for each line of fit.

Sum of squared residuals for $y = 0.25x + 29.0$: _____

Sum of squared residuals for $y = 0.25x + 28.8$: _____

C Which line has the smaller sum of squared residuals?

_____

REFLECT

1. Analyze Relationships How does squaring a residual affect its value?

_____

_____

_____

2. Suppose the residuals for a line of fit for a data set are 2.6, 2.3, −2.3, and −2.5, and the residuals for a second line of fit are 0.6, 0.2, −0.2, and −0.4.

a. Which line fits the data better? How can you tell?

_____

b. Would the sum of the residuals or the sum of the squared residuals be a better measure of the quality of fit? Explain.

_____

_____

_____

_____

_____

_____

Math On the Spot

my.hrw.com

Comparing Squared Residuals

The quality of a line of fit can be evaluated by finding the sum of the squared residuals. The closer the sum of the squared residuals is to 0, the better the line fits the data.

EXAMPLE 1   FL   S-ID.2.6b

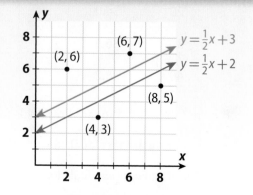

The data in the table below are graphed at right along with two possible lines of fit. For each line, find the sum of the squares of the residuals. Which line is a better fit?

x	2	4	6	8
y	6	3	7	5

STEP 1 Find the residuals of each line.

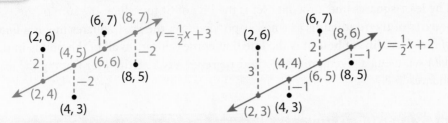

x	y (actual)	y predicted by $y = \frac{1}{2}x + 3$	residual for $y = \frac{1}{2}x + 3$	y predicted by $y = \frac{1}{2}x + 2$	residual for $y = \frac{1}{2}x + 2$
2	6	4	2	3	3
4	3	5	−2	4	−1
6	7	6	1	5	2
8	5	7	−2	6	−1

STEP 2 Square the residuals and find their sum.

$$y = \frac{1}{2}x + 3: (2)^2 + (-2)^2 + (1)^2 + (-2)^2 = 4 + 4 + 1 + 4 = 13$$

$$y = \frac{1}{2}x + 2: (3)^2 + (-1)^2 + (2)^2 + (-1)^2 = 9 + 1 + 4 + 1 = 15$$

The sum of the squares for $y = \frac{1}{2}x + 3$ is smaller, so it provides the better fit for the data.

REFLECT

3. **What If?** Suppose the data pair (5, 4) was added to the data set. Which of the two lines would fit the data better now?

_____

_____

YOUR TURN

4. Find the sum of the squares of the residuals for the data above using the line $y = \frac{1}{2}x + 4$. How good is this fit?

_____

_____

_____

Animated Math

my.hrw.com

Personal Math Trainer

Online Assessment and Intervention

my.hrw.com

Performing Linear Regression

The **least-squares line** for a data set is the line of fit for which the sum of the squares of the residuals is as small as possible. So, the least-squares line is a *line of best fit*. A **line of best fit** is the line that comes closest to all of the points in the data set, using a given process. **Linear regression** is a method for finding the least-squares line.

EXAMPLE 2  **FL** **S-ID.2.6a**

The table shows latitudes and average temperatures for several cities. Use a calculator to estimate the average temperature in Vancouver, Canada at 49.1°N

City	Latitude	Average temperature (°C)
Barrow, Alaska	71.2° N	−12.7
Yakutsk, Russia	62.1° N	−10.1
London, England	51.3° N	10.4
Chicago, Illinois	41.9° N	10.3
San Francisco, California	37.5° N	13.8
Yuma, Arizona	32.7° N	22.8
Tindouf, Algeria	27.7° N	22.8
Dakar, Senegal	14.0° N	24.5
Mangalore, India	12.5° N	27.1

Use your calculator to find an equation for a line of best fit.

STEP 1   Press the **STAT** key and select **1:Edit**. Enter the latitudes in column **L1** and the average temperatures in column **L2**.

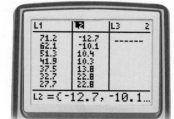

STEP 2   Press **STAT** **PLOT** to create a scatter plot of the data.

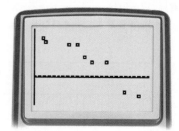

STEP 3 Press **STAT** again and choose **CALC**. From the menu choose **4:LinReg(*ax* + *b*)**. The calculator will display the slope, *a*, and the *y*-intercept, *b*, of the line of best fit. The screen also displays values for the correlation coefficient *r* and r^2.

STEP 4 Round the values for *a* and *b* and write the equation for the best fit line: $y \approx -0.693x + 39.11$.

STEP 5 Press **Y=**, then enter the best fit equation you found in Step 4, then press **GRAPH**. The calculator graphs the line.

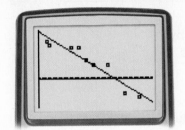

Use the equation to estimate the average temperature in Vancouver, Canada at 49.1° N.

$$y \approx -0.693x + 39.11$$

$$\approx -0.693(49.1) + 39.11 \qquad \textit{Substitute the given value for x.}$$

$$\approx 5.1 \qquad \textit{Solve.}$$

The average temperature in Vancouver should be near 5° C.

> **Math Talk**
> **Mathematical Practices**
>
> Nashville is 5.7° south of Chicago. What estimate would you give for its average temperature?

REFLECT

5. Interpret the slope and *y*-intercept of the equation from the calculator. For each degree of latitude, how does the temperature change?

_____

_____

_____

_____

_____

YOUR TURN

6. Use the equation from Example 1 to estimate the average temperature at Munich, Germany at 48.1° N.

_____

Personal Math Trainer

Online Assessment and Intervention

⊙ my.hrw.com

Follow the steps to evaluate lines of fit for the data set given in the table.
(Explore Activity)

x	1	2	3	6
y (actual)	3	6	4	5
y predicted by $y=\frac{3}{4}x+3$				
Residual				
Squared residual				

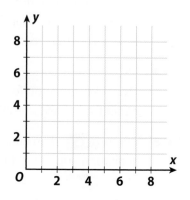

1. Make a scatter plot of the data in the table.

2. Graph the line of fit $y=\frac{3}{4}x+3$ on the scatter plot.

3. Calculate the y-values predicted by $y=\frac{3}{4}x+3$, and write them in the table.

4. Calculate the residuals and squared residuals, and write them in the table.

5. What is the sum of the squares of the residuals for the line

   $y=\frac{3}{4}x+3$? _____

6. Draw a new line of fit on the scatter plot, find its equation, and calculate
   the sum of squared residuals for your line. Which line is a better fit?
   Explain. (Example 1)

   _____

   _____

   _____

7. Use your calculator to find an equation for a line of best fit. (Example 2)

   _____

ESSENTIAL QUESTION CHECK-IN

8. How can you use a graphing calculator to find the line of best fit for a bivariate
   data set?

   _____

   _____

8.3 Independent Practice

FL S-ID.2.6, S-ID.2.6a, S-ID.2.6b, S-ID.2.6c

Personal
Math Trainer

Online
Assessment and
my.hrw.com   Intervention

9. The table gives the distance in meters of the gold medal-winning discus throw between 1920 and 1964. When appropriate, use a graphing calculator to solve the problems below.

Olympic Games year	Gold medal discus throw distance (m)
1920	44.685
1924	46.155
1928	47.32
1932	49.49
1936	50.48
1940	No Olympics
1944	No Olympics
1948	52.78
1952	55.03
1956	56.36
1960	59.18
1964	61.00

a. What are the independent variable and dependent variable in this data set?

_____

_____

b. In which column on the graphing calculator will you represent: years? distance? Write the first 3 entries for each column.

_____

_____

c. Enter your data. What values does the calculator give for the slope, intercept, and correlation coefficient? Write the best fit equation for the data set.

_____

_____

_____

d. Draw a Conclusion How good was the fit of the equation you wrote for this data? Explain.

_____

_____

e. Suppose the Olympics had been held in 1940 and 1944. What distance

would you predict for each year? _____

f. Make a Prediction In the 2012 London Olympics, Robert Harting of Germany took the Gold Medal with a throw of 68.27 m. Was this distance greater or less than the best fit equation would predict? Explain.

_____

_____

Work Area

10. The table shows average test scores for eight different students in history and science.

History	90	70	75	100	90	85	80	90
Science	80	75	72	95	92	82	80	92

a. Make a scatter plot of the data.

b. Use a calculator to find the best fit line. Graph the line, and write its equation here.

_____

c. **Draw Conclusions** How strong is the correlation between a student's test scores in history and a student's test scores in science? Explain.

_____

_____

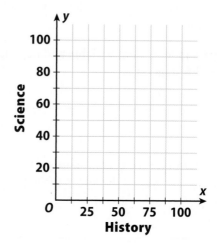

d. Roger's test scores in history were higher than his scores in science. The table shows how long Roger studied for his tests. Do the data support the conclusion that Roger could have scored higher in science if he had studied more? Explain your reasoning.

Test	1	2	3	4	5
History (hours studied)	2.75	3.5	4.00	3.75	5.50
Science (hours studied)	2.25	1.25	1.4	0.75	2.25

_____

_____

_____

_____

_____

_____

_____

Ready to Go On?

Personal
Math Trainer

Online
Assessment and
Intervention

my.hrw.com

8.1 Correlation

Estimate the correlation coefficient for each scatter plot.

1.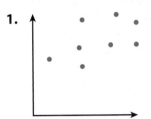

_____

2.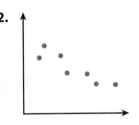

_____

3.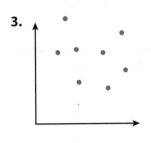

_____

8.2 Fitting Lines to Data

The table gives data for the average salary, in millions of dollars, of players on Major League Baseball teams and the number of wins each team had in 2012.

4. Make a scatter plot of the data.

Team	Salary	Wins
Arizona Diamondbacks	$2.6	81
Toronto Blue Jays	$2.7	73
Milwaukee Brewers	$3.8	83
Detroit Tigers	$4.6	88
Texas Rangers	$4.6	93
Los Angeles Angels	$5.3	89
New York Yankees	$6.2	95

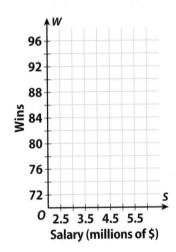

8.3 Linear Regression

5. Use your calculator to find the line of best fit for the data.

Graph the line on the scatter plot. _____

? ESSENTIAL QUESTION

6. How can you use statistical methods to find relationships between variables?

_____

_____

_____

Module 8 Quiz   **271**

Personal
Math Trainer

Online
Assessment and
Intervention

Selected Response

1. Variables x and y have a strong negative correlation. Which of the following is true of the value of y at points x and $x + 1$?

   Ⓐ y at $x + 1 < y$ at x

   Ⓑ y at $x + 1 > y$ at x

   Ⓒ y at $x + 1 = y$ at x

   Ⓓ y at $x + 1 < 0$

2. In which of the following examples is correlation most likely to be due to causation?

   Ⓐ The temperature of water is correlated with the amount of sugar that dissolves in it.

   Ⓑ A full moon is correlated with high rates of crime.

   Ⓒ A new moon is correlated with low rates of crime.

   Ⓓ Use of air conditioning is correlated with the amount of lemonade people drink.

3. Which linear function is its own inverse?

   Ⓐ $y = 3x$ Ⓒ $x + y = 7$

   Ⓑ $x + 2y = 4$ Ⓓ $y = x + 1$

4. What is the equation for a line that passes through points $(10, 4)$ and $(6, -4)$?

   Ⓐ $y = 2x + 4$ Ⓒ $y = 0.5x + 4$

   Ⓑ $y = 0.75x + 16$ Ⓓ $y = 2x - 16$

5. Shandra graphed the points $(2, 6)$, $(3, 3)$, $(4, 5)$, $(5, 2)$ on a coordinate plane. Which equation provides the best fit for the data?

   Ⓐ $y = 3x + 12$ Ⓒ $y = -2x + 12$

   Ⓑ $y = -2x - 12$ Ⓓ $y = -3x + 8$

6. The table shows four data pairs. What is the sum of the squared residuals for the line of fit with equation $y = 3x - 2$?

x	1	2	4	6
y	1.5	3.25	8.5	14.5

   Ⓐ 5.31

   Ⓑ 6.25

   Ⓒ 12.25

   Ⓓ 11.0

Mini-Tasks

7. The table shows the median number of text messages sent per day by people of different ages.

Age	20	30	40	50	60
Number of Texts	50	20	10	6	2

   a. Use your calculator to find the equation for a line of best fit for the data. Write the equation and graph the line on the scatter plot.

   _____

   b. Would it be reasonable to use your model to predict the number of text messages sent by 10-year-olds? Explain.

   _____

   _____

   _____

   _____

   _____

   _____

   _____

Systems of Equations and Inequalities

MODULE **9**

? ESSENTIAL QUESTION

How are the graphs of systems of linear equations and inequalities related to their solutions?

ⓞ my.hrw.com

Real-World Video

A Mars rover is sent into space to land on Mars. This requires planning the trajectory of the rover to intersect with the orbit of Mars. Systems of equations are used to find the intersection of graphs.

GO DIGITAL
my.hrw.com

my.hrw.com

Go digital with your write-in student edition, accessible on any device.

Math On the Spot

Scan with your smart phone to jump directly to the online edition, video tutor, and more.

Animated Math

Interactively explore key concepts to see how math works.

Personal Math Trainer

Get immediate feedback and help as you work through practice sets.

Are YOU Ready?

Complete these exercises to review skills you will need for this module.

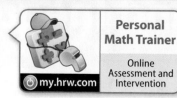

Graph Functions

EXAMPLE Graph $y = 2x - 4$.
  1. Make a table of values.
  2. Plot the ordered pairs.
  3. Draw a line through the points.

x	y
0	−4
2	0
−2	−8

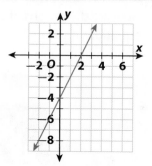

Graph each function.

1. $y = 3x + 6$

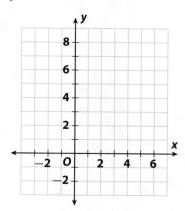

2. $y = -x + 5$

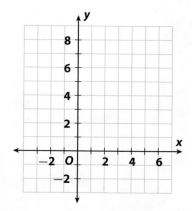

Combine Like Terms

EXAMPLE Simplify $2x + 3 + 3x$.
  $2x + 3x + 3$ Combine like terms.
  $5x + 3$

Simplify each expression.

3. $-4y + (-2y) + 6 - 4$

4. $12x - (-4) - 3x$

5. $9 - 10c + 4c$

6. $9t + (-12t) - 6s + 3s$

7. $-7x - 5y - (-7x) + 2y$

8. $4a + 5b + 3 - (6a + 5b + 8)$

Reading Start-Up

Visualize Vocabulary

Use the ✔ words to complete the chart.

Word	Example
	$y = 2x - 5$
	$y < 2x - 5$
	(x, y)
	$(0, y)$
	$(x, 0)$

Vocabulary

Review Words

  Distributive Property
  (Propiedad distributiva)

✔ linear equation *(ecuación lineal)*

✔ linear inequality *(desigualdad lineal)*

✔ ordered pair *(par ordenado)*

  solution of a linear equation in two variables *(solución de una ecuación lineal en dos variables)*

✔ x-intercept *(intersección con el eje x)*

✔ y-intercept *(intersección con el eje y)*

Preview Words

  elimination method

  solution of a system of linear equations

  solution of a system of linear inequalities

  substitution method

  system of linear equations

Understand Vocabulary

To become familiar with some of the vocabulary terms in the module, read the description and write the term described. You may refer to the module, the glossary, or a dictionary.

1. The word *system* means "a group." How do you think a system of linear equations is different from a linear equation?

_____

_____

2. What does the word eliminate mean? What might the *elimination* method refer to when solving mathematical equations?

_____

_____

3. A solution of a linear equation was the ordered pair that made the equation true. Modify this to define solution of a linear inequality .

_____

Active Reading

Tri-Fold Before beginning the module, create a tri-fold to help you learn the concepts and vocabulary in this module. Fold the paper into three sections. Label the columns "What I Know," "What I Want to Know," and "What I Learned." Complete the first two columns before you read. After studying the module, complete the third column.

Unpacking the Standards

Understanding the standards and the vocabulary terms in the standards will help you know exactly what you are expected to learn in this module.

FL A-REI.3.6

Solve systems of linear equations exactly and approximately (e.g., with graphs), focusing on pairs of linear equations in two variables.

Key Vocabulary

system of linear equations *(sistema de ecuaciones lineales)*
A system of equations in which all of the equations are linear.

What It Means to You

You can solve systems of equations to find out when two relationships involving the same variables are true at the same time.

UNPACKING EXAMPLE A-REI.3.6

Find the solution of the system of equations.

$$\begin{cases} y = 2x - 3 \\ y = -\frac{1}{2}x + 2 \end{cases}$$

The solution of the system is the point (x, y) that satisfies both equations simultaneously. On a graph, it is the point at which the lines intersect, $(2, 1)$.

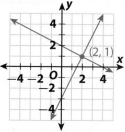

FL A-CED.1.3

Represent constraints by ... inequalities ... and interpret solutions as viable or nonviable options in a modeling context.

Key Vocabulary

inequality *(desigualdad)*
A statement that compares two expressions by using one of the following signs: $<, >, \leq, \geq$, or $\neq$.

solution of an inequality in one variable *(solución de una desigualdad en una variable)*
A value or values that make the inequality true.

What It Means to You

You can use inequalities to represent limits on the values in a situation so that the solutions make sense in a real-world context.

UNPACKING EXAMPLE A-CED.1.3

Anyone riding the large water slide at a the park must be at least 40 inches tall.

Let h represent a person's height.

Height is at least 40 inches.
$$h \qquad \geq \qquad 40$$

Visit **my.hrw.com** to see all **Florida Math Standards** unpacked.

my.hrw.com

Solving Linear Systems by Graphing

FL A-REI.3.6

Solve systems of linear equations exactly and approximately (e.g., with graphs), focusing on pairs of linear equations in two variables. *Also A-CED.1.3*

ESSENTIAL QUESTION

How can you find the solution of a system of linear equations by graphing?

Solving a Linear System by Graphing

A **system of linear equations,** also called a *linear system*, consists of two or more linear equations that have the same variables. A **solution of a system of linear equations** with two variables is an ordered pair that satisfies all of the equations in the system. The values of the variables in the ordered pair make each equation in the system true.

Math On the Spot
my.hrw.com

Systems of linear equations can be solved by graphing and by using algebraic methods. In this lesson you will learn to solve linear systems by graphing the equations in the system and analyzing how those graphs are related.

EXAMPLE 1

FL A-REI.3.6

Solve the system of linear equations below by graphing. Check your answer.

$$\begin{cases} -x + y = 3 \\ 2x + y = 6 \end{cases}$$

STEP 1 Find the intercepts for each equation, plus a third point for a check. Graph each line.

$-x + y = 3$ $\qquad$ $2x + y = 6$

x-intercept: -3 $\qquad$ x-intercept: 3

y-intercept: 3 $\qquad$ y-intercept: 6

third point: $(3, 6)$ $\quad$ third point: $(-1, 8)$

STEP 2 Find the point of intersection.

The two lines appear to intersect at $(1, 4)$.

STEP 3 Check to see if $(1, 4)$ makes both equations true.

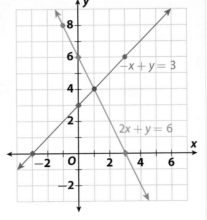

$-x + y = 3$ $\qquad$ $2x + y = 6$

$-(1) + 4 \overset{?}{=} 3$ $\qquad$ $2(1) + 4 \overset{?}{=} 6$

$3 = 3 \checkmark$ $\qquad\qquad$ $6 = 6 \checkmark$

The solution is $(1, 4)$.

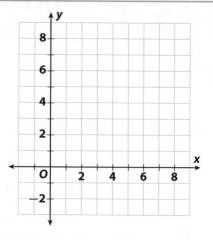

YOUR TURN

1. Solve the system of linear equations below by graphing. Check your answer.
    $$\begin{cases} x + y = 8 \\ x - y = 2 \end{cases}$$

    Solution: _____

Special Systems of Linear Equations

When a system of equations consists of two lines that intersect in one point, as shown in Figure 1 below, there is exactly one solution to the system.

If two linear equations in a system have the same graph, as shown in Figure 2, the graphs are coincident lines, or the same line. There are infinitely many solutions of the system because every point on the line represents a solution of both equations.

A system with at least one solution is a consistent system. Consistent systems can either be independent or dependent.

- An independent system has exactly one solution. The graph of an independent system consists of two intersecting lines.
- A dependent system has infinitely many solutions. The graph of a dependent system consists of two coincident lines.

When the two lines in a system do not intersect, as shown in Figure 3, they are parallel lines. There are no ordered pairs that satisfy both equations, so there is no solution. A system that has no solution is an inconsistent system.

The table below summarizes how systems of linear equations can be classified.

Classification of Systems of Linear Equations			
Classification	**Consistent and Independent**	**Consistent and Dependent**	**Inconsistent**
Number of Solutions	Exactly one	Infinitely many	None
Description	Different slopes	Same slope, same y-intercept	Same slope, different y-intercepts
Graph	Figure 1	Figure 2	Figure 3

EXAMPLE 2

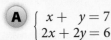

FL A-REI.3.6

Use the graph to solve each system of linear equations. Classify each system.

A $\begin{cases} x + y = 7 \\ 2x + 2y = 6 \end{cases}$

The lines do not intersect and appear to be parallel lines.

This system has no solution. The system is inconsistent.

B $\begin{cases} 2x + 2y = 6 \\ x + y = 3 \end{cases}$

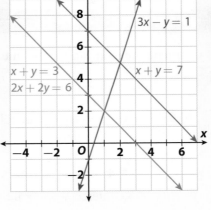

The equations have the same graph, so the graphs are coincident lines.

This system has infinitely many solutions. The system is consistent and dependent.

REFLECT

2. Use the graph above to identify two lines that represent a linear system with exactly one solution. What are the equations of the lines? Explain your reasoning.

_____

_____

Math Talk
Mathematical Practices

Why is the greatest possible number of solutions one for a system of linear equations whose graph shows two distinct lines?

YOUR TURN

Graph each system of linear equations. Classify each system.

3. $\begin{cases} 2x + 2y = 8 \\ x - y = 4 \end{cases}$

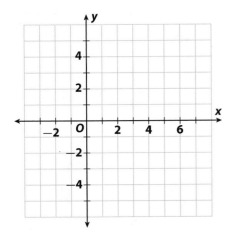

_____

_____

4. $\begin{cases} y = 2x - 4 \\ y = 2x + 6 \end{cases}$

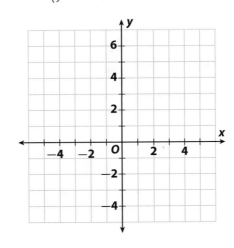

_____

_____

Personal Math Trainer

Online Assessment and Intervention

⊙ my.hrw.com

Estimating a Solution by Graphing

You can estimate a solution for a linear system by graphing and then check your estimate to determine if it is an approximate solution.

 EXAMPLE 3  FL A-REI.3.6

Estimate the solution for the linear system by graphing.

$$\begin{cases} x + 2y = 2 \\ 2x - 3y = 12 \end{cases}$$

STEP 1 Graph each equation by finding intercepts.

$x + 2y = 2$	$2x - 3y = 12$
x-intercept: 2	x-intercept: 6
y-intercept: 1	y-intercept: -4

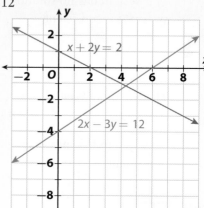

STEP 2 Find the point of intersection.

The two lines appear to intersect at about $\left(4\frac{1}{4}, -1\frac{1}{8}\right)$.

STEP 3 Check if $\left(4\frac{1}{4}, -1\frac{1}{8}\right)$ is an approximate solution.

$$x + 2y = 2 \qquad\qquad 2x - 3y = 12$$

$$4\frac{1}{4} + 2\left(-1\frac{1}{8}\right) \overset{?}{=} 2 \qquad 2\left(4\frac{1}{4}\right) - 3\left(-1\frac{1}{8}\right) \overset{?}{=} 12$$

$$4\frac{1}{4} + \left(-2\frac{1}{4}\right) \overset{?}{=} 2 \qquad\qquad 8\frac{1}{2} - \left(-3\frac{3}{8}\right) \overset{?}{=} 12$$

$$2 = 2 \checkmark \qquad\qquad\qquad 11\frac{7}{8} \approx 12 \checkmark$$

The point $\left(4\frac{1}{4}, -1\frac{1}{8}\right)$ does not make both equations true, but it is acceptable since $11\frac{7}{8}$ is close to 12. So, $\left(4\frac{1}{4}, -1\frac{1}{8}\right)$ is an approximate solution.

YOUR TURN

5. Estimate the solution for the linear system by graphing.

$$\begin{cases} x - y = 3 \\ x + 2y = 4 \end{cases}$$

Approximate solution:

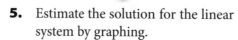

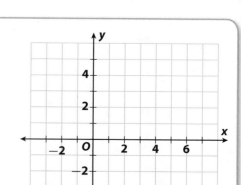

Guided Practice

Solve the system of linear equations by graphing. Check your answer. (Example 1)

1. $\begin{cases} x - y = 7 \\ 2x + y = 2 \end{cases}$

$x - y = 7$

x-intercept: _____

y-intercept: _____

$2x + y = 2$

x-intercept: _____

y-intercept: _____

The solution of the system is _____.

Does your solution check in both original equations? _____

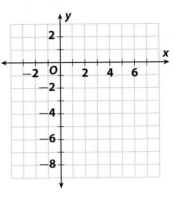

Use the graph to solve and classify each system of linear equations. (Example 2)

2. $\begin{cases} x + y = -1 \\ -2x + 2y = -2 \end{cases}$

Is the system consistent?

_____

Is the system independent?

_____

Solution: _____

3. $\begin{cases} -x + y = 3 \\ -2x + 2y = -2 \end{cases}$

Is the system consistent?

_____

Solution: _____

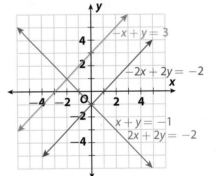

Estimate the solution for the system of linear equations by graphing. (Example 3)

4. $\begin{cases} x + y = -1 \\ 2x - y = 5 \end{cases}$

$x + y = -1$

x-intercept: _____

y-intercept: _____

$2x - y = 5$

x-intercept: _____

y-intercept: _____

The two lines appear to intersect at

_____.

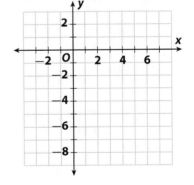

? ESSENTIAL QUESTION CHECK-IN

5. How does graphing help you solve a system of linear equations?

_____

_____

_____

9.1 Independent Practice

Personal Math Trainer

Online Assessment and Intervention

my.hrw.com

FL A-REI.3.6, A-CED.1.3

Solve each system of linear equations by graphing. Check your answer.

6. $\begin{cases} x - y = -2 \\ 2x + y = 8 \end{cases}$

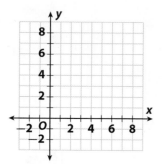

Solution: _____

7. $\begin{cases} x - y = -5 \\ 2x + 4y = -4 \end{cases}$

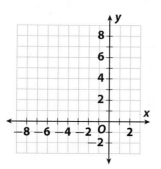

Solution: _____

8. $\begin{cases} x + 2y = -8 \\ -2x - 4y = 4 \end{cases}$

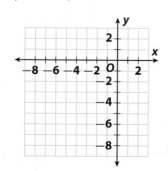

Solution: _____

Estimate the solution for the linear system by graphing.

9. $\begin{cases} x + y = 5 \\ x - 3y = 3 \end{cases}$

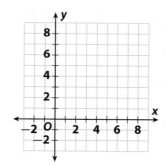

Approximate solution: _____

Graph each system. Then classify it as *consistent and independent*, *consistent and dependent*, or *inconsistent*.

10. $\begin{cases} x + 2y = 6 \\ x = 2 \end{cases}$

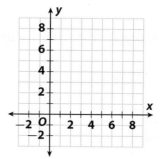

_____

11. $\begin{cases} 2x - y = -6 \\ 4x - 2y = -12 \end{cases}$

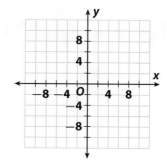

_____

12. Use the graphed system below to find an approximate solution. Then write a system of equations that represents the system.

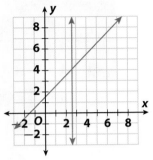

_____

_____

13. Communicate Mathematical Ideas When a system of linear equations is graphed, how is the graph of each equation related to the solutions of that equation?

_____

_____

_____

_____

_____

14. Critical Thinking Write *sometimes*, *always*, or *never* to complete the following statement:

If the equations in a system of linear equations have the same slope, there are _____ infinitely many solutions for the system.

_____

15. Suppose you use the graph of a system of linear equations to estimate the solution. Explain how you would check your estimate to determine if it is an approximate solution.

_____

_____

_____

_____

_____

_____

16. Without graphing, describe the graph of this linear system of equations.

$$\begin{cases} x = 3 \\ y = 4 \end{cases}$$

What is the solution of the linear system?

_____

_____

_____

_____

_____

_____

17. How can you recognize a dependent system of equations by analyzing the equations in the

system? _____

_____

_____

18. How would you classify a system of equations whose graph is composed of two lines with different slopes and the same y-intercepts? What is the solution to the system?

_____

_____

_____

19. Sophie and Marcos are each saving for new bicycles. So far, Sophie has $10 saved and can earn $5 per hour walking dogs. Marcos has $4 saved and can earn $8 per hour at his family's plant nursery. After how many hours of work will Sophie and Marcos have saved the same amount? What will that amount be? Use the system of equations below to complete the graph.

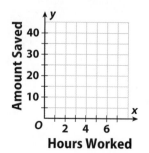

Sophie: $y = 5x + 10$

Marcos: $y = 8x + 4$

_____

20. **Represent Real-World Problems** Cora ran 1 mile last week and will run 7 miles per week from now on. Hana ran 2 miles last week and will run 4 miles per week from now on. The system of linear equations $\begin{cases} y = 7x + 1 \\ y = 4x + 2 \end{cases}$ can be used to represent this situation. Explain what x and y represent in the equations.

_____

_____

_____

FOCUS ON HIGHER ORDER THINKING

Work Area

21. **Explain the Error** Jake was asked to give an example of an inconsistent system of linear equations. He wrote the system shown below. Explain Jake's error.

$$\begin{cases} y = 2x - 4 \\ y = x - 4 \end{cases}$$

_____

_____

_____

22. **Draw Conclusions** The equations in a system of linear equations have different slopes and the same y-intercept. Can you find the solution without graphing? Explain.

_____

_____

_____

_____

Solving Linear Systems by Substitution

FL A-REI.3.6

Solve systems of linear equations exactly and approximately (e.g., with graphs), focusing on pairs of linear equations in two variables. *Also A-CED.1.3*

ESSENTIAL QUESTION

How can you solve a system of linear equations by using substitution?

EXPLORE ACTIVITY   FL   A-REI.3.6

Solve by Substituting

In the system of linear equations shown below, the value of y is given. You can use this value of y to find the value of x and the solution of the system.

$$\begin{cases} y = 3 \\ x + y = 5 \end{cases}$$

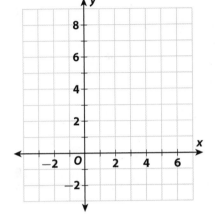

A Substitute the value for y in the second equation and solve for x.

$$x + y = 5$$

$$x + \boxed{} = 5$$

$$x = \boxed{}$$

B You know the values of x and y. What is the solution of the system?

Solution: ($\boxed{}$, $\boxed{}$)

C Graph the system of linear equations. How do your solutions compare?

_____

D Use substitution to find the values of x and y in this system of linear equations. Once you find the value for x, substitute it either original equation to find the value for y.

$$\begin{cases} y = 2x \\ 2x + 3y = 40 \end{cases}$$

Solution: ($\boxed{}$, $\boxed{}$)

REFLECT

1. For the system in part D, what equation did you get after substituting $2x$ for y in $2x + 3y = 40$ and simplifying?

_____

2. How could you check your solution in part D?

_____

_____

Solve a Linear System by Substitution

The **substitution method** is used to solve systems of linear equations by solving an equation for one variable and then substituting the resulting expression for that variable into the other equation. The steps for this method are as follows:

1. Solve one of the equations for one of its variables.

2. Substitute the expression from Step 1 into the other equation and solve for the other variable.

3. Substitute the value from Step 2 into either original equation and solve to find the value of the variable in Step 1.

EXAMPLE 1

 FL A-REI.3.6

My Notes

Solve the system of linear equations by substitution. Check your answer.

$$\begin{cases} -3x + y = 1 \\ 4x + y = 8 \end{cases}$$

STEP 1 Solve an equation for one variable.

$-3x + y = 1$ *Select one of the equations.*
$y = 3x + 1$ *Solve for the variable y. Isolate y on one side.*

STEP 2 Substitute the expression for y in the other equation and solve.

$4x + 3x + 1 = 8$ *Substitute the expression for the variable y.*
$7x + 1 = 8$ *Combine like terms.*
$7x = 7$ *Subtract 1 from each side.*
$x = 1$ *Divide each side by 7.*

STEP 3 Substitute the value of x you found into one of the equations and solve for the other variable, y.

$-3(1) + y = 1$ *Substitute the value of x into the first equation.*
$-3 + y = 1$ *Simplify.*
$y = 4$ *Add 3 to each side.*

So, (1, 4) is the solution of the system.

STEP 4 Check the solution by graphing.

$-3x + y = 1$ $4x + y = 8$
x-intercept: $-\frac{1}{3}$ x-intercept: 2
y-intercept: 1 y-intercept: 8

The point of intersection is (1, 4).

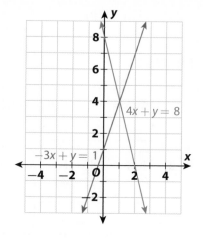

REFLECT

3. **Justify Reasoning** Is it more efficient to solve $-3x + y = 1$ for x? Why or why not?

_____

_____

4. What is another way to check your solution?

_____

_____

 YOUR TURN

Solve each system of linear equations by substitution. Check your answer.

5. $\begin{cases} 2x + y = 5 \\ \quad\ y = x - 4 \end{cases}$

Solution: _____

6. $\begin{cases} \quad\ x + 3y = 4 \\ -x + 2y = 6 \end{cases}$

Solution: _____

Solving Special Systems by Substitution

You can use the substitution method for systems of linear equations that have infinitely many solutions and for systems that have no solutions.

EXAMPLE 2

FL   A-REI.3.6

Solve each system of linear equations by substitution.

A $\begin{cases} \quad\ x - y = -2 \\ -x + y = 4 \end{cases}$

STEP 1 Solve $x - y = -2$ for x: $x = y - 2$

STEP 2 Substitute the resulting expression into the other equation and solve.

$-(y - 2) + y = 4$ Substitute.

$2 \neq 4$ Simplify.

The resulting equation is false, so the system has no solutions.

STEP 3 Graph the equations to provide more information.

The graph shows that the lines are parallel and do not intersect.

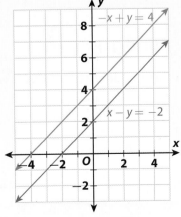

B $\begin{cases} 2x + y = -2 \\ 4x + 2y = -4 \end{cases}$

STEP 1 Solve $2x + y = -2$ for y: $\qquad y = -2x - 2$

STEP 2 Substitute the resulting expression into the other equation and solve.

$4x + 2(-2x - 2) = -4$ Substitute.

$\qquad 4x - 4x - 4 = -4$ Use the Distributive Property.

$\qquad\qquad\quad -4 = -4$ Simplify.

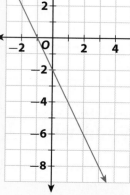

The resulting equation is true so the system has infinitely many solutions.

STEP 3 Graph the equations to provide more information.

The graphs are the same line, so the system has infinitely many solutions.

REFLECT

7. In part B of Example 2, why is it more efficient to solve and substitute for y than to solve and substitute for x?

_____

_____

_____

8. Give two possible solutions of the system in part B of Example 2. How are all the solutions of this system related to one another?

_____

_____

_____

Personal Math Trainer

Online Assessment and Intervention

ⓞ my.hrw.com

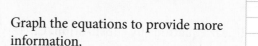

YOUR TURN

Solve each system of linear equations by substitution.

9. $\begin{cases} x + 3y = 6 \\ 2x + 6y = 12 \end{cases}$

Solution: _____

_____

10. $\begin{cases} 2x - y = -1 \\ 2x - y = -4 \end{cases}$

Solution: _____

_____

Modeling with Linear Systems

You can use a system of linear equations and its graph to model many real-world situations.

EXAMPLE 3 Real World   FL A-REI.3.6, A-CED.1.3

One family fitness center has a $50 enrollment fee and costs $30 per month. Another center has no enrollment fee and costs $40 per month. In how many months will both fitness centers cost the same? What will that cost be? Write an equation for each option. Let t represent the total amount paid and m represent the number of months.

	Total cost	is	**enrollment fee**	plus	cost per month	times	months.
Option 1	t	$=$	50	$+$	30	$\cdot$	m
Option 2	t	$=$	0	$+$	40	$\cdot$	m

STEP 1 $t = 50 + 30m$ *Write the system of equations.*
         $t = 40m$

STEP 2 $50 + 30m = 40m$ *Substitute $50 + 30m$ for t in the second equation.*

         $\underline{-30m \quad -30m}$ *Subtract $30m$ from each side.*
             $50 = 10m$

         $\dfrac{50}{10} = \dfrac{10m}{10}$ *Divide each side by 10.*

             $5 = m$

STEP 3 $t = 40m$ *Write one of the original equations.*
           $= 40(5)$ *Substitute 5 for m.*
           $= 200$

STEP 4 $(5, 200)$ *Write the solution as an ordered pair.*

In 5 months, the total cost for each option will be the same, $200.

> **Math Talk**
> **Mathematical Practices**
>
> In a graph of the system of equations, why must the values of the variables be greater than or equal to zero?

YOUR TURN

11. One high-speed Internet provider has a $30 setup fee and charges $40 per month. Another provider has a $60 setup fee and charges $30 per month. In how many months will the cost be the same?

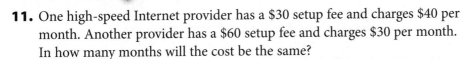

Personal Math Trainer

Online Assessment and Intervention

my.hrw.com

Solve each system of linear equations by substitution. Check your answer. (Examples 1 and 2)

1. $\begin{cases} y = x + 5 \\ 4x + y = 20 \end{cases}$

STEP 1 Find the value of x.

$$4x + y = 20$$

$$4x + \boxed{} = 20$$

$$\boxed{}x = \boxed{}$$

$$x = \boxed{}$$

STEP 2 Find the value of y.

$$y = x + 5$$

$$y = \boxed{} + 5$$

$$y = \boxed{}$$

Solution: _____

2. $\begin{cases} x + 2y = 6 \\ 2x + 4y = 12 \end{cases}$

STEP 1 Solve $x + 2y = 6$ for x.

$$x = \boxed{}$$

STEP 2 Substitute that expression for x into $2x + 4y = 12$.

$$2(\boxed{}) + 4y = 12$$

$$\boxed{} - \boxed{}y + \boxed{}y = 12$$

$$\boxed{} = 12$$

Solution: _____

_____

Solve each system of linear equations by substitution. Check your answer. (Examples 1 and 2)

3. $\begin{cases} x + 2y = 7 \\ 4x + 3y = 3 \end{cases}$

Solution: _____

4. $\begin{cases} 2x - y = -4 \\ 2x - 2y = -10 \end{cases}$

Solution: _____

5. $\begin{cases} y = 2x \\ y = 3x - 3 \end{cases}$

Solution: _____

6. The Blanco family is deciding between two lawn-care services. Evergreen charges a $49 startup fee, plus $29 per month. Great Grass charges a $25 startup fee, plus $37 per month. In how many months will both lawn-care services cost the same? What will that cost be? (Example 3)

_____

? **ESSENTIAL QUESTION CHECK-IN**

7. Explain how you can solve a system of linear equations by substitution.

_____

_____

_____

_____

9.2 Independent Practice

FL A-REI.3.6, A-CED.1.3

Personal
Math Trainer

Online
Assessment and
Intervention

my.hrw.com

For each linear system, tell whether it is more efficient to solve for x and then substitute for x or to solve for y and then substitute for y. Explain your reasoning. Then solve the system.

8. $\begin{cases} 6x - 3y = 15 \\ x + 3y = -8 \end{cases}$

_____

_____

_____

_____

Solution: _____

9. $\begin{cases} 3x - y = -1 \\ 5x - y = 3 \end{cases}$

_____

_____

_____

Solution: _____

For each system of linear equations, write the expression you could substitute for x. Then solve the system.

10. $\begin{cases} 2x - y = 6 \\ x + y = -3 \end{cases}$

_____

Solution: _____

11. $\begin{cases} x - 2y = 0 \\ 4x - 3y = 15 \end{cases}$

_____

Solution: _____

12. **Communicate Mathematical Ideas** The solution of a system of two linear equations yields the equation $0 = 3$. Describe what the graph of the system looks like.

_____

_____

_____

13. Use *one solution, no solutions,* or *infinitely many solutions* to complete this statement.

When the solution of a system of linear equations yields the equation $4 = 6$, the system has _____.

_____

14. **Represent Real-World Problems** Ella buys a book and a pen for $14. The cost of the book is $2 more than twice the cost of the pen. Write a system of linear equations for the situation. Then find the cost of each item. Let x represent the cost of the pen, and let y represent the cost of the book.

_____

_____

_____

15. **Interpret the Answer** The perimeter of a rectangular picture frame is 66 inches. The length is 3 inches greater than the width. The system of linear equations used to represent the situation is shown below.

$\begin{cases} 2x + 2y = 66 \\ x + 3 = y \end{cases}$

Name the dimension represented by each variable.

_____

_____

16. Kim and Leon exercise a total of 20 hours each week. Leon exercises 2 hours less than 3 times the number of hours Kim exercises. How many hours does each exercise?

_____

17. Multi-Step Use the receipts below to write and solve a system of linear equations to find the cost of a large popcorn bucket and the cost of a small drink.

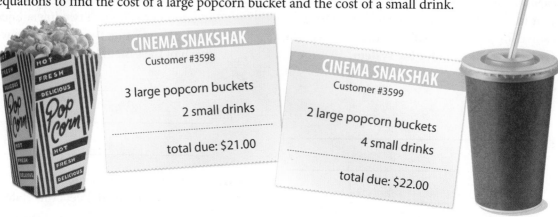

CINEMA SNAKSHAK
Customer #3598

3 large popcorn buckets
2 small drinks

total due: $21.00

CINEMA SNAKSHAK
Customer #3599

2 large popcorn buckets
4 small drinks

total due: $22.00

_____

_____

 FOCUS ON HIGHER ORDER THINKING

Work Area

18. Multiple Representations For the first equation in the system of linear equations below, write an equivalent equation without denominators. Then solve the system.

$$\begin{cases} \dfrac{x}{2} + \dfrac{y}{3} = 6 \\ x - y = 2 \end{cases}$$

_____

19. Critical Thinking Is it possible for a system of three linear equations to have one solution? If so, give an example.

_____

_____

_____

_____

20. Draw Conclusions Solve the system of linear equations below. What does the solution tell you about the graph of the system?

$$\begin{cases} x - 2y = -4 \\ 4y = 2x + 8 \end{cases}$$

_____

_____

Solving Linear Systems by Adding or Subtracting

FL A-REI.3.6
Solve systems of linear equations exactly and approximately (e.g., with graphs), focusing on pairs of linear equations in two variables. Also A-CED.1.3

ESSENTIAL QUESTION

How can you solve a system of linear equations by using addition and subtraction?

EXPLORE ACTIVITY

FL A-REI.3.6

Exploring the Effects: Adding Equations

Remember that the sum of a number and its opposite is zero. You can use that fact to help you solve some systems of linear equations.

A Look at the system of linear equations below.

$$\begin{cases} x - 3y = -15 \\ 5x + 3y = -3 \end{cases}$$

What do you notice about the coefficients of the y-terms.

_____

B What is the sum of $-3y$ and $3y$? How do you know?

_____

C Find the sum of the two equations by combining like terms.

$$\begin{array}{rrr} x & -3y & = -15 \\ +5x & +3y & = \underline{-3} \end{array}$$

$$\boxed{} + \boxed{} = \boxed{}$$

D Use the resulting equation from part C to find the value of x.

$$x = \boxed{}$$

E Use the value of x to find the value of y. What is the solution of the system?

$$y = \boxed{}$$ Solution: _____

REFLECT

1. When you add $5x + 3y$ to $x - 3y$ and add -3 to -15, how do you know that the resulting sums are equal?

_____

_____

_____

EXPLORE ACTIVITY *(cont'd)*

2. How could you check your solution in part E?

_____

_____

Math On the Spot
my.hrw.com

Solving a Linear System by Adding or Subtracting

The **elimination method** is another method used to solve a system of linear equations. In this method, one variable is *eliminated* by adding or subtracting the two equations of the system to obtain a single equation in one variable. The steps for this method are as follows:

1. Add or subtract the equations to eliminate one variable, and then solve for the other variable.

2. Substitute the value into either original equation to find the value of the eliminated variable.

3. Write the solution as an ordered pair.

EXAMPLE 1
 FL A-REI.3.6

Solve each system of linear equations using the indicated method. Check your answer.

 A Solve the system of linear equations below by adding.

$$\begin{cases} 4x - 2y = 12 \\ x + 2y = 8 \end{cases}$$

STEP 1 Add the equations.

$4x - 2y = 12$ Write the equations so that like terms are aligned.

$\underline{+\ x + 2y = 8}$ Notice that the terms $-2y$ and $2y$ are opposites.

$5x + 0 = 20$ Add to eliminate the variable y.

$5x = 20$ Simplify.

$x = 4$ Divide each side by 5.

STEP 2 Substitute the value of x into one of the equations and solve for y.

$x + 2y = 8$ Use the second equation.

$4 + 2y = 8$ Substitute 4 for the variable x.

$2y = 4$ Subtract 4 from each side.

$y = 2$ Divide each side by 2.

My Notes

STEP 3 Write the solution as an ordered pair.

$(4, 2)$ is the solution of the system.

STEP 4 Check the solution by graphing.

$4x - 2y = 12$ $x + 2y = 8$

x-intercept: 3 x-intercept: 8

y-intercept: -6 y-intercept: 4

The point of intersection is $(4, 2)$.

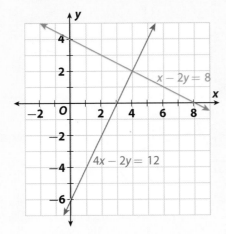

B Solve the system of linear equations below by subtracting.

$$\begin{cases} 2x + 6y = 6 \\ 2x - y = -8 \end{cases}$$

STEP 1 Subtract the equations.

$2x + 6y = 6$ Write the equations so that like terms are aligned.

$\underline{-(2x - y = -8)}$ Notice that both equations contain the term $2x$.

$0 + 7y = 14$ Subtract to eliminate the variable x.

$7y = 14$ Simplify.

$\dfrac{7y}{7} = \dfrac{14}{7}$ Divide each side by 7.

$y = 2$ Simplify.

STEP 2 Substitute the value of y into one of the equations and solve for x.

$2x - y = -8$ Use the second equation.

$2x - 2 = -8$ Substitute 2 for the variable y.

$2x = -6$ Add 2 to each side.

$x = -3$ Divide each side by 2.

STEP 3 Write the solution as an ordered pair.

$(-3, 2)$ is the solution of the system.

STEP 4 Check the solution by graphing.

$$2x + 6y = 6 \qquad 2x - y = -8$$

x-intercept: 3 x-intercept: -4

y-intercept: 1 y-intercept: 8

The point of intersection is $(-3, 2)$.

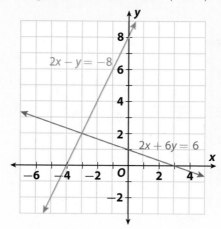

REFLECT

3. Draw Conclusions Can the system in part A be solved by subtracting one of the original equations from the other? Why or why not?

_____

_____

4. What If? In part B, what would happen if you added the original equations instead of subtracted?

_____

_____

_____

5. Justify Reasoning How can you decide whether to add or subtract to eliminate a variable in a linear system? Explain your reasoning.

_____

_____

_____

_____

YOUR TURN

Solve each system of linear equations by adding or subtracting.

6. $\begin{cases} 2x + 5y = -24 \\ 3x - 5y = 14 \end{cases}$

Solution: _____

7. $\begin{cases} 3x + 2y = 10 \\ 3x - y = 22 \end{cases}$

Solution: _____

8. $\begin{cases} 3x + 2y = 5 \\ x + 2y = -1 \end{cases}$

Solution: _____

9. $\begin{cases} 3x - y = -2 \\ -2x + y = 3 \end{cases}$

Solution: _____

Solving Special Systems

You can use the elimination method for systems of linear equations that have infinitely many solutions and for systems that have no solutions.

EXAMPLE 2 FL A-REI.3.6

Solve each system of linear equations by adding or subtracting.

A $\begin{cases} -4x - 2y = 4 \\ 4x + 2y = -4 \end{cases}$

STEP 1 Add the equations.

$$\begin{array}{r} -4x - 2y = 4 \\ +4x + 2y = -4 \\ \hline 0 + 0 = 0 \\ 0 = 0 \end{array}$$

Notice that the terms $-4x$ and $4x$ and $-2y$ and $2y$ are opposites.

Add to eliminate the variables.

Simplify.

The resulting equation is true so the system has infinitely many solutions.

STEP 2 Graph the equations to provide more information.

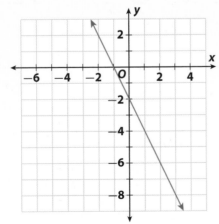

The graphs are the same line, so the system has infinitely many solutions.

$$\textcircled{B} \quad \begin{cases} x + y = -2 \\ x + y = 4 \end{cases}$$

STEP 1 Subtract the equations.

$$x + y = -2 \qquad \text{\textit{Write the equations so that like terms are aligned.}}$$

$$\underline{-(x + y) = -(4)} \qquad \text{\textit{Notice that both equations contain the terms } x \text{ and } y.}$$

$$0 + 0 = -6 \qquad \text{\textit{Subtract to eliminate the variables.}}$$

$$0 = -6 \qquad \text{\textit{Simplify.}}$$

The resulting equation is false, so the system has no solutions.

STEP 2 Graph the equations to provide more information.

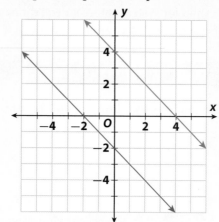

The graph shows that the lines are parallel and do not intersect.

Math Talk
Mathematical Practices

When a linear system has no solution, what happens when you try to solve the system by adding or subtracting?

REFLECT

10. Communicate Mathematical Ideas Suppose you solve a system of linear equations in which both variables are eliminated by subtraction. What is the solution of your system?

_____

_____

_____

YOUR TURN

Personal Math Trainer

Online Assessment and Intervention

my.hrw.com

Solve each system of linear equations by adding or subtracting.

11. $\begin{cases} 4x - y = 3 \\ 4x - y = -2 \end{cases}$

Solution: _____

_____

12. $\begin{cases} x - 6y = 7 \\ -x + 6y = -7 \end{cases}$

Solution: _____

_____

Modeling with Linear Systems

Some real-world situations can be modeled with systems of equations that can be solved by the elimination method.

Math On the Spot
my.hrw.com

EXAMPLE 3   FL A-REI.3.6, A-CED.1.3

Best Backyards is building a rectangular deck for a customer. The customer wants the perimeter to be 40 meters and the difference between twice the length and twice the width to be 4 meters. What will be the length and width of the deck?

Write an equation for each requirement.

Let l represent the length and w represent the width.

Perimeter:	Twice the length	plus	twice the width	is	40
	$2l$	$+$	$2w$	$=$	40

Difference:	Twice the length	minus	twice the width	is	4
	$2l$	$-$	$2w$	$=$	4

STEP 1 Add the equations.

$$2l + 2w = 40$$ Align like terms. Notice that the terms $2w$ and $-2w$ are opposites.

$$\underline{2l - 2w = 4}$$

$$4l + 0 \;\; = 44$$ Add to eliminate the variable w.

$$4l = 44$$ Simplify.

$$l = 11$$ Divide each side by 4.

STEP 2 Substitute the value of l into one of the equations and solve for w.

$$2l + 2w = 40$$ Use the first equation.

$$2(11) + 2w = 40$$ Substitute 11 for the variable l.

$$22 + 2w = 40$$ Simplify.

$$2w = 18$$ Subtract 22 from each side.

$$w = 9$$ Divide each side by 2.

STEP 3 Write the solution as an ordered pair.

$(l, w) = (11, 9)$ is the solution of the system.

The length of the deck will be 11 meters, and the width will be 9 meters.

YOUR TURN

13. Movies and More is having a one-day sale on certain movie DVDs and video games. You can buy 3 DVDs and 2 video games for $74. Or you can buy 5 DVDs and 2 video games for $98. Write and solve a system of equations to find the cost of one DVD and the cost of one video game.

_____

Guided Practice

Solve each system of linear equations by adding or subtracting. Check your answer. (Examples 1 and 2)

1. $\begin{cases} -5x + y = -3 \\ 5x - 3y = -1 \end{cases}$

STEP 1   Add the equations. Find the value of y.

$$-5x + y = -3$$
$$+5x - 3y = -1$$

$\boxed{} + \boxed{} = \boxed{}$

$y = \boxed{}$

STEP 2   Find the value of x.

$$-5x + y = -3$$

$-5x + \boxed{} = -3$

$-5x = \boxed{}$

$x = \boxed{}$

Solution: _____

2. $\begin{cases} 2x + y = -6 \\ -5x + y = 8 \end{cases}$

Solution: _____

3. $\begin{cases} 6x - 3y = 15 \\ 4x - 3y = -5 \end{cases}$

Solution: _____

4. $\begin{cases} -5x - y = -3 \\ -5x - y = -2 \end{cases}$

Solution: _____

5. A picture frame has a perimeter of 62 inches. The difference between the length and twice the width is 1 inch. What are the length and width of the frame? (Example 3)

_____

?   **ESSENTIAL QUESTION CHECK-IN**

6. When you solve a system of linear equations by adding or subtracting, what needs to be true about the variable terms in the equations?

_____

_____

9.3 Independent Practice

FL A-REI.3.6, A-CED.1.3

7. The sum of two numbers is 65. The difference of the two numbers is 27. Write and solve a system of linear equations to find the two numbers. Let x represent the greater number, and let y represent the lesser number.

System: _____

Greater number: _____

Lesser number: _____

8. The sum of the digits in a two-digit number is 12. The tens digit is 2 more than the ones digit. Write and solve a system of linear equations to find the number. Let x represent the tens digit, and let y represent the ones digit.

System: _____

Number: _____

9. **Justify Reasoning** Solve the system of equations below by substitution and by elimination.

$$\begin{cases} x + y = -4 \\ 2x + y = -3 \end{cases}$$

Which method do you prefer? Explain your reasoning.

Solution: _____

_____

_____

_____

10. Can you solve this system of linear equations by adding or subtracting? Why or why not?

$$\begin{cases} x + 2y = 7 \\ 4x + 3y = 3 \end{cases}$$

_____

_____

11. **Draw Conclusions** Use addition or subtraction to find the solution of the system below. What does the solution tell you about the graph of the solution of this system?

$$\begin{cases} x + y = 5 \\ x - 3y = 3 \end{cases}$$

Solution: _____

_____

_____

_____

12. A garden has a perimeter of 120 feet. The difference between the length and twice the width is 24 feet. Write a system of linear equations that represents this situation. Then solve the system to find the length and width of the garden.

System: _____

Length: _____

Width: _____

13. The sum of two angles is 90°. The difference between twice the larger angle and the smaller angle is 105°. Write a system of linear equations that represents this situation. Then solve the system to find the measures of the two angles.

System: _____

Larger angle: _____

Smaller angle: _____

14. Use *one solution, no solutions,* or *infinitely many solutions* to complete this statement.

When the solution of a system of linear equations yields the equation $4 = 4$, the

system has _____ .

15. **Multi-step** For a school play, Ricco bought 3 adult tickets and 5 child tickets for $40. Sasha bought 1 adult ticket and 5 child tickets for $25. Find the cost of an adult ticket and the cost of a child ticket. Then find how much Julia will pay for 5 adult tickets and 3 child tickets.

_____

_____

16. Bright Pools is building a rectangular pool at a new house. The perimeter of the pool has to be 94 feet, and the length has to be 2 feet more than twice the width.

    What will be the length and width of the pool?

    _____

 **FOCUS ON HIGHER ORDER THINKING**

Work Area

17. **Multiple Representations** You can use subtraction to solve the system of linear equations shown below.

$$\begin{cases} 2x + 4y = -4 \\ 2x - 2y = -10 \end{cases}$$

    Instead of subtracting $2x - 2y = -10$ from $2x + 4y = -4$, what equation can you add to get the same result? Explain.

    _____

    _____

18. **Explain the Error** Liang's solution of a system of linear equations is shown below.

$$\begin{cases} 3x - 2y = 12 \\ -x - 2y = -20 \end{cases}$$

$$3x - 2y = 12$$
$$\underline{+\ -x - 2y = -20}$$
$$2x \quad\quad = -8$$
$$x \quad\quad = -4$$

$$3x + 2y = 12$$
$$3(-4) + 2y = 12$$
$$2y = 24$$
$$y = 12$$

Solution: $(-4, 12)$

    Explain Liang's error and give the correct solution.

    _____

    _____

    _____

FL   A-REI.3.5

Prove that, given a system of two equations in two variables, replacing one equation by the sum of that equation and a multiple of the other produces a system with the same solutions. *Also A-CED.1.3, A-REI.3.6*

LESSON 9.4 Solving Linear Systems by Multiplying

How can you solve a system of linear equations by using multiplication and elimination?

EXPLORE ACTIVITY 1   FL   A-REI.3.5, A-REI.3.6

Understanding Linear Systems and Multiplication

A Graph this system of linear equations. Label each equation and find the solution.

$$\begin{cases} 2x - y = 1 \\ x + y = 2 \end{cases}$$

The solution of the system is _____.

B Use one of the equations in the system to write a new equation.

$x + y = 2$	Write the second equation in the system.
$2(x + y = 2)$	Multiply each term in the equation by 2.
$2x + 2y = 4$	Simplify.

C Graph the new equation. How is the graph of this equation related to the graphs of the original two equations?

_____

_____

REFLECT

1. **Draw Conclusions** What is true about the equations $x + y = 2$ and $2x + 2y = 4$?

_____

2. Could you solve the original system by using the elimination method? Explain. Could you solve a new system that contained the new equation and the first equation in the original system? Explain.

_____

_____

_____

Proving the Elimination Method with Multiplication

If you add the new equation you found in Explore Activity 1 and the first equation in the original system, you get a third equation. The graph of this new equation is shown at the right.

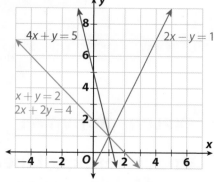

$$2x + 2y = 4$$
$$\underline{+ \ 2x - \ y = 1}$$
$$4x + \ y = 5$$

A Is the solution of the original system also a solution of the system formed by the equation $2x - y = 1$ and the third equation? Explain. _____

_____

B If the original system is $Ax + By = C$ and $Dx + Ey = F$, where A, B, C, D, E, and F are constants, then multiply the second equation by a nonzero constant k to get $kDx + kEy = kF$. Then add this equation to the first equation to get the third equation.

$$Ax + \quad\quad By = C$$
$$\underline{+ \ kDx + \quad\quad kEy = \quad kF}$$
$$(A + kD)x + (B + kE)y = C + kF$$

C Complete the following proof to show that if (x_1, y_1) is a solution of the original system, then it is also a solution of the new system below.

$$\begin{cases} Ax + By = C \\ (A + kD)x + (B + kE)y = C + kF \end{cases}$$

$Ax_1 + By_1 = C$	(x_1, y_1) is a solution of $Ax + By = C$.
$Dx_1 + Ey_1 = F$	(x_1, y_1) is a solution of $Dx + Ey = F$.
$\boxed{}(Dx_1 + Ey_1) = kF$	Multiplication Property of Equality
$kDx_1 + kEy_1 = kF$	Distributive Property
$C + kDx_1 + kEy_1 = \boxed{} + kF$	Addition Property of Equality
$Ax_1 + \boxed{} + kDx_1 + kEy_1 = C + kF$	Substitute $Ax_1 + By_1$ for C.
$Ax_1 + kDx_1 + \boxed{} + kEy_1 = C + kF$	Commutative Property of Addition
$(Ax_1 + kDx_1) + (By_1 + kEy_1) = C + kF$	Associative Property of Addition
$(A + kD)x_1 + (\boxed{} + kE)y_1 = C + kF$	Distributive Property

$(A + kD)x_1 + (B + kE)y_1 = C + kF$, so (x_1, y_1) is a solution of the new system.

Solving a Linear System by Multiplying One Equation

Math On the Spot
my.hrw.com

In some linear systems, neither variable can be eliminated by adding or subtracting the equations directly. In systems like these, you need to multiply one or both of the equations by a constant so that adding or subtracting the equations will eliminate one or more of the variables. The steps for this method are as follows:

1. Decide which variable to eliminate.

2. Multiply one or both equations by a constant so that adding or subtracting will eliminate that variable.

3. Solve the system using the elimination method.

EXAMPLE 1

 FL A-REI.3.5, A-REI.3.6

Solve the system of linear equations by multiplying. Check your answer.

$$\begin{cases} 3x + 8y = 7 \\ 2x - 2y = -10 \end{cases}$$

STEP 1 Multiply the second equation by a constant and then add the equations.

$4(2x - 2y = -10)$	Multiply each term in the second equation by 4 to get opposite y-coefficients.
$8x - 8y = -40$	
$\underline{+\ 3x + 8y = \quad 7}$	Add the first equation to the new equation.
$11x + 0y = -33$	Add the two equations.
$11x = -33$	Simplify.
$x = -3$	Divide each side by 11.

STEP 2 Substitute the value of x into one of the equations and solve for y.

$3x + 8y = 7$	Use the first equation.
$3(-3) + 8y = 7$	Substitute -3 for the variable x.
$-9 + 8y = 7$	Simplify.
$8y = 16$	Add 9 to each side.
$y = 2$	Divide each side by 8.

STEP 3 Write the solution as an ordered pair: $(-3, 2)$.

My Notes

STEP 4 Check the solution by graphing.

$$3x + 8y = 7 \qquad 2x - 2y = -10$$

x-intercept: $2\frac{1}{3}$ x-intercept: -5

y-intercept: $\frac{7}{8}$ y-intercept: 5

The point of intersection is $(-3, 2)$.

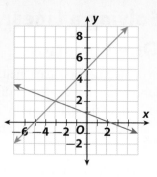

The solution of the system is $(-3, 2)$.

Personal Math Trainer
Online Assessment and Intervention
ⓞ my.hrw.com

Math On the Spot
ⓞ my.hrw.com

YOUR TURN

3. Solve the system of linear equations by multiplying. Check your answer.

$$\begin{cases} -3x + 4y = 12 \\ 2x + y = -8 \end{cases} \qquad \text{Solution: _____}$$

Solving a Linear System by Multiplying Both Equations

You may need to multiply both equations in a system before you can add or subtract.

EXAMPLE 2

FL   A-REI.3.6

Solve the system of linear equations by multiplying.

$$\begin{cases} -3x + 9y = -3 \\ 4x - 13y = 5 \end{cases}$$

STEP 1 Multiply both of the equations and add.

$$4(-3x + 9y = -3) \qquad \text{Multiply the first equation by 4.}$$

$$3(4x - 13y = 5) \qquad \text{Multiply the second equation by 3.}$$

$$-12x + 36y = -12 \qquad \text{Simplify the first equation.}$$

$$\underline{+12x - 39y = 15} \qquad \text{Simplify the second equation.}$$

$$-3y = 3 \qquad \text{Add the two equations.}$$

$$\frac{-3y}{-3} = \frac{3}{-3} \qquad \text{Divide each side by } -3.$$

$$y = -1 \qquad \text{Simplify.}$$

STEP 2   Substitute the value of y into one of the equations and solve for x.

$$4x - 13y = 5 \qquad \textit{Use the second equation.}$$

$$4x - 13(-1) = 5 \qquad \textit{Substitute} -1 \textit{ for the variable } y.$$

$$4x + 13 = 5 \qquad \textit{Simplify.}$$

$$4x = -8 \qquad \textit{Subtract 13 from both sides.}$$

$$x = -2 \qquad \textit{Divide each side by 4.}$$

Math Talk

Mathematical Practices

Describe how to find the numbers by which you would multiply both equations to eliminate a variable.

STEP 3   Write the solution as an ordered pair: $(-2, -1)$.

YOUR TURN

Solve each system of linear equations by multiplying. Check your answer.

4. $\begin{cases} 2x + 3y = -1 \\ 5x - 2y = -12 \end{cases}$

5. $\begin{cases} 5x - 2y = 11 \\ 3x + 5y = 19 \end{cases}$

Solution: _____

Solution: _____

Personal Math Trainer

Online Assessment and Intervention

⊕ my.hrw.com

Applying Linear Systems

EXAMPLE 3 Real World   **FL**   A-REI.3.6, A-CED.1.3

Math On the Spot

⊕ my.hrw.com

Jessica spent $14.85 to buy 13 flowers. The bouquet contained daisies, which cost $1.25 each, and tulips, which cost $0.90 each. How many of each type of flower did Jessica buy?

Total Number:	Number of daisies	plus	number of tulips	is	13
	d	+	t	=	13
Total Cost:	Cost of daisies	plus	cost of tulips	is	14.85
	$1.25d$	+	$0.90t$	=	14.85

STEP 1   Multiply the first equation by a constant and then subtract the equations.

$$0.90d + 0.90t = 11.70 \qquad \textit{Multiply the first equation by 0.90.}$$

$$\frac{-(1.25d + 0.90t) = -(14.85)}{-0.35d \qquad\quad = -3.15} \qquad \textit{Subtract the second equation.}$$

$$\frac{-0.35d}{-0.35} = \frac{-3.15}{-0.35} \qquad \textit{Divide each side by } -0.35.$$

$$d = 9 \qquad \textit{Simplify}$$

STEP 2 Substitute the value of d into one of the equations and solve for t.

$$d + t = 13 \qquad \textit{Use the first equation.}$$

$$(9) + t = 13 \qquad \textit{Substitute 9 for the variable d.}$$

$$t = 4 \qquad \textit{Simplify.}$$

Jessica bought 9 daisies and 4 tulips.

YOUR TURN

6. Roses are \$2.50 each and lilies are \$1.75 each. Ellis spent \$24.75 for 12 of the flowers. How many of each type of flower did he buy?

_____

Guided Practice

1. Solve the system of linear equations by multiplying. Check your answer. (Example 1)

$$\begin{cases} -2x + 2y = 2 \\ 5x - 6y = -9 \end{cases}$$

$\boxed{}\,x + \boxed{}\,y = 6$

$\dfrac{+5x - \qquad 6y = -9}{-x \qquad\quad = \boxed{}}$

Solution: _____

Solve each system of linear equations by multiplying. Check your answer. (Examples 1 and 2)

2. $\begin{cases} 3x + 3y = 12 \\ 6x + 11y = 14 \end{cases}$

Solution: _____

3. $\begin{cases} 4x + 3y = 11 \\ 2x - 2y = -12 \end{cases}$

Solution: _____

4. $\begin{cases} 3x + 8y = 17 \\ -2x + 9y = 3 \end{cases}$

Solution: _____

5. The length of a rectangle is 8 inches more than the width. The perimeter of the rectangle is 56 inches. Write and solve a system of linear equations to find the length and width of the rectangle. (Example 3)

_____

ESSENTIAL QUESTION CHECK-IN

6. Explain how you can solve a system of linear equations by using multiplication and elimination.

_____

_____

_____

9.4 Independent Practice

  A-REI.3.5, A-REI.3.6, A-CED.1.3

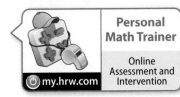

For each linear system, tell whether you would multiply the terms in the first or second equation in order to eliminate one of the variables. Give the number by which you could multiply. Then solve the system.

7. $\begin{cases} x + 3y = -14 \\ 2x + y = -3 \end{cases}$

Equation: _____

Number: _____

Solution: _____

8. $\begin{cases} 9x - 3y = 3 \\ -3x - 8y = 17 \end{cases}$

Equation: _____

Number: _____

Solution: _____

For each linear system, give the number by which you would multiply the terms in each equation in order to eliminate one of the variables. Then solve the system.

9. $\begin{cases} -3x + 2y = 4 \\ 5x - 3y = 1 \end{cases}$

First equation number: _____

Second equation number:

_____

Solution: _____

10. $\begin{cases} 5x + 2y = -1 \\ 3x + 7y = 11 \end{cases}$

First equation number: _____

Second equation number:

_____

Solution: _____

11. Critical Thinking Suppose you want to eliminate y in this system.

$\begin{cases} 2x + 11y = -3 \\ 3x + 4y = 8 \end{cases}$

What numbers would you need to multiply the two equations by to eliminate y? Why might you choose to eliminate x instead?

_____

_____

_____

_____

_____

_____

12. Represent Real-World Problems The Tran family is bringing 12 packages of buns to the neighborhood picnic. The hamburger buns cost $2.00 per package. The hot-dog buns cost $1.50 per package. They spent $20 for the buns. Write and solve a system of equations that can be used to find the number of packages of each type of bun they purchased.

System: _____

Hamburger buns: _____

Hot-dog buns: _____

13. Conrad drew 2 angles. Three times the measure of angle 1 is 30° more than 5 times the measure of angle 2. The sum of twice the measure of angle 1 and twice the measure of angle 2 is 180°. Find the measure of each angle.

Angle 1: _____

Angle 2: _____

14. Multi-step The school store is running a promotion on school supplies. Different supplies are placed on two shelves. You can purchase 3 items from shelf A and 2 from shelf B for $16. Or you can purchase 2 items from shelf A and 3 from shelf B for $14. How much more does one item on shelf A cost than an item on shelf B? Explain.

_____

_____

15. A local boys club sold 176 bags of mulch and made a total of $520. They did not sell any of the expensive cocoa mulch. Use the table to determine how many bags of each type of mulch they sold.

Mulch Prices			
Type of mulch	Cocoa	Hardwood	Pine Bark
Price	$4.75	$3.50	$2.75

_____

 FOCUS ON HIGHER ORDER THINKING

Work Area

16. Explain the Error A linear system has two equations, $Ax + By = C$ and $Dx + Ey = F$. A student multiplies the x- and y-coefficients in the second equation by a constant k to get $kDx + kEy = F$. The student then adds the result to $Ax + By = C$ to write a new equation.

a. What is the new equation that the student wrote?

_____

b. If the ordered pair (x_1, y_1) is a solution of the original system and not $(0, 0)$, will it also be a solution of the new equation? Why or why not?

_____

_____

_____

17. Critical Thinking Would you prefer to solve the system in Exercise 7 by using substitution? Explain your reasoning.

_____

_____

_____

_____

_____

LESSON 9.5

Solving Systems of Linear Inequalities

FL A-REI.4.12

Graph the . . . solution set to a system of linear inequalities in two variables as the intersection of the corresponding half-planes. *Also A-CED.1.3*

ESSENTIAL QUESTION

How do you solve a system of linear inequalities?

EXPLORE ACTIVITY

 **FL** A-REI.4.12

Graphing Linear Inequalities on the Same Coordinate Plane

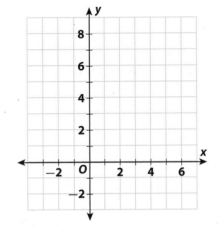

A Graph the inequality $x + y \leq 4$.

Did you shade above or below the boundary line?

_____

B Graph the inequality $x - y \geq 2$.

Did you shade above or below the boundary line?

_____

C Look at the region of your graph where the graphs of the two inequalities overlap. Choose three ordered pairs from that region. Test each pair in each inequality.

_____

Ordered pair	Satisfies $x + y \leq 4$?	Satisfies $x - y \geq 2$?
(,)		
(,)		
(,)		

REFLECT

1. If you test another ordered pair in the region where the graphs overlap, do you think it will satisfy one, both, or neither of the inequalities? Explain your reasoning.

_____

_____

2. **Draw Conclusions** An ordered pair that makes a linear inequality true is a solution of that linear inequality. What can you conclude about the ordered pairs in the region where the graphs overlap?

_____

_____

Lesson 9.5 **311**

Solving a System of Linear Inequalities by Graphing

A **system of linear inequalities** consists of two or more linear inequalities that have the same variables. The **solutions of a system of linear inequalities** are all the ordered pairs that make all the inequalities in the system true.

EXAMPLE 1 FL A-REI.4.12

Solve the system of inequalities by graphing. Check your answer.

$$\begin{cases} x + 2y > 2 \\ -x + y \le 4 \end{cases}$$

My Notes

STEP 1 Graph $x + 2y > 2$.

The equation of the boundary line is $x + 2y = 2$.

x-intercept: 2 y-intercept: 1

The inequality symbol is $>$, so use a dashed line.

Shade above the boundary line because $(0, 0)$ is *not* a solution of the inequality.

STEP 2 Graph $-x + y \le 4$.

The equation of the boundary line is $-x + y = 4$.

x-intercept: -4 y-intercept: 4

The inequality symbol is $\le$, so use a solid line.

Shade below the boundary line because $(0, 0)$ *is* a solution of the inequality.

STEP 3 Identify the solutions.

The solutions are the points in the region where the graphs overlap.

STEP 4 Check your answer by testing a point from each region.

Ordered pair	Satisfies $x + 2y > 2$?	Satisfies $-x + y \le 4$?	In the region where the graphs overlap?
$(0, 0)$			
$(2, 3)$			
$(-4, 2)$			
$(-2, 4)$			

REFLECT

3. Draw Conclusions How does testing specific ordered pairs tell you that the solution you graphed is correct?

_____

_____

4. Is $(-2, 2)$ a solution of the system of inequalities? Why or why not?

_____

_____

_____

5. Solve the system of inequalities by graphing. Check your answer.

$$\begin{cases} x - y \geq -1 \\ \quad y > 2 \end{cases}$$

Personal
Math Trainer

Online Assessment
and Intervention

⊙ my.hrw.com

Solving Systems of Inequalities Whose Graphs Have Parallel Boundary Lines

The graphs of linear inequalities in a system can have parallel boundary lines. Unlike in systems of *equations* containing parallel lines, this does not always mean the system of inequalities has no solution.

Math On the Spot

⊙ my.hrw.com

EXAMPLE 2

FL   A-REI.4.12

Graph each system of linear inequalities. Describe the solutions.

A $\begin{cases} -x + y > 3 \\ -x + y \leq -5 \end{cases}$

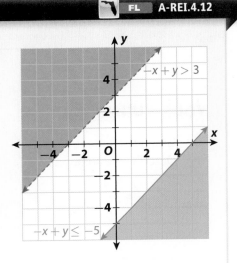

The two regions do not overlap.

The system has no solution.

B $\begin{cases} x + y > -4 \\ x + y > -1 \end{cases}$

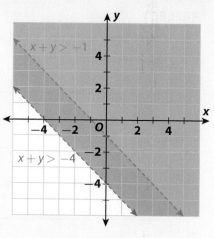

The solutions are all the points in the region where the graphs overlap. They are all the solutions of $x + y > -1$.

C $\begin{cases} -x + 3y \leq 3 \\ -x + 3y \geq -3 \end{cases}$

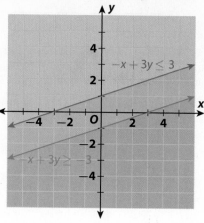

The solutions are all the points in the regions between the boundary lines and on the boundary lines.

REFLECT

6. Can the solution of a system of linear inequalities be a line? If so, give an example.

_____

_____

7. Does the system $3x - 2y < 4$ and $3x - 2y > 4$ have a solution? Explain.

_____

_____

_____

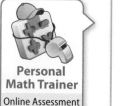

Personal Math Trainer

Online Assessment and Intervention

⏻ my.hrw.com

YOUR TURN

8. Graph the system of linear inequalities. Describe the solutions.

$\begin{cases} x - y < -1 \\ x - y \geq 3 \end{cases}$

Description: _____

_____

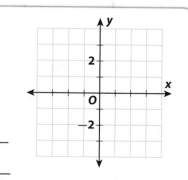

Modeling with Systems of Linear Inequalities

You can use a system of linear inequalities and its graph to model many real-world situations.

Math On the Spot
⊙ my.hrw.com

EXAMPLE 3    FL   A-REI.4.12, A-CED.1.3

Rosa is buying T-shirts and shorts. T-shirts cost $12 and shorts cost $20. She plans to spend no more than $120 and buy at least 4 items. Show and describe all possible combinations of the number of T-shirts and shorts she could buy. List two possible combinations.

STEP 1   Write a system of linear inequalities. Let t represent the number of T-shirts and s represent the number of shorts.

Total items:	$t + s \geq 4$	She wants to buy at least 4 items.
Total spent:	$12t + 20s \leq 120$	She wants to spend no more than $120.

STEP 2   Graph the system. The graph should be in only the first quadrant because the numbers of T-shirts and shorts are not negative.

Rosa's Options

STEP 3   Describe all of the possible combinations. Rosa could buy any combination of T-shirts and shorts represented by a point in the region where the graphs overlap. Answers must be whole numbers because she cannot buy part of a T-shirt or pair of shorts.

Math Talk
Mathematical Practices

How do you choose which region to select the combinations from?

STEP 4   List two possible combinations. Two possible combinations: 2 T-shirts and 3 shorts or (2, 3), 1 T-shirt and 5 shorts or (1, 5)

YOUR TURN

9. Sergio is building a garden. He wants the length to be at least 30 feet and the perimeter to be no more than 100 feet. Graph all possible dimensions of the garden. Is a length of 35 feet and a width of 10 feet a possible combination?

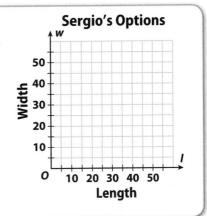

Sergio's Options

Personal Math Trainer

Online Assessment and Intervention

⊙ my.hrw.com

_____

Solve each system of linear inequalities by graphing. Describe the solutions. (Examples 1 and 2)

1. $\begin{cases} x - y \leq -3 \\ x - y > 3 \end{cases}$

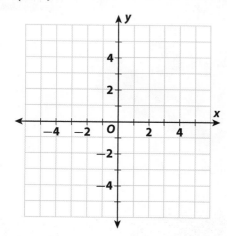

2. $\begin{cases} x + y \leq -2 \\ -x + y > 1 \end{cases}$

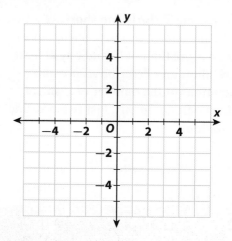

_____

_____

_____

_____

3. Jason is buying grapes for a picnic. Green grapes cost $2 a pound and red grapes cost $3 a pound. He plans to buy at least 4 pounds of grapes and spend no more than $20. List two possible combinations of the number of pounds of green and red grapes he could buy. (Example 3)

_____

_____

Jason's Options

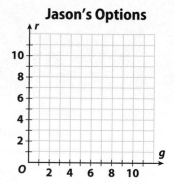

? **ESSENTIAL QUESTION CHECK-IN**

4. How do you solve a system of linear inequalities?

_____

_____

_____

_____

9.5 Independent Practice

FL A-REI.4.12, A-CED.1.3

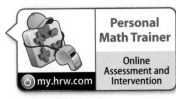

Personal
Math Trainer

Online
Assessment and
Intervention

my.hrw.com

Solve each system of linear inequalities by graphing. Name two ordered pairs that are solutions of the system.

5. $\begin{cases} y \geq -2 \\ 4x + y \geq 2 \end{cases}$

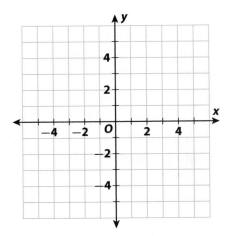

_____

6. $\begin{cases} x < 1 \\ 2x + y > 1 \end{cases}$

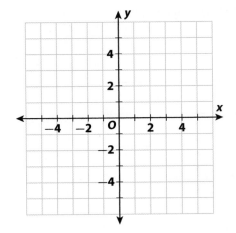

_____

7. $\begin{cases} 4x + y \geq 4 \\ 4x + y \geq -4 \end{cases}$

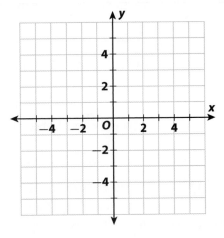

_____

8. The system of inequalities below defines the boundaries of a region in the plane. What inequality symbol or symbols could replace "?" to make the solution a triangular region?

$$\begin{cases} y \leq -x + 1 \\ y \geq \frac{1}{3}x - 3 \\ x \;\underline{\,?\,}\; -4 \end{cases}$$

_____

9. Describe the solutions of this system of linear inequalities. Then write a possible system for the graphed inequalities.

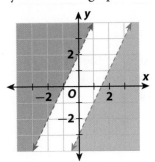

_____

_____

10. Critical Thinking Without graphing, describe the solution of $\begin{cases} x \geq 3 \\ y \leq 4 \end{cases}$.

_____

_____

11. Natalia is drawing a rectangle. She wants the width to be at least 10 inches and the perimeter to be no more than 72 inches.

   a. Write a system of inequalities that can be used to solve this problem.

   _____

   b. Give a possible length and width for the rectangle.

   _____

   c. Give a length and a width that cannot be used for the rectangle.

   _____

12. Leon works at a grocery store for $8 an hour. He also mows lawns for $10 an hour. He needs to earn at least $120 per week, but he does not want to work more than 20 hours per week. Use a system of inequalities to find a possible combination of hours he can work at the grocery store and mowing lawns in order to meet his goal.

_____

 FOCUS ON HIGHER ORDER THINKING

Work Area

13. Communicate Mathematical Ideas Is it possible for a system of two linear inequalities to have every point in the plane as a solution? Why or why not?

_____

_____

_____

_____

14. Graph the system of linear inequalities. Describe the solutions of the system.
$$\begin{cases} x + 4y > -4 \\ x + y \leq 2 \\ x - y \geq 2 \end{cases}$$

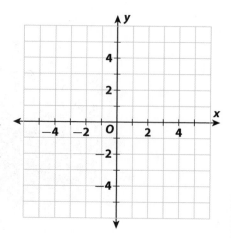

_____

_____

_____

_____

Ready to Go On?

9.1 Solving Linear Systems by Graphing

Solve each system of linear equations by graphing.

1. $\begin{cases} x - y = 5 \\ x + y = 3 \end{cases}$ Solution: _____

2. $\begin{cases} -x + y = 3 \\ -2x + y = 6 \end{cases}$ Solution: _____

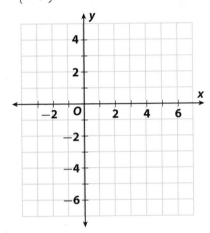

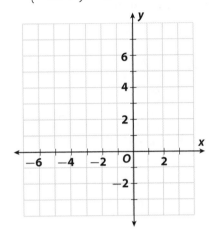

9.2 Solving Linear Systems by Substitution

Solve each system of linear equations by substitution.

3. $\begin{cases} x + y = -2 \\ 2x - 2y = 8 \end{cases}$ Solution: _____

4. $\begin{cases} x - 2y = -7 \\ 2x - 3y = -10 \end{cases}$ Solution: _____

9.3, 9.4 Solving Linear Systems by Elimination

Solve each system of linear equations by elimination.

5. $\begin{cases} x + 3y = 5 \\ 2x + 3y = 7 \end{cases}$ Solution: _____

6. $\begin{cases} 2x + 5y = 4 \\ 4x + 7y = 2 \end{cases}$ Solution: _____

9.5 Solving Systems of Linear Inequalities

7. Solve the system of linear inequalities by graphing.

$\begin{cases} 2x + y \leq 8 \\ 3x - y < 2 \end{cases}$

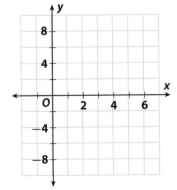

? ESSENTIAL QUESTION

8. How are the graphs of systems of linear equations and inequalities related to their solutions?

_____

_____

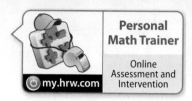
Selected Response

1. Which system of linear equations is represented by the graph below?

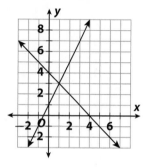

(A) $\begin{cases} x + y = 4 \\ 2x + y = 1 \end{cases}$ (C) $\begin{cases} x - y = 4 \\ 2x - y = -1 \end{cases}$

(B) $\begin{cases} x + y = 4 \\ 2x - y = -1 \end{cases}$ (D) $\begin{cases} x + y = 4 \\ x - 2y = 1 \end{cases}$

2. Julie is solving the linear system below by substitution.

$$\begin{cases} 2x + y = 7 \\ 3x - 2y = -7 \end{cases}$$

Which of the following would be a step in solving the system?

(A) Substitute $y + 7$ for x in $3x - 2y = -7$.

(B) Substitute $-y + 7$ for x in $3x - 2y = -7$.

(C) Substitute $-2x + 7$ for y in $3x - 2y = -7$.

(D) Substitute $2x - 7$ for y in $3x - 2y = -7$.

3. Which step can be taken to eliminate a variable from the linear system below?

$$\begin{cases} -4x + 2y = -2 \\ 4x - 3y = -1 \end{cases}$$

(A) Add to eliminate the variable x.

(B) Subtract to eliminate the variable x.

(C) Add to eliminate the variable y.

(D) Subtract to eliminate the variable y.

4. Which of the following equations describes a line with an x-intercept of 9?

(A) $-3x - 7y = -63$ (C) $3x + 2y = 9$

(B) $9x + y = 9$ (D) $-3x + 2y = -27$

5. Which ordered pair is a solution of $y > 2x - 3$?

(A) $(-1, -5)$ (C) $(2, 3)$

(B) $(1, -5)$ (D) $(2, -2)$

6. Which ordered pair is *not* a solution of the system of linear inequalities graphed below?

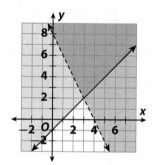

(A) $(1, 7)$ (C) $(3, 2)$

(B) $(2, 5)$ (D) $(4, 3)$

Mini-Tasks

7. Marco and Tam play video games a total of 15 hours each week. Marco plays 3 hours more than twice the number of hours Tam plays. Write a system of linear equations to represent the situation. How many hours do each play?

_____

_____

_____

Study Guide Review

Linear Functions

Key Vocabulary

linear function *(función lineal)*

linear equation *(ecuación lineal)*

standard form of a linear equation *(forma estándar de una ecuación lineal)*

x-intercept *(intersección con el eje x)*

y-intercept *(intersección con el eje y)*

rate of change *(tasa de cambio)*

rise *(distancia vertical)*

run *(distancia horizontal)*

slope *(pendiente)*

slope formula *(formula de pendiente)*

slope-intercept form *(forma de pendiente-intersección)*

family of functions *(familia de funciones)*

parent function *(función madre)*

parameter *(parámetro)*

? **ESSENTIAL QUESTION**

How do equations, graphs, tables, and word descriptions relate to linear functions?

EXAMPLE 1

Find the slope and the *y*-intercept of the line that is graphed below. Then, write the equation of the line in slope-intercept form.

The *y*-intercept is 2. Since the line goes through the points (0, 2) and (4, 4), the slope is $m = \frac{(4-2)}{(4-0)} = \frac{1}{2}$. So, the equation for the line in slope-intercept form is $y = \frac{1}{2}x + 2$.

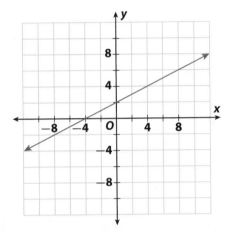

EXAMPLE 2

Find the slope of the line that has its *x*-intercept at 3 and its *y*-intercept at 4.

The intercepts give two points on the line, (3, 0) and (0, 4). Use these two points in the slope formula: $m = \frac{(4-0)}{(0-3)} = -\frac{4}{3}$.

EXERCISES

1. Tell whether the function given by $y - 3 = 2x$ is linear. Compare it to the linear function represented by the table below. Describe how the functions are alike and how they are different. (Lessons 6.1, 6.5)

x	1	2	3	4
y	1	3	5	7

_____

_____

2. Find the slope and the intercepts of the line from the graph. Then, write the equation of the line in slope-intercept form. (Lessons 6.2, 6.3, 6.7)

_____

_____

_____

_____

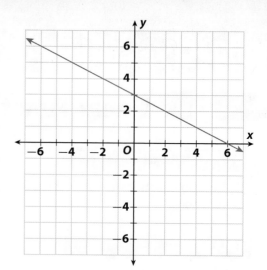

3. Find the slope of the line that has its x-intercept at -2 and its y-intercept at 7. (Lesson 6.4)

_____

4. Brandon's cell phone bill is given by $y = 0.15x + 5$ and Lisa's cell phone bill is given by $y = 0.20x + 25$, where x is the number of text messages each sends in a month. Interpret the meaning of 0.15 and 0.20 in these equations, and describe the difference between the graphs of the functions. (Lesson 6.6)

_____

_____

_____

_____

_____

MODULE **7** # Building Linear Functions

? **ESSENTIAL QUESTION**

How are mathematical operations related to solving linear equations and inequalities and creating new functions?

EXAMPLE 1

Add the linear functions $f(x) = 2x - 7$ and $g(x) = 4x + 3$ to get the linear function $h(x) = f(x) + g(x)$.

$f(x) + g(x) = (2x - 7) + (4x + 3)$ Substitute for $f(x)$ and $g(x)$.

$\qquad\quad = (2x + 4x) + (-7 + 3)$ Combine like terms.

$\qquad\quad = 6x - 4$ Simplify.

Key Vocabulary

arithmetic sequence
  (sucesión aritmética)

common difference
  (diferencia común)

inverse of a function
  (función inversa)

linear inequality in two
  variables *(desigualdad
  lineal en dos variables)*

solution of an inequality
  *(solución de
  una desigualdad)*

boundary line *(línea de límite)*

half-plane *(semiplano)*

EXAMPLE 2

The amount of money, A, that a tour guide earns in a day is given by $A = 20x + 40$, where x is the number of tours given by the guide. Find the number of tours given as a function of A.

$A = 20x + 40$	Start with A as a function of x.
$A - 40 = 20x$	Subtract.
$\frac{A}{20} - 2 = x$	Divide.
$x = \frac{A}{20} - 2$	Solve for x.

EXERCISES

Write a recursive rule and an explicit rule for each arithmetic sequence. (Lesson 7.1)

5. 8, 11, 14, 17, … _____

6. 10, 5, 0, −5, … _____

7. An employee earns a base salary of \$30,000 plus an additional \$2,000 for each project completed in a year. Her income tax rate is 15%. Write a function $S(x)$ for the salary earned for completing x projects in a year. Then write a function $T(x)$ for the tax owed by the employee for completing x projects in a year. (Lesson 7.2)

_____

_____

8. Find the inverse of the linear function $y = 7x + 3$. (Lesson 7.3)

_____

9. Graph the solution set for $4x + 2y > 5$. (Lesson 7.4)

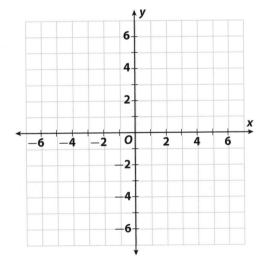

Modeling with Linear Functions

Key Vocabulary
bivariate data
scatter plot (*diagrama de dispersión*)
correlation (*correlación*)
correlation coefficient (*coeficiente de correlación*)
line of fit (*línea de ajuste*)
residual (*residual*)
residual plot (*parcela residual*)
interpolation (*interpolación*)
extrapolation
linear regression (*regresión lineal*)
least squares regression line (*mínimos cuadrados línea de regresión*)
line of best fit (*línea de mejor ajuste*)

? **ESSENTIAL QUESTION**

How can you use statistical methods to find relationships between sets of data?

EXAMPLE

Describe the correlation in the scatter plot below, and estimate the correlation coefficient.

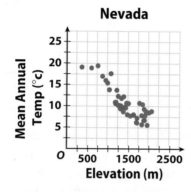

Nevada

The scatter plot shows a strong negative correlation. Points lie close to a line with a negative slope. The correlation coefficient is close to -1.

EXERCISES

10. The scatter plot shows a relationship between years of experience at a job and income earned. The line of best fit is $I = 1.32x + 25$, where I is income in thousands of dollars per year and x is years of experience. Estimate the correlation coefficient. Then, predict the income earned by someone with 40 years of experience. (Lessons 8.1, 8.2)

_____

11. The table below gives the ages, *t*, of boys on a middle-school basketball team and their shoe sizes, *s*. One student estimates that the line of best fit is given by $s = 0.8t + 0.5$. Use the table to compute the squares of the residuals for this line. (Lesson 8.3)

	$s = 0.8t + 0.5$			
t	*s* (actual)	*s* (predicted)	Residuals	Square of Residuals
10	9	8.5	0.5	0.25
11	7			
12	10			
13	12			
13	9.5			

Systems of Equations and Inequalities

Key Vocabulary

system of linear equations (*sistema de ecuaciones lineales*)

solution of a system of linear equations (*solución de un sistema de ecuaciones lineales*)

substitution method (*sustitución*)

elimination method (*eliminación*)

system of linear inequalities (*sistema de desigualdades lineales*)

solution of a system of linear inequalities (*solución de un sistema de desigualdades lineales*)

ESSENTIAL QUESTION

How are the graphs of systems of linear equations and inequalities related to their solutions?

EXAMPLE

Solve the system of linear equations.

$$\begin{cases} y = 3x + 1 \\ 2y - 3 = 4x \end{cases}$$

$2(3x + 1) - 3 = 4x$ Substitute the first equation into the second.

$6x - 1 = 4x$ Distribute.

$2x = 1$ Combine like terms.

$x = \frac{1}{2}$ Solve for x.

$y = 3(\frac{1}{2}) + 1$ Plug this solution into either equation to find y.

$y = \frac{5}{2}$

The solution is $(\frac{1}{2}, \frac{5}{2})$.

EXERCISES

12. Solve the system of equations by substitution. (Lesson 9.2)

$$\begin{cases} y - 2 = 4x \\ 5y - 2x = 1 \end{cases}$$

_____

Solve each system of equations by elimination. (Lessons 9.3, 9.4)

13. $\begin{cases} 4x + 6y = 38 \\ 4x - 2y = 14 \end{cases}$

14. $\begin{cases} 3x - 2y = 9 \\ 5x + y = 2 \end{cases}$

_____   _____

Solve each system of equations or inequalities by graphing.
(Lessons 9.1, 9.5)

15. $\begin{cases} y = 4x + 9 \\ y = 2x - 1 \end{cases}$ _____

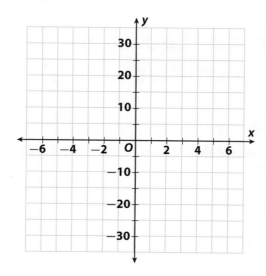

16. $\begin{cases} 4y \leq 15x + 40 \\ 2y + 50 \geq 25x \end{cases}$

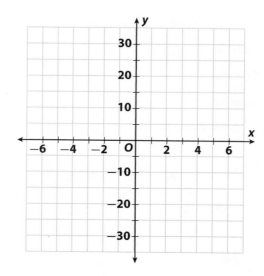

1. A gym charges a one-time sign-up fee and then a regular monthly fee. The cost of a membership as a function of the number of months as a member is shown for 2010 (red) and 2011 (blue) on the graph.

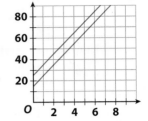

   a. What parameters of the graph represent the sign-up fee and the monthly fee? What are those values for the 2010 line?

   _____

   _____

   b. How did the membership costs change from 2010 to 2011? Explain how you can tell from the graphs.

   _____

   _____

   _____

2. **CAREERS IN MATH** **Environmental Scientist** To rate the fuel efficiency of a car, the following data were collected comparing the distance traveled to the amount of gasoline used on the trip.

fuel (gal)	1.3	7.5	3.9	2.1	10.8	3.3	6.7
dist. (mi)	42	223	109	58	330	97	188

   a. Draw a scatter plot representing this data, and then use linear regression to find the equation of the line of best fit.

   _____

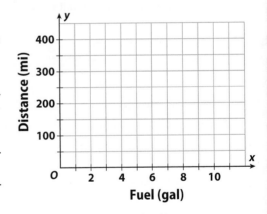

   b. What do the *x*-intercept and *y*-intercept represent?

   _____

   _____

   _____

   _____

   c. What is the slope of the line? What does it represent in this situation?

   _____

3. Amado, Kaylynn, and their friends want to rent a limousine for prom.
Louie's Limousine Company lists the costs from the table on their website.

Number of People	6	8	10	12
Cost	$62	$65	$69	$84

a. Amado thinks the equation for the line of best fit should be
$y = 3.5x + 38$, but Kaylynn thinks the equation should be $y = 4x + 35$.
Compare the residuals for each line by completing the table below.

x	y (actual)	y predicted by $y = 3.5x + 38$	residual for $y = 3.5x + 38$	y predicted by $y = 4x + 33$	residual for $y = 4x + 33$
6	62				
8	65				
10	69				
12	84				

b. Amado thinks that both lines fit the data equally well, because
$3 + 1 + 4 + 4 = 5 + 0 + 4 + 3$. Explain his error.

_____

_____

c. Which line fits the data better? Explain.

_____

_____

_____

d. Amado wants to have 16 people in the limousine. What is the best
estimate for the amount that each person will have to pay? Explain.

_____

_____

_____

e. If Kaylynn and Amado rent the limousine by themselves, estimate how
much each person would pay.

_____

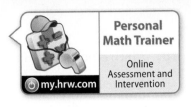

Personal Math Trainer

Online Assessment and Intervention

my.hrw.com

Selected Response

1. Which function is the inverse function of $f(x) = 3x - 1$?

Ⓐ $f(x) = 3x + 1$

Ⓑ $f(x) = \frac{1}{3}x + \frac{1}{3}$

Ⓒ $f(x) = \frac{1}{3}x - 1$

Ⓓ $f(x) = x + 3$

2. If the line of best fit for a scatter plot is given by $y = 3.18x - 6.27$, what is the predicted value of y when $x = 2$?

Ⓐ 5.12   Ⓒ 6.36

Ⓑ 0   Ⓓ 0.09

3. What is the slope of the line that has intercepts at $(0, 1)$ and $(-3, 0)$?

Ⓐ $\frac{1}{3}$ Ⓒ 3

Ⓑ -3 Ⓓ -1

4. Which arithmetic sequence is described by the explicit rule $f(n) = 2 - 3n$?

Ⓐ 1, 3, 5, 7, ...

Ⓑ $-1, -4, -7, -10, ...$

Ⓒ 3, 5, 7, 9, ...

Ⓓ 2, 5, 8, 11, ...

Hot Tip!

Eliminate unreasonable answer choices. Some choices may be too great or too small or have incorrect units.

5. What is the y-intercept of $2x + 5y = 15$?

Ⓐ $(0, 3)$

Ⓑ $(0, \frac{7}{2})$

Ⓒ $(3, 0)$

Ⓓ $(\frac{7}{2}, 0)$

6. Which inequality best represents the graph?

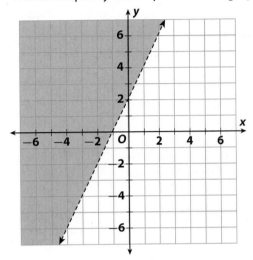

Ⓐ $2x + y > 3$

Ⓑ $-4x + y \leq 3$

Ⓒ $-3x + y < 2$

Ⓓ $-2x + y > 2$

7. If $f(x) = 3x - 4$ and $g(x) = -2x + 1$, which of the following represents $f(x) - g(x)$?

Ⓐ $h(x) = x - 3$

Ⓑ $h(x) = -5x + 5$

Ⓒ $h(x) = 5x - 5$

Ⓓ $h(x) = 2x + 3$

8. How many significant digits should the product of 22,312 cm and 12.5 cm have?

Ⓐ 2   Ⓒ 4

Ⓑ 3   Ⓓ 5

9. What is the solution for $3x - 1 > \frac{9x + 6}{3}$?

Ⓐ $x < -\frac{1}{2}$

Ⓑ $x > -\frac{1}{2}$

Ⓒ $x < \frac{1}{2}$

Ⓓ no solution

10. Which is not a linear function?

Ⓐ $y = 6x$

Ⓑ $y = x + 6$

Ⓒ $6y = x$

Ⓓ $xy = 6$

11. Between which two variables should a negative correlation be expected?

Ⓐ Age and value of a car

Ⓑ Age and height of a tree

Ⓒ A person's height and weight

Ⓓ A city's population and the number of letters in its name

12. The point $(1, 2)$ is a solution of which of the following systems of equations?

Ⓐ $y + 1 = x - 5; y = 2x$

Ⓑ $2y - 3 = x; x + y = 5$

Ⓒ $3y + x = 7; x - y = -1$

Ⓓ $2x + 2y = 2; 7x = 4y$

13. Which of the following is a solution to the system of inequalities $y > 3x - 1$ and $2x + y < 1$?

Ⓐ $(0, 5)$

Ⓑ $(-2, 3)$

Ⓒ $(4, 4)$

Ⓓ $(-1, -4)$

14. If a car is rented and driven x miles, which linear function describes the total amount owed to the car company which charges a flat rate of $200 plus $0.25 per mile?

Ⓐ $C(x) = 0.25x + 200$

Ⓑ $C(x) = 5x - 25$

Ⓒ $C(x) = 200x + 0.25$

Ⓓ $C(x) = 200.25x$

15. Which of the following is a solution to the system of equations $2x + 3y = 7$ and $4x - 2y = -2$?

Ⓐ $(2, 1)$

Ⓑ $(1, 3)$

Ⓒ $(5, -1)$

Ⓓ $(\frac{1}{2}, 2)$

Mini-Tasks

16. A 6-foot snowman is built and begins to melt, losing 6 inches of height per day.

a. Write an equation that represents the height y (in feet) after x days.

_____

b. Identify both the x- and y-intercept, and describe their real-world meanings.

_____

_____

_____

_____

17. The perimeter of a rectangle is 30 cm, and its height is 3 cm more than twice its width.

a. Write a system of linear equations for h and w that describes the situation.

_____

_____

b. Solve the system to find the height and width of the rectangle.

_____

_____

UNIT 2B

Exponential Relationships

MODULE 10

Exponential Functions and Equations

FL A-CED.1.1, F-IF.2.5, F-IF.3.7e, F-BF.1.2, F-BF.2.3, F-LE.1.2

MODULE 11

Modeling with Exponential Functions

FL A-CED.1.2, F-LE.1.1, F-LE.1.1a, F-LE.1.1b, F-LE.1.1c, F-LE.1.3, F-LE.2.5, S-ID.2.6a, S-ID.2.6b

CAREERS IN MATH

Statistician A statistician collects, analyzes, and interprets numerical data of all types. He or she also helps design surveys and experiments. A solid science background is beneficial when helping others design and interpret experiments; for example, monitoring the rise and decline of animal populations. If you're interested in a career as a statistician, you should study these mathematical subjects:

- Algebra
- Trigonometry
- Calculus

Research other careers that require the use of statistics to analyze and interpret data.

Unit 2B Performance Task

At the end of the unit, check out how **statisticians** use math.

Unit 2B **331**

Vocabulary Preview

Use the puzzle to preview key vocabulary from this unit. Unscramble the circled letters within the found words to answer the riddle at the bottom of the page.

```
T  V  R  T  G  H  Y  U  I  N  M  J  G  R  R  D  F  E  Z
E  D  E  G  A  X  C  E  E  T  S  J  A  M  M  T  T  C  T
J  X  D  E  Q  A  Z  F  X  C  F  H  U  F  P  V  Q  N  X
F  D (P) Y  T  L  Q  G  P  H  N  M  U  F  O  E  F  E  V
B  R  U  O  E  D  F  Q  O  E  D  S  W  S  I  T  P  U  O
V  Q  W  X  N  N  T  F  N  I  G  R  R  U  Q  F  H  Q  V
X  W  S  G  T  E  Z  V  E  U  F  D  S  V  Q  E  R  E  B
Z  D  E  F  G  Z  N  B (N) I  O  H  S  Q  E  D  R  S  S
U  F  D  Q  S  R  V  T  T  T  G  T  U  I  T  A  P  C  B
A  D  C  F  G  F  H  R  I  R  G  W  E  D  V  J  V  I  X
C  A  Q  W  S  G  E  W  A  A  T  S  H  J  C  I  T  R  C
A  V  B  G  F  Y  S  L  L  Z  L  G  F  Y  S  H  F (T) E
P  D  F  G  V  E  U  F  G  H  D  D  T  Z  H  D  A (E) D
L  D  Q  A  D  G  B  G  R  Y  Y  F  E  E  N  F  Q  M  O
J  D  E  W  S  L  E  R  O  G  T  Y  H  C  N  L  T  O  C
A  V  F  D  C  P  Z  A  W  W  S  A  S  X  A  V  H  E  C
C  O  M  M  O (N) R  A  T  I (O) T  R  F  G (Y) D  G  F
G  D  C  V  B  N  H  Y  H  R  S  E  D  R  F  T  G  H  Y
N  O  I  T  C  N  U  F  L  A  I (T) N  E  N  O  P  X  E
```

1. This occurs when a quantity increases by the same rate, in each time period (Lesson 10.2)

2. A function whose successive output values have a constant ratio for each unit increase in the input values (Lesson 10.1)

3. In a geometric sequence, the constant ratio of any term and the previous term (Lesson 10.3)

4. A sequence in which the ratio of consecutive terms is constant (Lesson 10.3)

5. This occurs when a quantity decreases by the same rate in each time period (Lesson 10.2)

Q: If the 3 in x^3 is an exponent, what is the 2 in y^2?

A: __ __ __ __ __ __ __ __ __ __ __

Exponential Functions and Equations

ESSENTIAL QUESTION

How can exponential functions be used to represent real-world situations?

Real-World Video

Scientists have found many ways to use radioactive elements that decay exponentially over time. Uranium-235 is used to power nuclear reactors, and scientists use Carbon-14 dating to calculate how long ago an organism lived.

my.hrw.com

GO DIGITAL
my.hrw.com

my.hrw.com

Go digital with your write-in student edition, accessible on any device.

Math On the Spot

Scan with your smart phone to jump directly to the online edition, video tutor, and more.

Animated Math

Interactively explore key concepts to see how math works.

Personal Math Trainer

Get immediate feedback and help as you work through practice sets.

Are YOU Ready?

Complete these exercises to review skills you will need for this module.

Personal Math Trainer

Online Assessment and Intervention

my.hrw.com

Exponents

EXAMPLE Write 10^4 as a multiplication of factors.

$$10^4 = 10 \times 10 \times 10 \times 10$$

10 is the base. It tells you the factor to multiply.
4 is the exponent. It tells you how many times the base is used as a factor. If the exponent is 0, remember that the product is 1.

Write each expression as a multiplication of factors.

1. 5^1 **2.** 9^0 **3.** 3^5

_____   _____   _____

4. 2^4 **5.** 6^3 **6.** a^2

_____   _____   _____

Evaluate Powers

EXAMPLE Evaluate 4^3.

$$4^3 = 4 \times 4 \times 4$$ Rewrite as repeated multiplication.

$$= 64$$ Evaluate.

Evaluate each power.

7. 8^2 **8.** 5^4 **9.** 6^0

_____   _____   _____

Properties of Exponents

EXAMPLE Simplify x^4x^5.

$$x^4x^5 = x^{4+5} = x^9$$ When multiplying numbers with the same base, add exponents.

Simplify.

10. x^3x **11.** $x^3y^4 \cdot y^3$ **12.** $5a^2b \cdot 6a^3b$

_____   _____   _____

Reading Start-Up

Visualize Vocabulary

Use the ✔ Review Words to complete the bubble map.

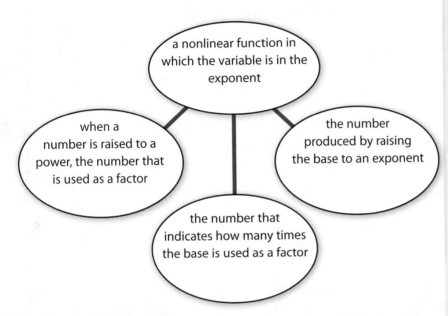

a nonlinear function in which the variable is in the exponent

when a number is raised to a power, the number that is used as a factor

the number produced by raising the base to an exponent

the number that indicates how many times the base is used as a factor

Understand Vocabulary

To become familiar with some of the vocabulary terms in the module, consider the following. You may refer to the module, the glossary, or a dictionary.

1. Occurs in an exponential function when the output gets smaller as the input gets larger.

   _____

2. Occurs in an exponential function when the output gets larger as the input gets larger.

   _____

Active Reading

Booklet Before beginning the module, create a booklet to help you learn the concepts in this module. Write the main idea of each lesson on each page of the booklet. As you study each lesson, write important details that support the main idea, such as vocabulary and formulas. Refer to your finished booklet as you work on assignments and study for tests.

MODULE 10
Unpacking the Standards

Understanding the standards and vocabulary terms in the standards will help you know exactly what you are expected to learn in this module.

 FL A-CED.1.2

Create equations in two or more variables to represent relationships between quantities; graph equations on coordinate axes with labels and scales.

Key Vocabulary

equation *(ecuación)*
A mathematical statement that two expressions are equivalent.

What It Means to You

Creating equations in two variables to describe relationships gives you access to the tools of graphing and algebra to solve the equations.

UNPACKING EXAMPLE A-CED.1.2

A customer spent $29 on a bouquet of roses and daisies. Roses cost $2.50 each and daisies cost $1.75 each.

r = number of roses in bouquet

d = number of daisies in bouquet

$$2.5r + 1.75d = 29$$

 FL F-IF.3.7E

Graph exponential… functions, showing intercepts and end behavior… .

Key Vocabulary

exponential function *(función exponencial)*
A function that can be written in the form $f(x) = ab^x$.

What It Means to You

You will learn to graph a new type of function, called an exponential function, in which successive output values have a constant ratio for each unit increase in the input values.

UNPACKING EXAMPLE F-IF.3.7E

Graph the function $f(x) = 2^x$.

Find points on the graph using a table, then graph the points and connect them with a smooth curve.

x	f(x)
−2	0.25
−1	0.5
0	1
1	2
2	4

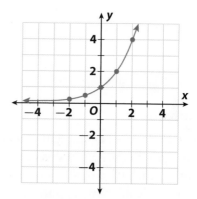

Visit **my.hrw.com** to see all **Florida Math Standards** unpacked.

my.hrw.com

FL   F-LE.1.2

Construct ... exponential
functions ... given a graph, a
description of a relationship, or
two input-output pairs (include
reading these from a table).
*Also F-IF.2.5, F-IF.3.7e, A-CED.1.2,
A-SSE.2.3c*

LESSON
10.1   Exponential Functions

ESSENTIAL QUESTION

How can you identify and represent an exponential function?

EXPLORE ACTIVITY      FL   A-SSE.2.3c

Zero and Negative Exponents

Complete the table, and examine the patterns.

Power	5^5	5^4	5^3	5^2	5^1	5^0	5^{-1}	5^{-2}
Values	3125	625	125	25	5			

$\div 5 \quad \div 5 \quad \div 5 \quad \div 5$

A What happens to the value of the power with each decrease of 1 in the exponent?

_____

B Show the pattern that you used to find the value for 5^0, 5^{-1}, and 5^{-2}.

_____

REFLECT

1. Communicating Mathematics Describe how to find the value of 5^{-2} without dividing the value of 5^{-1} by 5.

_____

_____

The properties of zero and negative exponents are given below.

Zero and Negative Exponents		
Words	**Algebra**	**Example**
Any nonzero number raised to the zero power is 1.	$c^0 = 1, c \neq 0$	$12^0 = 1$
Any nonzero number raised to a negative power is equal to 1 divided by the number raised to the opposite power.	$c^{-n} = \frac{1}{c^n}, c \neq 0$	$2^{-3} = \frac{1}{2^3} = \frac{1}{8}$

Representing an Exponential Function

A function whose successive output values have a *constant ratio* for each unit increase in the input values is an *exponential function*. An **exponential function** can be represented by an equation of the form $f(x) = ab^x$, where a, b, and x are real numbers, $a \neq 0$, $b > 0$, and $b \neq 1$. The constant ratio is the base b. When evaluating exponential functions, you will need to use the properties of exponents.

EXAMPLE 1

FL F-IF.3.7e

My Notes

Make a table for the function $f(x) = 2\left(\frac{2}{3}\right)^x$ using the input values $x = -2, -1, 0, 1, 2, 3$. Then graph the function using the ordered pairs from the table as a guide.

STEP 1 Make a table of values by calculating the function values for the given values of x.

x	$f(x)$	$(x, f(x))$
-2	$2\left(\frac{2}{3}\right)^{-2} = 2\left(\frac{1}{\left(\frac{2}{3}\right)^2}\right) = 2\left(\frac{1}{\frac{4}{9}}\right) = 2\left(\frac{9}{4}\right) = \frac{9}{2}$	$\left(-2, \frac{9}{2}\right)$
-1	$2\left(\frac{2}{3}\right)^{-1} = 2\left(\frac{1}{\left(\frac{2}{3}\right)^1}\right) = 2\left(\frac{1}{\frac{2}{3}}\right) = 2\left(\frac{3}{2}\right) = 3$	$(-1, 3)$
0	$2\left(\frac{2}{3}\right)^0 = 2(1) = 2$	$(0, 2)$
1	$2\left(\frac{2}{3}\right)^1 = 2\left(\frac{2}{3}\right) = \frac{4}{3}$	$\left(1, \frac{4}{3}\right)$
2	$2\left(\frac{2}{3}\right)^2 = 2\left(\frac{4}{9}\right) = \frac{8}{9}$	$\left(2, \frac{8}{9}\right)$
3	$2\left(\frac{2}{3}\right)^3 = 2\left(\frac{8}{27}\right) = \frac{16}{27}$	$\left(3, \frac{16}{27}\right)$

Math Talk

Mathematical Practices

Explain why $f(x)$ is a decreasing function.

STEP 2 Graph the function.

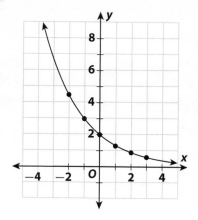

YOUR TURN

2. Find the value of the function $f(x) = 2\left(\frac{2}{3}\right)^x$ when $x = -3$. Graph the corresponding point on the coordinate grid on the preceding page.

_____

Writing an Equation from a Verbal Description

You can model a real-world exponential relationship by identifying the values of a and b in the function $f(x) = ab^x$.

EXAMPLE 2   FL   F-LE.1.2

When a piece of paper is folded in half, the total thickness doubles. Suppose an unfolded piece of paper is 0.1 millimeter thick. Write an equation for the total thickness, $t(n)$, as a function of the number of folds, n. Then use the function to determine the thickness of the paper after 5 folds and 8 folds.

STEP 1   Identify the values of a and b, and write the equation in the form $t(n) = ab^n$.

- The value of a is the thickness $t(n)$ before any folds are made (when $n = 0$), or 0.1 millimeter.
- Because the thickness doubles with each fold, the value of b (the constant ratio) is 2.
- The equation for the function is $t(n) = 0.1(2)^n$.

STEP 2   To find the thickness after 5 and 8 folds, evaluate the function for $n = 5$ and $n = 8$.

$$t(5) = 0.1(2)^5 = 0.1(32) = 3.2$$

$$t(8) = 0.1(2)^8 = 0.1(256) = 25.6$$

After 5 folds the paper is 3.2 millimeters thick.

After 8 folds, the paper is 25.6 millimeters thick.

Math Talk
Mathematical Practices

How can you tell that the function described in the example is an exponential function?

YOUR TURN

3. Write a function for the thickness of folding a piece of paper that is 0.2 millimeters thick, and determine the thickness after 3 and 7 folds.

_____

Writing an Equation from Input-Output Pairs

Many real-world situations can be modeled by exponential functions. Some of these situations can be easily observed and data from the observations can be used to write the corresponding exponential function.

EXAMPLE 3

 FL   F-LE.1.2

The height, $h(n)$, of a dropped ball is an exponential function of the number of bounces, n. On its first bounce, a certain ball reached a height of 15 inches. On its second bounce, the ball reached a height of 7.5 inches. Write an equation for the height of the ball, in inches, as a function of the number of bounces.

STEP 1   Divide successive function values, or heights, to find the value of b.
$$b = 7.5 \div 15 = 0.5$$

STEP 2   Use the value of b and a known ordered pair to find the value of a.

$h(n) = ab^n$	Write the general form.
$h(n) = a(0.5)^n$	Substitute the value for b.
$15 = a(0.5)^1$	Substitute the input and output values for the first bounce.
$15 = 0.5a$	Simplify.
$30 = a$	Solve for a.

STEP 3   Write an equation for the function: $h(n) = 30(0.5)^n$.

REFLECT

4. **Justify Reasoning** Use unit analysis to explain why b is a unit-less factor in Step 2 above.

_____

_____

5. **What If?** Show that using the values for the second bounce will give the same result for a.

_____

_____

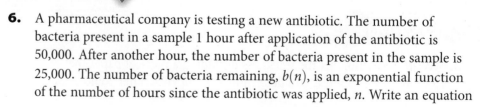

YOUR TURN

6. A pharmaceutical company is testing a new antibiotic. The number of bacteria present in a sample 1 hour after application of the antibiotic is 50,000. After another hour, the number of bacteria present in the sample is 25,000. The number of bacteria remaining, $b(n)$, is an exponential function of the number of hours since the antibiotic was applied, n. Write an equation

for the number of bacteria remaining after n hours. _____

1. Make a table of values for the function $f(x) = 2^x$ and graph the function. (Example 1)

x	$f(x) = 2^x$	$(x, f(x))$
−3	$f(\cdot\ ) = 2\quad =$	
−2	$f(\quad) = 2\quad =$	
−1	$f(\quad) = 2\quad =$	
0	$f(\ ) = 2\quad =$	
1	$f(\ ) = 2\quad =$	
2	$f(\ ) = 2\quad =$	
3	$f(\ ) = 2\quad =$	

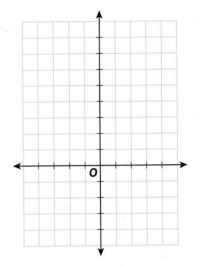

Use two points to write an equation for each function shown. (Examples 2 and 3)

2.

x	−3	−2	−1	0
f(x)	8	4	2	1

$\dfrac{f(-1)}{f(-2)} = \boxed{}$, so $b = \boxed{}$

$a = f\left(\boxed{}\right) = \boxed{}$

$f(x) = \boxed{}$

3.

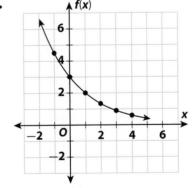

$f(x) =$ _____

? ESSENTIAL QUESTION CHECK-IN

4. How can you determine the values of a and b from a description of an exponential function of the form $f(x) = ab^x$?

_____

_____

10.1 Independent Practice

FL   F-LE.1.2, A-CED.1.2, A-SSE.2.3c, F-IF.2.5, F-IF.3.7e

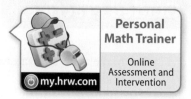

Personal
Math Trainer

Online
Assessment and
Intervention

my.hrw.com

Make a table of values and a graph for each function.

5. $f(x) = 2\left(\frac{3}{4}\right)^x$

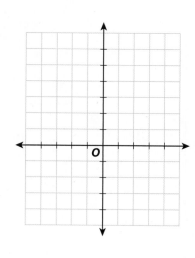

x	f(x)
−3	
−2	
−1	
0	
1	
2	
3	

6. $f(x) = 0.9(0.6)^x$

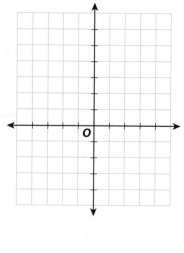

x	f(x)
−3	
−2	
−1	
0	
1	
2	
3	

Use two points to write an equation for the function shown.

7.

x	1	2	3	4
f(x)	8	6.4	5.12	4.096

_____

8.

x	−1	0	1	2
f(x)	0.75	3	12	48

_____

9.

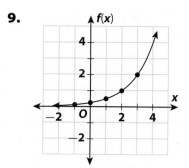

_____

10.

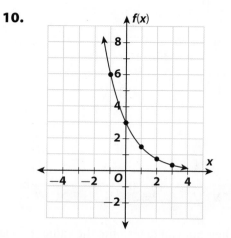

_____

11. Look for a Pattern As the x-values of an exponential function increase by a constant amount, the values of the function are multiplied by the constant ratio, b. What is the value of b in the function below?

x	$f(x)$
−1	1.5
0	3
1	6
2	12

Value of b: _____

12. The area of the top surface of an 8.5 inch by 11 inch piece of paper is a function of the number of times it is folded in half.

a. Identify the value of a. What does it represent in this situation?

Value of a: _____

_____

_____

b. Write an equation for the function that models this situation. Explain why this is an exponential function.

Equation: _____

_____

_____

c. What is the area of the top surface after 4 folds? Round to the nearest tenth of a square inch.

_____

d. **What if?** What would the equation be if the original piece of paper had dimensions 11 inches by 17 inches? Compare this with the equation in Part b.

Equation: _____

_____

_____

13. Suppose you do a favor for 3 people. Then you ask each of them to do a favor for 3 more people, passing along the request that each person who receives a favor does a favor for 3 more people. Suppose you do 3 favors on Day 1, each recipient does 3 favors on Day 2, and so on.

a. Complete the table for the first five days.

Day (n)	Favors $f(n)$
1	3
2	9
3	
4	
5	

b. Write an equation for the exponential function that models this situation.

_____

c. According to the model, how many favors will be done on Day 10? Explain your reasoning.

_____

_____

_____

_____

_____

_____

d. What would the equation be if everyone did a favor for 4 people rather than 3 people?

_____

14. Write an equation for the function whose graph is shown at the right.

_____

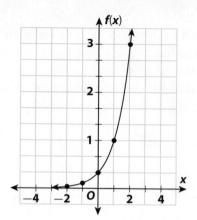

FOCUS ON HIGHER ORDER THINKING

Work Are

15. **Draw Conclusions** Assume that the domain of the function $f(x) = 3(2)^x$ is the set of all real numbers. What is the range of the function? Explain.

_____

_____

16. **Find the Error** Kaylee needed to write the equation of an exponential function from points on the graph of the function. To determine the value of b, Kaylee chose the ordered pairs $(1, 6)$ and $(3, 54)$ and divided 54 by 6. She determined that the value of b was 9. What error did Kaylee make?

_____

_____

_____

_____

17. **What If?** An exponential function has been defined as a function that can be represented by the equation $f(x) = ab^x$, where a, b, and x are real numbers, $a \neq 0$, $b > 0$, and $b \neq 1$. Why must it be specified that $b \neq 1$? What would the graph of the function look like if $b = 1$?

_____

_____

_____

_____

_____

LESSON 10.2 Exponential Growth and Decay

FL **F-LE.1.1c**

Recognize situations in which a quantity grows or decays by a constant percent rate per unit interval relative to another. Also *A-SSE.2.3c, F-IF.2.4, F-IF.2.5, F-IF.3.7, F-IF.3.7e, F-IF.3.8b, F-LE.1.2, F-LE.2.5*

? ESSENTIAL QUESTION

How can exponential functions model a changing quantity?

Exponential Growth

Exponential growth occurs when a quantity increases by the same rate *r* in each unit of time *t*. When this happens, the value of the quantity at any given time can be calculated as a function of the rate and the original amount. Because the function value increases as time increases, exponential growth functions are examples of **increasing functions**.

Math On the Spot
⊙ my.hrw.com

> ### Exponential Growth
>
> An exponential growth function has the form $y = a(1 + r)^t$, where $a > 0$.
>
> *y* represents the final amount.
>
> *a* represents the original amount.
>
> *r* represents the rate of growth expressed as a decimal.
>
> *t* represents time.

The exponential growth form $y = a(1 + r)^t$ is equivalent to the form $y = ab^x$, with $b = 1 + r$, $b > 1$ and *x* replaced by *t*.

EXAMPLE 1   FL   F-LE.1.1c, F-IF.2.5

A painting is sold for the first time for \$1400, and the value increases by 9% each year after it is sold. Write an exponential growth function to model this situation. Then find the value of the painting in 25 years. Graph the function. State the domain and range of the function. What does the *y*-intercept represent in the context of the problem?

STEP 1 Write the exponential growth function for this situation.

$y = a(1 + r)^t$ Write the formula.

$= 1400(1 + 0.09)^t$ Substitute 1400 for *a* and 0.09 for *r*.

$= 1400(1.09)^t$ Simplify.

STEP 2 Find the value in 25 years.

$y = 1400(1.09)^t$

$= 1400(1.09)^{25}$ Substitute 25 for *t*.

$\approx 12{,}072.31$ Use a calculator and round to the nearest hundredth.

After 25 years, the painting will be worth approximately $12,072.31.

STEP 3 Create a table of values to graph the function.

t	y	(t, y)
0	1400	(0, 1400)
1	1526	(1, 1526)
2	1663.34	(2, 1663.34)
3	1813.04	(3, 1813.04)
4	1976.21	(4, 1976.21)
5	2154.07	(5, 2154.07)
25	12072.31	(25, 12072.31)

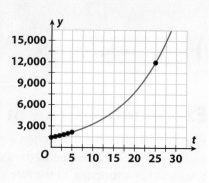

STEP 4 Determine the domain and the range of the function.

The input values represent years after a painting was sold for the first time. The values cannot be negative.

The domain is the set of real numbers t such that $t \geq 0$.

The output values represent the value of the painting in dollars. These values cannot be negative. Also, since this is an increasing function, the values cannot be less than the initial value of the painting.

The range is the set of real numbers y such that $y \geq 1400$.

STEP 5 The y-intercept is the value of y when $t = 0$. In the context of this problem, $t = 0$ is the time when the painting first sold. Therefore, the y-intercept represents the value of the painting when it was first sold.

Math Talk

Mathematical Practices

What is the value of the common ratio between two function values that have t-values that differ by 1? Give examples.

YOUR TURN

1. A sculpture is increasing in value at a rate of 8% per year, and its value in 2008 was $1200. Write an exponential growth function to model this situation. Then find the sculpture's value in 2014. Graph the function.

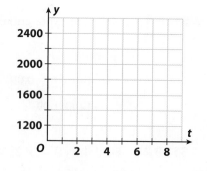

_____

_____

Exponential Decay

Exponential decay occurs when a quantity decreases by the same rate r in each unit of time t. Just like exponential growth, the value of the quantity at any given time can be calculated as a function of the rate and the original amount. Because the function value decreases as time increases, exponential decay functions are examples of **decreasing functions.**

Math On the Spot

my.hrw.com

> ### Exponential Decay
>
> An exponential decay function has the form $y = a(1 - r)^t$, where $a > 0$.
>
> y represents the final amount.
>
> a represents the original amount.
>
> r represents the rate of decay as a decimal.
>
> t represents time.

Notice an important difference between exponential growth functions and exponential decay functions. For exponential growth, the value inside the parentheses will be greater than 1 because r is added to 1 and $r > 0$. For exponential decay, the value inside the parentheses will be less than 1 because r is subtracted from 1 and $r > 0$.

The exponential decay form $y = a(1 - r)^t$ is equivalent to the form $y = ab^x$, with $b = 1 - r$, $0 < b < 1$ and x replaced by t.

EXAMPLE 2   **FL**   F-LE.1.1c, F-IF.2.5

The population of a town is decreasing at a rate of 1% per year. In 2005 there were 1300 people. Write an exponential decay function to model this situation. Then find the population in 2013. Graph the function. State the domain and range of the function. What does the *y*-intercept represent in the context of the problem?

STEP 1   Write the exponential decay function.

$$y = a(1 - r)^t$$
$$= 1300(1 - 0.01)^t \qquad \text{Substitute 1300 for } a \text{ and } 0.01 \text{ for } r.$$
$$= 1300(0.99)^t \qquad \text{Simplify.}$$

STEP 2   Find the population in 2013.

2013 is 8 years after 2005, the year for which the initial value of the population is given. So $t = 8$.

$$y = 1300(0.99)^t$$
$$= 1300(0.99)^8 \qquad \text{Substitute 8 for } t.$$
$$\approx 1200 \qquad \text{Use a calculator.}$$

The population in 2013 is approximately 1200 people.

STEP 3   Create a table of values to graph the function.

t	y	(t, y)
0	1300	(0, 1300)
1	1287	(1, 1287)
2	1274	(2, 1274)
3	1261	(3, 1261)
4	1249	(4, 1249)
5	1236	(5, 1236)
8	1200	(8, 1200)

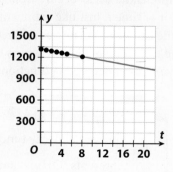

Note that while the graph may appear to be linear, it is not. The graph has this appearance because the population is declining at a slow rate.

STEP 4   Determine the domain and the range of the function.

The input values represent years after the initial population was given. The values cannot be negative.

The domain is the set of real numbers t such that $t \geq 0$.

The output values represent the population of the town. These values cannot be negative. Also, since this is a decreasing function, the values cannot be more than the initial population.

The range is the set of real numbers y such that $0 \leq y \leq 1300$.

STEP 5   The y-intercept is the value of y when $t = 0$. In the context of this problem, $t = 0$ is the year 2005. Therefore, the y-intercept represents the population of the town in 2005.

Math Talk

Mathematical Practices

What would a negative value of t represent in the context of Example 2?

YOUR TURN

2. The fish population in a local stream is decreasing at a rate of 3% per year. The original population was 48,000. Write an exponential decay function to model this situation. Then find the population after 7 years. Graph the function.

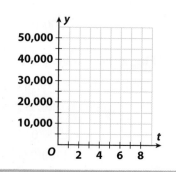

_____

Personal Math Trainer

Online Assessment and Intervention

⏻ my.hrw.com

Comparing Exponential Growth and Exponential Decay

You can use graphs to describe and compare exponential growth and exponential decay models over time.

 EXAMPLE 3 Real World | **FL** | **F-LE.1.1c**

The graph shows the value of two different shares of stock over the period of four years since they were purchased. The values have been changing exponentially. For each stock write the equation of the function that represents the value of the stock. Describe and compare the behaviors of the two stocks.

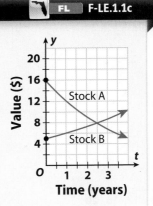

STEP 1 The graph for Stock A shows that the value of the stock is decreasing as time increases.

The initial value, when $t = 0$, is 16. The value when $t = 1$ is 12. Since $12 \div 16 = 0.75$, the function that represents the value of Stock A after t years is $A(t) = 16(0.75)^t$. $A(t)$ is an exponential decay function.

STEP 2 The graph for Stock B shows that the value of the stock is increasing as time increases.

The initial value, when $t = 0$, is 5. The value when $t = 1$ is 6. Since $6 \div 5 = 1.2$, the function that represents the value of Stock B after t years is $B(t) = 5(1.2)^t$. $B(t)$ is an exponential growth function.

STEP 3 The value of Stock A is going down over time. The value of Stock B is going up over time. The initial value of Stock A is greater than the initial value of Stock B. However, after about 2.5 years, the value of Stock B becomes greater than the value of Stock A.

Math Talk
Mathematical Practices

Is it likely that the function representing the value of Stock B can be used to predict its value for 30 years? Explain.

YOUR TURN

3. Two shares of two different stocks changed exponentially over a period of 3 years. For each stock, write the equation and function that represents the value of the stock. For Stock A, the initial value when $t = 0$ is 12. The value when $t = 1$ is 6. For stock B, the initial value when $t = 0$ is 4. The value when $t = 1$ is 6. Describe and compare the two stocks.

_____

_____

_____

_____

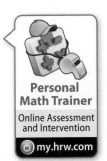
Personal Math Trainer

Online Assessment and Intervention

(○) my.hrw.com

Write an exponential growth or decay function to model each situation. Graph each function. Then find the value of the function after the given amount of time.

1. The cost of tuition at a college is $12,000 and is increasing at a rate of 6% per year; 4 years. (Example 1)

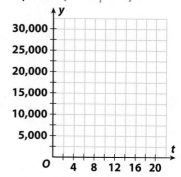

_____

2. The value of a car is $18,000 and is depreciating at a rate of 12% per year; 10 years. (Example 2)

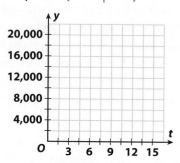

_____

3. The value of two parcels of land has been changing exponentially since they were purchased, as shown in the graph. Describe and compare the values of the two parcels of land. (Example 3)

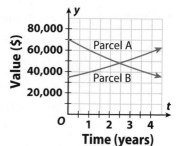

_____

_____

_____

_____

_____

_____

? ESSENTIAL QUESTION CHECK-IN

4. How can you tell from its graph whether a function represents exponential growth or exponential decay?

_____

_____

_____

_____

_____

10.2 Independent Practice

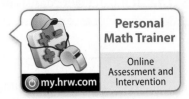

Personal Math Trainer

my.hrw.com

Online Assessment and Intervention

FL A-SSE.2.3c, F-IF.2.4, F-IF.2.5, F-IF.3.7, F-IF.3.7e, F-IF.3.8b, F-LE.1.1c, F-LE.1.2, F-LE.2.5

Write an exponential growth or decay function to model each situation. Graph each function. Then find the value of the function after the given amount of time.

5. The amount (to the nearest hundredth) of a 10-mg dose of a certain antibiotic decreases in your bloodstream at a rate of 16% per hour; 4 hours.

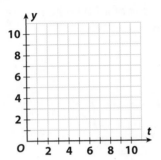

6. The number of student-athletes at a local high school is 300 and is increasing at a rate of 8% per year; 5 years.

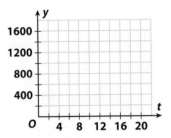

Write an exponential growth or decay function to model each situation. Then find the value of the function after the given amount of time.

7. Annual sales for a company are $149,000 and are increasing at a rate of 6% per year; 7 years. _____

8. The population of a town is 18,000 and is decreasing at a rate of 2% per year; 6 years. _____

9. The population of a small town is 1600 and is increasing at a rate of 3% per year; 10 years. _____

10. The value of a book is $58 and decreases at a rate of 10% per year; 8 years.

_____

11. A new savings account starts at $700 and increases at 1.2% yearly; 7 years.

_____

12. Mr. Nevin buys a car for $18,500. The value of the car depreciates 9% per year; 7 years. _____

13. If the domain consists of the set of all nonnegative real numbers, then for the graph of an exponential growth function, the y-intercept represents the

_____ value of the function. For the graph of an exponential

decay function, the y-intercept represents the _____ value of the function. Even though the graph of an exponential decay function is decreasing, if the initial value of the function is positive, the function will never

reach the _____ .

Work Area

14. Explain the Error Two students were asked to find the value of a $1000 item after 3 years. The item was depreciating at a rate of 40% per year. Who is incorrect? Explain the error.

$$1000(0.6)^3$$

$$\$216$$

Student A

$$1000(0.4)^3$$

$$\$64$$

Student B

_____

_____

_____

15. Make a Conjecture The value of a certain car can be modeled by the function $y = 20{,}000(0.84)^t$, where t is time in years. Will the value ever be zero? Explain.

_____

_____

_____

16. Communicate Mathematical Ideas Lynn says that it is always possible to look at a graph of an exponential function and determine whether it represents growth or decay. Nigel says he thinks it might not be. Who is correct? Explain.

_____

_____

_____

_____

_____

FL **F-LE.1.2**

Construct linear and exponential functions, including arithmetic and geometric sequences, given a graph, a description of a relationship, or two input-output pairs .... *Also, A-SSE.2.3c, F-BF.1.1, F-BF.1.1a, F-BF.1.2, F-IF.1.3, F-IF.3.8b, F-LE.1.1a*

ESSENTIAL QUESTION

How can a geometric sequence be described?

Writing General Rules for Geometric Sequences

In a **geometric sequence**, the ratio of consecutive terms is constant. The constant ratio is called the **common ratio**, often represented by r.

Math On the Spot
⏻ my.hrw.com

EXAMPLE 1 **FL** **F-BF.1.2**

Makers of Japanese swords in the 1400s repeatedly folded and hammered the metal to form layers. The folding process increased the strength of the sword.

The table shows how the number of layers depends on the number of folds. Write a recursive rule and an explicit rule for the geometric sequence represented by the table.

Number of Folds	n	1	2	3	4	5
Number of Layers	$f(n)$	2	4	8	16	32

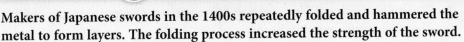

STEP 1 Find the common ratio by calculating the ratios of consecutive terms.

$$\frac{4}{2} = 2 \qquad\qquad \frac{8}{4} = 2$$

$$\frac{16}{8} = 2 \qquad\qquad \frac{32}{16} = 2$$

The common ratio, r, is 2.

STEP 2 Write a recursive rule for the sequence.

The first term is 2, so $f(1) = 2$.

All terms after the first term are the product of the previous term and the common ratio: $f(2) = f(1) \cdot 2, f(3) = f(2) \cdot 2, f(4) = f(3) \cdot 2, \ldots$

$f(n) = f(n - 1) \cdot 2$ for $n \geq 2$.

The recursive rule is stated by providing the first term and the rule for successive terms.

> This can be read as "each term in the sequence after the first term is equal to the previous term times two."

$f(1) = 2$

$f(n) = f(n - 1) \cdot 2$ for $n \geq 2$

STEP 3 Write an explicit rule for the sequence by writing each term as the product of the first term and a power of the common ratio.

n	$f(n)$
1	$2(2)^0 = 2$
2	$2(2)^1 = 4$
3	$2(2)^2 = 8$
4	$2(2)^3 = 16$
5	$2(2)^4 = 32$

Generalize the results from the table: $f(n) = 2 \cdot 2^{n-1}$.

REFLECT

1. **Draw Conclusions** How can you use properties of exponents to simplify the explicit rule found in Example 1?

_____

_____

_____

2. **Justify Reasoning** Explain how you know that the sequence 4, 12, 36, 108, 324, … is a geometric sequence.

_____

_____

3. **What If?** A geometric sequence has a common ratio of 5. The 6th term of the sequence is 30. What is the 7th term? What is the 5th term? Explain.

_____

_____

_____

_____

YOUR TURN

Personal
Math Trainer

Online Assessment
and Intervention

⏻ my.hrw.com

4. Write a recursive rule and an explicit rule for the geometric sequence represented by the table.

n	1	2	3	4	5
$f(n)$	2	6	18	54	162

_____

_____

Writing More General Rules for Geometric Sequences

FL   F-BF.1.2

Math On the Spot
my.hrw.com

Use the geometric sequence 6, 24, 96, 384, 1536, ... to help you write a recursive rule and an explicit rule for any geometric sequence. For the general rules, the values of n are consecutive integers starting with 1.

STEP 1 Find the common ratio.

Numbers	**Algebra**
6, 24, 96, 384, 1536, ...	$f(1), f(2), f(3), f(4), f(5), ...$
Common ratio = 4	Common ratio = r

STEP 2 Write a recursive rule.

Numbers	**Algebra**
$f(1) = 6$ and	Given $f(1)$,
$f(n) = f(n-1) \cdot 4$ for $n \geq 2$	$f(n) = f(n-1) \cdot r$ for $n \geq 2$

STEP 3 Write an explicit rule.

Numbers	**Algebra**
$f(n) = 6 \cdot 4^{n-1}$	$f(n) = f(1) \cdot r^{n-1}$

REFLECT

5. **Communicate Mathematical Ideas** The first term of a geometric sequence is 81 and the common ratio is $\frac{1}{3}$. Explain how you could find the 4th term of the sequence.

_____

6. What is the recursive rule for the sequence $f(n) = 5(4)^{n-1}$?

_____

YOUR TURN

7. Write a recursive rule and an explicit rule for the geometric sequence 128, 32, 8, 2, 0.5, ...

_____

_____

Personal Math Trainer

Online Assessment and Intervention

my.hrw.com

Writing a Geometric Sequence Given Two Terms

The explicit and recursive rules for a geometric sequence can also be written in *subscript notation*. In subscript notation, the subscript indicates the position of the term in the sequence. a_1, a_2, and a_3 are the first, second, and third terms of a sequence, respectively. In general, a_n is the *n*th term of a sequence.

EXAMPLE 3  **FL   F-LE.1.2**

The shutter speed settings on a camera form a geometric sequence where a_n is the shutter speed in seconds and *n* is the setting number. The fifth setting on the camera is $\frac{1}{60}$ second, and the seventh setting on the camera is $\frac{1}{15}$ second. Write an explicit rule for the sequence using subscript notation.

STEP 1   Identify the given terms in the sequence.

$a_5 = \frac{1}{60}$ The fifth term of the sequence is $\frac{1}{60}$.

$a_7 = \frac{1}{15}$ The seventh term of the sequence is $\frac{1}{15}$.

STEP 2   Find the common ratio.

$a_7 = a_6 \cdot r$ Write the recursive rule for a_7.

$a_6 = a_5 \cdot r$ Write the recursive rule for a_6.

$a_7 = a_5 \cdot r \cdot r$ Substitute the expression for a_6 into the rule for a_7.

$\frac{1}{15} = \frac{1}{60} \cdot r^2$ Substitute $\frac{1}{15}$ for a_7 and $\frac{1}{60}$ for a_5.

$4 = r^2$ Multiply each side by 60.

$2 = r$ Definition of positive square root

> ## Math Talk
> **Mathematical Practices**
>
> When finding the common ratio, why can you ignore the negative square root of 4 when solving $4 = r^2$?

STEP 3   Find the first term of the sequence.

$a_n = a_1 \cdot r^{n-1}$ Write the general explicit rule.

$\frac{1}{60} = a_1 \cdot 2^{5-1}$ Substitute $\frac{1}{60}$ for a_n, 2 for *r*, and 5 for *n*.

$\frac{1}{60} = a_1 \cdot 16$ Simplify.

$\frac{1}{960} = a_1$ Divide each side by 16.

STEP 4   Write the explicit rule.

$a_n = a_1 \cdot r^{n-1}$ Write the general explicit rule.

$a_n = \frac{1}{960} \cdot 2^{n-1}$ Substitute $\frac{1}{960}$ for a_1 and 2 for *r*.

Therefore, $a_n = \frac{1}{960} \cdot 2^{n-1}$.

YOUR TURN

8. The third term of a geometric sequence is $\frac{1}{54}$. The fifth term of the sequence is $\frac{1}{6}$. All terms of the sequence are positive numbers. Write an explicit rule for the sequence using subscript notation. _____

Relating Geometric Sequences and Exponential Functions

A geometric sequence is equivalent to an exponential function with a domain that is restricted to the positive integers. For an exponential function of the form $f(n) = ab^n$, recall that a represents the initial value and b is the common ratio. Compare this to $f(n) = f(1) \cdot r^{n-1}$, where $f(1)$ represents the initial value and r is the common ratio.

EXAMPLE 4

FL   F-LE.1.2

The graph shows the heights to which a ball bounces after it is dropped. Write an explicit rule for the sequence of bounce heights.

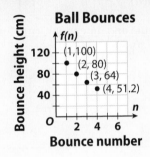

Ball Bounces

STEP 1   Represent the sequence in a table.

n	1	2	3	4
$f(n)$	100	80	64	51.2

STEP 2   Examine the sequence to determine whether it is geometric. The sequence is geometric because each term is the product of 0.8 and the previous term. The common ratio is 0.8.

STEP 3   Write an explicit rule for the sequence.

$f(n) = f(1) \cdot r^{n-1}$ Write the general rule.

$f(n) = 100 \cdot 0.8^{n-1}$ Substitute 100 for f(1) and 0.8 for r.

The sequence has the rule $f(n) = 100 \cdot 0.8^{n-1}$, where n is the bounce number and $f(n)$ is the bounce height.

YOUR TURN

9. The number of customers $f(n)$ projected to come into a new store in month number n is represented by the following table.

n	1	2	3	4
$f(n)$	1000	1500	2250	3375

Write an explicit rule for the sequence. _____

1. The table shows the beginning-of-month balances, rounded to the nearest cent, in Marla's saving account for the first few months after she made an initial deposit in the account. (Example 1)

Month	n	1	2	3	4
Account balance ($)	f(n)	2000	2010.00	2020.05	2030.15

   a. Explain how you know that the sequence of account balances is a geometric sequence.

   _____

   b. Write recursive and explicit rules for the sequences of account balances.

   Recursive rule: $f(1) = $ ⬚ , $f(n) = $ ⬚ · ⬚
   for $n \geq 2$

   Explicit rule: $f(n) = $ ⬚ · ⬚

2. Write a recursive rule and an explicit rule for the geometric sequence 9, 27, 81, 243. (Example 2)

   $\dfrac{27}{9} = $ ⬚ $\dfrac{81}{27} = $ ⬚ $\dfrac{243}{81} = $ ⬚

   Recursive rule: _____

   Explicit rule: _____

3. Write an explicit rule for the geometric sequence with terms $a_2 = 12$ and $a_4 = 192$. Assume that the common ratio r is positive. (Example 3)

   Explicit rule: _____

4. Write an explicit rule for the geometric sequence with terms $a_3 = 1600$ and $a_5 = 256$. Assume that the common ratio is positive. (Example 3)

   Explicit rule: _____

? ESSENTIAL QUESTION CHECK-IN

5. How can you write the explicit rule for a geometric sequence if you know the recursive rule for the sequence?

   _____

   _____

   _____

10.3 Independent Practice

 FL A-SSE.2.3c, F-BF.1.1, F-BF.1.1a, F-BF.1.2, F-IF.1.3, F-IF.3.8b, F-LE.1.1a, F-LE.1.2

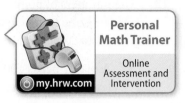

Personal Math Trainer

Online Assessment and Intervention

⏻ my.hrw.com

6. The graph shows the number of players in the first four rounds of the U.S Open women's singles tennis tournament.

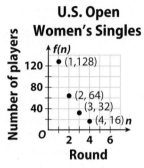

U.S. Open Women's Singles

a. Write an explicit rule for the sequence of players in each round.

_____

b. How many rounds are there in the tournament? (*Hint:* In the last round, only two players are left.)

_____

7. Write a recursive rule and an explicit rule for the geometric sequence $12, 3, \frac{3}{4}, \frac{3}{16}, \ldots$

Recursive rule: _____

Explicit rule: _____

Each rule represents a geometric sequence. If the given rule is recursive, write it as an explicit rule. If the rule is explicit, write it as a recursive rule. Assume that $f(1)$ is the first term of the sequence.

8. $f(n) = 6(3)^{n-1}$

_____

_____

9. $f(1) = 10; f(n) = f(n-1) \cdot 8$ for $n \geq 2$

_____

_____

Write an explicit rule for each geometric sequence based on the given terms from the sequence. Assume that the common ratio r is positive.

10. $a_2 = 50$ and $a_4 = 12.5$

_____

11. $a_3 = 24$ and $a_5 = 384$

_____

12. An economist predicts that the cost of food will increase by 4% per year for the next several years.

a. Use the economist's prediction to write an explicit rule for a geometric sequence that gives the cost in dollars of a box of cereal in year n that costs $3.20 in year 1.

_____

b. What is the fourth term of the sequence, and what does it represent in this situation?

_____

_____

13. The numbers of points that a player must accumulate to reach the next level of a video game form a geometric sequence, where $f(n)$ is the number of points needed to complete level n.

    a. A player needs 1000 points to complete level 2 and 8,000,000 to complete level 5. Write an explicit rule for the sequence.

        _____

    b. How many points are needed for level 7?

        _____

H.O.T.   **FOCUS ON HIGHER ORDER THINKING**

                                                                                                            Work Area

14. **Justify Reasoning** If a geometric sequence has a common ratio r that is negative, describe the terms of the sequence. Explain.

_____

_____

_____

_____

15. **Communicate Mathematical Ideas** If you are given the seventh term of a geometric sequence and the common ratio, how can you determine the second term of the sequence without writing an explicit rule or recursive rule? Explain.

_____

_____

_____

_____

_____

16. **Critique Reasoning** Miguel writes the following: 5, ___, 5, ___, …

He tells Alicia that what he has written represents a geometric sequence and asks Alicia to fill in the missing terms. Alicia says that the missing terms must both be 5. Miguel says that Alicia is incorrect. Who is correct? Explain.

_____

_____

_____

_____

Transforming Exponential Functions

FL **F-BF.2.3**

Identify the effect on the graph of replacing $f(x)$ by $f(x) + k$, $kf(x)$, $f(kx)$... for specific values of k (both positive and negative...) and illustrate an explanation of the effects on the graph using technology...

ESSENTIAL QUESTION

How does the graph of $f(x) = ab^x$ change when a and b are changed?

EXPLORE ACTIVITY 1   **FL** **F-BF.2.3**

Changing the Value of a in $f(x) = ab^x$

Recall that a family of functions is a set of functions whose graphs have basic characteristics in common. The most basic function of a family of functions is called the parent function. For exponential functions, every different base determines a different parent function for its own family of functions.

You can explore the behavior of an exponential function of the form $f(x) = ab^x$ by examining *parameters* a and b.

A Graph parent function $Y_1 = (1.5)^x$ and functions $Y_2 = 2(1.5)^x$ and $Y_3 = 3(1.5)^x$ on a graphing calculator. Use a viewing window from -5 to 5 for x and from -1 to 6 for y, using a scale of 1. Sketch the curves at right.

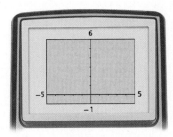

B Use the CALC feature while viewing the graphs to calculate the value of Y_1 when $x = -2$. Then use the up and down arrow keys to jump to the other curves and calculate their values when $x = -2$. Round to the nearest thousandth if necessary. Repeat this process until you have completed the table at the right.

x	Y_1	Y_2	Y_3
-2			
-1			
0			
1			
2			

A **vertical stretch** of a graph is the result of stretching the graph away from the x-axis. Each y-value of an (x, y) pair is multiplied by a factor $a > 1$.

A **vertical shrink** of a graph is the result of squeezing the graph towards the x-axis. Each y-value of an (x, y) pair is multiplied by a factor a such that $0 < a < 1$.

REFLECT

1. **Communicate Mathematical Ideas** Describe the graph of Y_2 as a vertical stretch or vertical shrink of the graph of Y_1 and identify the factor. In the same way, describe the graph of Y_2 using the graph of Y_1.

_____

_____

_____

FL F-BF.2.3

Changing the Value of b in $f(x) = b^x$

A Graph the functions $Y_1 = 1.2^x$ and $Y_2 = 1.5^x$ on a graphing calculator. Use a viewing window from -5 to 5 for x and from -2 to 5 for y, with a scale of 1 for both. Sketch the curves at right.

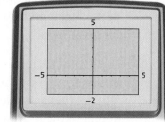

B Use the TBLSET and TABLE features to make a table of values starting at -2 with an increment of 1. Then complete the table. Round to the nearest thousandth if necessary.

C Which graph rises more quickly as x increases to the right of 0? Which graph falls, or approaches 0, more quickly as x decreases to the left of 0?

_____

_____

_____

x	Y_1	Y_2
-2	0.694	
-1		0.667
0		
1	1.2	1.5
2		

D Identify the y-intercepts of the graphs of Y_1 and Y_2.

_____

E Using the same window as above, graph the functions $Y_3 = 0.6^x$ and $Y_4 = 0.9^x$. Sketch the curves.

F Make a table of values starting at -2 with an increment of 1. Then complete the table.

X	Y_3	Y_4
-2	2.778	
-1		1.111
0		
1	0.6	0.9
2		

Math Talk

Mathematical Practices

For the graphs of Y_3 and Y_4, which graph rises more quickly as x decreases to the left of 0? Which graph falls more quickly as x increases to the right of 0?

REFLECT

2. **What If?** Consider the function $Y_5 = 1.3^x$. How will its graph compare with the graphs of Y_1 and Y_2? Discuss end behavior and the y-intercept.

_____

_____

_____

_____

Adding a Constant to an Exponential Function

Adding a constant to an exponential function causes the graph of the function to translate up or down, depending on the constant.

Math On the Spot
my.hrw.com

EXAMPLE 1

FL   F-BF.2.3

Describe the effect of transforming the function $f(x) = 1.5^x$ into $g(x) = 1.5^x + 2$.

Make a table of values for the functions and graph them. Round values in the table to the nearest thousandth.

x	f(x)	g(x)
−2	0.444	2.444
−1	0.667	2.667
0	1	3
1	1.5	3.5
2	2.25	4.25

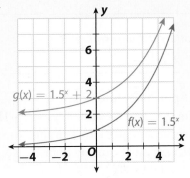

$g(x)$ is a vertical translation of $f(x)$ up 2 units.

Animated Math
my.hrw.com

YOUR TURN

3. Describe the effect of transforming the function $f(x) = 2^x$ into $g(x) = 2^x - 5$.

_____

Personal Math Trainer
Online Assessment and Intervention
my.hrw.com

In general, the constant that is added to an exponential function $f(x)$ determines the size and direction of the translation. For example, if $f(x) = 0.75^x$ and $h(x) = 0.75^x - 3$, then $h(x)$ is a vertical translation of $f(x)$ down 3 units.

The table below summarizes the general shapes of exponential function graphs.

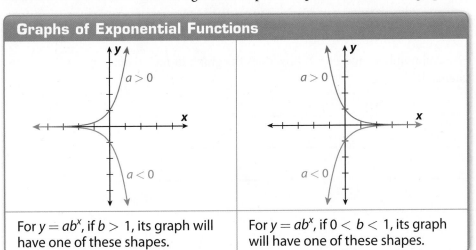

Graphs of Exponential Functions	
For $y = ab^x$, if $b > 1$, its graph will have one of these shapes.	For $y = ab^x$, if $0 < b < 1$, its graph will have one of these shapes.

Guided Practice

The graphs of the parent function $Y_1 = (0.5)^x$ and the function $Y_2 = 2(0.5)^x$ are shown at the right. Use the graphs for Exercises 1–4. (Explore Activity 1)

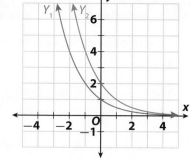

1. If Y_1 is written in the form $Y_1(x) = ab^x$, what is a? _____

2. If Y_2 is written in the form $Y_2(x) = ab^x$, what is a? _____

3. Look at the graphs. Are the values of Y_2 greater than or less than the values of Y_1?

   _____

4. Is Y_2 a *vertical stretch* or a *vertical shrink* of Y_1?

   _____

5. The function Y_3 is an exponential function. Use two points from the graph of the function to write an equation for Y_3. Then use a different value for b to write an equation for a function in the same family of functions that rises more quickly than Y_3 as x increases to the right of 0. (Explore Activity 2)

   _____

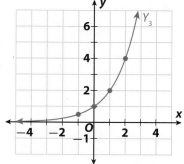

The graphs of the function $Y_5 = 1.2^x + 1$ and the function $Y_6 = 1.2^x + 3$ are shown at the right. Use the graphs for Exercises 6–7. (Example 1)

6. Which graph rises more quickly as x increases to the right of 0? Which graph falls, or approaches 0, more quickly as x decreases to the left of 0?

   _____

7. Y_6 is a vertical translation of Y_5. Tell the number of units Y_5 was translated and the direction of the translation.

   _____

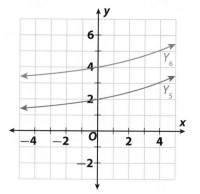

? ESSENTIAL QUESTION CHECK-IN

8. If a and b are positive real numbers and $b \neq 1$, how does the graph of $f(x) = ab^x$ change when b is changed?

   _____

   _____

   _____

   _____

10.4 Independent Practice

FL F-BF.2.3

Personal
Math Trainer

Online
my.hrw.com | Assessment and
Intervention

A parent function and a function in the same family are given. Tell whether the value of a or the value of b was changed in $f(x) = ab^x$.

9. $f(x) = (0.2)^x$ $f(x) = 2(0.2)^x$ _____

10. $f(x) = 3^x$ $f(x) = 3.5^x$ _____

11. $f(x) = 3^x$ $f(x) = 1.5(3)^x$ _____

Values of the parent function $Y_1 = (2.5)^x$ and the function $Y_2 = 0.5(2.5)^x$ are shown below.

x	Y_1	Y_2
-2	0.16	0.08
-1	0.4	0.2
0	1	0.5
1	2.5	1.25
2	6.25	3.125

12. How do the values in the table for Y_2 compare with the values for Y_1 for a given value of x?

_____

_____

_____

_____

13. Is Y_2 a *vertical stretch* or a *vertical shrink* of Y_1? Explain how you know.

_____

_____

_____

_____

Values of a parent function are shown below.

x	-2	-1	0	1	2
$f(x)$	4	2	1	0.5	0.25

14. Write an equation for the parent function.

_____

15. Write an equation for a function in the same family of functions whose graph will rise more quickly than the parent function as x decreases to the left of 0.

_____

The graphs of the function $Y_3 = 2^x + 4$ and the function $Y_4 = 2^x + 2$ are shown below.

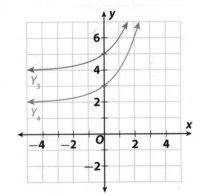

16. Identify the y-intercepts of Y_3 and Y_4.

_____

17. Justify Reasoning Did changing the constant in Y_3 to obtain Y_4 translate the graph of Y_3 up or down? Explain.

_____

_____

_____

18. Graph the functions $Y_1 = 0.6^x$ and $Y_2 = 0.3^x$ on a graphing calculator. Use a viewing window from -5 to 5 for x and from -2 to 8 for y, with a scale of 1 for both. Sketch the curves.

How does the graph of Y_1 compare with the graph of Y_2? Discuss end behavior and the y-intercept.

_____

_____

_____

_____

H.O.T. ⬛ **FOCUS ON HIGHER ORDER THINKING**

Work Area

19. Critical Thinking Describe how the graph of $f(x) = ab^x$ changes for a given positive value of a as you increase the value of b when $b > 1$. Discuss end behavior and the y-intercept.

_____

_____

_____

_____

20. Communicate Mathematical Ideas Consider the functions $Y_1 = (1.02)^x$ and $Y_2 = (1.03)^x$. Which function increases more quickly as x increases to the right of 0? How do the growth factors support your answer?

_____

_____

_____

_____

21. Communicate Mathematical Ideas Consider the functions $Y_1 = (0.94)^x$ and $Y_2 = (0.98)^x$. Which function decreases more quickly as x increases to the right of 0? How do the decay factors support your answer?

_____

_____

_____

_____

LESSON 10.5 Equations Involving Exponents

FL **A-CED.1.1**

Create equations and inequalities in one variable and use them to solve problems. Include equations arising from linear and quadratic functions, and simple rational and exponential functions. *Also A-CED.1.2, F-BF.1.1, F-BF.1.1a, F-LE.1.2*

ESSENTIAL QUESTION

How can you solve equations involving variable exponents?

EXPLORE ACTIVITY

FL **A-CED.1.1**

Exploring Equations Containing Exponents

The equation $2^x = 8$ has an exponent that is a variable. You can use what you know about powers to find the value of the variable.

A Write 8 as a power of 2.

$$2^x = 8$$

$$2^x = \boxed{} \cdot \boxed{} \cdot \boxed{}$$

$$2^x = \boxed{}^{\boxed{}}$$

B Suppose $x = 4$. Is $2^4 = 2^3$? Explain.

_____

Suppose $x = 3$. Is $2^3 = 2^3$? Explain.

_____

C What is the value of x? _____

REFLECT

1. Communicating Mathematical Ideas What do you notice about the bases of the expressions 2^x and 2^3?

_____

The Equality of Bases Property is given below.

Equality of Bases Property		
Words	**Algebra**	**Example**
Two powers with the same positive base other than 1 are equal if and only if the exponents are equal.	If $b > 0$ and $b \neq 1$, then $b^x = b^y$ if and only if $x = y$.	If $2^x = 2^9$, then $x = 9$. If $x = 9$, then $2^x = 2^9$.

Math On the Spot

my.hrw.com

Solving Equations by Equating Exponents

You can apply the properties of equations you already know and the Equality of Bases Property to solve equations involving exponents.

EXAMPLE 1

 FL A-CED.1.1

Solve each equation.

A $\frac{5}{2}(2)^x = 80$

$\frac{2}{5} \cdot \frac{5}{2}(2)^x = \frac{2}{5} \cdot 80$ Multiply to isolate the power $(2)^x$.

$(2)^x = 32$ Simplify.

$(2)^x = 2^5$ Write 32 as a power of 2.

$x = 5$ $b^x = b^y$ if and only if $x = y$.

B $4\left(\frac{5}{3}\right)^x = \frac{500}{27}$

$\frac{1}{4} \cdot 4\left(\frac{5}{3}\right)^x = \frac{1}{4} \cdot \frac{500}{27}$ Multiply to isolate the power.

$\left(\frac{5}{3}\right)^x = \frac{125}{27}$ Simplify.

$\left(\frac{5}{3}\right)^x = \left(\frac{5}{3}\right)^3$ Write the fraction as a power of $\frac{5}{3}$.

$x = 3$ $b^x = b^y$ if and only if $x = y$.

REFLECT

2. How can you check a solution?

_____

_____

3. Communicate Mathematical Ideas How can you work backward to write $\frac{125}{27}$ as a power of $\frac{5}{3}$?

_____

_____

4. Justify Reasoning Is it possible to solve the equation $2^x = 96$ using the method in Example 1? Why or why not?

_____

_____

_____

YOUR TURN

Solve each equation.

5. $\frac{2}{3}(3)^x = 54$

$x =$ _____

6. $6\left(\frac{5}{4}\right)^x = \frac{75}{8}$

$x =$ _____

7. $\frac{1}{2}(4)^x = 32$

$x =$ _____

8. $5(3)^x = 405$

$x =$ _____

Writing an Equation and Solving by Graphing

Some equations cannot be solved using the method in Example 1 because it isn't possible to write both sides of the equation as a whole number power of the same base. Instead, you can consider the expressions on either side of the equation as the rules for two different functions. You can then solve the original equation in one variable by graphing the two functions. The solution is the input value for the point where the two graphs intersect.

EXAMPLE 2 *Real World*   **FL**   F-BF.1.1, F-LE.1.2

A town has 78,918 residents. The population is increasing at a rate of 6% per year. The town council is offering a prize for the best prediction of how long it will take for the population to reach 100,000. Make a prediction.

STEP 1   Write an exponential model to represent the situation.

Let y represent the population and x represent time (in years).

$y = 78{,}918(1 + 0.06)^x$

STEP 2   Write an equation in one variable to represent the time, x, when the population reaches 100,000.

$100{,}000 = 78{,}918(1.06)^x$

STEP 3   Write functions for the expressions on either side of the equation.

$f(x) = 100{,}000$ *$f(x)$ is a constant function.*

$g(x) = 78{,}918(1.06)^x$ *$g(x)$ is an exponential growth function.*

STEP 4 Graph the functions on a graphing calculator. Let $Y_1 = f(x)$ and $Y_2 = g(x)$. Use a viewing window from -2 to 8 for x, using a scale of 1, and a viewing window from $-20{,}000$ to $200{,}000$ for y, using a scale of 20,000. Sketch the graphs.

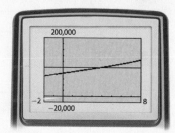

STEP 5 Use the intersect feature on the CALC menu to find the input value where the graphs intersect. (Do not round.)

The input value where the graphs intersect is 4.063245.

STEP 6 Use the input value to make a prediction as to the number of years until the population reaches 100,000.

The population will reach 100,000 in just over 4 years.

REFLECT

9. **Communicate Mathematical Ideas** Why is the input value of the intersection point of $f(x)$ and $g(x)$ the solution?

_____

_____

_____

_____

Math Talk

Mathematical Practices

Suppose the contest is announced on January 1. Explain how to predict the date on which the population will be 100,000.

YOUR TURN

There are 250 bass in a lake. The population is increasing at the rate of 20% per year. You want to make a prediction for how long it will take the population to reach 400.

10. Write an equation in one variable to represent the time, x, when the population reaches 400.

_____

11. Make a prediction for how long will it take for the bass population to reach 400. Round the answer to the nearest tenth of a year.

_____

Personal Math Trainer

Online Assessment and Intervention

my.hrw.com

Guided Practice

Solve each equation without graphing. (Example 1)

1. $\frac{3}{4}(6)^x = 162$

$(6)^x = \boxed{}$

$(6)^x = 6^{\boxed{}}$

$x = \boxed{}$

2. $3\left(\frac{5}{6}\right)^x = \frac{75}{36}$

$\left(\frac{5}{6}\right)^x = \boxed{}$

$\left(\frac{5}{6}\right)^x = \left(\frac{5}{6}\right)^{\boxed{}}$

$x = \boxed{}$

3. $7\left(\frac{1}{2}\right)^x = \frac{7}{8}$

$x =$ _____

4. $\frac{1}{5}(5)^x = 125$

$x =$ _____

5. $10(4)^x = 640$

$x =$ _____

Solve each equation by graphing. Round to the nearest hundredth. (Example 2)

6. $6^x = 100$

$x \approx$ _____

7. $7^x = 400$

$x \approx$ _____

8. $(2.5)^x = 100$

$x \approx$ _____

There are 225 wolves in a state park. The population is increasing at the rate of 15% per year. You want to make a prediction for how long it will take the population to reach 500. (Example 2)

9. Write an equation in one variable to represent the time, x, when the population

reaches 500. _____

10. Make a prediction for how long will it take for the wolf population to reach 500.

Round the answer to the nearest tenth of a year. _____

? ESSENTIAL QUESTION CHECK-IN

11. How can you solve equations involving variable exponents?

_____

_____

_____

_____

10.5 Independent Practice

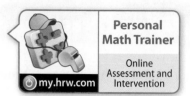

FL A-CED.1.1, A-CED.1.2, F-BF.1.1, F-BF.1.1a, F-LE.1.2

Personal Math Trainer

Online Assessment and Intervention

my.hrw.com

Solve each equation without graphing.

12. $8(3)^x = 648$

$x =$ _____

13. $\frac{1}{5}(5)^x = 5$

$x =$ _____

14. $3\left(\frac{3}{10}\right)^x = \frac{27}{100}$

$x =$ _____

15. $6(5)^x = 750$

$x =$ _____

16. $\frac{3}{4}\left(\frac{2}{3}\right)^x = \frac{4}{27}$

$x =$ _____

17. $\frac{1}{2}\left(\frac{1}{5}\right)^x = \frac{1}{50}$

$x =$ _____

18. What did you do first to solve the equation $\frac{1}{5}(5)^x = 5$ in Exercise 13?

_____

Solve each equation by graphing. Round to the nearest hundredth.

19. $6^x = 150$

$x \approx$ _____

20. $5^x = 20$

$x \approx$ _____

21. $3^x = 100$

$x \approx$ _____

22. $(5.5)^x = 40$

$x \approx$ _____

23. Write the constant function and the exponential function you graphed in order to solve the equation $5^x = 20$ in Exercise 20.

constant function: $f(x) =$ _____

exponential function: $g(x) =$ _____

24. Can you solve the equation $30 = (1.5)^x$ using the method shown in Example 1? Explain.

_____

_____

Use the equation $2^x = 16$ for Exercises 25–27.

25. Solve the equation using properties of equations and the Equality of Bases Property.

$x =$ _____

26. Solve the equation by graphing a constant function and an exponential function on the coordinate plane below.

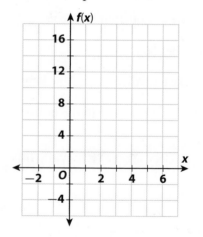

$x =$ _____

27. How do your solutions in Exercises 26 and 25 compare?

_____

28. Justify Reasoning Which method do you prefer for solving the equation $2^x = 16$? Explain.

_____

_____

_____

_____

_____

29. Which method would be better for solving the equation $2^x = 20$? Explain.

_____

_____

_____

There are 175 deer in a state park. The population is increasing at the rate of 12% per year. You want to make a prediction for how long it will take the population to reach 300.

30. Write an equation in one variable to represent the time, x, when the population reaches 300.

_____

_____

31. Write the constant function and the exponential function you will graph to find the time, x, when the population reaches 300.

constant function: $f(x) =$ _____

exponential function: $g(x) =$ _____

32. Graph the functions from Exercise 31 on a graphing calculator. Sketch the graphs below.

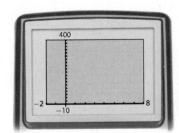

33. Explain how you can use the graphs to find the time when the population reaches 300.

_____

_____

_____

_____

34. Make a prediction for how long it will take for the deer population to reach 300. Round the answer to the nearest tenth of a year.

_____

A city has 175,000 residents. The population is increasing at the rate of 10% per year. You want to make a prediction for how long it will take the population to reach 300,000.

35. Write an equation in one variable to represent the time, x, when the population reaches 300,000.

_____

_____

36. Make a prediction for how long will it take for the population to reach 300,000. Round the answer to the nearest tenth of a

year. _____

37. What If? Suppose there are 350,000 residents of another city. The population of this city is decreasing at a rate of 3% per year. Which city's population will reach 300,000 sooner? Explain.

_____

_____

_____

_____

_____

38. Last year a debate club sold 972 fundraiser tickets on their most successful day. This year the 4 club officers plan to match that number on a single day as follows.

To start off, on Day 0, each of the 4 officers will sell 3 tickets and ask each buyer to sell 3 more tickets the next day. Every time a ticket is sold, the buyer of the ticket will be asked to sell 3 more tickets the next day.

If the plan works, on what day will the number of tickets sold be 972?

a. Write an equation in one variable to model the situation. _____

b. If the plan works, on what day will the number sold be 972? _____

 **FOCUS ON HIGHER ORDER THINKING**

Work Area

39. Explain the Error Jean and Marco each solved the equation $9(3)^x = 729$. Which is incorrect? Explain your reasoning.

	Jean
	$9(3)^x = 729$
	$\frac{1}{9} \cdot 9(3)^x = \frac{1}{9} \cdot 729$
	$3^x = 81$
	$3^x = 3^4$
	$x = 4$

	Marco
	$9(3)^x = 729$
	$(3)^x = 9 \cdot 729$
	$3^x = 6{,}561$
	$3^x = 3^8$
	$x = 8$

_____

_____

_____

_____

40. Critical Thinking Without solving, determine which of the following equations has a greater solution. Explain your reasoning.

$$\frac{1}{3}(3)^x = 243 \qquad\qquad \frac{1}{3}(9)^x = 243$$

_____

_____

_____

_____

_____

_____

Ready to Go On?

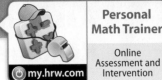

10.1 Exponential Functions

Use two points to write an equation for each function shown.

1.

x	−2	−1	0	1	2
f(x)	2.5	5	10	20	40

_____

2.

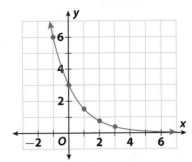

_____

10.2 and 10.3 Exponential Growth and Decay, and Geometric Sequences

Write an exponential growth or decay function to model each situation. Then find the value of the function after the given amount of time.

3. An antique car is worth $35,000, and its value grows by 6% per year; 8 years.

_____

4. The student enrollment is 980 students and decreases by 1.3% per year; 7 years.

_____

If the given rule is recursive, write it as an explicit rule. If the rule is explicit, write it as a recursive rule. Assume that $f(1)$ is the first term of the sequence.

5. $f(1) = 4.5; f(n) = f(n - 1) \cdot 6$ for $n \geq 2$

_____

6. $f(n) = 0.6(7)^{n-1}$

_____

10.4 and 10.5 Transforming Exponential Functions and Equations Involving Exponents

7. Describe the effect of replacing $f(x) = 4^x$ by $g(x) = 4^x + 1$.

_____

8. Solve $5\left(\frac{1}{3}\right)^x = \frac{5}{27}$ without using a calculator.

_____

? ESSENTIAL QUESTION

9. How can exponential functions be used to represent real-world situations?

_____

_____

_____

Selected Response

1. Which is the graph of an exponential function with initial value 8 and common ratio 0.5?

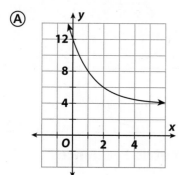

Ⓐ

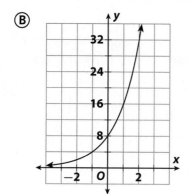

Ⓑ

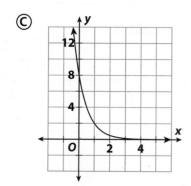

Ⓒ

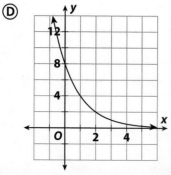

Ⓓ

2. What is the 5th term of the sequence defined by $f(n) = 5(n - 2)$?

Ⓐ 3   Ⓒ 10

Ⓑ 5   Ⓓ 15

3. What is the slope of the line whose equation is $2x - 3y = 5$?

Ⓐ $-\frac{3}{5}$ Ⓒ $\frac{2}{3}$

Ⓑ $-\frac{2}{3}$ Ⓓ $\frac{3}{2}$

4. David deposits $500 in a savings account. The value grows at a rate of 2% per year. What is the value of the savings account after 5 years?

Ⓐ $451.96

Ⓑ $552.04

Ⓒ $1,244.16

Ⓓ $2,550.00

5. What is the solution to the equation $5\left(\frac{1}{2}\right)^x = 160$?

Ⓐ -5

Ⓑ -4

Ⓒ 4

Ⓓ 5

Mini-Task

6. The monthly incomes for the first five months of Yuri's tutoring business are $500, $750, $1125, $1687.50, and $2531.25.

a. Write the explicit rule for the sequence of monthly incomes.

_____

b. If Yuri's monthly incomes continue to follow this sequence, in what month will his monthly income reach $4,000?

_____

Modeling with Exponential Functions

MODULE
11

LESSON 11.1
Exponential Regression

FL A-CED.1.2, F-LE.2.5, S-ID.2.6a, S-ID.2.6b

LESSON 11.2
Comparing Linear and Exponential Models

FL F-LE.1.1, F-LE.1.1a, F-LE.1.1b, F-LE.1.1c, F-LE.1.3

? ESSENTIAL QUESTION

When do you use exponential functions to model real-world data?

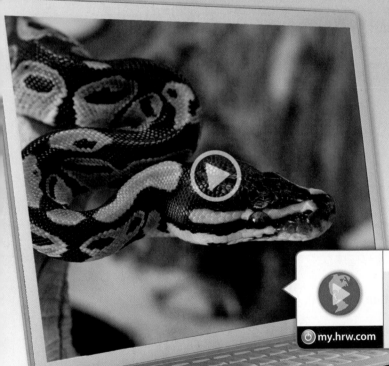

Real-World Video

Pythons originally kept as pets but later released into the Florida ecosystem find themselves in an environment with no natural predators and prey ill-equipped to evade or defend itself. As a result, the python population can grow exponentially, causing havoc among local wildlife and pets.

my.hrw.com

GO DIGITAL

my.hrw.com

my.hrw.com

Go digital with your write-in student edition, accessible on any device.

Math On the Spot

Scan with your smart phone to jump directly to the online edition, video tutor, and more.

Animated Math

Interactively explore key concepts to see how math works.

Personal Math Trainer

Get immediate feedback and help as you work through practice sets.

Are YOU Ready?

Complete these exercises to review the skills you will need for this module.

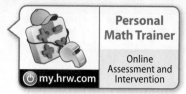

Personal Math Trainer

my.hrw.com

Online Assessment and Intervention

Percent Problems

EXAMPLE What is 108% of $500?

$$\downarrow \quad \downarrow \quad \downarrow \quad \downarrow \quad \downarrow$$
$$x \; = 1.08 \; \times \; 500 \qquad \text{Translate.}$$
$$x = (1.08)(500) \qquad \text{Simplify.}$$
$$x = 540$$

Simplify each expression.

1. What is 103% of $800?

2. What is 95% of 15,000 people?

3. What is 84% of 200 milligrams?

4. What is 105% of 105% of $30,000?

Function Tables

EXAMPLE Generate ordered pairs for the function $y = 3x + 2$ for $x = 0, 1, 2, 3$.

x	y = 3x + 2	y
0	$y = 3(0) + 2 = 2$	2
1	$y = 3(1) + 2 = 5$	5
2	$y = 3(2) + 2 = 8$	8
3	$y = 3(3) + 2 = 11$	11

Generate ordered pairs for each function for $x = 0, 1, 2, 3, 4$.

5. $y = 25{,}000 + 1050x$

x	y
0	
1	
2	
3	
4	

6. $y = 25{,}000(1.04)^x$

x	y
0	
1	
2	
3	
4	

Reading Start-Up

Vocabulary

Review Words

correlation coefficient
(coeficiente de correlación)

✓ exponential function
(función exponencial)

✓ linear function
(función lineal)

✓ regression equation
(ecuación de regresión)

residual *(residuo)*

scatter plot
(diagrama de dispersión)

Visualize Vocabulary

Use the Review Words with a check next to them to complete the Venn diagram.

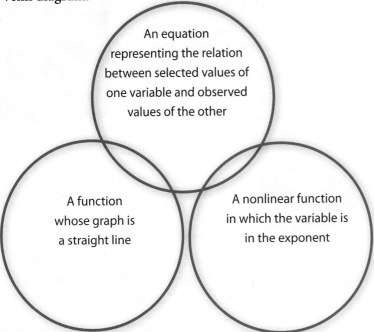

An equation representing the relation between selected values of one variable and observed values of the other

A function whose graph is a straight line

A nonlinear function in which the variable is in the exponent

Understand Vocabulary

Use some of the vocabulary terms in this module to answer the following questions. You may refer to the module, the glossary, or a dictionary.

1. The _____ provides an indication of how well the regression model fits the data.

2. The term scatter plot refers to a type of graph. What do you think a *scatter plot* looks like?

_____

Active Reading

Double-Door Fold Create a double-door fold to help you understand the concepts in this module. Label one flap "Exponential Model" and the other flap "Comparing Linear and Exponential Models." As you study the lessons, write important ideas under the appropriate flap.

MODULE 11
Unpacking the Standards

Understanding the standards and related vocabulary terms will help you know exactly what you are expected to learn in this module.

 FL S-ID.2.6a

Fit a function to the data; use functions fitted to data to solve problems in the context of the data.

Key Vocabulary

function *(función)*
An input-output relationship that has exactly one output for each input

What It Means to You

You can use a function to approximate the relationship between two variables.

UNPACKING EXAMPLE S-ID.2.6A

This table shows the number of Blu-ray discs Clarissa has sold each year since she opened her video store in 2006.

Years since 2006	0	1	2	3	4	5	6
Number of Blu-rays sold	27	117	252	313	395	423	573

Enter the data from the table on a graphing calculator. Use the calculator's linear regression feature to find the model of the data. This data can be represented by the linear function $f(x) = 85.46x + 43.61$.

FL F-LE.1.1

Distinguish between situations that can be modeled with linear functions and with exponential functions.

Key Vocabulary

exponential function *(función exponencial)*
A non-linear function in which the variable is in the exponent

linear function *(función lineal)*
A function that has a graph that is a straight line

What It Means to You

You can determine whether a linear or exponential function is best to model a set of real-world data.

UNPACKING EXAMPLE F-LE.1.1

The value of a $15,000 car decreases by $1000 each year.

The amount of decrease, $1000, remains constant. The value of the car for the first 3 years is: $15,000, $15,000 − $1000 = $14,000, and $14,000 − $1000 = $13,000, respectively. This shows a linear function.

The value of a $15,000 car decreases by 10% each year.

The percent of decrease, 10%, remains constant. But the amount of decrease changes each year based on the value of the car that year. The value of the car for the first 3 years is: $15,000, $15,000 × 0.90 = $13,500, and $13,500 × 0.9 = $12,150, respectively. This shows an exponential function.

Visit **my.hrw.com** to see all **Florida Math Standards** unpacked.

my.hrw.com

11.1 Exponential Regression

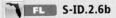

FL **S-ID.2.6a**
Fit a function to the data; use functions…to solve problems in the context of the data.

FL **S-ID.2.6b**
Informally assess the fit of a function by plotting and analyzing residuals. *Also A-CED.1.2, F-LE.2.5*

ESSENTIAL QUESTION

How can you use exponential regression to model data?

Fitting an Exponential Function to Data

This lesson will explore data that is best approximated by an exponential function of the form $y = f(x) = ab^x$.

Math On the Spot
⏻ my.hrw.com

EXAMPLE 1 Real World   FL **S-ID.2.6a**

Use a calculator to find an exponential function model for the data.

Number of Internet hosts							
Years since 2001	0	1	2	3	4	5	6
Number (millions)	110	147	172	233	318	395	433

STEP 1   Enter the data from the table on a graphing calculator, with years since 2001 (the *x*-value) in List 1 and the number of Internet hosts (the *y*-value) in List 2. Then, graph the data as a scatter plot.

Choose scatter plot with no line

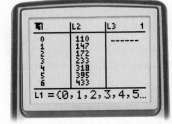  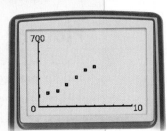

The points in the scatter plot follow an upward curve. An exponential function might fit the data better than a linear model.

STEP 2   Use the exponential regression feature.

Math Talk
Mathematical Practices

What is the growth rate for the exponential model?

Round the values of *a* and *b* to write the function $y = 113(1.27)^x$.
Because the *r* value is close to 1, the model is a good fit.

REFLECT

1. Communicate Mathematical Ideas Which parameter, a or b, represents the initial value of y? Explain how you know.

_____

_____

_____

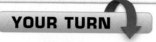

2. Use your calculator to find an exponential function that models the average number of text messages a month for the data shown.

Average Number of Monthly Text Messages							
	2006 (Q4)	2007 (Q1)	2007 (Q2)	2007 (Q3)	2007 (Q4)	2008 (Q1)	2008 (Q2)
Quarter Years	0	1	2	3	4	5	6
Average Number	108	129	172	193	218	288	357

EXPLORE ACTIVITY

FL S-ID.2.6b

Plotting and Analyzing Residuals

Recall that a residual is the difference between the actual y-value in the data set and the predicted y-value. Residuals can be used to assess how well a model fits a data set. If a model fits the data well, then:

- The numbers of positive and negative residuals are roughly equal.
- The residuals are randomly distributed about the x-axis on a residual plot.
- The absolute value of the residuals is small relative to the data values.

Analyze the residuals of the exponential model found in Example 1.

A The portion of the regression model and scatter plot corresponding to the second data point of the Internet host data is shown. Label the actual y-value from the data as y_d, and label the y-value predicted by the model as y_m. Find the difference between these values ($y_d - y_m$), and then place the result in the residual column for $x = 1$ in the chart on the next page.

B On your calculator, enter the regression equation as the rule for equation Y_1. Then view the table to find the y-values predicted by model (y_m). Record the results in the table on the right.

C Now complete the residuals column by subtracting the predicted values from the actual values.

D Set up a residual scatter plot of the data and graph it. (The residuals data will automatically be saved as Plot 2. Adjust the viewing window as needed.) Plot the points on the graph provided.

Number of Internet hosts (millions)			
x	Actual value y_d	Predicted value y_m	Residual $y_d - y_m$
0	110	113	−3
1	147	143	
2	172		
3	233		
4	318		
5	395		
6	433		

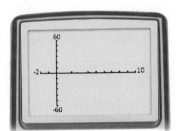

REFLECT

3. **Multiple Representations** What does the residual plot reveal about the fit of the model? Does this agree with the correlation coefficient?

_____

_____

_____

_____

_____

4. **Look for Patterns** What can you infer about the accuracy of the model as it moves further away from the initial value? Explain.

_____

_____

_____

_____

The first two columns of the table show the population of Arizona (in thousands) in each census from 1900–2000. (Example 1 and Explore Activity)

1. Find an exponential function model for the data. Plot the remaining data points on the screen below and sketch the regression curve.

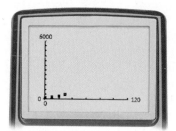

2. Round the parameters a and b to four significant digits. The regression equation is:

$$y = f(x) = \boxed{} \times \boxed{}^{x}$$

The regression equation approximates the Arizona population in 1900 to

be _____ people and the growth rate

to be _____, meaning the population

increases by _____% each year.

Arizona population in thousands (y)			
Years since 1900 (x)	Actual y_d	Predicted y_m	Residual $y_d - y_m$
0	123		
10	204		8
20	334	283	
30	436		
40	499		−88
50	750	847	
60	1302		
70	1771		
80	2718		178
90	3665		
100	5131	5281	

3. Round the value of the correlation coefficient to three significant digits.

$r = \boxed{}$, suggesting the model ⟨ **is / is not** ⟩ a good approximation of the population data.

4. Complete the Arizona population table by filling in the remaining y_m and $y_d - y_m$ values. Use the regression model stored in your calculator to obtain the y_m values. Round to the nearest whole number.

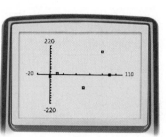

5. Complete the residual plot in which five of the residuals have already been plotted.

6. How can you use exponential regression to model data?

_____

_____

_____

11.1 Independent Practice

FL S-ID.2.6a, S-ID.2.6b, A-CED.1.2, F-LE.2.5

Personal Math Trainer

Online Assessment and Intervention

⊙ my.hrw.com

7. Multistep In 2012, the number of Internet hosts was reported to be 888 million. Consider how this compares to the model found in Example 1.

a. Based on the model, predict the number of Internet hosts for 2012. Compare the values obtained from reading the table, tracing the graph, and calculating using the regression equation.

_____

_____

_____

_____

_____

_____

b. Does the residual for 2012 meet the good-fit requirement of being small relative to the data? Explain.

_____

_____

_____

c. Discuss the likely accuracy of the number of Internet hosts predicted for 2025. Explain your answer.

_____

_____

_____

_____

_____

8. What if? Use a graphing calculator to model the Arizona population data on page 384 through **linear** regression.

a. Describe the shape of the residual plot and explain what this suggests about the fit of the model.

_____

_____

_____

_____

_____

b. Would the correlation coefficient lead you to draw the same conclusion regarding how well the model approximates the data? Explain.

_____

_____

_____

_____

_____

9. Make a Prediction Use the exponential regression model of the Arizona population data to predict the year in which the state's population will first exceed 15,000. Explain how you arrived at your answer.

_____

_____

_____

_____

10. Interpret the Answer The concentration of ibuprofen in a person's blood was plotted each hour. An exponential model fit the data with $a = 400$ and $b = 0.71$. Interpret these parameters.

_____

_____

_____

H.O.T. FOCUS ON HIGHER ORDER THINKING

11. Critique Reasoning The absolute values of the residuals in Mark's regression model are less than 20. Working on a different data set, Sandy obtained residuals in the hundreds. This led Mark to conclude his model is a better fit than Sandy's. Explain why Mark is wrong to base his critique of their regression models on the values of the residuals.

_____

_____

_____

_____

12. Make a Conjecture When Chris used exponential regression on the Arizona population data on page 384, he obtained the following results: $a = 186$, $b = 1.026$, $r = 0.813$. When he reviewed the data in his lists, he found he had entered a number incorrectly. Is it more likely that his error was in entering the final value too high or too low? Justify your reasoning.

_____

_____

_____

_____

13. Draw Conclusions Madelyn has recorded the number of bacteria on her growth plate every hour for three hours. She finds that a linear model fits her data better than the expected exponential model. What should she do to improve her model?

_____

_____

_____

_____

LESSON
11.2
Comparing Linear and Exponential Models

FL **F-LE.1.1**

Distinguish between situations
that can be modeled with linear
functions and with exponential
functions. *Also F-LE.1.1a,
F-LE.1.1b, F-LE.1.1c, F-LE.1.3*

ESSENTIAL QUESTION

How can you recognize when to use a linear or exponential model?

EXPLORE ACTIVITY 1   FL **F-LE.1.1b, F-LE.1.1c**

Comparing Constant Change and Constant Percent Change

Suppose that you are offered a job that pays $1000 the first month with a raise every month after that. You can choose a $100 raise or a 10% raise. Which option would you choose? What if the raise were 8%, 6%, or 4%?

A Find the monthly salaries for the first three months. Record the results in the table, rounded to the nearest dollar.

- For the $100 raise, enter 1000 into your graphing calculator, press Enter, enter +100, press ENTER, and then press ENTER repeatedly.
- For the 10% raise, enter 1000, press ENTER, enter × 1.10, press ENTER, and then press ENTER repeatedly.
- For the other raises, multiply by 1.08, 1.06, or 1.04.

	Monthly Salary After Indicated Monthly Raise				
Month	**$100**	**10%**	**8%**	**6%**	**4%**
0	$1000	$1000	$1000	$1000	$1000
1	$1100	$1100	$1080	$1060	$1040
2					
3					

B For each option, find how much the salary changes each month, both in dollars and as a percent of the previous month's salary. Record the values in the table.

	Change in Salary per Month for Indicated Monthly Raise									
Interval	**$100**		**10%**		**8%**		**6%**		**4%**	
	$	**%**	**$**	**%**	**$**	**%**	**$**	**%**	**$**	**%**
0 – 1	$100	10%	$100	10%	$80	8%	$60	6%	$40	4%
1 – 2										
2 – 3										

C Continue the calculations you did in Part A until you find the number of months it takes for each salary with a percent raise to exceed the salary with the $100 raise. Record the number of months in the table below.

Number of Months Until Salary with Percent Raise Exceeds Salary with $100 Raise			
10%	8%	6%	4%
2			

REFLECT

1. **Analyze Relationships** Compare and contrast the salary changes per month for the alternative raise options. Explain the source of any differences.

_____

_____

_____

2. **Justify Reasoning** Which raise option would you choose? What would you consider when deciding? Explain your reasoning.

_____

_____

_____

Math On the Spot

⏻ my.hrw.com

Comparing Linear and Exponential Functions

When comparing raises, a fixed dollar increase can be modeled by a linear function and a fixed percent increase can be modeled by an exponential function. Using a calculator to graph these functions can help you compare them.

EXAMPLE 1

FL   F-LE.1.1, F-LE.1.3

Compare the two salary plans listed. Will Job B ever have a higher monthly salary than Job A? If so, after how many months will this occur?

- Job A: $1000 for the first month with $100 raise every month thereafter
- Job B: $1000 for the first month with a 1% raise every month thereafter

STEP 1   Write functions that represent the monthly salaries.

Let t represent the number of elapsed months.

Job A: $S_A(t) = 1000 + 100t$ *linear function*

Job B: $S_B(t) = 1000 \times 1.01^t$ *exponential function*

STEP 2 Graph the functions on a calculator using Y_1 for Job A and Y_2 for Job B.

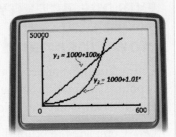

Animated Math
🔘 my.hrw.com

STEP 3 Estimate the number of months it takes for the salaries to become equal, using the intersect feature of the calculator.

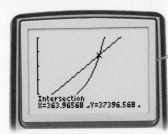

At $x \approx 364$ months, the salaries are equal.

STEP 4 Go to the estimated intersection point in the Table feature. Find the first x-value at which Y_2 exceeds Y_1.

At $x = 364$, $Y_2 > Y_1$

Job B will have a higher monthly salary than Job A at 364 months.

REFLECT

3. **Draw Conclusions** Which job offers a monthly salary that reflects a constant change, and which offers a monthly salary that reflects a constant percent change?

_____

_____

_____

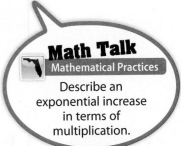

Math Talk
Mathematical Practices

Describe an exponential increase in terms of multiplication.

YOUR TURN

4. Companies A and B each have 50 employees. If Company A increases its workforce by 2 employees per month, and Company B increases its workforce by an average of 2% per month, will Company B ever have more employees than company A? If so, when?

_____

_____

Personal Math Trainer

Online Assessment and Intervention

🔘 my.hrw.com

How Linear and Exponential Functions Grow

Linear functions undergo a constant change (change by equal differences) while exponential functions undergo a constant percent change (change by equal factors). Now you will explore the proofs of these statements.

A Complete the proof that linear functions grow by equal differences over equal intervals.

Given: $x_2 - x_1 = x_4 - x_3$

f is a linear function of the form $f(x) = mx + b$

Prove: $f(x_2) - f(x_1) = f(x_4) - f(x_3)$

Proof:

1. $x_2 - x_1 = x_4 - x_3$ *Given*

2. $m(x_2 - x_1) = \boxed{}(x_4 - x_3)$ *Mult. Prop. of Equality*

3. $mx_2 - \boxed{} = mx_4 - \boxed{}$ *Distributive Property*

4. $mx_2 + b - mx_1 - b =$ *Add. & Sub. Prop. of Equality*

$mx_4 + \boxed{} - mx_3 - \boxed{}$

5. $f(x_2) - f(x_1) = $ _____   *Definition of f(x)*

B Complete the proof that exponential functions grow by equal factors over equal intervals.

Given: $x_2 - x_1 = x_4 - x_3$

g is an exponential function of the form $g(x) = ab^x$

Prove: $\dfrac{g(x_2)}{g(x_1)} = \dfrac{g(x_4)}{g(x_3)}$

Proof:

1. $x_2 - x_1 = x_4 - x_3$ *Given*

2. $b^{(x_2 - x_1)} = b^{(x_4 - x_3)}$ *If $x = y$, then $b^x = b^y$.*

3. $\dfrac{b^{x_2}}{b^{x_1}} = \dfrac{b^{x_4}}{\boxed{}}$ *Quotient of Powers Prop.*

4. $\dfrac{ab^{x_2}}{ab^{x_1}} = \dfrac{ab^{x_4}}{\boxed{}}$ *Mult. Prop. of Equality*

5. $\dfrac{g(x_2)}{g(x_1)} = \dfrac{g(x_4)}{\boxed{}}$ *Definition of g(x)*

Choosing a Modeling Function

Both linear equations and exponential equations and their graphs can model real-world situations. Example 2 presents how to select the correct model.

Math On the Spot
⏻ my.hrw.com

EXAMPLE 2  FL **F-LE.1.1, F-LE.1.3**

A gas had an initial pressure of 150 torr. Its pressure was then measured every 5 seconds for 25 seconds. Determine whether the change in pressure over time is best described by an increasing or decreasing function, and whether it is a linear or exponential function. Find the regression equation.

STEP 1 Determine how the dependent variable changes. Pressure decreases over time.

STEP 2 Determine if the dependent variable appears to change by equal differences or by equal factors over equal intervals.

Pressure of gas over time		Change per interval	
time (s)	pressure (torr)	difference $P(t_n) - P(t_{n-1})$	factor $\dfrac{P(t_n)}{P(t_{n-1})}$
0	150	—	—
5	117	−33	0.78
10	90	−27	0.77
15	70	−20	0.78
20	56	−14	0.80
25	41	−15	0.73

The factor changes are close to equal while the difference changes are not, suggesting an exponential regression model should be used.

STEP 3 Perform the exponential regression analysis, and evaluate the fit.

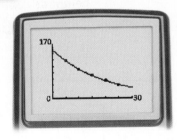  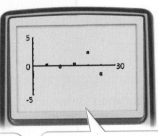

r-value suggests a good fit.

Analysis of residuals suggests a good fit.

The regression equation is $P(t) = 151(0.950)^t$.

YOUR TURN

5. The volume of a gas was measured as the temperature was increased from 173 K to 423 K in 50 K intervals. The gas volumes recorded, starting at 173 K, were 16, 21, 26, 30, 36, and 40 cm³. Determine whether the data is best described by an increasing or decreasing function, and whether it is linear or exponential. Find the regression equation.

Personal Math Trainer

Online Assessment and Intervention

⏻ my.hrw.com

1. Centerville has 2500 residents and Easton has 2000 residents. Centerville's population decreases by 80 people per year and Easton's population decreases by 3% per year. Will Easton ever have a greater population than Centerville? If so, when? (Example 1)

If t is time in years from now, Centerville's population is given by the equation

$$P_C(t) = \boxed{} - \boxed{}\, t$$

and Easton's population is given by the equation

$$P_E(t) = \boxed{} \times \boxed{}^{\,t}$$

Graph both functions on your calculator. The functions intersect at $t \approx$ _____.

Using the Table feature on your calculator, find the first x-value at which Easton's population is greater than Centerville's.

Easton's population will exceed Centerville's after _____ years. At this time,

Centerville will have _____ residents, and Easton will have _____ residents.

Complete each statement with the correct function from the table.
(Explore Activity 1, Example 2)

2. _____ decreases by a constant amount per interval, so it is

a(n) _____ function.

3. _____ decreases by a constant percent per interval, so it is

a(n) _____ function.

4. An equation for the linear function is:

_____

5. An equation for the exponential function is:

_____

x	$f(x)$ height of ball after each bounce	$g(x)$ number of cookies remaining each day
0	200	300
1	150	288
2	113	276
3	84	264
4	63	252
5	47	240

? **ESSENTIAL QUESTION CHECK-IN**

6. How can you recognize when to use a linear or exponential model?

_____

_____

_____

11.2 Independent Practice

FL   F-LE.1.1, F-LE.1.1a, F-LE.1.1b, F-LE.1.1c, F-LE.1.3

Personal Math Trainer

Online Assessment and Intervention

my.hrw.com

Without graphing, tell whether each quantity is changing at a constant rate per unit of time, at a constant percent rate per unit of time, or neither. Justify your reasoning.

7. Amy received a $15,000 interest-free loan from her parents and agreed to make monthly payments of $150.

_____

_____

8. Carla's salary is $50,000 in her first year on a job plus a 1% commission on sales.

_____

_____

_____

_____

9. Enrollment at school is 976 students initially and then increases 2.5% each year thereafter.

_____

_____

_____

10. **Draw Conclusions** Maria would like to put $500 in savings for a 5-year period. Should she choose a simple interest account which pays an interest rate of 12% of the principal (initial amount) each year or compounded interest account which pays 12% annual interest compounded monthly?

_____

_____

_____

11. **Critical Thinking** Will an exponential growth function always eventually exceed a linear growth function? Explain.

_____

_____

_____

_____

_____

_____

_____

12. **Interpret the Answer** Westward and Middleton each have 40,000 residents. Westward's population decreases by 900 people per year and Middleton's population decreases by 2% per year.

a. Sketch the functions on the screen provided. Label the functions and include the scale.

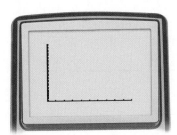

b. Will Westward ever have a greater population than Middleton? If so, when? Explain your reasoning.

_____

_____

_____

H.O.T. | **FOCUS ON HIGHER ORDER THINKING**

Work Area

13. Critique Reasoning Jordan analyzed the following data showing the number of cells in a bacteria culture over time.

Time (min)	0	6.9	10.8	13.5	15.7	17.4
Cells	8	16	24	32	40	48

He concluded that since the number of cells showed a constant change and the time did not, that neither a linear function nor an exponential function modeled the number of cells over time well. Was he correct? Explain how you know.

_____

_____

_____

14. Check for Reasonableness In Example 2, an exponential function was chosen to model the data even though the dependent variable did not change by exactly the same factor in every interval.

a. Do you think this was the best model for the real-world data? Justify your reasoning.

_____

_____

_____

b. Another parameter of the data to consider is the average rate of change (AROC), which is the slope of the line that passes through any two consecutive data points. How does the AROC change for the data in Example 2? Is this more consistent with an exponential or linear function? Explain.

_____

_____

_____

Ready to Go On?

11.1 Exponential Regression

The first two columns of the table show the population of box turtles in a Tennessee zoo over a period of 5 years.

1. Use a graphing calculator to find an exponential function model for the data. Round to the nearest thousandth.

   _____

2. Use the model to predict the number of box turtles in the sixth year.

   _____

   _____

   _____

Population of box turtles			
Year (x)	Actual (y_d)	Predicted (y_m)	Residual ($y_d - y_m$)
1	21	22	−1
2	27		
3	33		
4	41		
5	48		

3. Complete the chart using the observed and predicted values for the number of box turtles. Round to the nearest whole number.

11.2 Comparing Linear and Exponential Models

4. Julio is offered jobs with two different companies.

   Company A is offering $2000 a month for the first month with a $50 raise every month after. Company B is offering $2000 a month for the first month with a 2% raise every month after.

   Write functions that represent the monthly salary at each company, and use the functions to determine which company will have a higher monthly salary after 2 years.

   Company A _____

   Company B _____

   _____

❓ ESSENTIAL QUESTION

5. When do you use exponential functions to model real-world data?

   _____

   _____

MODULE 11 MIXED REVIEW

Assessment Readiness

Personal
Math Trainer

Online
Assessment and
Intervention

my.hrw.com

Selected Response

1. Kalinda kept track of the number of minutes she spent exercising for several days.

Days	1	2	3	4	5
Minutes	15	22	19	35	29

Which scatter plot represents Kalinda's data?

Ⓐ
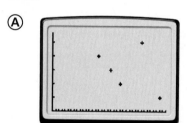

Ⓑ
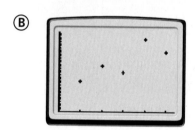

Ⓒ
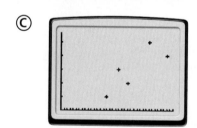

Ⓓ
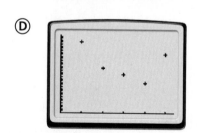

2. You know $f(x) = -5x + 4$ and $g(x) = 2x - 1$. What is $h(x) = f(x) - g(x)$?

Ⓐ $h(x) = -7x + 5$ Ⓒ $h(x) = -3x + 3$

Ⓑ $h(x) = -7x + 3$ Ⓓ $h(x) = 7x - 5$

3. Which of the following correlation coefficients indicates a weak positive correlation?

Ⓐ -0.1 Ⓒ 0.65

Ⓑ 0.1 Ⓓ 0.85

4. Another term for a "best fit" line is

Ⓐ correlation coefficient

Ⓑ residual

Ⓒ regression equation

Ⓓ slope

5. What is the value of the exponential function $f(x) = 2 \cdot \left(\frac{1}{3}\right)^x$ when $x = -2$?

Ⓐ 18 Ⓒ $\frac{2}{9}$

Ⓑ -18 Ⓓ $\frac{-2}{9}$

6. Which function represents a salary after m months with an initial salary of $1200 per month and a monthly raise of 5%?

Ⓐ $S(m) = 1200 + 5m$

Ⓑ $S(m) = 1200 \times 1.05^m$

Ⓒ $S(m) = 1200 \times 0.05^m$

Ⓓ $S(m) = 1200 + 0.05m$

Mini-Tasks

7. Use a graphing calculator to write both a linear regression equation and an exponential regression equation to represent the information in problem 1. Is either equation a good fit? Explain.

_____

_____

_____

_____

_____

_____

_____

Study Guide Review

Exponential Functions and Equations

Key Vocabulary

common ratio
 (razón común)
exponential growth
 (crecimiento exponencial)
exponential decay
 (disminución exponencial)
exponential function
 (función exponencial)
geometric sequence
 (sucesión geométrica)

? ESSENTIAL QUESTION

How can exponential functions be used to represent real-world situations?

EXAMPLE 1

James bought several shares of two different stocks. The graph below shows the value of Stock A and Stock B over time.

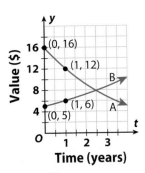

A Write the exponential decay function, $f(t)$, for the price of Stock A.

STEP 1 $b = 12 \div 16 = 0.75$

STEP 2 $f(n) = ab^n$

$f(n) = a(0.75)^n$

$12 = a(0.75)^1$

$12 = 0.75a$

$a = 16$

STEP 3 $f(t) = ab^t$

$f(t) = 16(0.75)^t$

B Write the exponential growth function, $g(t)$, for the price of Stock B.

STEP 1 $b = 6 \div 5 = 1.2$

STEP 2 $g(n) = ab^n$

$g(n) = a(1.2)^n$

$6 = a(1.2)^1$

$6 = 1.2a$

$a = 5$

STEP 3 $f(t) = ab^t$

$f(t) = 5(1.2)^t$

EXAMPLE 2

Write a recursive rule and an explicit rule for the geometric sequence
$6, -24, 96, -384\ldots$. Determine the sixth term in the sequence.

Identify the first term: 6

Calculate the common ratio: $-24 \div 6 = -4$

Recursive rule: $f(1) = 6, f(n) = f(n-1) \times (-4)$ for $n \geq 2$

Explicit rule: $f(n) = 6 \times (-4)^{n-1}$

Use the explicit rule to find the sixth term: $f(6) = 6 \times (-4)^{6-1} = -6144$

EXAMPLE 3

The graphs of three exponential functions, Y_1, Y_2, and Y_3, are provided. Based on the graphs, identify the parameter changes relative to Y_1 and write the equations of all three functions.

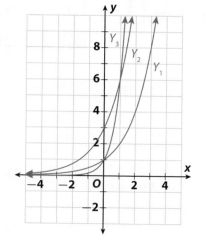

The graph of Y_1 has the points (0, 1) and (1, 2), indicating the y-intercept is 1 and the factor change in y is 2. The equation of this function is $Y_1 = f(x) = 1 \times 2^x$ or $f(x) = 2^x$.

The graph of Y_2 has the points (0, 3) and (1, 6). This indicates a of Y_2 is three times a of Y_1. The factor change in y is the same as that of Y_1 ($\frac{6}{3} = 2$) so the bases are equal. The equation of this function is $Y_2 = f(x) = (3 \times 1) \times 2^x$ or $f(x) = 3 \times 2^x$.

The graph of Y_3 has the points (0, 1) and (1, 6). The factor change in y is triple that of Y_1, indicating b of Y_2 is three times b of Y_1 and visualized in the steeper slope of the graph. Both functions have the same y-intercept. The equation of this function is $Y_3 = f(x) = (3 \times 2)^x$ or $f(x) = 6^x$.

EXERCISES

An invasive plant species was introduced into a lake in 2002. Two years later, the invasive plant population was recorded at 42 plants; 3 years after the introduction, the plants numbered 55; and after 4 years, their population totaled 72 plants. (Lesson 10.1, 10.2)

1. Determine the common ratio to the nearest tenth and the initial invasive plant population in 2002 to the nearest tenth. Write the function corresponding to the data described. [Let 2002 correspond to $x = 0$.]

_____

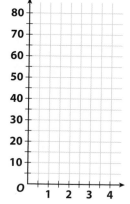

2. Construct an x-y scatter plot of the data for the first five years, including the initial population value, on the graph provided.

3. Is the data represented by an exponential growth or exponential decay function? What is the percent rate of change? Explain.

_____

_____

_____

_____

_____

4. Based on the model, what will the invasive plant population be in 2012? Explain.

_____

_____

The number of players after each round of an online video game tournament is shown in the table. (Lesson 10.3)

Round	Number of Players
1	3840
2	2573
3	1724
4	1155

5. Write the recursive and explicit rules for the geometric sequence.

_____

_____

6. Determine how many players remain after the 11th round.

_____

The graphs of three exponential functions, Y_1, Y_2, and Y_3, are provided. (Lessons 10.4, 10.1)

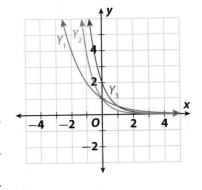

7. Which two functions have the same parameter b? How do their a-values differ? Justify your conclusions.

_____

_____

_____

_____

_____

_____

8. Which two functions have the same parameter a? How do their b-values differ? Justify your conclusions.

_____

_____

_____

_____

9. Write the function representing each graph.

_____

The equation $10 \times 4^x = 640$ can be solved by equating exponents or by graphing each side of the equation as the rule for a function. (Lesson 10.5)

10. Solve by equating exponents. Explain your process.

_____

_____

_____

11. Solve by graphing on a graphing calculator. Sketch your functions on the graph provided and indicate how the value of the exponent is determined from this information.

_____

_____

_____

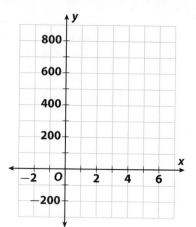

Modeling with Exponential Functions

? ESSENTIAL QUESTION

When do you use exponential functions to model real-world data?

EXAMPLE 1

Job A has a salary plan beginning at $1000 for the first month with a $100 raise every month thereafter. The salary plan of Job B also starts at $1000 the first month, but includes a 1% raise every month thereafter. Determine if a linear or exponential growth function applies to each salary plan and write the corresponding function (let t represent the number of elapsed months). Using a graphing calculator, determine how many months it will take for Job B to have a higher monthly salary than Job A.

The rate of change of the salary in Job A is a constant $100 per monthly interval, consistent with linear growth. The equation of the representative function is $S_A(t) = 1000 + 100t$.

The rate of change of the salary in Job B is a constant factor of 1% per monthly interval, thus the actual dollar amount of the change increases each month. This is consistent with exponential growth. The equation of the representative function is $S_B(t) = 1000 \times 1.01^t$.

Graph the functions as Y_1 and Y_2. The point of intersection gives an estimate of the month in which the salaries are equal. This information is then used to search the table for a more precise value of x. At $x = 364$ is the first month in which the salary of Job B ($37409) will exceed that of Job A ($37400).

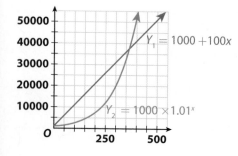

EXERCISES

12. Jan has $1200 to start an investment account. Investment plan A will pay 1.3% of the monthly principal. Investment plan B will pay $24 per month. Write the functions that represent the monthly account balances; let t represent the number of elapsed months. Graph the functions using a calculator. Sketch the functions on the graph provided; include axis labels and the coordinates of intersection. Compare and contrast the benefits of each plan. (Lesson 11.2)

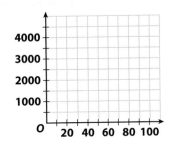

_____

_____

_____

_____

_____

The table shows the temperature of a pizza over three-minute intervals after taking it out of the oven. (Lessons 11.1, 11.2)

Time (min)	0	3	6	9	12	15	18	21
Temperature (°F)	450	350	290	230	190	150	130	110

13. Based on the data, explain why an exponential model is predicted to be a better fit than a linear model.

_____

_____

_____

14. Use technology to find an exponential function model for the data. Report the parameters in the equation to two significant digits. Assess the fit of the model based on the correlation coefficient and the residual plot. Using the regression model, predict how long it will take the pizza to cool down to a room temperature of 70°F.

_____

_____

_____

_____

_____

_____

1. Seymour invests in a 5-year CD. Over the 5-year period, the CD earns a fixed annual interest rate, compounded once per year. The equation $V(t) = 3000(1.049)^t$ gives the value $V(t)$, in dollars, of the CD after t years.

a. Explain what the numerical parameters in the equation represent.

_____

_____

_____

b. Compare the interest earned after 5 years of compounded interest to the interest earned after 5 years at the same interest rate per year if the interest is earned only on the principal amount.

_____

_____

2. **CAREERS IN MATH** **Statistician** When researching data concerning caribou populations in the Arctic, Lee uncovered some archives of old caribou populations, shown in the table.

a. Use a graphing calculator to find an exponential function that models the data.

_____

b. Complete the table below.

Year	Population
1975	2812
1976	2880
1977	2970
1978	3130
1979	3281
1980	3437
1981	3906
1982	4590

Years Since 1972	Actual y_d	Predicted y_m	Residual $y_d - y_m$
0	2812		
1	2880		
2	2970		
3	3130		
4	3281		
5	3437		
6	3906		
7	4590		

c. Use the data to make an inference about the accuracy of the model.

_____

UNIT 2B MIXED REVIEW

Assessment Readiness

Selected Response

1. Which data set exhibits exponential decay?

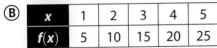

Ⓐ
x	1	2	3	4	5
f(x)	3	6	12	24	48

Ⓑ
x	1	2	3	4	5
f(x)	5	10	15	20	25

Ⓒ
x	1	2	3	4	5
f(x)	8	4	2	1	0.5

Ⓓ
x	1	2	3	4	5
f(x)	10	8	6	4	2

2. An online music sharing club has 5060 members. The membership is increasing at a rate of 2% per month. In approximately how many months will the membership reach 10,000?

Ⓐ 3.7 months

Ⓑ 34.4 months

Ⓒ 48.8 months

Ⓓ 98.8 months

3. Solve $7(\frac{1}{2})^x = \frac{7}{8}$ for x.

Ⓐ 4

Ⓑ 3

Ⓒ $\frac{1}{4}$

Ⓓ −3

4. During the first month of school, 89 students were attending after-school activities. However, attendance declined by 5% per month over the school year. Which function represents the number of students attending after t months?

Ⓐ $A(t) = 89 + 0.05t$

Ⓑ $A(t) = 89 \times (0.05)^t$

Ⓒ $A(t) = 89 \times (0.95)^t$

Ⓓ $A(t) = 89 \times (1.05)^t$

5. Which function best represents the graph?

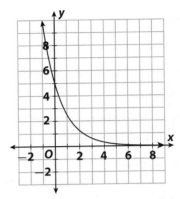

Ⓐ $f(x) = 2.5 \times 0.7^x$

Ⓑ $f(x) = 2.5 \times 1.4^x$

Ⓒ $f(x) = 5 \times 0.5^x$

Ⓓ $f(x) = 5 \times 2^x$

6. Which statement is true regarding the functions Y_1 and Y_2?

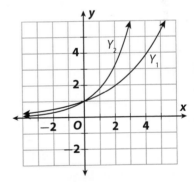

Ⓐ Y_2 has a larger a-value than Y_1.

Ⓑ Y_2 has a larger b-value than Y_1.

Ⓒ Y_2 has different a- and b-values than Y_1.

Ⓓ Y_2 has a constant added to the Y_1 function.

7. What is the 12th term in the geometric sequence 3, −9, 27, −81…? Assume $f(1) = 3$ is the first term.

Ⓐ −531,441   Ⓒ 531,441

Ⓑ −177,147   Ⓓ 1,594,323

Hot Tip! If a test item does not require a diagram as part of the answer, use the given information to create your own.

8. Which statement describes the residual plot associated with an exponential growth model that is a good fit?

Ⓐ The residuals form a parabolic pattern.

Ⓑ Every positive residual is followed by a negative one.

Ⓒ There are more positive residuals than negative ones.

Ⓓ The residuals get larger as x increases, but remain small relative to the y-values.

9. Which inequality represents the situation: "Alex has at most $45 to spend on a basketball, including 8% tax?"

Ⓐ $p + 0.08p < 45$

Ⓑ $p + 0.08p > 45$

Ⓒ $p + 0.08p \geq 45$

Ⓓ $p + 0.08p \leq 45$

10. Which ordered pair is *not* a solution to $2x + 3y = 12$?

Ⓐ $(0, 4)$

Ⓑ $(3, 2)$

Ⓒ $(2, 3)$

Ⓓ $(6, 0)$

11. The cost to ship a package is $C(w) = 0.23w + 7$, where w is the weight in pounds. Write the inverse function to find the weight of a package as a function $w(C)$ of the cost.

Ⓐ $w(C) = \frac{C - 7}{0.23}$

Ⓑ $w(C) = \frac{C + 7}{0.23}$

Ⓒ $w(C) = 0.23C + 7$

Ⓓ $w(C) = -0.23C - 7$

Mini-Tasks

12. The table shows the number of phone calls made per day (in millions) in years since 1940.

Years, x	0	10	20	30	40
Calls, y	98.8	171	288	494	853

a. Fit a function to the data using four significant digits. Tell whether it is exponential or linear.

_____

b. Graph the function below. Label the axes.

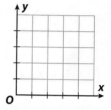

c. Identify what the y-intercept represents.

_____

_____

d. Use a graphing calculator to make a residual plot. Does the model fit the data well? Explain.

_____

_____

_____

_____

e. Predict the calls per day in 1975 and in 1995. Which is more likely to be accurate? Explain.

_____

_____

_____

_____

_____

UNIT 3
Statistics and Data

MODULE **12**

Descriptive Statistics
FL   S-ID.2.5

MODULE **13**

Data Displays
FL   S-ID.1.1,
S-ID.1.2, S-ID.1.3, S-ID.1.4

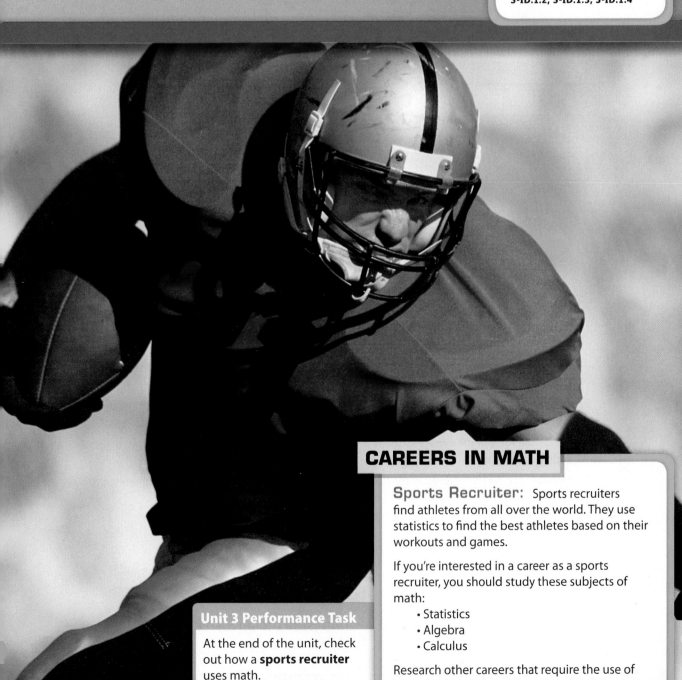

CAREERS IN MATH

Sports Recruiter: Sports recruiters find athletes from all over the world. They use statistics to find the best athletes based on their workouts and games.

If you're interested in a career as a sports recruiter, you should study these subjects of math:
- Statistics
- Algebra
- Calculus

Research other careers that require the use of statistics to make decisions.

Unit 3 Performance Task

At the end of the unit, check out how a **sports recruiter** uses math.

Unit 3   **405**

Vocabulary Preview

Use the puzzle to preview key vocabulary from this unit. Unscramble the circled letters to answer the riddle at the bottom of the page.

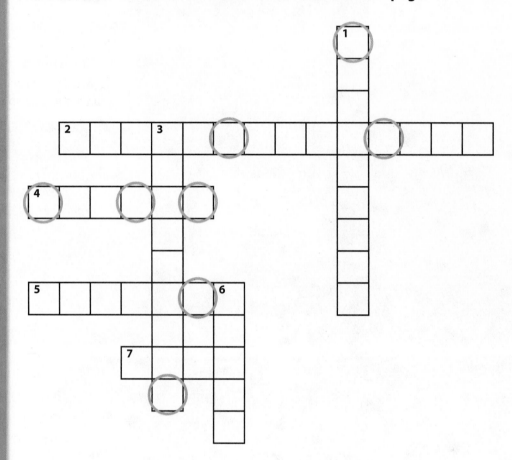

Across

2. a table that lists items by frequency (Lesson 12.1)

4. the middle value or the average of the two middle values (Lesson 13.1)

5. a value that is far from the rest of the data (Lesson 13.2)

7. the sum of all data values divided by the number of values (Lesson 13.1)

Down

1. a bar graph using intervals and frequency (Lesson 13.3)

3. the median of the upper or lower half of a data set (Lesson 13.1)

6. the difference between the greatest and least value (Lesson 13.1)

Q: Why might the average statistician lose his friends?

A: ___ ___ ___ ___ ___ ___ ___ ___ ___ ___

Descriptive Statistics

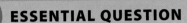

? ESSENTIAL QUESTION

How can you summarize two categories of categorical data and recognize associations and trends between two categories of categorical data?

Real-World Video

With emotions riding high, it can be difficult to evaluate popular opinion concerning personal preferences such as favorite sports teams. Polls and surveys use a methodical, mathematical approach to reduce or eliminate bias.

my.hrw.com

© Daniel Padavona/Shutterstock

GO DIGITAL
my.hrw.com

my.hrw.com

Go digital with your write-in student edition, accessible on any device.

Math On the Spot

Scan with your smart phone to jump directly to the online edition, video tutor, and more.

Animated Math

Interactively explore key concepts to see how math works.

Personal Math Trainer

Get immediate feedback and help as you work through practice sets.

Are YOU Ready?

Complete these exercises to review skills you will need for this module.

Fractions, Decimals, and Percents

EXAMPLE Write $\frac{5}{40}$ as a decimal.

$5 \div 40 = 0.125$ *Divide 5 by 40.*

$\frac{5}{40} = 0.125$

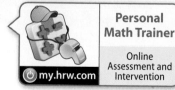

Personal Math Trainer

Online Assessment and Intervention

my.hrw.com

Write each fraction as a decimal.

1. $\frac{12}{48}$

_____

2. $\frac{9}{30}$

_____

3. $\frac{25}{40}$

_____

4. $\frac{6}{16}$

_____

Write each decimal as a percent.

5. 0.65

_____

6. 0.07

_____

7. 0.092

_____

8. 0.122

_____

Write each fraction as a percent.

9. $\frac{7}{20}$

_____

10. $\frac{15}{80}$

_____

11. $\frac{2}{25}$

_____

12. $\frac{65}{125}$

_____

Tables and Charts

EXAMPLE Use the table below to find the number of marbles that are blue or red.

$15 + 12 = 27$ *Add the number of blue marbles to the number of red marbles.*

The table shows the colors of all the marbles Arturo owns.

13. How many of Arturo's marbles are white, orange, or blue?

_____

14. How many marbles does Arturo own in all?

_____

15. What percent of Arturo's marbles are white, orange, or blue?

_____

Color	Number of Marbles
Red	15
Blue	12
White	6
Orange	2
Green	10
Purple	5

Reading Start-Up

Vocabulary

Review Words

✓ correlation (*correlación*)

✓ scatter plot (*diagrama de dispersión*)

✓ two-variable data (*data de dos variables*)

Preview Words

categorical data

conditional relative frequency

frequency table

joint relative frequency

marginal relative frequency

quantitative data

relative frequency

two-way frequency table

Visualize Vocabulary

Complete the concept map using the Review Words.

| Data that involves two variables describing the same set of items. _____ _____ | → | A group of plotted points that shows the relationship between two variables. _____ _____ | → | The amount of relationship existing between two variables. _____ _____ |

Understand Vocabulary

Draw a line to match the Preview Word with its definition.

Preview Words

1. frequency table

2. joint relative frequency

3. relative frequency

Definitions

- A relative frequency that is found by dividing a frequency that is not in the Total row or the Total column by the grand total

- Data that can be expressed with categories such as male/female, analog/digital, citizen/alien and so on

- A table that lists the number of times, or frequency, that each data value occurs

- For a category in a frequency table, the frequency of the category divided by the total of the frequencies

Active Reading

Two-Panel Flip Chart Create a Two-Panel Flip Chart to help you understand the concepts in this module. Label each flap with the title of one of the lessons in the module. As you study each lesson, write important ideas under the appropriate flap. Include any examples that will help you remember the concepts later when you look back at your notes.

MODULE 12
Unpacking the Standards

Understanding the standards and the vocabulary terms in the standards will help you know exactly what you are expected to learn in this module.

FL S-ID.2.5

Summarize categorical data for two categories in two-way frequency tables. Interpret relative frequencies in the context of the data (including joint, marginal, and conditional relative frequencies). Recognize associations and trends in the data.

Key Vocabulary

frequency table *(tabla de frecuencia)*
A table that lists the number of times, or frequency, that each data value occurs.

joint relative frequency *(frecuencia relativa conjunta)*
A relative frequency that is found by dividing a frequency that is not in the Total row or the Total column by the grand total.

marginal relative frequency *(frecuencia relativa marginal)*
A relative frequency that is found by dividing a row total or column total by the grand total.

conditional relative frequency *(frecuencia relativa condicional)*
A relative frequency that is found by dividing a frequency that is not in the Total row or the Total column by the frequency's row total or column total.

Visit **my.hrw.com** to see all **Florida Math Standards** unpacked.

my.hrw.com

What It Means to You

Two-way frequency tables give you a visual way to organize data categorized by two different variables so that you can more easily identify relationships.

UNPACKING EXAMPLE S-ID.2.5

The two-way frequency table below shows the numbers of households in a study that own a dog, a cat, or both.

| | Owns a Cat | | |
Owns a Dog	Yes	No	Total
Yes	15	24	39
No	18	43	61
Total	33	67	100

Here are a few conclusions you can draw from the table.

- $\frac{39}{100}$, or 39%, of households own a dog; $\frac{33}{100}$, or 33%, own a cat.

- $\frac{15}{100}$, or 15%, own a dog and a cat; $\frac{43}{100}$, or 43%, own neither.

- Of dog owners, $\frac{15}{39}$, or about 38.5%, also own a cat.

- Of cat owners, $\frac{15}{33}$, or about 45.5%, also own a dog.

You can also show the data in a two-way *relative* frequency table by dividing each number by the grand total and expressing the answer as a percent.

joint relative frequency

| | Owns a Cat | | |
Owns a Dog	Yes	No	Total
Yes	15%	24%	39%
No	18%	43%	61%
Total	33%	67%	100%

This cell should always be 100% in a two-way relative frequency table.

marginal relative frequencies

Two-Way Frequency Tables

FL S-ID.2.5

Summarize categorical data for two categories in two-way frequency tables. Interpret relative frequencies in the context of the data (including joint, marginal, and conditional relative frequencies). Recognize possible associations and trends in the data.

ESSENTIAL QUESTION

How can categorical data for two categories be summarized?

EXPLORE ACTIVITY

FL S-ID.2.5

Categorical Data and Frequencies

Data that can be expressed with numerical measurements is **quantitative data**. In this lesson you will examine *qualitative data*, or **categorical data**, which cannot be expressed using numbers. Data describing gender, model of car owned, or marital status are examples of categorical data.

A Circle the categorical data variable. Justify your choice.

temperature   weight   height   color

_____

_____

B Identify whether the given data is categorical or quantitative.

large, medium, small _____

120 ft^2, 130 ft^2, 140 ft^2 _____

C A **frequency table** shows how often each item occurs in a set of categorical data. Use the categorical data listed on the left to complete the frequency table.

Ways Students Get to School
bus, car, walk, car, car, car, bus, walk, walk, walk, bus, bus, car, bus, bus, walk, bus, car, bus, car

Way	Frequency
bus	
car	
walk	

REFLECT

1. How did you determine the numbers for each category in the

Frequency column? _____

_____

2. What must be true about the sum of the frequencies in a frequency table?

_____

Math On the Spot

⏻ my.hrw.com

Animated
Math

⏻ my.hrw.com

My Notes

Constructing a Two-Way Frequency Table

If you have a data set with two categorical variables, you can list the frequencies of the paired values in a **two-way frequency table**.

EXAMPLE 1

 **FL** S-ID.2.5

In a survey, Jenna asked 40 randomly selected students whether they preferred dogs, cats, or other pets. She also recorded the gender of each student. The results are shown in the two-way frequency table below. Each entry is the frequency of students who prefer a certain pet and are a certain gender. For instance, 8 girls prefer dogs as pets. Complete the table.

STEP 1 Find the row totals.

Girl: $8 + 7 + 1 = 16$

Boy: $10 + 5 + 9 = 24$

	Preferred Pet			
Gender	**Dog**	**Cat**	**Other**	**Total**
Girl	8	7	1	16
Boy	10	5	9	24
Total	18	12	10	40

STEP 2 Find the column totals.

Dog: $8 + 10 = 18$

Cat: $7 + 5 = 12$

Other: $1 + 9 = 10$

STEP 3 Find the grand total.

Sum of row totals $= 16 + 24 = 40$

Sum of column totals $= 18 + 12 + 10 = 40$

Both sums equal the grand total. So grand total $= 40$

REFLECT

3. Look at the totals for each row. Was Jenna's survey evenly distributed among boys and girls? _____

4. Look at the totals for each column. Which pet is preferred most? Justify your answer. _____

_____

5. Complete the two-way frequency table.

	Preferred Fruit			
Grade	**Apple**	**Orange**	**Banana**	**Total**
9th grade	19	12	23	
10th grade	22	9	15	
Total				

Personal
Math Trainer

Online Assessment
and Intervention

⏻ my.hrw.com

Reading a Two-Way Frequency Table

You can extract information about paired categorical variables by reading a two-way frequency table.

EXAMPLE 2

FL   S-ID.2.5

One hundred students were surveyed about which beverage they chose at lunch. The results are shown in the two-way frequency table below. Fill in the missing information.

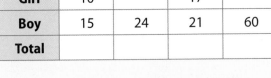

Gender	Lunch Beverage			
	Juice	Milk	Water	Total
Girl	10		17	
Boy	15	24	21	60
Total				

STEP 1   Find the total number of girls.

$100 - 60 = 40$ *Subtract the number of boys from 100.*

There are 40 girls in total.

STEP 2   Find the number of girls who chose milk.

$40 - 10 - 17 = 13$ *Subtract the number of girls who chose juice and the number who chose water from the total number of girls, 40.*

The number of girls who chose milk is 13.

Math Talk
Mathematical Practices

Which lunch beverage is the least preferred? How do you know?

STEP 3   Find the totals for each beverage and check that the grand total equals the total number of students surveyed (100). Complete the table.

Gender	Lunch Beverage			
	Juice	Milk	Water	Total
Girl	10	13	17	40
Boy	15	24	21	60
Total	25	37	38	100

YOUR TURN

6. One hundred students were surveyed about whether they played video games. The results are shown in the two-way frequency table. Complete the table.

Gender	Play Video Games		
	Yes	No	Total
Girl	34	19	53
Boy		9	
Total			

In Exercises 1 and 2, identify whether the data is categorical or quantitative. (Explore Activity)

1. gold medal, silver medal, bronze medal _____

2. 100 m, 200 m, 400 m _____

3. A theater company asked its members to bring in canned food for a food drive. Use the categorical data to complete the frequency table. (Explore Activity)

Cans Donated to Food Drive
peas, corn, peas, soup, corn, corn, soup, soup, corn, peas, peas, corn, soup, peas, corn, peas, corn, peas, corn, soup, corn, peas, soup, corn, corn

Cans	Frequency
soup	
peas	
corn	

4. Antonio surveyed 60 of his classmates about their participation in school activities and whether they have a part-time job. The results are shown in the two-way frequency table below. Complete the table. (Example 1)

	Activities				
Have a Job	**Clubs only**	**Sports only**	**Both**	**Neither**	**Total**
Yes	12	13	16	4	
No	3	5	5	2	
Total					

5. Marta surveyed 100 students about whether they like swimming or bicycling. Complete the two-way frequency table shown. (Example 2)

	Like Swimming		
Like Bicycling	**Yes**	**No**	**Total**
Yes	65	16	81
No		6	
Total			

How many of the students surveyed

like swimming but not bicycling? _____

ESSENTIAL QUESTION CHECK-IN

6. How can categorical data for two categories be summarized?

_____

12.1 Independent Practice

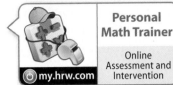

Personal Math Trainer

Online Assessment and Intervention

my.hrw.com

FL S-ID.2.5

Identify whether the given data is categorical or quantitative.

7. 75°, 79°, 82° _____

8. juice, soda, water _____

Two hundred students were asked to name their favorite science class. The results are shown in the two-way frequency table. Use the table for Exercises 9 and 10.

	Favorite Science Class			
Gender	Biology	Chemistry	Physics	Total
Girl	42	39	23	104
Boy		45	32	
Total				

9. How many boys were surveyed? Explain how you found your answer.

_____

_____

10. Complete the table. How many more girls than boys chose Biology as their favorite science class? Explain how you found your answer.

_____

_____

_____

The results of a survey of 150 students about whether they own an electronic tablet or a laptop are shown in the two-way frequency table below. Use the table for Exercises 11 and 12.

	Device				
Gender	Electronic tablet	Laptop	Both	Neither	Total
Girl	15	54		9	88
Boy		35	8	5	
Total					

11. Complete the table. Do the surveyed students own more laptops or more

electronic tablets? _____

12. Which group had more people answer the survey: boys, or students who own only an electronic tablet? Explain.

_____

_____

13. **Critical Thinking** Teresa surveyed 100 students about whether they like pop music or country music. Out of the 100 students surveyed, 42 like pop only, 34 like country only, 15 like both pop and country, and 9 do not like either pop or country. Use this data to complete the two-way frequency table below.

Like Country	Like Pop		
	Yes	No	Total
Yes			
No			
Total			

14. The table shows the results of a survey about students' preferred frozen yogurt flavor. Complete the table and use it to complete the statement below.

Gender	Preferred Flavor			
	Vanilla	Chocolate	Strawberry	Total
Girl		15	18	45
Boy	17	25		
Total				100

Students preferred _____ the most and _____ the least.

Work Area

15. **Multiple Representations** Use the data in Exercise 13 to complete the Venn diagram below.

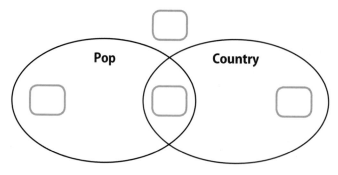

16. **Justify Reasoning** Charles surveyed 100 boys about their favorite color. Of the 100 boys surveyed, 44 preferred blue, 25 preferred green, and 31 preferred red. Can you make a two-way frequency table from the survey results? Explain your reasoning. _____

_____

_____

12.2 Relative Frequency

FL S-ID.2.5

Summarize categorical data for two categories in two-way frequency tables. Interpret relative frequencies in the context of the data (including joint, marginal, and conditional relative frequencies). Recognize possible associations and trends in the data.

ESSENTIAL QUESTION How can you recognize possible associations and trends between two categories in categorical data?

EXPLORE ACTIVITY   FL S-ID.2.5

Relative Frequencies

To show what part of a data set each category in a frequency table makes up, you can convert the data to *relative frequencies*. The **relative frequency** of a category is the frequency of the category divided by the total of all the frequencies.

The frequency table below shows the results of a survey Kenesha took at school. She asked 80 randomly selected students whether they preferred basketball, football, or soccer.

Preferred Sport	Basketball	Football	Soccer	Total
Frequency	20	32	28	80

A Convert this frequency table to a relative frequency table that uses decimals. Divide each number in the frequency table by the total to obtain the corresponding relative frequency as a decimal. Record the results in the table below.

Preferred Sport	Basketball	Football	Soccer	Total
Relative Frequency	$\frac{20}{80} = 0.25$			

B Convert the frequency table to a relative frequency table that uses percents.

Preferred Sport	Basketball	Football	Soccer	Total
Relative Frequency	25%			

REFLECT

1. Explain what the numerator and denominator of the ratio $\frac{20}{80}$ refer to in part A.

_____

_____

_____

2. What types of numbers can you use to write relative frequencies?

_____

Math On the Spot

⏻ my.hrw.com

Two-Way Relative Frequency Tables

You can obtain the following relative frequencies from a two-way frequency table:

- A **marginal relative frequency** is found by dividing a row total or a column total by the grand total. It tells what portion of the total has a specified characteristic.
- A **joint relative frequency** is found by dividing a frequency that is not in the Total row or the Total column by the grand total. It tells what portion of the total has both of two specified characteristics.

EXAMPLE 1  FL S-ID.2.5

My Notes

For her survey about sports preferences, Kenesha also recorded the gender of each student. The results are shown in the two-way frequency table below. Create a two-way relative frequency table for Kenesha's data.

	Preferred Sport			
Gender	**Basketball**	**Football**	**Soccer**	**Total**
Girl	6	12	18	36
Boy	14	20	10	44
Total	20	32	28	80

To find the joint relative frequencies and marginal relative frequencies, divide each number in the two-way frequency table by the grand total. Write the quotients as decimals.

joint relative frequency: 7.5% of students surveyed are girls who prefer basketball.

marginal relative frequency: 45% of students surveyed are girls.

	Preferred Sport			
Gender	**Basketball**	**Football**	**Soccer**	**Total**
Girl	$\frac{6}{80} = 0.075$	$\frac{12}{80} = 0.15$	$\frac{18}{80} = 0.225$	$\frac{36}{80} = 0.45$
Boy	$\frac{14}{80} = 0.175$	$\frac{20}{80} = 0.25$	$\frac{10}{80} = 0.125$	$\frac{44}{80} = 0.55$
Total	$\frac{20}{80} = 0.25$	$\frac{32}{80} = 0.4$	$\frac{28}{80} = 0.35$	$\frac{80}{80} = 1$

To check your work, add the joint relative frequencies in each row or column. Verify that the sum equals the row or column's marginal relative frequency.

Girl row:	$0.075 + 0.15 + 0.225 = 0.45$
Boy row:	$0.175 + 0.25 + 0.125 = 0.55$
Basketball column:	$0.075 + 0.175 = 0.25$
Football column:	$0.15 + 0.25 = 0.4$
Soccer column:	$0.225 + 0.125 = 0.35$

YOUR TURN

3. Find the joint relative frequency of students surveyed who like jogging and like aerobics. Express your answer as a decimal and as a percent.

_____

	Like Aerobics		
Like Jogging	Yes	No	Total
Yes	7	14	21
No	12	7	19
Total	19	21	40

Personal Math Trainer

Online Assessment and Intervention

🕐 **my.hrw.com**

Conditional Relative Frequencies

Another type of relative frequency is *conditional relative frequency,* which describes what portion of a group with a given characteristic also has another specified characteristic. A **conditional relative frequency** is found by dividing a frequency that is not in the Total row or the Total column by the total for that row or column.

Math On the Spot

🕐 **my.hrw.com**

EXAMPLE 2
FL S-ID.2.5

From Kenesha's two-way frequency table about preferred sports, you know that 36 students surveyed were girls and 28 students surveyed prefer soccer. You also know that 18 students surveyed are girls who prefer soccer. Use this information to find each conditional relative frequency.

A Find the conditional relative frequency that a student surveyed prefers soccer, given that the student is a girl. Express your answer as a decimal and as a percent.

$\frac{18}{36} = 0.5$, or 50%   *Divide the number of girls who prefer soccer by the total number of girls.*

The conditional relative frequency is 0.5, or 50%. This means that 50% of girls surveyed prefer soccer.

B Find the conditional relative frequency that a student surveyed is a girl, given that the student prefers soccer. Express your answer as a decimal and as a percent.

$\frac{18}{28} \approx 0.643$, or about 64.3%   *Divide the number of girls who prefer soccer by the number of students who prefer soccer.*

The conditional relative frequency is about 0.643, or 64.3%. This means that about 64.3% of students who prefer soccer are girls.

REFLECT

4. **Communicate Mathematical Ideas** In part A, why was the number of girls who prefer soccer not divided by 80, the grand total?

_____

_____

_____

My Notes

YOUR TURN

5. From Kenesha's table, you know that 44 students surveyed were boys, 20 students preferred basketball, and 14 students were boys who prefer basketball. Find the conditional relative frequency that a student surveyed is a boy, given that the student prefers basketball. Express your answer as a

decimal and as a percent. _____

Finding Possible Associations

Two-way frequency tables can be analyzed to locate possible associations or patterns in the data.

EXAMPLE 3

Kenesha is interested in the question, "Does gender influence what type of sport people prefer?" If there is no influence, then the distribution of gender within each sport preference will roughly equal the distribution of gender within the whole group. Analyze the results of Kenesha's survey from Example 1. Determine which sport each gender is more likely to prefer.

A Analyze the data about the girls that were surveyed.

STEP 1 Identify the percent of all students surveyed who are girls.

$$\frac{36}{80} = 0.45 = 45\%$$

STEP 2 Determine each conditional relative frequency.

Basketball: Of the 20 students who prefer basketball, 6 are girls. Percent who are girls, given a preference for basketball:

$$\frac{6}{20} = 0.3 = 30\%$$

Football: Of the 32 students who prefer football, 12 are girls. Percent who are girls, given a preference for football:

$$\frac{12}{32} = 0.375 = 37.5\%$$

Soccer: Of the 28 students who prefer soccer, 18 are girls. Percent who are girls, given a preference for soccer:

$$\frac{18}{28} \approx 0.643 = 64.3\%$$

STEP 3 Interpret the results by comparing each conditional relative frequency to the percent of all students surveyed who are girls.

Basketball: 30% is less than 45%
Girls are less likely than boys to prefer basketball.

Football: 37.5% is less than 45%
Girls are less likely than boys to prefer football.

Soccer: 64.3% is greater than 45%
Girls are more likely than boys to prefer soccer.

B Analyze the data about boys that were surveyed.

STEP 1 Identify the percent of all students surveyed who are boys. Subtract the percent for girls from 100%.

$$100\% - 45\% = 55\%$$

STEP 2 Determine each conditional relative frequency for boys. Subtract each percent for girls from 100%.

Basketball: 100% − 30% = 70%
70% of students who prefer basketball are boys.

Football: 100% − 37.5% = 62.5%
62.5% of students who prefer football are boys.

Soccer: 100% − 64.3% = 35.7%
35.7% of students who prefer soccer are boys.

STEP 3 Interpret the results by comparing each conditional relative frequency to the percent of all students surveyed who are boys.

Basketball: 70% is more than 55%
Boys are more likely than girls to prefer basketball.

Football: 62.5% is more than 55%
Boys are more likely than girls to prefer football.

Soccer: 35.7% is less than 55%
Boys are less likely than girls to prefer soccer.

Math Talk
Mathematical Practices

If sport preference were completely uninfluenced by gender, about how many girls would prefer each sport? Explain.

YOUR TURN

6. Steven asks 40 students whether they regularly eat breakfast. Of the 25 students who regularly eat breakfast, 9 are boys. Of the 15 who do not regularly eat breakfast, 10 are boys. Which gender is more likely to eat breakfast?

_____

Personal Math Trainer

Online Assessment and Intervention

my.hrw.com

The results of a survey of 40 students and the foreign language they are studying are shown in the two-way frequency table. Use the data for Exercises 1 and 2.

Gender	Foreign Language			
	Chinese	French	Spanish	Total
Girl	2	8	12	22
Boy	4	1	13	18
Total	6	9	25	40

1. Complete the two-way relative frequency table below using decimals.
(Explore Activity and Example 1)

Gender	Foreign Language			
	Chinese	French	Spanish	Total
Girl	$\frac{2}{40} = 0.05$	$\frac{8}{40} =$		
Boy				$\frac{18}{40} = 0.45$
Total		$\frac{9}{40} = 0.225$		

2. Give each conditional relative frequency as a percent. (Example 2)

a. The conditional relative frequency that a student surveyed is studying Chinese, given that the student is a boy:

$$\frac{\text{number of boys studying Chinese}}{\text{total number of boys surveyed}} = \frac{4}{18} \approx \boxed{}$$ _____

b. The conditional relative frequency that a student surveyed is a girl, given

that the student is studying Spanish: _____

3. Determine which gender is more likely to study each foreign language.
(Example 3)

_____

_____

ESSENTIAL QUESTION CHECK-IN

4. How can you recognize possible associations and trends between two categories in categorical data?

_____

_____

_____

12.2 Independent Practice

FL S-ID.2.5

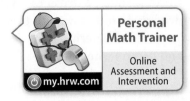

Personal
Math Trainer

Online
Assessment and
Intervention

my.hrw.com

Jasmine surveyed 80 students about their after-school activities. She recorded her results in the two-way frequency table below. Use the data for Exercises 5–12.

Gender	Activity			Total
	Sports	Clubs	Other	
Girl	9	21	8	38
Boy	22	8	12	42
Total	31	29	20	80

5. Create a two-way relative frequency table for the data using decimals.

Gender	Activity			Total
	Sports	Clubs	Other	
Girl				
Boy				
Total				

6. Find the relative frequency, expressed as a percent, of surveyed students who have clubs as their activity.

_____

7. Is the relative frequency of surveyed girls that have sports as their activity a joint relative frequency or a marginal relative frequency? Explain.

_____

_____

_____

_____

8. Find the joint relative frequency of surveyed students who are boys and have clubs as their activity. _____

9. Find the marginal relative frequency of surveyed students who have sports as their activity. _____

10. **What If?** Jasmine surveys 10 more students. Of these, 6 are boys and all 6 boys have sports as their activity. None of the new girls have sports as their activity. How does this new data change the marginal relative frequency of surveyed students who have sports as their activity?

_____

11. Find the conditional relative frequency that a surveyed student has clubs as their activity, given that the student is a girl. Express your answer as a decimal and a percent. Explain how you found your answer.

_____

_____

_____

_____

12. Find the conditional relative frequency that a surveyed student is a boy, given that the student has an activity other than sports or clubs. Express your answer as a decimal and a percent. Explain how you found your answer.

_____

_____

_____

_____

In some states, a driver of a vehicle may not use a handheld cell phone while driving. In one state with this law, 250 randomly selected drivers were surveyed to determine the association between drivers who know the law and drivers who obey the law. The results are shown in the table below.

Obeys Law	Knows Law		
	Yes	No	Total
Yes	160	45	205
No	25	20	45
Total	185	65	250

13. Give each conditional relative frequency as a percent.

   a. The conditional relative frequency that a driver surveyed obeys the handheld cell phone law, given that the driver knows the law:

      _____

   b. The conditional relative frequency that a driver surveyed knows the handheld cell phone law, given that the driver obeys the law:

      _____

   c. The conditional relative frequency that a driver surveyed obeys the law, given that the driver does not know the law:

      _____

14. Is there any association between the drivers who know the handheld cell phone law and drivers who obey the handheld cell phone law? Explain.

_____

_____

H.O.T.   **FOCUS ON HIGHER ORDER THINKING**

Work Area

15. Analyze Relationships Explain the difference between a relative frequency and a conditional relative frequency in a two-way frequency table.

_____

_____

_____

16. Explain the Error For the data about handheld cell phone laws above, Chelsea found the conditional frequency that a driver surveyed does not know the law, given that the driver obeys the law, by dividing 45 by 250. Explain Chelsea's error.

_____

_____

Ready to Go On?

12.1 Two-Way Frequency Tables

The results of a survey of 150 students about the type of movie they prefer are shown in the two-way frequency table. Use the table for Exercises 1 and 2.

1. Complete the table. How many boys were surveyed? _____

2. How many girls like science fiction movies? _____

Gender	Preferred Movie Type			
	Comedy	Drama	Science fiction	Total
Girl	24	33		72
Boy		12	36	
Total				

12.2 Relative Frequency

Use the data in the two-way frequency table above for Exercises 3 and 4.

3. Complete the two-way relative frequency table for the data using decimals.

4. Find the conditional relative frequency that a student surveyed is a boy, given that the student prefers comedy.

_____

Gender	Preferred Movie Type			
	Comedy	Drama	Science fiction	Total
Girl				
Boy				
Total				

5. Use the data to identify which gender is more likely to prefer comedy. Explain.

_____

_____

_____

? ESSENTIAL QUESTION

6. How can you recognize possible associations between two categories of categorical data?

_____

_____

_____

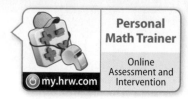

Selected Response

The results of a survey of 80 students about whether they prefer rice or a vegetable as a side with their meal are shown in the two-way frequency table below. Use the table for Questions 1–3.

	Preferred Side		
Gender	Rice	Vegetable	Total
Girl	20	?	46
Boy	16	18	?
Total	?	44	80

1. How many girls prefer vegetables?

Ⓐ 18   Ⓒ 26

Ⓑ 20   Ⓓ 33

2. What is the difference between the number of girls surveyed and the number of boys surveyed?

Ⓐ 4   Ⓒ 34

Ⓑ 12   Ⓓ 36

3. How many students surveyed prefer rice as a side?

Ⓐ 16   Ⓒ 36

Ⓑ 20   Ⓓ 44

4. What is the degree of $12x^4y^2$?

Ⓐ 2   Ⓒ 6

Ⓑ 4   Ⓓ 12

5. Which product equals $4x^2 - 36$?

Ⓐ $(2x - 6)(2x + 6)$

Ⓑ $(4x + 36)(x - 1)$

Ⓒ $(2x + 6)^2$

Ⓓ $(2x - 6)^2$

Derrick surveyed 40 of his classmates by asking each student whether his or her favorite subject is Math, English, or another subject. His results are shown in the two-way frequency table below. Use the table for Questions 6–9.

	Favorite Subject			
Gender	Math	English	Other	Total
Girl	11	10	3	24
Boy	5	4	7	16
Total	16	14	10	40

6. What is the joint relative frequency of surveyed students who are girls that prefer English?

Ⓐ 0.075   Ⓒ 0.175

Ⓑ 0.1   Ⓓ 0.25

7. What is the marginal relative frequency of surveyed students who prefer Math?

Ⓐ 4%   Ⓒ 22.5%

Ⓑ 17.5%   Ⓓ 40%

Mini-Tasks

8. Find the conditional relative frequency that a surveyed student prefers English, given that the student is a boy.

_____

9. Describe how gender is related to favorite subject.

_____

_____

_____

_____

Data Displays

? ESSENTIAL QUESTION

How can data sets be displayed and compared, and what statistics can be gathered using the display?

Real-World Video

In baseball, there are many options for how a team executes a given play. The use of statistics for in-game decision making sometimes reveals surprising strategies that run counter to the common wisdom.

my.hrw.com

GO DIGITAL

my.hrw.com

my.hrw.com

Go digital with your write-in student edition, accessible on any device.

Math On the Spot

Scan with your smart phone to jump directly to the online edition, video tutor, and more.

Animated Math

Interactively explore key concepts to see how math works.

Personal Math Trainer

Get immediate feedback and help as you work through practice sets.

427

Are YOU Ready?

Complete these exercises to review skills you will need for this module.

Solve Proportions

EXAMPLE

$$\frac{3}{4} = \frac{x}{12}$$

$4x = 36$ Cross-multiply.

$x = 9$ Solve for the unknown.

Solve each proportion.

1. $\frac{15}{9} = \frac{3}{x}$

2. $\frac{10}{20} = \frac{x}{100}$

3. $\frac{250}{1500} = \frac{x}{100}$

4. $\frac{32}{10} = \frac{4}{x}$

5. $\frac{3}{4} = \frac{x}{200}$

6. $\frac{15}{18} = \frac{x}{42}$

Compare and Order Real Numbers

EXAMPLE   Compare. Write $<$, $>$, or $=$.

20 ◯ 13   20 is greater than 13.

Compare. Write $<$, $>$, or $=$.

7. -18 ◯ -17

8. $\frac{2}{3}$ ◯ $\frac{1}{2}$

9. 0.75 ◯ $\frac{9}{12}$

10. 0.16 ◯ 0.8

Fractions, Decimals, and Percents

EXAMPLE   Write the equivalent decimal.

$\frac{1}{2} = 0.5$ Divide the numerator by the denominator.

$45\% = 0.45$ Write the percent over 100 and convert to a decimal.

Write the equivalent percent.

$\frac{1}{4} = 0.25 \times 100 = 25\%$ Convert to a decimal and then multiply by 100.

Write the equivalent decimal.

11. $\frac{3}{5} = $ _____

12. $8\% = $ _____

13. $\frac{3}{4} = $ _____

Write the equivalent percent.

14. $0.2 = $ _____

15. $\frac{1}{10} = $ _____

16. $0.36 = $ _____

Reading Start-Up

Visualize Vocabulary

Use the Review Words to complete the chart.

Word	Definition	Example
	The number of times a data value occurs in a set of data	Henry's goals in each game: 0, 1, 1, 3, 2, 0, 1, 0, 2, 1, 1
	Numerical measurements gathered from a survey or experiment	Quiz grades: 78, 82, 85, 90, 88, 79
	Data that is qualitative in nature	"liberal," "moderate," or "conservative"

Example table within first row:

Goals	Frequency
0	3
1	5
2	2
3	1

Vocabulary

Review Words
- ✓ categorical data *(datos categóricos)*
- ✓ frequency *(frecuencia)*
- frequency table *(tabla de frecuencia)*
- ✓ quantitative data *(datos cuantitativos)*

Preview Words
- box plot
- dot plot
- first quartile (Q_1)
- histogram
- interquartile range
- mean
- median
- normal curve
- normal distribution
- outlier
- quartiles
- range
- skewed to the left
- skewed to the right
- symmetric
- third quartile (Q_3)

Understand Vocabulary

To become familiar with some of the vocabulary terms in the module, consider the following. You may refer to the module, the glossary, or a dictionary.

1. In a _____ distribution, a vertical line can be drawn and the result is a graph divided in two parts that are approximate mirror images of each other.

2. A _____ is a bar graph used to display the frequency of data divided into equal intervals.

3. A _____ is a data representation that uses a number line and x's or dots to show frequency. A _____ displays a five-number summary of a data set.

Active Reading

Layered Book Before beginning the module, create a Layered Book to help you organize what you learn. Write a vocabulary term or new concept on each page as you proceed. Under each tab, write the definition of the term and an example of the term or concept. See how the concepts build on one another.

Unpacking the Standards

Understanding the standards and the vocabulary terms in the standards will help you know exactly what you are expected to learn in this module.

Use statistics appropriate to the shape of the data distribution to compare center (median, mean) and spread (interquartile range, standard deviation) of two or more different data sets.

Key Vocabulary

mean *(media)*
The average of the data values.

median *(mediana)*
The middle value when values are listed in numerical order.

interquartile range *(rango intercuartil)*
A measure of the spread of a data set, obtained by subtracting the first quartile from the third quartile.

What It Means to You

You can use the mean and median of data sets to compare the centers of the data sets. You can use the range, interquartile range, or standard deviation to compare the spreads of the data sets.

UNPACKING EXAMPLE S-ID.1.2

The lengths in feet of the alligators at a zoo are 9, 7, 12, 6, and 10. The lengths in feet of the crocodiles at the zoo are 13, 10, 8, 19, 18, and 16.

What is the difference between the mean length of the crocodiles and the mean length of the alligators?

Alligators: $\dfrac{9 + 7 + 12 + 6 + 10}{5} = 8.8$

Crocodiles: $\dfrac{13 + 10 + 8 + 19 + 18 + 16}{6} = 14$

$14 - 8.8 = 5.2 \text{ ft}$

FL **S-ID.1.1**

Represent data with plots on the real number line (dot plots, histograms, and box plots).

Key Vocabulary

dot plot *(diagrama de puntos)*
A data representation that uses a number line and x's or dots to show frequency.

 Visit **my.hrw.com** to see all **Florida Math Standards** unpacked.

What It Means to You

You can represent data sets using various models and use those models to interpret the information.

UNPACKING EXAMPLE S-ID.1.1

Class Scores on First Test (top) and Second Test (bottom)

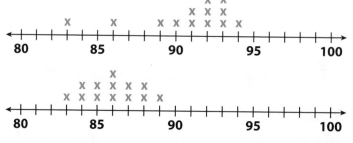

How do the medians of the two sets of test scores compare?

Look at each dot plot and locate the median. The median for the first test (92) is higher than the median for the second test (86).

Measures of Center and Spread

FL S-ID.1.2

Use statistics appropriate to the shape of the data distribution to compare center (median, mean) and spread (interquartile range, standard deviation) of two or more different data sets.

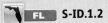

ESSENTIAL QUESTION

How can you describe and compare data sets?

EXPLORE ACTIVITY   FL S-ID.1.2

Exploring Data Sets

Caleb and Kim have bowled three games. Their scores are shown in the chart below.

Name	Game 1	Game 2	Game 3	Average score
Caleb	151	153	146	
Kim	122	139	189	

A Complete the table by finding each player's average score. How do the average scores compare?

_____

B Whose game is more consistent? Explain why.

_____

_____

C Suppose that in a fourth game, Caleb scores 150 and Kim scores 175. How would that affect your conclusions about the average and consistency of their scores?

_____

_____

REFLECT

1. **Draw Conclusions** Do you think the average is an accurate representation of the three games that Caleb and Kim played? Why or why not?

_____

_____

_____

_____

Math On the Spot

my.hrw.com

Measures of Center: Mean and Median

Two commonly used *measures of center* for a set of numerical data are the mean and median. Measures of center represent a central or typical value of a data set.

- The **mean** is the sum of the values in the set divided by the number of values in the set.
- The **median** is the middle value in a set when the values are arranged in numerical order.

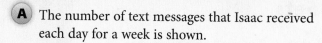

EXAMPLE 1

FL S-ID.1.2

Find the mean and the median for each set of values.

A The number of text messages that Isaac received each day for a week is shown.

$$47, 49, 54, 50, 48, 47, 55$$

Mean:
$$47 + 49 + 54 + 50 + 48 + 47 + 55 = 350$$ Find the sum.
$$\frac{350}{7} = 50$$ Divide the sum by the number of data values.

Median:
$$47, 47, 48, \mathbf{49}, 50, 54, 55$$ Order values, then find the middle value.

Mean: 50 text messages a day;
Median: 49 text messages a day

B The amount of money Elise earns in tips per day for six days is listed below.

$$\$75, \$97, \$360, \$84, \$119, \$100$$

Mean:
$$75 + 97 + 360 + 84 + 119 + 100 = 835$$ Find the sum of the data values.
$$\frac{835}{6} = 139.1\overline{66}$$ Divide the sum by the number of data values.
$$\approx \$139.17$$

Median:
$$75, 84, \mathbf{97}, \mathbf{100}, 119, 360$$ Order values, then find the mean of the two middle numbers.
$$\frac{97 + 100}{2} = 98.5$$

Mean: $139.17 a day; Median: $98.50 a day

Math Talk

Mathematical Practices

For part B, which measure of center better describes Elise's tips? Explain.

YOUR TURN

2. Niles scored 70, 74, 72, 71, 73, and 96 on his six geography tests. Find the mean and median.

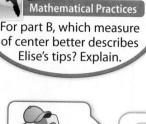

Personal Math Trainer

Online Assessment and Intervention

my.hrw.com

Measures of Spread: Range and IQR

Measures of spread describe how data values are spread out from the center. Two commonly used *measures of spread* for a set of numerical data are the range and interquartile range.

- The **range** is the difference between the greatest and the least data values.
- **Quartiles** are values that divide a data set into four equal parts. The **first quartile (Q_1)** is the median of the lower half of the set, the second quartile is the median of the whole set, and the **third quartile (Q_3)** is the median of the upper half of the set.
- The **interquartile range (IQR)** of a data set is the difference between the third and first quartiles. It represents the range of the middle half of the data.

$$\text{Range: } 9 - 1 = 8$$
$$\text{IQR: } 7 - 3 = 4$$

$$1, 2, 2, 3, 3, 4, 4, \ 5, \ 6, 6, 7, 7, 8, 8, 9$$

First quartile (Q_1): 3 | Third quartile (Q_3): 7

Median (Q_2): 5

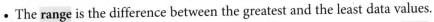

EXAMPLE 2 (Real World)   FL S-ID.1.2

The April high temperatures for five years in Boston are 77 °F, 86 °F, 84 °F, 93 °F, and 90 °F. Find the median, range, and IQR for the set.

Find the median.

77, 84, 86, 90, 93   *Order the values and identify the middle value.*

The median is 86.

Find the range.

Range = 93 − 77 = 16

Find the interquartile range. When finding the quartiles, do not include the median as part of either the lower half or the upper half of the data.

This is the lower half.

77, 84, 86, 90, 93

This is the median.

This is the upper half.

$Q_1 = \frac{77 + 84}{2} = 80.5$ and $Q_3 = \frac{90 + 93}{2} = 91.5$

Find the difference between Q_3 and Q_1: IQR = 91.5 − 80.5 = 11

Math Talk
Mathematical Practices

Why is the IQR less than the range?

YOUR TURN

3. Find the median, range, and interquartile range for this data set.

21, 31, 26, 24, 28, 26 _____

Personal Math Trainer

Online Assessment and Intervention

my.hrw.com

Measures of Spread: Standard Deviation

Standard deviation, another measure of spread, represents the average of the distances between individual data values and the mean.

The formula for finding the standard deviation of the data set $x_1, x_2, \ldots, x_n$ is:

$$\text{standard deviation} = \sqrt{\frac{(x_1 - \bar{x})^2 + (x_2 - \bar{x})^2 + \ldots + (x_n - \bar{x})^2}{n}}$$

where $\bar{x}$ is the mean of the set of data, and n is the number of data values.

EXAMPLE 3    **FL** **S-ID.1.2**

Calculate the standard deviation for the temperature data from Example 2.

The April high temperatures were 77, 86, 84, 93, 90.

STEP 1 Find the mean. $\text{Mean} = \dfrac{77 + 86 + 84 + 93 + 90}{5} = \dfrac{430}{5} = 86$

STEP 2 Complete the table.

Data value, x	Deviation from mean, $x - \bar{x}$	Squared deviation, $(x - \bar{x})^2$
77	$77 - 86 = -9$	$(-9)^2 = 81$
86	$86 - 86 = 0$	$0^2 = 0$
84	$84 - 86 = -2$	$(-2)^2 = 4$
93	$93 - 86 = 7$	$7^2 = 49$
90	$90 - 86 = 4$	$4^2 = 16$

STEP 3 Find the mean of the squared deviations.

$$\text{Mean} = \frac{81 + 0 + 4 + 49 + 16}{5} = \frac{150}{5} = 30$$

STEP 4 Take the square root of the mean of the squared deviations. Use a calculator, and round to the nearest tenth.

$$\text{Square root of mean} = \sqrt{30} \approx 5.5$$

The standard deviation is about 5.5.

Math Talk

Mathematical Practices

In terms of the data values used, what makes calculating the standard deviation different from calculating the range?

Personal Math Trainer

Online Assessment and Intervention

my.hrw.com

YOUR TURN

4. Find the standard deviation to the nearest tenth for a data set with the following values: 122, 139, 189.

_____

Comparing Data Sets

Numbers that characterize a data set, such as measures of center and spread, are called **statistics**. They are useful when comparing large sets of data.

Math On the Spot

⏻ my.hrw.com

EXAMPLE 4 ▨ **FL** **S-ID.1.2**

The tables below list the average ages of players on 15 teams randomly selected from the 2010 teams in the National Football League (NFL) and Major League Baseball (MLB). Calculate the mean, median, interquartile range, and standard deviation for each data set, and describe how the average ages of NFL players compare to those of MLB players.

NFL Players' Average Ages, by Team
25.8, 26.0, 26.3, 25.7, 25.1, 25.2, 26.1, 26.4, 25.9, 26.6, 26.3, 26.2, 26.8, 25.6, 25.7

MLB Players' Average Ages, by Team
28.5, 29.0, 28.0, 27.8, 29.5, 29.1, 26.9, 28.9, 28.6, 28.7, 26.9, 30.5, 28.7, 28.9, 29.3

STEP 1 On a graphing calculator, enter the two sets of data into two lists, L_1 and L_2.

> Examine the data as you enter the values.

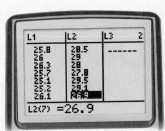

STEP 2 Use the "1-Var Stats" feature to find statistics for the data in lists L_1 and L_2. Your calculator may use the following notations:

Mean: $\bar{x}$

Median: Med

Standard deviation: σx

Scroll down to see the median, Q_1, and Q_3. Calculate the interquartile range by subtracting Q_1 from Q_3.

	Mean	Median	IQR ($Q_3 - Q_1$)	Standard Deviation
NFL	25.98	26.00	0.60	0.46
MLB	28.62	28.70	1.10	0.91

STEP 3 Compare the corresponding statistics for the NFL data and the MLB data. The mean and median are lower for the NFL than for the MLB; so we can conclude that NFL players tend to be younger than MLB players.

The IQR and standard deviation are smaller for the NFL; so we know that the ages of NFL players are closer together than those of MLB players.

Personal
Math Trainer

Online Assessment
and Intervention

my.hrw.com

YOUR TURN

5. a. The average member ages for every gym in Newman County are: 21, 23, 28, 28, 31, 32, 32, 35, 37, 39, 41, 41, 44, 45. Calculate the mean, median, interquartile range, and standard deviation for the data set.

_____

b. The following statistics describe the average member ages at gyms in Oldport County: mean = 39, median = 39, IQR = 9, and standard deviation = 6.2. Describe how the ages of gym members in Oldport County compare to those of gym members in Newman County.

_____

_____

_____

Guided Practice

There are 28, 30, 29, 26, 31, and 30 students in a school's six Algebra 1 classes. There are 34, 31, 39, 31, 35, and 34 students in the school's six Spanish classes. (Explore Activity and Examples 1–2)

1. Find the mean, median, range and interquartile range for the number of students in an Algebra 1 class.

   mean: _____   median: _____

   range: _____   IQR: _____

2. Find the standard deviation to the nearest tenth for the number of students in an Algebra 1 class, and find the standard deviation to the nearest tenth for the number of students in a Spanish class. (Example 3)

   Algebra class: _____   Spanish class: _____

3. Draw a conclusion about the typical size of an Algebra 1 class and the typical size of a Spanish class. (Example 4)

   _____

   _____

ESSENTIAL QUESTION CHECK-IN

4. How can you describe and compare data sets?

   _____

   _____

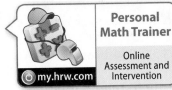

Personal Math Trainer

Online Assessment and Intervention

my.hrw.com

13.1 Independent Practice

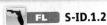

FL S-ID.1.2

Find the mean, median, and range of each data set.

5. 75, 63, 89, 91

_____

6. 19, 25, 31, 19, 34, 22, 31, 34

_____

Find the mean, median, range, and interquartile range for this data set.

13, 14, 18, 13, 12, 17, 15, 12, 13,
19, 11, 14, 14, 18, 22, 23

7. Mean: _____

8. Median: _____

9. Range: _____

10. Interquartile range: _____

The numbers of members in six yoga clubs are: 80, 74, 77, 71, 75, 91. Use this data set for questions 11–13.

11. Explain the steps for finding the standard deviation of the set of membership numbers.

_____

_____

_____

_____

_____

_____

12. Find the standard deviation of the number of members to the nearest tenth. _____

13. **Explain the Error** Suppose a person in the club with 91 members transfers to the club with 71 members. A student claims that the measures of center and the measures of spread will all change. Correct the student's error.

_____

_____

_____

_____

_____

14. **Represent Real-World Problems**
Lamont's bowling scores were 153, 145, 148, and 166 in four games. For each question, choose the mean, median, or range, and give its value.

a. Which measure gives Lamont's average

score? _____

b. Which measure should Lamont use to convince his parents that he's skilled enough to join a bowling league? Explain.

_____

_____

_____

_____

c. Lamont bowls one more game. Give an example of a score that would convince Lamont to use a different measure of center to persuade his parents. Explain.

_____

_____

_____

15. **Represent Real-World Problems** The table lists the heights (in centimeters) of 8 males and 8 females on the U.S. Olympic swim team, all randomly selected from the team that participated in the 2008 Olympic Games in Beijing, China.

Heights of Olympic male swimmers	196	188	196	185	203	183	183	196
Heights of Olympic female swimmers	173	170	178	175	173	180	180	175

a. Use a graphing calculator to complete the table below.

	Center		Spread	
	Mean	Median	IQR $(Q_3 - Q_1)$	Standard deviation
Olympic male swimmers				
Olympic female swimmers				

b. What can you conclude about the heights of Olympic male swimmers and Olympic female swimmers?

_____

_____

_____

16. **What If?** If all the values in a set are increased by 10, does the range also increase by 10? Explain.

_____

_____

17. **Communicate Mathematical Ideas** Jorge has a data set with the following values: 92, 80, 88, 95, and x. If the median value for this set is 88, what must be true about x? Explain.

_____

_____

18. **Critical Thinking** If the value for the median of a set is not found in the data set, what must be true about the data set? Explain.

_____

_____

_____

FL S-ID.1.3

Interpret differences in shape, center, and spread in the context of the data sets, accounting for possible effects of extreme data points (outliers). *Also S-ID.1.1, S-ID.1.2*

LESSON 13.2 Data Distributions and Outliers

ESSENTIAL QUESTION Which statistics are most affected by outliers, and what shapes can data distributions have?

Using Dot Plots to Display Data

A **dot plot** is a data representation that uses a number line and x's, dots, or other symbols to show frequency. Dot plots are sometimes called line plots.

EXAMPLE 1 Real World   FL S-ID.1.1

Math On the Spot
my.hrw.com

Twelve employees at a small company make the following annual salaries (in thousands of dollars):

25, 30, 35, 35, 35, 40, 40, 40, 45, 45, 50, 60

Choose an appropriate scale for the number line. Create a dot plot of the data by putting an X above the number line for each time that value appears in the data set.

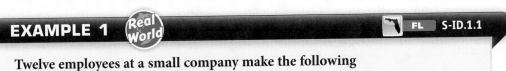
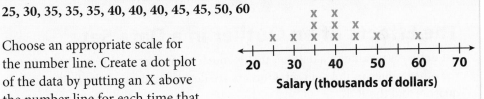

Salary (thousands of dollars)

REFLECT

1. Recall that quantitative data consists of numbers, such as counts or measurements. Qualitative data is expressed in categories, such as attributes or preferences. Is it appropriate to use a dot plot for displaying quantitative data, qualitative data, or both? Explain.

_____

_____

2. **Analyze Relationships** How can you use a dot plot to find the median value? What is the median salary at the company?

_____

_____

_____

3. When you examine the dot plot above, which data value appears most unlike the other values? Explain.

_____

_____

YOUR TURN

4. A cafeteria offers items at seven different prices. John counted how many items were offered at each price one week. Make a dot plot of the data.

Price ($)	1.50	2.00	2.50	3.00	3.50	4.00	4.50
Items	3	3	5	8	6	5	3

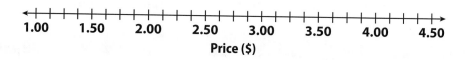

Price ($)

EXPLORE ACTIVITY FL S-ID.1.1

The Effects of an Outlier in a Data Set

An **outlier** is a value in a data set that is much greater or much less than most of the other values in the data set. Outliers are determined using the first or third quartile and the IQR.

How to Identify an Outlier
A data value x is an outlier if $x < Q_1 - 1.5(IQR)$ or if $x > Q_3 + 1.5(IQR)$.

Suppose the list of salaries in the previous example is expanded to include the owner's salary, which is $150,000. Now the list of salaries is: 25, 30, 35, 35, 35, 40, 40, 40, 45, 45, 50, 60, 150.

A Create a dot plot for the revised data set. Choose an appropriate scale for the number line.

Salary (thousands of dollars)

B Is the owner's salary an outlier? Determine if $150 > Q_3 + (1.5)IQR$.

$Q_3 =$ _____ $\qquad Q_1 =$ _____

$IQR =$ _____

$Q_3 + (1.5)IQR =$ _____

Is 150 an outlier? _____

EXPLORE ACTIVITY (cont'd)

C Complete the table to see how the owner's salary changes the data set. Use a calculator and round to the nearest hundredth, if necessary.

	Mean	Median	Range	IQR	Standard deviation
Set without 150					
Set with 150					

D Complete each sentence by stating whether the statistic increased, decreased, or stayed the same when the data value 150 was added to the original data set. If the statistic increased or decreased, say by what amount.

The mean _____ .

The median _____ .

The range _____ .

The IQR _____ .

The standard deviation _____ .

REFLECT

5. Critical Thinking Explain why the median was unaffected by the outlier 150.

_____

_____

_____

_____

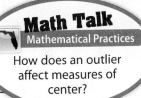

Math Talk
Mathematical Practices

How does an outlier affect measures of center?

6. Is the value 60 an outlier of the data set including 150? Use the inequalities at the beginning of the Explore Activity to support your answer.

_____

_____

YOUR TURN

Use the following data set to solve each problem: 21, 24, 3, 27, 30, 24

7. Is there an outlier? If so, identify the outlier. _____

8. Determine how the outlier affects the mean, median, and range of the data.

_____

_____

Personal Math Trainer

Online Assessment and Intervention

⟳ my.hrw.com

Comparing Data Distributions

A data distribution can be described as **symmetric**, **skewed to the left**, or **skewed to the right**, depending on the general shape of the distribution in a dot plot or other data display.

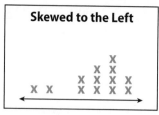

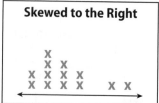

EXAMPLE 2

 FL S-ID.1.1

The data table shows the number of miles run by members of two track teams during one day. Make a dot plot and determine the type of distribution for each team. Explain what the distribution means for each.

Miles	3	3.5	4	4.5	5	5.5	6
Members of Team A	2	3	4	4	3	2	0
Members of Team B	1	2	2	3	4	6	5

Make dot plots of the data.

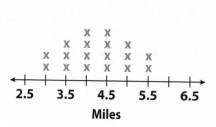

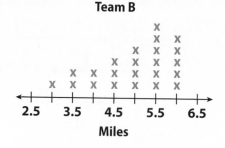

The data for team A show a symmetric distribution. The distances run are evenly distributed about the mean.

The data for team B show a distribution skewed to the left. Most team members ran a distance greater than the mean.

REFLECT

9. Will the mean and median in a symmetric distribution always be approximately equal? Explain.

_____

_____

10. Will the mean and median in a skewed distribution always be approximately equal? Explain.

_____

_____

My Notes

YOUR TURN

11. Create a dot plot for the data. Describe the distribution as skewed to the left, skewed to the right, or symmetric.

Miles	3	3.5	4	4.5	5	5.5	6
Members of Team C	2	2	3	3	3	2	2

Team C

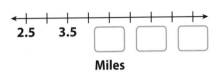

2.5   3.5   ☐ ☐ ☐

Miles

This distribution is _____.

Guided Practice

The list gives the grade level for each member of the marching band at JFK High. (Example 1)

9, 10, 9, 12, 11, 12, 10, 10, 11, 10, 10, 9, 11, 9, 11, 10, 12, 9, 11

1. Make a dot plot of the data.

JFK High Marching Band Member Grade Levels

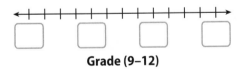

☐   ☐   ☐   ☐

Grade (9–12)

2. Determine whether the data set {7, 10, 54, 9, 12, 8, 5} has an outlier. Then determine the effect of the outlier. (Explore Activity)

   a. Determine if $54 > Q_3 + (1.5)$IQR.

   $Q_3 =$ _____ $Q_1 =$ _____

   IQR = _____

   $Q_3 + (1.5)$IQR = _____

   Is 54 an outlier? _____

b. Complete the table.

	Mean	Median	Range
Set without 54			
Set with 54			

c. How does the outlier affect the mean, the median, and the range?

_____

_____

Use the dot plots below to answer Exercises 3–6. (Example 2)

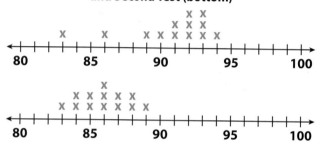

Class Scores on First Test (top)
and Second Test (bottom)

3. How do the medians of the two sets of test scores compare?

_____

_____

4. For which test is the distribution of scores symmetric? _____

5. For which test is the median greater than the mean? _____

6. Which measure of center is appropriate for comparing the two sets

of test scores? _____

ESSENTIAL QUESTION CHECK-IN

7. Which statistics are most affected by outliers, and what shapes can data distributions have?

_____

_____

_____

_____

Name _____ Class _____ Date _____

13.2 Independent Practice

 FL S-ID.1.1, S-ID.1.2, S-ID.1.3

Personal
Math Trainer

my.hrw.com

Online
Assessment and
Intervention

Rounded to the nearest $50,000, the values
(in thousands of dollars) of homes sold by a
realtor are listed below. Use the data set for
Exercises 8–12.

300 250 200 250 350

400 300 250 400 300

8. Use the number line to create a dot plot for
the data set.

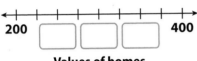

**Values of homes
(thousands of dollars)**

9. Suppose the realtor sells a home with a value
of $650,000. Which statistics are affected
when 650 is included in the data set?

_____

_____

10. Would 650 be considered an outlier? Explain.

_____

_____

_____

11. Find the mean and median for the data set
with and without the data value 650.

_____

_____

12. If 650 is included in the data set, why might
the realtor want to use the mean instead of
the median when advertising the typical
value of homes sold?

_____

_____

13. Represent Real-World Problems The table
shows Chloe's scores on math tests in each
quarter of the school year.

Chloe's Scores			
I	**II**	**III**	**IV**
74	77	79	74
78	75	76	77
82	80	74	76
76	75	77	78
85	77	87	85

a. Use the number line below to create a
dot plot for all of Chloe's scores.

Chloe's test scores

b. Complete the table below for the data set.

Mean	Median	Range	IQR	Standard deviation

c. Identify any outliers in the data set.

_____

d. Which of the statistics from the table
above would change if the outliers were
removed?

_____

_____

_____

e. Describe the shape of the distribution.

_____

14. Critical Thinking Magdalene and Peter conducted the same experiment. Both of their data sets had the same mean. Both made dot plots of their data that showed symmetric distributions, but Peter's dot plot shows a greater IQR than Magdalene's dot plot. Identify which plot below belongs to Peter and which belongs to Magdalene.

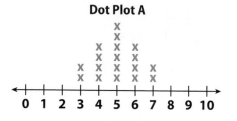

Dot Plot A

Dot Plot B

_____

15. Justify Reasoning Why will outliers always have an effect on the range?

_____

_____

_____

_____

16. Explain the Error Chuck and Brenda are discussing the distribution of the dot plot shown. Brenda says that if you add some families with 5 or 6 siblings then there will be a symmetric distribution. Explain her error.

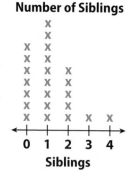

Number of Siblings

Siblings

_____

_____

_____

_____

_____

17. Critique Reasoning Victor thinks that only the greatest and the least values in a data set can be outliers, since an outlier must be much greater or much less than the other values. Is he correct? Explain.

_____

_____

_____

LESSON
13.3 Histograms

FL S-ID.1.1

Represent data with plots on the real number line (dot plots, histograms, and box plots).

ESSENTIAL QUESTION

How can you estimate statistics from data displayed in a histogram?

Understanding Histograms

Like a dot plot, a **histogram** uses a number line to display data. The number line on a histogram groups the data values into equal intervals, and uses the heights of bars to indicate the frequency of data values within each interval. (Recall that the frequency of a data value is the number of times it occurs.)

A Look at the histogram of "Scores on a Math Test". Which axis indicates the frequency?

_____

_____

B What does the horizontal axis indicate, and how is it organized?

_____

_____

_____

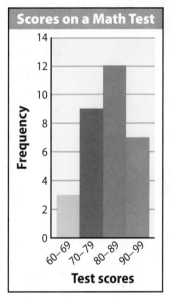

Scores on a Math Test

C How many students had test scores in the

interval 60–69? _____ between 70 and 79? _____

REFLECT

1. What statistical information can you tell about a data set by looking at a histogram? What statistical information cannot be determined by looking at a histogram?

_____

_____

2. How many test scores were collected? How do you know?

_____

_____

_____

Creating a Histogram

When creating a histogram, make sure that the bars are of equal width and that they touch without overlapping. Create a frequency table to help organize the data before constructing the histogram.

EXAMPLE 1

 FL **S-ID.1.1**

Listed below are the ages of the 100 U.S. senators at the start of the 112th Congress on January 3, 2011. Create a histogram for this data set.

39, 39, 42, 44, 46, 47, 47, 47, 48, 49, 49, 49, 50, 50, 51, 51, 52, 52, 53, 53, 54, 54, 55, 55, 55, 55, 55, 55, 56, 56, 57, 57, 57, 58, 58, 58, 58, 58, 59, 59, 59, 59, 60, 60, 60, 60, 60, 60, 60, 61, 61, 62, 62, 62, 63, 63, 63, 63, 64, 64, 64, 64, 66, 66, 66, 67, 67, 67, 67, 67, 67, 67, 68, 68, 68, 68, 69, 69, 69, 70, 70, 70, 71, 71, 73, 73, 74, 74, 74, 75, 76, 76, 76, 76, 77, 77, 78, 86, 86, 86

> The data values range from 39 to 86, so use an interval width of 10 and start the first interval at 30.

STEP 1 Create a frequency table.

- It may be helpful to organize the data by listing from least to greatest.
- Decide the interval width and where to start the first interval.
- Use the data to complete the table. When done, check that the sum of the frequencies is 100.

Age interval	Frequency
30–39	2
40–49	10
50–59	30
60–69	37
70–79	18
80–89	3

STEP 2 Use the frequency table to create the histogram.

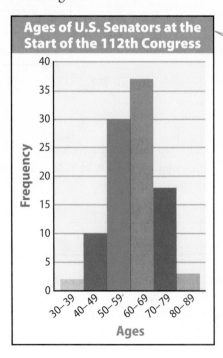

> Remember to give the graph a title and label both axes.

REFLECT

3. Describe the shape of the distribution of senators' ages. Explain.

_____

_____

_____

_____

_____

YOUR TURN

4. Listed below are the scores from a golf tournament.

68, 78, 76, 71, 69, 73, 72, 74, 76, 70, 77, 74, 75, 76, 71

a. Complete the frequency table.

Golf scores	Frequency
68 – 70	
71 – 73	
74 – 76	
77 – 79	

b. Complete the histogram.

Golf Tournament Scores

**Personal
Math Trainer**

Online Assessment
and Intervention

my.hrw.com

Math On the Spot

my.hrw.com

Estimating Statistics from a Histogram

You can estimate statistics by studying a histogram. Reasonable estimates of the mean, median, IQR, and standard deviation can be based on information provided by a histogram.

EXAMPLE 2

FL S-ID.1.1

Look at the histogram from Example 1. Estimate the mean and the median ages from the histogram.

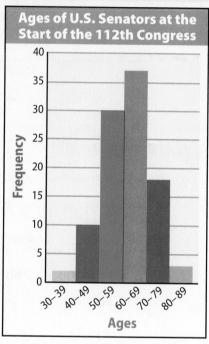

Ages of U.S. Senators at the Start of the 112th Congress

A To estimate the mean, first find the midpoint of each interval and multiply by the frequency. Sum the results and divide by the total number of values.

1st interval:
$(35)(2) = 70$

2nd interval:
$(45)(10) = 450$

3rd interval:
$(55)(30) = 1650$

4th interval:
$(65)(37) = 2405$

5th interval:
$(75)(18) = 1350$

6th interval:
$(85)(3) = 255$

Mean: $\dfrac{70 + 450 + 1650 + 2405 + 1350 + 255}{100}$

$= \dfrac{6180}{100} \approx 62$

A good estimate for the mean of this set is 62.

> **Math Talk**
> **Mathematical Practices**
>
> What is represented by the product of the midpoint of an interval and the frequency of that interval?

B To estimate the median, you need to estimate the average of the 50th and 51st numbers in the ordered set.

First, use the histogram to find which interval contains these values. There are 42 values in the first 3 intervals, so the 50th and 51st values will be in the interval 60–69.

The median is the average of the 8th and 9th value in this interval. This interval has 37 values. To estimate how far into this interval the median is located, find $\frac{8.5}{37} \approx 0.23$, or 23%, of the interval width, 10. Then add the result to the interval's least value, 60.

$(0.23)10 + 60 \approx 62$

A good estimate for the median of this set is 62.

REFLECT

5. Are these estimates of the mean and median reasonable? Explain.

_____

_____

6. The histogram shows the ages of teachers at Plainsville High School. Estimate the teachers' mean and median ages from the histogram.

_____

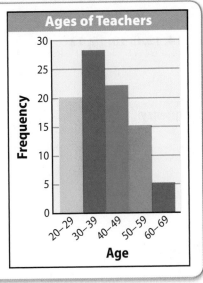

Ages of Teachers

Personal
Math Trainer

Online Assessment
and Intervention

⏻ my.hrw.com

Guided Practice

The histogram shows the 2004 Olympic results for women's weightlifting. Medals were awarded to the three athletes who lifted the most weight. (Explore Activity)

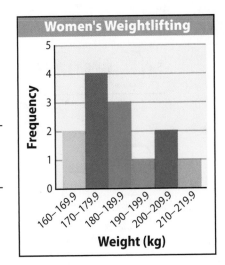

Women's Weightlifting

1. How many women lifted between 160 and 169.9 kg?

_____

2. How many women lifted between 170 and 209.9 kg?

_____

3. Tara Cunningham from the United States lifted 172.5 kg. Did she win a medal for this lift? Explain.

_____

_____

_____

4. Can you determine which weight earned the silver medal? Explain.

_____

_____

_____

The length (in full days) of Maria's last 15 vacations are given.
(Examples 1 and 2)

4, 8, 6, 7, 5, 4, 10, 6, 7, 14, 12, 8, 10, 15, 12

5. Make a frequency table.

Days	Frequency
4–6	
7–9	
10–12	
13–15	

6. Create a histogram using the frequency table.

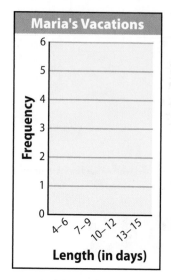

7. Estimate the mean from the histogram.

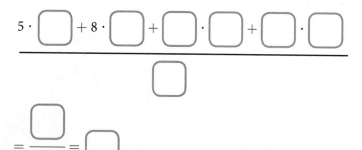

Multiply the midpoint value of each interval by its frequency. Divide the sum of those products by the total number of values.

The mean calculated from the data set is about _____, so the estimate is [very close / not very close].

Calculate the mean of the given data and compare your estimate to the calculated mean.

? ESSENTIAL QUESTION CHECK-IN

8. How can you estimate statistics from data displayed in a histogram?

_____

_____

_____

_____

13.3 Independent Practice

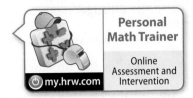

FL S-ID.1.1

The heights of the students in Marci's karate class are shown on the histogram below. Use the histogram for Exercises 9 and 10.

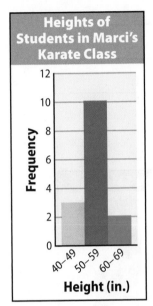

9. How many students are in Marci's karate class?

_____

10. Describe the shape of the distribution.

_____

_____

11. Represent Real-World Problems The breathing intervals of gray whales are shown below. Use the frequency table to make a histogram for the data.

Breathing Intervals (min)	
Interval	Frequency
5–7	4
8–10	7
11–13	7
14–16	8

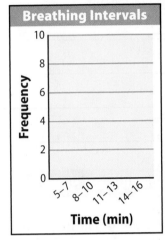

The ages of the first 44 U.S. presidents on the date of their first inauguration are shown in the histogram below. Use the histogram for Exercises 12 and 13.

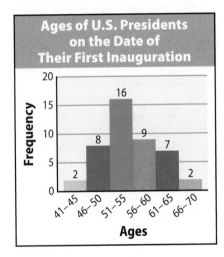

12. Communicate Mathematical Ideas Describe the shape of the distribution. Is it approximately symmetric, skewed to the right, or skewed to the left? Explain.

_____

_____

_____

_____

13. Use the histogram to estimate the mean and median age of presidents at their first inauguration.

  a. Mean presidential age at first inauguration: _____

  b. Median presidential age at first inauguration: _____

14. **Communicate Mathematical Ideas** Describe how you could estimate the IQR using a histogram.

_____

_____

_____

_____

H.O.T. **FOCUS ON HIGHER ORDER THINKING**

15. **Justify Reasoning** The frequencies of starting salary ranges for college graduates are shown in the histogram.

Bobby says the mean is found in the following way:

$$\frac{25 + 35 + 45 + 55}{4} = \frac{160}{4} = 40.$$

What is his error?

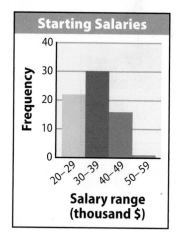

Starting Salaries

Frequency / Salary range (thousand $)

_____

_____

_____

_____

_____

16. **Critical Thinking** Margo's assignment is to make a data display of some data she finds in a newspaper. She found a frequency table with the intervals shown at the right.

Explain why attempting to draw a histogram using the given intervals would be problematic.

Age
Under 18
18–30
31–54
55 and older

_____

_____

_____

_____

FL | S-ID.1.1
Represent data with plots on the real number line (dot plots, histograms, and box plots). Also S-ID.1.2

Math On the Spot
⏻ my.hrw.com

? ESSENTIAL QUESTION

How can you compare data sets using box plots?

Constructing a Box Plot

A **box plot** can be used to show how the values in a data set are distributed. You need five values to make a box plot: the minimum (or least value), first quartile, median, third quartile, and maximum (or greatest value).

EXAMPLE 1 | FL | S-ID.1.1

The numbers of runs scored by a softball team in 20 games are given. Use the data to make a box plot.

3, 4, 8, 12, 7, 5, 4, 12, 3, 9, 11, 4, 14, 8, 2, 10, 3, 10, 9, 7

STEP 1   Order the data from least to greatest.

2, 3, 3, 3, 4, 4, 4, 5, 7, 7, 8, 8, 9, 9, 10, 10, 11, 12, 12, 14

STEP 2   Identify the five needed values. Those values are the minimum, first quartile, median, third quartile, and maximum.

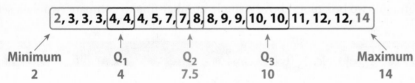

STEP 3   Draw a number line and plot a point above each of the five needed values. Draw a box whose ends go through the first and third quartiles, and draw a vertical line through the median. Draw horizontal lines from the box to the minimum and maximum.

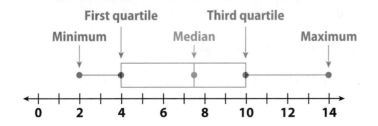

Animated Math
⏻ my.hrw.com

Shutterstock

REFLECT

1. The lines that extend from the box in a box plot are sometimes called "whiskers." What part (lower, middle, or upper) and about what percent of the data does the box represent? What part and about what percent does each "whisker" represent?

_____

_____

2. Which measures of spread can be determined from the box plot, and how are they found? Calculate each measure.

_____

_____

Personal Math Trainer

Online Assessment and Intervention

⏱ my.hrw.com

YOUR TURN

3. Use the data to make a box plot.

13, 14, 18, 13, 12, 17, 15, 12, 13, 19, 11, 14, 14, 18, 22, 23

Math On the Spot

⏱ my.hrw.com

Comparing Data Using Box Plots

You can plot two box plots above a single number line to compare two data sets.

EXAMPLE 2 (Real World) FL S-ID.1.1

The box plots show the ticket sales, in millions of dollars, for the top 25 movies of 2000 and 2007. Use the box plots to compare the data sets.

A Identify the set with the greater median.

The median for 2000 is about 125. The median for 2007 is about 170. The data set for 2007 has the greater median.

© Houghton Mifflin Harcourt Publishing Company • Image Credits: ©Stuart Miles/

B Identify the set with the greater interquartile range.

The length of the box for 2007 is greater than the length of the box for 2000. The data set for 2007 has a greater interquartile range.

C About how much greater were the ticket sales for the top movie in 2007 than for the top movie in 2000?

2007 maximum: about $335 million   Read the maximum values from the box plots.

2000 maximum: about $260 million

$$335 - 260 = 75$$ Find the difference between the maximum values.

The ticket sales for the top movie in 2007 were about $75 million more than for the top movie in 2000.

Math Talk
Mathematical Practices

Explain how to find which data set has a smaller range.

REFLECT

4. **Analyze Relationships** Use the box plots to compare the median and shape of the two data distributions.

_____

_____

_____

_____

YOUR TURN

The box plots show the scores, in thousands of points, of two players of a video game.

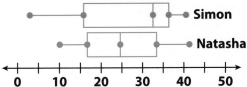

5. Which data set has a greater median? _____

6. Which data set has the greater interquartile range? _____

7. Which player had a higher top score? About how much higher was it than

the other player's top score? _____

_____

Personal Math Trainer

Online Assessment and Intervention

my.hrw.com

Guided Practice

Use the data to make a box plot. (Example 1)

1. 25, 28, 26, 16, 18, 15, 25, 28, 26, 16

    a. Order the data from least to greatest.

    _____

    b. Identify the median and the first and third quartiles.

    Median = _____

    First quartile = _____

    Third quartile = _____

    c. Identify the minimum and maximum.

    Minimum = _____

    Maximum = _____

    d. Construct the box plot.

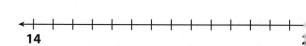

The box plots show the prices, in dollars, of athletic shoes at two sports apparel stores. Use the box plots for Exercises 2 and 3. (Example 2)

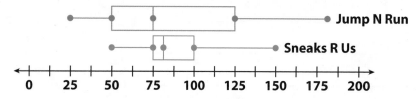

2. Which store has the greater median price? About how much greater?

_____

3. Which store has the smaller interquartile range? What does this tell you about the data sets?

_____

_____

? ESSENTIAL QUESTION CHECK-IN

4. How can you compare data sets using box plots?

_____

_____

_____

_____

13.4 Independent Practice

Personal
Math Trainer

Online
Assessment and
Intervention

my.hrw.com

FL S-ID.1.1, S-ID.1.2

The finishing times of two runners for several
one-mile races, in minutes, are shown below.
Use the box plots for Exercises 5–7.

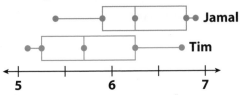

5. Who has the faster median time?

_____

6. Who has the slowest time?

_____

7. Overall, who is the faster runner? Explain.

_____

_____

The table below shows the scores that Gabrielle
and Marcus each earned the last 15 times they
played a board game together. Use the table to
complete Exercises 8–10.

Gabrielle	150, 195, 180, 225, 120, 135, 115, 220, 190, 185, 230, 170, 160, 200, 120
Marcus	170, 155, 175, 200, 190, 165, 170, 180, 160, 175, 155, 170, 160, 180, 175

8. Create a box plot for each data set on the
number line below.

9. Which set has the higher median?

_____

10. Which set has more scores that are close to
the median? Explain.

_____

_____

_____

_____

_____

The number of traffic citations given daily by
two police departments over a two-week period
is shown. Use the box plots for Exercises 11–13.

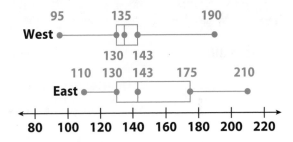

11. Which department gave the greatest
number of citations in a day? How
much higher was that number than
the greatest number given by the other

department? _____

12. What is the difference in the median
number of citations given by the two

departments? _____

13. Detective Costello says that it looks like the
mean numbers of citations per day given
by the two departments are about the same
because the range looks similar. Is she
correct? Explain.

_____

_____

The box plots show the prices of vehicles at a used-car dealership.

Prices (in Thousands of Dollars) of Cars and SUVs

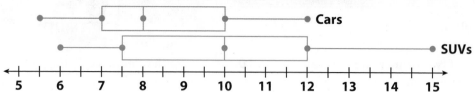

14. Suppose the dealership acquires a used car that it intends to sell for $15,000. Would the price of the car be an outlier? Explain.

_____

15. Compare the distribution of SUV prices with the distribution of car prices.

_____

_____

_____

 **FOCUS ON HIGHER ORDER THINKING**

Work Area

Dolly and Willie's scores are shown. Use the box plots for Exercises 16 and 17.

First Quarter Assignments

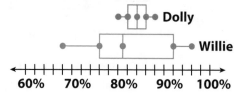

16. Dolly claims that she is the better student. What statistics make Dolly seem like the better student? Explain.

_____

_____

17. Willie claims that he is the better student. What statistics make Willie seem like the better student? Explain.

_____

_____

18. **Critical Thinking** Suppose the minimum in a data set is the same as the first quartile. How would this affect a box plot of the data? Explain.

_____

_____

13.5 Normal Distributions

FL S-ID.1.4

Use the mean and standard deviation of a data set to fit it to a normal distribution and to estimate population percentages. Use calculators, spreadsheets, and tables to estimate areas under the normal curve. *Also S-ID.1.1*

ESSENTIAL QUESTION

How can you use characteristics of a normal distribution to make estimates and probability predictions about the population that the data represents?

EXPLORE ACTIVITY 1   FL S-ID.1.4

Investigating Symmetric Distributions

A bell-shaped, symmetric distribution with a tail on each end is called a **normal distribution.**

Use a graphing calculator and the infant birth weight data in the table below to determine if the set represents a normal distribution.

Birth Weight (kg)				
3.3	3.6	3.5	3.4	3.7
3.6	3.5	3.4	3.7	3.5
3.4	3.5	3.2	3.6	3.4
3.8	3.5	3.6	3.3	3.5

A Enter the data into a graphing calculator. Calculate the "1-Variable Statistics" for the distribution of baby weights.

Mean $\bar{x} \approx$ _____

Standard deviation $\sigma x \approx$ _____

Median = _____

$\text{IQR} = Q_3 - Q_1 =$ _____

B Plot a histogram.

- Turn on a statistics plot, select the histogram option, and enter the birth weights as data.
- Set the viewing window to display one bar per data value. Use the values shown at the right.
- Use the calculator to generate the histogram by pressing GRAPH. You can obtain the heights of the bars by pressing TRACE and using the arrow keys.

C Sketch the histogram on the grid below. Label the axes and the bar intervals.

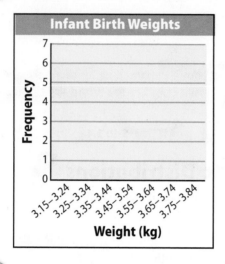

D Could this data be described by a normal distribution? Explain.

_____

_____

REFLECT

1. Which intervals on the histogram had the fewest values? Which interval had the greatest number of values?

_____

_____

_____

2. Make a Conjecture For this normal distribution, the mean and the median are the same. Is this true for every normal distribution? Explain.

_____

_____

_____

_____

3. Counterexamples Allison thinks that every symmetric distribution must be bell-shaped. Provide a counterexample to show that she is incorrect.

_____

_____

_____

FL S-ID.1.4

Investigating a Symmetric Relative Frequency Histogram

The table gives the frequency of each weight from the data set used in Explore Activity 1.

Weight (kg)	3.2	3.3	3.4	3.5	3.6	3.7	3.8
Frequency	1	2	4	6	4	2	1

A Convert the frequency table above to a relative frequency table by using the fact that there are 20 data values.

Weight (kg)	3.2	3.3	3.4	3.5	3.6	3.7	3.8
Relative frequency	$\frac{1}{20} = 0.05$						

What is the sum of the relative frequencies? _____

B Sketch a relative frequency histogram. The heights of the bars now indicate relative frequencies.

C Recall from Explore Activity 1 that the mean of this data set is 3.5 and the standard deviation is 0.14. By how many standard deviations does a birth weight of 3.2 kg differ from the mean? Justify your answer.

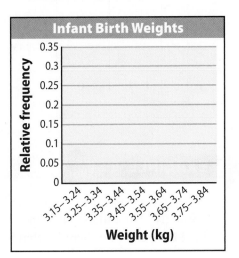

_____

_____

_____

_____

REFLECT

4. a. Identify the interval of values that are within one standard deviation of the mean. What percent of the values in the set are in this interval?

_____

_____

b. Identify the interval of values that are within two standard deviations of the mean. What percent of the values in the set are in this interval?

_____

_____

Finding Areas Under a Normal Curve

The smaller the intervals are in a symmetric, bell-shaped relative frequency histogram, the closer the shape of the histogram is to a curve, called a *normal curve*.

Math Talk

Mathematical Practices

Could a data set create a curve other than a normal curve?

Properties of Normal Curves

A **normal curve** has the following properties:

- 68% of the data fall within 1 standard deviation of the mean.
- 95% of the data fall within 2 standard deviations of the mean.
- 99.7% of the data fall within 3 standard deviations of the mean.

The symmetry of a normal curve allows you to separate the area under the curve into eight parts and know what percent of the data is contained in each part.

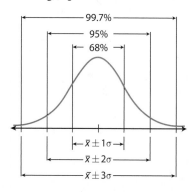

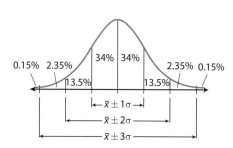

EXAMPLE 1

 FL S-ID.1.4

The masses (in grams) of pennies minted in the United States after 1982 are normally distributed with a mean of 2.50 g and a standard deviation of 0.02 g. Find the percent of pennies that have a mass between 2.46 g and 2.54 g.

Find the distance between 2.46 and the mean. $2.50 - 2.46 = 0.04$ g; 0.04 g is twice the standard deviation of 0.02 g, so 2.46 g is 2 standard deviations below the mean.

Find the distance between 2.54 and the mean. $2.54 - 2.50 = 0.04$ g; so 2.54 g is 2 standard deviations above the mean.

95% of the data in a normal distribution fall within 2 standard deviations of the mean.

95% of pennies have a mass between 2.46 g and 2.54 g.

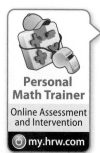
YOUR TURN

5. Find the percent of pennies that have a mass between 2.48 g and 2.52 g.

_____

Using a Normal Curve to Find Probabilities

Knowing the percentages of data under sections of a normal curve allows you to make predictions about the larger population that a normally distributed sample of data represents.

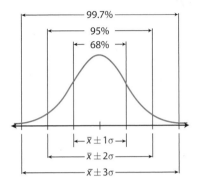

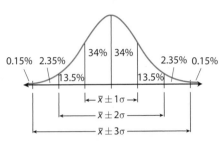

Math On the Spot
my.hrw.com

EXAMPLE 2 *Real World*   FL S-ID.1.4

The masses of pennies minted in the United States after 1982 are normally distributed with a mean of 2.50 g and a standard deviation of 0.02 g. Find the probability that a randomly chosen penny has a mass greater than 2.52 g.

STEP 1 Determine the distance between 2.52 and the mean.
The mean is 2.50; 2.52 − 2.50 = 0.02.

Determine how many standard deviations this distance is.
The distance of 0.02 equals the standard deviation, so 2.52 is 1 standard deviation above the mean.

STEP 2 Look at the parts of the curve that are more than 1 standard deviation above the mean. Identify what percent of the data is contained in the area under each part.

13.5%, 2.35%, 0.15%

STEP 3 The total probability is the sum of the probabilities for each part of the curve. Express the probability as a percent and as a decimal.

13.5% + 2.35% + 0.15% = 16%

The probability is 16%, or 0.16.

My Notes

YOUR TURN

6. Find the probability that a randomly chosen penny has a mass less than or equal to 2.50 g.

_____

Personal Math Trainer

Online Assessment and Intervention

my.hrw.com

Suppose the scores on a test given to all juniors in a school district are normally distributed with a mean of 74 and a standard deviation of 8. Find the following. (Examples 1 and 2)

1. The percent of juniors whose score is no more than 90

_____

2. The percent of juniors whose score is between 58 and 74

_____

3. The percent of juniors whose score is at least 74

_____

4. The percent of juniors whose score is below 66

_____

5. The probability that a randomly chosen junior has a score above 82

_____

6. The probability that a randomly chosen junior has a score between 66 and 90

_____

7. The probability that a randomly chosen junior has a score below 74

_____

8. The probability that a randomly chosen junior has a score above 98

_____

? ESSENTIAL QUESTION CHECK-IN

9. How do you find percents of data and probabilities of events associated with normal distributions?

_____

_____

_____

_____

_____

_____

13.5 Independent Practice

  S-ID.1.4, S-ID.1.1

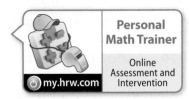

10. A normal distribution has a mean of 10 and a standard deviation of 1.5.

    a. In which interval do 95% of the data fall?

    _____

    b. In which interval do 68% of the data fall?

    _____

Suppose the heights (in inches) of adult males in the United States are normally distributed with a mean of 72 inches and a standard deviation of 2 inches. Find each of the following.

11. The percent of men who are no more than 68 inches tall

_____

12. The percent of men who are between 70 and 72 inches tall

_____

13. The percent of men who are at least 76 inches tall

_____

14. The probability that a randomly chosen man is more than 72 inches tall

_____

15. The probability that a randomly chosen man is between 68 and 76 inches tall

_____

16. The probability that a randomly chosen man is less than 76 inches tall

_____

17. Ten customers at Fielden Grocery were surveyed about how long they waited in line to check out. Their wait times, in minutes, are shown below.

16	15	10	7	5
5	4	3	3	2

    a. What is the mean of the data set?

    _____

    b. How many data points are below the mean, and how many are above the mean?

    _____

    _____

    c. Do the data appear to be normally distributed? Explain.

    _____

    _____

    _____

    _____

    _____

    _____

18. Kori is analyzing a normal data distribution, but the data provided is incomplete. Kori knows that the mean of the data is 120, and that 84% of the data values are less than 130. Find the standard deviation for this data set.

_____

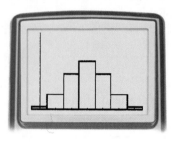 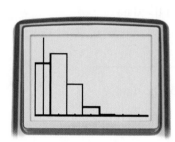

H.O.T. FOCUS ON HIGHER ORDER THINKING

Work Area

19. **Critical Thinking** The calculator screen on the left shows the probability distribution for the number of "heads" that come up when six coins are flipped. The screen on the right shows the probability distribution for the number of 1s that come up when six dice are rolled. For which distribution is it reasonable to use a normal curve as an approximation? Why?

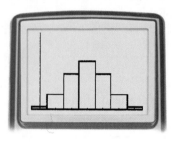 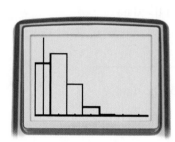

_____

_____

_____

Suppose the upper arm length (in centimeters) of adult males in the United States is normally distributed with a mean of 39.4 cm and a standard deviation of 2.3 cm.

20. **Justify Reasoning** What percent of adult males have an upper arm length between 34.8 and 41.7 cm? Explain how you got your answer.

_____

_____

_____

_____

_____

21. **Communicate Mathematical Ideas** Explain how you can determine whether a set of data is normally distributed.

_____

_____

_____

_____

_____

_____

Ready to Go On?

13.1 Measures of Center and Spread

1. The high temperatures in degrees Fahrenheit on 11 days were 68, 71, 75, 74, 75, 71, 73, 71, 72, 74, and 79. Find the mean, median, and range.

   _____

13.2 Data Distributions and Outliers

2. Describe the shape of the distribution. If a data point with a value of 3.0 inches is added, how will the median change?

   _____

   _____

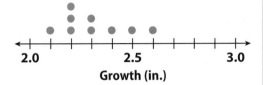

Growth (in.)

13.3 and 13.4 Histograms and Box Plots

3. Use the table showing the average number of hours of sleep for people at different ages to create a histogram.

Age	3–9	10–13	14–18	19–30	31–45	46–50
Sleep (h)	11	10	9	8	7.5	6

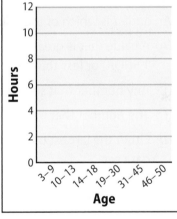

4. Find the range and the IQR of the data in the box plot.

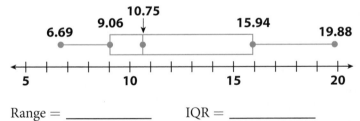

   Range = _____   IQR = _____

13.5 Normal Distributions

5. Suppose compact fluorescent light bulbs last, on average, 10,000 hours. The standard deviation is 500 hours. What percent of light bulbs burn out within

   11,000 hours? _____

? ESSENTIAL QUESTION

6. How can data sets be displayed and compared, and what statistics can be

   gathered using the display? _____

   _____

Assessment Readiness

Personal Math Trainer

Online Assessment and Intervention

my.hrw.com

Selected Response

1. Which value is always represented on a box plot?

   Ⓐ Mean   Ⓒ Frequency

   Ⓑ Median   Ⓓ Standard deviation

2. The mean score on a test is 50. Which CANNOT be true?

   Ⓐ Half the scores are 0, and half the scores are 100.

   Ⓑ The range is 50.

   Ⓒ Half the scores are 25, and half the scores are 50.

   Ⓓ Every score is 50.

3. An outlier is which of the following?

   Ⓐ A value that is greater than $Q_3 + 1.5(IQR)$ or less than $Q_1 - 1.5(IQR)$

   Ⓑ Any number that seems out of place

   Ⓒ The number that occurs most often

   Ⓓ Either the largest or smallest value in a data set

4. The box in a box plot represents which of the following?

   Ⓐ median   Ⓒ middle 50%

   Ⓑ mean   Ⓓ upper 50%

5. What is $\frac{1}{3^{-3}}$ simplified?

   Ⓐ 9   Ⓒ $\frac{1}{9}$

   Ⓑ 27   Ⓓ $\frac{1}{27}$

6. What is the correct factorization of $2x^2 + 5x - 7$?

   Ⓐ $(2x - 7)(x + 1)$

   Ⓑ $(2x + 7)(x - 1)$

   Ⓒ $(2x - 1)(x + 7)$

   Ⓓ $(2x + 1)(x - 7)$

7. Which is the interquartile range of the box plot shown?

   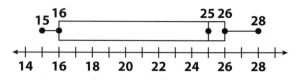

   Ⓐ 25   Ⓒ 13

   Ⓑ 16   Ⓓ 10

Mini-Tasks

8. Michael is collecting data on the growth of plants after one week. He planted nine seeds of two different types of plants and recorded his data in the table below.

Growth of Plants (in.)								
Type A	2.1	2.2	2.2	2.2	2.3	2.3	2.4	2.5	2.6
Type B	1.9	2.0	2.0	2.1	2.1	2.1	2.2	2.2	2.3

   a. Create a box plot for both types of plant.

   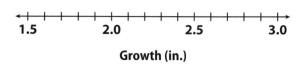

   Growth (in.)

   b. Describe the shape of each distribution.

   _____

   _____

   _____

   c. Which data value(s) occur(s) most often for each type of plant?

   _____

   _____

Study Guide Review

Descriptive Statistics

Key Vocabulary

categorical data *(datos categóricos)*

conditional relative frequency *(frecuencia relativa condicional)*

frequency table *(tabla de frecuencia)*

joint relative frequency *(frecuencia relativa conjunta)*

marginal relative frequency *(frecuencia relativa marginal)*

quantitative data *(datos cuantitativos)*

relative frequency *(frecuencia relativa)*

? ESSENTIAL QUESTION

How can you summarize two categories of categorical data and recognize associations and trends between two categories of categorical data?

EXAMPLE 1

In a survey, Quan asked 100 randomly selected students whether they preferred winter, spring, summer, or fall. He also recorded the gender of each student. The results are shown in the two-way frequency table below. Complete the table.

Gender	Preferred Season				
	Winter	Spring	Summer	Fall	Total
Girl	8	12	25	5	?
Boy	9	5	30	6	?
Total	?	?	?	?	?

Find the total for each gender by adding the frequencies in each row. Write the row totals in the Total column.

Find the total for each preferred season by adding the frequencies in each column. Write the column totals in the Total row.

Find the grand total, which is the sum of the row totals as well as the sum of the column totals. Write the grand total in the lower-right corner of the table (the intersection of the Total column and the Total row.)

Gender	Preferred Season				
	Winter	Spring	Summer	Fall	Total
Girl	8	12	25	5	50
Boy	9	5	30	6	50
Total	17	17	55	11	100

EXAMPLE 2

Does gender influence a student's preference for a particular season?

Use the data from Quan's survey to create a two-way relative frequency table. Find the joint relative frequencies and marginal relative frequencies by dividing each number in the frequency table by the grand total. Write the quotients as decimals.

Gender	Preferred Season				
	Winter	Spring	Summer	Fall	Total
Girl	$\frac{8}{100} = 0.08$	$\frac{12}{100} = 0.12$	$\frac{25}{100} = 0.25$	$\frac{5}{100} = 0.05$	$\frac{50}{100} = 0.5$
Boy	$\frac{9}{100} = 0.09$	$\frac{5}{100} = 0.05$	$\frac{30}{100} = 0.3$	$\frac{6}{100} = 0.06$	$\frac{50}{100} = 0.5$
Total	$\frac{17}{100} = 0.17$	$\frac{17}{100} = 0.17$	$\frac{55}{100} = 0.55$	$\frac{11}{100} = 0.11$	$\frac{100}{100} = 1$

Determine each conditional relative frequency to find what percent of the students who prefer each season are girls. Compare each percentage to the percent of surveyed students who are girls (50%).

Winter: $\frac{8}{17} \approx 0.47 = 47\%$

Spring: $\frac{12}{17} \approx 0.71 = 71\%$

Summer: $\frac{25}{55} \approx 0.45 = 45\%$

Fall: $\frac{5}{11} \approx 0.45 = 45\%$

All of the percentages are close to 50% except spring. According to the survey, girls are more likely than boys to prefer spring.

EXERCISES

The results of a survey asking 40 students the number of siblings they have are shown in the two-way relative frequency table below. (Lessons 16.1, 16.2)

1. Complete the table.

Gender	Siblings				
	0	1	2	3+	Total
Freshman	$\frac{6}{40} =$ ___	$\frac{7}{40} =$ ___	$\frac{6}{40} =$ ___	$\frac{3}{40} =$ ___	$\frac{}{40} =$ ___
Seniors	$\frac{4}{40} =$ ___	$\frac{8}{40} =$ ___	$\frac{4}{40} =$ ___	$\frac{2}{40} =$ ___	$\frac{}{40} =$ ___
Total	$\frac{}{40} =$ ___	$\frac{}{40} =$ ___	$\frac{}{40} =$ ___	$\frac{}{40} =$ ___	$\frac{}{40} =$ ___

2. Analyze the data to decide if freshman are more likely or less likely than seniors to have zero siblings. Explain.

_____

_____

_____

Key Vocabulary

box plot *(gráfica de mediana y rango)*

dot plot *(diagrama de acumulación)*

histogram *(histograma)*

interquartile range *(rango entre cuartiles)*

mean *(media)*

median *(mediana)*

normal curve *(curva normal)*

normal distribution *(distribución normal)*

outlier *(valor extremo)*

quartiles *(cuartil)*

range *(rango)*

symmetric *(simétrico)*

? ESSENTIAL QUESTION

How can data sets be displayed and compared and what statistics can be gathered using the display?

EXAMPLE 1

Estimate the mean, median, and standard deviation of the heights from the histogram.

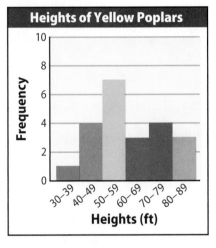

Heights of Yellow Poplars

Find the estimated mean.

30–39: 35; 1   *Find the midpoint of each range.*

40–49: 45; 4   *Find the frequency of each range.*

50–59: 55; 7

60–69: 65; 3

70–79: 75; 4

80–89: 85; 3

$$\frac{35 \times 1 + 45 \times 4 + 55 \times 7 + 65 \times 3 + 75 \times 4 + 85 \times 3}{22} \approx 61$$

Multiply each midpoint by the frequency for that interval, and then find the mean of those values.

Find the estimated standard deviation.

30–39: $(35 - 61)^2 = 676$ *Subtract the estimated mean from the midpoint of each range and square it.*

40–49: $(45 - 61)^2 = 256$

50–59: $(55 - 61)^2 = 36$

60–69: $(65 - 61)^2 = 16$

70–79: $(75 - 61)^2 = 196$

80–89: $(85 - 61)^2 = 576$

$$\sqrt{\frac{676 \times 1 + 256 \times 4 + 36 \times 7 + 16 \times 3 + 196 \times 4 + 576 \times 3}{22}} \approx 14$$

Multiply each square by the frequency for the corresponding interval, and then find the mean of the products. Take the square root of the result.

Find the estimated median.

The median value will be the mean of the 11th value and the 12th value in the ordered set. This falls in the 50–59 range.

This interval has seven values. Since the previous intervals together contain five values, the median will be the mean of the 6th and 7th values in the interval 50–59. Estimate the median as the sum of the interval's least value, 50, and $\frac{1}{7}$ of the interval width, 10, multiplied by the mean of 6 and 7, 6.5

$50 + \left(\frac{1}{7} \times 10 \times 6.5 \right) \approx 59.3$, so 59 is a good estimate for the median.

EXAMPLE 2

The heights of pine trees in a forest are given. Use the data to make a box plot.
18, 13, 22, 25, 27, 32, 35, 60, 36, 16, 26, 24, 31, 46, 38, 29, 23, 19, 42, 34

Order the data from least to greatest.
13, 16, 18, 19, 22, 23, 24, 25, 26, 27, 29, 31, 32, 34, 35, 36, 38, 42, 46, 60

Find the **minimum**, first quartile, median, third quartile, and **maximum**.

Remember, you may have to calculate the mean of two numbers when finding the median and the first and third quartiles.

$\text{median} = \frac{27 + 29}{2} = 28$

$\text{first quartile} = \frac{22 + 23}{2} = 22.5$

$\text{third quartile} = \frac{35 + 36}{2} = 35.5$

Plot these points above a number line and draw the box plot.

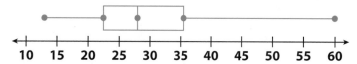

EXAMPLE 3

Suppose the heights of professional basketball players in the United States are distributed normally, with a mean of 79 inches and a standard deviation of 4 inches. Find the percent of players that have a height between 71 and 75 inches.

How far below the mean is 71 inches?
$79 - 71 = 8$ inches

How many standard deviations is this?
The standard deviation is 4 inches, so 8 inches is 2 standard deviations.

How far below the mean is 75 inches?
$79 - 75 = 4$ inches

How many standard deviations is this?
The standard deviation is 4 inches, so 4 inches is 1 standard deviation.

Look at the following graph to find what percent of the data distribution falls under the curve between 1 and 2 standard deviations below the mean.

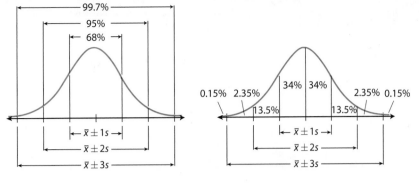

This is the third section of the second graph, which includes 13.5% of the data values.

EXERCISES

The histogram represents the test scores in two different math classes. (Lesson 17.3)

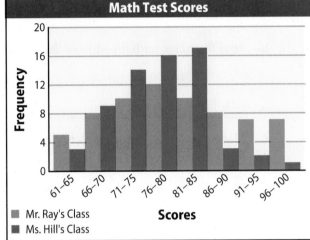

1. Which class has a greater median?

   _____

2. Which class has a greater standard deviation?

   _____

The following box plot represents the amount people spend at two different movie theaters. (Lessons 17.1, 17.2, 17.4)

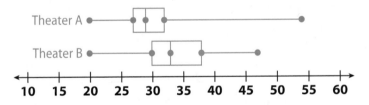

3. Which set has a greater median? _____

4. Which set has a greater interquartile range? _____

5. Is the maximum value for Theater A, 54, an outlier? Explain.

   _____

   _____

6. Suppose the mean 40-yard dash time of professional football players is 4.41 seconds with a standard deviation of 0.15 seconds. Assume normal distribution. What is the percent of players who run the 40-yard dash in between 4.11 and 4.41 seconds? (Lesson 17.5)

   _____

1. **CAREERS IN MATH** Sports Recruiter The data table shows the 40-yard dash times of two running backs over a week.

	1	2	3	4	5	6	7
Athlete A	4.21	4.18	4.28	4.15	4.19	4.18	4.25
Athlete B	4.15	4.31	4.24	4.41	4.26	4.24	4.31

a. Find the mean and median for both athletes' times.

_____

_____

b. Find the range for both athletes' times.

_____

_____

c. Make a box plot for each athlete's data set. Use the same number line for both box plots.

d. Are any of the values in either set outliers? Explain.

_____

_____

e. Find the standard deviation for both athletes' times.

_____

_____

f. Which athlete would you choose to be your team's running back? Explain.

_____

_____

_____

_____

UNIT 3 MIXED REVIEW

Assessment Readiness

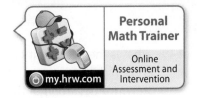

Personal
Math Trainer

Online
Assessment and
Intervention

my.hrw.com

Selected Response

The results of a survey of how many students are in each math class are: 18, 19, 20, 20, 21, 19, 21, 22, 20. Use the data for Items 1–5.

1. Which of the following is the correct dot plot?

   Ⓐ
   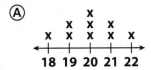

   Ⓑ
   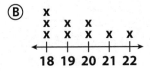

   Ⓒ
   ```
                      x
              x  x  x
         x  x  x  x  x
         +--+--+--+--+--+
         18 19 20 21 22
   ```

   Ⓓ
   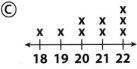

2. What is the distribution of the data?

   Ⓐ symmetric   Ⓒ skewed right

   Ⓑ skewed left   Ⓓ even

3. What is the mean of the data?

   Ⓐ 19   Ⓒ 20.5

   Ⓑ 20   Ⓓ 21

4. What is the standard deviation of the data?

   Ⓐ 2.00   Ⓒ 1.15

   Ⓑ 1.55   Ⓓ 1.33

5. If a new class was reported to have 30 students, how would this affect the statistics?

   Ⓐ both the mean and median would go up

   Ⓑ both the mean and median would stay the same

   Ⓒ only the median would go up

   Ⓓ only the mean would go up

The results of a survey of 40 students about whether they prefer to draw or sing are shown in the two-way frequency table below. Use the table for Items 6–9.

Gender	Preferred		
	Draw	Sing	Total
Girl	18	?	24
Boy	12	4	?
Total	?	10	40

6. How many girls prefer to sing?

   Ⓐ 6   Ⓒ 24

   Ⓑ 18   Ⓓ 10

7. How many boys were surveyed?

   Ⓐ 40   Ⓒ 18

   Ⓑ 12   Ⓓ 16

8. How many students prefer to draw?

   Ⓐ 30   Ⓒ 12

   Ⓑ 18   Ⓓ 10

Gather as much information from the diagram as you can but remember that the diagram can appear misleading.

9. Does it appear as though gender influences preference for drawing or singing?

   Ⓐ yes

   Ⓑ no

10. What is the interquartile range of the plot shown?

    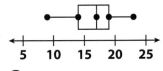

    Ⓐ 5   Ⓒ 12

    Ⓑ 9   Ⓓ 15

11. What is the probability that a randomly chosen data point would be within one standard deviation of the mean? Assume normal distribution.

Ⓐ 34% Ⓒ 99.7%

Ⓑ 95% Ⓓ 68%

12. Which of the following is not needed when making a box plot?

Ⓐ mean Ⓒ median

Ⓑ minimum Ⓓ third quartile

13. Simplify $(3x^3 + 2y^2)(12x + y)$.

Ⓐ $36x^4 + 2y^3$

Ⓑ $6x^3y^2 + 12xy$

Ⓒ $72x^4y^3$

Ⓓ $36x^4 + 24xy^2 + 3x^3y + 2y^3$

14. What is the slope of the line that has intercepts at $(0, 5)$ and $(-1, 0)$?

Ⓐ -5 Ⓒ $\frac{1}{5}$

Ⓑ 5 Ⓓ $-\frac{1}{5}$

15. Which ordered pair is a solution to $-3x + 2y > 9$?

Ⓐ $(3, 9)$ Ⓒ $(3, -6)$

Ⓑ $(0, -3)$ Ⓓ $(-3, 1)$

Mini-Task

16. Jeremy had these scores on his weekly quizzes in History class:

93, 85, 88, 100, 84, 82, 95, 95, 91, 92, 98, 100, 68, 67, 80

a. Use the data to make a frequency table.

66–70	
71–75	
76–80	
81–85	
86–90	
91–95	
96–100	

b. Draw a histogram based on your frequency table.

c. Find the mean and median of Jeremy's scores. Round to the nearest whole number if needed.

_____

d. Describe how you would estimate the mean and median based on your histogram.

_____

_____

_____

_____

_____

_____

_____

_____

_____

_____

Polynomial Expressions and Equations

CAREERS IN MATH

Investigator An investigator is called upon to evaluate and determine the cause of traffic accidents. Investigators use math to calculate a vehicle's stopping distance, which allows them to determine how fast the vehicle was traveling at the time of the accident.

If you're interested in a career as an investigator, you should study these mathematical subjects:
- Algebra
- Geometry
- Trigonometry
- Calculus

Research other careers that require the use of mathematical formulas to understand real-world scenarios.

Unit 4 Performance Task

At the end of the unit, check out how an **Investigator** uses math.

Vocabulary Preview

Use the puzzle to preview key vocabulary from this unit. Unscramble each of the clue words. Copy the letters in the numbered cells to answer the riddle.

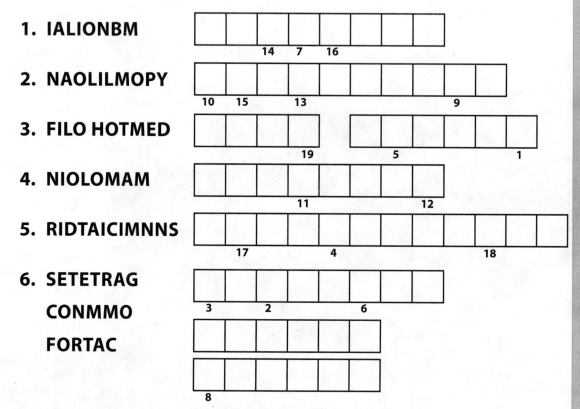

1. **IALIONBM**

2. **NAOLILMOPY**

3. **FILO HOTMED**

4. **NIOLOMAM**

5. **RIDTAICIMNNS**

6. **SETETRAG CONMMO FORTAC**

1. Two monomial terms separated by addition or subtraction (Lesson 14.1)
2. A sum or difference of two or more monomials (Lesson 14.1)
3. A method for multiplying two binomials (Lesson 14.4)
4. A number, variable, or product of numbers and variables that has a whole number exponent (Lesson 14.1)
5. Tells how many real solutions a quadratic equation will have (Lesson 16.6)
6. The greatest factor shared by two or more whole numbers (Lesson 15.1)

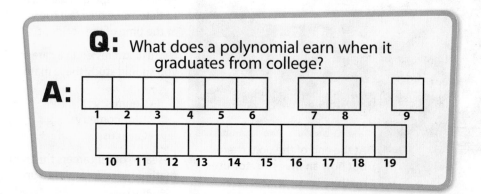

Q: What does a polynomial earn when it graduates from college?

A:

Polynomials and Operations

ESSENTIAL QUESTION

How are polynomials like other number systems, such as whole numbers and integers?

Real-World Video

Vehicles, such as planes and cars, are aerodynamically tested in a wind tunnel. The complex factors involved in wind tunnel testing can be modeled with polynomial functions.

my.hrw.com

G⊙ DIGITAL
my.hrw.com

my.hrw.com

Go digital with your write-in student edition, accessible on any device.

Math On the Spot

Scan with your smart phone to jump directly to the online edition, video tutor, and more.

Animated Math

Interactively explore key concepts to see how math works.

Personal Math Trainer

Get immediate feedback and help as you work through practice sets.

Are YOU Ready?

Complete these exercises to review skills you will need for this module.

Personal Math Trainer

Online Assessment and Intervention

my.hrw.com

Distributive Property

EXAMPLE
$$4(5 - 2) = 4(5) + 4(-2)$$ Apply $a(b + c) = ab + ac$.
$$= 20 - 8$$ Simplify.
$$= 12$$

$$-2(3 + x) = (-2)(3) + (-2)(x)$$ Apply $a(b + c) = ab + ac$.
$$= -6 - 2x$$ Simplify.

Simplify each expression.

1. $3(x + 2)$ **2.** $7(y - 5)$ **3.** $(3 - 2x)8$ **4.** $2(-x - 3)$

_____ _____ _____ _____

5. $-6(-4x + 1)$ **6.** $(8 - 5x)(-4)$ **7.** $-3(x - 5)$ **8.** $-8(-6x - 9)$

_____ _____ _____ _____

Combine Like Terms

EXAMPLE
$$18 + 7y - 8 - 5y$$
$$18 - 8 + 7y - 5y$$ Reorder.
$$18 - 8 = 10$$ Subtract.
$$7y - 5y = (7 - 5)y = 2y$$ Add.
$$10 + 2y$$ Simplify.

Simplify each expression by combining like terms.

9. $5x + 15 + 2x$ **10.** $6a + 9 - 4a - 11$ **11.** $-5 + c - 10 + 3d$

_____ _____ _____

12. $22y - 15y + y - 15z$ **13.** $45 - 12 + 15x - 12y + 3x$ **14.** $-n + 15 + 4m - 18o - 1$

_____ _____ _____

15. $-8a - 4b + 18a - 5c + 2c - 12d + e - 45d + 4c$

_____

Reading Start-Up

Visualize Vocabulary

Use the Reviews Words with a check next to them to complete the chart.

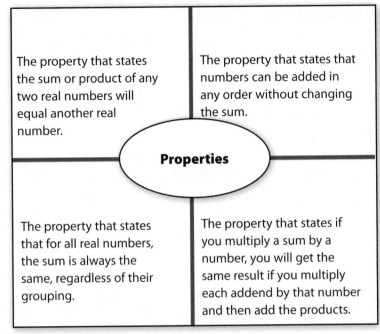

The property that states the sum or product of any two real numbers will equal another real number.	The property that states that numbers can be added in any order without changing the sum.
Properties	
The property that states that for all real numbers, the sum is always the same, regardless of their grouping.	The property that states if you multiply a sum by a number, you will get the same result if you multiply each addend by that number and then add the products.

Vocabulary

Review Words

✓Associative Property
(Propiedad asociativa)

✓Commutative Property
(Propiedad conmutativa)

✓Closure Property
(Propiedad cerradura)

✓Distributive Property
(Propiedad distributiva)

like terms
(términos similares)

properties of exponents
(propiedades de exponentes)

terms (términos)

Preview Words

binomial

degree of a polynomial

FOIL method

monomial

polynomial

trinomial

Understand Vocabulary

To become familiar with some of the vocabulary terms in the module, consider the following. You may refer to the module, the glossary, or a dictionary.

1. The prefix *tri-* is used to identify an item that has three parts, such as a *triangle* or a *tricycle*. What do you think a **trinomial** might be?

   _____

2. The prefix *poly-* is used to identify an item with many elements, such as a *polygon*. What do you think a **polynomial** might be?

   _____

Active Reading

Layered Book Before beginning the module, create a layered book to help you learn the concepts in this module. Label each flap with lesson titles from this module. As you study each lesson, write important ideas, such as vocabulary and formulas under the appropriate flap. Refer to your finished layered book as you work on exercises from this module.

MODULE 14

Unpacking the Standards

Understanding the standards and vocabulary terms in the standards will help you know exactly what you are expected to learn in this module.

 FL **A-APR.1.1**

Understand that polynomials form a system analogous to the integers, namely, they are closed under the operations of addition, subtraction, and multiplication; add, subtract, and multiply polynomials.

Key Vocabulary

monomial *(monomio)*
A number or product of numbers and variables with whole-number exponents, or a polynomial with one term.

What It Means to You

You will learn how to perform addition, subtraction, and multiplication on monomials and polynomials.

UNPACKING EXAMPLE A-APR.1.1

What is the sum, difference, and product of the polynomials $-4x^2$ and $3x^2 + 7x - 8$?

Sum	Difference	Product
$-4x^2$ $\underline{+3x^2 + 7x - 8}$ $-x^2 + 7x - 8$	$-4x^2$ $\underline{-(3x^2 + 7x - 8)}$ $-7x^2 - 7x + 8$	$-4x^2(3x^2 + 7x - 8)$ $= (-4x^2)(3x^2) +$ $\quad (-4x^2)(7x) - (-4x^2)8$ $= -12x^4 - 28x^3 + 32x^2$

 FL **A-SSE.1.2**

Use the structure of an expression to identify ways to rewrite it.

Key Vocabulary

polynomial *(polynomio)*
A monomial or a sum or difference of monomials.

What It Means to You

Expressions can be written many different ways.

UNPACKING EXAMPLE A-SSE.1.2

Pam wrote the polynomial $k^2 - 9$ while Sam wrote $(k - 3)^2$. Pam claimed that the two expressions were equivalent. Sam disagreed. Who was right?

Expand Sam's expression:

$$(k - 3)^2 = (k - 3)(k - 3)$$

Using the FOIL method:

$$(k - 3)(k - 3) = k^2 - 3k - 3k + 9$$

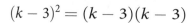

$$= k^2 - 6k + 9$$

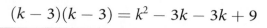

Sam was right. The two expressions are not equivalent.

 Visit **my.hrw.com** to see all **Florida Math Standards** unpacked.

 my.hrw.com

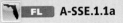
LESSON 14.1 Understanding Polynomials

ESSENTIAL QUESTION

What are polynomial expressions, and how do you simplify them?

EXPLORE ACTIVITY  FL A-SSE.1.1a

Identifying Monomials

A **monomial** is a number, variable, or product of numbers and variables that have whole number exponents. A monomial cannot have more than one term, and it cannot have a variable in its denominator.

Monomials				Not Monomial		
5	x	$-7xy$	$0.5x^4$	$-0.3x^{-2}$	$4x - y$	$\dfrac{2}{x^3}$

Complete the table to identify which terms are monomials.

Term	Is this a monomial?	Explain your reasoning.
$3bc$	yes	$3bc$ is the product of a number, 3, and the variables b and c.
x^3		x^3 is the product of a number, 1, and the variable x with a whole-number exponent.
$\sqrt{Z}$	no	
2^5		
$\dfrac{6}{k^2}$	no	
$4x + 7$		

REFLECT

1. **Communicate Mathematical Ideas** Explain why $16^{\frac{1}{2}}$ is a monomial, but $x^{\frac{1}{2}}$ is not a monomial.

_____

_____

_____

Classifying Polynomials

A **polynomial** can be one monomial, or the sum or difference of more than one monomial. Polynomials are classified by the number of terms: a monomial has one term, a **binomial** has two terms, and a **trinomial** has three terms. Polynomials are also classified by the **degree of a polynomial**, which is the greatest sum of the exponents in each term.

EXAMPLE 1

Classify each polynomial by its degree and the number of terms.

A $6x^3 - 5x^2y^2$

Degree: 4

Binomial

> $6x^3$ has degree 3, and $5x^2y^2$ has degree 4.
>
> There are 2 terms.
> $6x^3 - 5x^2y^2$ is a 4th degree binomial.

> Find the degree of each term by adding the exponents of the variables in that term. The greatest degree is the degree of the polynomial.

B $3^5 + 2n^2 + 8n$

Degree: 2

Trinomial

> 3^5 has degree 0, $2n^2$ has degree 2 and $8n$ has degree 1.
>
> There are 3 terms.
>
> $3^5 + 2n^2 + 8n$ is a 2nd degree trinomial.

REFLECT

2. Is $x^3y^2 + x^{0.5}$ a polynomial? Justify your answer.

_____

_____

_____

YOUR TURN

Classify each polynomial by its degree and the number of terms.

3. $4xy^2 + 3x^2y^2 + 5xy$

_____

4. $8ab^2 - 4a^2b$

_____

5. $15g^2h + 3g^2$

_____

6. $4p^2q^2 + 3q^5 + 5pq$

_____

Simplifying Polynomials

You can simplify polynomials by combining the like terms. *Like terms* are monomials that have the same variables that are raised to the same powers.

Math On the Spot

my.hrw.com

Like terms:

- Same variable
- Same power

$$r^2 + 2r^3 + 3r^2$$

Unlike terms:

- Different power

EXAMPLE 2

FL A-APR.1.1

Combine like terms to simplify each polynomial.

My Notes

A $3r^3 - 2r^2 + 5r^2 - 4r^3$

$3r^3 - 4r^3 - 2r^2 + 5r^2$ Rearrange in descending order of exponents.

$3r^3 - 4r^3 - 2r^2 + 5r^2$ Identify like terms.

$r^3(3 - 4) + r^2(-2 + 5)$ Combine using the Distributive Property.

$-1r^3 + 3r^2$ Simplify.

$3r^2 - r^3$

B $p^2q^5 - 4p^5q^4 - 4p^2q^5 + 3p^5q^4$

$-4p^5q^4 + 3p^5q^4 + p^2q^5 - 4p^2q^5$ Rearrange in descending order of exponents.

$-4p^5q^4 + 3p^5q^4 + p^2q^5 - 4p^2q^5$ Identify like terms.

$p^5q^4(-4 + 3) + p^2q^5(1 - 4)$ Combine using the Distributive Property.

$(-1)p^5q^4 + (-3)p^2q^5$ Simplify.

$-p^5q^4 - 3p^2q^5$

REFLECT

7. Can you think of a way to simplify like terms without using the Distributive Property? Explain.

_____

_____

_____

8. Simplify $5r^3 - r^2s + 6 - 3r^2s - 1r^3 + 2^5$

_____

9. Simplify $7a^2 - ab - 75 - 5ab + 1a^2 + 5^3$

_____

Evaluating Polynomials

You can use a polynomial to define a function, and you can evaluate the function by substituting values for the polynomial's variable.

EXAMPLE 3   FL   F-IF.1.2

An aerial firework is launched from a 6-foot-high platform with initial speed 200 ft/s. The polynomial $-16t^2 + 200t + 6$ gives the height in feet that the firework will rise in t seconds. How high will the firework rise if it has a 5-second fuse?

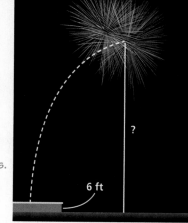

$-16t^2 + 200t + 6$	*Write the expression.*
$-16(5)^2 + 200(5) + 6$	*The time is 5 seconds.*
$-16(25) + 200(5) + 6$	*Use order of operations.*
$-400 + 1000 + 6 = 606$	

The firework will rise 606 feet.

REFLECT

10. Critical Thinking Kaylynn says that the expression $-16t^2 + 200t + 50$ can be used to model the height in feet after t seconds of a firework that is launched 100 feet off the ground. Is she correct? Explain.

_____

_____

11. An aerial firework is launched from a 20-foot-high platform, with initial speed 200 ft/s. If the polynomial $-16t^2 + 200t + 20$ gives the height in feet that the firework will rise in t seconds, how high will a firework with a 4-second fuse rise?

_____

Determine whether each term is a monomial. Give justification for your answer. (Explore Activity)

1. Is $3x^2y$ a monomial? _____ Justify your answer.

_____

_____

2. Is $2xy + 7x$ a monomial? _____ Justify your answer.

_____

Classify each polynomial by its degree and the number of terms. (Example 1)

3. $8x^2 - 3y + 7$

_____

4. $2x^6y - 8x^3y^3$

_____

Simplify each polynomial. (Example 2)

5. $2y^3 - y^2 + 2y^4 + 7y^3$

_____

6. $2mn^3 - 11n^3 + 5mn^3 + 2n^3$

_____

7. $6d^3 - 5d^2 + 2d - 5d^3 - 8d^2$

_____

8. $j^3k^2 + 10j^2k^3 + 5j^3k^2 - 7j^2k^3$

_____

Solve the problem by evaluating the polynomial. (Example 3)

9. Nate's architectural client said she wanted the width of every room in her house increased by 2 feet and the length decreased by 5 feet. The polynomial $2w^2 - w - 10$ gives the area of any room in the house with w representing the room's width. The width of the kitchen is 16 feet. What is the area of the kitchen?

_____

ESSENTIAL QUESTION CHECK-IN

10. What are polynomial expressions, and how do you simplify them?

_____

_____

_____

_____

14.1 Independent Practice

FL A-SSE.1.1a, A-APR.1.1, F-IF.1.2

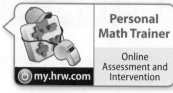

Personal Math Trainer

Online Assessment and Intervention

my.hrw.com

Identify each expression as a monomial, a binomial, trinomial, or none of the above. Write the degree of each expression.

11. $2z^2 - 5z - 10$

_____

12. $24x^2y$

_____

13. $5a^2b^3 - 4a^2b^3 + 2a^4b^3$

_____

14. $9q + \dfrac{4q}{5p} - 3p^2$

_____

Simplify each expression.

15. $3q^2 + 20 - 6q^2 - 17$

_____

16. $4k + 9k^2 - 13 - 6k - 4k^2$

_____

17. $6(x^2 + 2x - 3xy) + 8xy$

_____

18. $5t^2s^4 - 4ts^3 + 4ts + 2ts^3 + 7t^2s^4$

_____

19. $(3r^2 + 4)(2r - 1) - 8r^3 + 6r^2$

_____

20. $3p^2q + 3p(2p^2 + 2pq - 4) + 5p^3$

_____

21. **Make a Prediction** The number of cells in a bacteria colony increases according to the expression $t^2 - 4t - 4$ with t representing the time in seconds that the colony is allowed to grow at 20°C and $t^2 - 3t - 4$ when the colony grows at 30°C.

a. After 1 minute, which will be greater in number, a colony at 20°C or 30°C? Explain.

_____

_____

_____

b. After 10 minutes, how will the colonies compare in size? Explain.

_____

_____

_____

_____

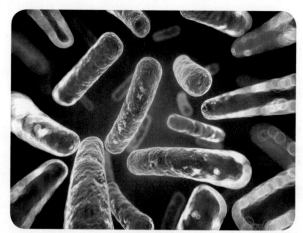

c. Which colony will have one million cells first? To the nearest minute, how long would it take to reach this size? Explain how you got your answer.

_____

_____

_____

_____

22. The polynomial $s^3 - \left(\frac{4}{3}\right)(3.14)\left(\frac{s}{2}\right)^3$ describes how much waste is made from carving a cube with side length s into the largest possible sphere.

a. How much waste is made from carving a cube into a sphere when $s = 6$ ft?

_____

b. How much waste is made from carving a cube into a sphere when $s = 12$ ft?

_____

Determine the polynomial that has the greater value for the given value of x.

23. $5x^2 - 2x + 6$ or $5x^2 - 6x + 2$, for $x = 8$

_____

24. $9x^3 - 3x^2 + 8$ or $3x^3 - 8x^2 + 9$, for $x = 2$

_____

25. $3x^3 - 8x^2 + x$ or $2x^3 + 17$, for $x = 3$

_____

26. A book store has a Valued Customer Club which gives its members discounts. The table shows the polynomials that are used to determine the total cost of an online order for people who belong to the Valued Customer Club and people who do not.

Valued Customer Club members	Non-members
$10.95x + 2.50$, where x is the number of books ordered	$12.50x + 4.50$, where x is the number of books ordered

a. How much do members pay for an online order of 8 books? _____

b. How much do non-members pay for an online order of 6 books? _____

c. Do members and non-members ever pay the same amount for an order of x books? Explain.

_____

_____

_____

27. Explain the Error Enrique thinks that the polynomial $4x^3 - 8x^2 + 9x$ has a degree of 16, since $4 \times 3 = 12$, $8 \times 2 = 16$, and $9 \times 1 = 9$. Explain his error, and determine the correct degree.

_____

_____

28. Multi-step Claire and Richard are both artists who use square canvases. Claire uses the polynomial $50x^2 + 250$ to decide how much to charge for her paintings and Richard uses the polynomial $40x^2 + 350$ to decide how much to charge for his paintings. In each polynomial, x is the height of the painting in feet.

a. How much does Claire charge for a 20-foot-tall painting? _____

b. How much does Richard charge for a 15-foot-tall painting? _____

c. To the nearest tenth, for what height will both Claire and Richard charge the same amount for a painting? Explain how to find the answer.

_____

d. When both Claire and Richard charge the same amount for a painting,

how much does each charge? _____

FOCUS ON HIGHER ORDER THINKING

Work Area

29. Justify Reasoning Carson says that the lowest degree a polynomial can have is 1. Gillian says that the lowest degree a polynomial can have is 0. Who is correct? Explain.

_____

_____

_____

30. Analyze Relationships A right triangle has height h and base $h + 4$. Write an expression that represents the area of the triangle. Then calculate the area of a triangle with a height of 12 cm.

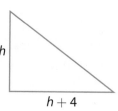

_____

31. Explain the Error Sewell says that the expression $(x + 1)^2$ will be greater than $(x - 1)^2$ for all values of x because $x + 1$ will always be greater than $x - 1$. Explain why Sewell is wrong. Give an example to show his error.

_____

_____

_____

LESSON 14.2 Adding and Subtracting Polynomials

FL A-APR.1.1

Understand that polynomials form a system analogous to the integers, namely, they are closed under the operations of addition, subtraction, and multiplication; add, subtract, and multiply polynomials.

ESSENTIAL QUESTION

How do you add and subtract polynomials?

EXPLORE ACTIVITY 1

FL A-APR.1.1

Properties of Addition

The Commutative Property of addition states that changing the order in which terms are added will not affect the answer. For example,

$5x + 4 = 4 + 5x$, and $-2 + 6x = 6x + (-2)$.

The Associative Property of addition states that changing the way in which terms are grouped will not affect the answer. For example,

$3 + (7 + 2x) = (3 + 7) + 2x$, and $(5 - 2x) + 6x = 5 + (-2x + 6x)$.

Identify the property being used to change the expression at each step.

A $45x + (8 + 15x)$
$45x + (15x + 8)$

This step changes the _____ of the terms, so the _____ Property of addition is used.

$(45x + 15x) + 8$

This step changes the _____ of the terms, so the _____ Property of addition is used.

$60x + 8$

B $(4h + 30) + (8 + 6h)$
$4h + (30 + 8) + 6h$

This step changes the _____ of the terms, so the _____ Property of addition is used.

$(30 + 8) + 4h + 6h$

This step changes the _____ of the terms, so the _____ Property of addition is used.

$38 + 10h$

REFLECT

1. Why isn't there a Commutative Property for subtraction as well as for addition? Explain using an example.

_____

_____

_____

Adding Polynomials

The Commutative and Associative properties are useful when adding polynomials. Remember, when adding terms, the order in which they are added and the way in which they are grouped does not affect the answer.

EXAMPLE 1

 FL A-APR.1.1

My Notes

Add.

A $(6x^2 + 5x + 2) + (-4x^2 + 3x - 7)$

$$\begin{array}{r} (6x^2 + 5x + 2) \\ +(\underline{-4x^2 + 3x - 7}) \\ 2x^2 + 8x - 5 \end{array}$$

Rewrite the problem vertically.

Add like terms.

B $(3a^3 - 2a + 4a^2 - 14) + (5a + 6 - 5a^3)$

$(3a^3 + 4a^2 - 2a - 14) + (-5a^3 + 5a + 6)$

Reorder using the Commutative Property. Write terms in order of degree.

$(3a^3 - 5a^3) + 4a^2 + (-2a + 5a) + (-14 + 6)$

Group like terms using the Associative Property.

$(-2a^3) + 4a^2 + (3a) + (-8)$

Add like terms.

$-2a^3 + 4a^2 + 3a - 8$

REFLECT

2. Analyze Relationships What is the key similarity between the vertical and horizontal method of adding polynomials?

_____

_____

_____

YOUR TURN

Find each sum.

3. $(-7x^2 + 3) + (-x^2)$

_____

4. $(5x^2 - 2x + 3) + (x^2 + x + 2)$

_____

5. $-6x^2 + (3x^2 + 5x)$

_____

6. $(x^2 - x - 1) + (6x - 3)$

_____

Distributive Property

The Distributive Property states that multiplying a number by a sum is the same thing as multiplying the number by each part of the sum, then adding the results. For example, $8(3x + 2) = (8)(3x) + (8)(2)$.

Use the Distributive Property to find the opposite of each polynomial.

A $3d^2 - 5d + 7$

$-1(3d^2 - 5d + 7)$　　　　　　　　　Multiply the polynomial by

　　　　　　　　　　　　　　　　　　　_____ to find the opposite.

$(-1)(\boxed{}) + (\boxed{})(-5d)$　　Use the Distributive Property

$+ (-1)(\boxed{})$　　　　　　　　to multiply _____ by each
　　　　　　　　　　　　　　　　　　　part of the sum.

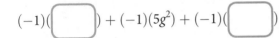 $\boxed{}d^2 + \boxed{}d - \boxed{}$

B $-4g^3 + 5g^2 - 9$

$-1(-4g^3 + 5g^2 - 9)$　　　　　　　　Multiply the polynomial by

　　　　　　　　　　　　　　　　　　　_____ to find the opposite.

$(-1)(\boxed{}) + (-1)(5g^2) + (-1)(\boxed{})$　Use the Distributive Property

　　　　　　　　　　　　　　　　　　　to multiply _____ by each
　　　　　　　　　　　　　　　　　　　part of the sum.

 $\boxed{}g^3 - \boxed{}g + \boxed{}$

REFLECT

7. Critical Thinking Describe how a polynomial and its opposite are alike, and how they are different.

_____

_____

_____

_____

8. Does the Distributive Property work for multiplication in a form like $a(b \cdot c)$? Explain using an example.

_____

_____

_____

Math On the Spot

⏻ my.hrw.com

My Notes

Subtracting Polynomials

When subtracting polynomials, remember to use the Distributive Property. A negative sign outside of a set of parentheses will reverse the sign of every term inside the parentheses.

EXAMPLE 2
FL   A-APR.1.1

Subtract.

A $(5n^2 + 4n + 3) - (2n^2 - 6n + 8)$

$$\begin{array}{r}(5n^2 + 4n + 3) \\ -(2n^2 - 6n + 8) \\ \hline \end{array}$$ Rewrite the problem vertically, with terms in columns.

$$\begin{array}{r}(5n^2 + 4n + 3) \\ -2n^2 + 6n - 8 \\ \hline \end{array}$$ Distribute the negative sign.

$$3n^2 + 10n - 5$$ Combine like terms.

B $(-3b + 4b^3 + 9 - 7b^2) - (-6b^2 + 2 - b^3)$

$(4b^3 - 7b^2 - 3b + 9) - (-b^3 - 6b^2 + 2)$ Reorder using the Commutative Property. Write terms in order of degree.

$4b^3 - 7b^2 - 3b + 9 + b^3 + 6b^2 - 2$ Distribute the negative sign.

$(4b^3 + b^3) + (-7b^2 + 6b^2) - 3b + (9 - 2)$ Group the like terms.

$(5b^3) + (-1b^2) - 3b + (7)$

$5b^3 - b^2 - 3b + 7$

REFLECT

9. How is subtracting polynomials different than adding polynomials?

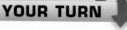

_____

_____

YOUR TURN

Find each difference.

10. $(4m^3 - m^2n + 6m^3) - (5m^2n - 1m^3 + 7mn^2)$

_____

11. $(2x^3y - 6y + 7x^3) - (6y + 2x^3 - 3x^3y)$

_____

12. $(3x^2 + 6x^3 - 7) - (8x^3 - 2x^2 + 5 - 4x)$

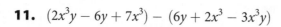

_____

Personal Math Trainer

Online Assessment and Intervention

⏻ my.hrw.com

Modeling with Polynomials

When solving problems by modeling, be sure to choose the correct operation for combining the polynomials.

EXAMPLE 3  FL A-APR.1.1

Math On the Spot
my.hrw.com

Suppose the cost in dollars of producing x toothbrushes is given by the polynomial $400,000 + 3x$ and the revenue generated from sales is given by the polynomial $20x - 0.00004x^2$.

STEP 1 Write a polynomial expression for the profit from making and selling x toothbrushes.

$(20x - 0.00004x^2) - (400,000 + 3x)$ Profit = Revenue − Cost

$20x - 0.00004x^2 + (-400,000 - 3x)$ Add the opposite.

$20x - 0.00004x^2 - 400,000 - 3x$ Associative Property.

$-0.00004x^2 + 17x - 400,000$ Combine like terms.

STEP 2 Find the profit for selling 200,000 toothbrushes.

$-0.00004x^2 + 17x - 400,000$

$-0.00004(200,000)^2 + 17(200,000) - 400,000$

$1,400,000$

The profit is $1,400,000 or $1.4 million.

REFLECT

13. If the toothbrush company sold 10,000 toothbrushes, how much would the company gain or lose?

_____

YOUR TURN

The profit from a company's factory in North Dakota is given by $n^2 - 15n + 23$. The company's profit from their factory in Florida is given by $n^2 - 20n - 14$. In both, n equals the number of goods produced in the factory.

14. Write a polynomial that represents the difference in profits between the two plants.

_____

15. Write a polynomial that represents the total profits of the two plants.

_____

Personal
Math Trainer

Online Assessment
and Intervention

my.hrw.com

Guided Practice

Identify whether the Commutative or the Associative Property is being used for each step. (Explore Activity 1)

1. $(5d^2 + 2d) + 3d^2$

$(2d + 5d^2) + 3d^2$ _____ Property

$2d + (5d^2 + 3d^2)$ _____ Property

$2d + 8d^2$

Add or subtract using the vertical method. (Example 1 and Example 2)

2. $(5bc^2 + 3bc + 3b) - (4bc^2 - 8bc - 2b)$

$5bc^2 + 3bc + 3b$

$\underline{-4bc^2 + 8bc + 2b}$

_____

3. $(9g^2 + 6g - 3) + (9g^2 - 6g + 3)$

$9g^2 + 6g - 3$

$\underline{+9g^2 - 6g + 3}$

_____

Add or subtract using the horizontal method. (Example 1 and Example 2)

4. $(13m^2 - m + 1) - (-10m^2 - 7m + 2)$

$13m^2 - m + 1$ _____

_____

5. $(-y^2 + 11y - 2) + (-6y^2 + 6y - 5)$

$-y^2 + 11y - 2$ _____

_____

Use the Distributive Property to find the opposite of the polynomial $-13x^3 + 12 - 6x.$ (Explore Activity 2)

6. $(-1)(-13x^3 + 12 - 6x)$

$(-1)(\boxed{}x^3) + (\boxed{})(12) + (-1)(\boxed{}x)$

$\boxed{}x^3 - \boxed{} + \boxed{}x$

7. The volume of a rectangular prism, in cubic inches, is given by the expression $x^3 + 3x^2 - 5x + 7$. The volume of a smaller rectangular prism is given by the expression $5x^3 - 6x^2 - 7x - 14$. How much greater is the volume of the larger rectangular prism? (Example 3)

large prism − small prism $= (x^3 + 3x^2 - 5x + 7) - (5x^3 - 6x^2 - 7x - 14)$

_____

? ESSENTIAL QUESTION CHECK-IN

8. How do you add and subtract polynomials?

_____

_____

_____

14.2 Independent Practice

FL A-APR.1.1

Add or subtract.

9. $(6^2 - 51 + 2) + (-12^2 - 8 + 22)$

_____

10. $(-13^2 + 100 - 29) + (5^3 + 80 - 44)$

_____

11. $(10p^2 - 2p + 1) + (-5p^2 - 3p + 12)$

_____

12. $(-6x^2 + 11x - 2) + (-6x^2 + 6x - 4)$

_____

13. $(-d^2 + 19d - 8) - (-5d^2 - 6d + 12)$

_____

14. $(8r^3s^2 + 6rs^2 + 6r) - (4r^3s^2 - 2rs^2 - 5r)$

_____

15. $(-3z^2 + 16z - 8) + (-3z^2 - 6z + 13)$

_____

16. $(8w^3t^2 + 6wt^2 + 6w) - (4w^3t^2 - 2wt^2 - 3w)$

_____

17. $(6x^2 + 7x - 2) + (3x^2 - 4x - 7)$

_____

18. $(18n^2 + n + 1) - (15n^2 - 4n - 11)$

_____

19. $(-5a^2 + 15a - 8) - (-5a^2 - 7a + 12)$

_____

20. $(7q^3r^2 + 14qr^2 + 21q) - (14q^3r^2 - 3qr^2 - 5q)$

_____

21. **Interpret the Answer** The water height of a pool is determined by $8g^2 + 3g - 4$, the rate that the pool is filled, and $9g^2 - 2g - 5$, the rate that water leaves the pool, where g represents the number of gallons entering or leaving the pool per minute.

a. Write an expression that determines the height of the water in the pool.

_____

b. What will be the height of the water if $g = 1, 2, 3,$ and 4?

_____

_____

c. To the nearest tenth, at which value for g will the water reach its greatest height? Explain.

_____

22. In square inches, the area of the square is $4x^2 - 2x - 6$ and the area of the triangle $2x^2 + 4x - 5$. What polynomial represents the area of the shaded region?

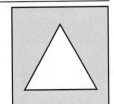

_____

23. Analyze Relationships The area of the shaded triangle is $5x^2 + 3x - 4$. What is the area of the entire figure?

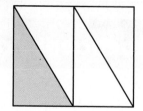

_____

Work Area

24. Communicate Mathematical Ideas Hallie subtracted a quantity from the polynomial $3y^2 + 8y - 16$ and ended up with the expression $(y + 2)(y - 2)$. What quantity did Hallie subtract? Explain how you got your answer.

_____

_____

_____

25. Explain the Error Geoffrey thinks that the sum of $5x^2y^3 + 6x + 7y$ and $8y + 4x^3y^2 + 2x$ is $9x^2y^3 + 8x + 15y$. Explain Geoffrey's error, and find the correct sum.

_____

_____

26. Analyze Relationships Write a polynomial that represents the difference between the perimeter of a square and the circumference of a circle that have side length and diameter of the same length, x. What is the difference when x is 9 inches?

_____

27. Critical Thinking Sherman has two sequences. The first sequence is described by the explicit rule $f(n) = 15n - 6$ and the second sequence is described by the explicit rule $f(n) = 4n + 11$. Find the sum of the 20th term in each sequence.

_____

28. Persevere in Problem Solving John has yellow and green cubes, each with side length c. Eight yellow cubes are glued together to make a larger cube. An even larger cube is made by gluing on green cubes until no yellow cubes can be seen. The large green cube has a side length of $4c$. Write an expression for the volume of the green cubes.

_____

_____

_____

_____

Multiplying Polynomials by Monomials

 **FL** **A-APR.1.1**

Understand that polynomials form a system analogous to the integers, namely, they are closed under the operations of addition, subtraction, and multiplication; add, subtract, and multiply polynomials.

ESSENTIAL QUESTION

How can you multiply polynomials by monomials?

EXPLORE ACTIVITY  **FL** **A-APR.1.1**

Modeling Polynomial Multiplication

You can use algebra tiles to model the multiplication of a monomial by a polynomial.

> **Rules**
>
> 1. The first factor goes on the left side of the grid, the second factor on the top.
> 2. Fill in the grid with tiles that have the same height as tiles on the left and the same length as tiles on the top.
> 3. Follow the key on the right. The product of two tiles of the same color is positive; the product of two tiles of different colors is negative.

A Use algebra tiles to find $2(x + 1)$.

KEY

⊞ = positive variable

⊟ = negative variable

⊞ = 1   ⊟ = −1

STEP 1 Fill in the factors.

Place the factor 2 on the left.
Place the factor $x + 1$ on the top.

STEP 2 Fill in the grid.

Fill in the grid according to Rule 2 above.
Draw the missing tiles.

STEP 3 Count the positive and negative tiles in the grid.

x tiles: _____

1 tiles: _____

Expression: _____

B Use algebra tiles to find $2x(x - 3)$.

STEP 1 Fill in the factors.

Remember, the first factor goes on the left side and the second factor goes on the top row.

STEP 2 Fill in the grid.

Fill in the grid according to Rule 2.
Draw the tiles.
Positives are yellow, negatives are red.

STEP 3 Count the positive and negative tiles in the grid.

x^2 tiles: _____

x tiles: _____

1 tiles: _____

expression: _____

REFLECT

1. How do the tiles illustrate the idea of x^2 visually?

_____

_____

2. How does the grid illustrate the Distributive Property? Explain.

_____

_____

_____

_____

Multiplying Monomials

When multiplying monomials, you may have to multiply variables with exponents. Recall the Product of Powers Property, which states that $a^m \times a^n = a^{(m+n)}$.

Math On the Spot
my.hrw.com

EXAMPLE 1  FL A-APR.1.1

Multiply.

A $(2x^4)(-3x^5)$

$(2 \cdot -3)(x^4 \cdot x^5)$ *Group factors that use the same variable.*

$(2 \cdot -3)(x^{4+5})$ *Product of Powers Property*

$-6x^9$ *Simplify.*

B $(8g^2h^5)(6gh^3)$

$(8 \cdot 6)(g^2 \cdot g)(h^5 \cdot h^3)$ *Group factors that use the same variable.*

$(8 \cdot 6)(g^{2+1})(h^{5+3})$ *Product of Powers Property*

$48g^3h^8$ *Simplify.*

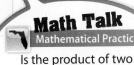

Math Talk
Mathematical Practices

Is the product of two monomials always a monomial? Explain.

REFLECT

3. What can you conclude about the order of factors in multiplication?

_____

_____

4. Explain the Error Felicity reasons that $g^2 \cdot g^{0.5} = g^1$, since $2 \cdot 0.5 = 1$. Explain her error and find the correct product for $g^2 \cdot g^{0.5}$.

_____

_____

5. Communicate Mathematical Ideas If $x^8 \cdot x^y = x$, what is the value of y? Explain.

_____

_____

YOUR TURN

Find the products.

6. $12x^5(5x^4)$ _____

7. $6a^4b(4a^3b^2)$ _____

8. $(6a^2b^5)(3ab)$ _____

9. $(4k^2d^5)(9d^3j^2)$ _____

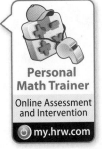

Personal
Math Trainer

Online Assessment
and Intervention

my.hrw.com

Multiplying a Polynomial by a Monomial

Remember, the Distributive Property states that multiplying a term by a sum is the same thing as multiplying the term by each part of the sum, then adding the results.

EXAMPLE 2

 FL   A-APR.1.1

Find each product.

A $4(5x^2 + 3x + 1)$

$4(5x^2 + 3x + 1)$ Distribute 4.

$4(5x^2) + 4(3x) + 4(1)$ Regroup and multiply.

$20x^2 + 12x + 4$ Simplify.

B $2x\,(3x^2 + 2x - 4)$

$2x(3x^2 + 2x - 4)$ Distribute 2x. Remember, $2x = 2x^1$.

$2x^1(3x^2) + 2x^1(2x^1) - 2x^1(4)$ Regroup.

$6x^{1+2} + 4x^{1+1} - 8x^1$ Multiply and combine exponents.

$6x^3 + 4x^2 - 8x$ Simplify.

REFLECT

10. Explain when to distribute and when not to distribute when multiplying monomials and polynomials.

_____

_____

_____

_____

YOUR TURN

Find each product.

11. $(4m^3n^2)(5m^2n - 3mn - 2)$

_____

12. $2a^2(5b^2 + 3ab + 6a + 1)$

_____

13. $3ab(2a^2b + 6ab^2 + 8b)$

_____

Application of Multiplying Polynomials and Monomials

Math On the Spot
my.hrw.com

Knowing how to multiply polynomials and monomials is useful when solving real-world problems.

EXAMPLE 3  FL A-APR.1.1

Chrystelle is making a planter box with a square base. She wants the height of the box to be 3 inches more than the length. If she needs the volume of the box to be as close as possible to 6,000 in^3, what should the length of the box be to the nearest whole inch?

STEP 1 Define terms and write what you know.

length of side $= s$

height $= s + 3$

volume $=$ side $\cdot$ side $\cdot$ height

$= (s \cdot s)(s + 3)$

$= s^2(s + 3) = s^3 + 3s^2$

STEP 2 Make a plan.

Chrystelle wants the volume of the planter to be as close as possible to 6000 in^3, so you need to find a value for s that gives a product that is close to 6000 in^3.

s	$s^3 + 3s^2$
15	$15^3 + 3(15)^2 = 4050$
16	$16^3 + 3(16)^2 = 4864$
17	$17^3 + 3(17)^2 = 5780$
18	$18^3 + 3(18)^2 = 6804$

STEP 3 Select the best answer.

6,000 is closer to 5780 than it is to 6804, so the length of the planter should be 17 inches.

REFLECT

14. **What If?** Explain how the answer would change if Chrystelle wanted the volume as close as possible to 4,400 in^3.

_____

_____

YOUR TURN

15. David needs a piece of paper where the length is 4 inches more than the width, and the area is as close as possible to 50 in^2. To the nearest whole inch, what should the measurements be for the piece of paper?

_____

Personal Math Trainer

Online Assessment and Intervention

my.hrw.com

Shutterstock

Guided Practice

Use the algebra tiles to find the product of polynomials. (Explore Activity)

1. What multiplication problem is being modeled? _____

2. Fill in the grid.

3. What is the product? _____

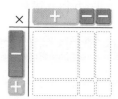

Find the product of the monomials. (Example 1)

4. $d^5f^2(16d^3e^4f^2)$

$= (\boxed{} \cdot \boxed{})$

$ (\boxed{} \cdot \boxed{})$

$= \underline{}$

5. $-13r^3s^5(-3rs^2)$

$= \underline{}$

$= \underline{}$

Find the product of the monomials and polynomials. (Example 2)

6. $5(2k^2 + k + 3)$

$5(\boxed{}) + 5(\boxed{}) + 5(\boxed{})$

_____

7. $8t(3t^2 + 5ts + 2s)$

$\boxed{}(\boxed{}) + \boxed{}(\boxed{}) + 8t(\boxed{})$

_____

8. A jeweler sells gems at a cost in dollars per centigram that is 4 more than 6 times the weight of the gem in centigrams. Thus, a gem that weighs w centigrams will be sold at a price of $6w + 4$ dollars per centigram — meaning that a larger, heavier gem will cost more per centigram than a smaller gem. If the jeweler sold a single gem for about $2500, what did the gem weigh to the nearest centigram? (Example 3)

_____

? ESSENTIAL QUESTION CHECK-IN

9. How can you multiply polynomials by monomials?

_____

_____

_____

14.3 Independent Practice

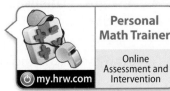

FL A-APR.1.1

Find each product.

10. $4x(3x^3y^4)$

_____

11. $-0.5m(-16m^4n^2)$

_____

12. $8a^2 b^4(-7a^3b^2)$

_____

13. $5(2k^2 + k + 4)$

_____

14. $9j(6k^2 - 2k + 13j)$

_____

15. $9a^2 b^2(-4a^3b^5)$

_____

16. $3i(3i^2 + 3ig + 3i^2g^2)$

_____

17. $-2t(3t^3 + 7ts + 5s)$

_____

18. $0.25de^2(-4d^2 + 12de^2 - 8d^2e)$

_____

19. $-6v^2w^3 (v^2 - 11v^2w^5 + 6w^4)$

_____

20. $7a^3b^4 (-3a^2 + 8ab^2 - 7a^2b)$

_____

21. $-10x^4y^4 (x^4 - 4x^4y^4 + 4y^3)$

_____

22. **Interpret the Answer** A construction engineer needs to make 25 square concrete slabs with sides of length x feet and height $x - 3$ feet. If the engineer can use at most 350,000 ft^3 of concrete, what should the dimensions of each slab be, to the nearest foot?

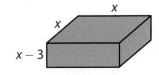

a. Write an expression for the volume of all the slabs.

_____

b. What should x equal, to the nearest foot?

_____

23. A fish market sells sushi-grade tuna having a length of f feet at a price of $4f - 2$ dollars per foot, meaning that the larger the fish is, the greater its price per foot will be. If the market made $552 selling a single tuna, what was the length of the fish?

_____

24. Analyze Relationships The target heart rate for a fit person of age a exercising at p percent of his or her heart rate is determined by the expression $\frac{1}{2}p(418 - a)$ for women and $\frac{1}{2}p(400 - a)$ for men. What is the difference between the target heart rates for a fit woman and a fit man?

_____

 **FOCUS ON HIGHER ORDER THINKING**

25. Represent Real World Problems Arthur found a pot full of beans on the stove in his restaurant that had a volume of 1413 in³. One of his cooks had emptied 10 cans of beans into the pot and left. To reproduce the recipe, Arthur needs to identify the beans that were used. At the store he finds several brands of beans in differently sized cans, all with radius r and height $r + 2$. To the nearest whole inch, find the dimensions of the cans that the cook used and explain how you got your answer.

_____

_____

_____

_____

_____

_____

26. Persevere in Problem Solving On the first day of a road trip, Daniel drove at an average speed of $5x$ miles per hour, and he drove for $x^2 + 15$ minutes. Find an expression that describes how many miles Daniel drove. Explain how you got your answer.

_____

_____

_____

_____

27. Justify Reasoning Is there any value for x that would make the statement $(x + 3)^3 = x^3 + 3^3$ true? Give an example to justify your answer.

_____

_____

_____

_____

14.4 Multiplying Polynomials

FL A-APR.1.1

Understand that polynomials form a system analogous to the integers, namely, they are closed under the operations of addition, subtraction, and multiplication; add, subtract, and multiply polynomials. *Also A-SSE.1.2*

ESSENTIAL QUESTION

How can you multiply binomials and polynomials?

EXPLORE ACTIVITY   FL A-APR.1.1

Modeling Binomial Multiplication

Using algebra tiles to model the product of two binomials is very similar to using algebra tiles to model the product of a monomial and a polynomial.

Rules

1. The first factor goes on the left side of grid, the second factor on the top.

2. Fill in the grid with tiles that have the same height as tiles on the left and the same length as tiles on the top.

3. Follow the key on the right. The product of two tiles of the same color is positive; the product of two tiles of different colors is negative.

KEY

 = positive variable

= negative variable

$\boxed{+} = 1$ $\boxed{-} = -1$

Use the tiles to find $(x + 1)(x - 2)$.

STEP 1   Fill in the factors, then fill in the grid.
Count the positive and negative tiles in the grid.

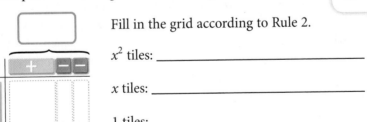

Fill in the grid according to Rule 2.

x^2 tiles: _____

x tiles: _____

1 tiles: _____

STEP 2   Remove any zero pairs.

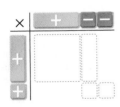

$x + (-x) = 0$, so these tiles represent a zero pair.

Remove one x tile and one $-x$ tile from the grid.

STEP 3 Recount the tiles in the grid and write the expression.

x^2 tiles: _____

x tiles: _____

1 tiles: _____

Expression: _____

REFLECT

1. **Communicate Mathematical Ideas** How can you tell when tiles form a zero pair?

_____

_____

2. Is it possible for more than one pair of tiles to form a zero pair? Explain.

_____

_____

Math On the Spot

my.hrw.com

Multiplying Binomials

You can use the Distributive Property to multiply two binomials.

$$(x + y)(x + z) = x(x + z) + y(x + z) = x^2 + xz + xy + yz$$

Another way to use the Distributive Property is the FOIL method. The FOIL method uses the Distributive Property to multiply terms of the binomials in this order: First terms, Outer terms, Inner terms, and Last terms.

$$(x + y)(x + z) = x^2 + xz + xy + yz$$

EXAMPLE 1

 FL   A-APR.1.1

Multiply.

A $(x^2 + 3)(x + 2)$

Use the FOIL method.

$(x^2 + 3)(x + 2) = (x^2 + 3)(x + 2)$ F Multiply the **first** terms. Result: x^3

$= (x^2 + 3)(x + 2)$ O Multiply the **outer** terms. Result: $2x^2$

$= (x^2 + 3)(x + 2)$ I Multiply the **inner** terms. Result: $3x$

$= (x^2 + 3)(x + 2)$ L Multiply the last terms. Result: 6

Add the results.

$$(x^2 + 3)(x + 2) = x^3 + 2x^2 + 3x + 6$$

$$\uparrow \quad \uparrow \quad \uparrow \quad \uparrow$$

$$\text{F} \quad \text{O} \quad \text{I} \quad \text{L}$$

B $(3x^2 - 2x)(x + 5)$

Use the FOIL method.

$(3x^2 - 2x)(x + 5) = (3x^2 - 2x)(x + 5)$ F Multiply the **first** terms. Result: $3x^3$

$= (3x^2 - 2x)(x + 5)$ O Multiply the **outer** terms. Result: $15x^2$

$= (3x^2 - 2x)(x + 5)$ I Multiply the **inner** terms. Result: $-2x^2$

$= (3x^2 - 2x)(x + 5)$ L Multiply the **last** terms. Result: $-10x$

Add the results. Group like terms.

$$(3x^2 - 2x)(x + 5) = 3x^3 + 15x^2 - 2x^2 - 10x = 3x^3 + 13x^2 - 10x$$

$$\uparrow \quad \uparrow \quad \uparrow \quad \uparrow$$

$$\text{F} \quad \text{O} \quad \text{I} \quad \text{L}$$

REFLECT

3. The FOIL method finds the sum of four partial products. Why does the result from part B only have three terms?

_____

_____

4. Analyze Relationships Would you use the FOIL method for numeric expressions like $(5 + 3)(7 + 2)$? Explain.

_____

_____

YOUR TURN

Multiply.

5. $(x + 4)(x - 3)$

6. $(2n + 6)(n + 3)$

_____

Personal Math Trainer

Online Assessment and Intervention

my.hrw.com

Multiplying Polynomials

To multiply polynomials with more than two terms, you can use the Distributive Property several times.

EXAMPLE 2

FL A-APR.1.1

Multiply.

A $(x + 2)(x^2 - 5x + 4)$

$(x + 2)(x^2 - 5x + 4) = x(x^2 - 5x + 4) + 2(x^2 - 5x + 4)$

$= x(x^2 - 5x + 4) + 2(x^2 - 5x + 4)$ Distribute.

$= x(x^2) + x(-5x) + x(4) + 2(x^2)$
$\quad + 2(-5x) + 2(4)$ Write products of terms.

$= x^3 - 5x^2 + 4x + 2x^2 - 10x + 8$ Simplify.

$= x^3 - 3x^2 - 6x + 8$ Combine like terms.

B $(3x - 4)(-2x^3 + 5x - 6)$

$(3x - 4)(-2x^3 + 5x - 6) = 3x(-2x^3 + 5x - 6) - 4(-2x^3 + 5x - 6)$ Distribute.

$= 3x(-2x^3) + 3x(5x) + 3x(-6)$
$\quad - 4(-2x^3) - 4(5x) - 4(-6)$ Write products of terms.

$= -6x^4 + 15x^2 - 18x + 8x^3$
$\quad -20x + 24$ Simplify.

$= -6x^4 + 8x^3 + 15x^2$
$\quad -38x + 24$ Combine like terms.

REFLECT

7. Communicate Mathematical Ideas Why can't you use the FOIL method when you multiply a binomial by a trinomial? Describe a FOIL-like method for multiplying a binomial by a trinomial.

_____

_____

_____

My Notes

YOUR TURN

Multiply.

8. $(x - 5)(x^2 + 4x - 6)$

9. $(3x + 1)(x^3 + 4x^2 - 7)$

_____   _____

Special Products of Binomials

Binomial products of the form $(a + b)^2$, $(a - b)^2$, and $(a + b)(a + b)$ are often called *special products*. You can use the FOIL method or the rules below to find special products.

Math On the Spot

my.hrw.com

Special Product Rules	
Sum and difference	$(a + b)(a - b) = a^2 - b^2$
Square of a binomial	$(a + b)^2 = a^2 + 2ab + b^2$ $(a - b)^2 = a^2 - 2ab + b^2$

EXAMPLE 3

FL   A-APR.1.1, A-SSE.1.2

Find each product.

A $(x - 3)^2$

$(x - 3)\ (x - 3)$ Use the FOIL method.

$x^2 - 3x - 3x + 3^2$ Combine like terms.

$x^2 - 6x + 9$ Simplify.

Animated Math

my.hrw.com

B $(a + b)^2$

$(a + b)\ (a + b)$ Use the FOIL method.

$a^2 + ab + ab + b^2$ Combine like terms.

$a^2 + 2ab + b^2$ Simplify.

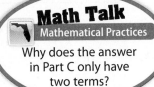

Math Talk

Mathematical Practices

Why does the answer in Part C only have two terms?

C $(n + 3)(n - 3)$

$n^2 - 3^2$ Use the Sum and Difference Rule.

$n^2 - 9$ Simplify.

YOUR TURN

Find each product.

10. $(x + 5)^2$ **11.** $(2p - 3)^2$ **12.** $(3s + 1)(3s - 1)$

_____   _____   _____

13. $(2x + 5)(2x - 5)$ **14.** $(3g + 6)^2$ **15.** $(4t - 8)^2$

_____   _____   _____

Personal Math Trainer

Online Assessment and Intervention

my.hrw.com

Use algebra tiles to find each product. (Explore Activity)

1. $(x - 2)(x + 3)$

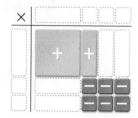

_____

2. $(2x - 1)(x + 3)$

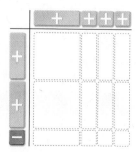

_____

Use the FOIL method to find each product. (Example 1)

3. $(x - 3)(x - 5)$

$\boxed{} - \boxed{}x - \boxed{}x + \boxed{}$

_____

4. $(y + 9)(y - 3)$

$\boxed{} - \boxed{}y + \boxed{}y - \boxed{}$

_____

5. $(4a - 4)(2a + 1)$

$\boxed{} + \boxed{}a - \boxed{}a - \boxed{}$

_____

6. $(3g + 2h)(-5g + 6h)$

$\boxed{} + \boxed{}gh - \boxed{}hg + 12\boxed{}$

_____

Find each product. (Example 2 and Example 3)

7. $(x + 3)(x^2 - 2x + 1)$

$(x\boxed{} - \boxed{}x^2 + \boxed{}x)$

$+ (\boxed{}x^2 - \boxed{}x + 3)$

_____

8. $(4k - 3)(-k^3 + 6k - 4)$

$(\boxed{} + \boxed{}k^2 - \boxed{}k)$

$+ (\boxed{}k^3 - \boxed{}k + 12)$

_____

9. $(2b + 7)(2b - 7)$

_____

10. $(5x + 1)(5x + 1)$

_____

? ESSENTIAL QUESTION CHECK-IN

11. How can you multiply binomials and polynomials?

_____

_____

14.4 Independent Practice

 FL A-APR.1.1, A-SSE.1.2

Personal Math Trainer

Online Assessment and Intervention

my.hrw.com

Use the distributive or FOIL method to find the product.

12. $(m + 3)(m + 7)$

13. $(y + 8)(y - 6)$

14. $(x - 12)(x - 4)$

15. $(z + 6)(2z + 1)$

16. $(4r + 7)(r - 2)$

17. $(3i + 7)(2i + 5)$

18. $(v + d)(-v + d)$

19. $(c + 7d)(c - 3d)$

20. $(3p + 5q)(-3p + q)$

21. Trina has two brothers. One brother is 7 years older than Trina and the other brother is 7 years younger than Trina. The product of her brothers' ages is 95.

   a. If x represents Trina's age, write an equation to describe the product of her

      brothers' ages. _____

   b. Solve the equation for x. How old is Trina? _____

22. Ociel has designed a square mural that measures 10 feet on each side. Bill has also designed a square mural, but his measures y feet shorter on each side.

   a. Write an expression to represent the area of Bill's mural. _____

   b. How much smaller than Ociel's mural is Bill's mural? Explain.

23. **Explain the Error** Mika thinks that $(7x^2 - 12y^3)^2$ is equal to $49x^4 - 84x^2y^3 + 144y^6$. Explain her error, and find the correct product.

24. Represent Real-World Problems Joanna, the line manager at
Smedley Electronics, works 14 hours a week more than her line
workers and gets paid $6.50 more per hour. Line workers work h
hours per week and get paid d dollars per hour.

a. Write an expression for how much a line worker gets paid
each week and how much Joanna gets paid each week.

_____

b. Write an expression for how much more Joanna gets paid each
week than one of her line workers.

_____

_____

c. If a line worker gets paid $576 for a 36-hour week, how much does Joanna
get paid for that same week?

_____

_____

 **FOCUS ON HIGHER ORDER THINKING**

Work Area

25. Critical Thinking The product of 3 consecutive odd numbers is 2145. Write an
expression for finding the numbers, then find the numbers.

_____

_____

26. Represent Real-World Problems The town swimming pool is d feet deep.
The width of the pool is 10 feet greater than 5 times the depth. The length of
the pool is 25 feet greater than the width.

a. Write and simplify an equation to represent the volume of the pool.

_____

_____

b. If the pool holds 51,000 ft^3 of water, what are the dimensions of the pool?

_____

27. Multi-step Explain how to find a general rule for the product $(a + b)^3$.

_____

_____

_____

Ready to Go On?

Personal
Math Trainer

Online
Assessment and
Intervention

my.hrw.com

14.1 Understanding Polynomials

Simplify each polynomial.

1. $a^2 + 12a - 7 - 3a^2 - 5a + 8$ _____

2. $7x^3y^2 + 3xy^2 + 6x - 9x^3y^2 + 2xy^2 + 5x - 1$ _____

14.2 Adding and Subtracting Polynomials

Add or subtract.

3. $(3x^2 - 6x + 2) - (8x + 6 - 5x^2)$

_____

4. $(3a^2b - 6ab^2 + 2a) + (4ab^2 - 3b - 2a^2b)$

_____

14.3 Multiplying Polynomials by Monomials

Multiply.

5. $4e(4e^2 + 5eg + 6e^2g^2)$

_____

6. $-2u(4u^3 + 5u^2s^2 + 6s)$

_____

14.4 Multiplying Polynomials

Multiply.

7. $(5c + 7)(5c - 7)$

_____

8. $(6y^2 - 3y)^2$

_____

9. $(9p^2 - 3q)(4p^3 - 5)$

_____

10. $\left(\frac{1}{4}c^2 + 2d\right)(-12c + 8d)$

_____

? ESSENTIAL QUESTION

11. How are polynomials like other number systems such as whole numbers and integers?

_____

_____

_____

_____

Assessment Readiness

Selected Response

1. What is the degree of the expression $7x^2y^3 + 5x^4y^3$?

Ⓐ 5 because the coefficient of $5x^4y^3$ is 5.

Ⓑ 6 because the sum of the y exponents is 6.

Ⓒ 7 because the sum of the exponents of $5x^4y^3$ is 7.

Ⓓ 6 because the sum of the x exponents is 6.

2. The sum of two trinomials _____.

Ⓐ must be another trinomial.

Ⓑ can be a monomial, a binomial, a trinomial, or another kind of polynomial.

Ⓒ can be a trinomial or a polynomial but cannot be a binomial or monomial.

Ⓓ cannot be a trinomial.

3. Which of the following is NOT true of the product of $\frac{2}{3}a^2(3b^2 + 9b + 6a)$ when simplified?

Ⓐ It has a term with a coefficient of 2.

Ⓑ It has a term of degree 4.

Ⓒ It has a term with an exponent of 3.

Ⓓ It has a fractional coefficient.

4. The product of two terms is $4x^2 - 9b^2$. What are the two terms?

Ⓐ $(2x - 3b)$ and $(2x + 3b)$

Ⓑ $(2x - 3b)$ and $(2x - 3b)$

Ⓒ $(2x - 3b)^2$

Ⓓ $(-2x + 3b)$ and $(2x + 3b)$

5. Michael wants to eliminate the variable y from the system below by adding.

$$\begin{cases} 7x - 6y = 8 \\ 2x + 2y = 6 \end{cases}$$

First, he will have to multiply one of the equations by a number. Which step will enable him to eliminate y by adding?

Ⓐ Multiply each term in $2x + 2y = 6$ by 3.

Ⓑ Multiply each term in $2x + 2y = 6$ by -3.

Ⓒ Multiply each term in $7x - 6y = 8$ by 3.

Ⓓ Multiply each term in $7x - 6y = 8$ by -3.

6. Which of the following regression equations represents a town with an initial population of 58,000 people and an annual growth rate of approximately 3%?

Ⓐ $y = 58{,}000 \times 1.03x$

Ⓑ $y = 58{,}000(1.03)^x$

Ⓒ $y = 58{,}000(3)^x$

Ⓓ $y = 58{,}000x^{1.03}$

Mini-Tasks

7. A cinder block with a hole in its center has the dimensions shown.

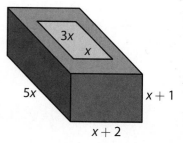

a. Write an expression that represents the volume of the hole in the center of the cinder block.

_____

b. Write an expression that represents the volume of the solid part of the cinder block.

_____

Factoring Polynomials

? ESSENTIAL QUESTION

How can you factor expressions of the form $ax^2 + bx + c$?

Real-World Video

Ruling out common elements in a scientific experiment is similar to removing common factors in an equation: logically, whatever is common to two samples can't be the cause of differences between them.

 my.hrw.com

Shutterstock

GO DIGITAL
my.hrw.com

my.hrw.com

Go digital with your write-in student edition, accessible on any device.

Math On the Spot

Scan with your smart phone to jump directly to the online edition, video tutor, and more.

Animated Math

Interactively explore key concepts to see how math works.

Personal Math Trainer

Get immediate feedback and help as you work through practice sets.

Are YOU Ready?

Complete these exercises to review skills you will need for this module.

Factors

EXAMPLE List the factors of 12.

1, 12
3, 4
2, 6

Any whole number that can be multiplied by another whole number to get 12 is a factor of 12.

List the factors of each number.

1. 8

2. 10

3. 30

_____   _____   _____

Multiply Monomials and Polynomials

EXAMPLE Multiply.

$6x(2x + 5)$
$6x(2x) + 6x(5) = 12x^2 + 30x$

Apply the Distributive Property.

Multiply.

4. $10(x - 5)$

5. $3h(h^2 j + 2h^2)$

6. $y(7y^3 - 4y^2 - 1)$

_____   _____   _____

Multiply Binomials

EXAMPLE Find the product.

$(x + 3)(x + 8)$

First: $x \cdot x = x^2$
Outer: $x \cdot 8 = 8x$
Inner: $3 \cdot x = 3x$
Last: $3 \cdot 8 = 24$
$x^2 + 8x + 3x + 24 = x^2 + 11x + 24$

Use FOIL to multiply each term in the first binomial by each term in the second binomial.

Find each product.

7. $(b - 7)(b + 1)$

8. $(2p - 5)(p - 1)$

9. $(3n + 4)(2n + 3)$

_____   _____   _____

Reading Start-Up

Vocabulary

Review Words

✓ binomial *(binomio)*

✓ constant *(constante)*

✓ factor *(factor)*

  prime factor *(factor primo)*

✓ trinomial *(trinomio)*

Preview Words

  greatest common factor (GCF)

Visualize Vocabulary

Fill in the missing information in the chart below.

Word	Definition	Examples
factor		$12 = 3 \cdot 4$ 3 and 4 are factors of 12. $xy = x \cdot y$ x and y are factors of xy.
binomial	a polynomial with ☐ terms	
	a polynomial with ☐ terms	
constant		$4, 0, \pi$

Understand Vocabulary

To become familiar with some of the vocabulary in the module, consider the following. You may refer to the module, the glossary, or a dictionary.

1. The largest common factor of two or more given numbers is the

_____.

2. The _____ of monomials is the product of the greatest integer and the greatest power of each variable that divide evenly into each monomial.

Active Reading

Four-Corner Fold Before beginning the module, create a Four-Corner Fold to help you organize what you learn. Use one flap for each lesson in the module. As you study the module, note important facts, examples, and formulas on the flaps. Look for similarities and differences between the lessons. Use your FoldNote to complete assignments and to study for tests.

Unpacking the Standards

Understanding the standards and the vocabulary terms in the standards will help you know exactly what you are expected to learn in this module.

 FL A-SSE.1.2

Use the structure of an expression to identify ways to rewrite it.

Key Vocabulary

greatest common factor (*máximo común divisor de una expresión*)
Factors that are shared by two or more whole numbers are called common factors. The greatest of these common factors is the greatest common factor.

What It Means to You

You can rewrite expressions by factoring out common factors and working FOIL in reverse.

UNPACKING EXAMPLE A-SSE.1.2

Martown Park has an area of $(x^2 - 3x - 18)$ feet. If the width is $(x + 3)$ feet, what is the length?

$$lw = \text{area}$$

$$\boxed{\text{length?}} \, (x + 3) = (x^2 - 3x - 18)$$

think about FOIL in reverse:

$$\boxed{(x + \text{or} - ?)} (x + 3) = (x^2 - 3x - 18)$$

The missing value and 3 need to have a sum of -3, which means the binomial needs to be $(x - \mathbf{6})$.

The length is $(x - 6)$ feet.

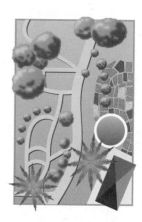

 **FL A-SSE.2.3**

Choose and produce an equivalent form of an expression to reveal and explain properties of the quantity represented by the expression.

What It Means to You

You can use patterns to recognize and rewrite expressions to reveal properties of the expression.

UNPACKING EXAMPLE A-SSE.2.3

Factor $25m^2 - 16n^2$.

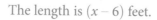

$$25m^2 - 16n^2$$

perfect square   difference   perfect square

This binomial is the difference of two squares, so it factors as

$$(5m - 4n)(5m + 4n)$$

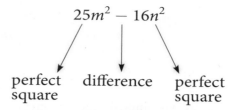

Visit **my.hrw.com** to see all **Florida Math Standards** unpacked.

my.hrw.com

LESSON
15.1 Factoring Polynomials

FL A-SSE.1.2
Use the structure of an expression to identify ways to rewrite it. *Also A-SSE.2.3*

ESSENTIAL QUESTION

How can you use the greatest common factor to factor polynomials?

EXPLORE ACTIVITY   FL A-SSE.1.2

Factoring and Greatest Common Factor

Factors that are shared by two or more whole numbers are called *common factors*. The greatest of these common factors is called the **greatest common factor**, or GCF.

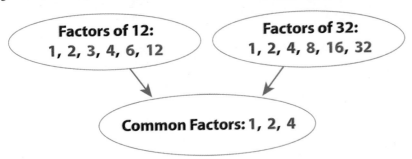

Factors of 12:
1, 2, 3, 4, 6, 12

Factors of 32:
1, 2, 4, 8, 16, 32

Common Factors: 1, 2, 4

The greatest of the common factors is 4.

Use the greatest common factor (GCF) and the Distributive Property to factor the expression $30x + 18$.

A Write out the prime factors of each term.

$30x + 18 = 2 \cdot$ _____ $\cdot$ _____ $\cdot\, x + 2 \cdot$ _____ $\cdot$ _____

B Circle the common factors.

$30x + 18 = \;\; 2 \;\; \cdot$ _____ $\cdot$ _____ $\cdot\, x + \;\; 2 \;\; \cdot$ _____ $\cdot$ _____

C Write the expression as the product of the GCF and a sum.

$30x + 18 = ($ _____ $) ($ _____ $x +$ _____ $)$

REFLECT

1. Will you get a completely factored expression if you factor out a common factor that is not the GCF? Explain.

_____

_____

2. Is the expression $2(3x - 4x)$ completely factored? Explain.

_____

_____

Greatest Common Factor of Monomials

To find the GCF of monomials, factor each coefficient and write all powers of variables as products. Then find the product of the common factors.

EXAMPLE 1  **FL** **A-SSE.1.2**

Find the GCF of each pair of monomials.

A $3x^3$ and $6x^2$

$3x^3 = 3 \cdot x \cdot x \cdot x$ *Factor each coefficient and write powers as*

$6x^2 = 2 \cdot 3 \cdot x \cdot x$ *products. Find the common factors.*

$\downarrow \quad \downarrow \quad \downarrow$

$3 \cdot x \cdot x$ *Find the product of the common factors.*

The GCF of $3x^3$ and $6x^2$ is $3x^2$.

B $4x^2$ and $5y^3$

$4x^2 = 2 \cdot 2 \cdot x \cdot x$ *Factor each coefficient and write powers as*

$5y^3 = 5 \cdot y \cdot y \cdot y$ *products.*

Since there are no common factors other than 1, the GCF of $4x^2$ and $5y^3$ is 1.

Math Talk

Mathematical Practices

Does factoring an expression change its value?

REFLECT

3. **Analyze Relationships** If two terms contain the same variable raised to different powers, to what power will the variable be raised in the GCF?

_____

4. Can the GCF of two positive numbers be greater than both numbers? Explain.

_____

_____

YOUR TURN

Find the GCF of each pair of monomials.

5. $18g^2$ and $27g^3$

_____

6. $16a^6$ and $9b$

_____

7. $15g^4$ and $45g^3$

_____

8. $9ab$ and $16bc$

_____

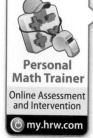

Factoring by Using the GCF

Remember that the Distributive Property states that $ab + ac = a(b + c)$.
Use the Distributive Property to factor out the GCF of the terms in a polynomial
to write the polynomial in factored form.

Math On the Spot
my.hrw.com

EXAMPLE 2

FL A-SSE.1.2

Factor each polynomial. Check your answer.

A $10y^3 + 20y^2 - 5y$

$\qquad 2y^2(5y) + 4y(5y) - 1(5y)$ The GCF is $5y$.

$\qquad\qquad 5y(2y^2 + 4y - 1)$ Use the Distributive Property.

Check:

$\qquad\qquad 5y(2y^2 + 4y - 1)$

$\qquad\qquad 10y^3 + 20y^2 - 5y$ ✓ The product is the original polynomial.

B $-12x - 8x^2$ Both coefficients are negative.

$\quad -1(12x + 8x^2)$ Factor out -1.

$\quad -1[3(4x) + 2x(4x)]$ The GCF of $12x$ and $8x^2$ is $4x$.

$\quad -1[4x(3 + 2x)]$ Use the Distributive Property.

$\quad -1(4x)(3 + 2x)$ Use the Associative Property.

$\quad -4x(3 + 2x)$

Check:

$\quad -4x(3 + 2x) = -12x - 8x^2$ ✓ The product is the original polynomial.

REFLECT

9. Can the polynomial $5x^2 + 7$ be factored? Explain.

_____

_____

YOUR TURN

Factor each polynomial. Check your answer.

10. $-28y^2 - 12y^5$

11. $8x^4 + 4x^3 - 2x^2$

_____   _____

**Personal
Math Trainer**

Online Assessment
and Intervention

my.hrw.com

Math On the Spot

⏻ my.hrw.com

My Notes

Factoring Out a Common Binomial Factor

Sometimes the GCF of the terms in an expression is a binomial. Such a GCF is called a common binomial factor. You factor out a common binomial factor the same way you factor out a monomial factor.

EXAMPLE 3
FL A-SSE.1.2

Factor each expression.

A $7(x - 3) - 2x(x - 3)$

$7(x - 3) - 2x(x - 3)$ $(x - 3)$ is a common binomial factor.

$(x - 3)(7 - 2x)$ Factor out $(x - 3)$.

B $-t(t^2 + 4) + (t^2 + 4)$

$-t(t^2 + 4) + (t^2 + 4)$ $(t^2 + 4)$ is a common binomial factor.

$-t(t^2 + 4) + 1(t^2 + 4)$ $(t^2 + 4) = 1(t^2 + 4)$

$(t^2 + 4)(-t + 1)$ Factor out $(t^2 + 4)$.

C $5x(x + 3) - 4(3 + x)$

$5x(x + 3) - 4(3 + x)$ $(3 + x) = (x + 3)$, so $(x + 3)$ is a common binomial factor.

$5x(x + 3) - 4(x + 3)$

$(x + 3)(5x - 4)$ Factor out $(x + 3)$.

D $-3x^2(x + 2) + 4(x - 7)$

$-3x^2(x + 2) + 4(x - 7)$ There are no common factors.

The expression cannot be factored.

Personal Math Trainer

Online Assessment and Intervention

⏻ my.hrw.com

YOUR TURN

Factor each expression, if possible.

12. $7x(2x + 3) + (2x + 3)$

13. $-4x(x + 2) + 9(x + 2)$

14. $7(3t - 2) + 2t^2(2t - 3)$

15. $5t(t + 6) - 8(6 + t)$

Factoring by Grouping

Some polynomials can be factored by grouping. When a polynomial has four terms, you may be able to make two groups and factor the GCF from each.

Math On the Spot
my.hrw.com

EXAMPLE 4

FL A-SSE.1.2

Factor each polynomial by grouping. Check your answer.

A $12a^3 - 9a^2 + 20a - 15$

$(12a^3 - 9a^2) + (20a - 15)$ Group terms that have a common number or variable as a factor.

$3a^2(4a - 3) + 5(4a - 3)$ Factor out the GCF of each group.

$3a^2(4a - 3) + 5(4a - 3)$ $(4a - 3)$ is a common factor.

$(4a - 3)(3a^2 + 5)$ Factor out $(4a - 3)$.

Check:

$(4a - 3)(3a^2 + 5)$ Multiply using FOIL.

$4a(3a^2) + 4a(5) - 3(3a^2) - 3(5)$

$12a^3 + 20a - 9a^2 - 15$

$12a^3 - 9a^2 + 20a - 15 ✓$ The product is the original polynomial.

B $2g^4 + 10g^3 + g + 5$

$(2g^4 + 10g^3) + (g + 5)$ Group terms.

$2g^3(g + 5) + 1(g + 5)$ Factor out the GCF of each group.

$2g^3(g + 5) + 1(g + 5)$ $(g + 5)$ is a common factor.

$(g + 5)(2g^3 + 1)$ Factor out $(g + 5)$.

Check:

$(g + 5)(2g^3 + 1)$ Multiply using FOIL.

$g(2g^3) + g(1) + 5(2g^3) + 5(1)$

$2g^4 + g + 10g^3 + 5$

$2g^4 + 10g^3 + g + 5 ✓$ The product is the original polynomial.

YOUR TURN

Factor each polynomial. Check your answer.

16. $6b^3 + 8b^2 + 9b + 12$ **17.** $4r^3 + 24r + r^2 + 6$

Personal Math Trainer

Online Assessment and Intervention

my.hrw.com

Factoring with Opposites

Recognizing opposite binomials can help you factor polynomials. The binomials $(5 - x)$ and $(x - 5)$ are opposites, because $(5 - x) = -1(x - 5)$.

EXAMPLE 5   **FL**   A-SSE.1.2

My Notes

Factor the polynomial by grouping and using opposites. Check your answer.

$3x^3 - 15x^2 + 10 - 2x$

$(3x^3 - 15x^2) + (10 - 2x)$ *Group terms.*

$3x^2(x - 5) + 2(5 - x)$ *Factor out the GCF of each group.*

$3x^2(x - 5) + 2(-1)(x - 5)$ *Write $(5 - x)$ as $-1(x - 5)$.*

$3x^2(x - 5) - 2(x - 5)$ *Simplify.*

$(x - 5)(3x^2 - 2)$ *Factor out $(x - 5)$.*

Check:

$(x - 5)(3x^2 - 2)$ *Multiply using FOIL.*

$x(3x^2) - x(2) - 5(3x^2) - 5(-2)$

$3x^3 - 2x - 15x^2 + 10$

$3x^3 - 15x^2 + 10 - 2x$ ✓   *The product is the original polynomial.*

REFLECT

18. Critique Reasoning Inara thinks that the opposite of $(a - b)$ is $(a + b)$, since addition and subtraction are opposites. Is she correct? Explain.

_____

_____

YOUR TURN

Factor each polynomial. Check your answer.

19. $15x^2 - 10x^3 + 8x - 12$ **20.** $8y - 8 - x + xy$

_____   _____

21. $48n^6 - 18n^5 - 56n + 21$ **22.** $8t^4 - 48t^3 - 3t + 18$

_____   _____

Write the expression as a product of the greatest common factor and a sum. (Explore Activity)

1. $15y^3 + 20y$

    a. Write out the prime factors of each term.

        $15y^3 + 20y = 3 \cdot \underline{\quad} \cdot \underline{\quad} \cdot \underline{\quad} \cdot y + 2 \cdot \underline{\quad} \cdot \underline{\quad} \cdot y$

    b. Circle the common factors.

        $15y^3 + 20y = 3 \cdot \underline{\quad} \cdot \underline{\quad} \cdot \underline{\quad} \cdot \left(y\right) + 2 \cdot \underline{\quad} \cdot \underline{\quad} \cdot \left(y\right)$

    c. Write the product of the GCF and a sum.

        $15y^3 + 20y = (\underline{\quad\quad})(\underline{\quad\quad} y^2 + \underline{\quad\quad})$

Find the GCF of each pair of monomials. (Example 1)

2. $9s$ and $63s^3$

    $9s \;\; = 3 \cdot \Box \cdot \Box$

    $63s^3 = 3 \cdot \Box \cdot 7 \cdot \Box \cdot \Box \cdot \Box$

    The GCF of $9s$ and $63s^3$ is _____.

3. $-14y^3 + 28y^2$

    $-14y^3 = \boxed{}$

    $28y^2 = \boxed{}$

    The GCF of $-14y^3$ and $28y^2$ is _____.

Factor each polynomial. Check your answer. (Example 2)

4. $-18y^3 - 7y^2 - y$

    $-y\left(\Box y^2 + \Box + 1\right)$

5. $9d^2 - 18$

    $\Box \left(d^2 - \Box\right)$

6. $6x^4 - 2x^3 + 10x^2$

    _____

7. $36t^3 + 63$

    _____

Factor each expression. (Example 3)

8. $4s(s + 6) - 5(s + 6)$

    $\left(\boxed{}\right)(s + 6)$

9. $-3(2 + b) + 4b(b + 2)$

    $\left(\boxed{}\right)\left(\boxed{}\right)$

10. $(6z)(z + 8) + (z + 8)$

    _____

11. $8w(5 - w) + 3(w - 5)$

    _____

Factor each polynomial. Check your answer. (Example 4)

12. $9x^3 + 18x^2 + x + 2$

$(9x^3 + \boxed{}) + (\boxed{})$

$\boxed{}(x + \boxed{}) + \boxed{}(\boxed{})$

$(\boxed{})(\boxed{})$

13. $2m^3 + 4m^2 + 6m + 12$

$(\boxed{} + 4m^2) + (\boxed{})$

$\boxed{}(m + \boxed{}) + \boxed{}(m + \boxed{})$

$(m + \boxed{})(\boxed{})$

$2(m + \boxed{})(\boxed{})$

14. $10x^3 - 40x^2 + 14x - 56$

_____

15. $2n^5 - 2n^4 + 7n^2 - 7n$

_____

Factor each polynomial. Check your answer. (Example 5)

16. $2r^2 - 6r + 12 - 4r$

$(2r^2 - \boxed{}) + (\boxed{})$

$\boxed{}(\boxed{} - 3) + \boxed{}(\boxed{})$

$2r(r - 3) + 4\boxed{}(\boxed{})$

$(\boxed{})(\boxed{})$

$\boxed{}(\boxed{})(\boxed{})$

17. $14q^2 - 21q + 6 - 4q$

$(\boxed{}) + (\boxed{})$

$7q(\boxed{}) + 2(\boxed{})$

$7q(\boxed{}) + 2\boxed{}(\boxed{})$

$(\boxed{})(\boxed{})$

18. $6c - 48 + 40c^2 - 5c^3$

_____

19. $3x^3 - 27x^2 + 45 - 5x$

_____

? **ESSENTIAL QUESTION CHECK-IN**

20. How can you use the greatest common factor to factor polynomials?

_____

_____

_____

_____

15.1 Independent Practice

FL A-SSE.1.2, A-SSE.2.3

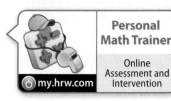

Personal
Math Trainer

Online
Assessment and
Intervention

my.hrw.com

21. Find the GCF of $-64n^4$ and $24n^2$.

_____

Factor each expression or state if it cannot be factored.

22. $13q^4 + 2p^2$

_____

23. $14n^3 + 7n + 7n^2$

_____

24. $2b(b + 3) + 5(b + 3)$

_____

25. $4(x - 3) - x(y + 2)$

_____

26. $7r^3 - 35r^2 + 6r - 30$

_____

27. Explain how to check that a polynomial has been factored correctly.

_____

_____

_____

_____

28. Samantha is making necklaces using 54 glass beads and 18 clay beads. Each necklace will have the same number of beads, but only one type of bead. If she puts the greatest possible number of beads on each necklace, how many necklaces can she make?

_____

29. After t years, the amount of money in a savings account that earns simple interest is $P + Prt$, where P is the starting amount and r is the yearly interest rate. Factor this expression.

_____

30. Addi has 36 jazz CDs and 48 country CDs. She wants to store as many CDs as possible on each shelf of a cabinet, while putting the same number of CDs on each shelf but not mixing jazz and country CDs on the same shelf. How many CDs can go on each shelf and how many shelves does she need?

_____

_____

31. The solar panel on Mandy's calculator has an area of $(7x^2 + x)$ cm^2. Factor this polynomial to find possible expressions for the dimensions of the solar panel.

_____

_____

_____

32. A model rocket is fired vertically into the air at 320 ft/s. The expression $-16t^2 + 320t$ gives the rocket's height after t seconds. Factor this expression.

_____

33. The area of a triangle is $\frac{1}{2}(x^3 - 2x + 2x^2 - 4)$. The height h is $x + 2$. Write an expression for the base b of the triangle. (*Hint*: Area of a triangle $= \frac{1}{2}bh$)

_____

34. José is making berry tarts for a party. He has 72 raspberries and 108 blueberries. Each tart will have the same number of berries, but only one kind of berry. If he puts the greatest possible number of berries in each tart, how many tarts can he make and how many berries will be in each tart?

_____

_____

35. The area of a rectangle is represented by the polynomial $x^2 + 3x - 6x - 18$.

   a. Find possible expressions for the length and width of the rectangle.

_____

   b. What are the length, width, and area of the rectangle if $x = 12$?

_____

 FOCUS ON HIGHER ORDER THINKING

Work Area

36. Critical Thinking Show two methods of factoring the expression $3a - 3b - 4a + 4b$. Is the result the same?

_____

_____

_____

37. Explain the Error Audrey and Owen came up with two different answers when they factored the expression $3n^3 - n^2$. Who was correct? Explain the error.

Owen	Audrey
$3n^3 - n^2$	$3n^3 - n^2$
$n^2(3n) - n^2(0)$	$n^2(3n) - n^2(1)$
$n^2(3n - 0)$	$n^2(3n - 1)$

_____

38. Communicating Mathematical Ideas Describe how to find the area of the figure. Show each step and write your answer in factored form.

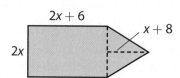

_____

_____

_____

_____

FL   A-SSE.1.2

Use the structure of an expression to identify ways to rewrite it. *Also A-SSE.2.3*

ESSENTIAL QUESTION

How can you factor expressions of the form $x^2 + bx + c$?

EXPLORE ACTIVITY 1

FL   A-SSE.1.2

Exploring Factors of $x^2 + bx + c$ when c is Positive

You know how to multiply binomials using FOIL. In this lesson, you will learn how to reverse this process and factor trinomials into two binomials.

Use algebra tiles to factor $x^2 + 7x + 6$.

A Identify the tiles you need to model the expression.

_____ x^2-tile(s), _____ x-tile(s), and _____ unit tile(s)

B Arrange the algebra tiles on the grid. Place the _____ x^2-tile in

the upper left corner, and arrange the _____ unit tiles in two rows and three columns in the lower right corner.

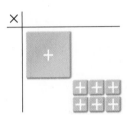

C Fill in the empty spaces on the grid with x-tiles. Only _____ x-tiles fit on the grid, so this arrangement is not correct.

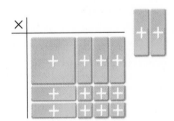

D Rearrange the unit tiles into a rectangle with different dimensions.

What is the length and width of the new rectangle? _____

E Fill in the empty spaces on the grid with x-tiles.

All _____ x-tiles were used, so this arrangement is correct.

$x^2 + 7x + 6 = (x + \boxed{})(x + \boxed{})$

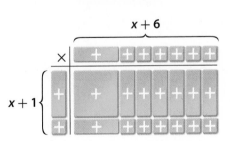

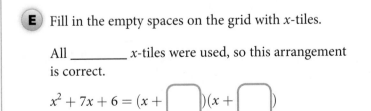

REFLECT

1. Finn checks the answer by multiplying and gets $x^2 + 1x + 6x + 6$. He believes he must have made a multiplication error. Is he correct? Explain.

_____

_____

2. What If? The second arrangement of unit tiles was a rectangle 1 tile high and 6 tiles wide. Could the arrangement have used a rectangle 6 tiles high and 1 tile wide? Explain.

_____

_____

3. Critical Thinking Are there any other ways to factor the polynomial $x^2 + 7x + 6$ besides $(x + 1)(x + 6)$? Explain.

_____

_____

EXPLORE ACTIVITY 2  **FL** A-SSE.1.2

Exploring Factors of $x^2 + bx + c$ when c is Negative

When using algebra tiles to factor polynomials, you may have to use both negative and positive tiles.

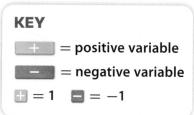

> **KEY**
>
> ☐ + ☐ = **positive variable**
>
> ☐ − ☐ = **negative variable**
>
> ⊞ = 1   ⊟ = −1

Animated Math

⏻ my.hrw.com

Use algebra tiles to factor $x^2 + x - 2$.

A Identify the tiles you need to model the expression.

_____ positive x^2-tile

_____ positive x-tile

_____ negative unit tiles

B The unit tiles will be placed on a grid to form a rectangle. List all the factor

pairs for 2: _____

C Arrange the algebra tiles on the grid. Place the

_____ positive x^2-tile in the upper left

corner, and arrange the _____ negative
unit tiles in the lower right corner.

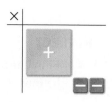

D Fill in the empty spaces on the grid with

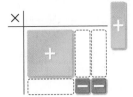

x-tiles. There is _____ positive
x-tile to place on the grid, so there will

be _____ empty places for
x-tiles.

E Fill the empty places with zero pairs.
A zero pair is two tiles that add to 0.

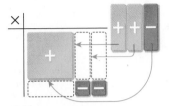

Add 1 positive _____ and

1 negative _____ to the grid.

F The empty spaces on the grid were
completely filled by zero pairs, so this
arrangement is correct.

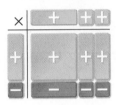

$x^2 + x - 2 = (x + \boxed{})(x - \boxed{})$

REFLECT

4. Analyze Relationships Why were the unit tiles not rearranged when the
x-tile did not complete the grid?

_____

_____

_____

_____

5. Why were both positive x-tiles placed in the top row?

_____

_____

_____

Factoring Trinomials

When factoring a polynomial in the form $x^2 + bx + c$, you are looking for two
binomials in the form $(x + n)$ and $(x + m)$, where n and m are a pair of numbers
whose product is c and whose sum is b.

So the first step is to find factor pairs of c. Always pay attention to the sign of c.
If c is positive, find factors of c that both have the same sign. If c is negative, find
one positive factor and one negative factor.

Math On the Spot

⊙ my.hrw.com

EXAMPLE 1   FL   A-SSE.1.2

A Factor $x^2 - 7x + 12$.

STEP 1 List factor pairs of c and find the sum of each pair. Since $c = 12$, which the c here is positive, use factor pairs where both factors have the same sign.

Factors of 12	Sum of Factors
1 and 12	$1 + 12 = 13$
2 and 6	$2 + 6 = 8$
3 and 4	$3 + 4 = 7$
−1 and −12	$(-1) + (-12) = -13$
−2 and −6	$(-2) + (-6) = -8$
−3 and −4	$(-3) + (-4) = -7$

−7 is the sum that you're looking for.

STEP 2 Use the factor pair whose sum equals b to factor the polynomial.

$$x^2 - 7x + 12 = (x - 3)(x - 4)$$

B Factor $x^2 + 4x - 45$.

STEP 1 List factor pairs of c and find the sum of each pair. Since $c = -45$, which is negative, use factor pairs where one factor is positive and the other factor is negative.

Factors of −45	Sum of Factors
1 and −45	$1 + (-45) = -44$
3 and −15	$3 + (-15) = -12$
5 and −9	$5 + (-9) = -4$
9 and −5	$9 + (-5) = 4$

4 is the sum that you're looking for. You can stop here.

STEP 2 Use the factor pair whose sum equals b to factor the polynomial.

$$x^2 + 4x - 45 = (x + 9)(x - 5)$$

REFLECT

6. When factoring a trinomial of the form $x^2 + bx + c$ where c is negative, one binomial factor contains a positive factor of c and one contains a negative factor of c. How do you know which factor of c should be positive and which should be negative?

_____

_____

_____

YOUR TURN

Factor each trinomial.

7. $x^2 - 11x + 30$

_____

8. $x^2 + 5x + 4$

_____

9. $x^2 - 5x - 14$

_____

10. $x^2 - x - 6$

_____

11. $x^2 + 4x - 21$

_____

12. $x^2 + 2x - 15$

_____

Personal Math Trainer

Online Assessment and Intervention

my.hrw.com

Guided Practice

1. Use algebra tiles to factor $x^2 + 6x + 8$. (Explore Activity 1)

   a. Identify the tiles you will need to model the expression.

      _____ x^2-tile _____ x-tiles _____ unit tiles

   b. This arrangement does not model the correct factors because it needs _____ x-tiles to fill the grid.

   c. This arrangement models the correct factors because it needs _____ x-tiles to fill the grid.

   d. $x^2 + 6x + 8 = (x + \boxed{})(x + \boxed{})$

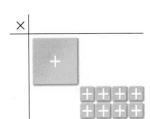

2. Use algebra tiles to factor $x^2 - 4x - 5$. (Explore Activity 2)

   a. Identify the tiles you will need to model the expression.

      _____ positive x^2-tile _____ negative x-tiles _____ negative unit tiles

   b. This arrangement has space for _____ x-tiles. You will have to add a _____ of x-tiles.

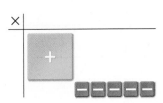

   c. $x^2 - 4x - 5 = (x - \boxed{})(x + \boxed{})$

3. Factor the polynomial $x^2 - 10x + 9$. (Example 1)

a. Complete the table with factor pairs of c.

Factors of 9	Sum of Factors
1 and _____	$1 + 9 = 10$
3 and _____	$3 + $ _____ $= $ _____
−1 and _____	$-1 + ($ _____ $) = $ _____
_____ and _____	_____ $+$ _____ $= $ _____

The factor pair whose sum equals b is _____ and _____.

b. $x^2 - 10x + 9 = (x - \boxed{})(x - \boxed{})$

Factor each trinomial. (Example 1)

4. $x^2 + 6x + 9$

$(x + \boxed{})(x + 3)$

5. $x^2 - 5x + 4$

$(x - 1)(x - \boxed{})$

6. $x^2 - 3x - 18$

$(x + 3)(\boxed{})$

7. $x^2 + 14x + 40$

$(x + 4)(\boxed{})$

8. $x^2 + 9x - 36$

_____

9. $x^2 - 2x - 35$

_____

10. $x^2 - 7x - 30$

_____

11. $x^2 + 2x - 8$

_____

12. The length of a rectangular porch is $(x + 7)$ feet. The area of the porch is $(x^2 + 9x + 14)$ square feet. Factor the expression for the area in order to find an expression for the width of the porch.

_____

? **ESSENTIAL QUESTION CHECK-IN**

13. How can you factor expressions of the form $x^2 + bx + c$?

_____

_____

_____

15.2 Independent Practice

FL   A-SSE.1.2, A-SSE.2.3

Personal
Math Trainer

Online
Assessment and
Intervention

my.hrw.com

Factor each trinomial.

14. $x^2 - 2x - 15$

_____

15. $x^2 + 9x + 18$

_____

16. $x^2 + 13x - 30$

_____

17. $x^2 + 11x + 28$

_____

18. $x^2 - 10x - 24$

_____

19. $x^2 - 12x + 32$

_____

20. Write the polynomial modeled and then factor it.

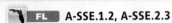

x^2	$-2x$
$4x$	-8

_____

_____

21. The area of a rectangle in square feet can be represented by $x^2 + 8x + 12$. The length is $(x + 6)$ ft. What is the width of the rectangle?

_____

_____

22. A homeowner wants to enlarge a rectangular closet that has an area of $(x^2 + 3x + 2)$ ft^2. The length is $(x + 2)$ ft. After construction, the area will be $(x^2 + 8x + 15)$ ft^2 with a length of $(x + 3)$ ft.

a. Find the dimensions of the closet before construction.

_____

_____

b. Find the dimensions of the closet after construction.

_____

_____

c. By how many feet will the length and width increase after construction?

_____

_____

23. Can all trinomials of the form $x^2 + bx + c$ be factored? Explain and defend your answer with an example.

_____

_____

_____

_____

24. Give a value of b that would make $x^2 + bx - 36$ factorable. Show the factorization.

_____

_____

25. Represent Real-World Problems The area of a rectangular fountain is $(x^2 + 12x + 20)$ ft^2. The width is $(x + 2)$ ft.

a. Find the length of the fountain.

_____

b. A 2-foot wide walkway is built around the fountain. Find the dimensions of the outside border of the walkway.

_____

c. Find the total area covered by the fountain and walkway.

_____

26. Give a value of b that would **not** make $x^2 + bx - 36$ factorable. Show that it cannot be factored.

_____

_____

![H.O.T.] **FOCUS ON HIGHER ORDER THINKING**

27. Justify Reasoning The area of a rectangle is $x^2 + 6x + 8$. The length is $(x + 4)$. Find the width of the rectangle. Is the rectangle a square? Explain.

_____

_____

28. Communicate Mathematical Ideas Rico says the expression $x^2 + bx + c$ is factorable when $b = c = 4$. Are there any other values where $b = c$ that make the expression factorable? Explain.

_____

_____

_____

_____

29. Critical Thinking Explain how to find all the possible positive values of b such that $x^2 + bx + 6$ can be factored into binomial factors. Write the possible trinomials.

_____

_____

_____

_____

_____

ESSENTIAL QUESTION

How can you factor expressions of the form $ax^2 + bx + c$?

Factoring $ax^2 + bx + c$ where $c > 0$

When you factor a polynomial in the form $ax^2 + bx + c$, the result will be the product of two binomial factors, in the form $(\boxed{}x + \boxed{})(\boxed{}x + \boxed{})$. The product of the two coefficients of x will be a, and the product of the two constant terms will be c. The sum of the products of the inner and outer terms will be bx.

Math On the Spot

⏻ my.hrw.com

Product = a — Product = c

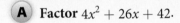

$$\left(\boxed{}\ x + \boxed{}\right)\left(\boxed{}\ x + \boxed{}\right) = ax^2 + bx + c$$

Sum of outer and inner products = b

EXAMPLE 1

FL A-SSE.1.2

A Factor $4x^2 + 26x + 42$.

STEP 1 Factor out any common factors of 4, 26, and 42.

$$4x^2 + 26x + 42 = 2(2x^2 + 13x + 21)$$

STEP 2 Make a table that lists the factor pairs for a and c. Find the value of b that results from each combination of factor pairs.

Factors of a $a = 2$	Factors of c $c = 21$	Outer Product + Inner Product
1 and 2	1 and 21	$(1)(21) + (2)(1) = 23$
1 and 2	3 and 7	$(1)(7) + (2)(3) = 13$
1 and 2	7 and 3	$(1)(3) + (2)(7) = 17$
1 and 2	21 and 1	$(1)(1) + (2)(21) = 43$

13 is the sum that you're looking for.

STEP 3 Use the combination of factor pairs that yields the correct value of b to factor the polynomial.

$$(1x + 3)(2x + 7) = (x + 3)(2x + 7)$$

$$4x^2 + 26x + 42 = 2(x + 3)(2x + 7)$$

B Factor $3x^2 - 26x + 35$.

STEP 1 Factor out any common factors of 3, −26, and 35.

3, −26, and 35 share no common factors other than 1.

STEP 2 Make a table that lists the factor pairs for a and c. Find the value of b that results from each combination of factor pairs.

Factors of a $a = 3$	Factors of c $c = 35$	Outer Product + Inner Product
1 and 3	−1 and −35	$(1)(-35) + (3)(-1) = -38$
1 and 3	−5 and −7	$(1)(-7) + (3)(-5) = -22$
1 and 3	−7 and −5	$(1)(-5) + (3)(-7) = -26$
1 and 3	−35 and −1	$(1)(-1) + (3)(-35) = -106$

STEP 3 Use the combination of factor pairs that yields the correct value of b to factor the polynomial.

> −26 is the sum that you're looking for.

$$3x^2 - 26x + 35 = (1x - 7)(3x - 5) = (x - 7)(3x - 5)$$

REFLECT

1. Critical Thinking When factoring $3x^2 - 26x + 35$, why should both factors of c be negative?

_____

_____

_____

_____

2. What If? If none of the factor pairs for a and c result in the correct value for b, what do you know about the polynomial?

_____

_____

YOUR TURN

Factor each polynomial.

3. $5x^2 - 14x + 8$

_____

4. $3x^2 + 11x + 6$

_____

5. $12x^2 - 48x + 45$

_____

6. $12x^2 + 62x + 70$

_____

7. $14x^2 + 33x + 18$

_____

8. $50x^2 - 165x + 135$

_____

Personal Math Trainer

Online Assessment and Intervention

my.hrw.com

Factoring $ax^2 + bx + c$ where $c < 0$

When factoring $ax^2 + bx + c$, if the value of c is negative, you know that one of the factors of c must be negative and one must be positive. Apply what you already know about factoring trinomials to this new situation.

Math On the Spot

my.hrw.com

EXAMPLE 2   FL A-SSE.1.2

A Factor $6x^2 - 21x - 45$.

STEP 1 Factor out any common factors of 6, –21, and –45.

$$6x^2 - 21x - 45 = 3(2x^2 - 7x - 15)$$

STEP 2 Make a table that lists the factor pairs for a and c. Since c is negative, one factor will be positive and the other will be negative.

Factors of a $a = 2$	Factors of c $c = -15$	Outer Product + Inner Product
1 and 2	1 and −15	$(1)(-15) + (2)(1) = -13$
1 and 2	3 and −5	$(1)(-5) + (2)(3) = 1$
1 and 2	5 and −3	$(1)(-3) + (2)(5) = 7$
1 and 2	15 and −1	$(1)(-1) + (2)(15) = 29$
1 and 2	−1 and 15	$(1)(15) + (2)(-1) = 13$
1 and 2	−3 and 5	$(1)(5) + (2)(-3) = -1$
1 and 2	−5 and 3	$(1)(3) + (2)(-5) = -7$
1 and 2	−15 and 1	$(1)(1) + (2)(-15) = -29$

−7 is the sum that you're looking for.

STEP 3 Use the combination of factor pairs that yields the correct value of b to factor the polynomial.

$$(1x - 5)(2x + 3) = (x - 5)(2x + 3)$$

$$6x^2 - 21x - 45 = 3(x - 5)(2x + 3)$$

B Factor $4x^2 + 4x - 35$.

STEP 1 Factor out any common factors for 4, 4, and –35.

4, 4, and –35 share no common factors other than 1.

STEP 2 Make a table that lists the factor pairs for a and c. Since c is negative, one factor will be positive and the other will be negative.

Factors of a $a = 4$	Factors of c $c = -35$	Outer Product + Inner Product
1 and 4	1 and −35	$(1)(-35) + (4)(1) = -31$
1 and 4	5 and −7	$(1)(-7) + (4)(5) = 13$
1 and 4	7 and −5	$(1)(-5) + (4)(7) = 23$
1 and 4	35 and −1	$(1)(-1) + (4)(35) = 139$
1 and 4	−1 and 35	$(1)(35) + (4)(-1) = 31$
1 and 4	−5 and 7	$(1)(7) + (4)(-5) = -13$
1 and 4	−7 and 5	$(1)(5) + (4)(-7) = -23$
1 and 4	−35 and 1	$(1)(1) + (4)(-35) = -139$
2 and 2	1 and −35	$(2)(-35) + (2)(1) = -68$
2 and 2	5 and −7	$(2)(-7) + (2)(5) = -4$
2 and 2	7 and −5	$(2)(-5) + (2)(7) = 4$
2 and 2	35 and −1	$(2)(-1) + (2)(35) = 68$

Math Talk

Mathematical Practices

How does the sign of c help you choose the correct factor pair for c?

STEP 3 Use the combination of factor pairs that yields the correct value of b to factor the polynomial.

4 is the sum that you're looking for.

$$4x^2 + 4x - 35 = (2x + 7)(2x - 5)$$

REFLECT

9. Critique Reasoning Rudy is factoring $14x^2 + 15x - 6$. He claims that 14, 15, and 6 share no common factors because 14 and 15 share no common factors. Is he correct? Explain.

_____

_____

_____

10. Make a Conjecture Using the information in the tables in Example 2, make a conjecture about what happens to b when you swap the positions of the plus and minus signs in the binomial factors.

_____

_____

Personal Math Trainer

Online Assessment and Intervention

my.hrw.com

YOUR TURN

Factor each polynomial.

11. $24x^2 + 32x - 6$

12. $9x^2 + 21x - 8$

_____   _____

1. Factor $3x^2 + 13x + 12$. **Check your answer.** (Example 1)

Complete the table for all factors of a and c.

Factors of a $a = 3$	Factors of c $c = 12$	Outer Product + Inner Product
1 and 3	1 and 12	$(1)(12) + (3)(1) = $ ____
1 and 3	2 and ____	$(1)($____$) + ($____$)(2) = 12$
1 and 3	____ and ____	$(1)($____$) + (3)($____$) = $ ____
1 and 3	____ and ____	$(1)($____$) + ($____$)(4) = $ ____
1 and 3	____ and ____	$(1)($____$) + ($____$)($____$) = $ ____
1 and 3	____ and 1	$(1)(1) + ($____$)($____$) = 37$

The factored form of $3x^2 + 13x + 12$ is $(x + \boxed{})(\boxed{}x + \boxed{})$.

2. Factor $8x^2 - 2x - 6$. **Check your answer.** (Example 2)

8, -2, and -6 have a common factor of _____, so $8x^2 - 2x - 6 = \boxed{}(4x^2 - x - 3)$

Complete the table for all factors of a and c.

Factors of a $a = 4$	Factors of c $c = -3$	Outer Product + Inner Product
1 and 4	1 and -3	$(1)(-3) + (4)(1) = 1$
1 and ____	3 and ____	$(1)($____$) + (4)($____$) = $ ____
1 and ____	____ and ____	$(1)($____$) + ($____$)($____$) = $ ____
1 and ____	____ and ____	$(1)($____$) + ($____$)($____$) = $ ____
2 and ____	____ and ____	$(2)($____$) + ($____$)(1) = $ ____
____ and ____	3 and ____	$(2)($____$) + (2)(3) = 4$

The factored form of $8x^2 - 2x - 6$ is $\boxed{}(x - \boxed{})(4x + \boxed{})$.

? ESSENTIAL QUESTION CHECK-IN

3. How can you factor expressions of the form $ax^2 + bx + c$?

_____

_____

15.3 Independent Practice

FL   A-SSE.1.2, A-SSE.2.3

Personal Math Trainer

Online Assessment and Intervention

my.hrw.com

Factor each trinomial, if possible. Check your answer.

4. $30x^2 + 35x - 15$

_____

5. $6x^2 - 29x + 9$

_____

6. $30x^2 + 82x + 56$

_____

7. $5z^2 + 17z + 6$

_____

8. $30d^2 + 7d - 15$

_____

9. $2y^2 - 11y + 14$

_____

10. $-4g^2 + 11g + 20$

_____

11. $9n^2 + 3n + 1$

_____

12. How is factoring a trinomial in the form $ax^2 + bx + c$ similar to factoring a trinomial in the form $x^2 + bx + c$? How is it different?

_____

_____

_____

_____

_____

13. The area of a soccer field is $(24x^2 + 100x + 100)$ m². The width of the field is $(4x + 10)$ m. What is the length?

_____

14. Find all the possible values of b such that $3x^2 + bx - 2$ can be factored.

_____

15. Write the polynomial modeled, and then factor it.

_____

_____

16. **Representing Real-World Problems** The attendance at a team's basketball game can be approximated with the polynomial $-5x^2 + 80x + 285$, where x is the number of wins the team had in the previous month.

a. Factor the polynomial completely.

_____

b. Estimate the attendance if the team won 4 games in the previous month.

_____

17. **Multiple Representations** Kyle stood on a bridge and threw a rock up and over the side. The height of the rock, in meters, can be approximated by $-5t^2 + 5t + 24$, where t is the time in seconds after Kyle threw it. Completely factor the expression.

_____

18. A triangle has an area of $\frac{1}{2}(4x^2 + 29x + 30)$ ft^2. If the base of the triangle is $(x + 6)$ ft, find the height of the triangle.

_____

19. **Draw Conclusions** If a polynomial in the form $ax^2 + bx + c$ has $a = b = c = 1$, can the expression be factored? Explain.

_____

_____

_____

_____

20. **Counterexamples** Marc thinks the only time a polynomial in the form $ax^2 + bx + c$ cannot be factored is when at least one of the values for a, b, or c is a prime number. Find a counterexample to Marc's statement.

_____

_____

21. Shruti has a rectangular picture frame with an area of $30x^2 + 5x - 75$ cm^2.

  a. Find the width of the frame when the height is $(3x + 5)$ cm. _____

  b. Find the width of the frame when the height is $(2x - 3)$ cm. _____

  c. Find the width of the frame when the height is 5 cm. _____

22. **Communicate Mathematical Ideas** Has the expression $(3x + 7)(6x + 3)$ been completely factored? Explain.

_____

_____

_____

23. **Explain the Error** Luna performed the work shown below to factor the polynomial $24x^2 + 18x + 3$. Explain her error, and find the correctly factored form.

$$24x^2 + 18x + 3 = 3(8x^2 + 6x + 0)$$
$$= 3(8x^2 + 6x)$$
$$= 3(2x)(4x + 3)$$

_____

_____

_____

24. The length of Rebecca's rectangular garden was two times the width, w. Rebecca increased the length and width of the garden so that the area of the new garden is $(2w^2 + 7w + 6)$ square yards. By how much did Rebecca increase the length and the width?

_____

25. The height in feet above the ground of a football that has been thrown or kicked can be described by the expression $-16t^2 + vt + h$ where t is the time in seconds, v is the initial upward velocity, and h is the initial height in feet.

a. Write an expression for the height of a football at time t when the initial upward velocity is 20 feet per second and the initial height is 6 feet.

_____

b. Factor your expression from part **a**.

_____

c. Find the height of the football after 1 second.

_____

 FOCUS ON HIGHER ORDER THINKING

26. **Critical Thinking** Find a value of m that will make the trinomial factorable. Is there more than one possible value? Explain.

$$x^2 + mx + 80$$

_____

_____

_____

27. **Explain the Error** Frank has factored the polynomial $2x^2 + 13x + 12$ as $(x + 1)(x + 12)$. Explain his error.

_____

_____

_____

28. **What If?** Can the polynomial $4x^2 + 0x - 25$ be factored? Explain.

_____

_____

_____

Factoring Special Products

FL A-SSE.1.2

Use the structure of an expression to identify ways to rewrite it. *Also A-SSE.2.3*

ESSENTIAL QUESTION

How can you use special products to aid in factoring?

EXPLORE ACTIVITY FL A-SSE.1.2

Factoring a Perfect-Square Trinomial

When you use algebra tiles to factor a polynomial, you must arrange the unit tiles on the grid in a rectangle. Sometimes, you can arrange the unit tiles to form a square.

Use algebra tiles to factor $x^2 + 6x + 9$.

A Identify the tiles you need to model the expression.

_____ x^2-tile _____ x-tiles _____ unit tiles

B The unit tiles will be placed on a grid to form a square. Which

factor pair for 9 will arrange the tiles in a square? _____

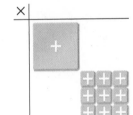

C Arrange the algebra tiles on the grid. Place the _____

x^2-tile in the upper left corner, and arrange the _____ unit tiles in the lower right corner.

D Fill in the empty spaces on the grid with x-tiles.

All _____ x-tiles were used, so this arrangement is correct.

$x^2 + 6x + 9 = (x + \boxed{})(x + \boxed{})$

Now, use algebra tiles to factor $x^2 - 8x + 16$.

E Identify the tiles you need to model the expression.

_____ positive x^2-tile _____ negative x-tiles

_____ positive unit tiles

F The unit tiles will be placed on a grid to form a square. Which factor

pair for 16 will arrange the tiles in a square? _____

G Arrange the algebra tiles on the grid.

Place the _____ positive
x^2-tile in the upper left corner, and

arrange _____ positive unit tiles
in the lower right corner.

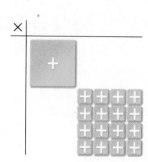

H Fill in the empty spaces on the grid

with x-tiles. All _____ negative
x-tiles were used, so this
arrangement is correct.

$x^2 - 8x + 16 =$

$(x - \boxed{})(x - \boxed{})$

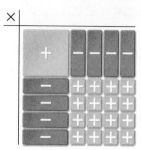

Math Talk

Mathematical Practices

How would the algebra
tile grid change if its
factored form was
$(x + 4)(x + 4)$?

REFLECT

1. **What If?** Suppose that the middle term in $x^2 + 6x + 9$ was changed from $6x$ to $10x$. How would this affect the way you factor the polynomial?

_____

_____

_____

2. If the unit tiles are arranged in a square when factoring with algebra tiles, what will be true about the binomial factors?

_____

_____

_____

Math On the Spot

⏻ my.hrw.com

Factoring Perfect-Square Trinomials

A perfect-square trinomial has either the form $a^2 + 2ab + b^2$ or the form $a^2 - 2ab + b^2$. Factor perfect-square trinomials according to the rules below.

Perfect-Square Trinomials	
Perfect-Square Trinomial	**Example**
$a^2 + 2ab + b^2 = (a + b)(a + b)$ $= (a + b)^2$	$x^2 + 6x + 9 = (x + 3)(x + 3)$ $= (x + 3)^2$
$a^2 - 2ab + b^2 = (a - b)(a - b)$ $= (a - b)^2$	$x^2 - 2x + 1 = (x - 1)(x - 1)$ $= (x - 1)^2$

EXAMPLE 1   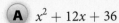 FL   A-SSE.1.2

Factor each perfect-square trinomial.

A $x^2 + 12x + 36$

    $x^2 + 2(x)(6) + 6^2$ *Rewrite in the form $a^2 + 2ab + b^2$.*

    $(x + 6)(x + 6)$ *Rewrite in the form $(a + b)(a + b)$.*

    The factored form of $x^2 + 12x + 36$ is $(x + 6)(x + 6)$, or $(x + 6)^2$.

B $4x^2 - 12x + 9$

    $(2x)^2 - 2(2x)(3) + 3^2$ *Rewrite in the form $a^2 - 2ab + b^2$.*

    $(2x - 3)(2x - 3)$ *Rewrite in the form $(a - b)(a - b)$.*

    The factored form of $4x^2 - 12x + 9$ is $(2x - 3)(2x - 3)$, or $(2x - 3)^2$.

C $36x^2 + 180x + 225$

    $9(4x^2 + 20x + 25)$ *Factor out the GCF of the terms.*

    $9[(2x)^2 + 2(2x)(5) + 5^2]$ *Rewrite in the form $a^2 + 2ab + b^2$.*

    $9(2x + 5)(2x + 5)$ *Rewrite in the form $(a + b)(a + b)$.*

    The factored form of $36x^2 + 180x + 225$ is $9(2x + 5)(2x + 5)$, or $9(2x + 5)^2$.

My Notes

REFLECT

3. Lee says that the trinomial $4x^2 + 15x + 9$ is a perfect-square trinomial, because $4x^2$ and 9 are both perfect squares. Is Lee correct? Explain.

_____

_____

4. Wendy checked the answer to Example 1A. Her work is shown below. Explain her error.

$$(x + 6)^2 = x^2 + 6^2 = x^2 + 36$$

_____

_____

_____

5. Perfect-square trinomials can be in the form $a^2 + 2ab + b^2$ or $a^2 - 2ab + b^2$. Why is the b^2 term always positive?

_____

_____

YOUR TURN

Factor each perfect-square trinomial.

6. $x^2 + 6x + 9$

_____

7. $25x^2 + 60x + 36$

_____

8. $36x^2 - 12x + 1$

_____

9. $16x^2 - 16x + 4$

_____

10. $9x^2 - 18x + 9$

_____

11. $4x^2 + 24x + 36$

_____

Factoring a Difference of Squares

What does "difference of two squares" mean?

$$x^2 - 100$$

square   difference   square

A polynomial is a difference of two squares if:

- It has two terms, one subtracted from the other.
- Both terms are perfect squares.

$$4x^2 \quad - \quad 9$$
$$2x \cdot 2x - 3 \cdot 3$$

The difference of two squares can be written as the product $(a + b)(a - b)$.

Difference of Two Squares	
Difference of Two Squares	**Example**
$a^2 - b^2 = (a + b)(a - b)$	$x^2 - 9 = (x + 3)(x - 3)$

EXAMPLE 2

FL   A-SSE.1.2

Factor each difference of squares.

A $x^2 - 81$

$x^2 - 9^2$ Rewrite in the form $a^2 - b^2$.

$(x + 9)(x - 9)$ Rewrite in the form $(a + b)(a - b)$.

The factored form of $x^2 - 81$ is $(x + 9)(x - 9)$.

B $16q^2 - 9p^4$ Remember $(a^m)^n = a^{mn}$.

$(4q)^2 - (3p^2)^2$ Rewrite in the form $a^2 - b^2$.

$(4q + 3p^2)(4q - 3p^2)$ Rewrite in the form $(a + b)(a - b)$.

The factored form of $16q^2 - 9p^4$ is $(4q + 3p^2)(4q - 3p^2)$.

C $4y^4 - 25y^2$

$y^2(4y^2 - 25)$ Factor out the GCF of the terms.

$y^2[(2y)^2 - 5^2]$ Rewrite in the form $a^2 - b^2$.

$y^2(2y + 5)(2y - 5)$ Rewrite in the form $(a + b)(a - b)$.

The factored form of $4y^4 - 25y^2$ is $y^2(2y + 5)(2y - 5)$.

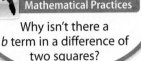

Math Talk
Mathematical Practices

Why isn't there a b term in a difference of two squares?

REFLECT

12. How can you recognize a difference of two squares?

_____

_____

_____

YOUR TURN

Factor each difference of squares.

13. $1 - 4x^2$

_____

14. $16x^2 - 4y^6$

_____

15. $p^8 - 49q^6$

_____

Personal Math Trainer

Online Assessment and Intervention

⏻ my.hrw.com

Guided Practice

For each trinomial, draw algebra tiles to show the factored form, then write the factored form. (Explore Activity)

1. $x^2 - 10x + 25$

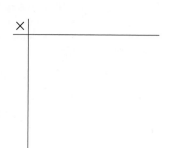

2. $x^2 + 8x + 16$

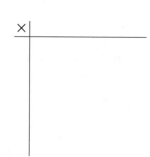

_____

_____

Factor each perfect-square trinomial. (Example 1)

3. $9x^2 + 18x + 9$

_____

4. $25x^2 + 20x + 4$

_____

5. $64x^2 - 12x + 1$

_____

6. $4x^2 + 24x + 36$

_____

7. $16x^4 - 24x^2 + 9$

_____

8. $25x^2 + 10x + 1$

_____

Factor each difference of two squares. (Example 2)

9. $s^2 - 16$

_____

10. $81 - 144x^4$

_____

11. $x^8 - 49$

_____

12. $400x^4 - 484x^2$

_____

13. $49x^6 - 36y^2$

_____

14. $25t^2 - 64$

_____

? **ESSENTIAL QUESTION CHECK-IN**

15. How can you use special products to aid in factoring?

_____

_____

_____

_____

_____

15.4 Independent Practice

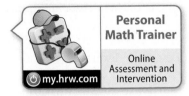

Personal Math Trainer

Online Assessment and Intervention

my.hrw.com

Determine whether each polynomial is a perfect-square trinomial or the difference of two squares. Then factor each expression.

16. $4x^2 - 20x + 25$

_____

17. $16b^2 - 169c^6$

_____

_____

18. $49x^2 + 140x + 100$

_____

19. $4x^2 - 36$

_____

_____

20. An architect is designing square windows with an area of $(x^2 + 20x + 100)$ ft². The dimensions of the windows are of the form $ax + b$, where a and b are whole numbers.

a. Find the dimensions of each square window. _____

b. Find an expression for the perimeter of a window. _____

c. Find the perimeter of a window when $x = 4$ ft. _____

21. **Critical Thinking** Sinea thinks that the fully factored form of the expression $(x^4 - 1)$ is $(x^2 - 1)(x^2 + 1)$. Is she correct? Explain.

_____

_____

_____

22. **Represent Real-World Problems** You are given a sheet of paper and asked to cut out a square piece with an area of $(4x^2 - 44x + 121)$ mm². The dimensions of the square have the form $ax - b$, where a and b are whole numbers.

a. Find the length of the one of the sides of the square you cut out.

_____

b. Find an expression for the perimeter of the square you cut out.

_____

c. Find the perimeter when $x = 41$ mm.

_____

23. Explain how to fully factor the expression $x^4 - 2x^2y^2 + y^4$.

_____

_____

_____

_____

_____

_____

_____

_____

24. A square poster has an area of $x^2 + 16x + 64$ square inches. Find the length of one side of the square.

_____

25. An artist framed a picture. The dimensions of the picture and frame are shown.

Completely factor the expression for the area of the frame.

_____

4x

2y

2y

4x

4x

26. Explain how to find the value of z if you know that $100x^2 + 120x + z$ is a perfect square trinomial.

_____

_____

_____

27. The area of a square is $(36d^2 - 36d + 9)$ in^2.

a. What expression represents the length of a side of the square?

_____

b. What expression represents the perimeter of the square? _____

c. What are the length of a side, the perimeter, and the area of the square when $d = 2$ in.?

_____

H.O.T. FOCUS ON HIGHER ORDER THINKING

Work Area

28. **Justify Reasoning** The area of a quadrilateral is $4x^2 + 16x + 16$, which is a perfect-square trinomial. Does the quadrilateral have to be a square? Explain.

_____

_____

29. **Explain the Error** When Jeremy factored $144x^2 - 40x + 100$, he first got $(12x + 10)(12x - 10)$, then he noticed a common factor, so he factored it further to get $2(6x + 5)(6x - 5)$. What was his error, and what is the correct factorization?

_____

_____

_____

30. **Multistep** Factor $5x^3 + x^2 - 20x - 12$.

_____

_____

Ready to Go On?

Personal
Math Trainer

my.hrw.com

Online
Assessment and
Intervention

15.1 Factoring Polynomials

Factor each expression. Check your answer.

1. $-14x - 12x^2$

2. $3x(x + 6) - 5(6 + x)$

3. $2x^3 - 12x^2 + 18 - 3x$

15.2 Factoring $x^2 + bx + c$

Factor each trinomial. Check your answer.

4. $x^2 - 20x + 19$

5. $n^2 + 13n + 36$

6. $x^2 - 4x - 21$

15.3 Factoring $ax^2 + bx + c$

Factor each trinomial. Check your answer.

7. $3n^2 - 26n + 35$

8. $6y^2 + 11y + 4$

9. $-4x^2 - 10x - 6$

15.4 Factoring Special Products

Determine whether each polynomial is a perfect-square trinomial or the difference
of two squares. Then factor each polynomial.

10. $4x^2 - 12x + 9$

11. $36n^2 + 24n + 4$

12. $4b^4 - 49b^2$

? ESSENTIAL QUESTION

13. How can you factor expressions of the form $ax^2 + bx + c$?

Assessment Readiness

Selected Response

1. Which is the complete factorization of $24x^3 - 12x^2$?

Ⓐ $6(4x^3 - 2x^2)$ Ⓒ $12x(2x^2 - x)$

Ⓑ $12(2x^3 - x^2)$ Ⓓ $12x^2(2x - 1)$

2. Which is a factor of $24x^2 - 49x + 2$?

Ⓐ $x - 2$

Ⓑ $x - 1$

Ⓒ $x + 1$

Ⓓ $x + 2$

3. The binomial $x - 3$ is **not** a factor of which of the following trinomials?

Ⓐ $2x^2 - x - 3$ Ⓒ $3x^2 - 6x - 9$

Ⓑ $2x^2 - 5x - 3$ Ⓓ $3x^2 - 10x + 3$

4. Which of the following is the complete factorization of $6a^3b + 3a^2b^3$?

Ⓐ $9a^5b^4$ Ⓒ $(6a^3b)(3a^2b^3)$

Ⓑ $3ab(2a^2 + ab^2)$ Ⓓ $3a^2b(2a + b^2)$

5. Which is the correct factorization of the polynomial $x^2 - 36$?

Ⓐ $(x - 6)(x - 6)$ Ⓒ $(x - 2)(x + 18)$

Ⓑ $(x + 4)(x - 9)$ Ⓓ $(x + 6)(x - 6)$

6. What value of b would make the trinomial $3x^2 + bx - 8$ factorable?

Ⓐ 3   Ⓒ 11

Ⓑ 10   Ⓓ 25

7. The population of a town is 88,000 and is increasing at a rate of 3% per year. At this rate, approximately what will the town's population be in 5 years?

Ⓐ 99,045   Ⓒ 102,016

Ⓑ 101,200   Ⓓ 264,000

8. Which of the following data sets is best described by a linear model?

Ⓐ $\{(2, 3), (1, 9), (0, 27), (-1, 81)\}$

Ⓑ $\{(-2, -2), (-3, -1), (-4, 1), (-5, 2)\}$

Ⓒ $\{(2, 6), (3, 3), (4, 0), (5, -3)\}$

Ⓓ $\{(2, 1), (3, 0), (4, -1), (5, 0)\}$

Mini-Tasks

9. A small rectangle is drawn inside a larger rectangle as shown.

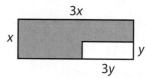

a. What is the area of each rectangle?

_____

b. What is the area of the shaded region?

_____

c. Factor the expression for the area of the shaded region.

_____

10. The area of a square is represented by $25z^2 - 40z + 16$.

a. What expression represents the length of a side of the square?

_____

b. What expression represents the perimeter of the square?

_____

c. Find the length of a side, the perimeter, and the area of the square when $z = 3$.

_____

Solving Quadratic Equations

ESSENTIAL QUESTION

How do you determine the best method for solving a quadratic equation or a system of equations?

Real-World Video

The designers of a fireworks display need to make precise timing calculations. An explosion too soon or too late could spell disaster!

my.hrw.com

PhotoDisc

GO DIGITAL
my.hrw.com

my.hrw.com

Go digital with your write-in student edition, accessible on any device.

Math On the Spot

Scan with your smart phone to jump directly to the online edition, video tutor, and more.

Animated Math

Interactively explore key concepts to see how math works.

Personal Math Trainer

Get immediate feedback and help as you work through practice sets.

Are YOU Ready?

Complete these exercises to review skills you will need for this module.

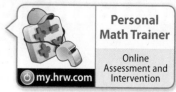

Personal Math Trainer

Online Assessment and Intervention

my.hrw.com

Simplify Polynomial Expressions

EXAMPLE $4r - 3r^2 + 2(6r + 5)$
$4r - 3r^2 + 12r + 10$ Multiply by 2.
$-3r^2 + 16r + 10$ Collect like terms.

Simplify each expression.

1. $8g - 5 + 2g^2 + 5g^2$

2. $3x - 5(x^2 + 3) - 2x^2$

Solve Multi-Step Equations

EXAMPLE   Solve $2x - 5 = 17$
$2x = 22$ Add 5 to both sides
$x = 11$ Divide both sides by 2.

Solve the following equations.

3. $2x + 7 = 0$

4. $14 - 3y = -7$

Multiply Binomials

EXAMPLE   Distributive Property
$(x + 2)(x - 5)$
$= x(x - 5) + 2(x - 5)$
$= x^2 - 5x + 2x - 10$
$= x^2 - 3x - 10$

FOIL
$(x + 2)(x - 5)$
  F O I L
$= x^2 - 5x + 2x - 10$
$= x^2 - 3x - 10$

Find each product.

5. $(x + 2)(x + 5)$

6. $(x - 7)(x + 2)$

7. $(3x - 8)(3x + 6)$

Factor Trinomials

EXAMPLE $x^2 + 7x - 18$
$= (x + \boxed{})(x + \boxed{})$
$= (x + 9)(x - 2)$

Factors of −18	Sum
−1 and 18	17 ✗
−2 and 9	7 ✓

Factor each polynomial completely.

8. $x^2 - 2x + 1$

9. $3x^2 - 22x + 7$

10. $x^2 - 7x - 18$

Reading Start-Up

Vocabulary

Review Words
- ✓ increasing function
  (*función de incremento*)
- ✓ perfect square
  (*cuadrado perfecto*)
- ✓ quadratic equation
  (*ecuación cuadrática*)
- ✓ square root
  (*raíz cuadrada*)
- ✓ system of equations
  (*sistema de ecuaciones*)

Preview Words
- discriminant
- completing the square
- properties of radicals
- quadratic formula

Visualize Vocabulary

Use the review words to complete the chart.

	a square of a whole number
	one of the two equal factors of a number
	a set of two or more equations that contain two or more variables
	an equation of the form $ax^2 + bx + c = 0$, where a is not 0
	a function where the y-value increases as the x-value increases

Understand Vocabulary

To become familiar with some of the vocabulary terms in the module, consider the following. You may refer to the module, the glossary, or a dictionary.

1. The _____ gives the solutions of a quadratic equation.

2. The _____ tells how many real solutions a quadratic equation will have.

3. _____ is a process that forms a perfect square trinomial.

Active Reading

Key-Term Fold Note Before beginning the module, create a key-term fold note to help you organize what you learn. Write a vocabulary term on each tab of the key-term fold. Under each tab, write the definition of the term.

Unpacking the Standards

Understanding the standards and the vocabulary terms in the standards will help you know exactly what you are expected to learn in this module.

 FL A-REI.2.4b

Solve quadratic equations by inspection, taking square roots, completing the square, the quadratic formula, and factoring, as appropriate, to the initial form of the equation.

Key Vocabulary

quadratic equation (ecuación cuadrática)

an equation of the form $ax^2 + bx + c = 0$, where $a \neq 0$

What It Means to You

You can solve quadratic equations by various methods. The best method to use depends upon the initial form of the equation.

UNPACKING EXAMPLE A-REI.2.4B

The equation $x^2 + x - 12 = 0$ can best be solved by factoring.

$$x^2 + x - 12 = 0$$
$$(x + 4)(x - 3) = 0$$
$$x + 4 = 0 \quad \text{or} \quad x - 3 = 0$$
$$x = -4 \quad \text{or} \quad x = 3$$

FL A-REI.3.7

Solve a simple system consisting of a linear equation and a quadratic equation in two variables, algebraically and graphically.

Key Vocabulary

system of equations (sistema de ecuaciones)

a set of two or more equations that contain two or more variables

What It Means to You

Given a linear equation and a quadratic equation, you can find 0, 1, or 2 ordered pairs that are solutions to both equations.

UNPACKING EXAMPLE A-REI.3.7

You can solve the system of equations algebraically.

$$y = x - 3 \text{ and } y = x^2 - 5x + 2$$

First, set the equations equal to each other and solve for x.

$$x - 3 = x^2 - 5x + 2$$
$$-3 = x^2 - 6x + 2$$
$$0 = x^2 - 6x + 5$$
$$0 = (x - 5)(x - 1)$$
$$x = 5 \text{ or } x = 1$$

Next, substitute the x values into one of the equations to find the y values.

$$y = 5 - 3 = 2 \text{ and } y = 1 - 3 = -2$$

So, the ordered pairs (5, 2) and (1, −2) are solutions of the system of equations.

Visit **my.hrw.com** to see all **Florida Math Standards** unpacked.

 my.hrw.com

LESSON 16.1 Solving Quadratic Equations Using Square Roots

FL A-REI.2.4b

Solve quadratic equations by inspection …, taking square roots … Recognize when the quadratic formula gives complex solutions… *Also* A-CED.1.1

? ESSENTIAL QUESTION

How can you solve quadratic equations using square roots?

EXPLORE ACTIVITY  **FL** A-REI.2.4b

Exploring Square Roots

A square root of a nonnegative number a is a real number b such that $b^2 = a$. For instance, 4 and -4 are square roots of 16 because $4^2 = 16$ and $(-4)^2 = 16$. Every positive real number a has two square roots: one positive, written $\sqrt{a}$, and one negative, written $-\sqrt{a}$.

The **Product Property of Radicals** states that for nonnegative a and b, $\sqrt{ab} = \sqrt{a} \cdot \sqrt{b}$.

> Read $\pm$ as "plus or minus."

$\pm\sqrt{45} = \pm\sqrt{9 \cdot 5}$ Rewrite 45 as a product using a perfect square.

$= \pm\sqrt{9} \cdot \sqrt{5}$ Use the product property.

$= \pm 3 \cdot \sqrt{5}$ The square root of 9 is 3.

The **Quotient Property of Radicals** states that for nonnegative a and positive b, $\sqrt{\frac{a}{b}} = \frac{\sqrt{a}}{\sqrt{b}}$.

$\pm\sqrt{0.07} = \pm\sqrt{\dfrac{7}{100}}$ Rewrite the decimal as a fraction.

$= \pm\dfrac{\sqrt{7}}{\sqrt{100}}$ Use the quotient property.

$= \pm\dfrac{\sqrt{7}}{10}$ The square root of 100 is 10.

Simplify each square root.

A $\pm\sqrt{16} = $ _____ or _____

B $\pm\sqrt{25} = $ _____ or _____

C   Use the Product Property of Radicals to evaluate:

$\pm\sqrt{12} = \pm\sqrt{(4 \cdot 3)} = \pm\sqrt{\boxed{}} \cdot \sqrt{3} = \pm 2 \cdot \sqrt{3}$

D   Use the Quotient Property of Radicals to evaluate: $\pm\sqrt{\dfrac{16}{4}} = \pm\dfrac{\sqrt{16}}{\sqrt{\boxed{}}} = \pm\dfrac{4}{\boxed{}} = \pm 2$

E   Use properties to evaluate:

$\pm\sqrt{0.27} = \pm\sqrt{\dfrac{\boxed{}}{100}} = \pm\dfrac{\sqrt{27}}{\sqrt{100}} = \pm\dfrac{\sqrt{\boxed{} \cdot \boxed{}}}{\boxed{}} = \bigcirc\dfrac{\sqrt{9} \cdot \sqrt{\boxed{}}}{10} = \pm\dfrac{3 \cdot \sqrt{\boxed{}}}{\boxed{}}$

EXPLORE ACTIVITY *(cont'd)*

REFLECT

1. **Analyze Relationships** Explain why $\sqrt{18}$ and $3\sqrt{2}$ are the same number.

   _____

   _____

2. **Communicate Mathematical Ideas** Explain why a must be non-negative when you find $\sqrt{a}$.

   _____

   _____

   _____

Math On the Spot

my.hrw.com

Solving a Quadratic Equation Using Square Roots

When solving an equation, you must perform the same operation on both sides in order to produce an equivalent equation; that is, to make sure it is still a true statement. The same property of equality applies for the operation of taking square roots.

EXAMPLE 1

FL   A-REI.2.4b

Solve $x^2 - 4 = 0$.

$$x^2 - 4 = 0$$
$$x^2 = 4 \qquad \text{Add 4 to both sides.}$$
$$x = \pm\sqrt{4} \qquad \text{Take the square root of both sides of the equation.}$$
$$x = \pm 2 \qquad \text{Simplify the square root.}$$

The solutions are 2 and -2.

Personal Math Trainer

Online Assessment and Intervention

my.hrw.com

YOUR TURN

Solve.

3. $x^2 - 9 = 0$

   _____

4. $x^2 - 64 = 0$

   _____

Special Cases

When solving quadratic equations that require more solution steps, the solutions may not be opposites, or the equations may not have real number solutions.

Math On the Spot
🔵 my.hrw.com

EXAMPLE 2

FL A-REI.2.4b

My Notes

A Solve $(x + 5)^2 = 36$ using square roots.

$$(x + 5)^2 = 36$$

$$x + 5 = \pm\sqrt{36}$$ Take the square root of both sides.

$$x + 5 = \pm 6$$ Simplify the square root.

$$x = \pm 6 - 5$$ Subtract 5 from both sides.

$$x = -6 - 5 \text{ or } x = 6 - 5$$ Solve for both cases.

$$x = -11 \qquad x = 1$$

The solutions are -11 and 1.

B Solve $2(x - 3)^2 = -32$.

$$2(x - 3)^2 = -32$$

$$(x - 3)^2 = -16$$ Divide both sides by 2.

Stop here. The square of a number is never negative, so this equation does not have real number solutions.

REFLECT

5. **What If?** How would the steps in part A change if 36 were replaced with 49?

_____

_____

_____

_____

YOUR TURN

Solve.

6. $(x - 2)^2 = 49$

7. $(x + 4)^2 = 81$

_____

_____

Personal Math Trainer

Online Assessment and Intervention

🔵 my.hrw.com

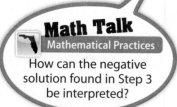

Math On the Spot

my.hrw.com

Solving Applied Equations

Real-world situations can sometimes be analyzed by solving a quadratic equation using square roots.

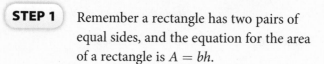

EXAMPLE 3 Real World

FL   A-CED.1.1, A-REI.2.4b

A contractor is building a fenced-in area at a daycare. The area will be rectangular with the length of its base equal to half the length of the height. The total area will be 5000 square feet. Determine the length of fencing the contractor will use.

STEP 1 Remember a rectangle has two pairs of equal sides, and the equation for the area of a rectangle is $A = bh$.

STEP 2 Substitute what you know into the equation and solve it.

$$5000 = \frac{1}{2}\, xx$$ Since we know that the base length is half the length of the height, we can substitute $\frac{1}{2}x$ for b and x for h. We can also substitute 5000 for A.

$$5000 = \frac{1}{2}\, x^2$$ Simplify.

$$10000 = x^2$$ Multiply by 2.

$$x = \pm 100$$ Take square roots of both sides.

STEP 3 Interpret the solution to the problem.

$x = 100$ and $x = -100$ are the solutions.

The answer must be positive, so we dismiss the negative result and obtain $x = 100$ feet of fence for the height.

Thus the length of fencing used will be $100 + 100 + 50 + 50 = 300$ feet.

Math Talk
Mathematical Practices

How can the negative solution found in Step 3 be interpreted?

Personal Math Trainer

Online Assessment and Intervention

my.hrw.com

YOUR TURN

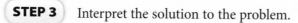

8. A rectangular picture has a height that is $\frac{1}{3}$ of the width. Find the width if the area of the picture is 300 cm². The formula for area of a rectangle is $A = bh$.

_____

Guided Practice

Simplify. (Explore Activity)

1. $\pm\sqrt{25}$ ____ 5, ☐

2. $\pm\sqrt{100}$ ____ ☐, −10

3. $\pm\sqrt{49}$ ____ ☐, ☐

4. $\pm\sqrt{63}$ ____

5. $\pm\sqrt{\frac{13}{25}}$ ____

6. $\pm\sqrt{\frac{36}{49}}$ ____

Solve each simple quadratic equation. (Example 1)

7. $2x^2 - 6 = 0$

$2x^2 = $ ☐

$x^2 = $ ☐

☐ = ☐

The solutions are ☐ and ☐ .

8. $y^2 = 81$

$y = $ ☐

$y = \pm 9$

The solutions are ☐ and ☐ .

Solve each quadratic equation. (Example 2)

9. $(x + 2)^2 = 64$

$x + 2 = $ ☐

$x + 2 = $ ☐ or $x + 2 = $ ☐

$x + 2 = 8$

$x = $ ☐

$x + 2 = -8$

$x = $ ☐

The two solutions for this equation are

☐ and ☐ .

10. $(x - 3)^2 = 49$

$x - 3 = \pm$ ☐

$x - 3 = $ ☐ or $x - 3 = $ ☐

$x - 3 = 7$

$x = $ ☐

$x - 3 = -7$

$x = $ ☐

The two solutions for this equation are

☐ and ☐ .

Solve each quadratic equation. (Example 2)

11. $(x + 4)^2 = 81$

$$x + 4 = \pm\sqrt{\boxed{}}$$

$$x + 4 = \boxed{} \quad \text{or } x + 4 = \boxed{}$$

$$x + 4 = 9 \qquad\qquad x + 4 = -9$$

$$x = \boxed{} \qquad\qquad x = \boxed{}$$

The two solutions for this equation are $\boxed{}$ and $\boxed{}$.

12. $4(x + 1)^2 = -100$

$$(x + 1)^2 = \boxed{}$$

There are _____ real number solutions for this equation.

13. A rectangular garden has a length that is $\frac{1}{4}$ of its width. Find the width of a garden if the area is 300 square meters. (Example 3)

Area of a rectangle $= \boxed{}$

$$300 = \frac{1}{4}w^2$$

$$w^2 = \boxed{}$$

$$w = \boxed{} \quad \text{or} \quad \boxed{}$$

The only reasonable solution for this problem is $\boxed{}$.

? ESSENTIAL QUESTION CHECK-IN

14. How can you solve quadratic equations using square roots?

_____

_____

_____

_____

_____

16.1 Independent Practice

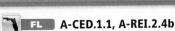 **FL** A-CED.1.1, A-REI.2.4b

Simplify.

15. $\pm\sqrt{144}$ _____

16. $\pm\sqrt{400}$ _____

17. $\pm\sqrt{4}$ _____

Choose either PP (Product Property) or QP (Quotient Property) to simplify. Then simplify.

18. $\pm\sqrt{32}$ _____

19. $\pm\sqrt{\dfrac{16}{25}}$ _____

20. $\pm\sqrt{75}$ _____

21. $\pm\sqrt{0.0025}$ _____

22. $\pm\sqrt{\dfrac{17}{169}}$ _____

23. $\pm\sqrt{54}$ _____

24. $\pm\sqrt{\dfrac{144}{36}}$ _____

25. $\pm\sqrt{48}$ _____

Solve the quadratic equations using square roots.

26. $x^2 - 25 = 0$ _____

27. $x^2 - 144 = 0$ _____

28. $x^2 - 400 = 0$ _____

29. $x^2 - 81 = 0$ _____

30. $x^2 - 100 = 0$ _____

Solve for x. Then check your answer.

31. $(x + 7)^2 = 49$

   a. Solve for x.

   _____

   b. Check your answer.

   _____

32. $(x - 3)^2 = 144$

   a. Solve for x.

   _____

   b. Check your answer.

   _____

   _____

33. $(x - 5)^2 = 81$

   a. Solve for x.

   _____

   b. Check your answer.

   _____

   _____

34. $(x + 3)^2 - 2 = 34$

   a. Solve for x.

   _____

   b. Check your answer.

   _____

   _____

35. A square field has an area of 100 square meters. What is the length of the square?

_____

36. A rectangular prism has a volume of 100 cm^3. The base of the prism is a square, and the height is the product of the length and width of the prism. Find the exact dimensions of the prism.

_____

_____

37. You have to decorate a cardboard sign with colored construction paper. The length of the sign is $\frac{1}{5}$ times the width of the sign, and the total area is 200 square centimeters.

   a. What is the width of the sign?

     _____

   b. What is the length of the sign?

     _____

38. **Explain the Error** Bob makes the following computation and gets stuck.

   $\sqrt{150} = \sqrt{10 \cdot 15} = \sqrt{10} \cdot \sqrt{15}$.

   a. What did Bob do wrong?

     _____

   b. How should he fix his error?

     _____

 FOCUS ON HIGHER ORDER THINKING

Work Area

39. **Draw Conclusions** The first floor of a house is 400 square feet. The width of the house is $\frac{1}{3}$ times the length of the house. What is the width of the house?

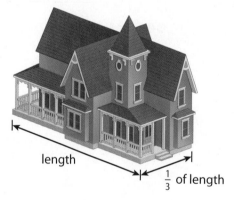

length

$\frac{1}{3}$ of length

     _____

     _____

40. **Explain** When solving the problem above, why didn't the student get a positive and a negative square root as answers?

     _____

     _____

41. **Communicate Mathematical Ideas** Write a quadratic equation with the solutions $+7$ and -7.

     _____

FL A-SSE.2.3a

Factor a quadratic expression to reveal the zeros of the function it defines. *Also A-CED.1.1, A-REI.2.4, A-REI.2.4b, A-SSE.2.3, F-IF.3.8, F-IF.3.8a*

LESSON 16.2 Solving $x^2 + bx + c = 0$ by Factoring

ESSENTIAL QUESTION

How can you use factoring to solve quadratic equations in standard form when $a = 1$?

EXPLORE ACTIVITY　　**FL** F-IF.3.8

Zero Product Property

For all real numbers a and b, the following is true.

Words	Sample Numbers	Algebra
If the product of two quantities equals zero, at least one of the quantities equals zero.	$5(0) = 0$ $(0)6 = 0$	If $ab = 0$, then $a = 0$ or $b = 0$.

Consider the equation $x^2 - 25 = 0$.

A Factor the left side as $\left(\boxed{} + \boxed{}\right)\left(\boxed{} - \boxed{}\right)$.

B Apply the Zero Product Property to $(x + 5)(x - 5) = 0$

$\boxed{} + \boxed{} = 0$　or　$\boxed{} - \boxed{} = 0$

$x = \boxed{}$　　or　　$x = \boxed{}$

The solutions of the equation $x^2 - 25 = 0$ are called the *zeros* of the related function $f(x) = x^2 - 25$ because they satisfy the equation $f(x) = 0$.

To see this, you can substitute 5 and -5 for x in $f(x) = x^2 - 25$.

The result is $f(5) = 0$ and $f(-5) = 0$.

REFLECT

1. **Analyze Relationships** Describe how to use the Zero Product Property to solve the equation $(x + 5)(x - 12) = 0$. Then identify the solutions.

_____

_____

_____

Applying the Zero Product Property to Functions

The Zero Product Property can help you solve for x when you are given a function.

My Notes

EXAMPLE 1

FL F-IF.3.8

Find the zeros of $f(x) = (x - 2)(x - 9)$.

STEP 1 Set $f(x)$ equal to zero.

$$(x - 2)(x - 9) = 0$$

STEP 2 Applying the Zero Product Property, either term can be equal to zero.

$$x - 2 = 0 \quad \text{or} \quad x - 9 = 0$$

STEP 3 Solve for x.

$$x = 2 \text{ or } x = 9$$

The zeros are 2 and 9.

REFLECT

2. Critique Reasoning Jodie was given the function $f(x) = (x - 1)(x + 2)$ and asked to find the zeros. The answer she provided was $x = -1$ and $x = 2$. Do you agree or disagree? Why?

_____

_____

3. What If? How would you find the zeros of the function $f(x) = -3(x + 5)$?

_____

_____

4. Communicate Mathematical Ideas Can you use the Zero Product Property to find the zeros of the function $f(x) = (1 + x) + (1 - 2x)$? Explain.

_____

Personal Math Trainer

Online Assessment and Intervention

my.hrw.com

YOUR TURN

5. Find the zeros of $f(x) = x(x + 8)$.

_____

Solving Quadratic Equations by Factoring

You can use the Zero Product Property to solve any quadratic equation written in standard form, $ax^2 + bx + c = 0$, provided the quadratic expression is factorable.

Math On the Spot
my.hrw.com

EXAMPLE 2
 FL F-IF.3.8

Solve $x^2 + 10x = -21$.

STEP 1 Write the equation in standard form.

$$x^2 + 10x + 21 = 0$$
Bring the constant term to the left hand side.

STEP 2 Find those factors of ac, whose sum equals b in the trinomial.

Factors of 21	Sum of Factors
1, 21	22
7, 3	10

Animated Math
my.hrw.com

STEP 3 Rewrite the equation by splitting the x-term according to the factors of the constant term, and simplify.

$$x^2 + 7x + 3x + 21 = 0$$
Split $10x$ into $7x$ and $3x$.

$$x(x + 7) + 3(x + 7) = 0$$
Factor out the common $(x + 7)$ from the first two and last two terms.

$$(x + 3)(x + 7) = 0$$
Use the Distributive Property.

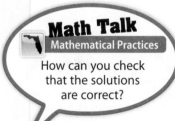
Math Talk
Mathematical Practices
How can you check that the solutions are correct?

STEP 4 Apply the Zero Product Property to find x.

$$x + 3 = 0 \text{ or } x + 7 = 0$$
Equate each factor with zero.

$$x = -3 \text{ or } x = -7$$

The solutions are -3 and -7.

YOUR TURN

Solve each equation.

6. $x^2 + 14x + 49 = 0$

7. $x^2 + 12x = -36$

Personal Math Trainer
Online Assessment and Intervention
my.hrw.com

Solving Applied Quadratic Equations

You can write quadratic equations for given situations and solve them by factoring.

EXAMPLE 3 Real World   **FL** **F-IF.3.8**

A golf ball is hit from a hill, and its height can be modeled by $h = -16t^2 + 32t + 48$, where h is height in feet and t is time in seconds. How long is the ball in the air?

STEP 1   Write the equation.
Substitute 0 for h for the height of the ball when it lands.

$h = -16t^2 + 32t + 48$
$0 = -16t^2 + 32t + 48$
$0 = t^2 - 2t - 3$ *Divide both sides by -16.*

STEP 2   Find those factors of ac, whose sum equals the b in the trinomial.

Factors of -3	Sum of Factors
$-3, 1$	-2
$3, -1$	2

STEP 3   Rewrite the equation by splitting the t-term according to the factors ac, and simplify.

$t^2 - 3t + t - 3 = 0$

$t(t - 3) + 1(t - 3) = 0$ *Factor $(t - 3)$ from the first two and last two terms.*

$(t + 1)(t - 3) = 0$ *Use the Distributive Property.*

STEP 4   Apply the Zero Product Property to find t.

$t + 1 = 0$ or $t - 3 = 0$ *Equate each factor with zero.*
$t = -1$ or $t = 3$

Since time cannot be a negative number, the ball is in the air for 3 seconds.

YOUR TURN

8.   Solve for t in the equation $h = -16t^2 + 32t + 128$.

_____

1. Find the zeros of the equation $x^2 - 49 = 0$. (Explore Activity)

    Factor the left side as $\boxed{}(x - 7) = 0$.

    Apply the Zero Product Property to $\boxed{} = 0$.

    $\boxed{} + \boxed{} = 0$ or $\boxed{} - \boxed{} = \boxed{}$

    $x = \boxed{}$ or $x = \boxed{}$

Find the zeros of each function. (Example 1)

2. $f(x) = (x + 1)(x - 1)$

    $-1, \boxed{}$

3. $f(x) = (x - 2)(x + 7)$

    $\boxed{}, -7$

4. $f(x) = (x + 3)(x - 6)$

    $\boxed{}, \boxed{}$

5. $\left(x + \frac{1}{2}\right)(x - 5) = 0$

    $\boxed{}, \boxed{}$

6. Solve $x^2 - 6x + 8 = 0$. (Example 2)

    $$x^2 - 6x + 8 = 0$$

    $$x^2 - 4x - 2x + 8 = 0$$

    $$x(x - \boxed{}) - \boxed{}(x - 4) = 0$$

    $$(x - 4)(x - \boxed{}) = 0$$

    $$x = \boxed{} \text{ or } \boxed{}$$

7. Solve $x^2 - 2x = 15$. (Example 2)

    $$x^2 - 2x = 15$$

    $$x^2 - 2x - 15 = \boxed{}$$

    $$x^2 - \boxed{}x + \boxed{}x - 15 = 0$$

    $$x(x - \boxed{}) + 3(x - \boxed{}) = 0$$

    $$(x - 5)(x + 3) = 0$$

    $$x = \boxed{} \text{ or } x = \boxed{}$$

8. The perimeter of a rectangle is 22 cm and its area is 24 square cm. What is the measure of its shorter side? (Example 3)

$$\text{Area} = l \times w = \boxed{}$$

$$l = \frac{24}{w}$$

$$\text{Perimeter} = 2l + 2w = 22$$

$$2\left(\frac{24}{w}\right) + 2\boxed{} = 22$$

$$\boxed{} + 2w^2 = 22w$$

$$w^2 - \boxed{}w + 24 = 0$$

$$\left(\boxed{} - \boxed{}\right)\left(\boxed{} - \boxed{}\right) = 0$$

$$w = \boxed{} \quad \text{or} \quad w = \boxed{}$$

The measure of the shorter side is $\boxed{}$ cm.

9. The height of an arrow after being shot directly upwards can be modeled by $h = -16t^2 + 128t$, where h is the height in feet and t is the time in seconds. Find the time it takes the arrow to fall to the ground. (Example 3)

$$h = -16t^2 + 128t$$

$$-16t^2 + 128t = 0$$

$$t^2 - \boxed{} = 0$$

$$\boxed{}\left(\boxed{} - \boxed{}\right) = 0$$

$$t = \boxed{} \quad \text{or} \quad t = \boxed{}$$

The time is $\boxed{}$ seconds.

? ESSENTIAL QUESTION CHECK-IN

10. How can you use factoring to solve quadratic equations in standard form when $a = 1$?

_____

_____

_____

_____

_____

16.2 Independent Practice

FL   A-CED.1.1, A-REI.2.4, A-REI.2.4b, A-SSE.2.3, A-SSE.2.3a, F-IF.3.8, F-IF.3.8a

Personal
Math Trainer

Online
Assessment and
Intervention

my.hrw.com

Find the zeros of each function.

11. $f(x) = (x - 4)(x + 2)$

_____

12. $f(x) = (x + 3)(x + 1)$

_____

13. $f(x) = (4x - 3)(2x - 1)$

_____

14. $f(x) = (x - a)(x - b)$

_____

Find the zeros of each function by first factoring the polynomial.

15. $f(y) = y^2 + 3y - 4$

_____

16. $f(p) = p^2 - 2p - 24$

_____

17. $f(z) = z^2 - 7z + 12$

_____

18. $f(q) = q^2 + 25q + 100$

_____

Solve each equation.

19. $x^2 + 7x = -10$

_____

20. $x^2 + 2x = 8$

_____

21. $x^2 + 2x + 1 = 0$

_____

22. $-2x^2 = 18 - 12x$

_____

23. Find three consecutive positive integers such that the product of the larger two is equal to twice the second integer plus twice the sum of all three integers.

_____

24. The height of a ball can be modeled by the function $h = -16t^2 + 16t + 32$, where h is the height in feet above the ground and t is the time in seconds. Find the time it takes the ball to reach the ground.

_____

25. The height of a flare can be approximated by the function $h = -t^2 + 5t + 6$, where h is the height in feet and t is the time in seconds. Find the time it takes the flare to hit the ground.

_____

26. The length of a rectangle is 1 ft less than 3 times the width. The area is 310 ft^2. Find the dimensions of the rectangle.

_____

27. The height of a fireworks rocket in meters can be approximated by $h = -5t^2 + 30t$, where h is the height in meters and t is time in seconds. Find the time it takes the rocket to reach the ground after it has been launched.

_____

28. A tee box is 64 feet above its fairway. When a golf ball is hit from the tee box with an initial vertical velocity of 48 ft/s, the following quadratic equation gives the time, t, in seconds when a golf ball is at height 0 feet on the fairway.
$0 = -16t^2 + 48t + 64$

a. Solve the quadratic equation by factoring to see how long the ball is in the air. _____

b. What is the height of the ball at 1.5 seconds? _____

c. Is the ball at its maximum height at 1.5 seconds? Explain.

_____

_____

29. Write an equation that could be used to find two consecutive even integers whose product is 24. Let x represent the first integer. Solve the equation and give the two integers.

_____

 **FOCUS ON HIGHER ORDER THINKING**

Work Area

30. Draw Conclusions A ball is thrown into the air from ground level. It follows an exact parabolic curve given by the equation $h = -2d^2 + 8d$, where h is the height, in meters, the ball reaches at distance d. At what distance from the point at which it is thrown will the ball reach its maximum height?

_____

_____

_____

31. Justify Reasoning Describe the relationships among the solutions of $x^2 - 4x - 12 = 0$, the zeros and x-intercepts of $y = x^2 - 4x - 12$, and the factors of $x^2 - 4x - 12$.

_____

_____

_____

32. Critique Reasoning Can you solve $(x - 2)(x + 3) = 5$ by solving $x - 2 = 5$ and $x + 3 = 5$? Why or why not?

_____

_____

_____

Solving $ax^2 + bx + c = 0$ by Factoring

FL   F-IF.3.8a

Use ... factoring ... a quadratic
function to show zeros ...
and interpret these in terms
of a context. *Also A-CED.1.1,
A-REI.2.4, A-REI.2.4b, A-SSE.2.3,
F-IF.3.8*

ESSENTIAL QUESTION

How can the quadratic equation $ax^2 + bx + c = 0$ be solved?

EXPLORE ACTIVITY  FL   F-IF.3.8a

Factoring $ax^2 + bx + c$

To multiply two binomials, add the products of the first terms, outside terms, inside terms, and last terms (FOIL).

As an example, $(3x + 1)(4x + 2) = (3x)(4x) + (3x)(2) + (1)(4x) + (1)(2) = 12x^2 + 10x + 2$. Notice that the 12 comes from multiplying the x coefficients, and the 2 comes from multiplying the constant terms.

So, to factor $ax^2 + bx + c$, find the factors of a and the factors of c, and check which pair gives the right value of b.

Factor $6x^2 + 13x + 5$.

A First, find the factors of 6: 6×1, ____ × ____

B Then, find the factors of 5: ____ × ____

C Combine these and FOIL:

$$(6x + \underline{\quad})(x + \underline{\quad}) = \underline{\quad}x^2 + \underline{\quad}x + \underline{\quad}$$

$$(6x + \underline{\quad})(x + \underline{\quad}) = \underline{\quad}x^2 + \underline{\quad}x + \underline{\quad}$$

$$(\underline{\quad}x + \underline{\quad})(\underline{\quad}x + \underline{\quad}) = \underline{\quad}x^2 + \underline{\quad}x + \underline{\quad}$$

$$(\underline{\quad}x + \underline{\quad})(\underline{\quad}x + \underline{\quad}) = \underline{\quad}x^2 + \underline{\quad}x + \underline{\quad}$$

D Determine the correct combination:

$$6x^2 + 13x + 5 = (\underline{\quad}x + \underline{\quad})\ (\underline{\quad}x + \underline{\quad})$$

REFLECT

1. Explain how this method works when factoring $x^2 + bx + c$.

_____

_____

Factoring and Using the Zero Product Property to Solve Quadratic Equations

Factoring can be used to solve quadratic equations. The Zero Product Property says that if $ab = 0$, then either $a = 0$ or $b = 0$. If the product of two factors is equal to zero, then one of the factors must be equal to zero.

My Notes

EXAMPLE 1   FL   A-REI.2.4

Solve the quadratic equation $3x^2 + 4x = x + 6$ by factoring.

STEP 1   Move everything to the left side of the equation to get 0 on the right side.

$$3x^2 + 4x - x - 6 = 0$$

STEP 2 $3x^2 + 3x - 6 = 0$ Combine like terms.

STEP 3 $(3x + 6)(x - 1) = 0$ Factor.

STEP 4 $3x + 6 = 0$ or $x - 1 = 0$ Use the Zero Product Property.

STEP 5 $x = -2$ or $x = 1$ Solve each equation.

REFLECT

2. What if the right-hand side was not zero before factoring?

_____

_____

_____

3. Communicate Mathematical Ideas Why is it necessary to rewrite the equation so that one side equals 0 before factoring?

_____

_____

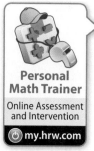

Personal Math Trainer

Online Assessment and Intervention

my.hrw.com

YOUR TURN

Solve each quadratic equation by factoring.

4. $14x^2 + 3x = 2x + 3$

_____

5. $8x^2 + 3 = 8x + 9$

_____

Special Cases

Factoring can be made easier by first taking out a common factor from every term, if there is one. Additionally, when possible, apply the factoring patterns.

Math On the Spot
my.hrw.com

Factoring Patterns

$(a-b)(a+b) = a^2 - b^2$	$(a+b)^2 = a^2 + 2ab + b^2$	$(a-b)^2 = a^2 - 2ab + b^2$

EXAMPLE 2

FL   A-REI.2.4, F-IF.3.8a

Solve each equation by factoring.

A
$$4x^2 + 4x - 8 = 0$$
$$4(x^2 + x - 2) = 0 \qquad \text{Take out a common factor.}$$
$$4(x + 2)(x - 1) = 0 \qquad \text{Factor inside parentheses.}$$
$$x = -2, 1 \qquad \text{Solve using Zero Product Property.}$$

B
$$9x^2 - 36 = 0$$
$$(3x - 6)(3x + 6) = 0 \qquad \text{Factor the difference of squares.}$$
$$x = 2, -2 \qquad \text{Solve using Zero Product Property.}$$

C
$$3x^2 + 6x + 3 = 0$$
$$3(x^2 + 2x + 1) = 0 \qquad \text{Take out a common factor.}$$
$$3(x + 1)^2 = 0 \qquad \text{Factor inside parentheses.}$$
$$x = -1 \qquad \text{Solve using Zero Product Property.}$$

REFLECT

6. Explain Describe another approach to solving the equation in part B.

_____

_____

_____

YOUR TURN

Solve each equation by factoring.

7. $5x^2 - 20 = 0$

8. $2x^2 - 8x + 8 = 0$

Personal Math Trainer

Online Assessment and Intervention

my.hrw.com

Solving Real-World Problems

Real-world situations can sometimes be modeled by quadratic equations.

EXAMPLE 3

FL   A-CED.1.1, A-REI.2.4, F-IF.3.8a

When a baseball player hits a pitch into the air, the height of the ball at time t is modeled by $h(t) = -16t^2 + v_0 t + h_0$, where v_0 is the initial upward velocity of the ball, and h_0 is the height at which the ball is hit. If a ball is 3 feet off the ground when it is hit with an initial velocity of 47 feet per second, how long will it be until the ball hits the ground?

STEP 1   Use the given information to write the equation.

$$-16t^2 + 47t + 3 = 0$$ *The ball hits the ground when the height is 0. This can be found by solving the equation.*

$$(16t + 1)(-t + 3) = 0$$ *Factor.*

STEP 2   Solve the equation, and interpret the solution to the problem.

The solutions are $t = -\frac{1}{16}$ and $t = 3$.

The answer should be positive, so $t = 3$ seconds.

Math Talk

Mathematical Practices

Why must the negative solution found in step 2 be disregarded?

REFLECT

9. **Communicate Mathematical Ideas** How is solving for the number of seconds it takes for the ball to hit the ground related to finding the zeros of a quadratic function?

_____

_____

_____

YOUR TURN

10. The profit earned by an electronics company for selling printers is modeled by the function $P(x) = -3x^2 + 33x - 72$, where x is the number of printers in hundreds, and P is measured in thousands of dollars. What two numbers of printers sold will result in zero profit?

_____

Solve each quadratic equation by factoring. (Example 1)

1. $7x^2 + 35x = 5x - 8$

$7x^2 + \boxed{}x + \boxed{} = 0$

$(7x + \boxed{})(x + \boxed{}) = 0$

$x = \boxed{}, \boxed{}$

2. $6x^2 - 10x + 5 = 3x$

$6x^2 - \boxed{}x + 5 = 0$

$(\boxed{}x - 5)(\boxed{}x - 1) = 0$

$x = \boxed{}, \boxed{}$

Solve each equation by factoring. (Example 2)

3. $4x^2 + 16x + 12 = 0$

$\boxed{}(x^2 + 4x + 3) = 0$

$\boxed{}(x + \boxed{})(x + \boxed{}) = 0$

$x = \boxed{}, \boxed{}$

4. $18x^2 - 18 = 0$

$\boxed{}(x^2 - 1) = 0$

$\boxed{}(x + \boxed{})(x - \boxed{}) = 0$

$x = \boxed{}, \boxed{}$

5. $11x^2 + 44x + 44 = 0$

$\boxed{}(x^2 + 4x + 4) = 0$

$\boxed{}(x + \boxed{})^2 = 0$

$x = \boxed{}$

6. $3x^2 - 30x + 75 = 0$

$\boxed{}(x^2 - 10x + 25) = 0$

$\boxed{}(x - \boxed{})^2 = 0$

$x = \boxed{}$

7. $12x^2 - 108 = 0$

$12(x^2 - \boxed{}) = 0$

$12(x + \boxed{})(x \boxed{} 3) = 0$

$x = \boxed{}, \boxed{}$

8. $5x^2 - 30x + 45 = 0$

$5(x^2 - \boxed{}x + \boxed{}) = 0$

$5(x - \boxed{})(x \boxed{} 3) = 0$

$x = \boxed{}$

9. $7x^2 = 70x - 175$

$7x^2 - 70x + \boxed{} = 0$

$7(x^2 - \boxed{}x + \boxed{}) = 0$

$7(x - \boxed{})(x \boxed{} 5) = 0$

$x = \boxed{}$

10. $2x^2 + 128 = -32x$

$2x^2 + 32x + 128 = 0$

$2(x^2 + \boxed{}x + \boxed{}) = 0$

$2(x + \boxed{})(x \boxed{} 8) = 0$

$x = \boxed{}$

11. The altitude of a model rocket launched into the air from a rooftop is given by the quadratic equation $A(t) = -16t^2 + 64t + 80$, where t is the time in seconds since launch, and A is measured in feet. At what time does the rocket land on the ground? (Example 3)

$$-16t^2 + 64t + 80 = 0$$

$$\boxed{}(t^2 - \boxed{}t - \boxed{}) = 0$$

$$\boxed{}(t + \boxed{})(t - \boxed{}) = 0$$

$$t = \boxed{}, \boxed{}$$

The rocket lands on the ground in _____ seconds.

12. A missile is fired with an initial upward velocity of 2320 feet per second. The height can be modeled by $h = -16t^2 + 2320t$, where h is the height in feet above the ground and t is the time in seconds. Find the time it takes the missile to reach a height of 40,000 feet. (Example 3)

$$-16t^2 + 2320t = 40{,}000$$

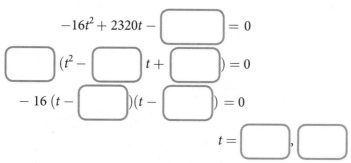

$$-16t^2 + 2320t - \boxed{} = 0$$

$$\boxed{}(t^2 - \boxed{}t + \boxed{}) = 0$$

$$-16(t - \boxed{})(t - \boxed{}) = 0$$

$$t = \boxed{}, \boxed{}$$

The missile will have a height of 40,000 feet at _____ seconds and

at _____ seconds.

13. What extra step is involved in factoring $ax^2 + bx + c = 0$ when a is not equal to 1?

_____

_____

_____

_____

16.3 Independent Practice

FL A-CED.1.1, A-REI.2.4, A-REI.2.4b, A-SSE.2.3, F-IF.3.8, F-IF.3.8a

Personal Math Trainer

Online Assessment and Intervention

my.hrw.com

Solve each quadratic equation by factoring.

14. $5x^2 - 10x = 9x + 4$

_____

15. $6x^2 - 8x = 2x - 4$

_____

16. $7x^2 - 1 = -50x - 8$

_____

17. $8x^2 - 4x = 2x + 9$

_____

Solve each equation by factoring.

18. $3x^2 - 48 = 0$

_____

19. $4x^2 = 16x$

_____

20. $2x^2 - 10x = -38x - 98$

_____

21. $9x^2 - 25x - 6 = 0$

_____

22. $11x^2 = 99$

_____

23. $25x^2 - 150x = -225$

_____

24. A ball is bounced off of the ground at time $t = 0$, and its height afterward is given (in cm) by the formula $h(t) = -490t^2 + 1470t$, where t is measured in seconds.

a. Write an equation to find when the height of the ball is 9.8 m (980 cm).

_____

b. Solve the equation by factoring.

_____

c. Explain why there are two solutions to this problem.

_____

_____

_____

25. As a satellite falls from outer space onto Mars, its distance in miles from the planet is approximated by the formula $D(t) = -4t^2 + 776$, where t is the number of minutes it has fallen.

a. Write an equation to find when the satellite will be 200 miles away from Mars.

_____

b. Solve the equation by factoring.

_____

c. Explain why only one of these solutions makes sense for this problem.

_____

_____

_____

26. A volleyball player sets the ball in the air, and the height of the ball after t seconds is given in feet by $h(t) = -16t^2 + 24t + 4$. A teammate wants to wait until the ball is 9 feet in the air before she spikes it.

a. Write an equation to find when the teammate should spike the ball.

_____

b. Solve the equation by factoring.

_____

c. Explain the meaning of each possible solution to this problem.

_____

_____

Work Area

27. Draw Conclusions The equation for the height of the volleyball in practice problem 26 was $h(t) = -16t^2 + 24t + 4$. After 2 seconds, this equation gives a height of -12 feet. How can this negative number be interpreted?

_____

_____

_____

28. Explain the Error In an attempt to solve the equation $3x^2 + 9x - 84 = 0$, a student factors to get $3(x + 7)(x - 4) = 0$. The student then reasons that, since there are three factors, by the Zero Product Property, there will be three solutions, one for each factor. Explain the error in the student's reasoning.

_____

29. Justify Reasoning What can be said about the factors of $ax^2 + bx + c$, if a and c are positive numbers and b is negative? Justify your answer.

_____

_____

30. Explain the Error To solve the equation $4x^2 = 4x$, a student first divides both sides by $4x$, and then claims the only solution is $x = 1$. Explain the mistake that the student made; what solution did he or she leave out?

_____

_____

Solving $x^2 + bx + c = 0$ by Completing the Square

FL   A-REI.2.4a

Use the method of completing the square to transform any quadratic equation in x into an equation of the form $(x - p)^2 = q$ that has the same solutions. Derive the quadratic formula from this form. *Also A-REI.2.4, A-REI.2.4b, A-SSE.1.1b, A-SSE.2.3b, F-IF.3.8, F-IF.3.8a*

ESSENTIAL QUESTION

How can you solve $x^2 + bx + c = 0$ without factoring?

EXPLORE ACTIVITY   FL   A-REI.2.4a

Visualizing Completing the Square

The diagram below represents the expression $x^2 + 6x + c$ with the constant term missing.

A Complete the diagram by filling the bottom-right corner with 1-tiles to form a square.

B How many 1-tiles did you add to the expression? _____

C Write the trinomial represented by the algebra tiles for the complete square.

$$x^2 + \boxed{}x + \boxed{}$$

D You should recognize this trinomial as an example of the special case $(a + b)^2 = a^2 + 2ab + b^2$. Recall that trinomials of this form are called perfect-square trinomials. Since the trinomial is a perfect square, you can factor it into two binomials that are the same.

$$x^2 + \boxed{}x + \boxed{} = (\boxed{} + \boxed{})^2$$

REFLECT

1. Look at the algebra tiles above. The x-tiles are divided equally, with three tiles on the right side and three tiles on the bottom side of the x^2-tile. How does the number 3 relate to the total number of x-tiles? How does the number 3 relate to the number of 1-tiles?

_____

2. **Communicate Mathematical Ideas** Suppose you want to complete the square for the expression $x^2 - 10x + c$. What would be the sign of the x-tiles? How many 1-tiles would you have?

_____

Completing the Square

Finding the value of c needed to make an expression such as $x^2 + 6x + c$ into a perfect square trinomial is called **completing the square**.

To complete the square for the expression $x^2 + bx + c$, replace c with $\left(\frac{b}{2}\right)^2$. The perfect-square trinomial is $x^2 + bx + \left(\frac{b}{2}\right)^2$, and it factors as $\left(x + \frac{b}{2}\right)^2$.

Using algebra tiles, half of the x-tiles are placed along the right side and half along the bottom side of the x-tile. The number of 1-tiles added is the square of the number of x-tiles on either side of the x^2-tile.

EXAMPLE 1

 **FL   A-REI.2.4**

Complete the square to form a perfect-square trinomial. Then factor the trinomial.

A $x^2 + 12x + c$

$b = 12$	Identify b.
$c = \left(\frac{b}{2}\right)^2 = \left(\frac{12}{2}\right)^2 = 36$	Find c.
$x^2 + 12x + 36$	Write the trinomial.
$(x + 6)^2$	Factor the trinomial.

B $z^2 - 26z + c$

$b = -26$	Identify b.
$c = \left(\frac{b}{2}\right)^2 = \left(\frac{-26}{2}\right)^2 = 169$	Find c.
$z^2 - 26z + 169$	Write the trinomial.
$(z - 13)^2$	Factor the trinomial.

REFLECT

3. Communicate Mathematical Ideas In part A, b is positive, and in part B, b is negative. Does this affect the sign of c? Why or why not?

_____

_____

_____

YOUR TURN

4. Complete the square for the expression $x^2 + 4x + c$, then factor the trinomial.

_____

Steps for Solving Quadratic Equations by Completing the Square

EXAMPLE 2   FL   A-REI.2.4a

Math On the Spot

⊙ my.hrw.com

Solve $x^2 + 14x = 15$.

$$x^2 + 14x = 15$$

$$\left(\frac{14}{2}\right)^2 = 7^2 = 49 \qquad \text{Find } \left(\frac{b}{2}\right)^2.$$

$$x^2 + 14x + 49 = 15 + 49 \qquad \text{Complete the square.}$$

$$(x + 7)^2 = 64 \qquad \text{Factor and simplify.}$$

$$x + 7 = \pm 8 \qquad \text{Take square root of both sides.}$$

$$x + 7 = 8 \text{ or } x + 7 = -8 \qquad \text{Write and solve two equations.}$$

$$x = 1 \text{ or } x = -15$$

> $(x + 7)(x + 7) =$ $(x + 7)^2$. So the square root of $(x + 7)^2$ is $x + 7$.

Check

$x^2 + 14x =$	15
$(1)^2 + 14(1)$	15
$1 + 14$	15
15	15

$x^2 + 14x =$	15
$(-15)^2 + 14(-15)$	15
$225 - 210$	15
15	15

REFLECT

5. **Communicate Mathematical Ideas**

   a. What method would you use to solve the equation $x^2 + 3x - 4 = 0$? Explain why you would use this method.

   _____

   _____

   _____

   b. What would you add to each side of the equation to complete the square?

   _____

YOUR TURN

6. Solve $x^2 - 2x - 1 = 0$.

   _____

Personal Math Trainer

Online Assessment and Intervention

⊙ my.hrw.com

Math On the Spot

my.hrw.com

Solving Applied Equations

EXAMPLE 3

FL   A-REI.2.4a

Jenny's rectangular garden has an area of 2816 square feet. The length of the garden is 20 feet longer than the width. Using the formula for the area of a rectangle, find the dimensions of her garden.

STEP 1   The **solution** will be the length and width of the garden.

List the important information:

- The total area of the garden is 2816 square feet.
- One side of the garden is 20 feet longer than the other side.

STEP 2   Set the formula for the area of a rectangle equal to 2816, the area of the garden. Solve the equation.

STEP 3   Let x be the width and $x + 20$ be the length.

Use the formula for area of a rectangle (length · width = area) and substitute values.

$$(x + 20) \cdot (x) = 2816 \qquad \text{Write the area equation.}$$

$$x^2 + 20x = 2816 \qquad \text{Simplify.}$$

$$\left(\frac{20}{2}\right)^2 = 10^2 = 100 \qquad \text{Find } \left(\frac{b}{2}\right)^2.$$

$$x^2 + 20x + 100 = 2816 + 100 \qquad \text{Add 100 to both sides.}$$

$$(x + 10)^2 = 2916 \qquad \text{Factor the perfect-square trinomial.}$$

$$x + 10 = \pm 54 \qquad \text{Take the square root of both sides.}$$

$$x + 10 = 54 \text{ or } x + 10 = -54 \qquad \text{Write and solve two equations.}$$

$$x = 44 \text{ or } x = -64$$

Math Talk
Mathematical Practices

Why is 100 added to each side of the equation $x^2 + 20x = 2{,}816$?

Since the width cannot be negative, the answer -64 can be discarded.

Therefore, the width is 44 feet, and the length is $44 + 20$, or 64 feet.

The length of the garden is 20 feet greater than the width. This checks because $44(64) = 2816$.

My Notes

REFLECT

7. What If? Suppose the area of Jenny's garden is 3500 square feet and the length is still 20 feet longer than the width. What would the dimensions of the garden be?

_____

_____

8. Critical Thinking Suppose you want to double the area of Jenny's garden by increasing the length and width by the same amount. What would the approximate new dimensions of the garden be?

_____

_____

9. Communicate Mathematical Ideas Can you solve the equation in step 3 by factoring? If so, show the steps.

_____

_____

_____

YOUR TURN

10. A landscaper is designing a rectangular brick patio. She has enough bricks to cover 144 square feet. She wants the length of the patio to be 10 feet greater than the width. What dimensions should she use for the patio?

_____

**Personal
Math Trainer**

Online Assessment
and Intervention

⏻ my.hrw.com

Guided Practice

Complete the square to form a perfect-square trinomial. (Example 1)

1. $x^2 + 14x + \boxed{}$

2. $x^2 - 4x + \boxed{}$

3. $x^2 - 3x + \boxed{}$

4. $x^2 + 12x + \boxed{}$

5. $x^2 - 14x + \boxed{}$

6. $x^2 + 18x + \boxed{}$

Solve each equation by completing the square. (Example 2)

7. $x^2 + 6x = -5$

$x^2 + 6x + \boxed{} = -5 + \boxed{}$

$(x + \boxed{})^2 = \boxed{}$

$x + \boxed{} = \pm \boxed{}$

$x = \boxed{}, \boxed{}$

8. $x^2 - 8x = 9$

$x^2 - 8x + \boxed{} = 9 + \boxed{}$

$(x - \boxed{})^2 = \boxed{}$

$x - \boxed{} = \pm \boxed{}$

$x = \boxed{}, \boxed{}$

9. $r^2 - 4r = 165$

$r^2 - 4r + \boxed{} = 165 + \boxed{}$

$(r - \boxed{})^2 = \boxed{}$

$r - \boxed{} = \pm \boxed{}$

$r = \boxed{}, \boxed{}$

10. $t^2 + 2t = 224$

$t^2 + 2t + \boxed{} = 224 + \boxed{}$

$(t + \boxed{})^2 = \boxed{}$

$t + \boxed{} = \pm \boxed{}$

$t = \boxed{}, \boxed{}$

11. $x^2 + 6x = 27$

_____

12. $x^2 + 4x = 6$

_____

13. Multi-Step The length of a rectangle is 4 meters longer than the width. The area of the rectangle is 80 square meters. Find the length and width. Round your answers to the nearest tenth of a meter. (Example 3)

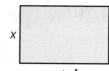

x

$x + 4$

_____

? ESSENTIAL QUESTION CHECK-IN

14. Consider solving an equation in the form $x^2 + bx = c$ by the completing the square. Typically, the first step is to find the value of $\left(\frac{b}{2}\right)^2$ and add it to both sides of the equation. How might your strategy differ when solving an equation such as $3x^2 - 24x = 27$?

_____

_____

_____

16.4 Independent Practice

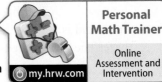

FL A-REI.2.4, A-REI.2.4a, A-REI.2.4b, A-SSE.1.1b, A-SSE.2.3b, F-IF.3.8, F-IF.3.8a

Complete the square to form a perfect-square trinomial.

15. $w^2 - 11w +$ _____

16. $c^2 - 14c +$ _____

Solve by completing the square.

17. $x^2 + 4x = 12$

_____

18. $x^2 + 6x = 16$

_____

19. $x^2 + 12x = -11$

_____

20. $x^2 - 12x = -26$

_____

21. $-x^2 + 4x + 12 = 0$

_____

22. $x^2 + 4x + 6 = 0$

_____

23. $4x^2 = 16x - 12$

_____

24.

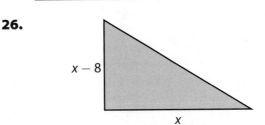

The length of Bill's backyard swimming pool is 60 feet longer than the width of the pool. The surface area of the water is 1600 square feet. What is the width and length of the pool?

_____

25. The height in feet, h, of a water-bottle rocket launched from a rooftop is given by the equation $h = -16t^2 + 320t + 32$, where t is the time in seconds. After the rocket is fired, how long will it take to return to the ground? Solve by completing the square. Round your answer to the nearest tenth of a second.

_____

26.

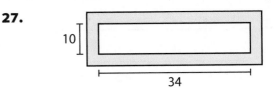

The height of a right triangle is 8 inches less than the length of its base. The area of the triangle is 90 square inches. What is the height and base of the triangle?

_____

_____

27.

10

34

Workmen created a roped-off border of width x around a 34-by-10-foot rectangular museum display to house Egyptian artifacts, as shown. The combined area of the display and the roped-off area is 640 square feet.

a. Write an equation for the combined area.

_____

b. Find the width of the roped-off area.

_____

28. The larger base of a trapezoid is three times as long as the shorter base, and the height of the trapezoid is 2 inches longer than the shorter base. The area of the trapezoid is 70 square inches. What is the length of the short base, x?

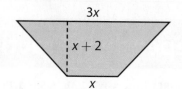

Work Area

29. Explain the Error While attempting to solve the equation $x^2 + 4x = 77$, the student made an error. Explain the mistake, and provide the correct answer(s).

$$x^2 + 4x = 77$$
$$x^2 + 4x + 4 = 77 + 4$$
$$(x + 2)^2 = 81$$
$$x + 2 = 9$$
$$x = 7$$

30. Communicate Mathematical Ideas Consider the right triangle shown at right. If the area is 96 square centimeters, briefly describe two separate methods you might use to find the length of the shorter leg, x.

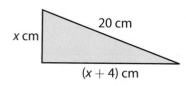

31. Justify Reasoning Using the method of completing the square, Sal is working to find the solution of the equation $x^2 + 6x = -10$. If his work is accurate, will he produce an answer that is a *real* number? Explain your reasoning.

Solving $ax^2 + bx + c = 0$ by Completing the Square

FL A-REI.2.4a

Use the method of completing the square to transform any quadratic equation in x into an equation of the form $(x - p)^2 = q$ that has the same solutions. Derive the quadratic equation from this form. *Also* *A-REI.2.4, A-REI.2.4b, A-SSE.1.1b*

ESSENTIAL QUESTION

How can you solve $ax^2 + bx + c = 0$ by completing the square when $a \neq 1$?

EXPLORE ACTIVITY  FL A-REI.2.4

Exploring Completing the Square when $a \neq 1$

Recall that quadratic expressions can be modeled using algebra tiles representing variable expressions and units. Visualizing a square with algebra tiles can help you understand what is really meant by completing the square. Use the diagram to answer A and B below.

A What is the expression represented by the tiles in the

diagram? _____

Complete the square by filling in the bottom-right corner with 1-tiles. How many 1-tiles did you add to the

diagram? _____

B Write the trinomial represented by the algebra tiles, including the completed square.

$$\boxed{} x^2 + \boxed{} x + \boxed{}$$

A perfect-square trinomial is the square of a binomial. The binomial is represented by one "side" of the algebra tile square. Use the algebra tiles to write the trinomial as the square of a binomial.

$$\boxed{} x^2 + \boxed{} x + \boxed{} = (\boxed{} x + \boxed{})^2$$

REFLECT

1. **Analyze Relationships** The coefficient of x^2 in the trinomial is 4. What is it about the number 4 that makes it possible to arrange the x^2-tiles in such a way that you can complete the square?

_____

_____

_____

_____

Math On the Spot

my.hrw.com

Completing the Square When *a* Is a Perfect Square

When *a* is a perfect square, completing the square is simpler than in other cases. Consider the case involving the algebra tiles in the Explore Activity: The number of 1-tiles needed to complete the square is equal to the square of *b* divided by four times *a*, or $\frac{b^2}{4a}$. This relationship is always the case when *a* is a perfect square.

EXAMPLE 1

 FL   A-REI.2.4a

Solve $4x^2 + 8x = 21$ by completing the square.

STEP 1   Add $\frac{b^2}{4a}$ to both sides of the equation.

$$4x^2 + 8x = 21$$
$$4x^2 + 8x + \frac{8^2}{4 \cdot 4} = 21 + \frac{8^2}{4 \cdot 4}$$
$$4x^2 + 8x + 4 = 21 + 4 = 25$$

STEP 2   Factor the left side of the equation as a perfect-square trinomial.

$$(2x + 2)^2 = 25$$

STEP 3   Apply the definition of a square root. Write two equations, and solve each equation to find the two solutions.

$$2x + 2 = \pm 5 \qquad \text{Take the square root of both sides of the equation.}$$
$$2x + 2 = 5 \text{ or } 2x + 2 = -5 \qquad \text{Rewrite as two equations.}$$
$$2x = 3 \text{ or } 2x = -7 \qquad \text{Solve for x.}$$
$$x = \frac{3}{2} \text{ or } x = -\frac{7}{2}$$

REFLECT

2. Why does *a* have to be a perfect square for this procedure to work?

_____

_____

_____

_____

My Notes

Personal
Math Trainer

Online Assessment
and Intervention

my.hrw.com

YOUR TURN

3. Solve $36x^2 + 36x = 7$ by completing the square.

_____

Completing the Square When *a* Is Not a Perfect Square

When the leading coefficient *a* is not a perfect square, you can transform the equation by multiplying both sides by a value such that *a* becomes a perfect square. Once *a* is a perfect square, proceed as in previous examples.

Math On the Spot
⏻ my.hrw.com

EXAMPLE 2

FL   A-REI.2.4a

Solve $2x^2 - 6x = 5$ by completing the square.

STEP 1   Since the coefficient of x^2 is 2, which is not a perfect square, multiply both sides by a value so the coefficient will be a perfect square, such as 2.

$$2(2x^2 - 6x) = 2(5)$$
$$4x^2 - 12x = 10$$

STEP 2   Add $\frac{b^2}{4a}$ to both sides of the equation. In this case, $\frac{b^2}{4a} = \frac{-12^2}{4 \cdot 4} = \frac{144}{16} = 9$.

$$4x^2 - 12x + 9 = 10 + 9 = 19$$

STEP 3   Factor the left side of the equation as a perfect-square trinomial.

$$(2x - 3)^2 = 19$$

STEP 4   Apply the definition of a square root. Write two equations, and solve each equation to find the two solutions:

$$2x - 3 = \pm\sqrt{19}$$ Take the square root of both sides.

$$2x - 3 = \sqrt{19} \text{ or } 2x - 3 = -\sqrt{19}$$ Rewrite as two equations.

$$2x = 3 + \sqrt{19} \text{ or } 2x = 3 - \sqrt{19}$$ Solve for x.

$$x = \frac{3 + \sqrt{19}}{2} \text{ or } x = \frac{3 - \sqrt{19}}{2}$$

> **Math Talk**
> Mathematical Practices
>
> Why is 2 the best value by which to multiply both sides of the equation before completing the square?

REFLECT

4. **Make a Conjecture** Would you get the same result for Example 2 if you divide each side by 2 in Step 1 and then complete the square? Explain.

_____

_____

YOUR TURN

5. Solve $3x^2 + 4x = 9$ by completing the square.

_____

Personal Math Trainer

Online Assessment and Intervention

⏻ my.hrw.com

Modeling Real-World Problems

Many real-world phenomena can be modeled using quadratic equations, and solving them by completing the square can be an effective way to answer questions about these situations.

EXAMPLE 3 FL A-REI.2.4a

My Notes

The height, h, of a baseball thrown into the air from a starting height of 5 feet with an initial velocity of 64 feet per second can be modeled using the equation $h = -16t^2 + 64t + 5$, where t represents time in seconds. How long will the ball remain in the air?

STEP 1 Set the equation equal to 0, and subtract the constant term from both sides so the equation will be in $ax^2 + bx = c$ format.

$$-16t^2 + 64t + 5 = 0$$

$$-16t^2 + 64t = -5$$

STEP 2 To complete the square, a must be positive (since the square root of a it will be a real number). To make a positive, multiply all three terms by -1.

$$16t^2 - 64t = 5$$

STEP 3 Add $\frac{b^2}{4a}$ to both sides of the equation. In this case, $\frac{b^2}{4a} = \frac{(-64)^2}{4 \cdot 16} = 64$.

$$16t^2 - 64t + 64 = 5 + 64 = 69$$

STEP 4 Factor the left side of the equation as a perfect-square trinomial.

$$(4t - 8)^2 = 69$$

STEP 5 Apply the definition of a square root. Write two equations, and solve each equation to find the two solutions:

$$4t - 8 = \pm\sqrt{69}$$ *Take the square root of both sides.*

$$4t - 8 = \sqrt{69} \text{ or } 4t - 8 = -\sqrt{69}$$ *Rewrite as two equations.*

$$4t = 8 + \sqrt{69} \text{ or } 4t = 8 - \sqrt{69}$$ *Solve for t.*

$$t = \frac{8 + \sqrt{69}}{4} \text{ or } t = \frac{8 - \sqrt{69}}{4}$$

As decimal approximations, $t = 4.077$ or -0.077. The negative solution can be discarded. The ball will remain in the air approximately 4.077 seconds.

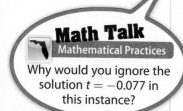

Math Talk

Mathematical Practices

Why would you ignore the solution $t = -0.077$ in this instance?

YOUR TURN

6. A baseball is thrown down from a 30-foot-high roof with an initial speed of 56 feet per second. The height, h, of the baseball can be modeled by the equation $h = -16t^2 - 56t + 30$, where t represents time in seconds. How long before the ball hits the ground?

_____

Guided Practice

Solve by completing the square. (Example 1)

1. $9x^2 + 30x = 16$

   $9x^2 + 30x + \boxed{} = 16 + \boxed{}$

   $\left(\boxed{}x + \boxed{}\right)^2 = \boxed{}$

   $\boxed{}x + \boxed{} = \pm\sqrt{\boxed{}}$

   $x = \boxed{}$ or $x = \boxed{}$

2. $25x^2 + 40x = 20$

   $25x^2 + 40x + \boxed{} = 20 + \boxed{}$

   $\left(\boxed{}x + \boxed{}\right)^2 = \boxed{}$

   $\boxed{}x + \boxed{} = \pm\sqrt{\boxed{}}$

   $x = \boxed{}$ or $x = \boxed{}$

Solve by completing the square. (Example 2)

3. $5x^2 - 6x = 11$

   $\boxed{} \cdot [5x^2 - 6x = 11]$

   $\boxed{}x^2 - \boxed{}x = \boxed{}$

   $\boxed{}x^2 - \boxed{}x + \boxed{} = \boxed{} + \boxed{}$

   $\left(\boxed{}x - \boxed{}\right)^2 = \boxed{}$

   $\boxed{}x - \boxed{} = \pm\sqrt{\boxed{}}$

   $x = \boxed{}$ or $x = \boxed{}$

4. $3x^2 + 8x = 5$

   $\boxed{} \cdot [3x^2 + 8x = 5]$

   $\boxed{}x^2 + \boxed{}x = \boxed{}$

   $\boxed{}x^2 + \boxed{}x + \boxed{} = \boxed{} + \boxed{}$

   $\left(\boxed{}x + \boxed{}\right)^2 = \boxed{}$

   $\boxed{}x + \boxed{} = \pm\sqrt{\boxed{}}$

   $x = \boxed{}$ or $x = \boxed{}$

5. $2x^2 - 3x = 20$

$\boxed{} \cdot [2x^2 - 3x = 20]$

$\boxed{}\, x^2 - \boxed{}\, x = \boxed{}$

$\boxed{}\, x^2 - \boxed{}\, x + \boxed{} = \boxed{} + \boxed{}$

$\left(\boxed{}\, x - \boxed{}\right)^2 = \boxed{}$

$\boxed{}\, x - \boxed{} = \pm\sqrt{\boxed{}}$

$\boxed{}\, x - \boxed{} = \pm\,\boxed{}$

$x = \boxed{}$ or $x = \boxed{}$

6. $3x^2 + 7x = 3$

$\boxed{} \cdot [3x^2 + 7x = 3]$

$\boxed{}\, x^2 + \boxed{}\, x = \boxed{}$

$\boxed{}\, x^2 + \boxed{}\, x + \boxed{} = \boxed{} + \boxed{}$

$\left(\boxed{}\, x + \boxed{}\right)^2 = \boxed{}$

$\boxed{}\, x + \boxed{} = \pm\sqrt{\boxed{}}$

$\boxed{}\, x + \boxed{} = \pm\,\boxed{}$

$x = \boxed{}$ or $x = \boxed{}$

7. The height, h, of a projectile launched from the top of a 50-foot hill, with an initial velocity of 24 feet per second can be modeled using the equation $h = -16t^2 + 24t + 50$, where t is the time in seconds. Complete the square to solve for t, and determine how long the projectile will be in the air. (Example 3)

$\boxed{}\, t^2 - \boxed{}\, t = \boxed{}$

$\boxed{}\, t^2 - \boxed{}\, t + \boxed{} = \boxed{}$

$\left(\boxed{}\, t - \boxed{}\right)^2 = \boxed{}$

$t = \dfrac{\boxed{} - \boxed{}}{\boxed{}}$ or $\dfrac{\boxed{} + \boxed{}}{\boxed{}}$

$t \approx \boxed{}$ seconds (The negative answer is not possible.)

? ESSENTIAL QUESTION CHECK-IN

8. When an equation is in the form $ax^2 + bx + c$, with $a \neq 1$, how can you solve for x without eliminating the coefficient of x^2?

_____

_____

16.5 Independent Practice

Personal
Math Trainer

Online
Assessment and
Intervention

my.hrw.com

Solve by completing the square.

9. $-x^2 + x + 6 = 0$ _____

10. $3x^2 - 6x - 9 = 0$ _____

Use the expression $\frac{b^2}{4a}$ to determine the constant that should be added to the expression to create a perfect-square trinomial.

11. $25x^2 + 10x$ _____

12. $100x^2 - 40x$ _____

Solve the following quadratic equations by completing the square.

13. $49x^2 + 28x = -3$ _____

14. $9x^2 - 18x = 7$ _____

15. $18x^2 + x = 5$ _____

16. $64x^2 + 16x = 14$ _____

17. $121x^2 - 110x = 4$ _____

Complete each trinomial so that it is a perfect square.

18. $x^2 + 18x + c$ _____

19. $x^2 + bx + 4$ _____

20. $x^2 - 100x + c$ _____

21. $x^2 - bx + \frac{81}{4}$ _____

22. $9x^2 - 24x + c$ _____

23. $25x^2 + 10x + c$ _____

24. $4x^2 - 6x + c$ _____

25. $49x^2 - 7x + c$ _____

Solve the following quadratic equations by completing the square.

26. $2x^2 + 10x = 12$ _____

27. $3x^2 - 8x = 3$ _____

28. $20x^2 - 12x = 11$ _____

29. $27x^2 + 18x = 4$ _____

30. Multi-Step A roped-off area of width x is created around a 30- by 10-foot rectangular museum display of Native American artifacts. The combined area of the display and the roped-off area is 800 square feet.

a. Write an equation for the combined

area. _____

b. Find the width of the roped-off area.

_____

31. A rocket is shot straight up from a 30-foot rooftop with an initial velocity of 128 feet per second. The height, h, of the rocket is given by the equation $h = -16t^2 + 128t + 30$, where t is the time elapsed in seconds.

a. How long will it take the rocket to return to the ground? Round your answer to the nearest tenth of a second.

_____

b. The maximum height that the rocket achieves is 286 feet. At what time does it reach that height? Round your answer to the nearest tenth of a second.

_____

32. During construction, a fuse is thrown straight down an elevator shaft from the thirty-seventh floor (370 feet above ground level) with an initial speed of 64 feet per second. The height, h, of the fuse is given by the equation $h = -16t^2 - 64t + 370$, where t is the time elapsed in seconds. How long will it take until the fuse hits the ground? Round your answer to the nearest tenth of a second.

_____

33. Represent Real-World Problems The length of a rectangular garden is 2 meters less than twice its width. If the area of the garden is 35 square meters, what are the dimensions of the garden? Round answers to the nearest tenth.

_____

Work Area

34. Draw Conclusions In the problem above, only one of two solutions is included as an answer. Why are certain solutions considered "extraneous"? Is one solution to a real-world problem involving a quadratic equation always thrown out?

_____

_____

_____

_____

_____

35. Find the Error Kendra was asked to solve $2x^2 + 14x = 27$ by completing the square. Her work is shown below. Where did she make her mistake?

$$2 \cdot [2x^2 - 14x = 27]$$

$$4x^2 - 28x = 54$$

$$4x^2 - 28x + 49 = 103$$

$$(2x - 7)^2 = 103$$

$$2x - 7 = \pm\sqrt{103}$$

$$2x = \sqrt{103} + 7 \text{ or } 2x = \sqrt{103} - 7$$

$$x = \frac{7 + \sqrt{103}}{2} \quad \text{or } x = \frac{-7 + \sqrt{103}}{2}$$

_____

_____

_____

LESSON

16.6 **The Quadratic Formula**

FL   A-REI.2.4b

Solve quadratic equations by
... completing the square,
the quadratic formula and
factoring, as appropriate to the
initial form of the equation. ...
Also A-REI.2.4, A-REI.2.4a

ESSENTIAL QUESTION

What is the quadratic formula, and how can you use it to solve quadratic
equations?

EXPLORE ACTIVITY    FL   A-REI.2.4a

Deriving the Quadratic Formula

In this Explore Activity, you will derive the quadratic formula, a formula that can
be used to solve any quadratic equation.

Solve the general form of a quadratic equation, $ax^2 + bx + c = 0$, $a \neq 0$, by
completing the square to find the values of x in terms of a, b and c.

A Write the standard form of a
quadratic equation.

$$ax^2 + bx + c = \boxed{}$$

Subtract c from both sides.

$$ax^2 + bx = \boxed{}$$

B Multiply both sides by $4a$ to make
the coefficient of x^2 a perfect square.

$$4a^2x^2 + \boxed{} = \boxed{}$$

C Add b^2 to both sides of the equation
to complete the square.

$$4a^2x^2 + 4abx + b^2 = -4ac + \boxed{}$$

D Factor the left side to write the
trinomial as the square of a
binomial. Simplify the right side.

$$\left(\boxed{} \right)^2 = b^2 - 4ac$$

E Take square roots of both sides.

$$\boxed{} = \pm\sqrt{\boxed{}}$$

F Subtract b from both sides.

$$2ax = \boxed{} \pm\sqrt{\boxed{}}$$

Divide both sides by $2a$ to solve for
x, remembering to include both
roots.

$$x = \frac{\boxed{} \pm\sqrt{\boxed{}}}{\boxed{}}$$

The formula you just derived, $x = \dfrac{-b \pm \sqrt{(b^2 - 4ac)}}{2a}$, is called the **quadratic formula**.

REFLECT

1. **What if?** If the derivation had begun by dividing each term by a, and then
manipulated to complete the square, what would the resulting binomial have
been? Does one derivation method appear to be simpler than the other? Explain.

Solving Quadratic Equations Using the Quadratic Formula

The "$\pm$" in the quadratic formula indicates that there are up to two possible solutions. The actual number of real solutions (zero, one, or two) can be determined by evaluating the **discriminant** of the quadratic formula, which is the part under the radical sign: $b^2 - 4ac$.

EXAMPLE 1  **FL** **A-REI.2.4b**

Solve using the quadratic formula.

A $2x^2 + 3x - 5 = 0$

$a = 2, b = 3, c = -5$ Identify a, b and c.

$x = \dfrac{-b \pm \sqrt{(b^2 - 4ac)}}{2a}$ Use the quadratic formula.

$x = \dfrac{-3 \pm \sqrt{3^2 - 4(2)(-5)}}{2(2)}$ Substitute the identified values into the quadratic formula.

$x = \dfrac{-3 \pm \sqrt{49}}{4}$ Simplify the discriminant and the denominator.

$x = \dfrac{-3 \pm 7}{4}$ Evaluate the square root.

$x = \dfrac{-3 + 7}{4}$ or $x = \dfrac{-3 - 7}{4}$ Write as two equations.

$x = 1$ or $x = \dfrac{-5}{2}$ Simplify both equations.

> Solutions are exact values.

Math Talk

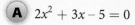
Mathematical Practices

How can you use substitution to check your solutions?

B $2x = x^2 - 4$

$x^2 - 2x - 4 = 0$ Write in standard form.

$a = 1, b = -2, c = -4$ Identify a, b and c.

$x = \dfrac{-(-2) \pm \sqrt{(-2)^2 - 4(1)(-4)}}{2(1)}$ Substitute the identified values into the quadratic formula.

$x = \dfrac{2 \pm \sqrt{20}}{2}$ Simplify the discriminant and the denominator.

$x = \dfrac{2 + \sqrt{20}}{2}$ or $x = \dfrac{2 - \sqrt{20}}{2}$ Write as two equations.

$x \approx 3.24$ or $x \approx -1.24$ Simplify using a calculator. Round to the hundredths place.

> Solutions are not exact values.

Personal Math Trainer

Online Assessment and Intervention

⏻ my.hrw.com

YOUR TURN

Solve using the quadratic formula. Round to the hundredths place.

2. $5x + 2 = 3x^2$

3. $2x^2 - 8x + 1 = 0$

_____   _____

EXAMPLE 2  FL A-REI.2.4b

Find the number of real solutions of each equation using the discriminant.

A $x^2 - 4x + 3 = 0$

$a = 1, b = -4, c = 3$	Identify a, b and c.
$b^2 - 4ac$	Use the discriminant.
$(-4)^2 - 4(1)(3)$	Substitute the identified values into the iscriminant.
$16 - 12 = 4$	Simplify.

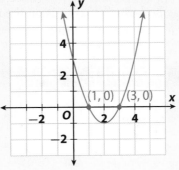

Since $b^2 - 4ac > 0$, the equation has 2 real solutions.

B $x^2 + 2x + 1 = 0$

$a = 1, b = 2, c = 1$	Identify a, b and c.
$b^2 - 4ac$	Use the discriminant.
$(2)^2 - 4(1)(1)$	Substitute the identified values into the discriminant.
$4 - 4 = 0$	Simplify.

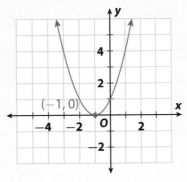

Since $b^2 - 4ac = 0$, the equation has 1 real solution.

C $x^2 - 2x + 2 = 0$

$a = 1, b = -2, c = 2$	Identify a, b and c.
$b^2 - 4ac$	Use the discriminant.
$(-2)^2 - 4(1)(2)$	Substitute the identified values into the discriminant.
$4 - 8 = -4$	Simplify.

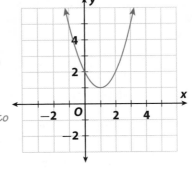

Since $b^2 - 4ac < 0$, the equation has NO real solutions.

YOUR TURN

Find the number of real solutions of each equation using the discriminant.

4. $9x^2 - 6x + 1 = 0$ **5.** $3x^2 + 10x + 2 = 0$ **6.** $x^2 + x + 1 = 0$

_____   _____   _____

_____   _____   _____

Math On the Spot

my.hrw.com

Solving Quadratic Equations Using Different Methods

There is no one correct way to solve a quadratic equation. The choice of method usually depends on the form of the equation, the coefficient values, and personal preference.

EXAMPLE 3

FL   A-REI.2.4b

Solve $x^2 + 7x + 6 = 0$ using the method indicated.

A Graphing

$$y = f(x) = x^2 + 7x + 6$$

Write the related quadratic function and graph.

$$y = 0 \text{ at } x = -6 \text{ and } -1$$

Find the x-intercepts.

Graphing always works to give approximate solutions.

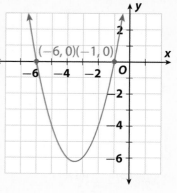

B Factoring

$$x^2 + 7x + 6 = 0$$

$$(x + 6)(x + 1) = 0$$ Factor.

$$x + 6 = 0 \text{ or } x + 1 = 0$$ Use the zero product property.

$$x = -6 \text{ or } x = -1$$ Solve each equation.

Factoring is useful when the equation is easily factored.

C Completing the square

$$x^2 + 7x + 6 = 0$$

$$x^2 + 7x = -6$$ Subtract the constant term from both sides.

$$x^2 + 7x + \frac{49}{4} = -6 + \frac{49}{4}$$ Add $\left(\frac{b}{2}\right)^2$ to both sides.

$$\left(x + \frac{7}{2}\right)^2 = \frac{25}{4}$$ Factor the left. Simplify the right.

$$x + \frac{7}{2} = \pm\frac{5}{2}$$ Take the square root of both sides.

$$x + \frac{7}{2} = \frac{5}{2} \text{ or } x + \frac{7}{2} = -\frac{5}{2}$$ Write as two equations.

$$x = -1 \text{ or } x = -6$$ Solve each equation.

Completing the square always works and is easiest if b is an even number.

My Notes

D Using the quadratic formula

$a = 1, b = 7, c = 6$ Identify a, b, and c.

$x = \dfrac{-(7) \pm \sqrt{(7)^2 - 4(1)(6)}}{2(1)}$ Substitute the identified values into the quadratic formula.

$x = \dfrac{-7 \pm \sqrt{25}}{2}$ Simplify the discriminant and the denominator.

$x = \dfrac{-7 + 5}{2}$ or $x = \dfrac{-7 - 5}{2}$ Evaluate the square root and write as two equations.

$x = -1$ or $x = -6$ Simplify both equations.

The quadratic formula always works. You can use it to find both exact and estimated solutions.

REFLECT

7. What are the disadvantages to solving a quadratic equation by graphing?

_____

_____

8. What are the disadvantages to solving a quadratic equation by factoring?

_____

_____

_____

9. What are the disadvantages to using the quadratic formula for solving a quadratic equation?

_____

_____

YOUR TURN

10. Solve $x^2 + x - 12 = 0$ using each method in Example 3.

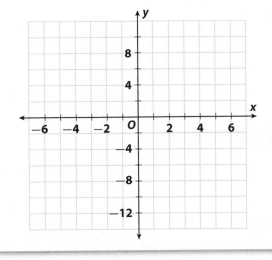

Personal Math Trainer

Online Assessment and Intervention

my.hrw.com

Solve using the quadratic formula, $x = \dfrac{-b \pm \sqrt{(b^2 - 4ac)}}{2a}$. (Example 1)

1. $6x^2 + 5x - 4 = 0$

$a = \boxed{}, b = \boxed{}, c = -4$

$x = \dfrac{-\boxed{} \pm \sqrt{5^2 - 4(\boxed{})(\boxed{})}}{2(\boxed{})}$

$x = \dfrac{-\boxed{} \pm \sqrt{\boxed{}}}{\boxed{}}$

$x = \dfrac{\boxed{} + \boxed{}}{\boxed{}}$, or $x = \dfrac{\boxed{} - \boxed{}}{\boxed{}}$

$x = \dfrac{\boxed{}}{2}$ or $x = \dfrac{\boxed{}}{3}$

2. $x^2 - 4x = -1$

$x^2 - 4x + \boxed{} = \boxed{}$

$a = 1, b = \boxed{}, c = \boxed{}$

$x = \dfrac{-\boxed{} \pm \sqrt{(\boxed{})^2 - 4(1)(\boxed{})}}{2(\boxed{})}$

$x = \dfrac{4 + \sqrt{\boxed{}}}{\boxed{}}$ or $x = \dfrac{\boxed{} - \sqrt{\boxed{}}}{2}$

$x \approx 3.73$ or $x \approx \boxed{}$

Find the number of real solutions using the discriminant, $b^2 - 4ac$. (Example 2)

3. $2x^2 - 2x + 3 = 0$

There are ____ real solutions.

4. $x^2 + 4x + 4 = 0$

There is ____ real solution.

5. $x^2 - 9x + 4 = 0$

There are ____ real solutions.

6. Which method would you use to solve the equation $x^2 + 4x + 3 = 0$? Explain your choice and give your solutions. (Example 3)

_____

_____

_____

_____

7. What is the quadratic formula, and how can you use it to solve quadratic equations?

_____

_____

16.6 Independent Practice

FL A-REI.2.4, A-REI.2.4a, A-REI.2.4b

Personal
Math Trainer

Online
Assessment and
Intervention

8. **Critique Reasoning** Dan said that if a quadratic equation does not have any real solutions, it is not a function. Critique his reasoning.

_____

_____

_____

_____

_____

9. **Interpret the Answer** A diver begins on a platform 10 meters above the surface of the water. The diver's height is given by the equation $h(t) = -4.9t^2 + 3.5t + 10$, where t is the time in seconds after the diver jumps.

a. How many real solutions does the equation have when the diver's height is 1 m? What are they? Round to the hundredths place.

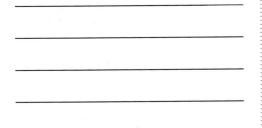

_____

_____

b. Do both solutions make sense in this situation? Explain.

_____

_____

_____

_____

_____

10. **Represent Real-World Problems** The height in meters of a model rocket on a particular launch can be modeled by the equation $h(t) = -4.9t^2 + 102t + 100$, where t is the time in seconds after its engine burns out 100 m above the ground.

a. Will the rocket reach a height of 600 m? What about 700 m? Use the discriminant to explain.

_____

_____

_____

_____

_____

b. How can graphing be used to check your answer in Part **a**?

_____

_____

_____

_____

c. How can the quadratic formula be used to determine how long the rocket stays

in the air? _____

_____

_____

_____

11. Communicate Mathematical Ideas Explain why a positive discriminant results in two real solutions.

_____

_____

12. Persevere in Problem Solving A gymnast, who can stretch her arms up to reach 6 feet, jumps straight up on a trampoline. The height of her feet above the trampoline can be modeled by the equation $h = -16x^2 + 12x$, where x is the time in seconds after her jump.

a. Do the gymnast's hands reach a height of 10 feet above the trampoline? Use the discriminant to explain. (*Hint*: Since h = height of feet, you must use the difference between the heights of the hands and feet.)

_____

_____

_____

_____

_____

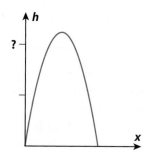

b. Use the discriminant to determine the maximum height she reaches. Explain your method.

_____

_____

_____

_____

_____

c. Solve the equation to determine the amount of time it takes her to reach her maximum height. Explain your method.

_____

_____

_____

_____

_____

Solving Systems of Linear and Quadratic Equations

FL A-REI.3.7

Solve a simple system consisting of a linear equation and a quadratic in two variables algebraically and graphically. *Also A-REI.2.4, A-REI.2.4b, F-IF.2.4*

ESSENTIAL QUESTION

How can you solve a system of equations when one equation is linear and the other is quadratic?

EXPLORE ACTIVITY

FL A-REI.3.7

Determining the Possible Number of Solutions

A system of one linear and one quadratic equation may have zero, one or two solutions.

A The graph of the quadratic function $f(x) = x^2 - 2x - 2$ is the U-shaped curve shown below. On the same coordinate plane, graph the following linear functions.

$$g(x) = -x - 2, \qquad h(x) = 2x - 6, \qquad j(x) = 0.5x - 5$$

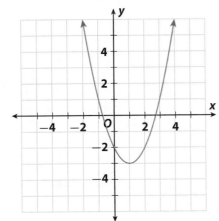

B Look at the graph of the system consisting of the quadratic function and $g(x)$.

How many solutions exist? _____

C Look at the graph of the system consisting of the quadratic function and $h(x)$.

How many solutions exist? _____

D Look at the graph of the system consisting of the quadratic function and $j(x)$.

How many solutions exist? _____

REFLECT

1. A system consisting of a quadratic equation and a linear equation can have

_____, _____, or _____ solutions.

Solving Systems Graphically

One way to solve a system is to graph both equations (or both functions) and then find the points where the graphs intersect. To graph a quadratic function in the form $f(x) = a(x - h)^2 + k$, you can use the fact that the turning point, called the *vertex*, of the U-shaped graph is at (h, k), and you can solve $f(x) = 0$ to find the curve's *x*-intercepts.

EXAMPLE 1

 FL   A-REI.3.7

Solve the system represented by the functions graphically.

$$f(x) = (x + 1)^2 - 4, \quad g(x) = 2x - 2$$

My Notes

STEP 1   Graph the quadratic function below. The vertex is the point $(-1, -4)$.

The *x*-intercepts are the points where $(x + 1)^2 - 4 = 0$.

$(x + 1)^2 = 4$

$x + 1 = \pm 2$ *Take the square root of both sides*

$x = 1 \text{ or } -3$ *Subtract 1 from both sides*

STEP 2   Graph the linear function on the same coordinate plane.

The y-intercept is −2 and the slope is 2

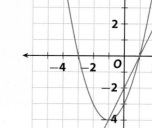

STEP 3   The solutions to the system are the points where the graphs intersect.

The two solutions are $(-1, -4)$ and $(1, 0)$.

REFLECT

2. If the linear function was $g(x) = 2x - 8$, how many solutions would the system have?

_____

_____

YOUR TURN

Solve each system represented by a pair of functions graphically.

3. $f(x) = -2(x + 2)^2 + 8, \, g(x) = 4x + 16$ _____

4. $f(x) = (x + 1)^2 - 9, \, g(x) = 6x - 12$ _____

Solving Systems Algebraically

Systems of equations can also be solved algebraically by using the substitution method.

Math On the Spot
my.hrw.com

EXAMPLE 2

FL A-REI.3.7

Solve the system from Example 1 algebraically.

STEP 1 Write both equations using y in place of the function notation.

$$y = (x + 1)^2 - 4, \, y = 2x - 2$$

STEP 2 Set the right hand sides equal to each other and solve for x.

$(x + 1)^2 - 4 = 2x - 2$

$x^2 + 2x - 3 = 2x - 2$ Simplify the left side.

$x^2 - 1 = 0$ Make one side equal zero.

$(x - 1)(x + 1) = 0$ Factor.

$x = 1$ or -1 Solve for x.

STEP 3 Substitute the x-values into the linear equation to find y.

$$y = 2(1) - 2 = 0$$

$$y = 2(-1) - 2 = -4$$

The solutions are $(1, 0)$ and $(-1, -4)$.

REFLECT

5. Why does Step 3 say to substitute into the linear equation? What if the x-values are substituted into the quadratic equation?

_____

_____

_____

6. Solve the following system of equations algebraically.

$$y = 3x^2 + 4x - 2, \, y = -20x - 23$$

_____

Personal
Math Trainer

Online Assessment
and Intervention

my.hrw.com

Solving Systems Using Technology

Systems of equations can be solved by graphing both equations on a calculator and using the Intersect feature.

EXAMPLE 3 FL A-REI.3.7

A rock climber is pulling his pack up the side of a cliff that is 175.5 feet tall at a rate of 2 feet per second. The height of the pack in feet after t seconds is given by $y = 2t$. The climber drops a coil of rope from directly above the pack. The height of the coil in feet after t seconds is given by $y = -16t^2 + 175.5$. At what time does the coil of rope hit the pack?

STEP 1 The system to be solved is
$$y_1 = 2t, y_2 = -16t^2 + 175.5$$

STEP 2 Enter these functions into a graphing calculator as Y_1 and Y_2, and graph both of them. Sketch the graphs on the coordinate plane.

STEP 3 Press 2nd and CALC, then select Intersect. Press Enter to select Y_1, then press Enter to select Y_2. Move the cursor near one of the intersections and press Enter to make a guess. The display will show the coordinates of the intersection. Repeat for the second intersection.

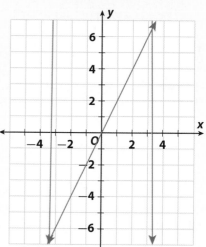

The intersection points are $(3.25, 6.5)$, $(-3.375, -6.75)$.

The coil hits the pack at $t = 3.25$ seconds.

YOUR TURN

7. A window washer is ascending the side of a building that is 520 feet tall at a rate of 3 feet per second. The elevation of the window washer after t seconds is given by $y = 3t$. A bucket of supplies is lowered to him from above. The height of the supplies in feet after t seconds is given by $y = -2t^2 + 520$. At what time do the supplies reach the window washer?

_____

Solve each system represented by a pair of functions graphically. (Example 1)

1. $f(x) = (x + 3)^2 - 4, g(x) = 2x + 2$

the vertex of $f(x)$ is at (⬜ , ⬜)

the x-intercepts are at $x =$ _____ , _____

$g(x)$ has slope _____ and intercept _____

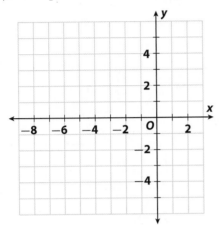

The solutions are _____.

2. $f(x) = x^2 - 1, g(x) = x - 2$

the vertex of $f(x)$ is at (⬜ , ⬜)

the x-intercepts are at $x =$ _____ , _____

$g(x)$ has slope _____ and intercept _____

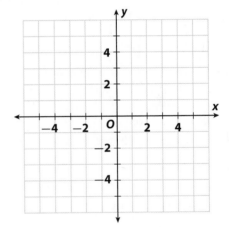

There are _____ real solutions.

3. $f(x) = (x - 4)^2 - 2, g(x) = -2$

the vertex of $f(x)$ is at (⬜ , ⬜)

the x-intercepts are at $x =$ _____ , _____

$g(x)$ has a slope of _____ and intercept _____

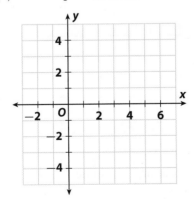

The solutions is _____.

4. $f(x) = -x^2 + 4, g(x) = -3x + 6$

the vertex of $f(x)$ is at (⬜ , ⬜)

the x-intercepts are at $x =$ _____ , _____

$g(x)$ has a slope of _____ and intercept _____

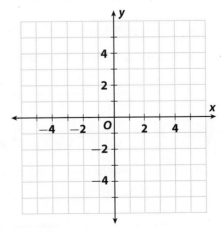

The solutions are _____.

Solve each system algebraically. (Example 2)

5. $f(x) = x^2 + 1, g(x) = 5$

$x^2 + 1 = \boxed{}$

$x^2 - \boxed{} = 0$

$x = \boxed{}$ or $\boxed{}$

the solutions are _____.

6. $f(x) = x^2 - 3x + 2, g(x) = 4x - 8$

$\boxed{} = 4x - 8$

$x^2 - \boxed{}\, x + \boxed{} = 0$

$(x + \boxed{})(x + \boxed{}) = 0$

$x = \boxed{}$ or $\boxed{}$

the solutions are _____.

7. $f(x) = (x - 3)^2, g(x) = 4$

$(x - 3)^2 = \boxed{}$

$x - \boxed{} = \pm \boxed{}$

$x = \boxed{}$ or $\boxed{}$

The solutions are _____.

8. $f(x) = -x^2 + 4x, g(x) = x + 2$

$-x^2 + 4x = \boxed{}$

$-x^2 + \boxed{}\, x - \boxed{} = 0$

$x = \dfrac{-b \pm \sqrt{b^2 - 4ac}}{2a}$

$= \dfrac{\boxed{} \pm \sqrt{3^2 - 4(\boxed{})(\boxed{})}}{2(-1)}$

$x = \dfrac{\boxed{} \pm \sqrt{\boxed{}}}{-2} = \dfrac{\boxed{} \pm 1}{-2}$

$x = \boxed{}$ or $\boxed{}$

The solutions are _____.

9. The height in feet of a skydiver t seconds after deploying her parachute is given by $h = -300t + 1000$. A ball is thrown up toward the skydiver, and after t seconds, the height of the ball in feet is given by $h = -16t^2 + 100t$. Use a graphing calculator to solve this system of equations, and then determine when the ball reaches the skydiver. (Example 3)

The two solutions to the system are _____ and _____.

The ball reaches the skydiver at time $t \approx$

_____

ESSENTIAL QUESTION CHECK-IN

10. How can the graphs of two functions be used to solve a system of a quadratic and a linear equation?

_____

_____

16.7 Independent Practice

Personal Math Trainer

Online Assessment and Intervention

my.hrw.com

FL A-REI.2.4, A-REI.2.4b, A-REI.3.7, F-IF.2.4

Solve each system represented by a pair of functions graphically.

11. $f(x) = -(x-2)^2 + 9$, $g(x) = 3x + 3$

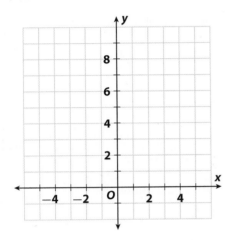

_____

12. $f(x) = 3(x+1)^2 - 1$, $g(x) = x - 4$

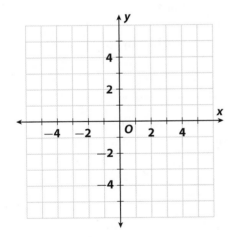

_____

Solve each systems of equations algebraically.

13. $y = 2x^2 - 5x + 6$, $y = 5x - 6$

_____

14. $y = x^2 + 7$, $y = -9x + 29$

_____

15. $y = 4x^2 + 45x + 83$, $y = 5x - 17$

_____

Answer the following questions with the help of a graphing calculator.

16. An elevator in a hotel moves at 20 feet per second. Leaving from the ground floor, its height in feet after t seconds is given by the formula $h = 20t$. A bolt comes loose in the elevator shaft above, and its height in feet after falling for t seconds is given by $h = -16t^2 + 200$.

a. Write the solution(s) to the system of equations which determines when the bolt hits the elevator.

_____

b. At what time does the bolt hit the elevator?

_____

c. At what height does the bolt hit the elevator?

_____

d. Explain why it makes sense for this problem to be modeled with a downward opening parabola?

_____

_____

_____

_____

17. A skeet shooter shoots a disk into the air. Its height in meters after t seconds is given by $h = -4.9t^2 + 30t$. Three seconds later, the shooter fires a bullet at the disk. The height of the bullet in meters after t seconds is given by $h = -4.9(t - 3)^2 + 400(t - 3)$.

    a. When does the bullet hit the disk?

    _____

    b. How high is the disk at that time?

    _____

    c. Begin solving the system algebraically and explain why there cannot be two solutions.

    _____

    _____

 FOCUS ON HIGHER ORDER THINKING

Work Area

18. Draw Conclusions A certain system of a linear and a quadratic equation has two solutions, $(2, 7)$ and $(5, 10)$. The quadratic equation is $y = x^2 - 6x + 15$. What is the linear equation? Explain.

_____

_____

19. Explain The Error A student is asked to solve the system of equations $y = x^2 + 2x - 7$ and $y - 2 = x + 1$. For the first step, the student sets the right hand sides equal to each other to get the equation $x^2 + 2x - 7 = x + 1$. Why does this not give the correct solution?

_____

20. Justify Reasoning It is possible for a system of two linear equations to have infinitely many solutions. Explain why this is not possible for a system with one linear and one quadratic equation.

_____

_____

_____

21. Explain the Error After solving the system of equations in problem 16, a student concludes that there are two different times that the bolt hits the elevator. What is the error in the student's reasoning?

_____

_____

Ready to Go On?

16.1–16.6 Solving Quadratic Equations

Solve each quadratic equation using the method stated. Round to the nearest hundredth, if necessary.

1. $(x + 5)^2 - 4 = 12$; square roots

_____

2. $3x^2 + 11x - 20 = 0$; factoring

_____

3. $x^2 - 4x + 4 = 0$; completing the square

_____

4. $5x^2 - 3x = 7$; quadratic formula

_____

5. $3x^2 = 48$; square roots

_____

6. $x^2 - 4x - 32 = 0$; factoring

_____

7. $x^2 - 8 = -7x$; completing the square

_____

8. $x^2 + 4x = 5$; quadratic formula

_____

9. $x^2 + 1 + 5x = 0$; quadratic formula

_____

10. $2x - 3 + x^2 = 0$; completing the square

_____

16.7 Solving Systems of Linear and Quadratic Equations

Solve each system of equations algebraically.

11. $2x + y = 4$; $y = x^2 - 2x + 1$

_____

12. $y = 3x - 2$; $x^2 - y = 6$

_____

? ESSENTIAL QUESTION

13. How do you determine the best method for solving a quadratic equation or a system of equations?

_____

_____

_____

_____

Assessment Readiness

Selected Response

1. How many solutions does the equation $4x^2 - 6x - 9 = 0$ have?

Ⓐ 0   Ⓒ 2

Ⓑ 1   Ⓓ 3

2. Which graph shows the system of equations $y = x - 4$ and $y = 2x^2 - 5$?

Ⓐ
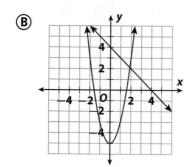

Ⓑ
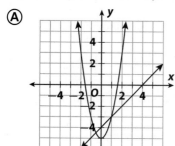

Ⓒ
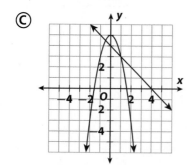

Ⓓ
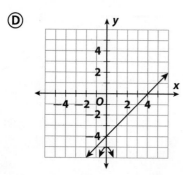

3. Which is a solution of $2x^2 + 4x - 6 = 0$?

Ⓐ −6   Ⓒ 1

Ⓑ −1   Ⓓ 3

4. Which function increases the fastest?

Ⓐ $y = 3x$ Ⓒ $y = 3x^2$

Ⓑ $y = 3^x$ Ⓓ $y = 3^{-x}$

5. Which of the following is used to find the solutions to a quadratic equation?

Ⓐ $a^2 + b^2 = c^2$ Ⓒ $b^2 - 4ac$

Ⓑ $\sqrt{a^2 + b^2}$ Ⓓ $x = \dfrac{-b \pm \sqrt{b^2 - 4ac}}{2a}$

6. Which point is the solution to the system of equations?

$$\begin{cases} 3x + y = 6 \\ \quad\ x = y + 2 \end{cases}$$

Ⓐ $(4, 2)$ Ⓒ $(2, -2)$

Ⓑ $(2, 0)$ Ⓓ $(3, 1)$

7. Which is the slope of the line $-2x + 4y = 8$?

Ⓐ $\frac{1}{2}$ Ⓒ -2

Ⓑ 2 Ⓓ $-\frac{1}{2}$

Mini-Tasks

8. a. Use any method to solve the equation $-17x + 32 = 11x^2 - 17$.

_____

b. Explain why you chose this method.

_____

_____

_____

_____

Study Guide Review

Key Vocabulary

binomial (*binomio*)
degree of a polynomial
  (*grado de un polinomio*)
FOIL method
  (*los primeros, los externos,*
  los internos y los ultimos)
monomial (*monomio*)
polynomial (*polinomio*)
trinomial (*trinomio*)

? ESSENTIAL QUESTION

How are polynomials like other number systems such as whole numbers and integers?

EXAMPLE 1

A new company is producing t-shirts for sale online. The cost, in dollars, to produce x t-shirts is modeled by the polynomial $350 + 2.5x$. The revenue the company generates from the sale of t-shirts can be modeled by the monomial $12x$. If 752 t-shirts have been sold, how much profit has the company generated?

$Profit = Revenue - Cost$ *Difference of costs and income*

$\quad = (12x) - (350 + 2.5x)$ *Substitute expressions.*

$\quad = (12x - 2.5x) - 350$ *Group like terms.*

$\quad = 9.5x - 350$ *Simplify.*

$Profit = 9.5(752) - 350$ *Substitute 752 for x.*

$\quad = 6{,}794$ *Simplify.*

EXAMPLE 2

Simplify the expression $(x + 3)(x^2 + 6x - 2) + (x^3 - 2x^2 - 5)$.

$$(x + 3)(x^2 + 6x - 2) = x(x^2 + 6x - 2) + 3(x^2 + 6x - 2)$$

$$= x(x^2) + x(6x) - x(2) + 3(x^2) + 3(6x) - 3(2)$$

$$= x^3 + 6x^2 - 2x + 3x^2 + 18x - 6$$

$$= x^3 + (6x^2 + 3x^2) + (18x - 2x) - 6$$

$$= x^3 + 9x^2 + 16x - 6$$

$$(x + 3)(x^2 + 6x - 2) + (x^3 - 2x^2 - 5) = (x^3 + 9x^2 + 16x - 6) + (x^3 - 2x^2 - 5)$$

$$= x^3 + 9x^2 + 16x - 6 + x^3 - 2x^2 - 5$$

$$= (x^3 + x^3) + (9x^2 - 2x^2) + 16x - (6 + 5)$$

$$= 2x^3 + 7x^2 + 16x - 11$$

1. The polynomial $0.5t^2 + 2t - 6$ represents the distance (in feet) a model
   car travels in t seconds. How far will the car travel in 5 seconds? (Lesson 14.1) _____

2. Add $(2x^2 + 3x - 4) + (5x^2 - 2x + 3)$. (Lesson 14.2) _____

3. Multiply $(3x + 7)(3x - 7)$. (Lesson 14.4) _____

4. Use the FOIL method to find the product $(x + 9)(x - 7)$.

   (Lesson 14.4) _____

MODULE 15 Factoring Polynomials

Key Vocabulary
greatest common factor
(maximo común divisor)

? ESSENTIAL QUESTION

How can you factor expressions of the form $ax^2 + bx + c$?

EXAMPLE 1

A carpenter is building square tables with the top surface area represented by
the trinomial $(x^2 + 8x + 16)$ ft². The side lengths of the tables are of the form
$ax + b$, where a and b are whole numbers. Find an expression to represent the
side lengths of the square tabletops.

Factor the polynomial: $x^2 + 8x + 16$

$$x^2 = x \cdot x, \ 16 = 4 \cdot 4, \text{ and } 8x = 2(4 \cdot x)$$
$$x^2 + 8x + 16 = (x + 4)^2$$

Each side length is represented by the expression $(x + 4)$ ft.

EXAMPLE 2

Factor $8x^2 + 52x + 60$.

STEP 1 Factor out any common factors.
$$8x^2 + 52x + 60 = 4(2x^2 + 13x + 15)$$

STEP 2 List all factor pairs for $a = 2$, and $c = 15$.

Factors of a $a = 2$	Factors of c $c = 15$	Outer Product + Inner Product
1 and 2	1 and 15	$(1)(15) + (2)(1) = 17$
1 and 2	3 and 5	$(1)(5) + (2)(3) = 11$
1 and 2	5 and 3	$(1)(3) + (2)(5) = 13$
1 and 2	15 and 1	$(1)(1) + (2)(15) = 31$

STEP 3 Use the correct factors of a and c to write the factored form.

$$8x^2 + 52x + 60 = 4(x + 5)(2x + 3)$$

EXERCISES

Factor each polynomial. (Lesson 15.1)

5. $5x^2 + 10x$ _____

6. $3x^2 - 12x - 6$ _____

Factor each trinomial. (Lessons 15.2 and 15.3)

7. $x^2 + 12x + 35$ _____

8. $x^2 - 3x - 54$ _____

9. $6x^2 + 29x + 28$ _____

10. $2x^2 - 9x - 18$ _____

11. Determine whether the trinomial $16x^2 + 40x + 25$ is a perfect square. If so, factor. If not, explain. (Lesson 15.4)

_____

MODULE **16** # Solving Quadratic Equations

Key Vocabulary
discriminant *(discriminante)*
end behavior
  (comportamiento extremo)
quadratic formula *(fórmula cuadrática)*

? ESSENTIAL QUESTION

How do you determine the best method for solving a quadratic equation or a system of equations?

EXAMPLE 1

Solve $(x - 3)^2 = 49$ using square roots.

$(x - 3)^2 = 49$

$x - 3 = \pm\sqrt{49}$ Take the square root of both sides.

$x - 3 = \pm 7$ Use $\pm$ to show both square roots.

$x = \pm 7 + 3$

$x = 7 + 3$ and $x = -7 + 3$

$x = 10$ $x = -4$ Simplify each equation.

The solutions are -4 and 10.

EXAMPLE 2

Solve the quadratic equation $-x^2 - 3 = x^2 - 21$ **by factoring.**
Verify using the quadratic formula.

$-x^2 - 3 - x^2 + 21 = 0$ Move all terms to one side.

$\qquad -2x^2 + 18 = 0$ Combine like terms.

$\qquad -2(x^2 - 9) = 0$ Factor.

$-2(x + 3)(x - 3) = 0$

$\qquad\qquad x = \pm 3$ Solve.

$x = \dfrac{0 \pm \sqrt{0 - 4(-2)(18)}}{2(-2)}$ Use the quadratic formula to verify.

$x = \pm \dfrac{\sqrt{144}}{-4}$

$x = \pm 3$

EXAMPLE 3

Solve the system $y = x^2 + 4x + 4$, $y = -2x - 4$ **algebraically.**

$x^2 + 4x + 4 = -2x - 4$ Set the right sides equal to each other.

$x^2 + 6x + 8 = 0$ Combine like terms.

$(x + 4)(x + 2) = 0$ Factor.

$x = -4 \text{ or } -2$ Solve.

EXERCISES

Solve each equation. (Lessons 16.1, 16.2, 16.3, 16.6)

3. $(3x + 3)^2 = 81$ _____

4. $5x^2 + 20x + 4 = 8 + x$ _____

Complete the square to solve each equation. (Lessons 16.3 and 16.4)

5. $x^2 - 8x = 20$ _____

6. $9x^2 - 12x = 45$ _____

7. Solve the system $y = x^2 - 16$, $y = x + 4$
    algebraically. Verify by graphing. (Lesson 16.7)

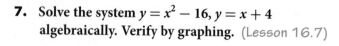

1. **CAREERS IN MATH** | Investigator The reaction distance, r, is the distance that a vehicle travels from the time the driver decides to stop until he or she applies the brakes. The braking distance, b, is the distance the vehicle travels once the brake is applied until it reaches a complete stop. Both distances are influenced by the initial speed of the vehicle. The stopping distance, s, is the sum of these.

$s = r + b$

$r = 1.47vt$, where v = speed (mi/h) and t = reaction time (s).

$b = 1.075 \dfrac{v^2}{a}$, where v = speed (mi/h) and a = deceleration rate (ft/s²).

a. Transportation departments typically use a reaction time of 2.5 seconds and a deceleration rate of 11.2 ft/s² to calculate stopping distance. Rewrite the reaction distance expression and the braking distance expression using these values. Round to the nearest thousandth. Note: The constants in these expressions include unit conversions so that the calculated distances are in feet.

_____

_____

b. Now write an expression to find the stopping distance.

_____

c. Evaluate your expressions from parts a. and b. to complete this table. Round to the nearest tenth.

Speed v (mi/h)	Reaction Distance r (ft)	Breaking Distance b (ft)	Stopping Distance s (ft)
20			
25			
30			
35			
40			
45			
50			
55			
60			

d. Suppose a skid mark is left from the time the brake is applied to the time the vehicle stops. Explain how to use the skid mark to determine how fast the vehicle was going.

_____

_____

_____

_____

_____

e. What impact would doubling the reaction time, *t,* have on the reaction distance?

_____

_____

_____

_____

Assessment Readiness

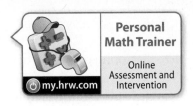

Personal Math Trainer

Online Assessment and Intervention

my.hrw.com

Selected Response

1. Which of the following is **not** a monomial?

Ⓐ $4x$

Ⓒ b^5

Ⓑ $7x^2y$

Ⓓ $ab^{0.4}$

2. What is the degree of this polynomial?
$7x^2y + 3xy + 7^4$

Ⓐ 4

Ⓒ 2

Ⓑ 1

Ⓓ 3

3. Which property of addition is illustrated by this expression?
$5x + (7x + 2x) = (5x + 7x) + 2x$

Ⓐ Associative

Ⓒ Distributive

Ⓑ Commutative

Ⓓ Identity

Hot Tip!

Try to solve the problem a second time using a different method to make sure your answer is correct.

4. What is the difference of $(22x^2 + 2x + 7)$ and $(7x^2 + 6x + 24)$?

Ⓐ $15x^2 + 4x + 17$

Ⓑ $6x^2 + 4x - 17$

Ⓒ $15x^2 - 4x + 17$

Ⓓ $15x^2 - 4x - 17$

5. What is the product of $8b$ and $(2ab + 4a + b)$?

Ⓐ $10ab^2 + 12ab + 8b^2$

Ⓑ $16ab + 32ab + 8b$

Ⓒ $16ab^2 + 28ab + 8b^2$

Ⓓ $16ab^2 + 32ab + 8b^2$

6. What is the product of $4x$ and $3x^2y$?

Ⓐ $12x^3y$

Ⓒ $12xy$

Ⓑ $12x^2y$

Ⓓ $7x^2y$

7. What is the product of $(x + 8)$ and $(x + 3)$?

Ⓐ $x^2 + 8x + 24$

Ⓒ $x^2 + 3x + 24$

Ⓑ $x^2 + 11x + 24$

Ⓓ $x^2 + 11x + 11$

8. What is the product of $(2x + 4)$ and $(-4x^2 + 3x + 7)$?

Ⓐ $8x^3 + 10x^2 + 26x + 28$

Ⓑ $-8x^3 - 10x^2 + 26x + 28$

Ⓒ $-18x^2 + 26x + 28$

Ⓓ $-4x^2 + 5x + 11$

9. Which of the following polynomials has special properties and produces a special pattern when factored?

Ⓐ $4x^2 + 20x + 25$ Ⓒ $4x + 10x + 26$

Ⓑ $4x^2 + 20x + 26$ Ⓓ $4x^2 + 10x + 25$

10. What is the GCF of $3x^2$ and $7y$?

Ⓐ $3x$

Ⓒ $7y$

Ⓑ 7

Ⓓ 1

11. How would the graphs of $f(x) = 2x + 6$ and $g(x) = 2x + 3$ compare if graphed on the same coordinate plane?

Ⓐ The graphs would intersect at $(0, 2)$.

Ⓑ The graph of $f(x)$ would be twice as steep as the graph of $g(x)$.

Ⓒ The graph of $f(x)$ would be 3 units above the graph of $g(x)$.

Ⓓ The graph of $f(x)$ would be 6 units above the graph of $g(x)$.

12. Factoring out which of the following factors from the expression $30x^3 + 6x^2 + 42x$ will result in a completely factored expression?

Ⓐ 3

Ⓒ 3x

Ⓑ 6

Ⓓ 6x

13. Which graph shows the system of equations $y_1 = x^2 + 6x + 9$ and $y_2 = 2x + 8$?

Ⓐ
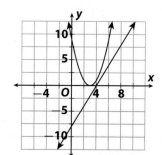

Ⓑ
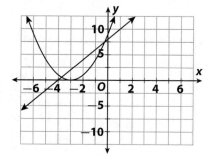

Ⓒ
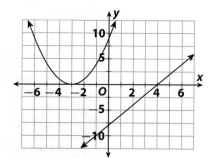

Ⓓ
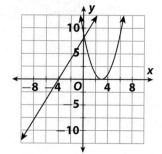

Mini-Tasks

14. The following diagram shows the floor plan of a theater stage.

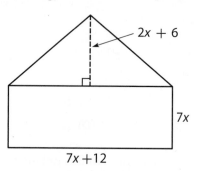

Find the area of the stage. Show each step and write your answer in factored form.

_____

_____

_____

_____

_____

_____

_____

_____

15. a. Use any method to solve the equation $0 = 4x^2 - 16x + 16$.

_____

b. Explain why you chose the method you used.

_____

_____

_____

Be sure to explain your answer fully and in complete sentences to get full credit for your response.

Functions and Modeling

CAREERS IN MATH

Skydiving Instructor: A skydiving instructor uses math to make models to analyze data and understand the effects of gravity on falling height and location.

If you're interested in a career as a skydiving instructor, you should study these mathematical subjects:
- Algebra
- Calculus
- Statistics

Research other careers that require the use of modeling data with mathematical functions.

Unit 5 Performance Task

At the end of the unit, check out how a **skydiving instructor** uses math.

Vocabulary Preview

Use the puzzle to preview key vocabulary from this unit. Unscramble each of the clue words. Copy the letters in the numbered cells to answer the riddle.

1. MXIAMMU

2. PIICEESEW CINTOUNF

3. VEXRET

4. BECU TOOR FOTNICNU

5. SEAQUR ROTO NUINOCFT

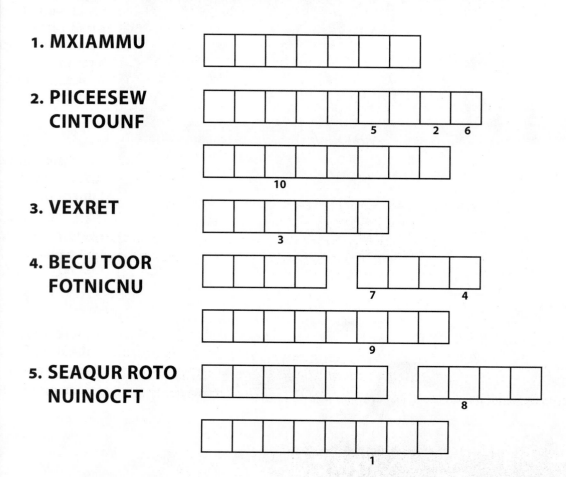

1. If a parabola opens downward, the y-value of the vertex (Lesson 17.4)
2. A function that has different rules for different parts of the domain (Lesson 18.1)
3. The point where two rays meet in the graph of an absolute value function (Lesson 18.2)
4. A function whose parent is $g(x) = \sqrt[3]{x}$. (Lesson 19.3)
5. A function whose parent is $g(x) = \sqrt{x}$. (Lesson 19.1)

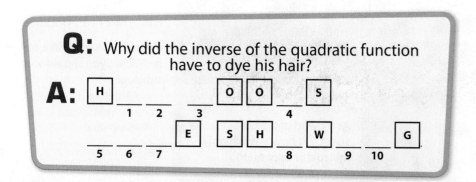

Q: Why did the inverse of the quadratic function have to dye his hair?

A: H _ _ _ _ O O _ S _ _ _ E S H _ W _ _ G.
    1   2 3   4   5 6 7   8   9 10

Quadratic Functions

ESSENTIAL QUESTION

How do quadratic functions relate to their graphs?

Real-World Video

Projectile motion describes the height of an object thrown or fired into the air. The height of a football, volleyball, or any projectile can be modeled by a quadratic equation.

⊙ my.hrw.com

GO DIGITAL

my.hrw.com

my.hrw.com

Go digital with your write-in student edition, accessible on any device.

Math On the Spot

Scan with your smart phone to jump directly to the online edition, video tutor, and more.

Animated Math

Interactively explore key concepts to see how math works.

Personal Math Trainer

Get immediate feedback and help as you work through practice sets.

Are YOU Ready?

Complete these exercises to review skills you will need for this module.

Symmetry

EXAMPLE If a figure coincides with itself when folded across a line, it has line symmetry. Use the line of symmetry provided to complete the figure.

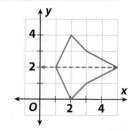

Use the line of symmetry provided to complete each figure.

1.

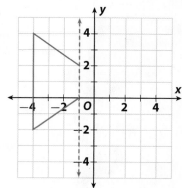

2.

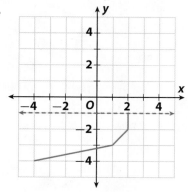

Function Tables

EXAMPLE Create a function table for $y = 3x + 4$.

x	y
0	4
1	7
2	10

Substitute the x-values into the equation and solve for y.

$y = 3(0) + 4 = 0 + 4 = 4$

Function tables example:

$y = 3(1) + 4 = 3 + 4 = 7$

$y = 3(2) + 4 = 6 + 4 = 10$

Complete the table for each function.

3. $y = 5x - 7$

x	y
−2	
0	
2	

4. $y = -8x$

x	y
−2	
0	
2	

5. $y = x^2 - 3$

x	y
−2	
0	
2	

Reading Start-Up

Visualize Vocabulary

Use the Review Words to complete the bubble map.

The set of points where x is in the domain and $y = f(x)$ is the

When a graph can be rotated or reflected and coincide in a coordinate plane with the original graph, it is said to have

A relation in which every input is paired with exactly one output is known as a

Vocabulary

Review Words

✓ function
(función)

✓ graph of a function
(gráfica de una función)

✓ symmetry
(simetría)

Preview Words

quadratic function

parabola

vertex of a parabola

maximum value

minimum value

zero of a function

axis of symmetry

Understand Vocabulary

To become familiar with some of the vocabulary terms in the module, consider the following definitions and select the term from the list of Preview Words that most applies. You may refer to the module, the glossary, or a dictionary.

1. The maximum or minimum value for a parabola.

_____

2. For the function f, any number x such that $f(x) = 0$.

_____

Active Reading

Tri-Fold Note Before beginning the module, create a Tri-Fold Note to help you organize what you learn. Write what you already know about quadratic functions on the first fold and what you want to learn on the second fold. As you read the module, take notes about what you have learned on the third fold to track your learning progress.

Unpacking the Standards

Understanding the standards and the vocabulary terms in the standards will help you know exactly what you are expected to learn in this module.

 FL **A-CED.1.2**

Create equations in two or more variables to represent relationships between quantities; graph equations on coordinate axes with labels and scales.

Key Vocabulary

equation *(ecuación)*
A mathematical statement that two expressions are equivalent.

What It Means to You

Creating equations in two variables to describe relationships gives you access to the tools of graphing and algebra to solve the equations.

UNPACKING EXAMPLE A-CED.1.2

A customer spent $29 on wristbands and gel watches. Wristbands cost $2.50 each and gel watches cost $1.75 each.

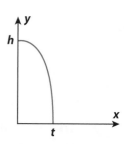

w = number of wristbands bought

g = number of gel watches bought

$$2.5w + 1.75g = 29$$

 FL **F-IF.2.4**

For a function that models a relationship between two quantities, interpret key features of graphs and tables in terms of the quantities, and sketch graphs showing key features given a verbal description of the relationship.

What It Means to You

Learning to interpret a graph enables a deep visual understanding of all sorts of relationships.

UNPACKING EXAMPLE F-IF.2.4

A cliff diver jumps into the ocean from a height of h feet and falls for t seconds before entering the water.

In this equation, the initial height would be the y-intercept and the time at which the diver entered the water would be represented by the x-intercept. As time increases, the height of the diver above the water decreases.

Visit **my.hrw.com** to see all **Florida Math Standards** unpacked.

my.hrw.com

Translating Quadratic Functions

FL   F-BF.2.3

Identify the effect on the graph of replacing $f(x)$ by $f(x) + k$, $k f(x)$, $f(kx)$, and $f(x + k)$ for specific values of k (both negative and positive)... find the value of k given the graphs... Also A-CED.1.2, F-BF.1.1, F-IF.1.2, F-IF.2.4

ESSENTIAL QUESTION

How does the graph of $f(x) = (x - h)^2 + k$ change as the constants h and k are changed?

EXPLORE ACTIVITY    FL   A-CED.1.2, F-IF.1.2

The Parent Quadratic Function

A **quadratic function** is a function that can be represented by an equation of the form $f(x) = ax^2 + bx + c$ where a, b, and c are constants and $a \neq 0$. Notice that the greatest exponent of the variable x is 2. The most basic quadratic function is $f(x) = x^2$. It is called the parent quadratic function.

A Complete the table of values below for the parent quadratic function.

B Plot the ordered pairs, and sketch the graph through the points with a curve.

x	$f(x) = x^2$
-3	$f(x) = x^2 = (-3)^2 = 9$
-2	
	1
0	0
1	
	4
3	

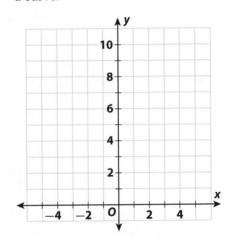

The U-shaped curve is called a **parabola**. The turning point on the parabola is called its **vertex**. The vertex occurs at $(0, 0)$ for this function.

REFLECT

1. a. What is the domain of $f(x) = x^2$? What is the range?

_____

_____

b. Communicate Mathematical Ideas What symmetry does the graph of $f(x) = x^2$ have? Why does it have this symmetry?

_____

_____

Vertical Translations

A **vertical translation** of a parabola is a shift of the parabola up or down, with no change in the shape of the parabola.

Vertical Translations of a Parabola

The graph of the function $f(x) = x^2 + k$ is the graph of $f(x) = x^2$ translated vertically.

- If $k = 0$, the graph is the graph of the parent function, $f(x) = x^2$.
- If $k > 0$, the graph of $f(x) = x^2$ is translated k units up.
- If $k < 0$, the graph of $f(x) = x^2$ is translated $|k|$ units down.

EXAMPLE 1

FL   F-BF.2.3, A-CED.1.2, F-IF.1.2

Graph each quadratic function.

A $g(x) = x^2 + 2$

x	$g(x) = x^2 + 2$
-3	11
-2	6
-1	3
0	2
1	3
2	6
3	11

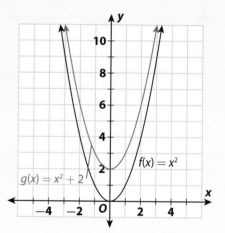

Plot the points from the table. Notice that the graph is identical to the graph of the parent function $f(x) = x^2$ but translated up 2 units.

B $g(x) = x^2 - 2$

x	$g(x) = x^2 - 2$
-3	7
-2	2
-1	-1
0	-2
1	-1
2	2
3	7

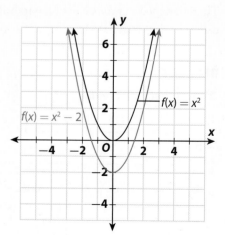

Notice that the graph is identical to the graph of the parent function but translated down 2 units.

REFLECT

2. Analyze Relationships How do the values in the table for $g(x) = x^2 + 2$ compare with the values in the table for the parent function $f(x) = x^2$?

_____

_____

3. Analyze Relationships How do the values in the table for $g(x) = x^2 - 2$ compare to the values in the table for the parent function $f(x) = x^2$?

_____

_____

YOUR TURN

Graph each quadratic function.

4. $f(x) = x^2 + 4$

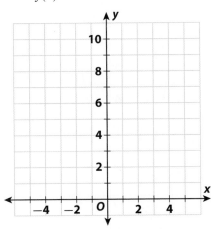

5. $f(x) = x^2 - 5$

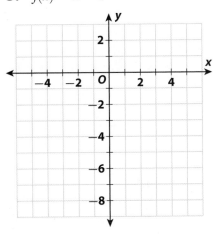

Personal Math Trainer

Online Assessment and Intervention

⏻ my.hrw.com

Horizontal Translations

A **horizontal translation** of a parabola is a shift of the parabola left or right, with no change in the shape of the parabola.

Math On the Spot

⏻ my.hrw.com

Horizontal Translations of a Parabola

The graph of the function $f(x) = (x - h)^2$ is the graph of $f(x) = x^2$ translated horizontally.

- If $h = 0$, the graph is the graph of the parent function, $f(x) = x^2$.
- If $h > 0$, the graph of $f(x) = x^2$ is translated h units to the right.
- If $h < 0$, the graph of $f(x) = x^2$ is translated $|h|$ units to the left.

EXAMPLE 2   FL   F-BF.2.3, A-CED.1.2, F-IF.1.2

Graph each quadratic function.

A $g(x) = (x - 1)^2$

x	$g(x) = (x - 1)^2$
−3	16
−2	9
−1	4
0	1
1	0
2	1
3	4

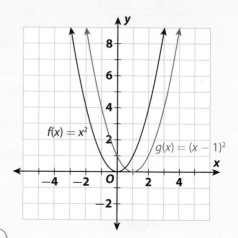

Plot the points from the table. Notice that the graph is identical to the graph of the parent function $f(x) = x^2$ but translated right 1 unit.

B $g(x) = (x + 1)^2$

x	$g(x) = (x + 1)^2$
−3	4
−2	1
−1	0
0	1
1	4
2	9
3	16

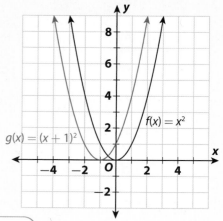

Notice that the graph is identical to the graph of the parent function but translated left 1 unit.

REFLECT

6. Analyze Relationships How do the values in the table for $g(x) = (x - 1)^2$ compare to the values in the table for the parent function $f(x) = x^2$?

_____

_____

7. Analyze Relationships How do the values in the table for $g(x) = (x + 1)^2$ compare to the values in the table for the parent function $f(x) = x^2$?

_____

_____

My Notes

YOUR TURN

Graph each quadratic function.

8. $f(x) = (x - 2)^2$

9. $f(x) = (x + 3)^2$

Personal Math Trainer

Online Assessment and Intervention

my.hrw.com

Writing a Quadratic Function Given a Graph

Math On the Spot

my.hrw.com

Translating a Parabola

The graph of the function $f(x) = (x - h)^2 + k$ is obtained from the graph of $f(x) = x^2$ by a combination of horizontal and vertical translations.

- If h and k are both 0, the graph is the graph of the parent function $f(x) = x^2$.
- If h is not 0, the value of h shifts the graph to the right or left.
- If k is not 0, the value of k shifts the graph up or down.
- The vertex of the parabola is at (h, k).

EXAMPLE 3

FL   F-BF.2.3, F-IF.1.2

Compare the graph of the parabola at the right to the graph of the parent function $f(x) = x^2$. Write an equation of the graph.

STEP 1 Notice the location of the vertex. The parent function has a vertex at (0, 0). This function has a vertex at (3, 2).

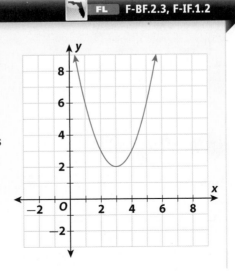

Lesson 17.1 **639**

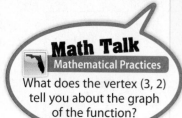

Math Talk

Mathematical Practices

What does the vertex (3, 2) tell you about the graph of the function?

STEP 2 Determine the values of h and k for the function $f(x) = (x - h)^2 + k$.

Since the vertex is at $(3, 2)$, $h = 3$ and $k = 2$. An equation of the parabola is $f(x) = (x - 3)^2 + 2$.

Personal Math Trainer

Online Assessment and Intervention

⏻ my.hrw.com

YOUR TURN

10. Compare the graph of the parabola at the right to the graph of the parent function $f(x) = x^2$. Write an equation of the graph.

_____

_____

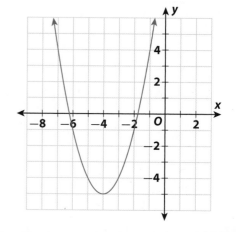

Guided Practice

Graph each quadratic function. (Examples 1 and 2)

1. $f(x) = x^2 + 3$

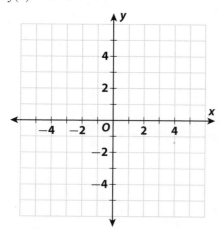

2. $f(x) = (x - 3)^2$

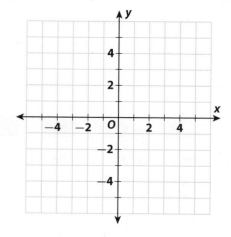

? ESSENTIAL QUESTION CHECK-IN

3. How does the graph of $f(x) = (x - h)^2 + k$ change as the constants h and k are

changed? _____

_____

_____

17.1 Independent Practice

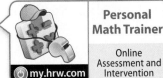

Personal Math Trainer

Online Assessment and Intervention

my.hrw.com

FL   F-BF.2.3, A-CED.1.2, F-BF.1.1, F-IF.1.2, F-IF.2.4

Determine the domain and range of the function.

4. $f(x) = (x - 3)^2$

_____

_____

_____

5. $f(x) = x^2 - 7$

_____

_____

_____

6. $f(x) = x^2 + 4$

_____

_____

_____

7. $f(x) = (x + 1)^2 - 6$

_____

_____

_____

8. The parabola at the right is a translation of the graph of the parent quadratic function $f(x) = x^2$.

a. How far has the parent function been translated horizontally? Vertically?

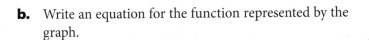

b. Write an equation for the function represented by the graph.

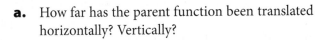

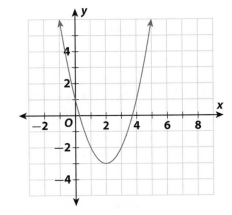

9. The graphs at the right show the heights of two birds as they begin to fly. Both graphs represent quadratic functions.

a. What is the starting height of each bird?

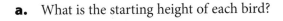

b. What is a possible function for each graph?

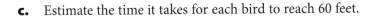

c. Estimate the time it takes for each bird to reach 60 feet.

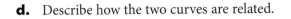

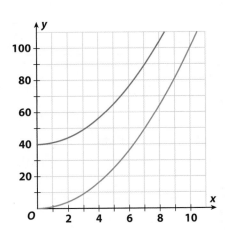

d. Describe how the two curves are related.

_____

_____

10. **Multiple Representations** Graph the following functions on a graphing calculator. Sketch the results on the coordinate grids provided below.

   a. $f(x) = (x + 1)^2$

   b. $g(x) = (x - 5)^2$.

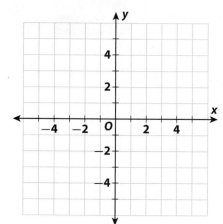

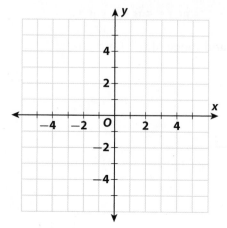

 FOCUS ON HIGHER ORDER THINKING

11. **Explain the Error** Nina is trying to write an equation for the function represented by a parabola that is a translation of the graph of $f(x) = x^2$. She finds that the graph has been translated 4 units to the right and 2 units up. She writes the function as $g(x) = (x + 4)^2 + 2$. Explain the error.

   _____

12. **Critical Thinking** A function is an *even* function if $f(-x) = f(x)$ for all x in the domain of the function. This means that the value of the function is the same when the function is evaluated for a number and for its opposite. The function $f(x) = x^2$ is an even function since you get the same value when you square $-x$ as you do when you square x. Are functions represented by vertical translations of the graph of $f(x) = x^2$ even functions? Are functions represented by horizontal translations of the graph of $f(x) = x^2$ even functions? Explain.

   _____

   _____

   _____

   _____

13. **Analyze Relationships** Describe how the effect of k on the graph of $f(x) = x^2 + k$ is similar to the effect of b on the graph of $f(x) = x + b$.

   _____

   _____

   _____

   _____

Stretching, Shrinking, and Reflecting Quadratic Functions

FL F-BF.2.3

Identify the effect on the graph of replacing $f(x)$ by $f(x) + k$, $k\,f(x)$, $f(kx)$, and $f(x + k)$ for specific values of k (both negative and positive)... find the value of k given the graphs... *Also A-CED.1.2, F-IF.1.2, F-IF.2.4*

ESSENTIAL QUESTION

How does the graph of $f(x) = ax^2$ change as the constant a is changed?

EXPLORE ACTIVITY FL F-BF.2.3, A-CED.1.2, F-IF.1.2

Examining Graphs of Functions of the Form $f(x) = ax^2$

A Complete the table of values for $f(x) = x^2$ and $g(x) = -x^2$.

x	$f(x) = x^2$	$g(x) = -x^2$
−3	9	−9
−2	4	
−1	1	
0	0	0
1	1	
2	4	
3	9	

B Graph the points from the table for $g(x) = -x^2$ and sketch the curve.

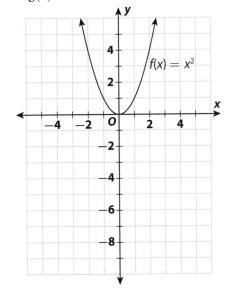

C Complete the table of values for $h(x) = 2x^2$.

x	$f(x) = x^2$	$h(x) = 2x^2$
−3	9	
−2	4	
−1	1	
0	0	
1	1	
2	4	
3	9	

D Graph the points from the table for $h(x) = 2x^2$ and sketch the curve below.

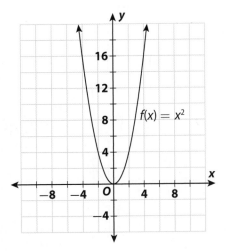

E The axis of symmetry in part B is still the y-axis, and the vertex is still $(0, 0)$. How is the new graph different from the old graph?

_____

F The axis of symmetry in part D is still the y-axis, and the vertex is still $(0, 0)$. How is the new graph different from the old graph?

_____

REFLECT

1. **Draw Conclusions** Based on the functions in the Explore Activity, how do you think $k(x) = \frac{1}{2}x^2$ differs from the parent function? Use a graphing calculator to verify your answer.

_____

_____

The quadratic parent function is $f(x) = x^2$.

The graphs of all other quadratic functions are transformations of the graph of $f(x) = x^2$.

For the parent function $f(x) = x^2$:

- The axis of symmetry is $x = 0$, or the y-axis.
- The vertex is $(0, 0)$.

The value of a in a quadratic equation of the form $y = ax^2$ determines not only the direction the parabola opens (upward or downward), but also the width of the parabola.

Math On the Spot
my.hrw.com

Graphing $g(x) = ax^2$ when $a > 0$

When $a > 0$, the graph of $g(x) = ax^2$ is a vertical stretch or vertical shrink of the parent function $f(x) = x^2$. The graph of $g(x)$ opens upward.

Vertical Stretch
$g(x) = ax^2$ with $a > 1$

Vertical Shrink
$g(x) = ax^2$ with $0 < a < 1$

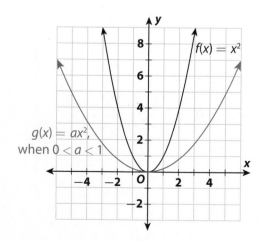

EXAMPLE 1
FL F-BF.2.3, A-CED.1.2, F-IF.1.2

Graph each quadratic function.

A $g(x) = 3x^2$

x	$g(x) = 3x^2$
−3	27
−2	12
−1	3
0	0
1	3
2	12
3	27

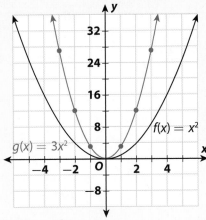

The graph of $g(x)$ is a vertical stretch of the parent function $f(x) = x^2$. The graph of $g(x)$ is narrower than the graph of $f(x)$.

B $g(x) = \frac{1}{3}x^2$

x	$g(x) = \frac{1}{3}x^2$
−3	3
−2	1.333
−1	0.333
0	0
1	0.333
2	1.333
3	3

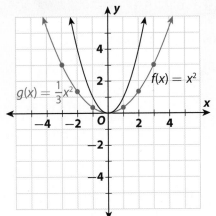

The graph of $g(x)$ is a vertical shrink of the parent function $f(x) = x^2$. The graph of $g(x)$ is wider than the graph of $f(x)$.

YOUR TURN

Graph each quadratic function.

2. $f(x) = 1.5x^2$

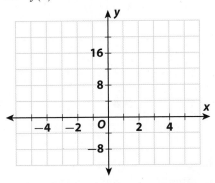

3. $f(x) = \frac{3}{4}x^2$

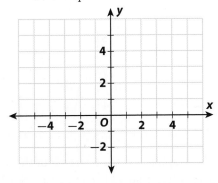

Personal Math Trainer

Online Assessment and Intervention

my.hrw.com

Math On the Spot

my.hrw.com

Graphing $g(x) = ax^2$ when $a < 0$

When $a < 0$, the graph of $g(x) = ax^2$ is a reflection across the x-axis of the parent function $f(x) = x^2$, followed by a vertical stretch or vertical shrink. The graph opens downward.

Vertical Stretch $g(x) = ax^2$ with $a < -1$

Vertical Shrink $g(x) = ax^2$ with $-1 < a < 0$

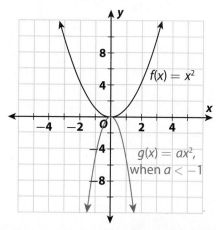

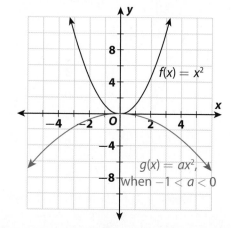

EXAMPLE 2   FL   F-BF.2.3, A-CED.1.2, F-IF.1.2

Graph each quadratic function.

A $g(x) = -2x^2$

x	$g(x) = -2x^2$
-3	-18
-2	-8
-1	-2
0	0
1	-2
2	-8
3	-18

B $g(x) = -\frac{1}{2}x^2$

x	$g(x) = -\frac{1}{2}x^2$
-3	-4.5
-2	-2
-1	-0.5
0	0
1	-0.5
2	-2
3	-4.5

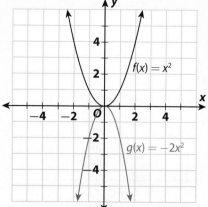

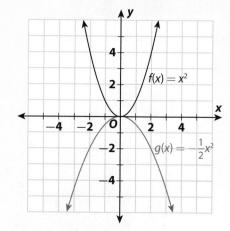

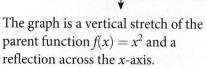

The graph is a vertical stretch of the parent function $f(x) = x^2$ and a reflection across the x-axis.

The graph is a vertical shrink of the parent function $f(x) = x^2$ and a reflection across the x-axis.

YOUR TURN

Graph each quadratic function.

4. $f(x) = -3x^2$

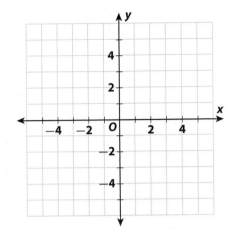

5. $f(x) = -\frac{3}{4}x^2$

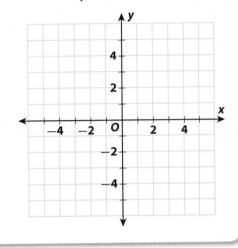

Writing a Quadratic Function Given a Graph

You can write a function rule for a parabola with its vertex at the origin by substituting the x- and y-values for any point on the parabola into $f(x) = ax^2$ and solving for a.

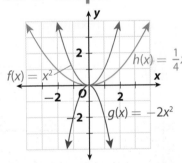

$f(x) = x^2$

$h(x) = \frac{1}{4}x^2$

$g(x) = -2x^2$

Math On the Spot

⏻ my.hrw.com

EXAMPLE 3   **FL**   F-BF.2.3, F-IF.1.2

The graph below represents a quadratic function of the form $f(x) = ax^2$. Write a rule for the function.

Use the point $(2, -1)$ to find a.

$y = ax^2$

$(-1) = a(2)^2$

$-1 = 4a$

$-\frac{1}{4} = a$

The rule is $f(x) = -\frac{1}{4}x^2$.

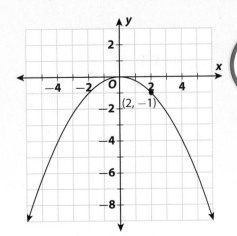

$(2, -1)$

Math Talk

Mathematical Practices

Why can you predict that the value of a is negative?

YOUR TURN

6. The graph below represents a quadratic function of the form $f(x) = ax^2$.
Write a rule for the function.

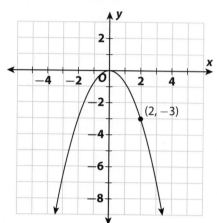

_____

Guided Practice

Graph each quadratic function. (Examples 1 and 2)

1. $f(x) = 0.6x^2$

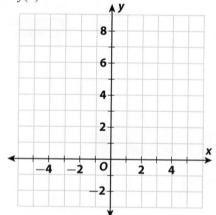

2. $f(x) = -2.5x^2$

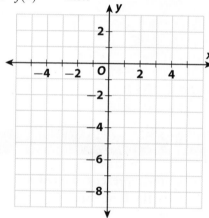

ESSENTIAL QUESTION CHECK-IN

3. How do the values of the constant a affect the graph of a parabola in the
function $g(x) = ax^2$?

_____

_____

_____

17.2 Independent Practice

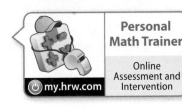

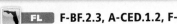

FL F-BF.2.3, A-CED.1.2, F-IF.1.2, F-IF.2.4

Order the functions from narrowest (most vertically stretched) to widest (most vertically shrunk).

4. $f(x) = -2x^2; g(x) = \frac{1}{2}x^2$ _____

5. $f(x) = \frac{3}{4}x^2; g(x) = -2x^2; h(x) = -8x^2$

_____

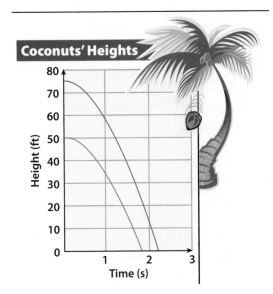

Coconuts' Heights

6. The graph compares the heights of two identical coconuts that fell from different trees.

a. Estimate the starting height of each coconut. _____

_____

b. If each graph is represented by a function of the form $f(x) = ax^2$, are the coefficients a positive or negative? Explain.

_____

_____

c. Estimate the time it takes for each coconut to reach the ground.

_____

_____

d. Describe how the two curves are related.

_____

_____

7. Multi-Step Give an example of a quadratic function that meets each description. Sketch the graph of your function.

a. Its graph has the same width as the graph of $f(x) = x^2$, but the graph opens downward.

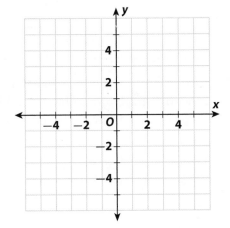

_____

b. Its graph opens downward but is narrower than the graph of $f(x) = x^2$.

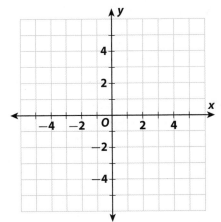

_____

8. **Draw Conclusions** In general, how does the y-coordinate of a point on the graph of $g(x) = \frac{1}{2}x^2$ compare with the y-coordinate of a point on the graph of $f(x) = x^2$ when the points have the same x-coordinate?

_____

_____

9. **Draw Conclusions** In general, how does the y-coordinate of a point on the graph of $h(x) = -2x^2$ compare to the y-coordinate of a point on the graph of $f(x) = x^2$ when the points have the same x-coordinate?

_____

_____

 **FOCUS ON HIGHER ORDER THINKING**

10. **Check for Reasonableness** The graph of $f(x) = ax^2$ is a parabola that passes through the point $(-2, 2)$. Kyle says that the value of a must be $-\frac{1}{2}$. Explain why this value of a is not reasonable.

_____

_____

11. **Critical Thinking** A quadratic function has a minimum value when the function's graph opens upward, and it has a maximum value when the function's graph opens downward. In each case, the minimum or maximum value is the y-coordinate of the vertex of the function's graph.

    Under what circumstances does the function $f(x) = ax^2$ have a minimum value? a maximum value? What is the minimum or maximum value in each case?

_____

_____

12. **Critical Thinking** A function is called an even function if $f(-x) = f(x)$ for all x in the domain of the function. Explain why the function $f(x) = ax^2$ is even for any value of a.

_____

_____

13. **Communicate Mathematical Ideas** Explain how you know, without graphing, what the graph of $g(x) = \frac{1}{10}x^2$ looks like.

_____

_____

_____

Combining Transformations of Quadratic Functions

FL · F-IF.3.7a

Graph linear and quadratic functions and show intercepts, maxima, and minima. *Also, A-CED.1.2, F-IF.1.2, F-IF.2.4, F-IF.3.7, F-BF.1.1, F-BF.2.3*

? ESSENTIAL QUESTION

How can you obtain the graph of $g(x) = a(x - h)^2 + k$ from the graph of $f(x) = x^2$?

EXPLORE ACTIVITY   FL F-IF.1.2, F-BF.2.3

Understanding Quadratic Functions of the Form $g(x) = a(x - h)^2 + k$

The function $f(x) = x^2$ is the parent function of the family of all quadratic functions. Every quadratic function can be represented by an equation of the form $g(x) = a(x - h)^2 + k$. The values of the parameters a, h, and k determine how the graph of the function compares to the graph of the parent function.

The sequence of graphs below shows how you can obtain the graph of $g(x) = 2(x - 3)^2 + 1$ from the graph of the parent quadratic function $f(x) = x^2$ using transformations.

A Graph $f(x) = x^2$. Then stretch the graph vertically by a factor

of _____ to obtain the graph of $y = 2x^2$. Graph the function.

B Translate the graph of $y = 2x^2$

right _____ units and up

_____ unit to obtain the graph of $g(x) = 2(x - 3)^2 + 1$.

Animated Math

my.hrw.com

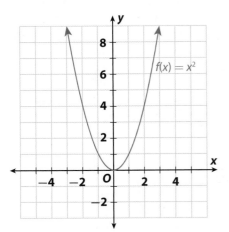

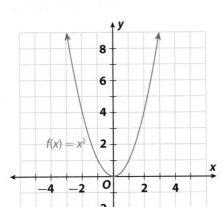

REFLECT

1. The vertex of the graph of $f(x) = x^2$ is _____ while the vertex of

the graph of $g(x) = 2(x - 3)^2 + 1$ is _____.

2. Using the equation $g(x) = 2(x - 3)^2 + 1$, find $g(4)$. Is $(4, g(4))$ on the curve you plotted?

_____

3. Using the equation $g(x) = 2(x - 3)^2 + 1$, find $g(5)$. Is $(5, g(5))$ on the curve you plotted?

_____

4. Using the equation $g(x) = 2(x - 3)^2 + 1$, find $g(2)$. Is $(2, g(2))$ on the curve you plotted?

_____

5. Make a Conjecture What is another way, besides the one in the Explore Activity, that you could use to graph the function $g(x) = 2(x - 3)^2 + 1$?

_____

_____

_____

Math On the Spot

my.hrw.com

Graphing $g(x) = a(x - h)^2 + k$

To graph a quadratic function of the form $g(x) = a(x - h)^2 + k$, first identify the vertex (h, k). Next, consider the sign of a to determine whether the graph opens upward or downward. If a is positive, the graph opens upward. If a is negative, the graph opens downward. Then generate two points on each side of the vertex. Using those points, sketch the graph of the function.

EXAMPLE 1

FL   F-IF.1.2, F-BF.2.3

Graph $g(x) = -3(x + 1)^2 - 2$.

My Notes

STEP 1   Identify and plot the vertex.

The vertex is at $(-1, -2)$.

STEP 2   Make a table for the function.

x	−3	−2	−1	0	1
g(x)	−14	−5	−2	−5	−14

STEP 3   Plot the points and draw a parabola through them.

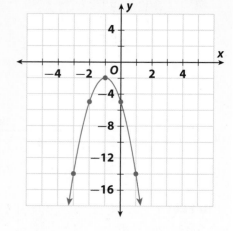

REFLECT

6. List the transformations of the graph of the parent function $f(x) = x^2$, in the order that you would perform them, to obtain the graph of $g(x) = -3(x + 1)^2 - 2$.

_____

_____

7. Justify Reasoning Before graphing $g(x) = -3(x + 1)^2 - 2$, would you have expected the graph to open upward or downward? Why?

_____

_____

8. What If? Suppose you changed the -3 in $g(x) = -3(x + 1)^2 - 2$ to -4. Which of the points identified in the example would change? What coordinates would they now have?

_____

_____

YOUR TURN

9. Graph $g(x) = -(x - 2)^2 + 4$.

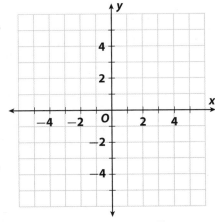

Personal Math Trainer

Online Assessment and Intervention

my.hrw.com

Writing a Quadratic Function Given a Graph

The graph of a parabola can be used to determine the corresponding quadratic function.

Math On the Spot

my.hrw.com

EXAMPLE 2 (Real World) | **FL** F-IF1.2, F-IF.2.4, F-BF.1.1, F-BF.2.3

A house painter standing on a ladder drops a paintbrush, which falls to the ground. The paintbrush's height above the ground (in feet) is given by a function of the form $f(t) = a(t - h)^2 + k$ where t is the time (in seconds) since the paintbrush was dropped.

My Notes

Use the graph to find an equation for $f(t)$.

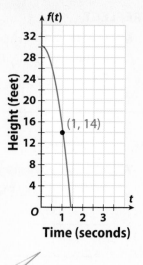

STEP 1 The vertex of the parabola is $(h, k) = (0, 30)$.

Substitute the values of h and k into the general equation for $f(t)$ to get $f(t) = a(t - 0)^2 + 30$, or $f(t) = at^2 + 30$.

STEP 2 From the graph you can see that $f(1) = 14$. Substitute 1 for t and 14 for $f(t)$ to determine the value of a for this function:

$$14 = a(1)^2 + 30$$

$$-16 = a$$

STEP 3 Write the equation for the function: $f(t) = -16t^2 + 30$.

> Only the portion of the parabola that lies in Quadrant I is shown because only nonnegative values of t and $f(t)$ make sense in this situation.

REFLECT

10. Multi-Step Using the graph, estimate how much time elapses before the paintbrush hits the ground: $t \approx$ _____

11. Check for Reasonableness Using the value of t from Question 10 and the equation for the height function from step 3 of the example, find the value of $f(t)$. How does this help you check the reasonableness of the equation?

_____

_____

_____

12. Why can't the value of $f(t)$ be negative in this situation?

_____

Personal Math Trainer

Online Assessment and Intervention

⏻ my.hrw.com

YOUR TURN

13. A diver jumps off a cliff into the sea below to search for shells. The diver's height above the sea (in feet) is given by a function of the form $f(t) = a(t - h)^2 + k$, where t is the time (in seconds) since the diver jumped. Use the graph to find an equation for $f(t)$.

$f(t) =$ _____

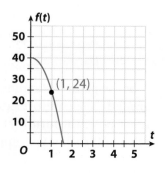

© Houghton Mifflin Harcourt Publishing Company • Image Credits: ©Inorsky/

Modeling the Height of an Object in Free Fall

The quadratic function $h(t) = -16t^2 + c$ can be used to approximate the height $h(t)$ in feet above the ground of a falling object t seconds after it is dropped from a height of c feet. This model is used only to approximate the height of falling objects because it does not account for air resistance, wind, and other real-world factors.

Math On the Spot
my.hrw.com

EXAMPLE 3   **FL** F-IF.1.2, F-IF.2.4, F-IF.3.7, F-IF.3.7a, F-BF.1.1

Two identical water balloons are dropped from different heights as shown in the diagram.

A Write the two height functions and compare their graphs.

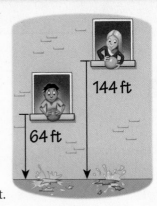

144 ft

64 ft

Animated Math

my.hrw.com

STEP 1 Write the height functions.

The constant c in the equation in the paragraph at the top of this page represents the original height.

$h_1(t) = -16t^2 + 64$ Dropped from 64 feet

$h_2(t) = -16t^2 + 144$ Dropped from 144 feet

Math Talk
Mathematical Practices

In part A, why was the window of the graphing calculator set for nonnegative values only?

STEP 2 Use a graphing calculator.

The graph of h_2 is a vertical translation of the graph of h_1. Since the balloon represented by h_2 is dropped from 80 feet higher than the one represented by h_1, the y-intercept of h_2 is 80 units higher than that of h_1.

$h_2(t) = -16t^2 + 144$

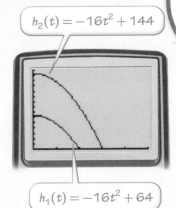

$h_1(t) = -16t^2 + 64$

B Use the graphs to tell how long it takes each water balloon to reach the ground.

The x-intercept of each graph indicates the amount of time it takes for the balloon to reach the ground.

The water balloon dropped from 64 feet reaches the ground in 2 seconds.
The water balloon dropped from 144 feet reaches the ground in 3 seconds.

REFLECT

14. **Represent Real-World Problems** Write the function for a water balloon that is dropped from a height of 50 feet. Explain.

_____

_____

YOUR TURN

15. Two baseballs are dropped, one from a height of 16 feet and the other from a height of 256 feet.

a. Write the two height functions.

_____

b. How long does it take each baseball to reach the ground?

_____

Guided Practice

Graph each quadratic function. (Example 1)

1. $f(x) = 2(x-2)^2 + 3$

2. $f(x) = -(x-1)^2 + 2$

3. A roofer working on a roof accidentally drops a hammer, which falls to the ground. The hammer's height above the ground (in feet) is given by a function of the form $f(t) = a(t-h)^2 + k$ where t is the time (in seconds) since the hammer was dropped. Use the graph to find an equation for $f(t)$. (Example 2)

_____

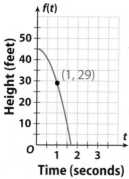

❓ ESSENTIAL QUESTION CHECK-IN

4. How can you use the values of a, h, and k, to obtain the graph of $g(x) = a(x-h)^2 + k$ from the graph of $f(x) = x^2$?

_____

_____

_____

17.3 Independent Practice

 FL A-CED.1.2, F-BF.1.1, F-BF.2.3, F-IF.1.2, F-IF.2.4, F-IF.3.7, F-IF.3.7a

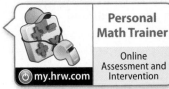

Personal
Math Trainer

Online
Assessment and
Intervention

Graph each quadratic function.

5. $f(x) = \frac{1}{2}(x-2)^2$

6. $f(x) = -\frac{1}{3}x^2 - 3$

7. $f(x) = 4(x+2)^2 - 3$

8. $f(x) = -\frac{1}{4}(x-1)^2 - 3$

9. Two tennis balls are dropped, one from a height of 16 feet and the other from a height of 100 feet.

a. Write the two height functions and use a graphing calculator to compare their graphs.

_____

_____

_____

_____

b. Use the graphs to tell how long it takes each tennis ball to reach the ground.

_____

_____

_____

10. A raindrop falls from a cloud at an altitude of 10,000 ft. Another raindrop falls from a cloud at an altitude of 14,400 ft.

a. Write the two height functions and use a graphing calculator to compare their graphs.

_____

_____

_____

b. Use the graphs to tell when each raindrop reaches the ground.

_____

_____

_____

_____

 FOCUS ON HIGHER ORDER THINKING

Work Area

11. **Explain the Error** Kevin says that the graph of the function $f(x) = -(x - 2)^2 + 3$ is a parabola that opens downward and has a vertex at $(3, 2)$. Explain the error.

_____

_____

12. **Make a Prediction** For what values of a and c will the graph of $f(x) = ax^2 + c$ have one x-intercept?

_____

_____

13. **Critical Thinking** Give an example of a quadratic function whose graph is wider than the graph of $f(x) = x^2$, opens downward, and has no x-intercepts.

_____

LESSON 17.4 Characteristics of Quadratic Functions

FL F-IF.2.4

For a function that models a relationship between two quantities, interpret key features of graphs and tables in terms of the quantities ... *Also F-IF.3.8*

ESSENTIAL QUESTION

How are the characteristics of quadratic functions related to the key features of their graphs?

EXPLORE ACTIVITY

FL F-IF.2.4

Explore Quadratic Functions

In this activity you will learn how to determine whether a function is a quadratic function by looking at its graph. If the graph of a function is a parabola, then the function is a quadratic function. If the graph of a function is not a parabola, then the function is not a quadratic function.

Use a graphing calculator to graph each of the functions. Set the viewing window to show -10 to 10 on both axes. Sketch the graph that you see on your calculator. Circle "yes" or "no" to tell whether each function is a quadratic function.

A $f(x) = x + 1$

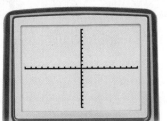

quadratic: yes   no

B $f(x) = -x^2 + 1$

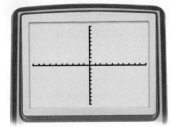

quadratic: yes   no

C $f(x) = 2x^2 - 1$

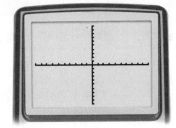

quadratic: yes   no

D $f(x) = x^3$

quadratic: yes   no

E $f(x) = \sqrt{x}$

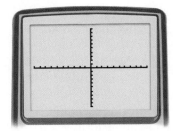

quadratic: yes   no

F $f(x) = 2^x$

quadratic: yes   no

REFLECT

1. **Communicate Mathematical Ideas** How can you determine whether a function is quadratic or not by looking at its graph?

_____

_____

_____

_____

2. **Make a Conjecture** Based on your observations, how can you tell if a function is a quadratic function by looking at the equation?

_____

_____

Math On the Spot

⏻ my.hrw.com

Identifying Quadratic Functions

If a function is quadratic, it can be represented by an equation of the form $y = ax^2 + bx + c$, where a, b, and c are real numbers and $a \neq 0$. This is called the standard form of a quadratic equation.

EXAMPLE 1

   FL   F-IF.3.8

Determine whether the function represented by each equation is quadratic. Explain.

A $y = -2x + 20$ *Compare to $y = ax^2 + bx + c$.*

This is not a quadratic function because $a = 0$.

B $y + 3x^2 = -4$

Rewrite the function in the form $y = ax^2 + bx + c$.

$$
\begin{aligned}
y + 3x^2 &= -4 \\
\underline{-3x^2 \qquad -3x^2} & \qquad \text{\footnotesize Subtract } 3x^2 \text{ from each side.}\\
y &= -3x^2 - 4 \qquad \text{\footnotesize } a = -3, b = 0, c = -4
\end{aligned}
$$

This is a quadratic function because a, b, and c are real numbers and $a \neq 0$.

C $-y + 2 + 4x^2 = 4x$

Rewrite the function in the form $y = ax^2 + bx + c$.

$$
\begin{aligned}
-y + 2 + 4x^2 &= 4x \\
y &= 4x^2 - 4x + 2 \qquad \text{\footnotesize } a = 4, b = -4, c = 2
\end{aligned}
$$

This is a quadratic function because a, b, and c are real numbers and $a \neq 0$.

My Notes

REFLECT

3. **Critical Thinking** Explain why the function represented by the equation $y = ax^2 + bx + c$ is quadratic only when $a \neq 0$.

_____

_____

4. **Communicate Mathematical Ideas** Why might it be easier to determine whether a function is quadratic when it is expressed in function notation?

_____

_____

YOUR TURN

Determine whether the function represented by each equation is quadratic. Explain.

5. $y - 4x + x^2 = 0$

6. $f(x) = 0.01 - 0.2x + x^2$

_____   _____

7. $x + 2y = 14x + 6$

8. $f(x) = \frac{1}{2}x - 4$

_____   _____

Personal Math Trainer

Online Assessment and Intervention

⊙ my.hrw.com

Maximum and Minimum Values

Every parabola has either a highest point or a lowest point, called the vertex. The y-coordinate of the highest point or lowest point is the maximum value or minimum value of the function represented by the parabola.

Math On the Spot

⊙ my.hrw.com

Minimum and Maximum Values		
Words	If $a > 0$, the parabola opens upward, and the y-value of the vertex is the **minimum** value of the function. If $a > 0$, the function has no maximum value.	If $a < 0$, the parabola opens downward, and the y-value of the vertex is the **maximum** value of the function. If $a < 0$, the function has no minimum value.

$y = x^2 + 6x + 9$

Vertex: $(-3, 0)$
Minimum: 0

$y = -x^2 + 6x - 4$

Vertex: $(3, 5)$
Maximum: 5

EXAMPLE 2   FL   F-IF.2.4

Determine the maximum or minimum value of each quadratic function from its graph or its equation.

A

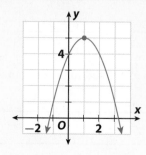

The parabola opens downward, so 5 is the maximum value.

B

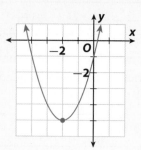

The parabola opens upward, so −5 is the minimum value.

C $y = 2(x + 1)^2 - 6$

The vertex (h, k) is $(-1, -6)$. Because $a > 0$, the parabola opens upward.

The minimum value of the function is −6.

D $y = -3(x - 4)^2 + 5$

The vertex (h, k) is $(4, 5)$. Because $a < 0$, the parabola opens downward.

The maximum value of the function is 5.

REFLECT

9. Critical Thinking How could you determine the maximum or minimum value if the equation of a quadratic function is given in standard form $y = ax^2 + bx + c$?

_____

YOUR TURN

Determine the maximum or minimum value of each quadratic function from its graph or its equation.

10.

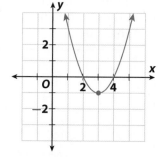

_____

11. $y = -(x - 5)^2 + 8$

_____

12. $y = 4(x + 2)^2 + 3$

_____

Personal Math Trainer

Online Assessment and Intervention

my.hrw.com

Zeros of a Function

A **zero of a function** is a value of x that makes the value of the function 0. The zeros of a function are the x-intercepts of the graph of the function. A quadratic function may have one, two, or no zeros.

> Recall that an x-intercept of a graph is the x-coordinate of the point where the graph crosses the x-axis. The value of y at an x-intercept is 0.

EXAMPLE 3 FL F-IF.2.4

Math On the Spot
my.hrw.com

Find the zeros of each quadratic function from its graph. Check your answers.

A $y = x^2 - x - 2$

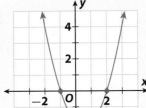

The zeros appear to be -1 and 2.

Check:

$y = x^2 - x - 2$

$y = (-1)^2 - (-1) - 2$

$\quad = 1 + 1 - 2 = 0$ ✔

$y = (2)^2 - (2) - 2$

$\quad = 4 - 2 - 2 = 0$ ✔

Animated Math
my.hrw.com

B $y = -2x^2 + 4x - 2$

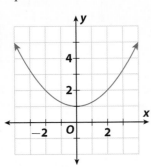

The only zero appears to be 1.

Check:

$y = -2x^2 + 4x - 2$

$y = -2(1)^2 + 4(1) - 2$

$\quad = -2(1) + 4 - 2$

$\quad = -2 + 4 - 2$

$\quad = 0$ ✔

C $y = \frac{1}{4}x^2 + 1$

The graph does not cross the x-axis, so this function has no zeros.

REFLECT

13. Critical Thinking If a quadratic function has only one zero, it has to occur at the vertex of the parabola. Using the graph of a quadratic function, explain why.

_____

_____

_____

Find the zeros of each quadratic function from its graph. Check your answers.

14. $y = -4x^2 - 2$

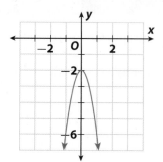

15. $y = x^2 - 6x + 9$

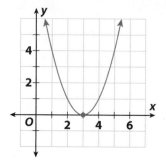

_____

_____

Math On the Spot

my.hrw.com

Axis of Symmetry

The vertical line that divides a parabola into two symmetrical halves is called its **axis of symmetry**. The axis of symmetry passes through the vertex of the parabola. You can use the zeros of a function to find the equation of the axis of symmetry of its graph.

Finding the Axis of Symmetry by Using Zeros

Words	Numbers	Graph
One Zero If a quadratic function has one zero, use the x-coordinate of the vertex to find the axis of symmetry.	Vertex: $(3, 0)$ Axis of symmetry: $x = 3$	
Two Zeros If a quadratic function has two zeros, use the average of the two zeros to find the axis of symmetry.	$\dfrac{-4+0}{2} = \dfrac{-4}{2} = -2$ Axis of symmetry: $x = -2$	

EXAMPLE 4    FL   F-IF.2.4

Sketch the axis of symmetry of each parabola and find its equation.

A

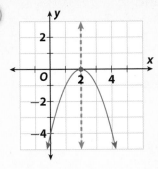

The function has one zero at $(2, 0)$, which is the vertex.

The axis of symmetry is $x = 2$.

B

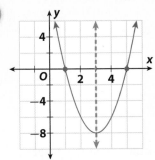

The function has two zeros, at $(1, 0)$ and $(5, 0)$, so use the average of the two zeros to the find the axis of symmetry.

$$\frac{1 + 5}{2} = \frac{6}{2} = 3 \qquad \textit{Find the average of 1 and 5.}$$

The axis of symmetry is $x = 3$.

YOUR TURN

Sketch the axis of symmetry of each parabola and find its equation.

16.

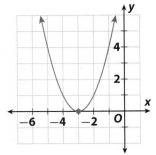

17.

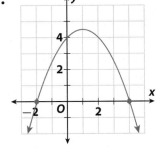

Personal
Math Trainer

Online Assessment
and Intervention

my.hrw.com

Determine whether the function represented by each equation is quadratic. (Example 1)

1. $y + 6x = 14$

2. $2x^2 + y = 3x - 1$

_____

_____

Determine whether each quadratic function has a minimum value or a maximum value. Then find the minimum or maximum value. (Example 2)

3.

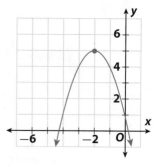

4. $y = (x + 11)^2 + 4$

_____

5. $y = -\frac{1}{2}(x - 1)^2 - 3$

_____

_____

Find the zeros of the quadratic function from its graph. Check your answers. (Example 3)

6. $y = 9 - x^2$

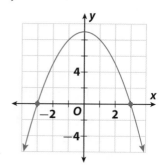

Sketch the axis of symmetry of the parabola and find its equation. (Example 4)

7.

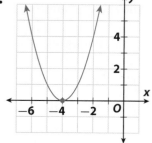

_____

_____

? ESSENTIAL QUESTION CHECK-IN

8. What can you tell about the graph of a parabola when the equation of the parabola is written in the form $y = a(x - h)^2 + k$?

_____

_____

_____

17.4 Independent Practice

 FL   F-IF.2.4, F-IF.3.8

Personal
Math Trainer

Online
Assessment and
Intervention

my.hrw.com

Determine whether each function is quadratic. Explain.

9. $x - 3x^2 + y = 5$

_____

10. $-2x + y = -3$

_____

For each quadratic function, determine whether it has a maximum value or a minimum value. Then determine the maximum or minimum value of the function from its graph or its equation.

11. $y = -\frac{1}{3}\left(x - \frac{1}{2}\right)^2 + \frac{1}{4}$ _____

12.

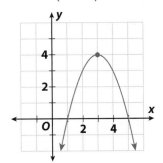

_____

Find the zeros of each quadratic function from its graph. Check your answers.

13. $y = \frac{1}{4}(x - 2)^2 + 2$

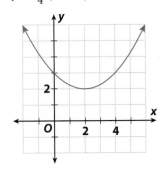

_____

14. $y = x^2 + 10x + 16$

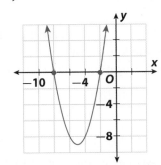

_____

Sketch the axis of symmetry of each parabola and find its equation.

15.

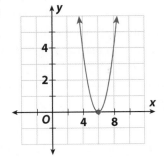

_____

16.

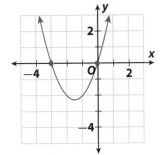

_____

17. Draw Conclusions What can be said about the axis of symmetry of the graph of the quadratic function represented by the equation $y = ax^2 + bx + c$ when $b = 0$?

_____

18. a. Critical Thinking If you are given the axis of symmetry of a quadratic function and know that the function has two zeros, how would you describe the location of the two zeros? Explain.

_____

_____

b. One zero of a given quadratic function is 6. The axis of symmetry for the graph of the quadratic function is $x = 7.5$. What is the other zero of this quadratic function?

_____

19. Explain the Error Martina rearranged the terms of a quadratic function and ended with $-y = -(x - 1)^2 - 3$. She stated that the graph of the function opened downward and that the function had a maximum value of -3. Assuming that Martina's work in rearranging the terms was correct, what was her error?

_____

20. Critical Thinking A quadratic function has two zeros. If the graph of the function opens downward, what can you say about the value of the function for input values less than the lesser zero, greater than the greater zero, and between the two zeros?

_____

_____

_____

_____

_____

_____

21. Make a Conjecture How could you find an equation of a quadratic function with zeros -3 and 1?

_____

_____

_____

LESSON 17.5

Solving Quadratic Equations Graphically

FL   A-REI.4.11

Explain why the *x*-coordinates of the points where the graphs of the equations $y = f(x)$ and $y = g(x)$ intersect are the solutions of the equation $f(x) = g(x)$; find the solutions approximately... *Also A-CED.1.1, A-CED.1.2, A.REI.2.4*

ESSENTIAL QUESTION

How can you use the graph of a quadratic function to solve a quadratic equation?

EXPLORE ACTIVITY  FL   A-REI.4.11

Finding Points of Intersection of Lines and Parabolas

The graphs of three quadratic functions are shown.

Parabola A is the graph of $f(x) = x^2$.

Parabola B is the graph of $h(x) = x^2 + 4$.

Parabola C is the graph of $j(x) = x^2 + 8$.

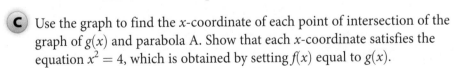

A On the same coordinate grid, graph the function $g(x) = 4$. What type of function is this? Describe its graph.

_____

B At how many points does the graph of $g(x)$ intersect each parabola?

Parabola A: _____ points of intersection

Parabola B: _____ points of intersection

Parabola C: _____ points of intersection

C Use the graph to find the *x*-coordinate of each point of intersection of the graph of $g(x)$ and parabola A. Show that each *x*-coordinate satisfies the equation $x^2 = 4$, which is obtained by setting $f(x)$ equal to $g(x)$.

_____

D Use the graph to find the *x*-coordinate of each point of intersection of the graph of $g(x)$ and parabola B. Show that each *x*-coordinate satisfies the equation $x^2 + 4 = 4$, which is obtained by setting $h(x)$ equal to $g(x)$.

_____

REFLECT

1. Describe how you could solve an equation like $x^2 + 2 = 11$ graphically.

_____

_____

_____

Solving Quadratic Equations Graphically, Method 1

You can solve a quadratic equation of the form $a(x - h)^2 + k = c$ by using the expressions on each side of the equation to define a function, graphing the functions, and finding the x-coordinates of the points of intersections of the graphs.

EXAMPLE 1

FL   A-REI.2.4

Solve $2(x - 4)^2 + 1 = 3$ by graphing.

STEP 1   Let $f(x) = 2(x - 4)^2 + 1$.

Let $g(x) = 3$.

STEP 2   Graph $f(x)$.

STEP 3   Graph $g(x)$.

STEP 4   Determine the points at which the graphs of $f(x)$ and $g(x)$ intersect.

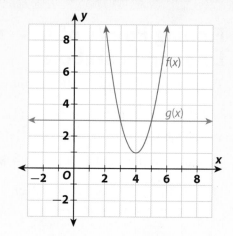

The graphs intersect in two locations: (3, 3) and (5, 3).

This means $f(x) = g(x)$ when $x = 3$ and $x = 5$.

Therefore, the solutions of the equation $f(x) = g(x)$ are 3 and 5.

So the solutions of $2(x - 4)^2 + 1 = 3$ are $x = 3$ and $x = 5$.

YOUR TURN

2.   Solve $3(x - 5)^2 - 2 = 10$ by graphing.

_____

Solving Quadratic Equations Graphically, Method 2

There is another way to solve a quadratic equation. First, write the related function for the quadratic equation by rewriting the equation so that one side is 0 and then replacing the 0 with y. Graph the related function and find the x-intercepts of the graph, which are the zeros of the function. The zeros of the function are the solutions of the original equation. Recall that a quadratic function may have two, one, or no zeros.

Solving Quadratic Equations by Graphing

Step 1 Write the related function.

Step 2 Graph the related function.

Step 3 Find the zeros of the related function.

EXAMPLE 2

FL   A-REI.2.4

Solve the equation $2x^2 - 5 = -3$ by graphing the related function.

STEP 1 Adding 3 to both sides of the equation produces the equation $2x^2 - 2 = 0$. The related function is $y = 2x^2 - 2$.

STEP 2 Make a table of values for the related function.

x	−2	1	0	1	2
y	6	0	−2	0	64

Graph the points represented by the table and connect the points.

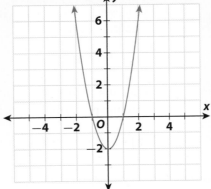

STEP 3 The zeros of the function are −1 and 1, so the solutions of the equation $2x^2 - 5 = -3$ are $x = -1$ and $x = 1$.

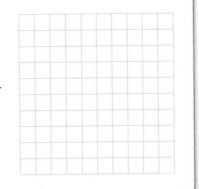

Math Talk

Mathematical Practices

How can you check that −1 and 1 are solutions of the equation $2x^2 - 5 = -3$?

YOUR TURN

3. Solve $6x + 8 = -x^2$ by graphing the related function.

_____

Personal Math Trainer

Online Assessment and Intervention

my.hrw.com

Modeling a Real-World Problem

Many real-world problems, particularly those involving the motion of falling objects near Earth's surface, can be modeled by quadratic functions.

 EXAMPLE 3 Real World

 FL A-CED.1.1, A-REI.2.4

While practicing a tightrope walk at a height of 20 feet, a circus performer slips and falls into a safety net 15 feet below. The function $h(t) = -16t^2 + 20$, where t represents time measured in seconds, gives the performer's height above the ground (in feet) as he falls. Write and solve an equation to find the amount of time before the performer lands in the net.

STEP 1 Write the equation that needs to be solved.

$$-16t^2 + 20 = 5$$

The performer falls into a net that is 15 feet below the tightrope, or 5 feet above the ground.

STEP 2 A graphing calculator requires that functions be entered in terms of x and y. In terms of x and y, the two functions that must be entered into the calculator are $y = -16x^2 + 20$ and $y = 5$.

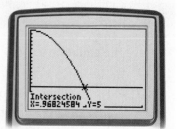

STEP 3 When setting a viewing window, decide what portion of each axis to use for graphing.

The calculator shows an x-value of 0.96824584 for the point of intersection, so a good approximation is x = 1.

STEP 4 Graph the two functions, and use the calculator's trace or intersect feature to find the amount of time before the performer lands in the net.

The performer lands in the net in about 1 second.

Math Talk
Mathematical Practices

The graphs also intersect to the left of the y-axis. Why is that point irrelevant to the problem?

Use $0 \le x \le 2$ and $0 \le y \le 20$. Only nonnegative values of x and y are meaningful.

REFLECT

4. Critical Thinking Why is only the x-value of the intersection point the solution to the equation?

_____

YOUR TURN

5. A squirrel is in a tree 46 feet off the ground and throws a chestnut that lands on a bush 36 feet below. The function $h(t) = -16t^2 + 46$, where t represents time measured in seconds, gives the height of the nut above the ground (in feet) as it falls. Write and solve an equation to find the amount of time before the nut lands on the bush.

_____

Interpreting Quadratic Models

Finding the solutions to a quadratic equation can be helpful in determining other information about the situation being modeled by the related function. For example, the solutions can be used to determine how long an event lasted or when a projectile reaches its greatest height.

Math On the Spot
⏱ my.hrw.com

EXAMPLE 4    **FL** A-CED.1.1, A-REI.2.4

A dolphin jumps out of the water. The quadratic function $y = -16x^2 + 20x$ models the dolphin's height (in feet) above the water after x seconds. How long is the dolphin out of the water?

Use the level of the water surface as 0. When the dolphin leaves the water, its height is 0 feet, and when the dolphin reenters the water, its height is 0 feet.

Solve $0 = -16x^2 + 20x$ to find the times when the dolphin leaves and reenters water.

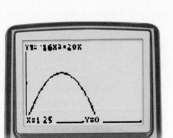

STEP 1   Write the related function for the equation $0 = -16x^2 + 20x$.

$y = -16x^2 + 20x$

STEP 2   Graph the function using a graphing calculator.

STEP 3   Use the calculator's trace function to estimate the zeros.

The zeros appear to be 0 and 1.25.

> Substituting 0 for x makes the right side of the equation equal to 0, so 0 is a solution.

Check $-16(1.25)^2 + 20(1.25) = -16(1.5625) + 25 =$
$-25 + 25 = 0$, so 1.25 is a solution.

The dolphin is out of the water for 1.25 seconds.

REFLECT

6. **Critical Thinking** How would you find the time it takes the dolphin to reach the highest point of his jump?

_____

_____

YOUR TURN

7. A baseball coach uses a pitching machine to simulate pop flies during practice. The quadratic function $y = -16x^2 + 80x$ models the height in feet of the baseball after x seconds. How long is the baseball in the air?

_____

Personal Math Trainer

Online Assessment and Intervention

⏱ my.hrw.com

1. Solve $(x + 2)^2 - 1 = 3$ by graphing. Indicate whether the solutions are exact or approximate. (Example 1)

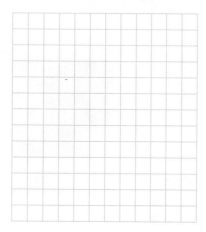

_____

2. Solve $x^2 + 5x + 4 = 0$ by graphing the related function. (Example 2)

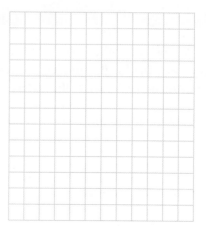

_____

3. A man standing at the edge of a cliff 106 feet high, drops a stick that gets caught on a tree limb 42 feet below. The function $h(t) = -16t^2 + 106$, where t represents the time measured in seconds, gives the height of the stick above the ground (in feet). Write and solve an equation to find the amount of time before the stick gets caught in the tree. (Example 3)

_____

4. Yosemite Falls in California consists of three smaller falls. The upper falls are 1430 feet high. The height $h(t)$ in feet of a water droplet falling from the top to the bottom of the upper falls is modeled by $h(t) = -16t^2 + 1430$, where t is time in seconds after it begins falling. Estimate the time that it takes a droplet to fall from the top to the bottom of the upper falls. (Example 4)

_____

_____

? ESSENTIAL QUESTION CHECK-IN

5. How are the solutions of a quadratic equation related to the graph of the related quadratic function?

_____

_____

17.5 Independent Practice

Personal Math Trainer

Online
Assessment and
Intervention

my.hrw.com

Solve each equation by graphing.

6. $-\frac{1}{2}x^2 + 2 = -4$

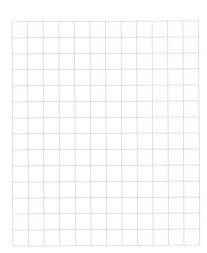

_____

7. $-(x-3)^2 - 2 = -6$

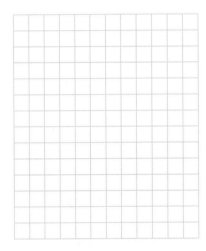

_____

8. As part of an engineering contest, a student who has designed a protective crate for an egg drops the crate from a window 18 feet above the ground. The height (in feet) of the crate as it falls is given by $h(t) = -16t^2 + 18$, where t is the time (in seconds) since the crate was dropped.

   a. Write and solve an equation to find the amount of time before the crate passes a window 10 feet directly below the window from which it was dropped.

_____

   b. Write and solve an equation to find the amount of time before the crate hits the ground.

_____

   c. Is the rate at which the crate falls constant? Explain.

_____

_____

_____

_____

9. A fireworks shell is fired from a mortar. Its height in feet is modeled by the function $h(t) = -16(t - 7)^2 + 784$, where t is the time in seconds. If the shell does not explode, how long will it take to return to the ground?

_____

10. A baseball is dropped from an airplane 500 feet above the ground. The height (in feet) above the ground is modeled by the function $h(t) = -16t^2 + 500$, where t is the time in seconds.

   a. What is the height of the ball after 2 seconds? _____

   b. How long will it take for the ball to fall to a height of 100 feet above

       ground? _____

   c. How long will it take the ball to reach the ground?

   _____

H.O.T. | FOCUS ON HIGHER ORDER THINKING

11. Counterexamples Pamela says that if the graph of a quadratic function opens upward, then the related quadratic equation has two solutions. Provide a counterexample to Pamela's claim.

_____

_____

_____

12. Critical Thinking Explain why a quadratic equation in the form $ax^2 - c = 0$, where $a > 0$ and $c > 0$, will always have two solutions. Explain why a quadratic equation in the form $ax^2 + c = 0$, where $a > 0$ and $c > 0$, will never have any real-number solutions.

_____

_____

_____

_____

13. Explain the Error Rodney was given the function $h(t) = -16t^2 + 50$ representing the height (in feet) above ground of a water balloon t seconds after being dropped from a roof 50 feet above the ground. He was asked to find how long it took the balloon to fall 20 feet. Rodney used the equation $-16t^2 + 50 = 20$ to solve the problem. What was Rodney's error?

_____

_____

_____

Comparing Linear, Quadratic, and Exponential Models

FL F-LE.1.3

Observe using graphs and tables that a quantity increasing exponentially eventually exceeds a quantity increasing linearly, quadratically, or (more generally) as a polynomial function. *Also F-IF.2.6, F-LE.1.1, F-LE.1.1b, F-LE.1.1c*

ESSENTIAL QUESTION

How can you decide which function type to use when modeling?

EXPLORE ACTIVITY 1    **FL**   **F-LE.1.1**

Examining the End Behavior of Linear and Quadratic Functions

The **end behavior** of a function is the behavior of the graph of the function as x approaches infinity and as x approaches negative infinity. The notation for end behavior is:

$$x \rightarrow \infty, f(x) \rightarrow ?$$

$$x \rightarrow -\infty, f(x) \rightarrow ?$$

"As x approaches infinity, what does $f(x)$ approach?"   and   "as x approaches negative infinity, what does $f(x)$ approach?"

A Look at the graph to see which direction the function is headed as x approaches positive and negative infinity.

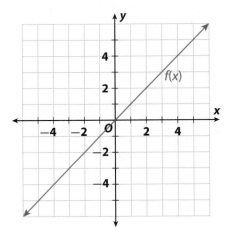

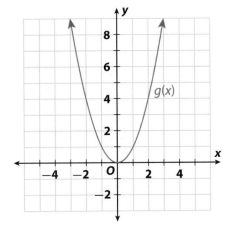

For the linear graph, as x approaches positive infinity, $f(x)$ is approaching

_____ and as x approaches negative infinity,

$f(x)$ is approaching _____.

For the quadratic graph, as x approaches positive infinity, $g(x)$ approaches

_____ and as x approaches negative infinity,

$g(x)$ approaches _____.

B Write the end behavior for both graphs.

Linear: As $x \to \infty$, $f(x) \to$ ☐. As $x \to -\infty$, $f(x) \to$ ☐.

Quadratic: As $x \to \infty$, $g(x) \to$ ☐. As $x \to -\infty$, $f(x) \to$ ☐.

REFLECT

1. What is the end behavior of $y = 7x - 11$?

_____

_____

_____

2. What is the end behavior of $y = 5x^2 + x - 8$?

_____

_____

EXPLORE ACTIVITY 2    **FL** F-IF.2.6

Examining the End Behavior of Linear, Quadratic, and Exponential Functions

Examining end behavior of a function requires looking at the x-values as they become large and positive or large and negative, and looking at their corresponding y-values.

A Fill in the missing values in the table.

Linear		Quadratic		Exponential	
x	$L(x) = 5x - 2$	x	$Q(x) = 5x^2 - 2$	x	$E(x) = 5^x - 2$
1	3	1	3	1	3
2	8	2	18	2	
3	13	3	43	3	123
4		4	78	4	623
5	23	5		5	3,123
6	28	6	178	6	15,623
7	33	7	243	7	
8	38	8	318	8	390,623

We want to determine which function "grows" the fastest. In other words, although all 3 functions have positive infinity as their end behaviors as x approaches infinity, which function approaches infinity the quickest?

B To determine rates of growth, determine the successive differences. Fill out the missing parts in the chart below.

Linear		Quadratic		Exponential	
x	$L(x+1) - L(x)$	x	$Q(x+1) - Q(x)$	x	$E(x+1) - E(x)$
1	5	1	15	1	20
2	5	2	25	2	
3		3	35	3	500
4	5	4		4	2500
5	5	5	55	5	
6	5	6	65	6	62,500
7	5	7		7	312,500

C Which function above is growing the fastest? _____

REFLECT

3. Which of the following functions' y-values will increase the quickest as x approaches infinity?

    a. $y_1 = 125x + 2$ **b.** $y_2 = 99x^2 + 51x + 1000$ **c.** $y_3 = 2^x$

_____

Comparing Function Families

For linear, quadratic, and exponential functions, certain patterns emerge as to when and where the functions increase and decrease on specific intervals.

EXPLORE ACTIVITY 3    **FL** **F-LE.1.3**

Math On the Spot
my.hrw.com

A Complete the table of values below and determine if each linear function is increasing or decreasing.

x	$f(x) =$ $6x - 5$	x	$g(x) =$ $2x + 7$	x	$h(x) =$ $-4x + 3$	x	$k(x) =$ $-x + 8$
3		3		3		3	
4		4		4		4	
5		5		5		5	
6		6		6		6	

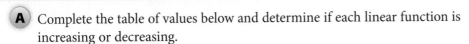

    $f(x)$ increasing $g(x)$ _____ $h(x)$ _____ $k(x)$ _____

Math Talk
Mathematical Practices

If a function is linear, what do you know about the difference in its y-values?

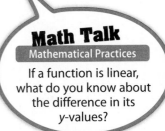

B What part of a linear function tells you if it is increasing or decreasing?

_____

C Complete the table below and determine if each quadratic function is increasing, decreasing, or both.

x	$f(x) = 3x^2 - 1$	x	$g(x) = x^2 - x$	x	$h(x) = -4x^2 + 5$	x	$k(x) = -x^2 + 8$
−1	2	−1	2	−1	1	−1	7
0		0		0		0	
1		1		1		1	
2		2		2		2	
3		3		3		3	

$f(x)$ both $g(x)$ _____ $h(x)$ _____ $k(x)$ _____

D Which of the quadratics above are always increasing or always decreasing?

_____

E Are all quadratics always increasing/decreasing, or do they switch back and forth?

_____

F Complete the table of values below and determine if each exponential function is increasing, decreasing, or both.

x	$f(x) = 2^x + 1$	x	$g(x) = -3^x + 4$	x	$h(x) = 5^x - 8$	x	$k(x) = -7 \cdot 3^x + 1$
0		0		0		0	
1		1		1		1	
2		2		2		2	
3		3		3		3	

$f(x)$ increasing $g(x)$ _____ $h(x)$ _____ $k(x)$ _____

G What part of the function tells you if it is increasing/decreasing?

_____

H Will the function $h(x) = 19^x - 10$ always increase or always decrease?

_____

4. Will the function $f(x) = 6^x - 5$ always increase or always decrease?

_____

Choosing a Function Model

Linear, quadratic, and exponential functions can be used in business, medicine, and other fields to model costs of products, disease growth/decay, and so on.

Math On the Spot
my.hrw.com

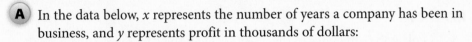

EXAMPLE 1   FL   F-LE.1.1

Analyze each set of data to find the type of function that best represents the data.

My Notes

A In the data below, x represents the number of years a company has been in business, and y represents profit in thousands of dollars:

x	$f(x+1) - f(x)$
1	3
2	5
3	7

STEP 1   Find the slope between consecutive points.

The slope is 2, 2, 2.

STEP 2   Find the type of function that can be modeled by the points $(1, 3)$, $(2, 5)$, $(3, 7)$, and $(4, 9)$.

The function is linear because the slope is constant.

B During an experiment, a strain of bacteria is found whose population is modeled by the following data:

Hours	Population
0	500
1	1000
2	2000
3	4000

STEP 1   Find the difference between consecutive points.

x	$f(x+1) - f(x)$
0–1	500
1–2	1000
2–3	2000

STEP 2 Take the second differences: $1000 - 500 = 500$; $2000 - 1000 = 1000$. The second differences are not the same.

STEP 3 Calculate the consecutive quotients, and tell what type of function models the data.

x	$\dfrac{f(x+1)}{f(x)}$
0–1	2
1–2	2
2–3	2

An exponential function best models the data.

REFLECT

5. Look at the difference in the y-values. Does the data represent a linear, quadratic, or exponential equation?

First Differences	Second Differences
$4 - 1 = 3$	$9 - 3 = 6$
$13 - 4 = 9$	$15 - 9 = 6$
$28 - 13 = 15$	$21 - 15 = 6$
$49 - 28 = 21$	$27 - 21 = 6$
$76 - 49 = 27$	$33 - 27 = 6$
$109 - 76 = 33$	$39 - 33 = 6$
$148 - 109 = 39$	N/A

_____

_____

6. If the differences between consecutive function values grow by a factor of 6, what type of function is it? _____

7. A function is found to have a constant second difference of 0. What type of function is it? _____

Personal Math Trainer
Online Assessment and Intervention
my.hrw.com

YOUR TURN

8. Data that is modeled by the points (3, 9), (4, 16), (5, 25), and (6, 36) can be best represented by what type of function? _____

9. Data that is modeled by the points (1, 6), (2, 18), (3, 54), and (4, 162) can be best represented by what type of function? _____

1. Determine the end behavior of $f(x) = 3^x$.

   a. $f(x + 1) = 3^{x+1} = 3^x \cdot 3 = 3f(x)$.
     Does the value of $f(x)$ increase or

     decrease as x increases? _____

   b. What happens to $f(x)$ as x approaches
     positive infinity?

     _____

2. Is this population data linear?

x (weeks)	y (population)
1	5
2	10
3	15
4	20
5	25

   Are the common differences constant?
   If so, what is the common difference?

   _____

3. Determine if the data is quadratic:
   $(0, -5), (1, -2), (2, 7), (3, 22), (4, 43)$

First difference	Second difference
3	
9	6
21	–

   _____

   _____

4. Determine the end behavior of
   $f(x) = 2x^2 + 3x - 7$.

   a. What type of function is this?

     _____

   b. What is the leading coefficient? _____

   c. What does this say about the end
     behavior?

     _____

5. The number of nuts produced by a walnut
   tree from years 3 to 7 is listed in the following
   table.

x (years)	y (nuts)
3	19
4	27
5	43
6	75
7	139

   a. Fill out the table of first differences.

First difference
8
32

   b. What do you notice about all the

     numbers? _____

   c. Does that tell you about the type of

     model that is exhibited? _____

6. How can you decide which function type to use when modeling?

   _____

17.6 Independent Practice

 FL F-IF.2.6, F-LE.1.1, F-LE.1.1b, F-LE.1.1c, F-LE.1.3

Determine if the following are linear, quadratic, exponential, or none of these.

7. $y = x - x^2$

_____

8. $y = 2(x - 3)^2$

_____

9. $y = 3^{x+2} + 12$

_____

10. $y = 7x + 11$

_____

11. $y = \left(\frac{2}{3}\right)^{3x} = 9$

_____

12. $(1, 2), (6, 27), (0, 5), (3, 8), (5, 11)$

_____

13. $(7, 38), (8, 45), (9, 52), (10, 59), (11, 66)$

_____

14. $(-1, 23), (0, 5), (1, 1), (2, 11), (3, 35)$

_____

15. $(1, -11), (2, 4), (3, 29), (4, 64), (5, 109)$

_____

16. $(4, 16), (5, 48), (6, 112), (7, 240), (8, 496)$

_____

17. A cannonball is fired from a stage at time $t = 0$, and its height afterward is given (in feet) by the function $y(t) = -16t^2 + 38t + 2$, where t is measured in seconds.

   a. Is this model linear, quadratic, or exponential?

_____

   b. How can you tell?

_____

18. A rocket is launched, and after t seconds its velocity (in feet per second) is given by the model $y(t) = 112t + 41$.

   a. Write a set of points from time $t = 0$ to $t = 5$.

_____

_____

   b. What will the velocity be at time $t = 9$?

_____

19. The population of bacteria is given by: $(0, 1), (1, 10), (2, 100), (3, 1,000), (4, 10,000)$

   a. List the differences from 1 to 10,000.

_____

   b. Is the data quadratic? If not, what is it?

_____

   c. If the function were written, where would the variable be?

_____

20. Return on a certain investment is modeled exponentially by the following data: $(4, 2), (5, 4), (6, 10), (7, 28), (8, 82)$

   a. Confirm that the data represents an exponential model.

_____

_____

   b. What is the next data point? _____

   c. What is the base of the model of this data? _____

21. The trajectory of a projectile fired from a ship is given in the table below.

x	y
6	52
7	67
8	84
9	103
10	124

a. Which model does the data represent?

_____

b. Which difference gave you this conclusion?

_____

c. What is this difference, and why is it unique?

_____

_____

22. A $50 investment is made and the data is listed below.

x (years)	y (dollars)
0	50
1	150
2	450
3	1,350
4	4,050

a. Is the data exponential?

_____

b. How can you tell?

_____

_____

_____

23. The amount of money (in thousands) a company spends on advertising is listed in the table by month.

x (months)	y (thousands)
3	14
4	27
5	44
6	65
7	90

a. Which model does the data represent?

_____

b. How much is spent in the 9th month?

_____

24. Which model does the data represent?
$(10, 51), (11, 57), (12, 63), (13, 69), (14, 75)$

_____

25. The rainfall (in inches) in a rainforest after x weeks is given by the following data:
$(5, 60), (6, 71), (7, 82), (8, 93), (9, 104)$

a. Which model does this data fit?

_____

b. How much rain will have fallen in the

13th week?? _____

26. Which model does this data fit?

x (miles)	y (cents)
4	14
5	50
6	94
7	146
8	206

_____

27. Explain the Error

x (miles)	y (cents)
7	183
8	233
9	289
10	351
11	419

To determine if the data represents a quadratic model, Jeff looks at the difference in the y-values: 50, 56, 62, 68.

He decides that since the differences are not constant, the model is not quadratic.

Explain the mistake he made.

_____

_____

_____

28. Justify Reasoning

a. Find the last row of the table of data.

x (days)	y (dollars)
0	1
1	$\frac{1}{2}$
2	$\frac{1}{4}$
3	$\frac{1}{8}$
4	$\frac{1}{16}$

b. Is the data linear, quadratic or exponential?

_____

c. What are the y-values changing by?

_____

d. Suppose that you had only the first three rows of data. Could another model fit the data?

_____

_____

Ready to Go On?

Personal
Math Trainer

Online
Assessment and
Intervention

my.hrw.com

17.1–17.3 Combining Transformations of Quadratic Functions

1. Write the function rule for a function whose graph is a transformation of the graph of $f(x) = x^2$ in the following ways: stretched vertically by a factor of 3, translated 2 units to the right and 3 units down. _____

17.4 Characteristics of Quadratic Functions

2. Given the quadratic function $f(x) = 2(x + 3.5)^2 - 4.5$, find the equation of the axis of symmetry, and find the zeros of the function. Determine whether the function has a maximum value or minimum value and determine that value.

   _____

17.5 Solving Quadratic Equations Graphically

3. Solve $4x^2 + 8x = 32$ by graphing. _____

4. The height of a fireworks rocket launched from a platform 35 meters above the ground can be approximated by $h = -5t^2 + 30t + 35$, where h is the height in meters and t is the time in seconds. Use a graph to find the time it takes the rocket to reach the ground after it is launched. _____

17.6 Comparing Linear, Exponential, and Quadratic Models

Describe the end behavior of each function (a) as x increases, and (b) as x decreases.

5. $y = 2x - 3$ _____

6. $y = -x^2 + 3x - 4$ _____

7. $y = 4^{-x}$ _____

8. Data that can be modeled by the points $(1, 9)$, $(2, 18)$, $(3, 36)$, and $(4, 72)$ can be represented by what type of function? _____

? ESSENTIAL QUESTION

9. What information does the graph of a quadratic function give you about the function?

   _____

   _____

MODULE 17 MIXED REVIEW

Assessment Readiness

Personal
Math Trainer

Online
Assessment and
Intervention

my.hrw.com

Selected Response

1. Which of the following is the complete factorization of $3x^2 - 12x - 36$?

   (A) $(3x - 6)(x - 6)$

   (B) $3(x + 2)(x - 6)$

   (C) $3(x - 2)(x + 6)$

   (D) $3(x - 6)(x - 2)$

2. Does the function $f(x) = -(x - 4)^2 + 2$ have a maximum value or a minimum value, and what is that value?

   (A) maximum, 4

   (B) maximum, 2

   (C) minimum, −2

   (D) minimum, −4

3. The graph shown is a transformation of the graph of $f(x) = x^2$. What is the equation of the function whose graph is shown?

   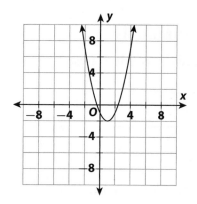

   (A) $f(x) = (x - 2)^2 + 1$

   (B) $f(x) = (x - 1)^2 + 2$

   (C) $f(x) = (x - 1)^2 - 2$

   (D) $f(x) = (x + 1)^2 - 2$

4. What is the solution to the system of linear equations?

   $2x + 3y = 7$

   $3x - 6y = -21$

   (A) $(1, -3)$

   (B) $(2, 1)$

   (C) $(3, 5)$

   (D) $(-1, 3)$

5. For which value of a will the graph of $f(x) = a(x - h)^2 + k$ be a reflection across the x-axis and a vertical shrink of $f(x) = x^2$?

   (A) 2

   (B) 1.5

   (C) −0.5

   (D) −2

Mini-Task

6. The quadratic function $f(x) = x^2 - 2x - 8$ can be used to solve the related quadratic equation $x^2 - 2x - 8 = 0$.

   a. Graph the quadratic function.

   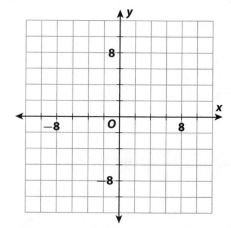

   b. What are the solutions to the quadratic equation?

   _____

Piecewise and Absolute Value Functions

? ESSENTIAL QUESTION

How do piecewise functions differ from other types of functions?

Real-World Video

Optimizing sales prices is key to running a successful retail business. Cost and pricing structures are rarely linear, instead taking 'jumps' at certain price points.

my.hrw.com

GO DIGITAL
my.hrw.com

my.hrw.com

Go digital with your write-in student edition, accessible on any device.

Math On the Spot

Scan with your smart phone to jump directly to the online edition, video tutor, and more.

Animated Math

Interactively explore key concepts to see how math works.

Personal Math Trainer

Get immediate feedback and help as you work through practice sets.

Are YOU Ready?

Complete these exercises to review skills you will need for this module.

Graph Linear Functions

EXAMPLE Graph the equation $y = -3x + 5$.

1. Substitute $x = 1$ into the equation.
   $y = -3(x) + 5$
   $y = -3(1) + 5$
   $y = -3 + 5$
   $y = 2$, so the point $(1, 2)$ is on the graph.

2. Repeat step 1 to find other points on the graph. Fill in the table shown.

x	1	0	−1	2
y	2	5	8	−1

3. Graph the points on the scale.

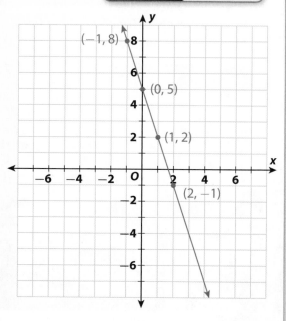

Graph the following equations on the grid shown.

1. $y = 2x + 1$

x	−1	0	1	2
y			3	

2. $y = -4x + 2$

x	−1	0	1	2
y				

3. $y = -2$

x	−1	0	1	2
y				

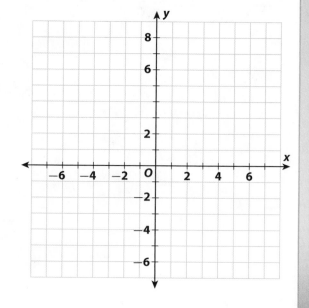

Reading Start-Up

Visualize Vocabulary

Use the Review Words to complete the Pyramid Chart. Write one word in each box.

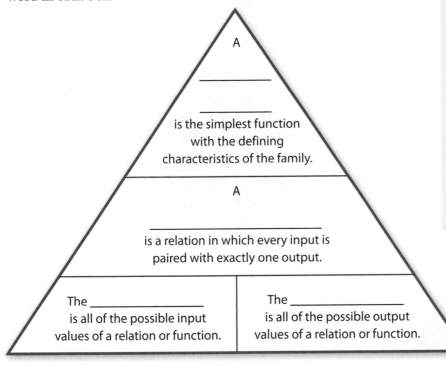

A

_____

_____

is the simplest function with the defining characteristics of the family.

A

_____

is a relation in which every input is paired with exactly one output.

The _____
is all of the possible input
values of a relation or function.

The _____
is all of the possible output
values of a relation or function.

Vocabulary

Review Words

  absolute value *(valor absoluto)*

✓ domain *(dominio)*

✓ function *(función)*

  integer *(entero)*

✓ parent function *(función de padres)*

✓ range *(rango)*

Preview Words

  absolute value function

  greatest integer function

  piecewise function

  step function

  vertex

Understand Vocabulary

To become familiar with some of the vocabulary terms in the module, consider the following. You may refer to the module, the glossary, or a dictionary.

1. The word *absolute* refers to an item that is not reduced or diminished in any way. How do you think this definition relates to an **absolute value function**?

   _____

2. The *step* is a discrete, discontinuous item that is separate from other items in a relation. What do you think a **step function** might be?

   _____

Active Reading

Three-Panel Flip Chart Before beginning the module, create a three-panel flip chart to help you organize what you learn. Label each flap with one of the lesson titles from this module. As you study each lesson, write important information like vocabulary and examples under the appropriate flap.

Unpacking the Standards

Understanding the standards and vocabulary terms in the standards will help you know exactly what you are expected to learn in this module.

 **F-IF.3.7b**

Graph square root, cube root, and piecewise-defined functions, including step functions and absolute value functions.

Key Vocabulary

piecewise function

(función a tramos)

A number or product of numbers and variables with whole-number exponents, or a polynomial with one term.

What It Means to You

You can see what a piecewise function looks like.

UNPACKING EXAMPLE F-IF.3.7B

The bank gives no interest for any account that has less than $1000 in it. Accounts of $1000 or greater are paid 3 percent interest. How do the rules for the function vary?

The function has two separate rules. Below $1000 one rule of no interest applies. At $1000 or more, a rule of 3 percent interest applies. A function with at least two different rules is a piecewise function.

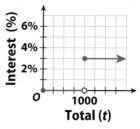

 F-BF.2.3

Identify the effect on the graph of replacing $f(x)$ by $f(x) + k$, $k\,f(x)$, $f(kx)$, and $f(x + k)$ for specific values of k (both positive and negative); find the value of k given the graphs. Experiment with cases and illustrate an explanation of the effects on the graph using technology.

What It Means to You

Glynnis created the graph shown by graphing $y = \frac{1}{2}x$, $y = x$, $y = 2x$, and $y = 4x$ all on the same grid. What pattern did she observe?

UNPACKING EXAMPLE F-BF.2.3

Glynnis realized that increasing the coefficient in front of x in the equation for each line increased the slope of the line.

From that, Glynnis could see that, for example, $y = 10x$ would be an extremely steep line, while $y = \frac{1}{10}x$ would be a line that was almost horizontal.

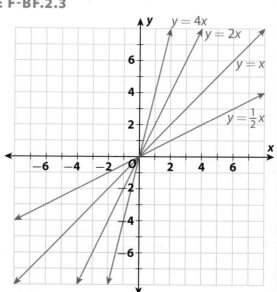

Visit **my.hrw.com** to see all **Florida Math Standards** unpacked.

my.hrw.com

LESSON
18.1 Piecewise Functions

FL F-IF.3.7b

Graph square root, cube root, and piecewise-defined functions, including step functions and absolute value functions. *Also A-CED.1.2, F-BF.1.1, F-IF.1.2, F-IF.2.4, F-IF.2.5, F-IF.3.7*

ESSENTIAL QUESTION

How are piecewise functions different from other functions?

Evaluating and Graphing Piecewise Functions

A piecewise function has different rules for different parts of its domain. To evaluate a piecewise function for a given value of x, substitute the value of x into the rule for the part of the domain that includes x.

Math On the Spot

my.hrw.com

EXAMPLE 1 FL F-IF.3.7b

A Find $f(-3)$, $f(4)$, $f(0.2)$, and $f(0)$ for $f(x) = \begin{cases} -x \text{ if } x < 0 \\ x + 1 \text{ if } x \geq 0 \end{cases}$

> A brace is used to write a piecewise function.

$f(-3) = -(-3)$ $-3 < 0$, so use the rule $f(x) = -x$.

$\quad\quad\quad = 3$ Write the value.

$f(4) = (4) + 1$ $4 \geq 0$, so use the rule $f(x) = x + 1$.

$\quad\quad = 5$ Write the value.

$f(0.2) = (0.2) + 1$ $0.2 \geq 0$, so use the rule $f(x) = x + 1$.

$\quad\quad\quad = 1.2$ Write the value.

$f(0) = (0) + 1$ $0 \geq 0$, so use the rule $f(x) = x + 1$.

$\quad\quad = 1$ Write the value.

B Make a table. Then graph $f(x) = \begin{cases} -x \text{ if } x < 0 \\ x + 1 \text{ if } x \geq 0 \end{cases}$

x	−3	−2	−1	−0.9	−0.1
f(x)	3	2	1	0.9	0.1

x	0	0.1	0.9	1	2
f(x)	1	1.1	1.9	2	3

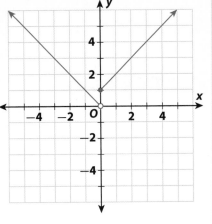

YOUR TURN

1. Graph the function defined by

$$f(x) = \begin{cases} -x - 2 \text{ if } x < 0 \\ x + 4 \text{ if } x \geq 0 \end{cases}$$

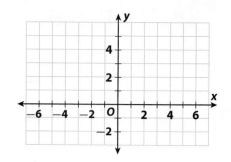

Evaluating and Graphing the Greatest Integer Function

The **greatest integer function** is the piecewise function defined so that $f(x)$ is the greatest integer less than or equal to x, represented by $[x]$. For example, $f(-2.1) = [-2.1] = -3$ since -3 is the greatest integer less than or equal to -2.1.

EXAMPLE 2   FL   F-IF.3.7b

Make a table and graph $f(x) = [x]$.

x	5	3.9	3.1	0.99	−0.2	−0.5	−2.1	−4.8
f(x)	5	3	3	0	−1	−1	−3	−5

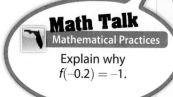

Math Talk
Mathematical Practices

Explain why
$f(-0.2) = -1$.

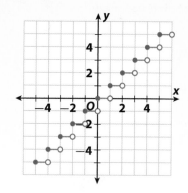

YOUR TURN

2. Graph the function defined by
$f(x) = -[x]$.

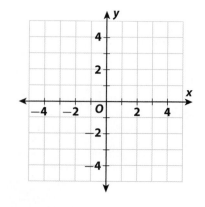

Writing and Graphing a Piecewise Function

Some real-world situations can be represented using a piecewise function.

EXAMPLE 3

FL   F-IF.2.4

Some engineering students have entered a contest for solar-powered electric cars. The cars must travel at a speed of 0.05 miles per minute for 3 minutes to reach a light source to recharge, stop for 1 minute to recharge, then increase their speed to 0.10 miles per minute for the final 2 minutes of their performance. Define and graph a function for the distance and time requirements.

Express d, the distance that a car has traveled in miles, as a function of t, the time in minutes that the car has traveled.

$$d(t) = \begin{cases} 0.05t & \text{if } 0 \leq t \leq 3 \\ 0.15 & \text{if } 3 < t \leq 4 \\ 0.15 + 0.10(t - 4) & \text{if } 4 < t \leq 6 \end{cases}$$

For the first 3 minutes, the car travels at 0.05 miles/min.

For the next 1 minute, distance is constant ($3 \times 0.05 = 0.15$).

For the final 2 minutes, the car travels at 0.10 miles/min

My Notes

Make a table of values for $d(t)$.

t	1	2	2.5	3	3.5	4	4.5	5	6
d(t)	0.05	0.1	0.125	0.15	0.15	0.15	0.20	0.25	0.35

Graph the function.

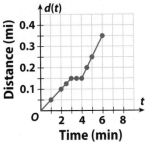

YOUR TURN

3. The cost of admission to a state fair is $4 for children less than 12 years old and $8 for everyone 12 and older. Define and graph a piecewise function that gives the cost of admission for a person who is x years old.

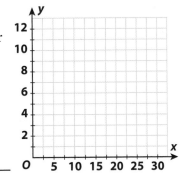

_____

Writing a Piecewise Function for a Graph

To define the piecewise function represented by a graph, write a rule for each part of the graph, and indicate the part of the domain to which each rule applies.

EXAMPLE 4   **FL**   **F-BF.1.1**

Define a piecewise function represented by the graph.

Write an equation for the ray on the left in $y = mx + b$ form.

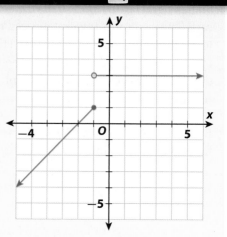

STEP 1   Find the slope, m, of the ray on the left. Use the points $(-2, 0)$ and $(-1, 1)$ and the slope formula.

$$m = \frac{y_2 - y_1}{x_2 - x_1} = \frac{1 - 0}{-1 - (-2)} = 1$$

My Notes

STEP 2   Substitute the value of one of the points on the ray back into the equation $y = mx + b$ using the slope you found.

$$y = mx + b$$
$$0 = (1)(-2) + b \qquad \text{Use } m = 1 \text{ and } (-2, 0).$$
$$0 = -2 + b$$
$$b = 2 \qquad\qquad\quad \text{Solve for } b.$$

STEP 3   Substitute m and b back into the equation.

$$y = mx + b$$
$$y = x + 2$$

Write an equation for the ray on the right in $y = mx + b$ form.

STEP 1   Find the slope, m, using points $(3, 3)$ and $(2, 3)$.

$$m = \frac{y_2 - y_1}{x_2 - x_1} = \frac{3 - 3}{3 - 2} = \frac{0}{1} = 0$$

STEP 2   Substitute the value of one of the points back into the equation $y = mx + b$ using the slope you found.

$$y = mx + b$$
$$3 = (0)(3) + b \qquad \text{Use } m = 0 \text{ and } (3, 3).$$
$$b = 3 \qquad\qquad\quad\; \text{Solve for } b.$$

STEP 3   Substitute m and b back into the equation.

$$y = mx + b$$
$$y = (0)x + 3$$
$$y = 3$$

Determine the domain for each part of the function.

Since the point $(-1, 1)$ is part of the ray on the left, the domain for the part of the function defined by $f(x) = x + 2$ is the set of real numbers less than or equal to -1.

The domain for the part of the graph on the right, which is defined by $f(x) = 3$, is the set of real numbers greater than -1.

This graph jumps from the ray on the left to the ray on the right at $x = -1$. This is called a point of **discontinuity**, a point where a graph is not continuous.

Define a piecewise function represented by the graph.

$$f(x) = \begin{cases} x + 2 \text{ if } x \leq -1 \\ 3 \text{ if } x > -1 \end{cases}$$

REFLECT

4. **Analyze Relationships** Which rule applies when the graph crosses the y-axis? The x-axis?

_____

_____

_____

5. Write an equation for the part of the graph on the left in $y = mx + b$ form.

_____

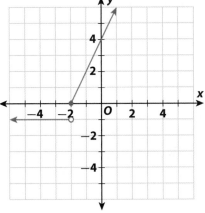

6. Write an equation for the part of the graph on the right in $y = mx + b$ form.

_____

7. Define a piecewise function represented by the graph.

_____

Personal Math Trainer

Online Assessment and Intervention

⏻ my.hrw.com

For each function, find $f(2), f(1), f(0), f(-2)$, and $f(-3)$.
Then graph the function. (Example 1)

1. $f(x) = \begin{cases} -x + 1 & \text{if } x < 1 \\ x & \text{if } x \geq 1 \end{cases}$

_____

_____

2. $f(x) = \begin{cases} -1 & \text{if } x \leq -1 \\ 2x + 2 & \text{if } x > -1 \end{cases}$

_____

_____

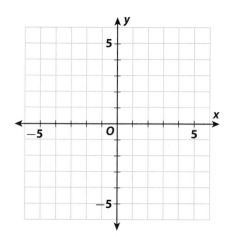

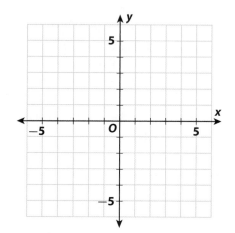

Complete the table for $f(x) = 2[x]$. Then graph the function. (Example 2)

3.

x	1	1.2	0.9	−1.2	−2.1
f(x)	2				

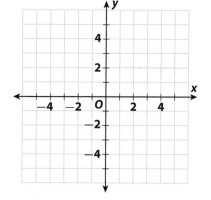

4. A parking garage charges $3 to park a car for less than 1 hour. The cost for parking for 1 hour or more is shown in the graph below. (Examples 3 and 4)

a. Graph the part of the function representing the cost of parking in the garage during the first hour.

b. Use the points $(2, 5)$ and $(3, 7)$ to write an equation for $C(t)$, the cost in dollars for parking t hours, when $t \geq 1$.

_____

c. $C(t) = \begin{cases} \underline{\hspace{2cm}} & \text{if } t < 1 \\ \underline{\hspace{2cm}} & \text{if } t \geq 1 \end{cases}$

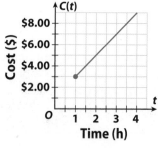

? ESSENTIAL QUESTION CHECK-IN

5. How are piecewise functions different from other functions?

_____

18.1 Independent Practice

FL A-CED.1.2, F-BF.1.1, F-IF.1.2, F-IF.2.4, F-IF.2.5, F-IF.3.7, F-IF.3.7a

Personal
Math Trainer

Online
Assessment and
Intervention

my.hrw.com

Graph each function.

6. $f(x) = \begin{cases} 3 & \text{if } x < -2 \\ x & \text{if } x \geq -2 \end{cases}$

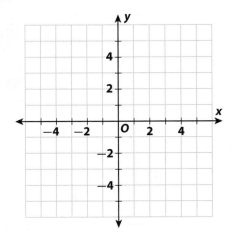

7. $f(x) = \begin{cases} 3x & \text{if } x \leq 2 \\ -3x + 8 & \text{if } x > 2 \end{cases}$

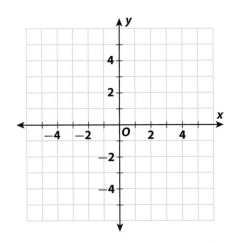

Define a piecewise function represented by the graph.

8. $f(x) = \begin{cases} \rule{3cm}{0.4pt} \\ \rule{3cm}{0.4pt} \end{cases}$

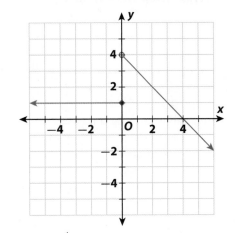

9. $f(x) = \begin{cases} \rule{3cm}{0.4pt} \\ \rule{3cm}{0.4pt} \end{cases}$

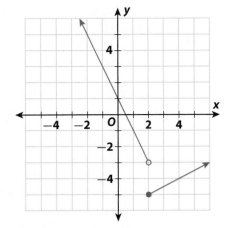

10. Explain the Error Deena looked at the functions shown in Exercises 6 through 9 and concluded that the domain of any piecewise function is the set of all real numbers. Is she correct? Explain.

_____

_____

_____

_____

11. Represent Real-World Problems At Maston Lake you can rent a kayak for $16 for the first 2 hours. Time greater than 2 hours is charged a rate of $4 an hour.

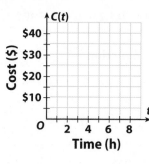

a. Make a graph representing $C(t)$, the cost in dollars of renting a kayak for t hours.

b. Write an equation for the part of the function where $0 < t \leq 2$.

_____

c. Write an equation for the part of the function where $t > 2$.

_____

d. $C(t) = \begin{cases} \underline{\hspace{3cm}} & \text{if } t \leq 2 \\ \underline{\hspace{3cm}} & \text{if } t > 2 \end{cases}$

12. Create a table and graph $f(x) = -2[x]$. Then graph the function.

x				
$f(x)$				

x				
$f(x)$				

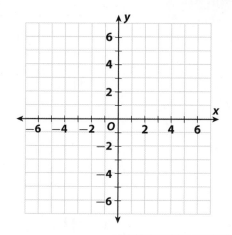

 **FOCUS ON HIGHER ORDER THINKING**

Work Area

13. Analyze Relationships The function $f(x) = \begin{cases} 6 & \text{if } x > 3 \\ 5x - 4 & \text{if } x \leq 3 \end{cases}$ has the same value for two different values for x, one of which is less than 3 and one that is greater than 3. The sum of the two values for x is 11. What are the two values?

_____

14. Explain the Error Margo created this graph of a piecewise function. Emilio told her that she must have made some kind of mistake. Did Margo make a mistake? Explain.

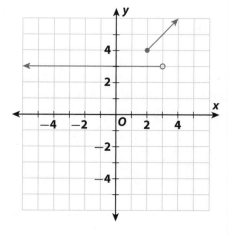

_____

_____

_____

_____

LESSON 18.2 Absolute Value Functions

FL F-IF.3.7b

Graph square root, cube root, and piecewise-defined functions, including step functions and absolute value functions. *Also F-IF.2.4, F-IF.3.7, F-BF.2.3*

ESSENTIAL QUESTION

What are the characteristics of an absolute value function?

EXPLORE ACTIVITY

FL F-IF.3.7b

Evaluating and Graphing Absolute Value Functions

As you just learned, a piecewise function has different rules for different parts of its domain. Is the **absolute value function** a piecewise function? Let's explore the properties of the absolute value function, $f(x) = |x|$.

A When $x \geq 0$: $|x| = x$ *Example:* $|3| = $ _____

     When $x < 0$: $|x| = $ _____   *Example:* $|-3| = -(-3) = $ _____

This can be expressed as a piecewise function: $f(x) = |x| = \begin{cases} -x \text{ if } x < 0 \\ x \text{ if } x \geq 0 \end{cases}$

B Complete the tables.

C Graph the absolute value function, $f(x) = |x|$.

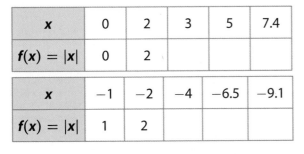

x	0	2	3	5	7.4
$f(x) = \|x\|$	0	2			

x	−1	−2	−4	−6.5	−9.1
$f(x) = \|x\|$	1	2			

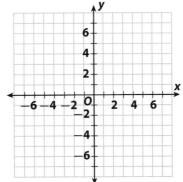

The function $f(x) = |x|$ is the **parent function** of absolute value functions. The graphs of absolute value functions are transformations of the graph you drew in part C.

REFLECT

1. What is the domain and range of the parent function, $f(x) = |x|$? Explain.

_____

_____

_____

Math Talk
Mathematical Practices

How do you think the "parent function" for absolute value got its name? Discuss.

2. **Look for a Pattern** With respect to shape and symmetry, what kind of pattern does the graph of $f(x) = |x|$ display?

_____

Math On the Spot

my.hrw.com

Characteristics of Absolute Value Functions

The graphs of absolute value functions have some features in common.

- The graphs are composed of two rays that meet at a common point, called the **vertex**. The vertex for both of the graphs above is at $(0, 2)$.
- The graphs are V-shaped and symmetrical about a vertical line passing through the vertex.

EXAMPLE 1

 FL F-IF.3.7b

Graph each function.

A $f(x) = |x| + 2$

STEP 1 Make a table.

x	0	1	−1	2	−2	5	−5
$f(x) = |x| + 2$	2	3	3	4	4	7	7

STEP 2 Graph the points.

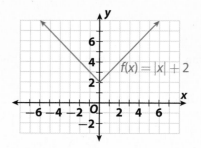

B $f(x) = -|x| + 2$

STEP 1 Make a table.

x	0	1	−1	2	−2	6	−6
$f(x) = -|x| + 2$	2	1	1	0	0	−4	−4

STEP 2 Graph the points.

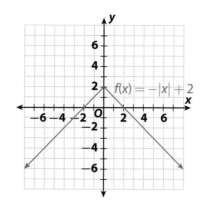

My Notes

3. **Analyze Relationships** How are the graphs in part A and part B related?

_____

YOUR TURN

4.   Graph $f(x) = -|x| + 1$.

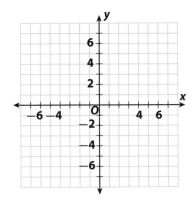

Personal Math Trainer

Online Assessment and Intervention

my.hrw.com

Transformations of Absolute Value Functions

Graphing additional absolute value functions can help you see how they are related to the parent function $f(x) = |x|$.

Math On the Spot

my.hrw.com

EXAMPLE 2   FL   F-IF.3.7b

Graph $f(x) = |x| + 1$, $g(x) = |x| + 5$, and $h(x) = |x| - 4$ on the same coordinate plane.

x	0	1	−1	2	−2	5	−5
$f(x) = |x| + 1$	1	2	2	3	3	6	6

x	0	1	−1	2	−2	7	−7
$g(x) = |x| + 5$	5	6	6	7	7	12	12

x	0	1	−1	3	−3	5	−6
$h(x) = |x| - 4$	−4	−3	−3	−1	−1	1	2

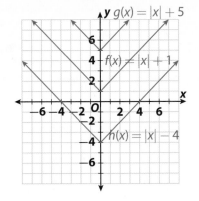

REFLECT

5. **Analyze Relationships** How are the graphs of $f(x) = |x| + 1$, $g(x) = |x| + 5$, and $h(x) = |x| - 4$ related to the graph of the parent absolute function?

_____

_____

6. Find the vertex, domain, and range for each function you graphed.

_____

_____

_____

_____

_____

YOUR TURN

7. Graph $f(x) = |x| + 3$, $g(x) = |x| - 3$, and $h(x) = |x| - 5$ on the same coordinate plane.

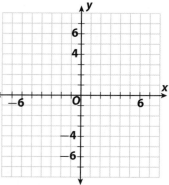

EXAMPLE 3

 **FL** **F-IF.3.7b**

Graph $f(x) = |x - 1|$, $g(x) = |x + 4|$, and $h(x) = |x - 4|$ on the same coordinate plane.

x	0	1	−1	2	−2	5	−5
$f(x) = \lvert x - 1 \rvert$	1	0	2	1	3	4	6

x	0	1	−1	2	−2	7	−7
$g(x) = \lvert x + 4 \rvert$	4	5	3	6	2	11	3

x	0	1	−1	3	−3	5	−5
$h(x) = \lvert x - 4 \rvert$	4	3	5	1	7	1	9

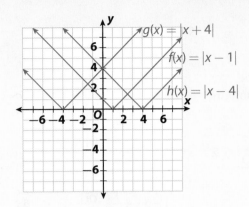
$g(x) = |x + 4|$
$f(x) = |x - 1|$
$h(x) = |x - 4|$

REFLECT

8. **Analyze Relationships** How are the graphs of $f(x) = |x - 1|$, $g(x) = |x + 5|$, and $h(x) = |x - 4|$ related to the graph of the absolute value parent function?

_____

_____

9. Find the vertex, domain, and range for each function you graphed.

_____

_____

_____

_____

_____

_____

YOUR TURN

10. Graph $f(x) = |x + 1|$, $g(x) = |x - 5|$, and $h(x) = |x + 5|$ on the same coordinate plane.

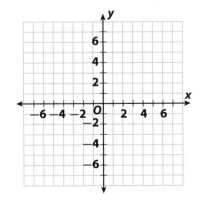

Personal Math Trainer

Online Assessment and Intervention

⊙ my.hrw.com

1. Complete the table of values below for the function $f(x) = |x| + 2$. Graph the function on the coordinate plane. (Example 1)

x	0	1	−1	2	−2
$f(x) = |x| + 2$	2		3		

x	3	−3	5	−5	−7
$f(x) = |x| + 2$					9

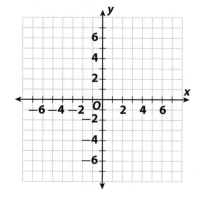

2. Complete the table of values below for the functions $g(x) = |x - 3|$ and $h(x) = -|x| + 1$. Graph both functions on the coordinate plane above. (Examples 2 and 3)

x	0	1	−1	2	−2	3	−3	4	−4	6
$g(x) = |x - 3|$	3									

x	0	1	−1	2	−2	3	−3	5	−5	6
$h(x) = -|x| + 1$	1									

3. Find the vertex, domain, and range for the function $f(x) = |x| + 2$ you graphed above. (Examples 2 and 3)

vertex: _____

domain: _____

range: _____

4. Find the vertex, domain, and range for the function $g(x) = |x - 3|$ you graphed above. (Examples 2 and 3)

vertex: _____

domain: _____

range: _____

? ESSENTIAL QUESTION CHECK-IN

5. What are the characteristics of the graph of an absolute value function?

_____

_____

_____

_____

18.2 Independent Practice

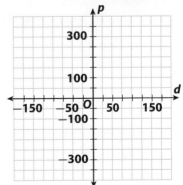

Personal Math Trainer

Online Assessment and Intervention

my.hrw.com

Graph each function. Identify the vertex, domain, and range.

6. $f(x) = |x| - 3$

vertex: _____

domain: _____

range: _____

_____

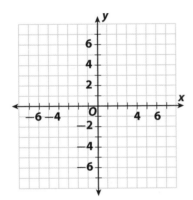

7. $g(x) = |x + 3|$

vertex: _____

domain: _____

range: _____

_____

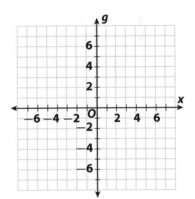

8. Represent Real-World Problems Montague National Bank is running a promotion in which customers get points for any transaction — positive deposits or negative withdrawals — that can be redeemed for prizes. Each transaction is awarded points equal to double the absolute value of its dollar value plus 100 bonus points.

a. Write an absolute value function $p(d)$ that gives the number of points that are awarded when a transaction of d dollars is made.

_____

b. Complete the table of values for $p(d)$.

d	+50	−50	+70	−70	6	−6
p(d)						

c. Graph $p(d)$ on the grid at the right.

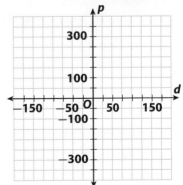

9. The speedometer on a car shows that the car is going 60 miles per hour. The function $e(x)$ defined by $e(x) = |x - 60|$ represents the error in the speed that the speedometer shows, where x is the actual speed of the car in miles per hour. For example, if the actual speed of the car is 70 miles per hour, the error in the speedometer display is $e(70) = |70 - 60| = |10| = 10$ miles per hour. Graph the function.

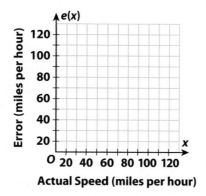

H.O.T. **FOCUS ON HIGHER ORDER THINKING**

Work Area

10. **Explain the Error** Terry is checking Randi's work. His comments are in red.

> Name: Randi Manietti
>
> #7 $f(x) = |x| - 5$
> $f(3) = -2$
>   Incorrect! Absolute
>   value functions have no
>   negative values.

Which student is correct? Explain.

_____

_____

_____

_____

11. **Critical Thinking** Give an example of an absolute value function that has only negative function values. Explain why all function values are negative.

_____

_____

_____

_____

Transforming Absolute Value Functions

FL   F-BF.2.3
Identify the effect on the graph of replacing $f(x)$ by $f(x) + k$, $k\,f(x)$, $f(kx)$, and $f(x + k)$ for specific values of k ... find the value of k given the graphs. Experiment with cases and illustrate an explanation of the effects on the graph using technology. Also F-IF.3.7, F-IF.3.7b

ESSENTIAL QUESTION

What is the effect of changing the parameters of an absolute value function?

EXPLORE ACTIVITY 1    FL   F-BF.2.3

Graphing Absolute Value Functions on a Graphing Calculator

You have learned how to graph an **absolute value function** by hand using ordered pairs from a table. Now try graphing the parent absolute value function, $f(x) = |x|$, on a graphing calculator. *Note: The steps for your calculator may vary.*

Recall that the graph of the *parent function* of absolute value functions is a V-shaped graph with its vertex at the point (0, 0).

A Graph the absolute value function, $y = |x|$.

> **STEP 1**   Enter the function as Y_1 by pressing **MATH** and using the Num menu. Choose the absolute value function.

> **STEP 2**   When you return to the function editor screen, type X.

> **STEP 3**   Press **GRAPH** to display the graph of $y = |x|$. Sketch the graph on the screen below, which shows $-15 \le x \le 15$ and $-10 \le y \le 10$.

B Now use your calculator to change the parameters of the parent function, $y = |x|$.

STEP 1 First add a constant to the parent function. Use your calculator to graph $y = |x| + 1$, $y = |x| + 4$, and $y = |x| - 5$, on the same graph. Sketch the graphs on the grid. Make sure that you place the vertex of each graph accurately.

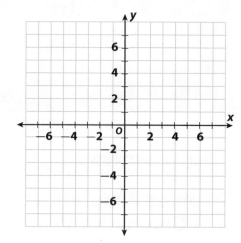

STEP 2 Now add a constant within the absolute value bars. Use your calculator to graph: $y = |x + 2|$, $y = |x - 6|$, and $y = |x + 6|$ on the same graph. Sketch the graphs on the grid.

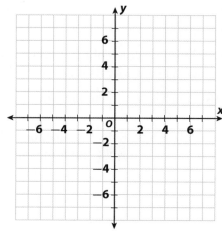

STEP 3 Now choose one of the functions from Step 1 or 2 above, but change the sign of the absolute value term. For example, you might choose to graph: $y = -|x| + 4$ and $y = -|x - 6|$. Sketch the graphs on the grid.

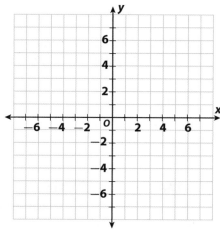

REFLECT

1. Draw Conclusions How does adding a constant term outside of the absolute value bars shift the graph of the function?

_____

_____

_____

2. Draw Conclusions How does adding a constant *inside* of the bars shift the graph of the function?

_____

_____

_____

FL   F-BF.2.3

Graphing Absolute Value Functions With Coefficients

> **Math Talk**
> Mathematical Practices
>
> How are the slopes of the rays that make up the graphs related to the coefficient of $|x|$?

You have seen how adding a constant to an absolute value function changes the graph of the function. Now you will explore the effects that coefficients of the absolute value term have on the graph.

A Use your calculator to graph $y = 2|x|$, $y = -3|x|$, and $y = 5|x|$ on the same graph. Sketch the graphs on the grid.

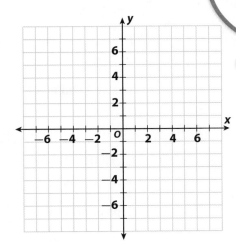

B Now see how fractional coefficients change the graphs. Graph $y = \frac{1}{2}|x|$, $y = \frac{1}{6}|x|$, and $y = \frac{3}{4}|x|$. Sketch the graphs on the grid.

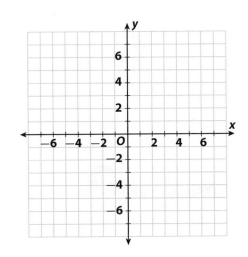

REFLECT

3. Draw Conclusions How do coefficients that are greater than 1 change the graph of an absolute value function?

_____

_____

4. Draw Conclusions How do fractional coefficients between 0 and 1 change the graph of an absolute value function?

_____

_____

Math On the Spot

my.hrw.com

Writing Equations Using Parameters

If you are given the graph of an absolute value function, you can write a rule for the function by identifying the parameters that have been used to transform the graph of the parent function. Start with the general form $f(x) = a|x - h| + k$ and substitute for the values of a, h, and k.

EXAMPLE 1

FL   F-BF.2.3

Write a function rule for the graph shown.

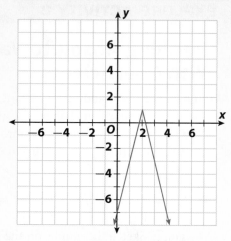

My Notes

STEP 1 Identify the coordinates of the vertex.

The vertex of the graph is (2, 1).

So $h = 2$ and $k = 1$.

STEP 2 Identify the slope of the rays.

Recall that the slope is the rise over the run.

slope of ray on left $= \frac{4}{1} = 4$; slope of ray on right $= -\frac{4}{1} = -4$

Since the graph opens downward, a is negative. Therefore, $a = -4$.

STEP 3 Substitute for a, h, and k in the general form.

$$f(x) = a|x - h| + k$$

$$f(x) = -4|x - 2| + 1$$

So, the function that is graphed is $f(x) = -4|x - 2| + 1$.

YOUR TURN

5. Write a function rule for the graph shown.

_____

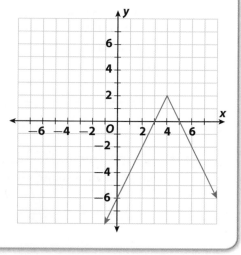

Personal Math Trainer

Online Assessment and Intervention

my.hrw.com

712   Unit 5

Graphing Using Parameters

EXAMPLE 2   FL   F-BF.2.3

Math On the Spot
my.hrw.com

Graph $f(x) = 2|x + 4| - 3$ without using a calculator or a table of values.

STEP 1   Identify h and k and identify the vertex of the graph.

The general form of an absolute value equation is $f(x) = a|x - h| + k$.

So $k = -3$ and $h = -4$.

The vertex of the graph is at $(-4, -3)$.

STEP 2   Graph the vertex.

Plot the vertex in purple.

STEP 3   Identify a and use it to graph the rays.

$a = 2$. So the graph opens upward.

The slope of the ray on the left is -2.

The slope of the ray on the right is 2.

Graph the rays.

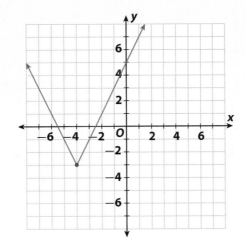

YOUR TURN

6.   Graph $f(x) = -3|x - 3| + 5$ without using a calculator or a table of values.

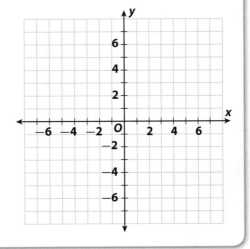

Personal
Math Trainer

Online Assessment
and Intervention

my.hrw.com

Use a calculator to graph both functions. Then sketch the functions on the coordinate plane. (Explore Activities 1 and 2)

1. $f(x) = |x| - 5$ and $g(x) = \frac{1}{2}|x| - 3$

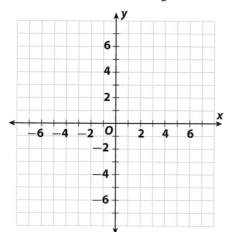

2. $g(x) = -2|x + 3|$ and $f(x) = 3|x - 4| + 1$

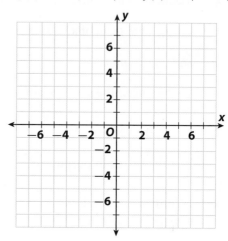

Find the vertex, the value of a, and a rule for the function represented by each graph. (Example 1)

3.

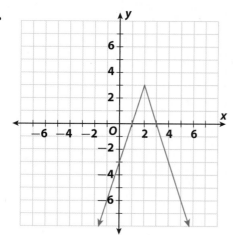

Vertex: _____

a: _____

$f(x) =$ _____

4.

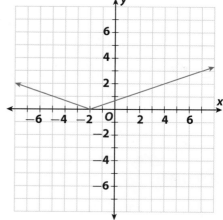

Vertex: _____

a: $\frac{1}{3}$

$g(x) = \frac{1}{3} \cdot$ _____

? ESSENTIAL QUESTION CHECK-IN

5. What is the effect of changing the parameters of an absolute value function?

_____

_____

18.3 Independent Practice

FL F-BF.2.3

Personal
Math Trainer
Online
Assessment and
Intervention
my.hrw.com

Use a calculator to graph both functions. Then sketch the functions on the coordinate plane.

6. $g(x) = 4|x - 1| - 2$ and
$f(x) = -4|x + 1| + 2$

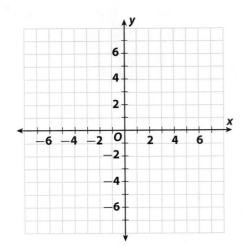

7. $f(x) = f(x) = \frac{1}{5}|x| + 2$ and $g(x) = -\frac{1}{5}|x + 2|$

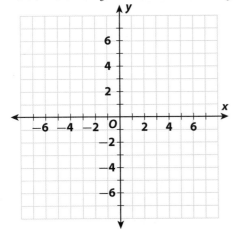

Find a rule for the function represented by each graph.

8.

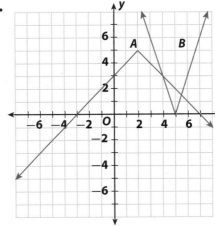

A: $f(x) =$ _____

B: $g(x) =$ _____

9.

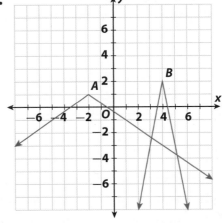

A: $f(x) =$ _____

B: $g(x) =$ _____

10. Explain the Error Ronaldo says that he needs only one piece of information to identify the range of an absolute value function—the constant term added to the absolute value term—such as the 3 in $f(x) = |x| + 3$. Explain why Ronaldo

is wrong. _____

_____

_____

11. Communicate Mathematical Ideas Jared drew the diamond shape shown on the coordinate grid by graphing two absolute value functions. What functions are represented by the graphs in Jared's drawing?

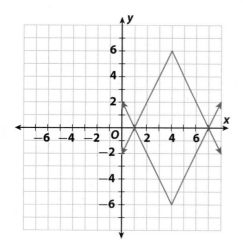

_____

Work Area

12. Justify Reasoning Each of the following functions is graphed on a coordinate grid with axes that go from −10 to 10. So the area of the coordinate grid is 400 square units. Order the functions in terms of the amount of area inside the V-shape that is created, from greatest to least. Explain your reasoning.

(a) $f(x) = |x|$ (b) $f(x) = 2|x|$ (c) $f(x) = |x| - 5$ (d) $f(x) = 2|x - 10|$

_____

_____

_____

_____

13. What If? Giselle created an absolute value equation whose graph is a V-shape that opens sideways rather than up or down. How did Giselle do it? Was her equation a function of x? Explain.

_____

_____

_____

_____

Ready to Go On?

18.1 Piecewise Functions

Graph each function.

1. $f(x) = \begin{cases} -2x \text{ if } x < 2 \\ -2x + 2 \text{ if } x \geq 2 \end{cases}$

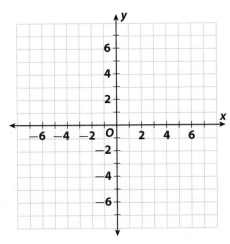

2. $f(x) = \begin{cases} -4 \text{ if } x \leq -2 \\ \frac{1}{2}x + 2 \text{ if } x > -2 \end{cases}$

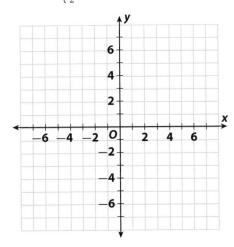

18.2 and 18.3 Absolute Value Functions and Transforming Absolute Value Functions

3. Graph: $f(x) = 3|x| - 5$

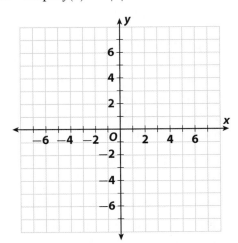

4. Write a rule for the graphed function.

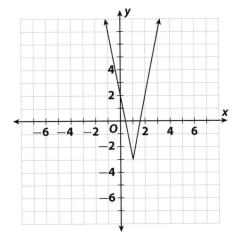

$g(x) = $ _____

? ESSENTIAL QUESTION

5. How do piecewise functions differ from other types of functions?

_____

_____

Personal Math Trainer

Online Assessment and Intervention

my.hrw.com

Selected Response

1. What is the value of x in $4(3^x) = 324$?

   Ⓐ 3   Ⓑ 4   Ⓒ 9   Ⓓ 81

2. How does the graph of $f(x) = (10)2^x - 1$ relate to $f(x) = 2^x$?

   Ⓐ vertical stretch and translation down

   Ⓑ vertical stretch and translation up

   Ⓒ vertical shrink and translation down

   Ⓓ vertical shrink and translation up

3. The graph shows costs for renting a power tool. Which function shows the cost of renting for more than 3 hours?

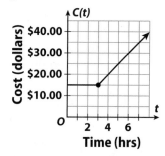

Time (hrs)

   Ⓐ $C(t) = 5(t - 3)$

   Ⓑ $C(t) = 5(t - 3) + 15t$

   Ⓒ $C(t) = 5t - 3$

   Ⓓ $C(t) = 5(t - 3) + 15$

4. What is the vertex of the graph of the equation $f(x) = 2|x - 6| + 9$?

   Ⓐ $(6, 9)$ Ⓒ $(2, 6)$

   Ⓑ $(2, 9)$ Ⓓ $(9, 6)$

5. Which of the following is true for the function $f(x) = -|x| + 3$?

   Ⓐ It has no negative values for y.

   Ⓑ It has only negative values for y.

   Ⓒ It has both positive and negative values for y.

   Ⓓ It has only whole-number values for y.

6. Which pair of functions form an "M-like" pattern when graphed on the same coordinate plane?

   Ⓐ $f(x) = -|x| + 3$ and $g(x) = -|x| - 3$

   Ⓑ $f(x) = -|x + 3|$ and $g(x) = -|x - 3|$

   Ⓒ $f(x) = |x| + 3$ and $g(x) = |x| - 3$

   Ⓓ $f(x) = 3|x|$ and $g(x) = -3|x|$

7. Zach drew a line segment from $(3, 3)$ to the point on the graph of $y = |x|$ where $x = -3$. Then he drew a line segment from $(3, 3)$ to the point on the graph of $y = |x| + 2$ where $x = 3$. Altogether, how long where the two line segments that Zach drew?

   Ⓐ 6 units   Ⓒ 8 units

   Ⓑ 12 units   Ⓓ 20 units

Mini-Tasks

8. Suppose your school is selling gourmet cookies door to door for $10 a box to raise money. Define a piecewise function $f(d)$ that indicates how much to pay a student (in dollars) for selling d boxes, satisfying the following conditions:

   • Students who sell 10 or fewer boxes are paid $1 per box.

   • Students who sell more than 10 boxes but fewer than 20 boxes are paid $1.50 per box for all boxes sold.

   • Students who sell 20 boxes or more are paid $2.50 per box for all boxes sold.

$$f(d) = \begin{cases} \underline{\hspace{4cm}} \\ \underline{\hspace{4cm}} \\ \underline{\hspace{4cm}} \end{cases}$$

Square Root and Cube Root Functions

? ESSENTIAL QUESTION

How do the square and cube root function families relate to their graphs?

Real-World Video

An audio engineer uses radical functions to calculate sound intensity, which decreases faster than linearly with distance.

⏻ my.hrw.com

GO DIGITAL
my.hrw.com

my.hrw.com

Go digital with your write-in student edition, accessible on any device.

Math On the Spot

Scan with your smart phone to jump directly to the online edition, video tutor, and more.

Animated Math

Interactively explore key concepts to see how math works.

Personal Math Trainer

Get immediate feedback and help as you work through practice sets.

Are YOU Ready?

Complete these exercises to review skills you will need for this module.

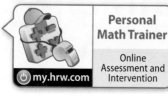

Squares and Square Roots

EXAMPLE Find the square root of 16.
$n = 4$ because $n^2 = 16$.

Finding the square of a number is the inverse operation of finding the square root.

Find the squares of the following numbers.

1. 8   **2.** −13   **3.** 50

_____ _____ _____

Find the square roots of the following numbers.

4. 9   **5.** 144   **6.** 225

_____ _____ _____

Function Tables

EXAMPLE Create a function table for $y = 4x - 1$.

x	y
0	−1
1	3
2	7

Insert the x values into the function and solve for y.
$y = 4(0) - 1 = 0 - 1 = -1$

7. Create a function table for $y = \sqrt{x} + 1$.

x	y
0	
1	
4	

8. Create a function table for $y = x^2 - 3$.

x	y
−2	
0	
5	

9. Create a function table for $y = 85$.

x	y
−4	
−2	
9	

10. Create a function table for $y = 5x + 4$.

x	y
−5	
−1	
3	

Reading Start-Up

Visualize Vocabulary

Use the Review Words to complete the bubble map. You may put only one word in each bubble.

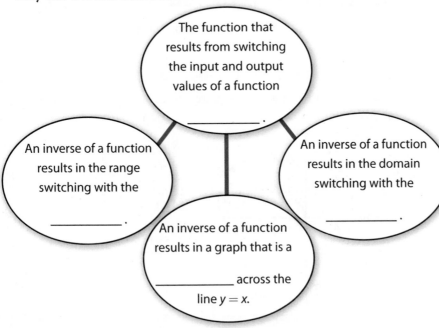

The function that results from switching the input and output values of a function

_____ .

An inverse of a function results in the range switching with the

_____ .

An inverse of a function results in the domain switching with the

_____ .

An inverse of a function results in a graph that is a

_____ across the line $y = x$.

Vocabulary

Review Words
- ✓ domain *(dominio)*
- ✓ inverse (of a function) *(función inversa)*
- parameter *(parámetro)*
- parent function *(función madre)*
- ✓ range *(rango)*
- ✓ reflection *(reflexión)*
- translation *(traslación)*

Preview Words
- cube root function
- square root function

Understand Vocabulary

To become familiar with some of the vocabulary terms in the module, consider the following. You may refer to the module, the glossary, or a dictionary.

1. A function whose rule contains a variable under a square-root sign.

_____

2. A function whose rule contains a variable under a cube-root sign.

_____

Active Reading

Layered Book Before beginning the module, create a Layered Book Note to help you organize what you learn. The four flaps of the layered book can summarize information into four pages, one for each lesson. Write details of each lesson on the appropriate flap to create a summary of the module.

MODULE 19
Unpacking the Standards
Understanding the standards and vocabulary terms in the standards will help you know exactly what you are expected to learn in this module.

 **F-IF.3.7b**

Graph square root, cube root, and piecewise-defined functions, including step functions and absolute value functions.

Key Vocabulary

function *(función)*
An input-output relationship that has exactly one output for each input.

What It Means to You

Creating graphs of different functions allows you to compare them visually.

UNPACKING EXAMPLE F-IF.3.7B

The shapes of the graphs of square and cube root parent functions are shown below.

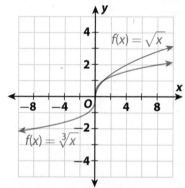

 F-BF.2.3

Identify the effect on the graph of replacing $f(x)$ by $f(x) + k$, $k\,f(x)$, $f(kx)$, and $f(x + k)$ for specific values of k (both positive and negative); find the value of k given the graphs. Experiment with cases and illustrate an explanation of the effects on the graph using technology.

Key Vocabulary

function notation *(notación de función)*
The notation used to describe a function.

What It Means to You

You can change a function by adding or multiplying by a constant. The result will be a new function that is a transformation of the original function.

UNPACKING EXAMPLE F-BF.2.3

The graph below shows examples of vertical translation of the function $f(x) = \sqrt{x}$ which occurs when a constant is added or subtracted to the function.

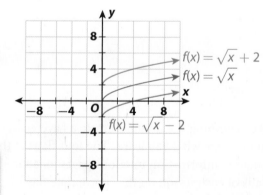

Visit **my.hrw.com** to see all **Florida Math Standards** unpacked.

my.hrw.com

FL   F-IF.3.7b

Graph square root, cube
root, and piecewise-defined
functions, including step
functions and absolute value
functions. *Also F-IF.3.7, F-IF.3.9*

 ESSENTIAL QUESTION

What function is the inverse of a quadratic function?

EXPLORE ACTIVITY (Real World)    FL   F-IF.3.9

Understanding One-to-One Functions

A function is **one-to-one** if each output of the function is paired with exactly one
input. Only one-to-one functions have inverses that are also functions.

Recall that the graph of $f^{-1}(x)$ is the reflection of the graph of $f(x)$ across the
line $y = x$.

Sketch the inverse of each function graphed below.

A
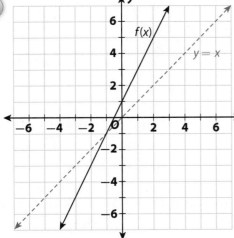

B
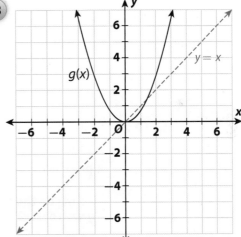

Linear functions with nonzero
slopes are always one-to-one,

so their inverses [**are / are not**]
functions.

Quadratic functions are not
one-to-one. The reflection
of the parabola labeled $g(x)$
across the line $y = x$

[**is / is not**] a function.

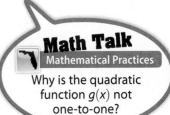

Math Talk
FL Mathematical Practices

Why is the quadratic
function $g(x)$ not
one-to-one?

REFLECT

1. Explain why the reflection of the graph of $g(x)$ across the line $y = x$ is not
    a function.

    _____

    _____

    _____

Graphing the Inverse of a Quadratic Function with Restricted Domain

EXAMPLE 1   FL   F-IF.3.7b

Graph the function $f(x) = 0.5x^2$ for the domain $x \geq 0$. Then graph its inverse, $f^{-1}(x)$, and write a rule for the inverse function.

STEP 1   Make a table of values to graph $f(x)$ for nonnegative values of x. Then use the table to graph the function.

x	$f(x) = 0.5x^2$
0	0
1	0.5
2	2
3	4.5
4	8

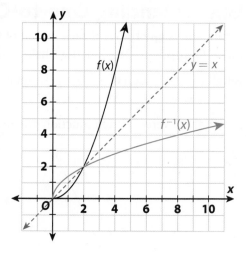

STEP 2   Make a table of values for $f^{-1}(x)$ by finding the image of each point on the graph of $f(x)$ after a reflection across the line $y = x$. To reflect a point across $y = x$, switch the x- and y-coordinates of the point.

Points on the graph of $f(x)$	(0, 0)	(1, 0.5)	(2, 2)	(3, 4.5)	(4, 8)
Points on the graph of $f^{-1}(x)$	(0, 0)	(0.5, 1)	(2, 2)	(4.5, 3)	(8, 4)

STEP 3   Use the table from Step 2 to graph $f^{-1}(x)$ on the grid in Step 1.

STEP 4   Write the rule for $f^{-1}(x)$.

$f(x) = 0.5x^2$

$y = \frac{1}{2}x^2$ Replace 0.5 with $\frac{1}{2}$ and $f(x)$ with y.

$2y = x^2$ Multiply both sides by 2.

$\sqrt{2y} = x$ Take the square root of both sides. Use the definition of positive square root.

$\sqrt{2x} = y$ Switch x and y to write the inverse.

$\sqrt{2x} = f^{-1}(x)$ Replace y with $f^{-1}(x)$.

The rule for the inverse function is $f^{-1}(x) = \sqrt{2x}$, for $x \geq 0$.

2. Graph the function $f(x) = x^2 + 2$ for the domain $x \geq 0$. Then graph its inverse, $f^{-1}(x)$, and write a rule for the inverse function.

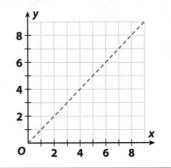

Personal Math Trainer

Online Assessment and Intervention

⏻ my.hrw.com

Domain of Square Root Functions

A quadratic function of the form $f(x) = ax^2$, where $x \geq 0$, is a one-to-one function, so its inverse is also a function. In general, the inverse of $f(x) = ax^2$ is the *square root function* $g(x) = \sqrt{\frac{x}{a}}$.

A square root function is a function whose rule involves $\sqrt{x}$. The parent square root function is $g(x) = \sqrt{x}$. The graph shows that $g(x) = \sqrt{x}$ is the inverse of $f(x) = x^2$ for $x \geq 0$.

A square root function is defined only for values of x that make the expression under the radical sign nonnegative.

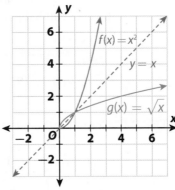

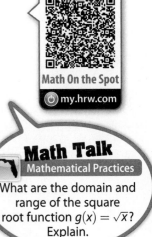

Math On the Spot

⏻ my.hrw.com

Math Talk
Mathematical Practices

What are the domain and range of the square root function $g(x) = \sqrt{x}$? Explain.

EXAMPLE 2   **FL**   F-IF.3.7b

Find the domain of the square root function $f(x) = \sqrt{x + 4} - 3$.

$f(x) = \sqrt{x + 4} - 3$

$x + 4 \geq 0$ The expression under the radical sign must be greater than or equal to 0.

$x \geq -4$ Solve the inequality. Subtract 4 from both sides.

The domain is the set of all real numbers greater than or equal to -4.

Find the domain of each square-root function.

3. $f(x) = \sqrt{3x - 5}$ **4.** $f(x) = 3\sqrt{x + 1}$

Personal Math Trainer

Online Assessment and Intervention

⏻ my.hrw.com

Modeling with Square Root Functions

EXAMPLE 3 Real World

FL F-IF.3.7b

The function $d(t) = 16t^2$ gives the distance d in feet that a dropped object falls in t seconds. Write and graph the inverse function $t(d)$ to find the time t in seconds it takes for an object to fall a distance of d feet. Then estimate how long it will take a penny dropped into a well to fall 48 feet.

My Notes

STEP 1 Write the inverse function.

The original function is a quadratic function with a domain restricted to $t \geq 0$. The function fits the pattern $f(x) = ax^2$ for $x \geq 0$, so its inverse will have the form $g(x) = \sqrt{\frac{x}{a}}$.

Original Function	Inverse Function
$d(t) = 16t^2$ for $t \geq 0$	$t(d) = \sqrt{\frac{d}{16}}$ for $d \geq 0$

STEP 2 Complete the table of values and use it to graph the function $t(d)$.

d	0	4	16	32	64	100
t	0	0.5	1	1.4	2	2.5

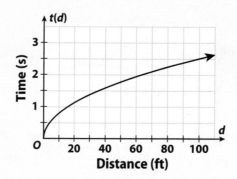

STEP 3 Use the function $t(d)$ to estimate how long it will take a penny to fall 48 feet.

$t(d) = \sqrt{\frac{d}{16}}$ Write the function.

$t(48) = \sqrt{\frac{48}{16}}$ Substitute 48 for d.

$t(48) = \sqrt{3}$ Simplify.

$t(48) \approx 1.73$ Use a calculator. Round to the nearest hundredth.

It will take about 1.73 seconds for a penny to fall 48 feet.

REFLECT

5. Explain why the domain is restricted to $t \geq 0$ for the original function $d(t) = 16t^2$.

_____

_____

6. Describe another way that you could find the time it would take a penny to fall 48 feet.

_____

_____

YOUR TURN

7. A company manufactures square tabletops that are covered by 16 square tiles. If s is the side length of each tile in inches, then the area A of a tabletop in square feet is given by $A(s) = \frac{1}{9}s^2$.

a. Write and graph the inverse function $s(A)$ to find the side length of the tiles in inches for a tabletop with an area of A square feet.

_____

b. What is the side length of the tiles that make up a tabletop with an area of 4 square feet?

_____

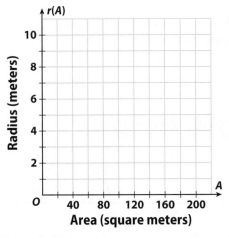

8. The function $A(r) = \pi r^2$ gives the area A in square meters of a circle with a radius of r meters.

a. Write and graph the inverse function $r(A)$ to find the radius in meters of a circle with an area of A square meters.

_____

b. Find the radius of a circular swimming pool that has a surface area of 120 square meters. Round to the nearest tenth.

_____

Personal Math Trainer

Online Assessment and Intervention

⊙ my.hrw.com

1. Complete the table of values to graph the function $f(x) = x^2 + 1$ for $x \geq 0$.
   Next, use the table to find four ordered pairs on the graph of the inverse
   function and draw its graph. Then write a rule for the inverse function.
   (Explore Activity and Example 1)

x	f(x)
0	1
1	
2	
3	

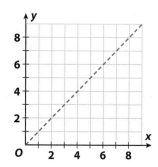

Ordered Pairs $f^{-1}(x)$
(1, 0)
(2,)

$f^{-1}(x) = $ _____

Find the domain of each square root function. (Example 2)

2. $y = 2\sqrt{4x - 1}$

   $\boxed{} \geq 0$

   $4x \geq \boxed{}$

   $x \geq \boxed{}$

3. $y = \sqrt{3(x - 3)} + 1$

   $\boxed{} \geq 0$

   $\boxed{} \geq 0$

   $3x \geq \boxed{}$

   $x \geq \boxed{}$

4. The function $a(r) = 3.14r^2$ approximates the area a in inches for a circle with
   radius of r inches. (Example 3)

   a. Write the inverse function $r(a)$.

   _____

   b. Use the inverse function to find the radius of a circle with an area of
      94.2 in^2. Round to the nearest tenth.

   _____

? ESSENTIAL QUESTION CHECK-IN

5. What is the inverse of a quadratic function?

   _____

   _____

   _____

19.1 Independent Practice

FL F-IF.3.7, F-IF.3.7b, F-IF.3.9

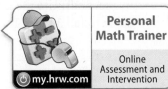

Personal
Math Trainer

Online
Assessment and
Intervention

my.hrw.com

Graph the function $f(x)$ for the domain $x \geq 0$. Then graph its inverse, $f^{-1}(x)$, and write a rule for the inverse function.

6. $f(x) = 2x^2, f^{-1}(x) = $ _____

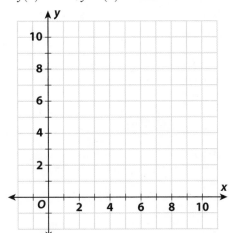

7. $f(x) = -x^2, f^{-1}(x) = $ _____

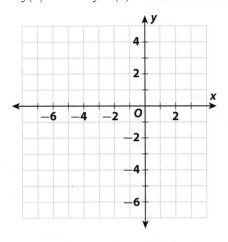

8. $f(x) = \frac{1}{3}x^2, f^{-1}(x) = $ _____

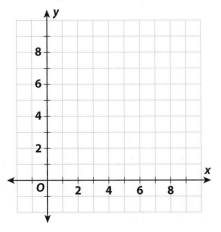

9. $f(x) = -\frac{1}{2}x^2, f^{-1}(x) = $ _____

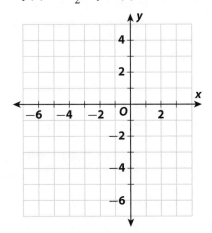

Find the domain of each square root function.

10. $f(x) = \sqrt{x-1},$ _____

11. $f(x) = \sqrt{2x+3} + 5,$ _____

12. $f(x) = \sqrt{2(x+1)},$ _____

13. $f(x) = 4 - \sqrt{3x-12},$ _____

14. $f(x) = \sqrt{2x-5},$ _____

15. $f(x) = \sqrt{4-3x},$ _____

16. Communicate Mathematical Ideas Explain how to find the domain of a square-root function. Why is the domain restricted for some square root functions?

_____

_____

_____

17. The function $d(t) = 16t^2$ gives the distance d in feet that a dropped object falls in t seconds. Use the inverse of the function to find how long it will take an apple to fall 32 feet. Round to the nearest hundredth.

_____

18. The function $A(s) = \pi r^2$ gives the area A in square feet of a circle with a radius of r feet. What is the radius of a circle with an area of 16π square feet?

_____

19. **Multi Step** The function $A(s) = s^2$ gives the area A in square meters for a square with a side of s meters. Write a formula for perimeter of a square in

terms of its area. _____

20. **Justify Reasoning** Consider the quadratic function $f(x) = x^2$.

a. Is $f(x)$ one-to-one? Explain.

_____

_____

b. How could you restrict the domain of $f(x)$ so that the inverse function, $f^{-1}(x)$, is one-to-one? Explain. Graph the function for the restricted domain.

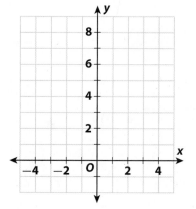

_____

_____

_____

Work Area

21. **Represent Real-World Problems** The formula for converting temperatures from degrees Fahrenheit F to degrees Celsius C is $C = \frac{5}{9}(F - 32)$. What is the inverse of this function? How can you use the inverse to find where the Celsius temperature equals the Fahrenheit temperature?

_____

_____

22. **Justify Reasoning** Why is a linear function not one to one if the slope is 0?

_____

_____

_____

LESSON
19.2
Transforming Square Root Functions

FL F-BF.2.3

Identify the effect on the graph of replacing $f(x)$ by $f(x) +$ k, $k\,f(x)$, $f(kx)$, and $f(x + k)$ for specific values of k (both positive and negative); find the value of k given the graphs... *Also F-IF.3.9.*

? **ESSENTIAL QUESTION**

How can you transform the parent square root function?

EXPLORE ACTIVITY 1   FL F-BF.2.3

Stretching and Shrinking Graphs

For a function in the form $g(x) = a\sqrt{x}$, the value of a indicates how the parent function $f(x) = \sqrt{x}$ is transformed.

A Complete the table for $g(x) = 3\sqrt{x}$.

x	$g(x) = 3\sqrt{x}$
0	
1	
4	
9	
16	

B Graph $g(x)$.

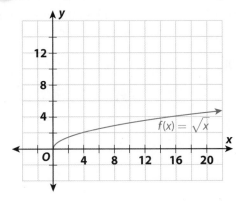

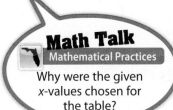

Math Talk
Mathematical Practices

Why were the given *x*-values chosen for the table?

C The graph of $g(x) = 3\sqrt{x}$ is a vertical *stretch* of the graph of the parent function. The stretch is a factor of 3 since each output is _____ times the output of the parent function.

D Complete the table for $h(x) = 0.5\sqrt{x}$.

x	$h(x) = 0.5\sqrt{x}$
0	
1	
4	
9	
16	

E Graph $h(x)$.

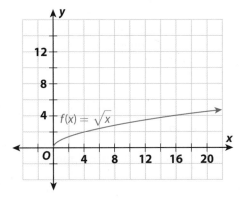

F The graph of $h(x) = 0.5\sqrt{x}$ is a vertical *shrink* of the graph of the parent function. The shrink is a factor of 0.5 since each output is _____ times the output of the parent function.

REFLECT

1. Interpret the Answer Complete the sentences for $f(x) = a\sqrt{x}$.

   a. When $|a| > 1$, the graph of $g(x)$ is a vertical _____ of the graph of the parent function.

   b. When $|a| < 1$, the graph of $g(x)$ is a vertical _____ of the graph of the parent function.

EXPLORE ACTIVITY 2   FL   F-BF.2.3, F-IF.3.9

Translating Graphs

In the previous activity, you explored how values of a in the function $f(x) = a\sqrt{x}$ affect the graph of the parent square root function. In this activity, you will explore how the values of h and k in the function $f(x) = \sqrt{x - h} + k$ affect the graph of the parent square root function.

A Complete the table for $g(x) = \sqrt{x + 4} - 3$.

x	$g(x) = \sqrt{x + 4} - 3$
−4	
−3	
0	
5	
12	

> Notice that the table uses x-values that result in perfect squares.

B Graph $g(x)$.

C The graph of $g(x) = \sqrt{x + 4} - 3$

   is a _____ of the graph of the parent function.

   The _____ is _____

   units to the left and _____ units down.

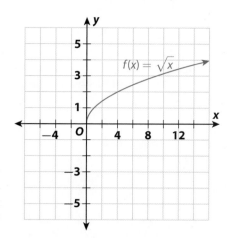

D Give the domain and range for $g(x)$.

   Domain: $x \geq$ _____

   Range: $y \geq$ _____

E Complete the table for $h(x) = \sqrt{x - 2} + 4$.

x	$h(x) = \sqrt{x - 2} + 4$
2	
3	
6	
11	
18	

> Notice that the table uses x-values that result in perfect squares.

F Graph $h(x)$.

G The graph of $h(x) = \sqrt{x - 2} + 4$

is a _____ of the graph of the parent function. The

translation is _____ units to

the _____ and _____

units _____.

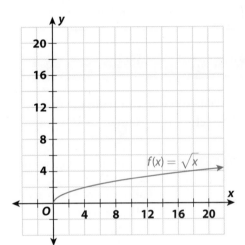

H Give the domain and range for $h(x)$.

Domain: $x \geq$ _____

Range: $y \geq$ _____

REFLECT

2. **Draw Conclusions** How can you determine the domain of $m(x) = \sqrt{x + 4} - 3$ by looking at its function rule?

_____

_____

_____

_____

3. **Make a Conjecture** Predict how different values of a in the function $f(x) = a\sqrt{x - h} + k$ will affect the range.

_____

_____

Writing the Equation of a Square Root Function

If the shape of the graph is shrunk or stretched and the graph moves left or right and/or up or down, this is a combination of transformations.

Transforming a Square Root Function

Any transformation has an equation of the form $f(x) = a\sqrt{x - h} + k$.

- If $a = 1$, $h = 0$, and $k = 0$, the graph is $f(x) = \sqrt{x}$.
- If h is not 0, then the value of h moves the graph right or left along the x-axis.
- If k is not 0, then the value of k moves the graph up or down along the y-axis.
- If a is not 1, then the graph of $f(x)$ is a shrink of the parent function if $a < 1$ and a stretch if $a > 1$.

EXAMPLE 1

Animated Math

🔘 my.hrw.com

My Notes

Write the function rule for the function represented by the graph.

STEP 1 Identify the function type.

The shape of the graph indicates a square root function.

STEP 2 Identify the values of h and k.

The endpoint $(0, 0)$ from the parent square function was translated to $(1, 3)$. So, $h = 1$ and $k = 3$.

The equation has the form $f(x) = a\sqrt{x - 1} + 3$.

STEP 3 Use the point $(5, 7)$ to identify a.

$$f(x) = a\sqrt{x - 1} + 3 \qquad \text{Substitute for } x \text{ and } y.$$
$$(7) = a\sqrt{(5) - 1} + 3 \qquad \text{Simplify the radical.}$$
$$7 = a\sqrt{4} + 3$$
$$7 = a(2) + 3 \qquad \text{Subtract 3 from both sides.}$$
$$4 = a(2) \qquad \text{Divide both sides by 2.}$$
$$2 = a$$

Substitute $a = 2$, $h = 1$, and $k = 3$ into the general function $f(x) = a\sqrt{x - h} + k$. The function is $f(x) = 2\sqrt{x - 1} + 3$.

REFLECT

4. The point $(0, 0)$ is on the graph of the parent square root function. How can you find the point on the square root function to which $(0, 0)$ is translated?

_____

_____

5. **Interpret the Answer** Does the graph in Example 1 represent a vertical stretch or a vertical shrink of the graph of the parent function? Does this agree with the value of a that you found? Explain.

_____

_____

_____

_____

YOUR TURN

Write the rule for the function represented by each graph.

6.

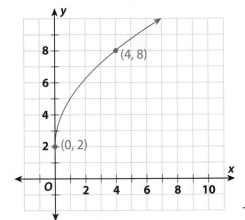

_____

7.

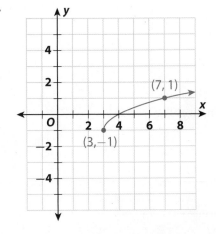

_____

Graph each square root function. Then describe the graph as a transformation
of the graph of the parent function, and give its domain and range.
(Explore Activities 1 and 2)

1. $g(x) = 0.5\sqrt{x + 2}$

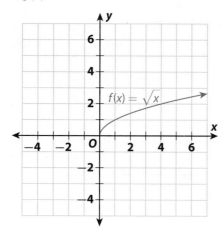

_____

_____

_____

2. $g(x) = -\sqrt{x} + 5$

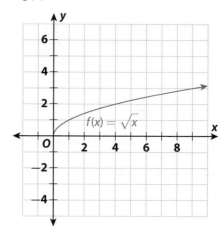

_____

_____

_____

3. Kyle drew this translation of the graph of the parent square
root function. (Example 1)

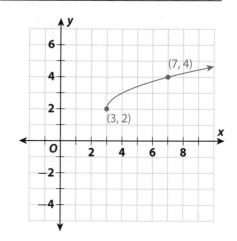

   a. How far has the graph of the parent function been

   translated horizontally? _____

   b. How far has the graph of the parent function been

   translated vertically? _____

   c. Write a rule for the function represented by the graph.

   _____

ESSENTIAL QUESTION CHECK-IN

4. What do the values of a, h, and k tell you about how the graph of
$f(x) = a\sqrt{x - h} + k$ is related to the graph of the parent function $f(x) = \sqrt{x}$?

_____

_____

_____

_____

19.2 Independent Practice

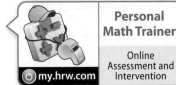

Personal Math Trainer

Online Assessment and Intervention

FL   F-BF.2.3, F-IF.3.9

my.hrw.com

Determine the domain and range of each function.

5. $f(x) = \sqrt{x - 3} + 2$

_____

_____

6. $f(x) = 3\sqrt{x + 2} + 1$

_____

_____

7. $f(x) = \sqrt{2x + 3}$

_____

_____

8. $f(x) = \sqrt{6 - 2x} + 3$

_____

_____

9. $f(x) = 5\sqrt{x + 0.5} + 3$

_____

_____

10. Multi-Step Write the function represented by the given transformation of the graph of $f(x) = \sqrt{x}$.

a. The graph is translated 3 units down.

_____

b. The graph is translated 3 units down and 2 units left.

_____

c. The graph is stretched by a factor of 5, translated 3 units down and 2 units left.

_____

11. Bill is a house painter. The graph shows the relationship between the number of square feet of paint, x, needed to cover a square wall, and the length in feet, y, of the square wall. The graph accounts for some paint that Bill may spill.

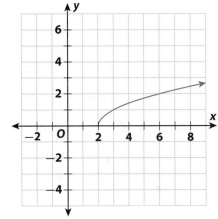

a. How much spillage is taken into account?

_____

_____

b. What function is represented by the graph?

_____

c. Estimate the length of the sides of the wall if enough paint was purchased to cover 40 square feet.

_____

d. Describe how the graph is related to the graph of the parent function.

_____

_____

_____

12. **Explain the Error** A student was trying to find the function for a graph of a translation of a square root function. She found the h value to be 2 and the k value to be 4. She writes the function as $f(x) = \sqrt{x - 4} + 2$. Explain the error.

_____

_____

 **FOCUS ON HIGHER ORDER THINKING**

Work Area

13. **Critical Thinking** What is the limitation of considering the square root function $f(x) = \sqrt{x}$ to be the inverse of the quadratic function $f(x) = x^2$? You might use a table or graph to help you think this through.

_____

_____

_____

_____

_____

_____

14. **Analyze Relationships** Describe how the effect that the value of k has on the graph of $f(x) = \sqrt{x} + k$ is similar to the effect that the value of b has on the graph of $f(x) = x + b$.

_____

_____

_____

15. **Multiple Representations** Which function has a greater minimum value, $f(x) = \sqrt{x - 4} - 1$ or the function whose graph is shown?

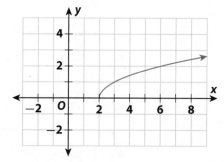

_____

_____

_____

19.3 Cube Root Functions

FL **F-IF.3.7b**

Graph square root, cube root, and piecewise-defined functions, including step functions and absolute value functions. *Also F-IF.3.7, F-IF.3.9*

ESSENTIAL QUESTION

What is the inverse of a cubic function?

EXPLORE ACTIVITY FL F-IF.3.7b

Understanding Cube Root Functions

The following activity will introduce you to the cube root function and its graph.

A Complete the table of values for the parent cubic function, $f(x) = x^3$, and use the table to complete the graph.

x	$f(x) = x^3$
−2	
−1	
0	
1	
2	

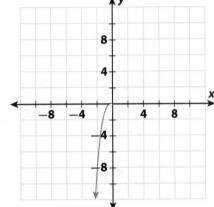

B Because $f(x)$ [**is / is not**] a one-to-one function, its inverse is also a function.

The inverse of $f(x) = x^3$ is the *cube root function* $g(x) = \sqrt[3]{x}$.

A **cube root function** is a function whose rule involves $\sqrt[3]{x}$. The parent cube root function is $g(x) = \sqrt[3]{x}$.

C Complete the table of values for the parent cube root function, $g(x) = \sqrt[3]{x}$. Use the table and the fact that the graphs of inverse functions are reflections across the line $y = x$ to graph the function $g(x)$.

x	$g(x) = \sqrt[3]{x}$
−8	
−1	
0	
1	
8	

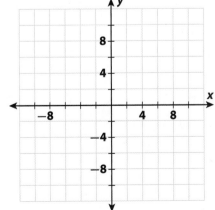

EXPLORE ACTIVITY *(cont'd)*

REFLECT

1. **Communicate Mathematical Ideas** Explain how the values in the tables for $f(x) = x^3$ and $g(x) = \sqrt[3]{x}$ show that the graphs of these functions are reflections of each other across the line $y = x$.

   _____

   _____

2. Is $g(x) = \sqrt[3]{x}$ also a one-to-one function? Explain.

   _____

3. **Analyze Relationships** What are the domain and range of $f(x) = x^3$? What are the domain and range of $g(x) = \sqrt[3]{x}$?

   _____

   _____

Graphing the Inverse of a Cubic Function

The graph of a function and the graph of its inverse are reflections of each other across the line $y = x$, so you can use the graph of a function to sketch the graph of its inverse.

EXAMPLE 1   FL   F-IF.3.7b

Graph the function $f(x) = 0.5x^3$. Then graph its inverse, $f^{-1}(x)$, and write a rule for the inverse function.

My Notes

STEP 1   Make a table of values and graph the function $f(x) = 0.5x^3$.

x	$f(x)$
−2	−4
−1	−0.5
0	0
1	0.5
2	4

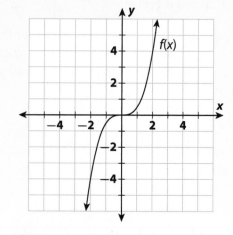

STEP 2 Find points on the graph of the inverse of $f(x)$ by finding the image of each point after a reflection across the line $y = x$.

Points on the graph of $f(x)$	$(-2, -4)$	$(-1, -0.5)$	$(0, 0)$	$(1, 0.5)$	$(2, 4)$
Points on the graph of $f^{-1}(x)$	$(-4, -2)$	$(-0.5, -1)$	$(0, 0)$	$(0.5, 1)$	$(4, 2)$

STEP 3 Use the table from Step 2 to graph $f^{-1}(x)$.

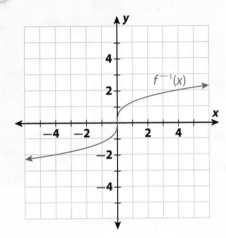

STEP 4 Write a rule for $f^{-1}(x)$.

$y = 0.5x^3$ Replace $f(x)$ with y. Solve for x.

$2y = x^3$ Multiply both sides by 2.

$\sqrt[3]{2y} = x$ Take the cube root of each side.

$\sqrt[3]{2x} = y$ Switch x and y to write the inverse.

$\sqrt[3]{2x} = f^{-1}(x)$ Replace y with $f^{-1}(x)$.

Math Talk
Mathematical Practices

How is the graph of a cube root function different from the graph of a square root function?

YOUR TURN

4. Graph the function $f(x) = 0.25x^3$. Then graph its inverse, $f^{-1}(x)$, and write a rule for the inverse function.

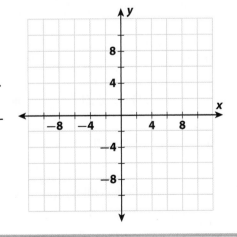

Personal Math Trainer

Online Assessment and Intervention

my.hrw.com

Modeling with Cube Root Functions

As with other types of functions, cube root functions can be used to model real-world situations.

EXAMPLE 2 Real World

FL   F-IF.3.7b

A pike is a type of freshwater fish. The function $w(L) = \frac{L^3}{3500}$ gives the approximate weight $w(L)$ in pounds of a pike with length L inches.

Write and graph the inverse function $L(w)$ to find the approximate length $L(w)$ in inches of a pike weighing w pounds. Then use your function to find the length of a 7-pound pike.

My Notes

STEP 1   Write the inverse function.

The original function is a cubic function.

It can be written in the form $f(x) = ax^3$ where $a = \frac{1}{3500}$.

Its inverse will have the form $g(x) = \sqrt[3]{\frac{x}{a}}$.

Original Function	Inverse Function
$w(L) = \frac{1}{3500}L^3$	$L(w) = \sqrt[3]{3500w}$

STEP 2   Make a table of values and use it to graph the function $L(w)$. Round the values of $L(w)$ to the nearest whole number.

w	0	1	2	3	4	5
L(w)						

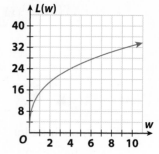

STEP 3   Use the function $L(w)$ to estimate the length of a 7-pound pike.

$L(w) = \sqrt[3]{3500w}$ Write the function.

$L(7) = \sqrt[3]{3500(7)}$ Substitute 7 for w.

$L(7) = \sqrt[3]{24,500}$ Simplify.

$L(7) \approx 29$ Use a calculator. Round to the nearest whole number.

So, a 7-pound pike will be about 29 inches long.

REFLECT

5. What is the reasonable domain and range of $L(w)$?

_____

_____

_____

_____

6. Interpret the Answer What is the significance in the context of the problem of the point at approximately $(6, 28)$ on the graph of $L(w)$?

_____

_____

7. Communicate Mathematical Ideas Describe what happens to the graph of $L(w)$ as the values of w increase. Is this true for all cube root functions?

_____

_____

_____

_____

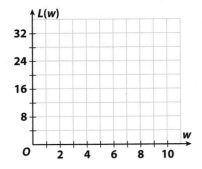

YOUR TURN

8. For another type of fish, the relationship between the weight $w(L)$ in pounds and the length L in inches is given by the function $w(L) = \frac{L^3}{2500}$. Write and graph the inverse function $L(w)$ to find the approximate length $L(w)$ in inches of a fish of this type weighing w pounds. Then find the length of a fish of this type that weighs 10 pounds.

_____

A 10-pound fish would be approximately _____ inches long.

Personal Math Trainer

Online Assessment and Intervention

⏻ my.hrw.com

Graph the function $f(x)$. Then graph its inverse, $f^{-1}(x)$, and write a rule for the inverse function. (Explore Activity and Example 1)

1. $f(x) = 2x^3$

$$y = 2x^3$$

$$\boxed{} = x^3$$

$$\boxed{} = x$$

$$\boxed{} = y$$

$$f^{-1}(x) = \underline{}$$

2. $f(x) = -x^3$

$$y = -x^3$$

$$\boxed{} = x^3$$

$$\boxed{} = x$$

$$\boxed{} = y$$

$$f^{-1}(x) = \underline{}$$

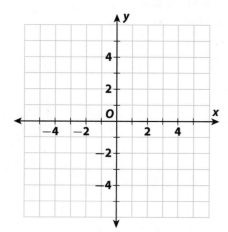

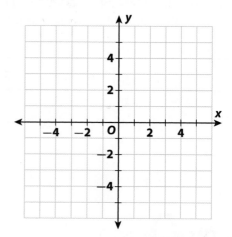

3. The function $V(r) = \frac{4}{3}\pi r^3$ gives the volume $V(r)$ in cubic inches of a sphere with a radius of r inches. (Example 2)

a. Write and graph the inverse function $r(V)$ to find the radius in inches of a sphere with a volume of V cubic inches. _____

b. To the nearest inch, what is the radius of a basketball with a volume of 455 cubic inches? _____

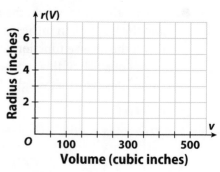

? ESSENTIAL QUESTION CHECK-IN

4. If you are given the rule for a cubic function, $f(x)$, what are two ways that you can graph its inverse function?

_____

_____

_____

19.3 Independent Practice

Personal
Math Trainer

Online
Assessment and
my.hrw.com   Intervention

 FL F-IF.3.7, F-IF.3.7b, F-IF.3.9

Graph $f(x)$. Then graph its inverse, $f^{-1}(x)$, and write a rule for the inverse function.

5. $f(x) = \frac{1}{4} x^3$

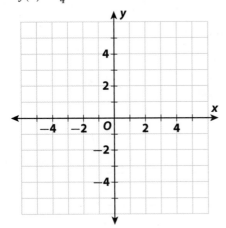

$f^{-1}(x) = $ _____

6. $f(x) = -\frac{1}{3} x^3$

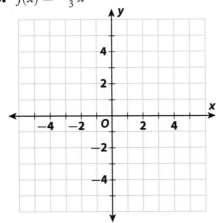

$f^{-1}(x) = $ _____

For each function, write a rule for the inverse function.

7. $g(x) = \sqrt[3]{\frac{x}{5}}$

_____

8. $h(x) = \sqrt[3]{\frac{5x}{2}}$

_____

_____

9. A company manufactures water tanks in the shape of rectangular prisms. The length of each tank is 3 times the width, and the height of each tank is twice the width.

a. Given that 1 cubic foot ≈ 7.48 gallons, write a function $c(w)$ that approximates the capacity in gallons of a tank with a width of w feet.

_____

_____

b. Write and graph the inverse function $w(c)$ to find the width in feet of a tank with a capacity of c gallons.

_____

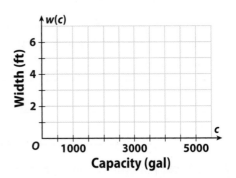

c. To the nearest foot, what is the width of a tank that has a capacity of 3000 gallons?

_____

_____

10. Communicate Mathematical Ideas
The graph of $f(x) = x(x + 1)(x - 1)$ is shown.

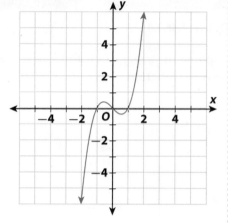

a. Is $f(x)$ a cubic function? Explain.

_____

_____

_____

_____

b. Is $f(x)$ a one-to-one function? Explain.

_____

_____

c. Does an inverse function for $f(x)$ exist? Explain.

_____

d. Give one way to restrict the domain of $f(x)$ so that an inverse function exists.

_____

11. Justify Reasoning Ellie is determining the inverse of $g(x) = \frac{27}{8}x^3$. She thinks that $g^{-1}(x) = \frac{2}{3}\sqrt[3]{x}$. Is she correct? Justify your answer.

_____

_____

_____

12. Critical Thinking Consider the restriction that you made to the domain of $f(x)$ in Exercise 10 so that the inverse function would exist. What effect does this restriction have on the range of the inverse function? Explain.

_____

_____

_____

_____

_____

_____

Transforming Cube Root Functions

FL F-BF.2.3

Identify the effect on the graph of replacing $f(x)$ by $f(x) + k$, $kf(x)$, $f(kx)$, and $f(x + k)$ for specific values of k (both positive and negative); find the value of k given the graphs...
Also F-IF.3.9

ESSENTIAL QUESTION

How can you transform the parent cube root function?

EXPLORE ACTIVITY 1　　**FL** F-BF.2.3

Stretching and Shrinking Graphs

$f(x) = \sqrt[3]{x}$ is the parent function from which other cube root functions are formed. You can transform the parent cube root function by changing the values of a, h, and k in the general form of the equation shown below.

$$f(x) = a\sqrt[3]{x - h} + k$$

A Complete the table for $g(x) = 3\sqrt[3]{x}$.

x	$g(x) = 3\sqrt[3]{x}$
−8	
−1	
0	
1	
8	

B Graph $g(x)$.

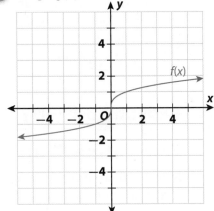

C The graph of $g(x)$ is a vertical _____ of the graph of the parent function by a factor of _____ .

D Complete the table for $h(x) = 0.5\sqrt[3]{x}$.

x	$h(x) = 0.5\sqrt[3]{x}$
−8	
−1	
0	
1	
8	

E Graph $h(x)$.

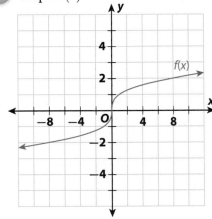

F The graph of $h(x)$ is a vertical _____ of the graph of the parent

function by a factor of _____ .

REFLECT

1. **Justify Reasoning** Explain how you know in part D that the graph of $h(x)$ is a vertical shrink of the graph of the parent function.

   _____

   _____

   _____

   _____

2. **Make a Conjecture** Complete the sentences for $f(x) = a\sqrt[3]{x}$ based on your observations from Explore Activity 1.

   • When $|a| > 1$, the graph of $f(x)$ is a vertical _____ of the graph of the parent function.

   • When $0 < |a| < 1$, the graph of $f(x)$ is a vertical _____ of the graph of the parent function.

EXPLORE ACTIVITY 2   FL   F-BF.2.3

Translating Graphs

New functions may also be formed by translating or reflecting the graph of the parent function.

A Complete the table for $g(x) = \sqrt[3]{x - 2} + 4$.

x	$g(x) = \sqrt[3]{x - 2} + 4$
−6	
1	
2	
3	
10	

B Graph $g(x)$.

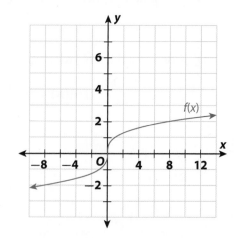

C The graph of $g(x)$ is a translation of the graph of the parent function 2 units

_____ and _____ units up. The domain

is _____ . The range is _____ .

D Complete the table for $h(x) = \sqrt[3]{x+3} - 2$.

E Graph $h(x)$.

x	$h(x) = \sqrt[3]{x+3} - 2$
−11	
−4	
−3	
−2	
5	

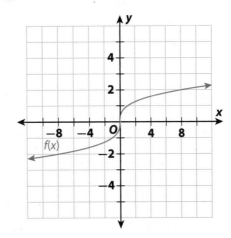

F The graph of $h(x)$ is a translation of the graph of the parent function 3

units _____ and _____ units down. The

domain is _____ . The range is _____ .

REFLECT

3. What are the values of h and k in $g(x) = \sqrt[3]{x-2} + 4$? What effect do h and k have on the graph of the function?

_____

_____

_____

_____

_____

_____

4. **Make a Conjecture** Complete the sentences for $f(x) = \sqrt[3]{x-h} + k$ based on your observations from Explore Activity 2.

• The graph of $f(x)$ is a translation of the parent function $|h|$ units

_____ if $h < 0$ and h units _____ if $h > 0$.

• The graph of $f(x)$ is a translation of the parent function $|k|$ units

_____ if $k < 0$ and k units _____ if $k > 0$.

Writing the Equation of a Cube Root Function

You can write the cube root function represented by a graph by identifying the values of *a*, *h*, and *k*.

EXAMPLE 1

FL   F-BF.2.3

Write the function rule for the function whose graph is shown below.

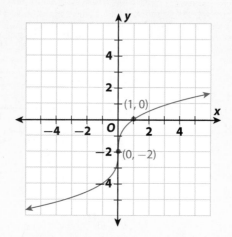

STEP 1   Identify the function type.

The shape of the graph indicates a cube root function.

STEP 2   Identify the values of *h* and *k*.

The point $(0, 0)$ from the graph of the parent cube root function was translated to $(0, -2)$.

Therefore, $h = 0$ and $k = -2$. So, the function is of the form $g(x) = a\sqrt[3]{x - 0} - 2$.

STEP 3   Use the point $(1, 0)$ to identify *a*.

$$g(x) = a\sqrt[3]{x - 0} - 2 \qquad \text{Function form}$$

$$0 = a\sqrt[3]{1 - 0} - 2 \qquad \text{Substitute 0 for } g(x) \text{ and 1 for } x.$$

$$0 = a\sqrt[3]{1} - 2$$

$$0 = a(1) - 2$$

$$2 = a$$

Substitute $h = 0$, $k = -2$, and $a = 2$ into the general function $f(x) = a\sqrt[3]{x - h} + k$. The function is $g(x) = 2\sqrt[3]{x} - 2$.

REFLECT

5. The point $(0, 0)$ is on the graph of the parent function. How can you find the point on the cube root function to which $(0, 0)$ is translated?

_____

_____

_____

_____

6. **Check for Reasonableness** Does the given graph represent a vertical stretch or a vertical shrink of the graph of the parent function? Does this agree with the value of a that was found? Explain.

_____

_____

_____

_____

YOUR TURN

7. Write the rule for the function represented by the graph.

_____

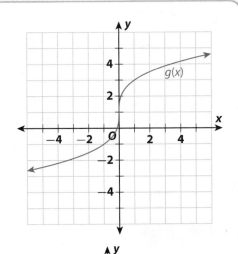

8. In the graph of the cube root function shown, are h and k positive or negative?

_____

_____

_____

_____

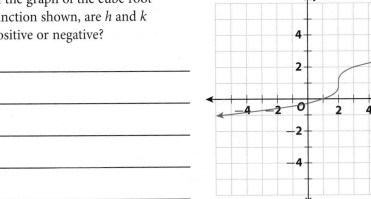

1. Graph the cube root function $g(x) = 2\sqrt[3]{x} - 4$. Then describe the graph as a transformation of the graph of the parent function shown, and give its domain and range. (Explore Activities 1 and 2)

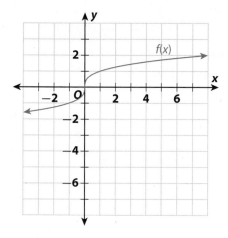

2. Write the rule for the function represented by the graph. (Example 1)

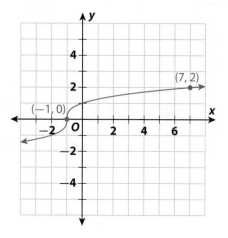

$f(x) =$ _____

_____

_____

Domain: _____

Range: _____

3. Explain how the graph of $g(x) = 2\sqrt[3]{x + 1} - 2$ is a transformation of the graph of the cube root parent function. (Explore Activities 1 and 2)

_____

_____

 ESSENTIAL QUESTION CHECK-IN

4. What do the values of a, h, and k tell you about how the graph of $f(x) = a\sqrt[3]{x - h} + k$ is related to the graph of the parent function $f(x) = \sqrt[3]{x}$?

_____

_____

_____

_____

_____

19.4 Independent Practice

FL F-BF.2.3, F-IF.3.9

Personal
Math Trainer

Online
Assessment and
my.hrw.com   Intervention

Graph each cube root function. Then describe the graph as a transformation of the graph of the parent function shown.

5. $g(x) = 0.2\sqrt[3]{x}$

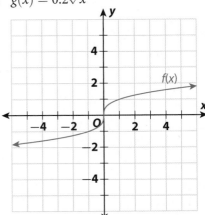

_____

_____

6. $g(x) = \sqrt[3]{x-3} + 1$

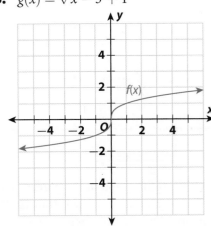

_____

_____

Write the rule for the function represented by each graph.

7.

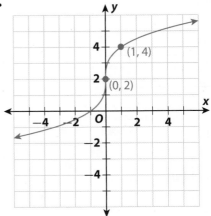

$f(x) = $ _____

8.

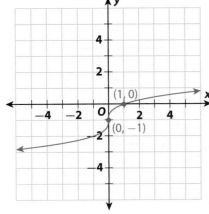

$f(x) = $ _____

9. What are the values of a, h, and k in the following function: $g(x) = 3 + \sqrt[3]{x+2}$?

_____

_____

_____

10. **Explain the Error** Kristen incorrectly described the graph of $g(x) = 0.3\sqrt[3]{x}$ as a vertical stretch of the graph of the parent function $g(x) = \sqrt[3]{x}$ by a factor of 0.3. What was her error?

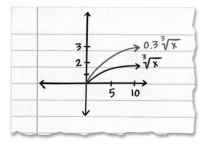

_____

_____

11. **What if?** If the graph of the parent function, $g(x) = \sqrt[3]{x}$, is stretched vertically by a factor of 2 and translated 2 units right and 3 units down, what would be the point where the curvature of the graph changes on the resulting graph?

_____

_____

12. **Explain the Error** To graph the function, $f(x) = \sqrt[3]{x-4}$, Dalton determined that the value of h was -4 and translated the graph of the parent function 4 units to the left. Explain why Dalton's translation was incorrect.

_____

_____

_____

_____

13. **Communicate Mathematical Ideas** Explain why square root functions have a limited domain and range, while both the domain and the range of cube root functions consist of all real numbers.

_____

_____

_____

_____

_____

Ready to Go On?

Personal
Math Trainer

my.hrw.com

Online
Assessment and
Intervention

19.1 Square Root Functions

Find the domain of each square root function.

1. $f(x) = \sqrt{x+5} - 2$

2. $f(x) = \sqrt{2x-6} - 1$

_____

_____

_____

_____

19.2 Transforming Square Root Functions

Describe the graph of each function as a transformation of the
graph of the parent function.

3. $f(x) = 2\sqrt{x-2}$

4. $f(x) = \frac{1}{3}\sqrt{x+1}$

_____

_____

_____

_____

19.3 Cube Root Functions

Write a rule for the inverse of each function.

5. $f(x) = -2x^3$

6. $f(x) = \frac{1}{6}x^3$

_____

_____

19.4 Transforming Cube Root Functions

7. Write the rule for the function
represented by the graph.

_____

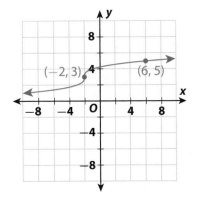

? **ESSENTIAL QUESTION**

8. What does the rule for a square root function
or a cube root function tell you about its graph?

_____

_____

_____

_____

_____

MODULE 19 MIXED REVIEW

Assessment Readiness

Personal
Math Trainer

Online
Assessment and
Intervention

my.hrw.com

Selected Response

1. For what values of a, h, and k does the function $y = a\sqrt{x - h} + k$ have a domain of all real numbers greater than or equal to -3 and a range of all real numbers less than or equal to 2?

Ⓐ $a = 1, h = 3, k = 2$

Ⓑ $a = -1, h = -3, k = 2$

Ⓒ $a = -1, h = -3, k = -2$

Ⓓ $a = 1, h = 3, k = -2$

2. What is the slope of the line through the points with coordinates $(3, -2)$ and $(2, 5)$?

Ⓐ -7 Ⓒ $\frac{1}{7}$

Ⓑ $-\frac{1}{7}$ Ⓓ 7

3. The graph shown is a transformation of the graph of $f(x) = \sqrt{x}$. What is the equation of the function whose graph is shown?

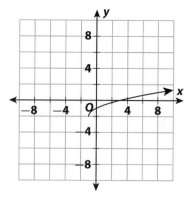

Ⓐ $f(x) = \sqrt{x + 1} - 2$

Ⓑ $f(x) = \sqrt{x + 1} + 2$

Ⓒ $f(x) = \sqrt{x - 2} - 1$

Ⓓ $f(x) = \sqrt{x - 1} + 2$

4. What is the 17th term of an arithmetic sequence whose first term is -2 and whose common difference is 5?

Ⓐ -87 Ⓒ 78

Ⓑ -82 Ⓓ 83

5. Which of the following is NOT a property of all normal curves?

Ⓐ 34% of the data fall within 1 standard deviation of the mean.

Ⓑ 68% of the data fall within 1 standard deviation of the mean.

Ⓒ 95% of the data fall within 2 standard deviations of the mean.

Ⓓ 99.7% of the data fall within 3 standard deviations of the mean.

6. What is the inverse function of $f(x) = \frac{1}{3}x + 2$?

Ⓐ $f^{-1}(x) = 3x - 2$

Ⓑ $f^{-1}(x) = \frac{1}{3}x - 2$

Ⓒ $f^{-1}(x) = 3x + 6$

Ⓓ $f^{-1}(x) = 3x - 6$

Mini-Tasks

7. a. Write a function for the volume of a cube whose side is s in centimeters.

_____

_____

b. Find the inverse of the function and describe what it represents.

_____

_____

c. You want to transform the inverse function rule in part b, so that it applies for measurements in inches. What type of transformation would this be? Justify your answer.

_____

_____

_____

Study Guide Review

? ESSENTIAL QUESTION

How do quadratic functions relate to their graphs?

EXAMPLE 1

Look at the graph of the quadratic function $g(x) = 4(x + 0.5)^2 - 9$. Find the minimum or maximum, zeros of the function, and the axis of symmetry.

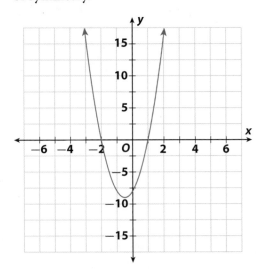

The graph opens upwards, so it has a minimum at $(-0.5, -9)$.

The zeros of the function are the x-values where the function intersects with the y-axis. These appear to be at $(-2, 0)$ and $(1, 0)$. These can be verified by substituting the x-values into the function.

The axis of symmetry on a parabola goes through the vertex. On this graph, the axis of symmetry is at $x = -0.5$.

EXAMPLE 2

What is the equation for the graph of the parabola?

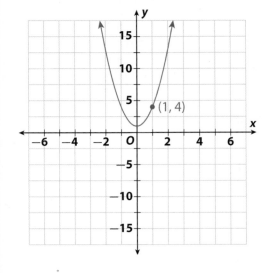

(1, 4)

You need to find a, h, and k in the equation $g(x) = a(x - h)^2 + k$. The vertex (h, k) is at $(0, 1)$. Substitute these values into the equation.

$$g(x) = a(x - 0)^2 + 1$$
$$g(x) = ax^2 + 1$$

Notice that $(1, 4)$ is on the graph. Substitute the values into the equation, and solve for a.

$$g(x) = ax^2 + 1$$
$$4 = a(1)^2 + 1$$
$$4 = a + 1$$

The equation is $g(x) = 3x^2 + 1$.

EXERCISES

1. Graph the equation $f(x) = -x^2 - 4x - 7$. Find the minimum or maximum, zeros, and axis of symmetry. (Lesson 17.4)

_____

_____

_____

2. Given the graph of the function, write the equation of the function. (Lessons 17.1, 17.2, 17.3)

_____

_____

_____

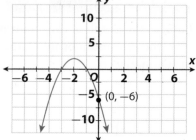
$(0, -6)$

3. A coconut tree is 64 feet tall and is dropping its fruit to the ground below. The function $h(t) = -16t^2 + 64$, where t represents time measured in seconds, gives the coconut's height above the ground (in feet) as it falls. How long does it take the coconut to reach the

ground? (Lesson 17.5) _____

MODULE 18 Piecewise and Absolute Value Functions

? ESSENTIAL QUESTION

How do piecewise functions differ from other types of functions?

Key Vocabulary

absolute value function
  (función de valor absoluto)
greatest integer function
  (función de entero mayor)
piecewise function _(función a tramos)_
step function _(función escalón)_
vertex of an absolute-value graph _(vértice de una gráfica de valor absoluto)_

EXAMPLE 1

Write the equation for the function whose graph is shown.

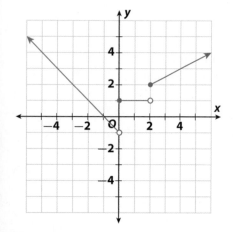

Write a rule for each part.

When $x < 0$: $y = -x - 1$

When $0 \le x < 2$: $y = 1$

When $x \ge 2$: $y = 0.5x + 1$

Write in bracket form.

$$f(x) = \begin{cases} -x - 1 & \text{when } x < 0 \\ 1 & \text{when } 0 \le x < 2 \\ 0.5x + 1 & \text{when } x \ge 2 \end{cases}$$

EXAMPLE 2

Graph each function.

a. $g(x) = 4|x|$ *Create a table of values for the function.*

x	−2	−1	0	1	2
$g(x) = 4|x|$	8	4	0	4	8

Graph the function on a coordinate plane.

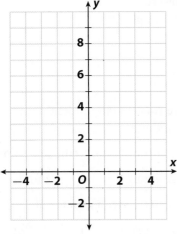

b. $g(x) = |x - 5| + 1$ *Create a table of values for the function.*

x	1	3	5	7	9
$g(x) = |x - 5| + 1$	5	3	1	3	5

Graph the function on a coordinate plane.

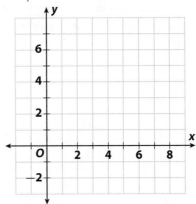

EXERCISES

On a trip, the Martez family travels at an average speed of 50 miles per hour for 3 hours, stops for 1.5 hours to eat, and resumes at an average speed of 60 miles per hour for 2 hours. (Lesson 18.1)

1. Write an equation for the function $d(t)$, where d is distance and t is time in hours.

---

2. Graph the function $g(x) = -\frac{3}{4}|x|$. (Lesson 18.2)

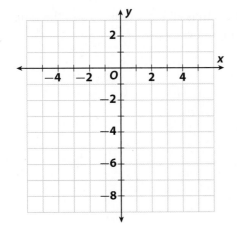

3. Write an equation for the function shown. (Lesson 18.3)

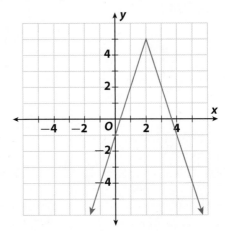

Square Root and Cube Root Functions

Key Vocabulary
cube root function
 (función de de raíz cúbica)
square root function
 (función de raíz cuadrada)

? ESSENTIAL QUESTION

How do the square and cube root function families relate to their graphs?

EXAMPLE 1

Graph each radical function with the parent function. Then describe the graph as a transformation of the graph of the parent function, and give its domain and range.

A $f(x) = 3\sqrt{x+1} - 2$

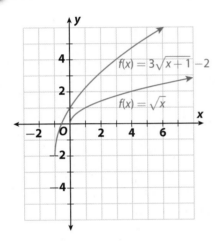

This is a square root function. Identify the values of h, k, and a in $f(x) = a\sqrt{x-h} + k$.

$h = -1$, a translation to the left 1 unit

$k = -2$, a translation down 2 units

$a = 3$, a stretch with a factor of 3

Domain: $\{x \mid x \geq -1\}$ Range: $\{y \mid y \geq -2\}$.

B $f(x) = -2\sqrt[3]{x-2} + 2$

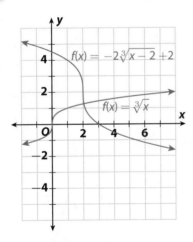

This is a cube root function. Identify the values of h, k, and a in $f(x) = a\sqrt[3]{x-h} + k$.

$h = 2$, a translation to the right 2 units

$k = 2$, a translation up 2 units

$a = -2$, a stretch with a factor of 2 and a reflection

The domain is all real numbers and the range is also all real numbers.

EXERCISES

Graph each radical function with the parent function. Then describe the graph as a transformation of the graph of the parent function, and give its domain and range. (Lessons 19.2, 19.4)

1. $f(x) = 3\sqrt{x+1}$

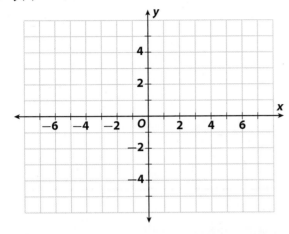

_____

_____

_____

2. $f(x) = 0.5\sqrt[3]{x} + 2$

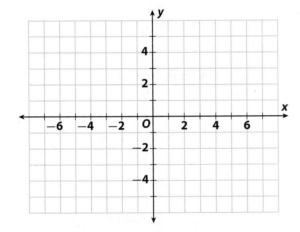

_____

_____

_____

Graph each function. Then graph the inverse of the function, and write a rule for the inverse function. (Lesson 19.1 and 19.3)

3. $f(x) = 2x^2 + 3$ for $x \geq 0$, $f^{-1}(x) = $ _____

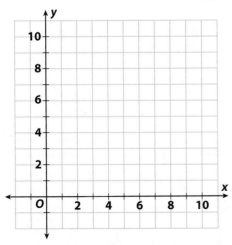

4. $f(x) = -3x^3, f^{-1}(x) =$ _____

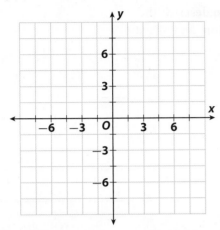

Unit 5 Performance Tasks

1. **CAREERS IN MATH** **Skydiving Instructor** Objects fall with an acceleration rate of -16 feet per second squared. A skydiving instructor needs to know how long it will take for the diver to reach the height at which the parachute should be opened. The diver jumped out of the plane at 12,500 feet.

a. Write an equation to representing this data, using x to represent time in seconds and y to represent the diver's height in feet.

_____

b. Draw a graph to represent the equation above.

c. What do the intercepts represent?

_____

_____

_____

_____

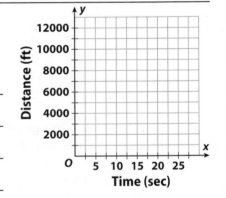

d. Assume the diver needs to open the parachute at a height of 2000 feet to land safely. Use the quadratic formula to estimate the time at which the diver should open the chute.

_____

_____

_____

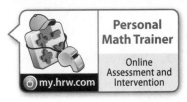

Personal
Math Trainer

Online
Assessment and
Intervention

my.hrw.com

Selected Response

1. For what values of a, h, and k does the function $y = a\sqrt{x - h} + k$ have a domain of all real numbers greater than or equal to -3, and a range of all real numbers less than or equal to -2?

(A) $a = -1, h = -3, k = 2$

(B) $a = -1, h = 3, k = -2$

(C) $a = 1, h = -3, k = 2$

(D) $a = 1, h = 3, k = -2$

2. The graph shown is a transformation of the graph of the cube root function. What is the equation of the function whose graph is shown?

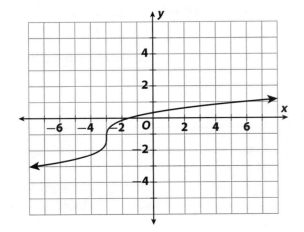

(A) $f(x) = \sqrt[3]{x + 3} - 1$

(B) $f(x) = \sqrt[3]{x + 3} + 2$

(C) $f(x) = \sqrt[3]{x - 3} - 1$

(D) $f(x) = \sqrt[3]{x - 3} + 2$

3. What is the slope of the line through the points with coordinates $(3, -2)$ and $(2, 5)$?

(A) -7 (C) $\frac{1}{7}$

(B) $-\frac{1}{7}$ (D) 7

4. What is equation of the function whose graph is shown?

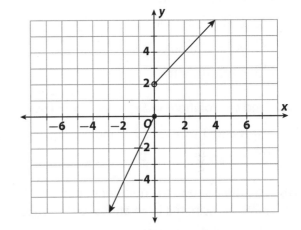

(A) $f(x) = \begin{cases} 2x & \text{when } x > 0 \\ x + 2 & \text{when } 0 \le x \end{cases}$

(B) $f(x) = \begin{cases} 2x & \text{when } x = 0 \\ x + 2 & \text{when } 0 \le x \end{cases}$

(C) $f(x) = \begin{cases} 2x & \text{when } x \le 0 \\ x + 2 & \text{when } 0 > x \end{cases}$

(D) $f(x) = \begin{cases} 2x & \text{when } x = 0 \\ x + 2 & \text{when } 0 > x \end{cases}$

If a test item does not have a diagram or graph, use the given information to sketch your own.

5. For which value of a will the graph of $y = a(x - h)^2 + k$ open upward and be a vertical stretch of the parent function?

(A) 5 (C) -3

(B) 0.7 (D) -0.2

6. Does the function $y = (x + 3)^2 - 5$ have a maximum value or a minimum value, and what is that value?

(A) maximum, -3 (C) minimum, -3

(B) maximum, -5 (D) minimum, -5

7. What is the domain of $y = \sqrt{x-3}$?

Ⓐ $\{x \mid x \geq 0\}$ Ⓒ $\{x \mid x \geq -3\}$

Ⓑ $\{x \mid x \geq 3\}$ Ⓓ $\{x \mid x > -3\}$

8. What type of transformation is $y = (x+3)^2$ of its parent function?

Ⓐ horizontal translation

Ⓑ vertical translation

Ⓒ vertical shrink

Ⓓ vertical stretch

9. Find the solutions of $5x^2 - 9x - 3 = 16x - 23$.

Ⓐ 4 and 3   Ⓒ 1 and 4

Ⓑ −1 and 3   Ⓓ −1 and 1

10. The table shows the number of people who have participated in an annual conference since it began in 2007.

Years since 2007, n	1	2	3
Participants, $p(n)$	12	36	108

Which function represents this situation?

Ⓐ $p(n) = \frac{1}{3}(4)^n$

Ⓑ $p(n) = 4(3)^n$

Ⓒ $p(n) = 4(\frac{1}{3})^n$

Ⓓ $p(n) = 3(4)^n$

11. Which of the following is the inverse of $f(x) = 3x + 4$?

Ⓐ $y = \frac{3x+4}{3}$

Ⓑ $y = \frac{x+4}{3}$

Ⓒ $y = \frac{3x-4}{3}$

Ⓓ $y = \frac{x-4}{3}$

Mini-Tasks

12. Consider the function $y = -\frac{2}{3}|x|$.

  a. Graph the function.

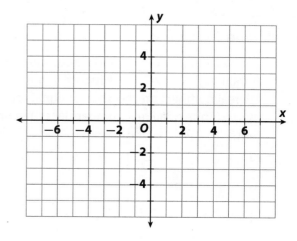

  b. What is the vertex? _____

  c. What is the domain?

_____

  d. What is the range? _____

  e. What would the equation be if the graph were moved up 2 units and left 4 units?

_____

_____

13. Explain the advantages and disadvantages of the methods of solving a system of linear and quadratic equations. Discuss algebraic, graphic, and technological methods.

_____

_____

_____

_____

_____

_____

_____

_____

_____

Solving Absolute Value Equations and Inequalities

FL A-CED.1.1
Create equations and inequalities in one variable and use them to solve problems. Include equations arising from linear and quadratic functions, and simple rational, absolute, and exponential functions.

ESSENTIAL QUESTION

How do you solve equations and inequalities that involve absolutevalue expressions?

EXPLORE ACTIVITY  FL A-CED.1.1

Solving Absolute Value Equations Graphically

The graphs of three absolute value functions are shown.

Graph A is $f(x) = |x|$.

Graph B is $h(x) = |x - 2|$.

Graph C is $j(x) = |x + 3|$.

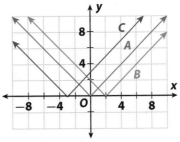

A On the same coordinate grid, graph the function $g(x) = 5$. What type of function is this? Describe its graph.

_____

B At how many points does the graph of $g(x)$ intersect each graph?

Graph A: _____ points of intersection

Graph B: _____ points of intersection

Graph C: _____ points of intersection

C Use the graph to find the x-coordinate of each point of intersection of the graphs of $h(x)$ and $g(x)$. Show that each x-coordinate satisfies the equation $|x - 2| = 5$, which is obtained by setting $h(x)$ equal to $g(x)$.

_____

D Use the graph to find the x-coordinate of each point of intersection of the graphs of $j(x)$ and $g(x)$. Show that each x-coordinate satisfies the equation $|x + 3| = 5$, which is obtained by setting $j(x)$ equal to $g(x)$.

_____

REFLECT

1. Describe how you could solve an equation like $|x + 4| = 9$ graphically.

_____

_____

_____

2. How many points of intersection exist for the graphs of $m(x) = |x| + 3$ and $n(x) = 3$? How many solutions does the equation $|x| + 3 = 3$ have? Explain.

_____

_____

_____

3. How many points of intersection exist for the graphs of $p(x) = |x| + 10$ and $q(x) = 2$? How many solutions does the equation $|x| + 10 = 2$ have? Explain.

_____

_____

_____

Math On the Spot

my.hrw.com

Solving Absolute Value Equations

To solve absolute value equations, perform inverse operations to isolate the absolute value expression. Then you must consider two cases.

Solving an Absolute Value Equation
1. Use inverse operations to isolate the absolute value expression.
2. Rewrite the resulting equation as two cases that do not involve absolute values.
3. Solve the equation in each of the two cases.

EXAMPLE 1

FL A-CED.1.1

Solve each equation.

A $|x| = 4$

$|x| = 4$ *Think: What numbers are 4 units from 0?*

Case 1	**Case 2**	*Rewrite the equation as two cases.*
$x = -4$	$x = 4$	

The solutions are -4 and 4.

B $4|x + 2| = 24$

$$\frac{4|x + 2|}{4} = \frac{24}{4}$$ Divide both sides by 4.

$$|x + 2| = 6$$ Think: What numbers are 6 units from 0?

Case 1	Case 2	
$x + 2 = -6$	$x + 2 = 6$	Rewrite the equation as two cases.
$\underline{-2-2}$	$\underline{-2-2}$	Subtract 2 from both sides.
$x = -8$	$x = 4$	

The solutions are -8 and 4.

Special Cases of Absolute Value Equations

Not all absolute value equations have two solutions. If the absolute value expression equals 0, there is one solution. If an equation states that an absolute value is negative, there are no solutions.

EXAMPLE 2   🏴 **FL**   **A-CED.1.1**

Solve each equation.

A $|x + 3| + 4 = 4$

$$|x + 3| + 4 = 4$$
$$\underline{-4-4}$$ Subtract 4 from both sides.
$$|x + 3| = 0$$

$$x + 3 = 0$$
$$\underline{-3-3}$$ There is only one case. Subtract 3 from both sides.
$$x = -3$$

B $5 = |x + 2| + 8$

$$5 = |x + 2| + 8$$
$$\underline{-8-8}$$ Subtract 8 from both sides.
$$-3 = |x + 2| \ ✗$$ Absolute value cannot be negative.

This equation has no solution.

YOUR TURN

Solve each equation.

6. $2 - |2x - 5| = 7$

7. $-6 + |x - 4| = -6$

_____

_____

Solving Absolute Value Inequalities

Absolute value inequalities are solved using the same steps as for solving absolute value equations. However, if you divide by a negative number, you must reverse the inequality symbol.

EXAMPLE 3

 **FL** A-CED.1.1

Solve each inequality. Graph the solution.

(A) $|x| + 3 < 12$

$|x| + 3 - 3 < 12 - 3$ Subtract 3 from both sides.

$|x| < 9$

$x > -9$ AND $x < 9$ Write as two cases.

$-9 < x < 9$

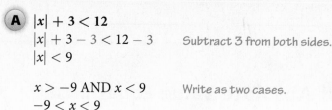

(B) $|x - 8| + 5 \geq 11$

$|x - 8| + 5 - 5 \geq 11 - 5$ Subtract 5 from both sides.

$|x - 8| \geq 6$

$x - 8 \leq -6$ OR $x - 8 \geq 6$ Write as two cases.

$x - 8 + 8 \leq -6 + 8$ OR $x - 8 + 8 \geq 6 + 8$ Add 8 to both sides.

$x \leq 2$ OR $x \geq 14$

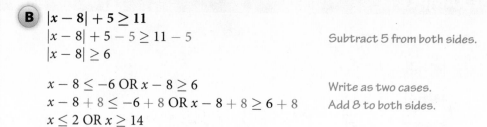

YOUR TURN

Solve each inequality.

8. $2|x| \leq 6$

9. $|x| + 10 > 12$

_____

_____

Solving Real-World Problems

Absolute value equations can be used to model and solve real-world problems.

Math On the Spot

my.hrw.com

EXAMPLE 4

FL A-CED.1.1

Sydney Harbour Bridge in Australia is 1149 meters long. Because of changes in temperature, the bridge can expand or contract by as much as 420 millimeters. Write and solve an absolute value equation to find the minimum and maximum lengths of the bridge.

First convert millimeters to meters: 420 mm = 0.42 m.

The length of the bridge can vary by 0.42 m, so find two numbers that are 0.42 units away from 1149 on a number line.

You can find these numbers by using the absolute value equation $|x - 1149| = 0.42$. Solve the equation by rewriting it as two cases.

Case 1	Case 2
$x - 1149 = -0.42$	$x - 1149 = 0.42$
$\underline{+ 1149 \quad + 1149}$	$\underline{+ 1149 \quad + 1149}$
$x = 1148.58$	$x = 1149.42$

Add 1149 to both sides of each equation.

The minimum length of the bridge is 1148.58 m, and the maximum length is 1149.42 m.

YOUR TURN

10. Sydney Harbour Bridge is 134 meters tall. The height of the bridge can rise or fall by 180 millimeters because of changes in temperature. Write and solve an absolute value equation to find the minimum and maximum heights of the bridge.

_____

_____

11. The diameter of a valve for the space shuttle must be within 0.001 mm of 5 mm. Write and solve an absolute value equation to find the minimum and maximum acceptable diameters of the valve.

_____

_____

Personal Math Trainer

Online Assessment and Intervention

my.hrw.com

Guided Practice

Solve each equation by graphing. (Explore Activity)

1. $|x + 1| = 3$

Graph the functions $f(x) = |x + 1|$

and $g(x) =$ _____.

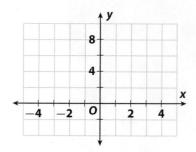

The solutions are $x =$ _____.

2. $2|x| = 4$

Graph the functions $f(x) =$ _____

and $g(x) =$ _____.

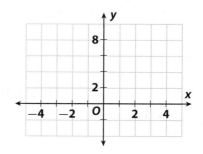

The solutions are $x =$ _____.

Solve each equation. (Examples 1 and 2)

3. $9 = |x + 5|$

_____

4. $|3x| + 2 = 8$

_____

5. $|x - 3| - 6 = 2$

_____

6. $|x + 4| = -7$

_____

7. $7 = |3x + 9| + 7$

_____

8. $5|x + 7| + 14 = 8$

_____

Solve each inequality. (Example 3)

9. $|3x| + 2 \leq 8$

_____

10. $|x + 2| > 7$

_____

11. $|x - 3| + 2 \geq 4$

_____

12. **Communication** Barry's walkie-talkie has a range of 2 mi. Barry is traveling on a straight highway and is at mile marker 207. Write and solve an absolute value equation to find the minimum and maximum mile marker from 207 that Barry's walkie-talkie will reach. (Example 4)

_____

? **ESSENTIAL QUESTION CHECK-IN**

13. How do you solve absolute value equations and inequalities?

_____

_____

_____

A1 Independent Practice

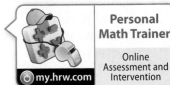

Personal Math Trainer

Online Assessment and Intervention

my.hrw.com

FL A-CED.1.1

Solve each equation or inequality.

14. $|2x - 4| = 22$

_____

15. $18 = 3|x - 1|$

_____

16. $3|x| - 12 = 18$

_____

17. $|x| + 6 = 12 - 6$

_____

18. $|x - 3| + 14 = 5$

_____

19. $3 + |x - 1| = 3$

_____

20. $|x| - 6 > 16$

_____

21. $|x + 1| - 7.8 \leq 6.2$

_____

22. $|x - 5| + 1 \leq 2$

_____

23. The two numbers that are 5 units from 3 on the number line are represented by

the equation $|n - 3| = 5$. What are these two numbers? _____

24. Write and solve an absolute value equation that represents two numbers x that are 2 units from 7 on a number line.

_____

25. A brick company guarantees to fill a contractor's order to within 5% accuracy. A contractor orders 1500 bricks. Write and solve an absolute value equation to find the maximum and minimum number of bricks guaranteed.

_____

26. Fill in the missing reasons to justify each step in solving the equation $3|2x + 1| = 21$.

Statements	Reasons
1. $3\|2x + 1\| = 21$	**1.** Given
2. $\|2x + 1\| = 7$	**2.**
3. $2x + 1 = -7$ or $2x + 1 = 7$	**3.** Definition of absolute value
4. $2x = -8$ or $2x = 6$	**4.**
5. $x = -4$ or $x = 3$	**5.**

27. A machine prints posters and then trims them to the correct size. The equation $|l - 65.1| = 0.2$ gives the maximum and minimum acceptable lengths for the posters in inches. Does a poster with a length of 64.8 inches fall within the acceptable range? Why or why not?

_____

_____

28. A nutritionist recommends that an adult male consume 55 grams of fat per day. It is acceptable for the fat intake to differ from this amount by at most 25 grams. Write and solve an absolute value inequality to find the range of fat intake that is acceptable.

_____

29. The thermostat for a sauna is set to 175 °F, but the actual temperature of the sauna may vary by as much as 12 °F. Write and solve an absolute value inequality to find the range of possible temperatures.

_____

_____

30. The minimum and maximum sound levels at a rock concert are 90 decibels and 95 decibels. Write an absolute value equation to model the situation.

_____

H.O.T. **FOCUS ON HIGHER ORDER THINKING**

Work Area

31. **Analyze Relationships** Tell whether each statement is sometimes, always, or never true. Justify your answer.

a. The value of $|x + 4|$ is equal to the value of $|x| + 4$.

_____

_____

b. The absolute value of a number is nonnegative.

_____

_____

32. **Critique Reasoning** Do you agree with the following statement: "To solve an absolute value equation, you need to solve two equations." Why or why not?

_____

_____

_____

_____

33. **Critical Thinking** Is there a value of a for which the equation $|x - a| = 1$ has exactly one solution? Explain.

_____

_____

_____

MODULE 1

LESSON 1.1

Your Turn

2. 31 oz **3.** 4 in. **4.** 676.5 cm
5. 5280 ft **7.** 2 **8.** 1 **9.** 3
12. perimeter: 15.9 ft; area: 16 ft²
13. 11 g/mL

Guided Practice

1. 177 mm; 176.5 mm and
<177.5 mm **2.** 10 ft; 9.5 ft and
<10.5 ft **3.** 71 cm; 70.5 cm and
<71.5 cm **4.** 19 in.; 18.5 in. and
<19.5 in. **5.** 4 **6.** 1 **7.** 5 **8.** 238.8;
38; ones; ones; 239 **9.** 3093.2; 38;
2; 2; 3100 **10.** 125.3; 4.71; 1.253;
4.71; 5.963; 4.71; hundredths
place: 5.96 m; speed = $\frac{\text{total distance}}{\text{time}}$
= $\frac{5.96 \text{ m}}{2.4 \text{ s}}$ = 2.48333... m/s; 2.4;
two; two; 2.5; 2.5 m/s **11.** When
performing calculations using
measurements, your answer
cannot be more precise than any
of the measurements provided.

Independent Practice

13. 8.5 lb **15.** millimeter,
centimeter, meter, decameter,
kilometer **17.** cups, pints, quarts,
gallons **19.** 57.2 **21.** 2.37
23. 1980 m **25.** Yes, he should
buy more paint. The actual
dimensions could be slightly
greater than 4 m by 20 m
depending upon the level
of precision Yoshi used in his
measurements. For example, if
the actual dimensions are 4.1 m
by 20.1 m, the area would
be 82.41 m², and more paint
would be needed. **27.** The 0 in
1.30 is a significant digit, so the
answer should be given to 3
significant digits, not 2. The area
is 1.69 m².

LESSON 1.2

Your Turn

3. 0.9 **4.** 0.1 **5.** 26 **6.** 10
8. 2.8 lb/ft **9.** 1848 ft/min
10. 10.4 in./min **11.** 132 ft/s
12. 34.7 m² **13.** 188 cm²
14. 11,664 in²

Guided Practice

1. multiply; 16.4 **2.** divide; 2.9
3. 3.28 ft/1 m **4.** 1 L/0.26 gal
5. 1 kg/2.2 lb mass
6. 1 L = 1000 mL

1 wk = 7 days   1 day = 24 hr
1 hr = 60 min   1 min = 60 s

$\frac{0.5 \text{ mL}}{1 \text{ s}} \cdot \frac{1 \text{ L}}{1000 \text{ mL}} \cdot \frac{60 \text{ s}}{1 \text{ min}} \cdot \frac{60 \text{ min}}{1 \text{ hr}} \cdot$
$\frac{24 \text{ h}}{1 \text{ day}} \cdot \frac{7 \text{ d}}{1 \text{ wk}}$ = 302.4 L/wk

1 significant digit(s); 300 L/wk

7. $\frac{3100 \text{ cm}^2}{1 \text{ min}} \cdot \left(\frac{0.39 \text{ in.}}{1 \text{ cm}}\right)^2 \cdot \frac{60 \text{ min}}{1 \text{ hr}}$
= $\frac{3100 \text{ cm}^2}{1 \text{ min}} \cdot \frac{0.1521 \text{ in}^2}{1 \text{ cm}^2} \cdot \frac{60 \text{ min}}{1 \text{ hr}}$
= $\frac{3100 \cdot 0.1521 \cdot 60 \text{ in}^2}{1 \text{ hr}}$
= 28,290.6 in²/hr

2; 28,000 **8.** Dimensional analysis
can be used to convert between
different units and different
measurement systems. This allows
you to work with measurements
in different units.

Independent Practice

9. F **11.** D **13.** C **15.** 17 feet
17. 31 mi/hr **19.** $3180.00.
21. Sample answer: A soft drink
company wanted to sell one
of its soft drinks in a country that
uses the metric system. If the
bottle contains 12 fluid ounces
of the soft drink, how many
liters should be indicated on the
label? Answer: 0.36 liter. **23.** The
student used the conversion
factor $\frac{3.28 \text{ ft}}{1 \text{ m}}$ instead of its square.
When converting areas, you must
account for the fact that area is
measured in square units.
Area: 23 ft².

MODULE 2

LESSON 2.1

Your Turn

3. 2 **4.** 5 **5.** 10 **6.** 8 **9.** 16
10. 125 **11.** 1 **12.** 10,000
13. 576 Calories

Guided Practice

1. 10 **2.** 10 **3.** 2 **4.** 8 **5.** 3 **6.** 7
7. 100 **8.** 81 **9.** 32 **10.** 16
11. 8 **12.** 16 **13.** 2.5 seconds
14. 3 units **15.** 4 units
16. The denominator represents
a root. For example, in the
expression $a^{\frac{m}{n}}$, the n represents
the nth root of a.

Independent Practice

17. 15 **19.** 5 **21.** 16
23. 1.5 seconds **25.** 0.25 second
27. 13 in. **29.** 15 mi **31.** Product
of Powers **33.** Power of a
Quotient **35.** Quotient of Powers
37. Sample answer:
$(4 \cdot 5)^3 = 4^3 \cdot 5^3$
39. Sample answer: $\frac{8^7}{8^5} = 8^2 = 64$
41. $2.5^{\frac{m}{n}} = 2.5^{\frac{1}{n} \cdot m}$
= $\left(2.5^{\frac{1}{n}}\right)^m = \left(\sqrt[n]{2.5}\right)^m$
$2.5^{\frac{m}{n}} = 2.5^{m \cdot \frac{1}{n}} = \left(2.5^m\right)^{\frac{1}{n}} = \sqrt[n]{2.5^m}$
The expressions show that you
can either take the nth root of 2.5
and then raise the result to the
mth power, or first raise 2.5 to the
mth power and then take the nth
root of the result.
43. $(a \cdot b)^n = (a \cdot b)(a \cdot b) \ldots$
$(a \cdot b)(a \cdot b)$, where there are n
factors of $(a \cdot b)$. The Associative
and Commutative Properties of
Multiplication allow the factors
a and b to be reordered and
regrouped so that there are n
factors of a grouped together
and n factors of b grouped
together, or $(a^n \cdot b^n)$.

LESSON 2.2

Your Turn
5. No. The sum of $2 + 2$ is 4, which is not a number in the set.
6. $\pi \div \pi = 1$

Guided Practice
1. yes **2.** no **3.** yes
4. $a \times b = \frac{p}{q} \times \frac{r}{s} = \frac{pr}{qs}$ Because pr and qs are integers, $\frac{pr}{qs}$ is a rational number. **5.** Then $b = \frac{r}{s}$, where r and s are integers and r and s are not 0. The product $a \times b$ must be either rational or irrational. Assume that the product $a \times b$ is rational. Then $a \times b = \frac{p}{q}$, where p and q are integers and q is not 0.

$a \times b = \frac{p}{q}$
$a \times b \cdot \frac{1}{b} = \frac{p}{q} \cdot \frac{1}{b} \quad (b \neq 0)$
$a = \frac{p}{q} \div b \quad (b \neq 0)$
$a = \frac{p}{q} \div \frac{r}{s} \quad (s \neq 0)$
$a = \frac{p}{q} \times \frac{s}{r} \quad (r \neq 0)$
$a = \frac{ps}{qr}$

The final equation shows that a is a rational number. But a is given as an irrational number. Therefore, the assumption the product $a \times b$ is rational is incorrect. So the product of an irrational number and a nonzero rational number is irrational. **6.** Find at least one counterexample.

Independent Practice
7. Sample answer: -1, and -5 **9.** none **11.** whole, integer, rational **13.** integer, rational **15.** whole, integer, rational **17.** closed **19.** not closed: $2 \times 2 = 4$ **21.** not closed: $-\frac{1}{2} \times \left(\frac{-1}{2}\right) = \frac{1}{4}$ **23.** not closed: $\sqrt{5} \times \sqrt{5} = 5$ **25.** closed **27.** For a rational number, the decimal form either repeats or terminates. For an irrational number, the decimal form neither repeats nor terminates. There are no other possibilities. **29.** 0; If a set is closed under subtraction, then for any number x in the set, $x - x = 0$, so 0 is also in the set.

MODULE 3

LESSON 3.1

Your Turn
5. 37 **6.** 200 **7.** About 16.7 mi/h

Guided Practice
1. terms: 7, 8p, $2r^3$; coefficients: 8, 2 **2.** terms: g^2, 14h, 10; coefficients: 1, 14
3. $(4x + y)^2 - 3z = (4 \cdot 2 + -1)^2$
$\qquad -3(5)$
$\qquad = (8 - 1)^2 - 15$
$\qquad = (49) - 15$
$\qquad = 34$
4a. The amount she earns in t hours. **b.** The terms are 60, 9t. The coefficient is 9. **c.** $\$60 + \$9(5)$ **d.** $60 + 45 = 105$ dollars **5.** To evaluate an algebraic expression, substitute the value(s) of the variable(s) into the expression and simplify using the order of operations. To interpret an algebraic expression, identify each term in the expression and describe what it represents.

Independent Practice
7. 18 **9.** 18 **11.** 10 **13.** -1
15a. Substitute 5 for x and -3 for y. $(x + y)^2 = 4$; $(x - y)^2 = 64$. $(x - y)^2$ is greater. **b.** Substitute -5 for x and -3 for y. $(x + y)^2 = 64$; $(x - y)^2 = 4$. $(x + y)^2$ is greater. **17.** The rate is 25 miles per hour. 15 minutes = 0.25 hour.
$d = rt$
$\quad = 25 \frac{miles}{hour} \cdot 0.25$ hour
$\quad = 6.25$ miles
19. Nina found that $(a + 1)^2$ is greater than $(a + 1)^3$ for any negative value of a except -1.

LESSON 3.2

Your Turn
4. 10x **5.** 25y **6.** 12r **7.** 3z
8. $2x + 9y^2$ **9.** $2n^3 + 3n^2$
10. $y^4 - 2y^2$ **11.** $-m^3 + m^2$ $+ 4n^2$ **15.** 20t **16.** $160
17. $9t + 10.50$

Guided Practice
1. The expressions $3(k - 3)$ and $3k - 9$; $9k - 9$ and $9(k - 1)$; and $3k + 3$ and $3 + 3k$ are equivalent.
2. 7x **3.** $8b + 4c$ **4.** $-8r$ **5.** 7g
6. 15x **7.** 4z **8.** $6m - 3n$
9. $3x + 3y$ **10.** 4z **11.** $8r^3 - r^2$
12. $8 + 3h^2$ **13.** $3a + 3b^2$
14. $4m - 28 + 15$
$\quad 4m - 13$
15. $10g + 7g - 8h$
$\quad 17g - 8h$
16. $4(m) - 4(2) + 3m$
$\quad 7m - 8$
17. $4x + 15x + 4y - x$
$\quad 18x + 4y$
18. $12 - 3(4) + 3(t) + 4t$
$\quad 7t$
19. $3g + 3(2) + -3(g) +$
$\quad 4(g) + 4(1)$
$\quad 4g + 10$
20. $3b + 2(4b) + 7$ Commutative Property.
$\quad 3b + 8b + 7$ Simplify.
$\quad 11b + 7$ Combine like terms.
21. Sample answer: $2w + 2(w + 2)$; $4w + 4$
22. You can simplify expressions by using the order of operations and combining like terms.

Independent Practice
23. Distributive Property
25. Commutative Property of Addition **27.** $8a + 7$
29. $2n - 48$ **31.** $14b + 3c - 3$
33a. $15 \frac{calories}{minute} \cdot r$ minutes number of calories burned when running. **b.** $60 - r$ represents the number of minutes she spends walking; $6(60 - r)$ is associated with calories **c.** $9r + 360$; calories **d.** When $r = 20$, it is 540; when $r = 30$, it is 630; when $r = 40$, it is 720; The greater the value of r, the greater the number of calories that are burned.
35. $7.5c - 10$; dollars **37.** 3.5 cups; when $c = 4$, the expression gives 31 cups; when $c = 3$, it yields 23 cups. Because 27 is halfway

between 23 and 31, c is 3.5.
39. Rectangle: $n(n + 2)$, or
$n^2 + 2n$; Square: $(n + 1)(n + 1)$, or
$n^2 + 2n + 1$; $n^2 + 2n \neq n^2 + 2n + 1$

LESSON 3.3

Your Turn
8. $1.075p$ **9.** $500 + 0.105s$
10. $0.80c$ **11.** $1.33p + 50$
14. $20 + 8w$ **15.** $120 + 100d$
16a. $800 - 30w$ dollars. **b.** \$560
17a. $50,000 - 2000m$ miles
b. 25 months

Guided Practice
1. $30 - 0.10t$
$30 - 0.1t$

2. total cost = hourly cost $\times$
number of hours + rental cost;
$20h + 3$; dollars **3.** $175 + 5h$;
dollars **4.** $21 + 4(y - 2)$ where y
represents dog years and $y > 2$
5a. $\frac{dollars}{week} \times$ weeks + dollars;
dollars **b.** $35 + 10w$ **c.** $355 - 10w$
6. First look for descriptive words
that indicate which arithmetic
operations are involved. Then
create a verbal model relating
the quantities. Finally, choose a
variable to represent the unknown
quantity, and write the expression.

Independent Practice
7a. $4(t + 7) + 2$ **b.** $4t + 30$

c. 42 °F **9a.** $\dfrac{t + (0.08 \cdot t) + 10}{3}$;
$\dfrac{1.08t + 10}{3}$ **b.** The variable, t,
represents the total cost of the
tickets. Units: dollars per person.
11. Since velocity $= \dfrac{meters}{second}$,

$\begin{aligned} accel. &= \frac{meters}{second} \div time \\ &= \frac{meters}{second} \cdot \frac{1}{seconds} \\ &= \frac{meters}{second^2} \end{aligned}$

meters per second squared
13. Sunil is correct. For a right
triangle, the base and height must
be the two smaller sides with the
hypotenuse being the largest side.
Monica incorrectly used the two
larger sides for her formula.

UNIT 1B Selected Answers

LESSON 4.1

Your Turn

1. $k = -1$ **2.** $m = 3$ **3.** $z = -1.5$
4. $m = -17$ **5.** $b = 2.25$ **6.** $n = -3$
7. $p = 1.5$ **8.** $t = 6$ **9.** infinitely
many solutions **10.** no solution
11. $p - 0.2p = 28.76$; $35.95

Guided Practice

1. Subtraction Property of
Equality, Division Property of
Equality; $x = -2$. **2.** Combine
like terms, Addition Property of
Equality, Division Property of
Equality; $y = 3$. **3.** $x = 5.5$ **4.** $b = 4$
5. $k = 9$ **6.** $n = -\frac{1}{5}$, or -0.2
7. $z = -8$ **8.** $r = 2$ **9.** no solutions;
the statement is false
10. infinitely many solutions; the
equation is an identity **11.** no
solutions; the statement is
false **12.** $12 - 2t = -4$; 8 P.M.
13. $7.50(20) - (7.50)(20)r = (6.75)$
(20); The rate is 0.10, or 10%.
14. To undo any operation, use
the opposite property of equality.
For example, you can undo
addition by using the Subtraction
Property of Equality.

Independent Practice

15. $y = 6$ **17.** $m = -2$
19. $z = \frac{9}{2}$, or 4.5 **21.** $a = -1$
23. $d = 4$ **25.** $a + (3a - 5) = 215$;
Aaron's score is 55, and David's
score is 160. **27.** $s + (2s + 4) = 28$;
One group has 8 students, and the
other group has 20 students.
29. $p + 0.08p = 37.80$; The jeans
cost $35. **31.** $2x + 9 = 25$; The
dimensions are 8 ft by 9 ft.
33a. length and width of the
garden; write an equation for
the perimeter of the garden and
then solve to find the length and
the width. **b.** Let w represent the

width of the garden. Then $w + 6$
represents the length of the
garden.
$$p = 2l + 2w$$
$$160 = 2(w + 6) + 2w$$
$$160 = 4w + 12$$
$$148 = 4w$$
$$37 = w$$
$A = 43 \cdot 37 = 1591$. The area is
1591 square feet.

LESSON 4.2

Your Turn

1. $n > \frac{1}{2}$

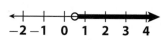

2. $h \le -2$

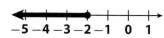

3. $m \ge 4$

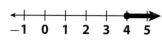

4. $s < 3$

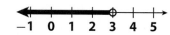

6. $t \le -0.7$

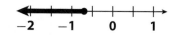

7. $y > \frac{9}{10}$

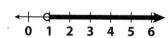

8. $x > -2$

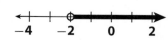

9. $y > -108$

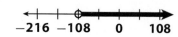

10. $3 > k$, so $k < 3$

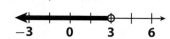

11. $a \ge -5$

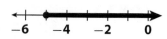

13. No solution

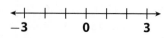

14. All real numbers are solutions.

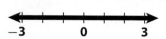

16. Ammon: 13 hours; Nakia:
16 hours

Guided Practice

1. $4 \le -9y + y$
$4 \le -8y$
$\dfrac{4}{-8} \ge \dfrac{-8y}{-8}$
$-\dfrac{1}{2} \ge y$

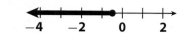

2. $7 - 4x < -1$
$\dfrac{+4x}{7} \quad \dfrac{+4x}{<-1 + 4x}$
$\dfrac{+1}{} \quad \dfrac{+1}{}$
$\dfrac{8}{4} < \dfrac{4x}{4}$
$x > 2$

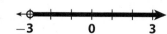

3. $d > -3$

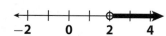

4. $k < -47$

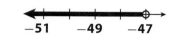

5. $m \ge -2$

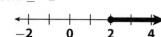

6. $a < -5$

7. no solution

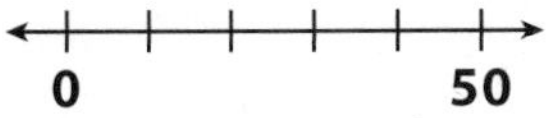

8. $y \geq -2$

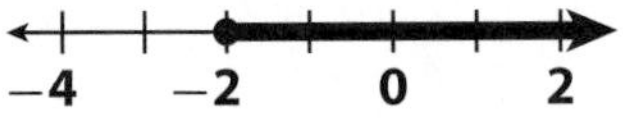

9. 20.5 hours.
10. at least 94 points **11.** To solve an inequality in one variable, use the properties of inequality to undo operations to isolate the variable. When multiplying or dividing both sides of an inequality by a negative number, reverse the inequality symbol.

Independent Practice

13. $0 > k$, so $k < 0$

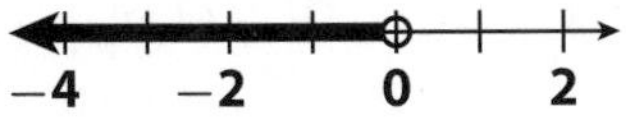

15. $m \leq 11$

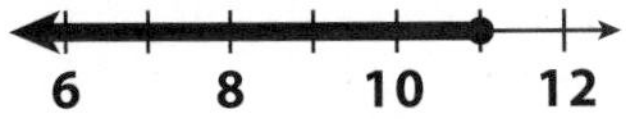

17. $q \leq \frac{1}{2}$

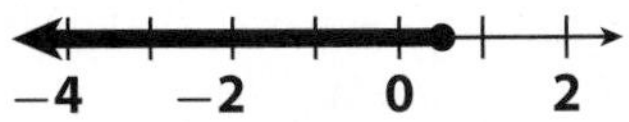

19. $-10.25 < x$, so $x > -10.25$

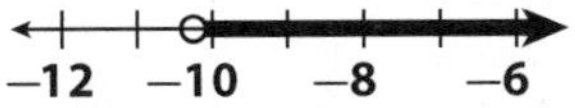

21. sometimes **23.** Fewer than 87 copies **25.** 18 gallons
27. when the job takes 4 or more hours **29.** No; the charges are the same at 4 hours.
31. Sample answer:

$-\frac{1}{3}x < -12$

$(-\frac{1}{3}x)(-3) > (-12)(-3)$

$x > 36$

LESSON 4.3

Your Turn

1. $b = P - a - c$ **2.** $h = \frac{V}{\pi r^2}$
4. $V = \frac{m}{D}$ **5.** $r = \frac{S}{2\pi h}$ **7.** $m = \frac{5}{2} - k$
8. $x = \frac{c+b}{a}$ **9.** $y = \frac{2x+14}{5}$ **10.** $s = \frac{3w}{4}$

Guided Practice

1. $t = \frac{d}{r}$ **2.** $l = \frac{V}{H}$ **3.** $h = \frac{SA - 2\pi r^2}{2\pi r^2}$
4. $h = \frac{2A}{a+b}$ **5.** $c = 3A - a - b$
6. $F = \frac{9}{5}C + 32$

7. You know the total cost and the item price and want to find the sales tax rate; $s = \frac{T-p}{p}$
8. $x = \frac{c}{b}$ **9.** $p = \frac{q - kn}{m}$
10. $r = \frac{a-b}{b}$ **11.** $t = \frac{A-P}{Pr}$
12. $y = mx + b$ **13.** $p = \frac{mq}{n}$
14. You use the properties of equality to undo operations to isolate the variable.

Independent Practice

15. $h = \frac{V}{\pi r^2}$ **17.** $n = \frac{S}{180} + 2$
19. $w = \frac{3V}{lh}$ **21.** $C = \frac{5}{9}(F - 32)$
23. $m = \frac{2p}{2k-1}$ **25.** $s = \frac{v+t}{r-u}$
27. $h = \frac{1}{g} - \frac{2}{3}$
29. $A = \left(x \cdot \frac{1}{2}x\right) + (x \cdot x)$

$= \frac{3}{2}x^2$

Solve $A = \frac{3}{2}x^2$ for x; $x = \sqrt{\frac{2}{3}A}$.
31. 10 inches **33a.** $l = \frac{P - 2w}{2}$
b. 18 cm **35a.** $s = 0.07c + 600$; where c is the cost of his sales.
b. \$2000

MODULE 5

LESSON 5.1

Your Turn

1. No **2.** Yes **3.** No **4.** No
6.

x	y = 20x + 15	(x, y)
3	y = 20(3) + 15	(3, 75)
5	y = 20(5) + 15	(5, 115)
7	y = 20(7) + 15	(7, 155)
9	y = 20(8) + 15	(8, 175)

Cost of Party

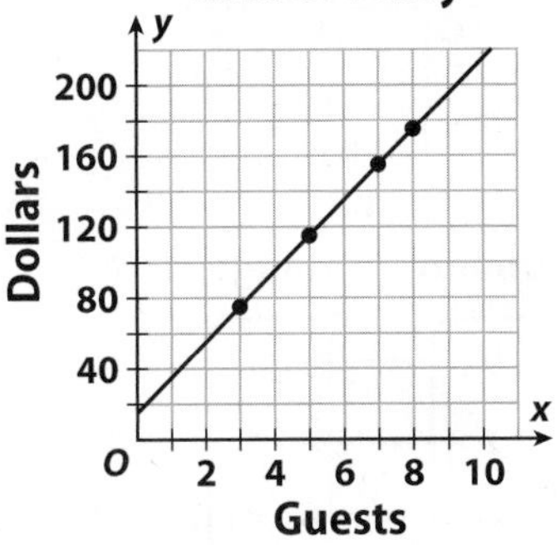

Guided Practice

1. $6(5) - 3(1) \stackrel{?}{=} 24$

$30 - 3 \stackrel{?}{=} 24$

$27 \stackrel{?}{=} 24$

(5, 1) is not a solution.

2. $6(0) - 3(-8) \stackrel{?}{=} 24$

$0 - 24 \stackrel{?}{=} 24$

$24 \stackrel{?}{=} 24$

(0, −8) is a solution.

3. Yes **4.** No **5.** No
6.

x	4x − 6 = y	(x, y)
−1	4(−1) − 6 = y	(−1, −10)
$-\frac{1}{2}$	$4\left(-\frac{1}{2}\right) - 6 = y$	$\left(-\frac{1}{2}, -8\right)$
0	4(0) − 6 = y	(0, −6)
2	4(2) − 6 = y	(2, 2)
4	4(4) − 6 = y	(4, 10)

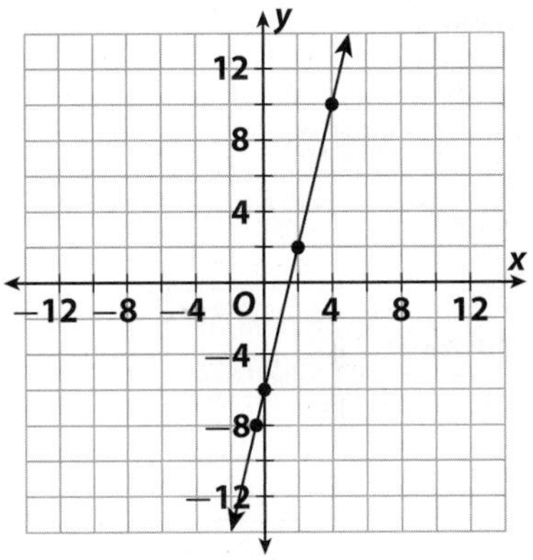

7. Savings

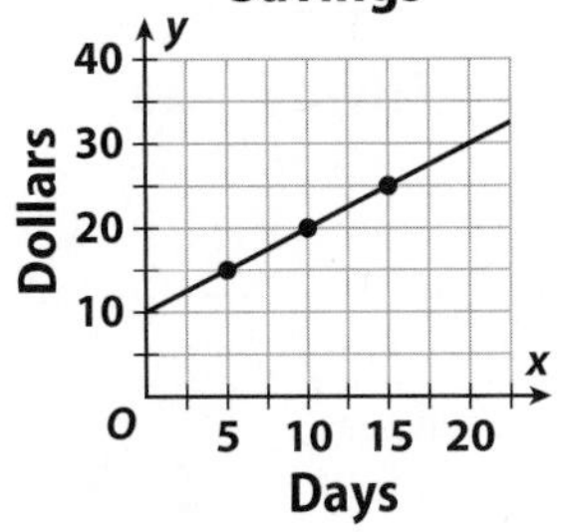

8. Every point on the graph is a solution to the linear equation.

Independent Practice

9. No;

$-5(4) + 2(8) \stackrel{?}{=} 4$

$-20 + 16 \stackrel{?}{=} 4$

$-4 \neq 4$

11. Yes;

$\frac{1}{3}(9) - 2(-2) \stackrel{?}{=} 7$

$3 + 4 \stackrel{?}{=} 7$

$7 = 7$

13a. Sample answer: (0, 200), (10, 120), (25, 0) **b.** Sample answer: (10, 120); This means that 10 seconds after the start of the race, Trish still has 120 meters left to run.

c. Sample answer: (10, 120);
$$8(10) + 120 \overset{?}{=} 200$$
$$200 = 200$$

d. Sample answer: (0, 0);
$$8(0) + 0 \overset{?}{=} 200$$
$$0 \neq 200$$

15. Sample answer: (100, 42); After 100 days, the pool has 42 m³ of water left. **17.** You can plot a few points so that you can draw the line. You can then find other solutions by identifying the coordinates of other points on the line.

LESSON 5.2

Your Turn

2.

Ranking	Prize, in Dollars
1	60
2	40
3	20
4	10

Trivia Prizes

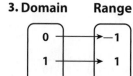

4.

x	f(x) = 4x + 6	(x, y)
0	f(0) = 6	(0, 6)
2	f(2) = 14	(2, 14)
3	f(3) = 18	(3, 18)
5	f(5) = 26	(5, 26)

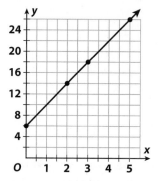

8. x = 3 **9.** x = −1

Guided Practice

1.

Domain	Range
0	−1
1	1
3	5

2.

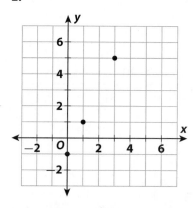

3. Domain   Range

4.

x	f(x) = 2x − 4	(x, y)
−2	f(−2) = 2(−2) − 4 = −8	(−2, −8)
0	f(0) = 2(0) − 4 = −4	(0, −4)
2	f(2) = 2(2) − 4 = 0	(2, 0)
4	f(4) = 2(4) − 4 = 4	(4, 4)

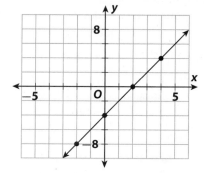

5. Step 1:
$$-2x + 4 = 2x - 8$$
$$\underline{+2x \qquad = +2x}$$
$$4 = 4x - 8$$

Step 2:
$$4 = 4x - 8$$
$$\underline{+8 = \qquad +8}$$
$$12 = 4x$$

Step 3:
$$\frac{12}{4} = \frac{4x}{4}$$
$$3 = x$$

The x-coordinate at the point of intersection is 3. So, f(x) = g(x) when x = 3.

6.

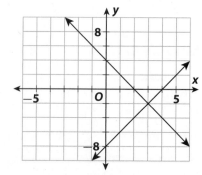

7. Functions can be represented by ordered pairs, mapping diagrams, tables, graphs, and equations.

Independent Practice

9. No; each input is paired with two outputs.

11a.

x	0	1	2	3	4	5
f(x)	5	4	3	2	1	0

b.

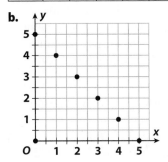

c. The domain is {0, 1, 2, 3, 4, 5}. The range is {0, 1, 2, 3, 4, 5}.
d. The points should not be connected because the x-values represent the number of downloaded songs, which will always be a whole number.
13a. $x = 15$; 15 months.
b. Sample answer: Find $f(15)$ and $g(15)$ and verify that they are equal. **c.** The graph of the two functions would look like two lines, which intersect at (15, 52.5). **15.** No, Fred is not correct; $f(3) = 45(3) - 40$
$= 135 - 40 = 95$
$g(3) = 85(3) - 110$
$= 255 - 110 = 145$.
After 3 weeks, Fred has earned $95, while George has earned $145.

LESSON 5.3

Your Turn

6.

n	f(n) = 3n + 1	f(n)
1	$f(1) = 3(1) + 1$	4
2	$f(2) = 3(2) + 1$	7
3	$f(3) = 3(3) + 1$	10
4	$f(4) = 3(4) + 1$	13

4, 7, 10, and 13.
7. 240 **8.** 134
10. 37, 34, 31, 28, 25, 22, 19, 16

Guided Practice

1. $f(4) = 14$ **2.** $f(7) = 23$

3.

n	f(n) = (n − 1)²	f(n)
1	$(1 - 1)^2$	0
2	$(2 - 1)^2$	1
3	$(3 - 1)^2$	4
4	$(4 - 1)^2$	9

4.

n	f(n) = 2n − 2	f(n)
1	$2(1) - 2$	0
2	$4 - 2$	2
3	$6 - 2$	4
4	$8 - 2$	6

5.

n	f(n)
1	$3\frac{1}{2}$
2	4
3	$4\frac{1}{2}$
4	5

6. $f(25) = \frac{1}{2}25 + 3 = 15.5$
7. $f(25) = \frac{25 - 3}{11} = 2$
8. The first 4 terms are 2, 8, 14, and 20.

n	f(n) = f(n − 1)₆	f(n)
1	1st term	2
2	$f(2 - 1) + 6 =$ $f(1) + 6$ $2 + 6 = 8$	8
3	$f(2) + 6 = 8 + 6$	14
4	$f(3) + 6 = 14 + 6$	20

9. Each position number n from the domain is associated with exactly one term $f(n)$ from the range.

Independent Practice

11. 4, 12, 24, and 40 **13.** 1, 3, 7, and 15 **15.** 6.2, 7.6, 4.8, and 10.4 **17.** −6 **19.** 2048
21a. $f(1) = 185$, $f(n) = f(n - 1) + 35$ for each positive whole number **b.** $360
23. $f(1) = 6.25$, $f(n) = f(n - 1) + 1.25$
25. Explicit rule: $f(n) = -3(n - 1) + 37$
Recursive rule: $f(1) = 37$, $f(n) = f(n - 1) - 3$
27a. $240 **b.** 8 months
29. Explicit rule: $f(n) = 2n$; Recursive rule: $f(1) = 2$ and $f(n) = f(n - 1) + 2$ for each whole number greater than 1.
31. Sample answer: $f(1) = 5$ and $f(n) = f(n - 1)$ for each whole number greater than 1.

LESSON 6.1

Your Turn

5. linear

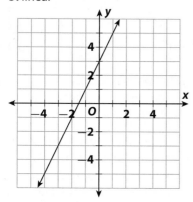

6. not linear

8. neither

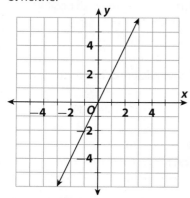

9. horizontal

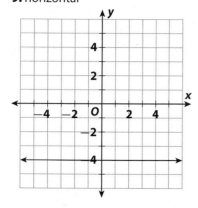

10. horizontal

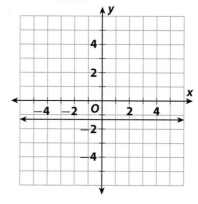

11. vertical

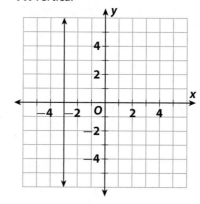

Guided Practice

1. $3y = 1$; horizontal

2. $5x + 0.1y = 4$; neither

3. $-\frac{1}{2}x = 14$; vertical

4.

x	y
0	−4
1	−1
2	2

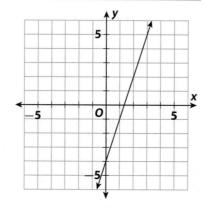

5a. Sample answer: {0, 1, 2, 3, 4, 5}; the numbers in the domain must be whole numbers. Andrea can only use the gift card 5 times, because $40 - 8(5) = 40 - 40 = 0$.
b. Sample answer: {40, 32, 24, 16, 8, 0} **6.** If the equation is in standard form, then the coefficients can indicate whether the graph will be a horizontal, a vertical line, or neither.

Independent Practice

7a. The function is $0x + y = 50,000$ or $y = 50,000$.

x	y
0	50,000
1000	50,000
2000	50,000

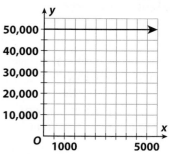

b. The function is $y = 20x$.

x	y
0	0
1000	20,000
2000	40,000

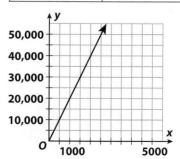

9. not a linear function **11.** linear function **13.** linear function
15. Sample answer: The Johnsons have a \$300,000 mortgage on their house. If they pay \$1500 per month, the function representing the amount of money they owe can be written as $M(n) = -300,000 + 1,500n$, where n is the number of payments they have made. **17.** The student plotted the points incorrectly, reversing the x- and y-coordinates.

LESSON 6.2

Your Turn
2. The x-intercept is -2. The y-intercept is 3.
3. The x-intercept is -10. The y-intercept is 6.
4a.

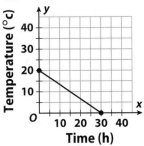

The x-intercept is 30. The y-intercept is 20. **b.** The x-intercept represents the number of hours that have elapsed when the temperature reaches 0°C; the y-intercept, the temperature at the beginning of the experiment.
6.

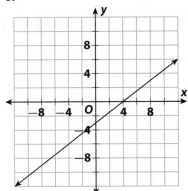

7.

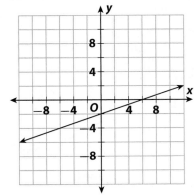

8. Sample answer: $(2, 1)$ and $(6, -1)$

Guided Practice
1. The x-intercept is -5. The y-intercept is 1. **2.** The x-intercept is 2. The y-intercept is -4. **3.** The x-intercept is -3. The y-intercept is -2. **4.** The x-intercept is 2. The y-intercept is -1. **5.** The x-intercept is 2. The y-intercept is 3. **6.** The x-intercept is 2. The y-intercept is 8.
7.

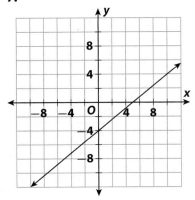

8.

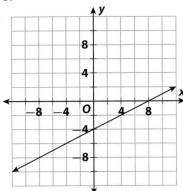

9. Often, the y-intercept is interpreted as what happened at

time = 0. The x-intercept is often interpreted as the time it took for the distance, temperature, etc. to reach 0.

Independent Practice
11a.

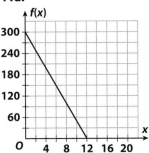

The x-intercept is 12. The y-intercept is 300. **b.** The x-intercept represents the amount of time it takes for the population to reach 0 fish; the y-intercept represents the population at the beginning of the stocking process when the time was 0 years.
13. Sample answer: Bridget has to answer the door to meet a postal employee. It takes her 5 seconds to reach the door, which is 60 feet away. The distance Bridget is from the door after x seconds is represented by y. **15.** $f(x) = 15 - 0.04x$; the x-intercept is 375 and it represents the distance that Kirsten can drive on 15 gallons of gas; the y-intercept is 15 and it represents the number of gallons of gas in the car when Kirsten left home.

LESSON 6.3

Your Turn
2. $-\frac{2}{5}$ **4.** $\frac{1}{2}$; positive **6.** 32; the slope of 32 means that the car was traveling at the rate 32 miles per hour.

Guided Practice
1. -3 **2.** 2 **3.** $\frac{1}{2}$ **4a.** -3 gallons per hour; -2 gallons per hour **b.** The difference in the rates of change shows that on average, the fuel was used more slowly between hours 1 and 3 than between

hours 0 and 1. **5.** negative
6. undefined **7.** zero **8.** positive
9. Sample answers: the rate that
a car is traveling; the rate that
gasoline is being used in a car.

Independent Practice
11. Sample answer: The rate
of change is about 20 files per
second. **13.** No; when lines have
the same slope, the ratio of the
rise to the run of those lines is the
same. The lines are not necessarily
in the same location.

LESSON 6.4

Your Turn
1. $-\frac{3}{4}$
4.

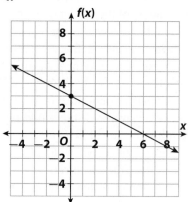

5.

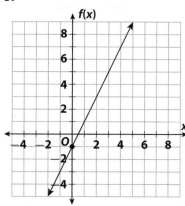

7.

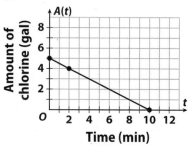

$A(t) = -\frac{1}{2}t + 5$
Domain: the set of all real
numbers t such that $0 \le t \le 10$
Range: the set of all real numbers
$A(t)$ such that $0 \le A(t) \le 5$

Guided Practice
1. $\frac{5}{2}$ **2.** 0 **3.** $\frac{1}{3}$ **4.** -2 **5.** The
y-intercept is 3. Plot the point
$(0, 3)$. The slope is -2. Use -2 as
the rise; then the run is 1. Begin
by moving down 2 unit(s). Then
move right 1 unit(s). Plot the
second point, $(1, 1)$.

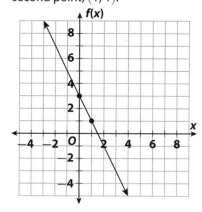

The domain is the set of real
numbers.
The range is the set of real
numbers.
6. The rate of change is the slope,
which can be substituted for m
in the slope-intercept form of the
equation.

Independent Practice
7. $-\frac{5}{3}$
9. $\frac{1}{2}$

11.

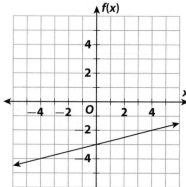

13.

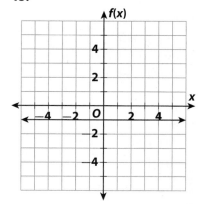

15. $y = -\frac{A}{B}x + \frac{C}{B}$; the slope is
$-\frac{A}{B}$; the y-intercept is $\frac{C}{B}$
17. Sample answer: Alyssa found
the correct slope and substituted
it for m in the equation $y = mx + b$.
However, she substituted the
x-intercept, 6, for b instead of
the y-intercept, 2. The correct
equation is $y = -\frac{1}{3}x + 2$.

LESSON 6.5

Your Turn
2. The two graphs have the same
slope (2), but their y-intercepts
are different. The y-intercept of
$f(x)$ is 0 and the y-intercept of $g(x)$
is 3. **3.** The slope of the graph of
$A(t)$ is 0.5, which is less than 2.5,
the slope of the graph of $K(t)$.

Guided Practice
1. Domain of $f(x)$: the set of all real
numbers from 0 to 5
Domain of $g(x)$: the set of all real

numbers from 0 to 5
Initial value of $f(x)$: -2
Initial value of $g(x)$: -2
Range of $f(x)$: the set of all real
numbers from -2 to 13
Range of $g(x)$: the set of all real
numbers from -2 to 18
2. 2.5 inches per hour; 2 more
inches per hour **3.** Plot the
ordered pairs in the table to
convert the representation to a
graph. Then you can compare the
slopes and intercepts of the two
graphs.

Independent Practice

5a. Domain of $f(x)$: the set of
all real numbers x such that
$-1 \le x \le 2$
Range of $f(x)$: the set of all
real numbers $f(x)$ such that
$-2 \le f(x) \le 7$
Domain of $g(x)$: the set of all real
numbers x such that $-2 \le x \le 3$
Range of $g(x)$: the set of all
real numbers $g(x)$ such that
$-5 \le g(x) \le 5$ **b.** For $f(x)$, the
slope is -3, and the y-intercept
is 4. For $g(x)$, the slope is 2, and
the y-intercept is -1. **7.** For a
line segment with a negative
slope, the initial value will be the
greatest value in the range. The
least value in the range will be
paired with the greatest value in
the domain. **9.** Sample answer:
I agree more with the second
student; In some contexts, a graph
or a table might be more useful
than a rule. If comparisons need
to be made, you can convert from
one form of representation to
another.

LESSON 6.6

Your Turn
10. The graph will have the same
slope, but it will intersect the
vertical axis at $(0, 0)$.

Guided Practice
1. Sample answer:

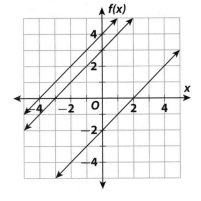

2. Sample answer:

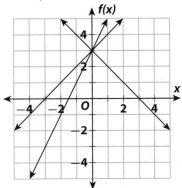

3. m. **4a.** green **b.** blue **c.** red
d. purple **5.** If b changes, the
y-intercept increases or decreases.
If m changes, the slope of the
graph gets either less or more
steep.

Independent Practice
7a. Sample answer:

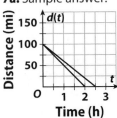

b. Sample answer:

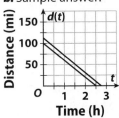

c. Sample answer: $d(t) = 150 -$
$40t$; In this function, 150
represents the initial distance

to be traveled, and -40 means
that the distance from his
destination is decreasing at
40 miles per hour.
9a. black line: $m = -\frac{1}{2}$, $b = 2$
b. blue line: $m = \frac{1}{3}$, $b = -3$
c. green line: $m = 2$, $b = \frac{1}{2}$
11. Marcus is correct; Unless
the y-intercept is the same
as the x-intercept, which can
only happen when both are 0,
changing the value of m while
leaving b unchanged will cause
the x-intercept to change.
13. Stephanie is correct. The
graph of $y = 3x + 2$ is a vertical
translation up 4 units of the graph
of $y = 3x - 2$, so the two graphs
are parallel.

LESSON 6.7

Your Turn
2. $f(x) = 4x - 2$ **3.** $f(x) = -3x + 5$
4. $f(x) = 6x$ **5.** $f(x) = 6$
7. $f(x) = 5x + 1$ **8.** $f(x) = -2x - 1$
9. $f(x) = \frac{1}{2}x - 3$ and $f(0) = -3$

Guided Practice
1. $f(x) = -\frac{3}{2}x + 1$ **2.** $f(x) = \frac{1}{2}x + 7$
3. $f(x) = -2x + 3$ **4.** You can use
two points to determine the slope
and then solve for the y-intercept
to write the function. If the slope
and the y-intercept are clear from
the graph, you can write the
function directly from them.

Independent Practice
5. $f(x) = -\frac{2}{3}x + 5$ **7.** $f(x) = \frac{3}{2}x - 3$
9. $f(x) = 2x - 1$ **11a.** $s(w) = 25w$
$+ 140$ **b.** The slope is 25. The
y-intercept is 140. **c.** Substitute
410 for $s(w)$ and solve for w; It will
take about 11 weeks. **13.** Sample
answers: $y = 2x - 3$, $2x - y = 3$
15. Andrew substituted the value
of the x-intercept instead of the
value of the y-intercept. He needs
to find the value of the y-intercept.
$f(x) = 3x + 6$.

MODULE 7

LESSON 7.1

Your Turn

1. recursive rule: $f(1) = 35$, $f(n) = f(n-1) + 12$ for $n \geq 2$; explicit rule: $f(n) = 35 + 12(n-1)$.
2. recursive rule: $f(1) = 20$, $f(n) = f(n-1) + 5$, for $n \geq 2$; explicit rule: $f(n) = 20 + 5(n-1)$
3. $f(n) = 20 + 15(n-1)$

Guided Practice

1. $f(1) = 6$,
$f(n) = f(n-1) + 1$ for $n \geq 2$
$f(n) = 6 + n - 1$
2. recursive rule: $f(1) = 3$,
$f(n) = f(n-1) + 4$, for $n \geq 2$;
explicit rule: $f(n) = 3 + 4(n-1)$.
3. $f(n) = 38 + 12(n-1)$ **4.** You need to know the first term, $f(1)$, and the common difference, d.

Independent Practice

5. recursive rule: $f(1) = 27$,
$f(n) = f(n-1) - 3$, for $n \geq 2$;
explicit rule: $f(n) = 27 - 3(n-1)$.
7. recursive rule: $f(1) = 9$,
$f(n) = f(n-1) + 15$, for $n \geq 2$;
explicit rule: $f(n) = 9 + 15(n-1)$.
9. recursive rule: $f(1) = 1$,
$f(n) = f(n-1) + 1.5$, for $n \geq 2$;
explicit rule: $f(n) = 1 + 1.5(n-1)$.
11. The fourth term is 10; the fortieth term is 118.
13. Write the general explicit rule as $f(n) = f(1) + d(n-1)$. Substitute 4 for $f(1)$ and 10 for d to solve: $f(6) = 4 + 10(6-1) = 4 + 50 = 54$ **15.** No; Cindy wrote an incorrect explicit rule because she switched the two values. The correct rule is $f(n) = 0.45 + 0.20 (n-1)$, and the cost of a 6-ounce letter is $f(6) = 0.45 + 0.20 (6-1) = \$1.45$. **17.** The difference between the 7th term and the 5th term will be twice the common difference. Find the difference between the 7th term

and the 5th term and divide the result by 2. $48 - 32 = 16$; $16 \div 2 = 8$ The common difference is 8.

LESSON 7.2

Your Turn

2. $h(x) = 2x + 6$; $j(x) = 4x + 2$
5. $h(x) = 28x - 14$ **6.** $h(x) = -6x + 33$ **7.** $h(x) = 7x - 4$
9. $f(t) = 9 + 3t$ **11.** $c(x) = 14 + 1.75x$

Guided Practice

1. $h(x) = (3x + 9) + (-2x + 5)$
$h(x) = (3x + -2x) + (9 + 5)$
$h(x) = x + 14$
2. $j(x) = (3x + 9) - (-2x + 5)$
$j(x) = (3x + 2x) + (9 - 5)$
$j(x) = 5x + 4$
3. $h(x) = (4)(2x + 3)$
$h(x) = 8x + 12$
4. $h(x) = (-2)(4x - 1)$
$h(x) = -8x + 2$
5. $f(x) = 195 - 5x$
6. $g(x) = 90 + 6x$ **7.** The rule for the sum of the functions is the sum of the rules for the two functions.

Independent Practice

9. $h(x) = 22x + 4$ **11.** $h(x) = 6x + 2$
13. $h(x) = 5x + 1$
15. $h(x) = -8x + 12$
17a. $R(t) = 2t - 500$
b. $D(t) = 10t + 400$ **c.** $T(t) = R(t) + D(t)$, $T(t) = 12t - 100$
19a. $j(x) = -3x + 3$ **b.** $k(x) = -3x + 3$ **c.** $l(x) = 0$ **d.** You can show that $f(x) \times [g(x) + h(x)] = [f(x) \times g(x)] + [f(x) \times h(x)]$ by using the Distributive Property. Since $j(x) = k(x)$, $j(x) - k(x) = 0$.
21a. $f(x) = -2x + 3$,
$g(x) = 3x - 2$
b. $h(x) = x + 1$, $j(x) = -5x + 5$
c. $h(3) > j(3)$ **23a.** $r(x) = 7 + 10x$
b. $h(x) = 82 - 5x$ **c.** $b(x) = 89 + 5x$
d. $\$109$ **e.** $\$124$ **25.** $g(x) = -3x - 3$

LESSON 7.3

Your Turn

3. $f^{-1}(x) = 3x + 18$
4. $f^{-1}(x) = 2x + 2$

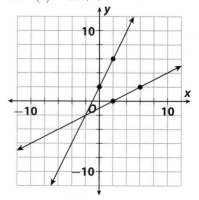

Guided Practice

1. To find values for $f(x)$, first you divide x by 2, then you subtract 3 from the result. The inverse operations in reverse order are add 3, then multiply by 2. The inverse function
$f^{-1}(x) = (x + 3)(2) = 2x + 6$
2. $y = x - 1$
$y + 1 = x$
$x + 1 = y$
$f^{-1}(x) = x + 1$
3. $y = x + 8$
$y - 8 = x$
$x - 8 = y$
$f^{-1}(x) = x - 8$
4. $f^{-1}(x) = -\frac{1}{4}x - 3$

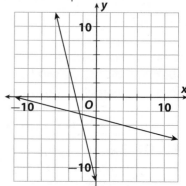

5. $f^{-1}(x) = \frac{1}{3}x + \frac{5}{3}$ or $\frac{(x+5)}{3}$

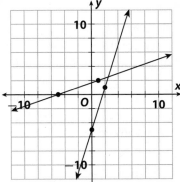

6. You can find the inverse of a linear function by using inverse operations to solve for x in terms of y and then switching the variables.

Independent Practice

7a. $f(x) = 8x + 6$

b. $f^{-1}(x) = \frac{x-6}{8}$

c. the total Carla pays for a pizza delivery

9. $f^{-1}(x) = \frac{9}{5}x + 32$ **11.** $f^{-1}(x) = -\frac{1}{3}x - 2$ or $f^{-1}(x) = \frac{(x+6)}{-3}$

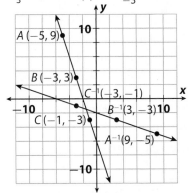

13. No; $f(x)$ contains the point $(0, 1)$, so the inverse of $f(x)$ must contain the point $(1, 0)$, which is not on the line for $g(x)$.

15a. $h^{-1}(x) = x + 5$

b. $j^{-1}(x) = \frac{x-9}{5}$ **c.** $k^{-1}(x) = \frac{x+9}{-5}$

17. Yes, an inverse function undoes the function, and its domain and range are the inverse of those of the function.

LESSON 7.4

Your Turn

2.

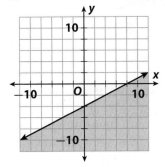

5.

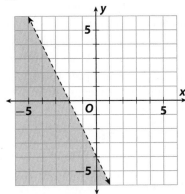

7. Let the amount of dry food equal x and the amount of wet food equal y. This gives us $4.50x + 1.50y \leq 15.00$.

8.

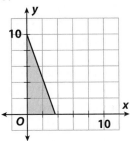

9. Sample answer: 1 bag of dry food and 6 cans of wet food; 2 bags of dry food and 4 cans of wet food

Guided Practice

1. $4y + 3x - y > -6x + 12$

$\underline{-3x \qquad\qquad -3x}$

$4y - y > -9x + 12$

$3y > -9x + 12$

$y > -3x + 4$

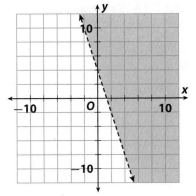

2. $5y + 3 < 2x$

$\underline{-3 \quad -3}$

$5y < 2x - 3$

$y < \frac{2}{5}x - \frac{3}{5}$

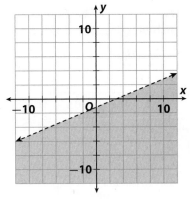

3. $15x + 20y \leq 140$ **4.** $y \leq 7 - \frac{3}{4}x$

5.

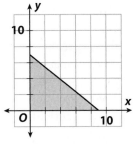

6. Sample answer: 4 chairs and 2 tables, or 2 chairs and 4 tables

7. Graph the related linear equation as a dashed or solid boundary line and shade the appropriate half-plane containing solutions.

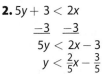

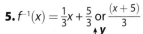

Independent Practice

9.

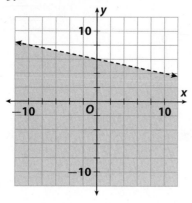

11a. $x + 12y \leq 60$ **b.** Subtract x from both sides. Then divide both sides by 12.
$y \leq 5 - \frac{1}{12}x$

c.

Point	Inequality	True? False?
$(6, 4)$	$(6) + 12(4)$ $= 54 \leq 60$	True
$(8, 5)$	$(8) + 12(5)$ $= 68 \leq 60$	False

d. Sandra can purchase 6 songs and 4 albums. **e.** No, because Sandra cannot buy a negative number of songs.

13a. $2.25x + 0.75y \leq 16.00$
b. They can travel $12\frac{1}{3}$ miles; substitute 3 for x in the inequality and solve for y: $y \leq 12\frac{1}{3}$
c. 3 passengers; substitute 10 for y in the inequality: $x \leq 3\frac{7}{9}$
Since the number of passengers has to be a whole number, at most 3 people can ride in the taxi
15. No; when you solve this equation for y, you must divide both sides of the equation by a negative number, which reverses the inequality symbol. $y \leq \frac{2}{3}x - 2$ Because the equation uses $\leq$, you must shade below the line.

MODULE 8

LESSON 8.1

Your Turn

3. Positive correlation; the number of participants is increasing over time. **4.** Close to 1; the data shown a strong positive correlation between year and number of participants.
5. Variables: time spent on Algebra homework and time spent on Biology homework; positive correlation. It is unlikely that one variable causes the other. The time spent on both subjects might be influenced by other common factors.

Guided Practice

1.

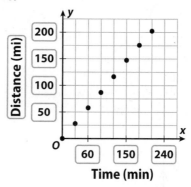

The x-value represents the time in minutes, and the y-value represents the distance in miles.
2. There is a strong positive correlation; As the time is increased, the distance traveled is also increased. **3.** 1 **4.** No. A decrease in temperature does not cause the distance traveled to increase, nor does distance traveled cause the temperature to drop. **5.** You can decide whether two variables have positive, negative, or no correlation by making a scatter plot. You can describe the strength of the correlation with a correlation coefficient.

Independent Practice

7. weak positive correlation; 0.5
9. no correlation, 0 **11.** negative correlation, -1 **13.** Sample answer: The number of ocelots in 2014 will probably be somewhere between 26 and 28.

LESSON 8.2

Your Turn

6.

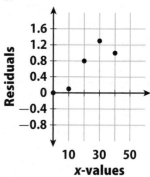

Sample answer: Two of the residuals are relatively large, and the residuals are not randomly distributed about the x-axis (none are below the axis). The line may not be a good fit.
8. 33.8 years old; interpolation
9. 42 years old; extrapolation

Guided Practice

1.

x	0	10	20	30	40
y	26.8	28.8	31.6	34.0	35.5

2.

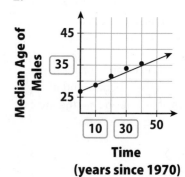

3. Sample answer: $y = 0.17x + 28.3$

4.

x	y Actual	y Predicted $y = 0.23x + 27$	Residual
0	26.8	$y = 27.0$	−0.2
10	28.8	$y = 29.3$	−0.5
20	31.6	$y = 31.6$	0
30	34.0	$y = 33.9$	0.1
40	35.5	$y = 36.2$	−0.7

5. $y + 0.23(25) + 27 \approx 32.75$
The median age for males in 1995 will be about 32.75 years old.
6. interpolation **7.** Make a scatter plot of the data, find the equation of a line of fit, and use residuals to evaluate the quality of fit.

Independent Practice
9.

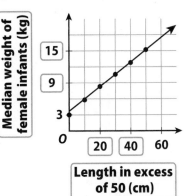

Length in excess of 50 (cm)

11. Sample answer: The residuals for $w = 0.244l + 3.4$:

w Predicted	Residual
3.4	0
5.84	−0.04
8.28	0.02
10.72	−0.12
13.16	−0.36
15.6	−0.4

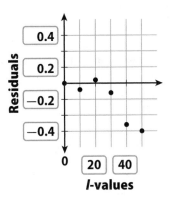

l-values

13. Sample answer: No. Infants and children do not continue to grow at the same rate indefinitely, so it is not reasonable to use the data for infants to predict the weight of a much larger child.
15. The line of fit would be shifted up by 0.2 kg; it would have the same slope, but its y-intercept would be 0.2 units greater.

LESSON 8.3
4. The sum of the squares of the residuals = 19.
Sample answer: The fit is not as good as the other two lines because the sum of the squares of the residuals is greater than the sums for those lines. **6.** $\approx 5.8°C$

Guided Practice
1. −4.

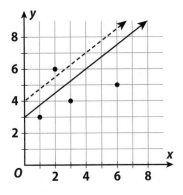

x	1	2	3	6
y	3	6	4	5
y predicted by $y = \frac{3}{4}x + 3$	3.75	4.5	5.25	7.5
Residual	−0.75	1.5	−1.25	−2.5
Squared residual	0.56	2.25	1.56	6.25

5. 10.62 **6.** Sample answer: For the dotted line on the graph, the sum of the squares of the residuals is 20.62. The first line was a better fit, because the sum of the squares of the residuals for that line was only 10.62. **7.** $y = 0.2143x + 3.857$
8. Sample answer: Enter the numerical data as lists using the STAT function and perform a linear regression on the data using the LinReg function.

Independent Practice
9a. The independent variable is year, and the dependent variable is distance. **b.** years: L1, 0, 4, 8; distance: L2, 44.685, 46.155, 47.32
c. The calculator expresses the slope as 0.34611403508772, the y-intercept as 44.63349122807, and the correlation coefficient (r) as 0.98956637439792. The best fit equation for the data set is $y \approx 0.346x + 44.63$. **d.** The equation written for this data was a very good fit. The value of r was close to 1, meaning that the data points are very close to the line.
e. 1940: 51.6 meters; 1944: 52.9 meters **f.** Less; Sample answer: The best fit line predicts that the 2012 winner would have a distance of 76.5 meters. Harting was considerably below this mark.

MODULE 9

LESSON 9.1

Your Turn
1. (5, 3)

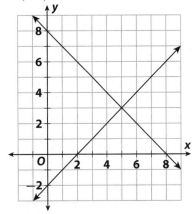

Selected Answers

3.

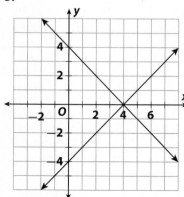

The system is consistent and independent.

4.

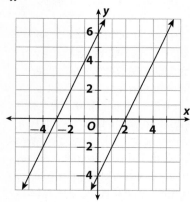

The system is inconsistent.

5. $\left(3\frac{1}{3}, \frac{1}{3}\right)$

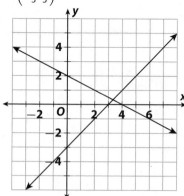

Guided Practice

1. $x - y = 7$
x-int: 7;
y-int: -7;
x-int: 1;
$2x + y = 2$
y-int: 2;
$(3, -4)$; yes

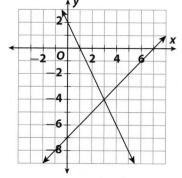

2. System consistent? Yes;
System independent? Yes;
$(0, -1)$
3. System consistent? No;
no solution
4. $x + y = -1$
x-intercept is -1;
y-intercept is -1;
$2x - y = 5$
x-intercept is 2.5;
y-intercept is -5;
$\left(1\frac{1}{3}, -2\frac{1}{3}\right)$

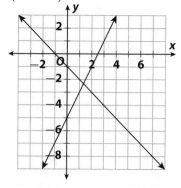

5. If the lines intersect in one point, you can solve the system by finding the coordinates of the point of intersection. If not, you can see that the system has either infinitely many solutions (coincident lines) or no solutions (parallel lines).

Independent Practice

7.

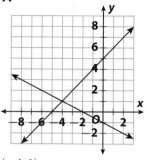

$(-4, 1)$

9.

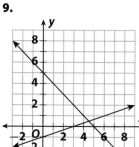

$\left(4\frac{1}{2}, \frac{1}{2}\right)$

11.

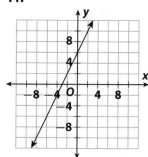

consistent and dependent
13. All solutions of a linear equation are represented by points on its graph; each point on the line corresponds to an ordered pair that makes the equation true.
15. Substitute the x- and y-values into both equations and compare the resulting values on the left and right sides of each equation. If the left and right values for each equation are close, the (x, y) pair is an approximate solution.
17. When you simplify the equations, they will have the same slope and y-intercept.

19.

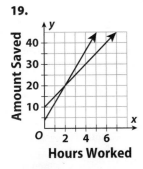

Hours Worked

After 2 hours of work, both Sophie and Marcos will have saved $20.
21. Sample answer: He should have written equations with the same slope and different y-intercepts.

LESSON 9.2

Your Turn

5. $(3, -1)$ **6.** $(-2, 2)$ **9.** infinitely many solutions **10.** no solutions **11.** The cost will be the same in 3 months.

Guided Practice

1. $4x + x + 5 = 20$
$5x = 15$
$x = 3$;
$y = 3 + 5$
$y = 8$
The solution is $(3, 8)$.
2. $x = -2y + 6$;
$2(-2y + 6) + 4y = 12$
$-4y + 12 + 4y = 12$
$12 = 12$
There are infinitely many solutions.
3. $(-3, 5)$ **4.** $(1, 6)$ **5.** $(3, 6)$ **6.** The cost will be the same in 3 months; The cost will be $136. **7.** Solve one equation for one variable and use the result to substitute into the other equation. Solve for the value of the other variable, then substitute that value into either equation to find the value of the first variable.

Independent Practice

9. Solve either equation for y first because the coefficient of y is -1. If solving for x first, each side

would have to be divided by a constant after isolating the x-term. The solution is $(2, 7)$.
11. Sample answer: $x = 2y$ The solution is $(6, 3)$.
13. no solutions. **15.** x represents the width and y represents the length. **17.** Sample answer: $3x + 2y = 21$ and $2x + 4y = 22$; cost of large popcorn bucket: $5; cost of small drink: $3 **19.** Yes; The solution will be a single ordered pair that is a solution of each of the equations. For example, the solution of the system containing the equations $2x - y = 4, x + y = -1$, and $y = -2x$, is $(1, -2)$.

LESSON 9.3

Your Turn

6. $(-2, -4)$ **7.** $(6, -4)$ **8.** $(3, -2)$
9. $(1, 5)$ **11.** no solution
12. infinitely many solutions
13. $3x + 2y = 74a$; $5x + 2y = 98$; A DVD costs $12. A video game costs $19.

Guided Practice

1. $0 + (-2y) = -4$
$y = 2$;
$-5x + 2 = -3$
$-5x = -5$
$x = 1$
The solution is $(1, 2)$.
2. $(-2, -2)$ **3.** $(10, 15)$
4. no solution **5.** The length is 21 inches. The width is 10 inches.
6. The equations must have at least one pair of variable terms that are the same or opposites.

Independent Practice

7. The system of equations is
$\begin{cases} x + y = 65 \\ x - y = 27 \end{cases}$;
The greater number is 46;
The lesser number is 19.
9. Solution: $(1, -5)$
Sample answer: elimination; the elimination method requires fewer steps than the substitution method. **11.** Solution: $\left(4\frac{1}{2}, \frac{1}{2}\right)$

or $(4.5, 0.5)$. The solution tells me that the two lines on the graph intersect at $(4.5, 0.5)$.
13. The system of equations is
$\begin{cases} x + y = 90 \\ 2x - y = 105 \end{cases}$; The larger angle measures 65°; The smaller angle measures 25°. **15.** An adult ticket costs $7.50. A child ticket costs $3.50; Julia will pay $48.
17. You can add $-2x + 2y = 10$; Subtracting is the same as adding the opposite.

LESSON 9.4

Your Turn

4. $(-4, 0)$ **5.** $(3, 2)$ **6.** 5 roses and 7 lilies

Guided Practice

1. $\begin{array}{r} -6x + 6y = 6 \\ + 5x - 6y = -9 \\ \hline -1x + 0 = -3 \\ -1x = -3 \\ x = 3 \end{array}$
Solution: $(3, 4)$
2. $(6, -2)$ **3.** $(-1, 5)$ **4.** $(3, 1)$
5. $2l + 2w = 56$; $l - w = 8$;
The length is 18 inches. The width is 10 inches. **6.** Multiply one or both equations so that one variable can be eliminated by using addition or subtraction, and then solve the system by elimination.

Independent Practice

7. Sample answer:
Equation: first
Number: -2
Solution: $(1, -5)$
9. Sample answer:
First equation number: 3
Second equation number: 2
Solution: $(14, 23)$ **11.** Sample answer: To eliminate y, you would multiply the first equation by 4 and the second by -11. To eliminate x, you could use 2 and -3 which are lesser numbers and easier to work with.

13. Angle 1: 60° Angle 2: 30°

15. They sold 48 bags of hardwood mulch and 128 bags of pine bark mulch. **17.** Sample answer: Yes. You can solve $x + 3y = -14$ for x and use that equation to substitute for x in $2x + y = -3$ to find the value of y. Then substitute that value of y into either equation to find the value of x.

LESSON 9.5

Your Turn

5.

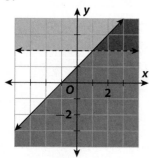

8.

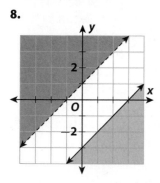

The two regions do not overlap, so the system has no solution.

9.

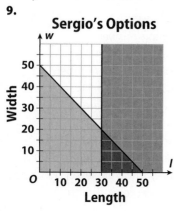

Sergio's Options

yes

Guided Practice

1.

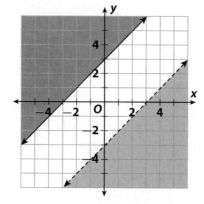

The system has no solutions.

2.

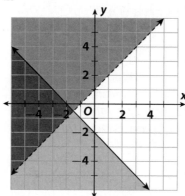

The solutions are the points in the region where the graphs overlap, including the points on the solid boundary line.

3.

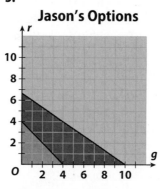

Jason's Options

Sample answer: 2 pounds of green grapes and 4 pounds of red grapes; 4 pounds of green grapes and 3 pounds of red grapes.

4. Graph each linear inequality in the system on the same coordinate plane. The solution of

the system is represented by the region where the graphs overlap.

Independent Practice

5.

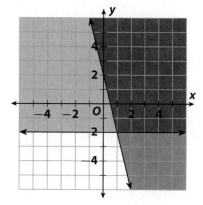

Sample pairs: $(2, 2)$ and $(4, -2)$

7.

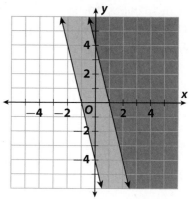

Sample pairs: $(1, 1)$ and $(4, 4)$

9. The graphs do not overlap, so the system has no solution;

Possible answer: $\begin{cases} 2x - y < -2 \\ 2x - y > 3 \end{cases}$

11a. $\begin{cases} x \geq 10 \\ 2x + 2y \leq 72 \end{cases}$ **b.** Sample answer: length: 15 inches; width 10 inches **c.** Sample answer: length: 25 inches; width 15 inches

13. No. Each boundary line divides the plane into two half-planes, each the solution of one of the inequalities. It is not possible for the two half-planes to overlap and completely cover the plane.

MODULE **10**

LESSON 10.1

Your Turn

2. $f(-3) = 6.75$

3. $t(n) = 0.2(2)^n$;
1.6 mm; 25.6 mm

6. $b(n) = 100,000(0.5)^n$

Guided Practice

1.

x	$f(x) = 2^x$	$(x, f(x))$
−3	$f(-3) = 2^{-3} = \frac{1}{8}$	$\left(-3, \frac{1}{8}\right)$
−2	$f(-2) = 2^{-2} = \frac{1}{4}$	$\left(-2, \frac{1}{4}\right)$
−1	$f(-1) = 2^{-1} = \frac{1}{2}$	$\left(-1, \frac{1}{2}\right)$
0	$f(0) = 2^0 = 1$	$(0, 1)$
1	$f(1) = 2^1 = 2$	$(1, 2)$
2	$f(2) = 2^2 = 4$	$(2, 4)$
3	$f(3) = 2^3 = 8$	$(3, 8)$

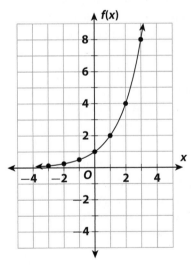

2. $\frac{f(-1)}{f(-2)} = \frac{2}{4} = 0.5$, so $b = 0.5$
$a = f(0) = 1$
$f(x) = (0.5)^x$

3. $f(x) = 3\left(\frac{2}{3}\right)^x$

4. a is the initial value of the function, when the input value is 0. b is the ratio of output values whose input values differ by 1.

Independent Practice

5.

x	f(x)
−3	$\frac{128}{27}$
−2	$\frac{32}{9}$
−1	$\frac{8}{3}$
0	2
1	$\frac{3}{2}$
2	$\frac{9}{8}$
3	$\frac{27}{32}$

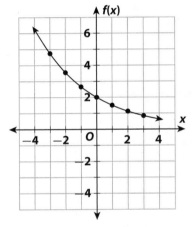

7. $f(x) = 10(0.8)^x$ **9.** $f(x) = \frac{1}{4}(2)^x$
11. 2
13a.

Day (n)	Favors f(n)
1	3
2	9
3	27
4	81
5	243

b. $f(n) = 3^n$. **c.** 59,049 favors.
Sample answer: The number of favors done on Day 10 is 3^{10}.
d. $f(n) = 4^n$ **15.** The range is the set of positive real numbers. Even for negative values of x, $f(x)$ is always positive.

17. If $b = 1$, then $f(x) = ab^x$ would be $f(x) = a(1)^x$. Raising 1 to any power that is a real number results in a value of 1. So the equation would become $f(x) = a(1) = a$, a constant. The graph of $f(x) = a$ is a horizontal line.

LESSON 10.2

Your Turn

1. $y = 1200(1.08)^t$;
$1,904.25

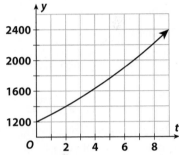

2. $y = 48,000(0.97)^t$;
The population after 7 years is 38,783.

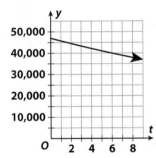

3. Stock A is $A(t) = 12(0.5)^t$ and Stock B is $B(t) = 4(1.5)^t$. The value of Stock A is decreasing and the value of Stock B is increasing. The initial value of Stock A is greater than the initial value of Stock B but eventually, the value of Stock B will be greater.

Guided Practice

1. $y = 12{,}000(1.06)^t$; $15,149.72

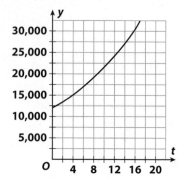

2. $y = 18{,}000(0.88)^t$; $5,013.02

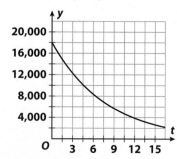

3. Parcel A's value is decreasing exponentially by about 14% each year. Parcel B's value is increasing exponentially by about 14% each year. Parcel A was worth more than Parcel B initially ($70,000 vs. $35,000), but after about 2.5 years, Parcel B is worth more than Parcel A.

4. If the graph slopes upward as the values on the horizontal axis increase, the function represents exponential growth. If the graph slopes downward as the values on the horizontal axis increase, the function represents exponential decay.

Independent Practice

5. $y = 10(0.84)^t$; 4.98 mg

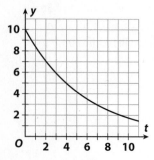

7. $y = 149{,}000(1.06)^7$; $224,040.91
9. $y = 1600(1.03)^{10}$; 2150
11. $y = 700(1.012)^7$; $760.96
13. least; greatest; horizontal axis **15.** Based on the function, the value will never be 0. The right side of the function equation is a product of positive numbers. So, the value can be close to 0, but not equal to 0.

LESSON 10.3

Your Turn

4. Recursive rule:
$f(1) = 2$,
$f(n) = f(n-1) \cdot 3$ for $n \geq 2$
Explicit rule: $f(n) = 2 \cdot 3^{n-1}$
7. Recursive rule:
$f(1) = 128$,
$f(n) = f(n-1) \cdot 0.25$ for $n \geq 2$
Explicit rule: $f(n) = 128 \cdot 0.25^{n-1}$
8. $a_n = \frac{1}{486} \cdot 3^{n-1}$
9. $f(n) = 1000 \cdot 1.5^{n-1}$

Guided Practice

1a. The ratio of consecutive balances is the same, 1.005.
b. Recursive rule:
$f(1) = 2000$,
$f(n) = f(n-1) \cdot 1.005$ for $n \geq 2$
Explicit rule:
$f(n) = 2000 \cdot 1.005^{n-1}$
2. $\frac{27}{9} = 3 \quad \frac{81}{27} = 3 \quad \frac{243}{81} = 3$
Recursive rule: $f(1) = 9$,
$f(n) = f(n-1) \cdot 3$ for $n \geq 2$
Explicit rule: $f(n) = 9 \cdot 3^{n-1}$
3. $a_n = 3 \cdot 4^{n-1}$
4. $a_n = 10{,}000 \cdot (0.4)^{n-1}$
5. Find the first term of the sequence and the common ratio in the two parts of the recursive rule, and use them to write an explicit rule.

Independent Practice

7. Recursive rule: $f(1) = 12$,
$f(n) = f(n-1) \cdot \frac{1}{4}$ for $n \geq 2$
Explicit rule: $f(n) = 12 \cdot \left(\frac{1}{4}\right)^{n-1}$
9. $f(n) = 10 \cdot 8^{n-1}$
11. $a_n = 1.5 \cdot 4^{n-1}$

13a. $f(n) = 50 \cdot 20^{n-1}$
b. 3,200,000,000 points
15. If you were given the second term, then you would get to the seventh term by multiplying by the common ratio five times, because geometric sequences are formed by multiplying a term by the common ratio to get the next term. So to get from the seventh term to the second, start with the seventh term and divide by the common ratio five times.

LESSON 10.4

Your Turn

3. $g(x)$ is a vertical translation of $f(x)$ down 5 units.

Guided Practice

1. 1 **2.** 2 **3.** greater than
4. vertical stretch **5.** $Y_3 = 2^x$;
Sample answer: $f(x) = 2.5^x$
6. Y_5 and Y_6 rise and fall at exactly the same rate. **7.** Y_5 was translated 2 units up. **8.** If $a > 0$ and $b > 1$, increasing the b-value makes the graph rise more quickly as x increases. For $a > 0$ and $0 < b < 1$, increasing the b-value makes the graph fall more gradually as x increases.

Independent Practice

9. a **11.** a **13.** Vertical shrink: for a given x-value, the graph of Y_2 is half as high as the graph of Y_1.
15. Sample answer: $f(x) = 0.25^x$
17. Down; the values of Y_4 are less than the values of Y_3.
19. The y-intercept equals a for all values of $b > 1$ because $ab^0 = a$. As the value of b increases, the graph rises more quickly as x increases to the right of 0 and it falls more quickly as x decreases to the left of 0. **21.** Y_1; Y_1 has the greater decay rate (6% rather than 2%); you would expect Y_1 to decrease more quickly as x increases to the right of 0.

LESSON 10.5

Your Turn
5. $x = 4$ **6.** $x = 2$ **7.** $x = 3$ **8.** $x = 4$
10. $400 = 250(1 + 0.2)^x$ or
$400 = 250(1.2)^x$ **11.** 2.6 years

Guided Practice
1.
$$\frac{3}{4}(6)^x = 162$$
$$\frac{4}{3} \cdot \frac{3}{4}(6)^x = \frac{4}{3} \cdot 162$$
$$(6)^x = 216$$
$$(6)^x = 6^3$$
$$x = 3$$

2.
$$3\left(\frac{5}{6}\right)^x = \frac{75}{36}$$
$$\frac{1}{3} \cdot 3\left(\frac{5}{6}\right)^x = \frac{1}{3} \cdot \frac{75}{36}$$
$$\left(\frac{5}{6}\right)^x = \frac{25}{36}$$
$$\left(\frac{5}{6}\right)^x = \left(\frac{5}{6}\right)^2$$
$$x = 2$$

3. $x = 3$ **4.** $x = 4$ **5.** $x = 3$ **6.** 2.57
7. $x \approx 3.08$ **8.** $x \approx 5.03$
9. $500 = 225(1.15)^x$
10. 5.7 years **11.** When the bases are equal, use the Equality of Bases Property. When the bases are not equal, graph each side of the equation as its own function and find the intersection.

Independent Practice
13. $x = 2$ **15.** $x = 3$ **17.** $x = 2$
19. $x \approx 2.80$ **21.** $x \approx 4.19$
23. constant function: $f(x) = 20$
exponential function: $g(x) = 5^x$
25. $x = 4$ **27.** They are the same.
29. Sample answer: Graphing, because 20 is not a whole number power of 2.
31. constant function: $f(x) = 300$
exponential function:
$g(x) = 175(1.12)^x$
33. You can find the intersection of the graphs to find the time when the population reaches 300.
35. $300,000 = 175,000(1 + 0.1)^x$ or
$300,000 = 175,000(1.1)^x$
37. The second city's population will reach 300,000 sooner, in about 5.1 years compared to 5.7 years.

39. Marco is incorrect. He did not multiply each side by $\frac{1}{9}$ to isolate the power $(3)^x$. He moved the 9 from the left side of the equation to the right side and multiplied.

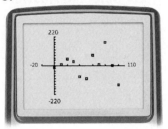

MODULE 11

LESSON 11.1

Your Turn
2. $y = 108.5(1.21)^x$

Guided Practice
1.

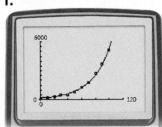

2. $y = f(x) = 135.9 \times 1.037^x$;
135,900; 1.037; 3.7%
3. $r = 0.997$; is
4.

y_m	$y_d - y_m$
136	−13
196	8
283	51
407	29
587	−88
847	−97
1221	81
1761	10
2540	178
3662	3
5281	−150

5.

6. You can use an exponential regression program to generate a function that models the data, and then analyze the residuals.

Independent Practice
7a. For $x = 11$, the table and rounded regression equation, $f(x) = 113 \times 1.27^{11}$, predict very similar results: 1.569 versus 1.566 billion. The trace predicts a result of 1.561 billion, which is also very close. **b.** $y_d - y_m = 665$ to 681; No, the residual is 75−77% of the actual value. **c.** The value predicted (35 billion) is likely to be very inaccurate. The accuracy of an exponential model decreases significantly the further from the origin it gets.
9. The year 2029. If the regression table is viewed in 1-year increments, the first y-value > 15,000 (15,264) occurs for $x = 129$.
11. It is the size of the residual relative to that of the data that is important. Sandy's data values may have been quite large relative to the data values Mark was using. **13.** She needs to gather data for longer than three hours. Exponential functions can appear linear, especially in the beginning.

LESSON 11.2

Your Turn
4. At $x = 65$ months, Company B will have more employees: 181 employees compared to Company A's 180 employees. **5.** increasing; linear; $f(x) = -0.61 + 0.097x$

Guided Practice

1. $P_C(t) = 2500 - 80t$;
$P_E(t) = 2000 \times 0.97^t$;
$t = 16$; 16 years;
Centerville: 1220;
Easton: 1229

2. $g(x)$; linear   **3.** $f(x)$; exponential

4. $g(x) = 300 - 12x$

5. $f(x) = 200 \times (0.75)^x$

6. A linear model should be used when the amount of increase or decrease in each interval is constant. An exponential model is appropriate when the increase per interval grows or the decrease per interval shrinks.

Independent Practice

7. Constant rate; She's paying a fixed dollar amount.   **9.** Constant percent rate. The number of students grows by the same 2.5% each year.   **11.** Yes, the graph of an exponential growth function eventually curves upward while a linear growth function continues in a straight line with a positive slope. Eventually the upward curve will intersect with and then exceed the line.   **13.** No, an exponential function is a good model. Graphing the data reveals an upward curve. Exponential regression gives an equation with $r = 0.9999$.

Selected Answers

MODULE 12

LESSON 12.1

Your Turn

5.

	Preferred Fruit			
Gr.	**A**	**O**	**B**	**T**
9	19	12	23	54
10	22	9	15	46
T	41	21	38	100

6.

	Play Video Games		
Gen.	**Y**	**N**	**T**
G	34	19	53
B	38	9	47
T	72	28	100

Guided Practice

1. categorical **2.** quantitative

3.

Cans	**Frequency**
soup	6
peas	8
corn	11

4.

	Activity				
Job	**C**	**S**	**B**	**N**	**T**
Y	12	13	16	4	45
N	3	5	5	2	15
T	15	18	21	6	60

5. 13

	Like Swimming		
Bic.	**Y**	**N**	**T**
Y	65	16	81
N	13	6	19
T	78	22	100

6. You can summarize categorical data for two categories in two-way frequency tables

Independent Practice

7. quantitative **9.** 96 boys; 104 of the 200 students were girls, so 200 − 104 or 96 of them were boys. **11.** laptops

13.

	Like Pop		
Co.	**Y**	**N**	**T**
Y	15	34	49
N	42	9	51
T	57	43	100

15.

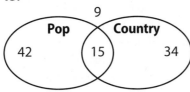

LESSON 12.2

Your Turn

3. 0.175, or 17.5% **5.** 0.7, or 70%
6. girls

Guided Practice

1.

	Foreign Language			
Gen.	**Chinese**	**French**	**Spanish**	**Total**
G	$\frac{2}{40} =$ 0.05	$\frac{8}{40} =$ 0.2	$\frac{12}{40} =$ 0.3	$\frac{22}{40} =$ 0.55
B	$\frac{4}{40} =$ 0.1	$\frac{1}{40} =$ 0.025	$\frac{13}{40} =$ 0.325	$\frac{18}{40} =$ 0.45
T	$\frac{6}{40} =$ 0.15	$\frac{9}{40} =$ 0.225	$\frac{25}{40} =$ 0.625	$\frac{40}{40} =$ 1

2a. 0.222; about 22.2% **b.** 48%
3. Boys are more likely than girls to study Chinese and Spanish, and girls are more likely than boys to study French. **4.** You can use relative frequencies to interpret associations and trends between two categories by comparing conditional relative frequencies to marginal relative frequencies.

Independent Practice

5.

	Activity			
Gen.	**S**	**C**	**O**	**T**
G	0.1125	0.2625	0.1	0.475
B	0.275	0.1	0.15	0.525
T	0.3875	0.3625	0.25	1

7. A joint relative frequency; it comes from dividing a frequency that is not in the Total row or the Total column by the grand total.
9. 0.3875, or 38.75%
11. About 0.553, or 55.3%; divide the number of girls who have clubs as their activity by the total number of girls.
13a. about 86.5% **b.** about 78% **c.** about 69%
15. A relative frequency is a frequency divided by the grand total. A conditional relative frequency is a frequency divided by the column or row total.

MODULE 13

LESSON 13.1

Your Turn

2. The mean is 76. The median is 72.5. **3.** median: 26; range: 10; IQR: 4 **4.** 28.4 **5a.** mean: 34.1; median: 33.5; IQR: 13; standard deviation: 7.2 **b.** Members of Oldport County gyms tend to be older than members of Newman County gyms, and the average ages at Oldport County gyms are less spread out.

Guided Practice

1. mean: 29; median: 29.5; range: 5; IQR: 2 **2.** Algebra class: 1.6; Spanish class: 2.7
3. A typical Spanish class has more students than a typical Algebra 1 class.

4. Use measures of center (mean and median) and measures of spread (range, IQR, and standard deviation) to compare data sets.

Independent Practice

5. mean: 79.5; median: 82; range: 28 **7.** 15.5 **9.** 12 **11.** Find the mean value. Then find the difference between the mean and each number. Next, square each deviation. Finally, find the mean of the six squared deviations and take the square root. **13.** The mean, median and IQR will not change, but the range decreases from 20 to 18, and the standard deviation decreases from 6.4 to 5.9.

15a.

Center		Spread	
Mean	Median	IQR $(Q_3 - Q_1)$	Standard deviation
191.3	192	12	7.0
175.5	175	6	3.4

b. The typical height of a male is greater than the typical height of a female. The heights of the females are more tightly clustered.
17. $x \le 88$; for 5 ordered values, the median is the 3rd. Since 95 and 92 are > 88, they must be 4th and 5th; so x must be $\le$ to the median.

LESSON 13.2

Your Turn

4.

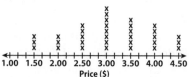

7. Yes; 3 **8.** The outlier decreases the mean from 25.2 to 21.5 and increases the range from 9 to 27. It has no effect on the median.
11. symmetric

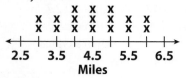

Guided Practice

1.

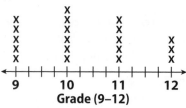

2a. 12; 7; 5; 19.5; yes
b.

Mean	Median	Range
8.5	8.5	7
15	9	49

c. The outlier increases the mean by 6.5, the median by 0.5, and the range by 42. **3.** The median for the first test, 92, is greater than the median for the second test, 86.
4. second test **5.** first test
6. median **7.** Outliers affect the mean more than the median, and outliers increase both the standard deviation and the IQR. Distributions can be symmetric, skewed to the left, or skewed to the right.

Independent Practice

9. mean, range, IQR, and standard deviation **11.** Without: mean = median = 300; With: mean ≈ 332, median = 300
13a.

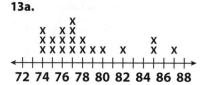

b.

Mean	78.1
Median	77
Range	13
IQR	4
Standard deviation	3.75

c. 87 **d.** The mean, range, and standard deviation would change.
e. Skewed to the right

15. Outliers always affect the range because one of the outliers will be either the highest or the lowest number in the data set, and the range is found by finding the difference between the highest and lowest numbers
17. No; if a data set has two outliers that are much greater than the other values, then the greatest and the second greatest values would both be outliers.

LESSON 13.3

Your Turn

4a.

Golf scores	Frequency
68–70	3
71–73	4
74–76	6
77–79	2

b.

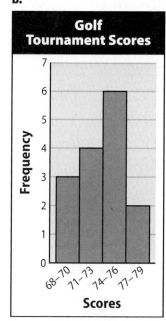

6. mean: 40; median: 39

Guided Practice

1. two **2.** ten **3.** No; only the three heaviest lifts get a medal, and 172.5 is not among the top three heaviest lifts. **4.** No; the silver medal was awarded for a lift between 200 and 209.9 kg, but there is no way to know the exact weight.

5.

Days	Frequency
4–6	5
7–9	4
10–12	4
13–15	2

6.

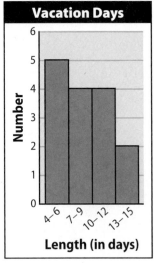

7. $\frac{5 \times 5 + 8 \times 4 + 11 \times 4 + 14 \times 2}{15}$
$= \frac{129}{15} = 8.6$; very close

8. Use the midpoint value and frequency for each interval to estimate the mean. To estimate the median, first identify the correct interval, then estimate where the value will be in the interval.

Independent Practice
9. 15

11.

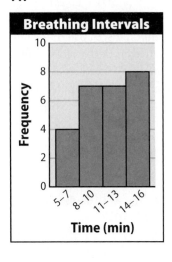

13a. 55 **b.** 55 **15.** He found the midpoint of each interval and divided their sum by the number of intervals, instead of multiplying the frequency by the midpoint for each interval and then dividing the sum of these products by the total number of data values.

LESSON 13.4

Your Turn

3.

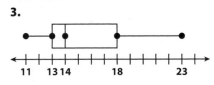

5. Simon's **6.** Simon's **7.** Natasha; about 1000 points

Guided Practice

1a. 15, 16, 16, 18, 25, 25, 26, 26, 28, 28 **b.** Median = 25; First quartile = 16; Third quartile = 26 **c.** Minimum = 15; Maximum = 28
d.

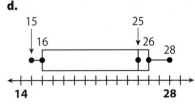

2. Sneaks R Us; about $6 greater **3.** Sneaks R Us; the middle 50% of prices don't vary as much at Sneaks R Us as at Jump N Run. **4.** By plotting two box plots on the same number line, you can compare the center, spread, and shape of the distributions.

Independent Practice

5. Tim **7.** Tim; his box plot is more toward the left than Jamal's. **9.** Gabrielle's **11.** East; 20 **13.** No; the range does not affect the mean of a set of data. **15.** The distribution of SUV prices is more symmetric than the distribution of car prices. The SUV prices have a greater median and are more spread out than the car prices.

17. Willie's set has the higher third quartile and maximum; his greatest 25% of scores are all higher than Dolly's highest score.

LESSON 13.5

Your Turn
5. 68% **6.** 0.5 or 50%

Guided Practice
1. 97.5% **2.** 47.5% **3.** 50% **4.** 0.16 or 16% **5.** 0.16 or 16% **6.** 0.815 or 81.5% **7.** 0.5 or 50% **8.** 0.0015 or 0.15% **9.** If a given data value is 1, 2, or 3 standard deviations from the mean, you can use the fact that 68% of the data are within 1 standard deviation of the mean, 95% of the data are within 2 standard deviations of the mean, and 99.7% of the data are within 3 standard deviations of the mean.

Independent Practice
11. 2.5% **13.** 2.5% **15.** 95% **17a.** 7 **b.** 6 data points are below, and 3 are above. **c.** No; the data set has 3 values greater than the mean but 6 values less than the mean, so the distribution is not symmetric. **19.** Use a normal curve for the distribution of heads when 6 coins are flipped, because the distribution is symmetric. **21.** First check that the distribution is symmetric. If so, find the mean value and the standard deviation of the set. Then verify that 68% of values are within 1 standard deviation, 95% of values are within 2 standard deviations, and 99.7% of values are within 3 standard deviations.

UNIT 4 Selected Answers

MODULE 14

LESSON 14.1

Your Turn

3. 4th degree trinomial **4.** 3rd degree binomial **5.** 3rd degree binomial **6.** 5th degree trinomial
8. $4r^3 - 4r^2s + 38$
9. $8a^2 - 6ab + 50$ **11.** 564 ft

Guided Practice

1. Yes; $3x^2y$ is the product of a number, 3, and variables with whole-number exponents.
2. No; a monomial has only one term. **3.** 2nd degree trinomial
4. 7th degree binomial
5. $2y^4 + 9y^3 - y^2$ **6.** $7mn^3 - 9n^3$
7. $d^3 - 13d^2 + 2d$ **8.** $6j^3k^2 + 3j^2k^3$
9. 486 sq ft **10.** A polynomial expression is an algebraic expression consisting of one or more monomials, which are products of numbers and variables with whole-number exponents. Simplify polynomials by combining like terms.

Independent Practice

11. trinomial; degree 2
13. trinomial; degree 7 **15.** $-3q^2 + 3$ **17.** $6x^2 + 12x - 10xy$
19. $-2r^3 + 3r^2 + 8r - 4$
21a. 20° C will have 3356 cells; 30° C will have 3416 cells, so 30° C will have 60 more bacteria.
b. 20° C will have 357,596 cells; 30° C will have 358,196 cells, so 30° C will have 600 more bacteria.
c. 30° C will reach 1,037,336 cells after 17 minutes. The answer was obtained by substituting values for the number of seconds into the 30° C expression, which always had a greater total than the 20° C expression.
23. $5x^2 - 2x + 6$ **25.** $2x^3 + 17$
27. Enrique multiplied the exponents by the coefficient of

each term. The correct degree is 3.
29. Gillian is correct. A polynomial can be a monomial, and a monomial can be a number. A polynomial that is a number would have no variables or exponents, so its degree would be 0.
31. For negative values of x, $(x + 1)^2$ will be less than $(x - 1)^2$. For example, when $x = -3$, $(x + 1)^2 = (-3 + 1)^2 = 4$, while $(x - 1)^2 = (-3 - 1)^2 = 16$.

LESSON 14.2

Your Turn

3. $-8x^2 + 3$ **4.** $6x^2 - x + 5$ **5.** $-3x^2 + 5x$ **6.** $x^2 + 5x - 4$ **10.** $11m^3 - 6 m^2n - 7mn^2$ **11.** $5x^3 + 5x^3y - 12y$
12. $-2x^3 + 5x^2 + 4x - 12$
14. $5n + 37$ **15.** $2n^2 - 35n + 9$

Guided Practice

1. Commutative Property; Associative Property
2. $bc^2 + 11bc + 5b$
3. $18g^2$ **4.** $13m^2 - m + 1 + 10m^2 + 7m - 2$ $23m^2 + 6m - 1$
5. $-y^2 + 11y - 2 - 6y^2 + 6y - 5 - 7y^2 + 17y - 7$
6. $(-1)(-13x^3) + (-1)(12) + (-1)(-6x)$
$13x^3 - 12 + 6x$
7. $-4x^3 + 9x^2 + 2x + 21$
8. To add polynomials, use the Commutative and Associative Properties to combine like terms. To subtract polynomials, distribute the minus sign to each term, and then combine.

Independent Practice

9. -143 **11.** $5p^2 - 5p + 13$ **13.** $4d^2 + 25d - 20$ **15.** $-6z^2 + 10z + 5$
17. $9x^2 + 3x - 9$ **19.** $22a - 20$
21a. $-g^2 + 5g + 1$ **b.** $g = 1$, height = 5 ft; $g = 2$, height = 7 ft; $g = 3$, height = 7 ft; $g = 4$, height = 5 ft; these values are found by

substituting the values of g into the expression found in part a.
c. The greatest water height (7.25 ft) occurs at $g = 2.5$.
23. $20x^2 + 12x - 16$
25. The terms $5x^2y^3$ and $4x^3y^2$ are not like terms. The correct sum is $4x^3y^2 + 5x^2y^3 + 8x + 15y$.
27. 385

LESSON 14.3

Your Turn

6. $60x^9$ **7.** $24a^7b^3$ **8.** $18a^3b^6$
9. $36d^8j^2k^2$ **11.** $20m^5n^3 - 12m^4n^3 - 8m^3n^2$ **12.** $10a^2b^2 + 6a^3b + 12a^3 + 2a^2$ **13.** $6a^3b^2 + 18a^2b^3 + 24ab^2$ **15.** 9 inches long, 5 inches wide

Guided Practice

1. $(-x + 1)(x - 2)$
2.

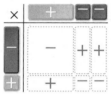

3. $-x^2 + 3x - 2$
4. $(1 \cdot 16)(d^5f^2 \cdot d^3e^4f^2)$
$= 16d^8e^4 f^4$
5. $(-13 \cdot -3)(r^3 \cdot r)(s^5 \cdot s^2) = 39r^4s^7$
6. $5(2k^2) + 5(k) + 5(3)$
$10k^2 + 5k + 15$
7. $8t(3t^2) + 8t(5ts) + 8t(2s)$
$24t^3 + 40t^2s + 16ts$
8. 20 centigrams **9.** Use the Distributive Property to distribute the monomial factor to each term of the polynomial. Simplify each product of monomials to obtain the final result.

Independent Practice

11. $8m^5n^2$ **13.** $10k^2 + 5k + 20$
15. $-36a^5b^7$ **17.** $-6t^4 - 14t^2s - 10ts$ **19.** $-6v^4w^3 + 66v^4w^8 - 36v^2w^7$ **21.** $-10x^8y^4 + 40x^8y^8 - 40x^4y^7$ **23.** 12 feet **25.** The volume

of a cylinder is the area of the circular base times the height, so the volume of each can is $\pi r^2 (r + 2)$. For 10 cans the total volume is $10 \cdot \pi r^2 (r + 2) = 10\pi r^3 + 20\pi r^2$. By substituting different values of r in this expression, we find that $r = 3$ gives a total volume of $1{,}413.7 \text{ in}^3$, so the cans had a radius of 3 inches and a height of $3 + 2 = 5$ inches. **27.** Yes, the statement would be true for $x = 0$ or $x = -3$; Sample answer: For -3: $(-3 + 3)^3 = 0$ and $(-3)^3 + 3^3 = -27 + 27 = 0$.

LESSON 14.4

Your Turn

5. $x^2 + x - 12$ **6.** $2n^2 + 12n + 18$
8. $x^3 - x^2 - 26x + 30$ **9.** $3x^4 + 13x^3 + 4x^2 - 21x - 7$ **10.** $x^2 + 10x + 25$
11. $4p^2 - 12p + 9$ **12.** $9s^2 - 1$
13. $4x^2 - 25$ **14.** $9g^2 + 36g + 36$
15. $16t^2 - 64t + 64$

Guided Practice

1. $x^2 + x - 6$ **2.** $2x^2 + 5x - 3$
3. $x^2 - 5x - 3x + 15$
  $x^2 - 8x + 15$
4. $y^2 - 3y + 9y - 27$
  $y^2 + 6y - 27$
5. $8a^2 + 4a - 8a - 4$
  $8a^2 - 4a - 4$
6. $-15g^2 + 18gh - 10hg + 12h^2$
  $-15g^2 + 8gh + 12h^2$
7. $(x^3 - 2x^2 + 1x) + (3x^2 - 6x + 3)$
  $x^3 + x^2 - 5x + 3$
8. $(-4k^4 + 24k^2 - 16k) + (3k^3 - 18k + 12)$
  $-4k^4 + 3k^3 + 24k^2 - 34k + 12$
9. $4b^2 - 49$ **10.** $25x^2 + 10x + 1$
11. Use FOIL to multiply binomials and a repeated use of the Distributive Property to multiply polynomials.

Independent Practice

13. $y^2 + 2y - 48$ **15.** $2z^2 + 13z + 6$
17. $6i^2 + 29i + 35$ **19.** $c^2 + 4cd - 21d^2$ **21a.** $(x + 7)(x - 7) = 95$
b. Trina is 12 years old.

23. Mika used the rule $(a - b)^2 = a^2 - ab + b^2$, but she should have used the rule $(a - b)^2 = a^2 - 2ab + b^2$. The correct product is $49x^4 - 168x^2y^3 + 144y^6$.
25. $n(n + 2)(n + 4)$ or $n^3 + 6n^2 + 8n$; 11, 13, 15
27. $(a + b)^3 = (a + b)(a + b)^2$, and $(a + b)^2 = a^2 + 2ab + b^2$, so $(a + b)^3 = (a + b)(a^2 + 2ab + b^2)$. If you distribute $(a + b)$, you get $(a + b)^3 = a^3 + 3a^2b + 3ab^2 + b^3$.

MODULE 15

LESSON 15.1

Your Turn

5. $9g^2$ **6.** 1 **7.** $15g^3$ **8.** b **10.** $-4y^2(7 + 3y^3)$ **11.** $2x^2(4x^2 + 2x - 1)$
12. $(7x + 1)(2x + 3)$ **13.** $(-4x + 9)(x + 2)$ **14.** cannot be factored **15.** $(5t - 8)(t + 6)$
16. $(2b^2 + 3)(3b + 4)$ **17.** $(4r + 1)(r^2 + 6)$ **19.** $(5x^2 - 4)(3 - 2x)$
20. $(8 + x)(y - 1)$ **21.** $(6n^5 - 7)(8n - 3)$ **22.** $(8t^3 - 3)(t - 6)$

Guided Practice

1a. $3 \cdot 5 \cdot y \cdot y \cdot y + 2 \cdot 2 \cdot 5 \cdot y$
b. $3 \cdot \circled{5} \cdot y \cdot y \cdot \circled{y} + 2 \cdot 2 \cdot \circled{5} \cdot \circled{y}$
c. $(5y)(3y^2 + 4)$
2. $3 \cdot 3 \cdot s$;
  $3 \cdot 3 \cdot 7 \cdot s \cdot s \cdot s$;
  $9s$
3. $-1 \cdot 2 \cdot 7 \cdot y \cdot y \cdot y$;
  $2 \cdot 2 \cdot 7 \cdot y \cdot y$;
  $14y^2$
4. $-y(18y^2 + 7y + 1)$ **5.** $9(d^2 - 2)$
6. $2x^2(3x^2 - x + 5)$ **7.** $9(4t^{3v} + 7)$
8. $(4s - 5)(s + 6)$ **9.** $(-3 + 4b)(2 + b)$ **10.** $(6z + 1)(z + 8)$
11. $(8w - 3)(5 - w)$
12. $(9x^3 + 18x^2) + (x + 2)$
  $9x^2(x + 2) + 1(x + 2)$
  $(9x^2 + 1)(x + 2)$
13. $(2m^3 + 4m^2) + (6m + 12)$
  $2m^2(m + 2) + 6(m + 2)$
  $(m + 2)(2m^2 + 6)$
  $2(m + 2)(m^2 - 3)$

14. $2(5x^2 + 7)(x - 4)$
15. $n(2n^3 + 7)(n - 1)$
16. $(2r^2 - 6r) + (12 - 4r)$
  $2r(r - 3) + 4(3 - r)$
  $2r(r - 3) + 4(-1)(r - 3)$
  $(r - 3)(2r - 4)$
  $2(r - 3)(r - 2)$
17. $(14q^2 - 21q) + (6 - 4q)$
  $7q(2q - 3) + 2(3 - 2q)$
  $7q(2q - 3) + 2(-1)(2q - 3)$
  $(7q - 2)(2q - 3)$
18. $(6 - 5c^2)(c - 8)$ **19.** $(3x^2 - 5)(x - 9)$ **20.** You can factor out the GCF of all the terms of the polynomial, or group the terms and factor out the GCF of pairs of terms.

Independent Practice

21. $8n^2$ **23.** $7n(2n^2 + 1 + n)$
25. cannot be factored
27. Apply the Distributive Property to the factored form and check if the product is the original polynomial. **29.** $P(1 + rt)$
31. Possible expressions for the dimensions are x cm and $(7x + 1)$ cm. **33.** $x^2 - 2$
35a. $(x - 6)$ and $(x + 3)$ **b.** length $= 15$, width $= 6$, area $= 90$
37. Audrey is correct. Owen said $n^2 = n^2 (0)$ instead of $n^2 = n^2(1)$

LESSON 15.2

Your Turn

7. $(x - 5)(x - 6)$
8. $(x + 1)(x + 4)$
9. $(x + 2)(x - 7)$
10. $(x + 2)(x - 3)$
11. $(x + 7)(x - 3)$
12. $(x + 5)(x - 3)$

Guided Practice

1a. 1; 6; 8 **b.** 9 **c.** 6
d. $(x + 4)(x + 2)$
2a. 1; 4; 5 **b.** 6; zero pair
c. $(x - 5)(x + 1)$

3a. -1 and -9

Factors of 9	Sum of Factors $= b$
1 and 9	$1 + 9 = 10$
3 and 3	$3 + 3 = 6$
-1 and -9	$-1 + (-9) = -10$
-3 and -3	$-3 + (-3) = -6$

b. $(x - 1)(x - 9)$
4. $(x + 3)(x + 3)$ **5.** $(x - 1)(x - 4)$
6. $(x + 3)(x - 6)$ **7.** $(x + 4)(x + 10)$
8. $(x + 12)(x - 3)$ **9.** $(x + 5)$
$(x - 7)$ **10.** $(x - 10)(x + 3)$
11. $(x - 2)(x + 4)$ **12.** $(x + 2)$
$(x + 7)$; The width of the porch
is $(x + 2)$ feet. **13.** Find a pair of
factors of c whose sum is b. The
factors of the polynomial will be
$(x + n)$ and $(x + m)$, where n and
m are those factors.

Independent Practice

15. $(x + 3)(x + 6)$ **17.** $(x + 4)$
$(x + 7)$ **19.** $(x - 4)(x - 8)$
21. The width is $(x + 2)$ ft. **23.** No,
not all trinomials have c terms
whose factors add up to b. For
example, $x^2 + 6x + 19$ cannot be
factored. **25a.** $(x + 10)$ ft
b. $(x + 6)$ ft by $(x + 14)$ ft
c. $x^2 + 20x + 84$ ft^2
27. $x^2 + 6x + 8 = (x + 4)(x + 2)$;
the width is $(x + 2)$; the rectangle is
not a square, because $(x + 2)$ is not
equal to $(x + 4)$. **29.** Find factors
of 6, and add each pair to find b.
Because c is positive, the factors will
have the same sign, and because
b is positive the signs will both be
positive. The factor pairs are 1 and
6, and 2 and 3. This produces $x^2 +$
$7x + 6$ and $x^2 + 5x + 6$.

LESSON 15.3

Your Turn

3. $(x - 2)(5x - 4)$ **4.** $(x + 3)$
$(3x + 2)$ **5.** $3(2x - 3)(2x - 5)$
6. $2(2x + 7)(3x + 5)$
7. $(7x + 6)(2x + 3)$
8. $5(2x - 3)(5x - 9)$ **11.** $2(2x + 3)$
$(6x - 1)$ **12.** $(3x + 8)(3x - 1)$

Guided Practice

1.

Factors of $a = 3$	Factors of $c = 12$	Outer + Inner $= b$
1 and 3	1 and 12	$(1)(12) + (3)(1) = 15$
1 and 3	2 and 6	$(1)(6) + (3)(2) = 12$
1 and 3	3 and 4	$(1)(4) + (3)(3) = 13$
1 and 3	4 and 3	$(1)(3) + (3)(4) = 15$
1 and 3	6 and 2	$(1)(2) + (3)(6) = 20$
1 and 3	12 and 1	$(1)(1) + (3)(12) = 37$

$(x + 3)(3x + 4)$

2. 2; $2(4x^2 - x - 3)$

Factors of $a = 4$	Factors of $c = -3$	Outer + Inner $= b$
1 and 4	1 and -3	$(1)(-3) + (4)(1) = 1$
1 and 4	3 and -1	$(1)(-1) + (4)(3) = 11$
1 and 4	-1 and 3	$(1)(3) + (4)(-1) = -1$
1 and 4	-3 and 1	$(1)(1) + (4)(-3) = -11$
2 and 2	1 and -3	$(2)(-3) + (2)(1) = -4$
2 and 2	3 and -1	$(2)(-1) + (2)(3) = 4$

$2(x - 1)(4x + 3)$ **3.** When $a \neq 1$,
examine factor pairs for a and c,
and find which arrangement of
factor pairs produces a sum of b.

Independent Practice

5. $(2x - 9)(3x - 1)$ **7.** $(z + 3)$
$(5z + 2)$ **9.** $(y - 2)(2y - 7)$
11. expression cannot be
factored **13.** $(6x + 10)$ m
15. $12x^2 - 11x - 5$; $(3x + 1)$
$(4x - 5)$ **17.** expression cannot be
factored **19.** No; If $a = b = c = 1$,
then b is positive, and the only
possible factor pair for a and for c
is 1 and 1. In the expression $(x + 1)$
$(x + 1)$, the sum of the products
of the inner and outer terms is $2x$,
not x. **21a.** $(10x - 15)$ cm
b. $(15x + 25)$ cm
c. $(6x^2 + x - 15)$ cm
23. When she factored out 3 in the
first step, the final term, should
be 1 instead of 0. The correctly
factored form is $3(2x + 1)(4x + 1)$.
25a. $-16t^2 + 20t + 6$
b. $-2(2t - 3)(4t + 1)$ **c.** 10 ft
27. Frank ignored the coefficient a
of x^2 and factored $x^2 + 13x + 12$.
The expression $2x^2 + 13x + 12$
cannot be factored.

LESSON 15.4

Your Turn

6. $(x + 3)(x + 3)$, or $(x + 3)^2$
7. $(5x + 6)(5x + 6)$, or $(5x + 6)^2$
8. $(6x - 1)(6x - 1)$, or $(6x - 1)^2$
9. $4(2x - 1)(2x - 1)$, or $4(2x - 1)^2$
10. $9(x - 1)(x - 1)$, or $9(x - 1)^2$
11. $4(x + 3)(x + 3)$, or $4(x + 3)^2$
13. $(1 + 2x)(1 - 2x)$ **14.** $4(2x + y^3)$
$(2x - y^3)$ **15.** $(p^4 + 7q^3)(p^4 - 7q^3)$

Guided Practice

1.

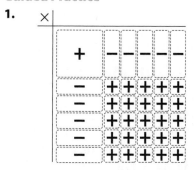

$(x - 5)(x - 5)$, or $(x - 5)^2$

2.

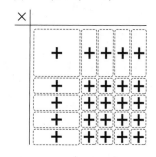

$(x + 4)(x + 4)$, or $(x + 4)^2$
3. $9(x + 1)^2$ **4.** $(5x + 2)^2$
5. $(8x - 1)^2$ **6.** $4(x + 3)^2$
7. $(4x^2 - 3)^2$ **8.** $(5x + 1)^2$
9. $(s + 4)(s - 4)$ **10.** $9(3 + 4x^2)$
$(3 - 4x^2)$ **11.** $(x^4 + 7)(x^4 - 7)$
12. $4x^2(10x + 11)(10x - 11)$
13. $(7x^3 + 6y)(7x^3 - 6y)$
14. $(5t + 8)(5t - 8)$
15. Check to see if a trinomial is
a perfect-square trinomial. If it is,
use the factoring rule that applies,
either $a^2 + 2ab + b^2 = (a + b)^2$
or $a^2 - 2ab + b^2 = (a - b)^2$. If a
binomial is the difference of two
squares, use the rule $a^2 - b^2 =$
$(a + b)(a - b)$ to factor it.

Independent Practice

17. difference of two squares; $(4b$
$+ 13c^3)(4b - 13c^3)$. **19.** difference

of two squares; $4(x + 3)(x - 3)$.
21. No, Sinea is not correct. The binomial $(x^2 - 1)$ is a difference of squares, so the fully factored form is $(x^2 + 1)(x + 1)(x - 1)$.
23. Use the rule for perfect square trinomials to factor $x^4 - 2x^2y^2 + y^4$ as $(x^2 - y^2)^2$. The binomial $(x^2 - y^2)$ is a difference of squares that can be factored as $(x + y)(x - y)$, so the fully factored form is $(x + y)^2$ $(x - y)^2$. **25.** $4(2x + y)(2x - y)$
27a. $(6d - 3)$ in. b. $4(6d - 3)$ in. **c.** 9 in.; 36 in.; 81 in^2
29. He factored out a 2 from both $(12x + 10)$ and $(12x - 10)$, which is the same as factoring out a 4 from the whole expression. It should be $4(6x + 5)(6x - 5)$.

MODULE **16**

LESSON 16.1

Your Turn

3. $x = 3$ or $x = -3$ **4.** $x = 8$ or $x = -8$ **6.** $x = 9$ or $x = -5$
7. $x = 5$ or $x = -13$ **8.** 30 cm

Guided Practice

1. 5, -5 **2.** 10, -10 **3.** 7, -7
4. $\pm 3 \cdot \sqrt{7}$ **5.** $\pm \frac{\sqrt{13}}{5}$ **6.** $\pm \frac{6}{7}$
7. $2x^2 = 6$
$\quad x^2 = 3$
$\quad x = \pm \sqrt{3}$
The solutions are $\sqrt{3}$ and $-\sqrt{3}$.
8. $y = \pm \sqrt{81}$
$\quad y = \pm 9$
The solutions are 9 and -9.
9. $x + 2 = \pm \sqrt{64}$
$\quad x + 2 = 8$ and $x + 2 = -8$
$\qquad x = 6$
$\qquad x = -10$
solutions: 6 and -10.
10. $x - 3 = \pm \sqrt{49}$
$\quad x - 3 = 7$ and $x - 3 = -7$
$\quad x - 3 = 7$
$\qquad x = 10$
$\quad x - 3 = -7$
$\qquad x = -4$
solutions: 10 and -4.

11. $x + 4 = \pm \sqrt{81}$
$\quad x + 4 = 9$ and $x + 4 = -9$
$\qquad x = 5 \qquad\qquad x = -13$
solutions: 5 and -13.
12. $(x + 1)^2 = -25$; There are 0 (or no) real-number solutions for this equation.
13. Area of a rectangle $= l \cdot w$
$\quad w^2 = 1200$
$\quad w = +34.64$ and -34.64
solution: 34.64 meters
14. You can solve quadratic equations using square roots by taking the square root of both sides of the equation. This allows you to determine the positive and negative numbers that solve the equation.

Independent Practice

15. 12 or -12 **17.** 2 or -2
19. Quotient Property; $\pm \frac{4}{5}$
21. Quotient Property; $\pm \frac{1}{20}$
23. Product Property; $\pm 3\sqrt{6}$
25. Product Property; $\pm 4\sqrt{3}$
27. $x = 12$ or $x = -12$ **29.** $x = 9$ or $x = -9$ **31a.** $x = 0$ or $x = -14$
b. $(0 + 7)^2 = 49$; $(-14 + 7)^2 = 49$
33a. $x = 14$ or $x = -4$
b. $(14 - 5)^2 = 81$; $(-4 - 5)^2 = 81$
35. 10 meters
37a. 31.62 centimeters
b. 6.32 centimeters
39. 11.5 feet
41. Sample answer: $x^2 - 49 = 0$

LESSON 16.2

Your Turn

5. 0, -8. **6.** $x = -7$
7. $x = -6$ **8.** $t = -2$ or $t = 4$

Guided Practice

1. Factor the left side as $(x + 7)$ $(x - 7) = 0$. Apply the Zero Product Property to $(x + 7)(x - 7) = 0$.
$\quad x + 7 = 0$ or $x - 7 = 0$
$\quad x = -7$ or $x = 7$
2. -1, 1 **3.** 2, -7 **4.** -3, 6 **5.** $-\frac{1}{2}$, 5
6. $x(x - 4) - 2(x - 4) = 0$
$\quad (x - 4)(x - 2) = 0$
$\qquad\qquad x = 4$ or $x = 2$

7. $x^2 - 2x - 15 = 0$
$\quad x^2 - 5x + 3x - 15 = 0$
$\quad x(x - 5) + 3(x - 5) = 0$
$\qquad (x - 5)(x + 3) = 0$
$\qquad\qquad x = 5$ or $x = -3$
8. Area $= l \times w = 24$ so $l = \frac{24}{w}$
$\quad 2\left(\frac{24}{w}\right) + 2w = 22$
$\qquad 48 + 2w^2 = 22w$
$\quad w^2 - 11w + 24 = 0$
$\quad (w - 3)(w - 8) = 0$
$\qquad\qquad w = 3$ or $w = 8$
The measure of the shorter side is 3 cm.
9. $t^2 - 8t = 0$
$\quad t(t - 8) = 0$
$\quad t = 0$ or $t = 8$
The time is 8 seconds.
10. You can find the factors of the constant term whose sum equals the coefficient of x, use those factors to factor the equation, and then use the Zero Product Property to solve.

Independent Practice

11. 4, -2 **13.** $\frac{3}{4}$, $\frac{1}{2}$ **15.** -4, 1
17. 3, 4 **19.** -5, -2 **21.** -1
23. 6, 7, 8 **25.** 6 seconds
27. 6 seconds **29.** $x(x + 2) = 24$
-6, -4 or 4, 6. **31.** The factors of $x^2 - 4x - 12$ are $(x - 6)(x + 2)$, so the zeros of the equation are 6 and -2. These are the values of x when y is zero, so they are the x-intercepts as well as the solutions of $x^2 - 4x - 12 = 0$.

LESSON 16.3

Your Turn

4. $x = -\frac{1}{2}$ or $x = \frac{3}{7}$ **5.** $x = -\frac{1}{2}$ or $x = \frac{3}{2}$ **7.** $x = 2$ or $x = -2$ **8.** $x = 2$
10. 300 or 800 printers sold

Guided Practice

1. $7x^2 + 30x + 8 = 0$
$\quad (7x + 2)(x + 4) = 0$
$\qquad x = -\frac{2}{7}, -4$
2. $6x^2 - 13x + 5 = 0$
$\quad (3x - 5)(2x - 1) = 0$
$\qquad x = \frac{5}{3}, \frac{1}{2}$
3. $4(x^2 + 4x + 3) = 0$
$\quad 4(x + 3)(x + 1) = 0$
$\qquad x = -3, -1$

UNIT 4 Selected Answers *(cont'd)*

4. $18(x^2 - 1) = 0$
$18(x + 1)(x - 1) = 0$
$x = -1, 1$
5. $11(x^2 + 4x + 4) = 0$
$11(x + 2)^2 = 0$
$x = -2$
6. $3(x^2 - 10x + 25) = 0$
$3(x - 5)^2 = 0$
$x = 5$
7. $12(x^2 - 9) = 0$
$12(x + 3)(x - 3) = 0$
$x = 3, -3$
8. $5(x^2 - 6x + 9) = 0$
$5(x - 3)(x - 3) = 0$
$x = 3$
9. $7x^2 - 70x + 175 = 0$
$7(x^2 - 10x + 25) = 0$
$7(x - 5)(x - 5) = 0$
$x = 5$
10. $2(x^2 + 16x + 64) = 0$
$2(x + 8)(x + 8) = 0$
$x = -8$
11. $-16(t^2 - 4t - 5) = 0$
$-16(t + 1)(t - 5) = 0$
$t = -1, 5$
The rocket lands on the ground in 5 seconds.
12. $-16t^2 + 2320t - 40{,}000 = 0$
$-16(t^2 - 145t - 2500) = 0$
$-16(t - 20)(t - 125) = 0$
$t = 20, 125$
20 seconds; 125 seconds
13. It is necessary to find all the factors of *a*, in addition to finding the factors of *c*, before seeing which combination works.

Independent Practice

15. $x = \frac{2}{3}, 1$ **17.** $x = -\frac{3}{4}, \frac{3}{2}$ **19.** $x = 0, 4$ **21.** $x = -\frac{2}{9}, 3$ **23.** $x = 3$ **25a.** $-4t^2 + 776 = 200$ **b.** $t = 12, -12$ **c.** $t = -12$ corresponds to a negative time fallen, so the answer is $t = 12$ minutes. **27.** If there were no floor and the ball kept falling, it would be 12 feet below ground level after 2 seconds.
29. The factors can both be written as $dx - e$, where *d* and *e* are both positive.

LESSON 16.4

Your Turn

4. $x^2 + 4x + 4$; $(x + 2)^2$
6. $x = 1 + \sqrt{2}$ or $x = 1 - \sqrt{2}$
10. width = 8 feet; length = 18 feet

Guided Practice

1. $x^2 + 14x + 49$ **2.** $x^2 - 4x + 4$
3. $x^2 - 3x + \frac{9}{4}$ **4.** $x^2 + 12x + 36$
5. $x^2 - 14x + 49$ **6.** $x^2 + 18x + 81$
7. $x^2 + 6x + 9 = -5 + 9$
$(x + 3)^2 = 4$
$x + 3 = \pm 2$
$x = -1, -5$
8. $x^2 - 8x + 16 = 9 + 16$
$(x - 4)^2 = 25$
$x - 4 = \pm 5$
$x = 9, -1$
9. $r^2 - 4r + 4 = 165 + 4$
$(r - 2)^2 = 169$
$r - 2 = \pm 13$
$r = 15, -11$
10. $t^2 + 2t + 1 = 224 + 1$
$(t + 1)^2 = 225$
$t + 1 = \pm 15$
$t = 14, -16$
11. $x = 3, -9$ **12.** $x = -2, \pm\sqrt{10}$ **13.** length = 11.2 meters, width = 7.2 meters **14.** First divide both sides of the equation by the coefficient of the squared term (in this case 3), then complete the square.

Independent Practice

15. $\frac{121}{4}$ **17.** $x = 2, -6$ **19.** $x = -1, -11$ **21.** $x = -2, 6$ **23.** $x = 1, 3$ **25.** $t = 20.1$ seconds **27a.** $(2x + 34)(2x + 10) = 640$ **b.** 3 feet **29.** The square roots of 81 are ± 9. Thus, there are two solutions: 7 and -11. **31.** No. When you take the square root of both sides, the right side becomes $\sqrt{-1}$. There is no real number whose square is -1.

LESSON 16.5

Your Turn

3. $\frac{1}{6}$ or $-\frac{7}{6}$ **5.** $x = \frac{-2 + \sqrt{31}}{3}$ or $x = \frac{-2 - \sqrt{31}}{3}$ **6.** $t \approx 0.47$ seconds

Guided Practice

1. $9x^2 + 30x + 25 = 16 + 25$
$(3x + 5)^2 = 41$
$3x + 5 = \pm\sqrt{41}$
$x = \frac{-5 + \sqrt{41}}{3}$ or $x = \frac{-5 - \sqrt{41}}{3}$
2. $25x^2 + 40x + 16 = 20 + 16$
$(5x + 4)^2 = 36$
$5x + 4 = \pm\sqrt{36}$
$x = -2$ or $x = \frac{2}{5}$
3. $5 \cdot [5x^2 - 6x = 11]$
$25x^2 - 30x = 55$
$25x^2 - 30x + 9 = 55 + 9$
$(5x - 3)^2 = 64$
$5x - 3 = \pm\sqrt{64}$
$x = \frac{11}{5}$ or $x = -1$
4. $3 \cdot [3x^2 + 8x = 5]$
$9x^2 + 24x = 15$
$9x^2 + 24x + 16 = 15 + 16$
$(3x + 4)^2 = 31$
$3x + 4 = \pm\sqrt{31}$
$x = \frac{-4 + \sqrt{31}}{3}$ or $x = \frac{-4 - \sqrt{31}}{3}$
5. $2 \times [2x^2 - 3x = 20]$
$4x^2 - 6x = 40$
$4x^2 - 6x + \frac{9}{4} = 40 + \frac{9}{4}$
$(2x - \frac{3}{2})^2 = \frac{169}{4}$
$2x - \frac{3}{2} = \pm\sqrt{\frac{169}{4}}$
$2x - \frac{3}{2} = \pm\frac{13}{2}$
$x = 4$ or $x = -\frac{5}{2}$
6. $3 \times [3x^2 + 7x = 3]$
$9x^2 + 21x = 9$
$9x^2 + 21x + \frac{49}{4} = 9 + \frac{49}{4}$
$(3x + \frac{7}{2})^2 = \frac{85}{4}$
$3x + \frac{7}{2} = \pm\sqrt{\frac{85}{4}}$
$3x + \frac{7}{2} = \pm\sqrt{\frac{85}{2}}$
$x = \frac{-7 + \sqrt{85}}{6}$ or $x = \frac{-7 - \sqrt{85}}{6}$
7. $16t^2 - 24t = 50$
$16t^2 - 24t + 9 = 59$
$(4t - 3)^2 = 59$
$t = \frac{3 - \sqrt{59}}{4}$ or $t = \frac{3 + \sqrt{59}}{4}$
$t \approx 2.67$ seconds (The negative answer is not possible.)
8. Multiply by a number so that the coefficient of x^2 will be a perfect square, then add $\frac{b^2}{4a}$ to both sides to begin solving.

Independent Practice

9. $x = -2$, or $x = 3$ **11.** 1 **13.** $x = -\frac{1}{7}$ or $x = -\frac{3}{7}$ **15.** $x = \frac{1}{2}$ or $x = -\frac{5}{9}$
17. $x = \frac{5 + \sqrt{29}}{11}$ or $x = \frac{5 - \sqrt{29}}{11}$

19. $b = 4$ or -4 **21.** $b = 9$ or -9
23. $c = 1$ **25.** $c = \frac{1}{4}$ **27.** $3, -\frac{1}{3}$
29. $x = \frac{-3 \pm \sqrt{21}}{9}$ **31a.** 8.2 seconds
b. 4.0 seconds **33.** width = 4.7
meters; length = 7.4 meters.
35. Kendra applied the symbol $\pm$
to the 7 rather than to $\sqrt{103}$,
to which it should have been
applied. The 7 should be positive
in both answers. The second
answer should be $x = \frac{7 - \sqrt{103}}{2}$.

LESSON 16.6

Your Turn

2. $-\frac{1}{3}$ or 2 **3.** 3.87 or 0.13
4. one real solution **5.** two real
solutions **6.** no real solutions
10.

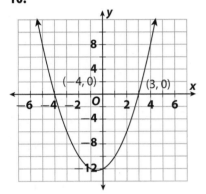

$x = -4$ or $x = 3$

Guided Practice

1. $a = 6, b = 5, c = -4$
$$x = \frac{-5 \pm \sqrt{5^2 - 4(6)(-4)}}{2(6)}$$
$$x = \frac{-5 \pm \sqrt{121}}{12}$$
$$x = \frac{-5 + 11}{12} \text{ or } x = \frac{-5 - 11}{12}$$
$$x = \frac{1}{2} \text{ or } x = \frac{-4}{3}$$
2. $x^2 - 4x + 1 = 0$
$a = 1, b = -4, c = 1$
$$x = \frac{-(-4) \pm \sqrt{(-4)^2 - 4(1)(1)}}{2(1)}$$
$$x = \frac{4 + \sqrt{12}}{2} \text{ or } x = \frac{4 - \sqrt{12}}{2}$$
$$x \approx 3.73 \text{ or } x \approx 0.27$$
3. There are 0 real solutions.
4. There is 1 real solution.

5. There are 2 real solutions.
6. Sample answer: I would use
factoring to solve, because the
equation is easily factorable and
therefore the method is less
times-consuming than using the
quadratic formula or completing
the square. The solutions are -1
and -3. **7.** The quadratic formula,
$x = \frac{-b \pm \sqrt{b^2 - 4ac}}{2a}$, gives the real
solutions (zero, one or two) to any
quadratic equation.

Independent Practice

9. a. Two real solutions: -1.04,
1.76 **b.** No. The solutions
represent the seconds after the
diver jumps, so the negative value
has no meaning in this context.
11. When $d > 0$, there are two
roots, thus two real solutions to
the quadratic equation.

LESSON 16.7

Your Turn

3. $(-4, 0), (-2, 8)$ **4.** $(2, 0)$
6. $(-1, -3), (-7, 117)$ **7.** 15.39
seconds

Guided Practice

1. The vertex of $f(x)$ is at $(-3, -4)$;
the x-intercepts are at $x = -1, -5$;
$g(x)$ has slope 2 and intercept 2.

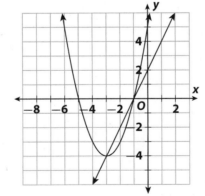

The solutions are $(-3, -4), (-1, 0)$.
2. The vertex of $f(x)$ is at $(0, -1)$;
the x-intercepts are at $x = 1, -1$;
$g(x)$ has slope 1 and intercept -2.

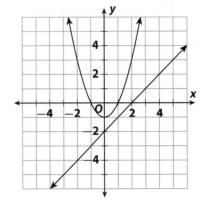

There are no (or 0) real solutions.
3. The vertex of $f(x)$ is at $(4, -2)$;
the x-intercepts are at
$x = 4 + \sqrt{2}, 4 - \sqrt{2}$; $g(x)$ has slope
0 and intercept -2.

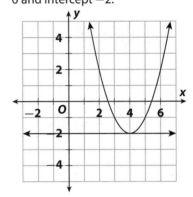

The solution is $(4, -2)$.
4. The vertex of $f(x)$ is at $(0, 4)$; the
x-intercepts are at $x = 2, -2$;
$g(x)$ has slope -3 and
intercept 6.

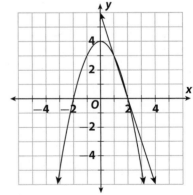

The solutions are $(2, 0), (1, 3)$.
5. $x^2 + 1 = 5$
$x^2 - 4 = 0$
$x = 2$ or -2
the solutions are $(2, 5), (-2, 5)$

6. $x^2 - 3x + 2 = 4x - 8$

$x^2 - 7x + 10 = 0$

$(x + (-2))(x + (-5)) = 0$

$x = 2$ or 5

the solutions are $(2, 0)$, $(5, 12)$

7. $(x - 3)^2 = 4$

$x - 3 = \pm 2$

$x = 5$ or 1

the solutions are $(1, 4)$, $(5, 4)$

8. $-x^2 + 4x = x + 2$

$-x^2 + 3x - 2 = 0$

$x = \frac{-b \pm \sqrt{b^2 - 4ac}}{2a}$

$= \frac{-3 \pm \sqrt{3^2 - 4(-1)(-2)}}{2(-1)}$

$x = \frac{-3 \pm \sqrt{1}}{-2} = \frac{-3 \pm 1}{-2}$

$x = 1$ or 2

the solutions are $(1, 3)$, $(2, 4)$

9. $(2.82, 154.74)$ and

$(22.18, -5654.74)$; 2.82 seconds

10. The *x*- and *y*-coordinates of the points of intersection of the two curves are solutions to the system of equations.

Independent Practice

11.

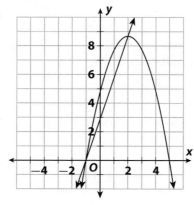

$(-1, 0)$, $(2, 9)$

13. $(2, 4)$, $(3, 9)$ **15.** $(-5, -42)$

17a. $t = 3.11$ seconds **b.** 45.9 feet

c. The $-4.9t^2$ term is eliminated through addition, leaving a linear equation with only one solution. **19.** Before equating, both equations must be solved for *y*. **21.** One solution involves a negative value of *t*, which would mean the bolt hit the elevator before it began to fall.

UNIT 5 Selected Answers

MODULE 17

LESSON 17.1

Your Turn

4.

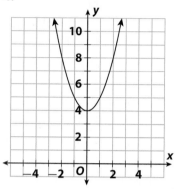

5.

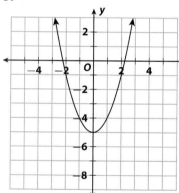

8.

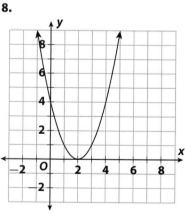

9.

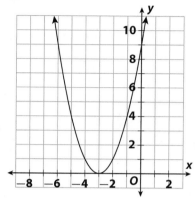

10. $y = (x + 4)^2 - 5$

Guided Practice

1.

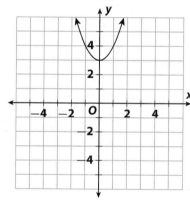

2.

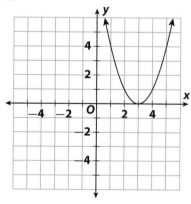

3. The graph of the parent function $f(x) = x^2$ will be translated h units to the right if h is positive and $|h|$ units to the left if h is negative. It will be translated k units up if k is positive and $|k|$ units down if k is negative.

Independent Practice

5. domain: the set of all real numbers; range: the set of real numbers y such that $y \geq -7$

7. domain: the set of all real numbers; range: the set of real numbers y such that $y \geq -6$

9a. green curve: 0 feet; blue curve: 40 feet **b.** green curve: $f(x) = x^2$; blue curve: $f(x) = x^2 + 40$. **c.** green curve: 8 seconds; blue curve: 5 seconds **d.** The blue curve is the green curve translated up 40 feet. **11.** Nina should have subtracted 4 from x in the equation instead of adding it.

13. The addition of k and b both result in vertical translations of the graphs of the related parent functions. The graph of $f(x) = x^2 + k$ is a vertical translation of the parabola $f(x) = x^2$, and the graph of $f(x) = x + b$ is a vertical translation of the line $f(x) = x$.

LESSON 17.2

Your Turn

2.

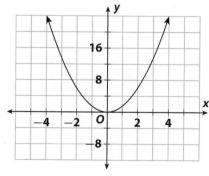

3.

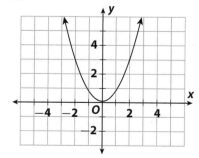

4.

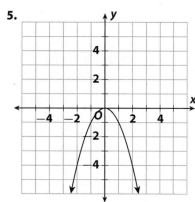

5.

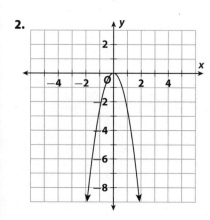

6. $f(x) = -\frac{3}{4}x^2$

Guided Practice

1.

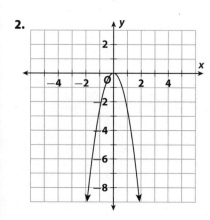

2.

3. The graph of the parent function $f(x) = x^2$ is stretched vertically if $|a| > 1$, and shrunk vertically if $|a| < 1$. The graph is reflected across the x-axis if $a < 0$.

Independent Practice

5. $h(x), g(x), f(x)$

7a. Sample answer: $f(x) = -x^2$

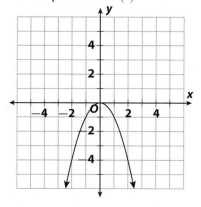

b. Sample answer: $f(x) = -2x^2$

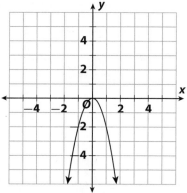

9. The y-coordinate of the point on the graph of $h(x)$ is -2 times the y-coordinate of the point on the graph of $f(x)$.

11. If $a < 0$, $f(x)$ has a maximum value. If $a > 0$, $f(x)$ has a minimum value. Since the vertex is $(0, 0)$ in either case, that value is 0.

13. Compared to the graph of the parent function $f(x) = x^2$, the graph of $g(x)$ would be wider (vertically shrunk). It will open upward because a is positive.

LESSON 17.3

Your Turn

9.

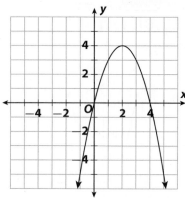

13. $f(t) = -16t^2 + 40$

15a. from 16 feet: $h_1(t) = -16t^2 + 16$; from 256 feet: $h_2(t) = -16t^2 + 256$ **b.** from 16 feet: 1 second; from 256 feet: 4 seconds

Guided Practice

1.

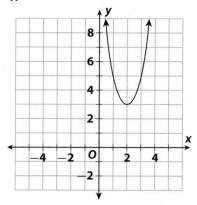

2.

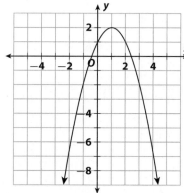

3. $f(t) = -16t^2 + 45$. **4.** The graph of $f(x) = x^2$ is stretched or shrunk by a factor of $|a|$, and reflected

across the x-axis if a is negative; it is translated h units horizontally and k units vertically.

Independent Practice
5.

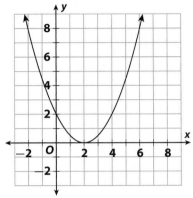

7.

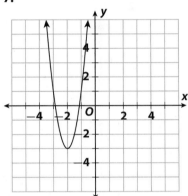

9a. The height functions are $h_1(t) = -16t^2 + 16$ and $h_2(t) = -16t^2 + 100$; Each graph is part of a parabola in the first quadrant, with vertex $(0, 16)$ for $h_1(t)$ and $(0, 100)$ for $h_2(t)$. The graph of $h_2(t)$ is the graph of $h_1(t)$ translated up 84 ft. **b.** From 16 feet: 1 second; from 100 feet: 2.5 seconds **11.** Kevin is right that the graph is a parabola that opens downward. However, the vertex is at $(2, 3)$, not $(3, 2)$. **13.** Sample answer: $f(x) = -\frac{1}{2}x^2 - 3$

LESSON 17.4

Your Turn
5. quadratic, $y = -x^2 + 4x$
6. quadratic, $f(x) = x^2 - 0.2x + 0.01$
7. not quadratic, $a = 0$ **8.** not quadratic, $a = 0$ **10.** minimum -1

---

11. maximum 8 **12.** minimum 3
14. no zeros **15.** 3 **16.** $x = -3$

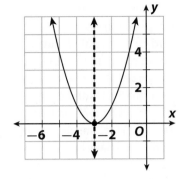

17. $x = 1$

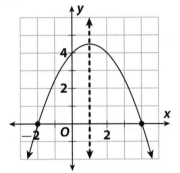

Guided Practice
1. not quadratic **2.** quadratic
3. maximum; 5 **4.** minimum; 4
5. maximum; -3 **6.** -3, 3
7. $x = -4$

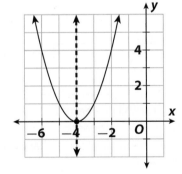

8. You can tell the location of the vertex, the equation of the axis of symmetry, and the maximum or minimum value of the function.

Independent Practice
9. quadratic, because it can be written as $y = 3x^2 - x + 5$, which is in the form $y = ax^2 + bx + c$, with $a \neq 0$. **11.** maximum; $\frac{1}{4}$
13. no zeros

---

15. $x = 6$

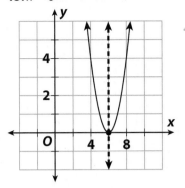

17. The axis of symmetry is the y-axis, or $x = 0$. **19.** Martina didn't divide by -1 to completely solve for y. The graph opens upward and has minimum value of 3. **21.** Sample answer: Find the product $(x - (-3))(x - 1)$, or $(x + 3)(x - 1)$. Then write a quadratic function using this product. So a possible quadratic function is $f(x) = x^2 + 2x - 3$.

LESSON 17.5

Your Turn
2. $x = 3$ and $x = 7$

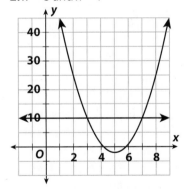

3. $x = -4$ and $x = -2$

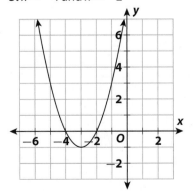

5. $-16t^2 + 46 = 10$;
1.5 seconds **7.** 5 seconds

Guided Practice

1.

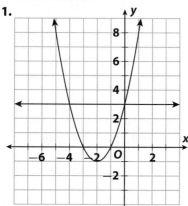

$x = -4$ and $x = 0$; exact.

2.

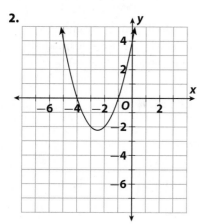

$x = -4$ and $x = -1$
3. $-16t^2 + 106 = 42$;
2 seconds **4.** approximately 9.5
seconds **5.** Any real solutions of
the quadratic equation are the
x-intercepts of the graph of the
related quadratic function.

Independent Practice

7.

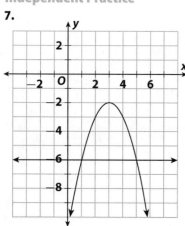

$x = 1$ and $x = 5$

9. 14 seconds **11.** Sample answers:
The graph of $f(x) = x^2$ opens
upward, but the related equation
$x^2 = 0$ has only one solution.
The graph of $f(x) = x^2 + 1$ opens
upward, but the related equation
$x^2 + 1 = 0$ has no real solutions.
13. Falling 20 feet means that the
balloon would have been
$50 - 20 = 30$ feet above ground,
and Rodney should have solved
the equation $-16t^2 + 50 = 30$.

LESSON 17.6

Your Turn

8. quadratic **9.** exponential

Guided Practice

1a. increases **b.** It approaches
infinity. **2.** Yes. The common
difference is 5. **3.** Yes. Second
differences are constant.
4a. quadratic **b.** 2 **c.** It is
increasing in both directions.
5a.

First Differences
8
16
32
64

b. They are all powers of 2.
c. Yes, this is exponential.
6. Examine the pattern of change
in the y-values.

Independent Practice

7. quadratic **9.** exponential
11. exponential **13.** linear
15. quadratic **17a.** quadratic
b. The highest power is 2.
19a. 9, 90, 900, 9000 **b.** No;
exponential **c.** in the exponent
21a. quadratic **b.** the second
difference **c.** The difference is 2.
Since it is constant, it is quadratic.
23a. quadratic **b.** $152,000
25a. linear **b.** 148 inches

27. He forgot to look at the second
differences. They are a constant 6,
so it is quadratic.

MODULE **18**

LESSON 18.1

Your Turn

1.

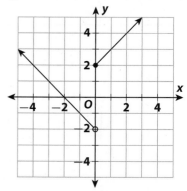

2.

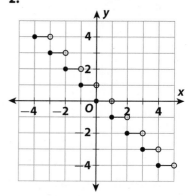

3. $f(x) = \begin{cases} 4 \text{ if } 0 < x < 12 \\ 8 \text{ if } x \geq 12 \end{cases}$

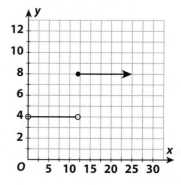

5. $y = -1$ **6.** $y = 2x + 4$
7. $f(x) = \begin{cases} 2x + 4 \text{ if } x \geq -2 \\ -1 \text{ if } x < -2 \end{cases}$

Guided Practice

1. $f(2) = 2, f(1) = 1, f(0) = 1,$
$f(-2) = 3, f(-3) = 4$

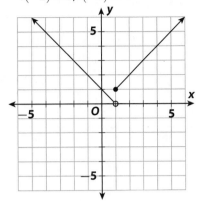

2. $f(2) = 6, f(1) = 4, f(0) = 2,$
$f(-2) = -1, f(-3) = -1$

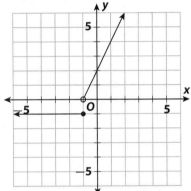

3.

x	1	1.2	0.9	−1.2	−2.1
f(x)	2	2	0	−4	−6

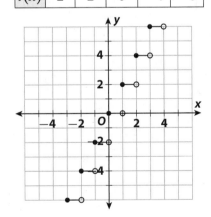

4a.

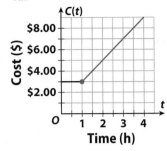

b. $C(t) = 2t + 1$

c. $C(t) = \begin{cases} 3 \text{ if } t < 1 \\ 2t + 1 \text{ if } t \geq 1 \end{cases}$

5. Piecewise functions have different rules for different parts of the domain.

Independent Practice

7.

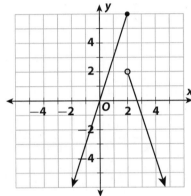

9. $f(x) = \begin{cases} \frac{1}{2}x - 6 & \text{if } x \geq 2 \\ -2x + 1 & \text{if } x < 2 \end{cases}$

11a.

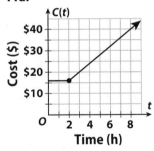

b. $C(t) = 16$

c. $C(t) = 4(t - 2) + \$16$ or
$C(t) = 4t + 8$

d. $C(t) = \begin{cases} 16 \text{ if } t \leq 2 \\ 4(t - 2) + 16 \text{ if } t > 2 \end{cases}$

13. 2 and 9

LESSON 18.2

Your Turn

4.

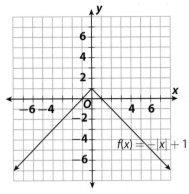

7.

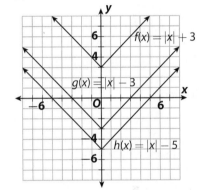

10.

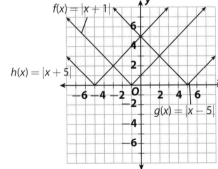

Guided Practice

1. and **2.**
$f(x)$: $(0, 2), (1, 3), (-1, 3), (2, 4), (-2, 5),$
$(3, 5), (-3, 5), (5, 7), (-5, 7), (-7, 9)$;
$g(x)$: $(0, 3), (1, 2), (-1, 4), (2, 1), (-2, 5),$
$(3, 0), (-3, 6), (4, 1), (-4, 7), (6, 3)$
$h(x)$: $(0, 1), (1, 0), (-1, 0), (2, -1),$
$(-2, -1), (3, -2), (-3, -2), (5, -4),$
$(-5, -4), (6, -5)$

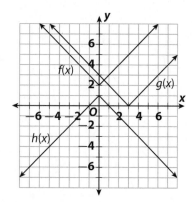

3. $(0, 2)$, all real numbers, $y \geq 2$
4. $(3, 0)$, all real numbers, $y \geq 0$
5. All absolute value functions are composed of two rays that meet at the vertex. All absolute value functions are symmetrical. The domain is always all real numbers, and the range is always limited.

Independent Practice
7. $(-3, 0)$, all real numbers x, real numbers $y \geq 0$

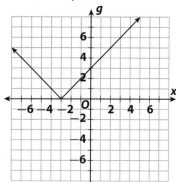

9.

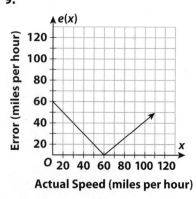

11. Answers may vary.
$a(x) = -|x| - 2$. Since the absolute value of x is nonnegative, $-|x| \leq 0$, so $-|x| - 2 \leq -2$.

LESSON 18.3

Your Turn
5. $y = -2|x - 4| + 2$
6.

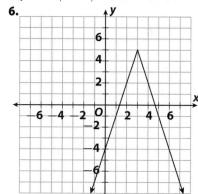

Guided Practice
1.

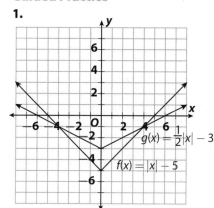

2.

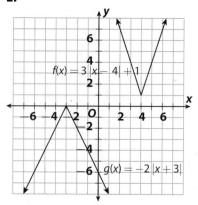

3. $(2, 3)$, -3, $f(x) = -3|x - 2| + 3$
4. Vertex: $(-2, 0)$; $a: \frac{1}{3}$;
$g(x) = \frac{1}{3} \times |x + 2|$
5. The parameters control the vertex location, the direction the graph opens, and the slope of the rays of the graph.

Independent Practice
7.

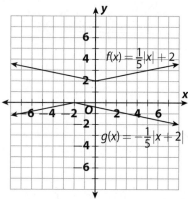

9a. $f(x) = -\frac{2}{3}|x + 2| + 1$
b. $f(x) = -5|x - 4| + 2$
11. $f(x) = 2|x - 4| - 6$ and $f(x) = -2|x - 4| + 6$ **13.** Giselle switched x- and y-values to get an equation such as $x = |y|$. The graph would open sideways. It would not be a function of x because it would have two y-values for the same value of x.

MODULE 19

LESSON 19.1

Your Turn
2.

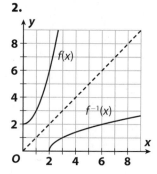

$f^{-1}(x) = \sqrt{x - 2}$ for $x \geq 2$ **3.** $x \geq \frac{5}{3}$
4. $x \geq -1$
7a. $s(A) = \sqrt{9A} = 3\sqrt{A}$
b. 6 inches **8a.** $r(A) = \sqrt{\frac{A}{P}}$
b. 6.2 meters

Guided Practice

1.

x	f(x)
0	1
1	2
2	5
3	10

Ordered Pairs $f^{-1}(x)$
(1, 0)
(2, 1)
(5, 2)
(10, 3)

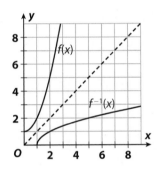

$f^{-1}(x) = \sqrt{x-1}$

2. $4x - 1 \geq 0$
$4x \geq 1$
$x \geq \frac{1}{4}$

3. $3(x - 3) \geq 0$ $4x - 1$
$3x - 9 \geq 0$
$3x \geq 0$
$x \geq 3$

4a. $r(a) = \sqrt{\frac{a}{3.14}}$ **b.** about 5.5
inches; $r(a) = \sqrt{\frac{a}{3.14}} = \sqrt{\frac{94.2}{3.14}} = \sqrt{30} \approx 5.5$ **5.** A square root
function is the inverse of a
quadratic function whose domain is
restricted. The inverse of $f(x) = ax^2$
for $x \geq 0$ is $f^{-1}(x) = \sqrt{\frac{x}{a}}$ for $x \geq 0$,
$a > 0$.

Independent Practice

7.

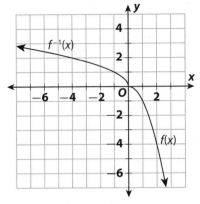

$f(x) = -x^2, f^{-1}(x) = \sqrt{-x}$

9.

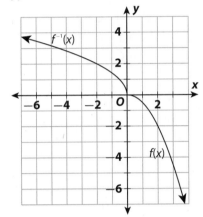

$f(x) = -\frac{1}{2}x^2, f^{-1}(x) = \sqrt{-2x}$
11. $x \geq -\frac{3}{2}$ **13.** $x \geq 4$ **15.** $x \leq \frac{4}{3}$
17. about 1.41 seconds
19. $P = 4\sqrt{A}$
21. $F = \frac{9}{5}C + 32$; If $F = C$,
solve $\frac{5}{9}(F - 32) = \frac{9}{5}F + 32$ for F.
The solution is -40∞.

LESSON 19.2

Your Turn
6. $f(x) = 3\sqrt{x} + 2$
7. $f(x) = \sqrt{x-3} - 1$

Guided Practice

1.

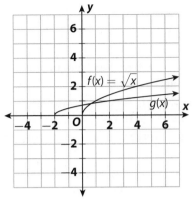

two units to the left, shrink;
Domain: $x \geq -2$;
Range: $y \geq 0$

2.

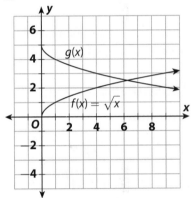

five units up, reflection;
Domain: $x \geq 0$;
Range: $y \leq 5$
3a. 3 to the right **b.** 2 up
c. $f(x) = \sqrt{x-3} + 2$
4. The graph will be translated to
the right if h is positive and to the
left if h is negative. The graph will
be translated up if k is positive and
down if k is negative. The graph
will stretch if $a > 1$ or shrink if
$a < 1$ and positive.

Independent Practice

5. Domain: $x \geq 3$
Range: $y \geq 2$
7. Domain: $x \geq -\frac{3}{2}$
Range: $y \geq 0$
9. Domain: $x \geq -0.5$
Range: $y \geq 3$

11a. enough to cover 2 square feet **b.** $f(x) = \sqrt{x-2}$ **c.** a little over 6 feet **d.** It is a translation of the graph of the parent function 2 units to the right.

13. The function $f(x) = \sqrt{x}$ is limited to the domain $x \geq 0$, so not every point (x, y) that belongs to the function $f(x) = x^2$ has a corresponding point (y, x) that belongs to the function $f(x) = \sqrt{x}$. This is further evidenced by the fact that the graph of $f(x) = \sqrt{x}$ is only a reflection of part of the graph of $f(x) = x^2$ in the line $y = x$. **15.** The graph has a greater minimum value, 0, than the minimum value of the function, -1.

LESSON 19.3

Your Turn

4.

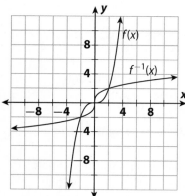

$f^{-1}(x) = \sqrt[3]{4x}$

8.

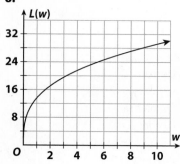

$L(w) = \sqrt[3]{2500w}$; approximately 29 inches long

Guided Practice

1. $\frac{y}{2} = x^3$

$\sqrt[3]{\frac{y}{2}} = x$

$\sqrt[3]{\frac{x}{2}} = y$

$f^{-1}(x) = \sqrt[3]{\frac{x}{2}}$

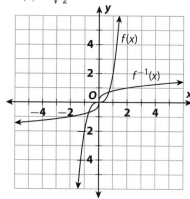

2. $-y = x^3$

$\sqrt[3]{-y} = x$

$\sqrt[3]{-x} = y$

$f^{-1}(x) = \sqrt[3]{-x}$

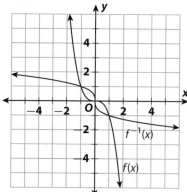

3a. $r(V) = \sqrt[3]{\frac{3}{4p}V}$

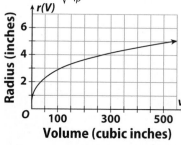

b. 5 inches **4.** You can graph $f(x)$ and reflect the graph over the line $y = x$ to produce the graph of $f^{-1}(x)$. Or you can start with the given function rule, solve for x, and switch the variables to find the rule for the inverse function, then graph.

Independent Practice

5.

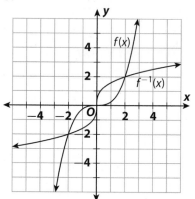

$f^{-1}(x) = \sqrt[3]{4x}$

7. $g^{-1}(x) = 5x^3$

9a. $c(w) = 44.88w^3$ **b.** $w(c) = \sqrt[3]{\frac{c}{44.88}}$

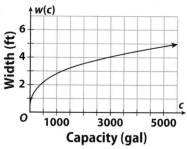

c. 4 feet **11.** yes; the inverse of $g(x) = \frac{27}{8}x^3$ is $g^{-1}(x) = \sqrt[3]{\frac{8}{27}x}$, which can be written as $g^{-1}(x) = \sqrt[3]{\left(\frac{2}{3}\right)^3 x}$. The term $\frac{2}{3}$ can be moved outside the radicand to show Ellie's answer, $g^{-1}(x) = \frac{2}{3}\sqrt[3]{x}$.

LESSON 19.4

Your Turn

7. $g(x) = 2\sqrt[3]{x} + 1$ **8.** h and k are both positive; the graph of the parent function has been translated to the right and up

Guided Practice

1.

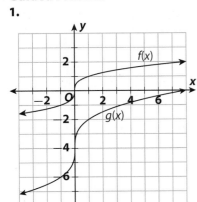

vertical stretch by a factor of 2; translation 4 units down; Domain: all real numbers; Range: all real numbers **2.** $f(x) = \sqrt[3]{x} + 1$

3. The parent function has been stretched vertically by a factor of 2, translated 1 unit to the left, and translated 2 units down.

4. If $|a| > 1$, then the graph of the parent function is stretched by a factor of a. If $0 < |a| < 1$, then the graph is shrunk by a factor of a. If h is positive, the graph is translated h units to the right. If h is negative, the graph is translated $|h|$ units to the left. If k is positive, the graph is translated k units up. If k is negative, the graph is translated $|k|$ units down.

Independent Practice

5.

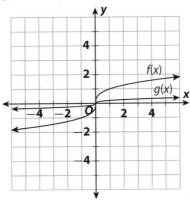

vertical shrink by a factor of 0.2 **7.** $f(x) = 2\sqrt[3]{x} + 2$ **9.** The value of a is 1. The value of h is -2, and the value of k is 3. **11.** The point where the curvature of the graph changes would be located at $(2, -3)$. **13.** In square root functions, the radicand must be nonnegative, so the domain, and hence, the range, are limited. In cube root functions, the radicand can be any number, so the domain and range consist of all real numbers.

Glossary/Glosario

ENGLISH	SPANISH	EXAMPLES
absolute value The absolute value of x is the distance from zero to x on a number line, denoted $\lvert x\rvert$. $\lvert x\rvert = \begin{cases} x & \text{if } x \geq 0 \\ -x & \text{if } x < 0 \end{cases}$	**valor absoluto** El valor absoluto de x es la distancia de cero a x en una recta numérica, y se expresa $\lvert x\rvert$. $\lvert x\rvert = \begin{cases} x & \text{si } x \geq 0 \\ -x & \text{si } x < 0 \end{cases}$	$\lvert 3\rvert = 3$ $\lvert -3\rvert = 3$
absolute-value equation An equation that contains absolute-value expressions.	**ecuación de valor absoluto** Ecuación que contiene expresiones de valor absoluto.	$\lvert x + 4\rvert = 7$
absolute-value function A function whose rule contains absolute-value expressions.	**función de valor absoluto** Función cuya regla contiene expresiones de valor absoluto.	$y = \lvert x + 4\rvert$
absolute-value inequality An inequality that contains absolute-value expressions.	**desigualdad de valor absoluto** Desigualdad que contiene expresiones de valor absoluto.	$\lvert x + 4\rvert > 7$
accuracy The closeness of a given measurement or value to the actual measurement or value.	**exactitud** Cercanía de una medida o un valor a la medida o el valor real.	
acute angle An angle that measures greater than 0° and less than 90°.	**ángulo agudo** Ángulo que mide más de 0° y menos de 90°.	
acute triangle A triangle with three acute angles.	**triángulo acutángulo** Triángulo con tres ángulos agudos.	
Addition Property of Equality For real numbers a, b, and c, if $a = b$, then $a + c = b + c$.	**Propiedad de igualdad de la suma** Dados los números reales a, b y c, si $a = b$, entonces $a + c = b + c$.	$\begin{aligned} x - 6 &= 8 \\ +6 \quad &+6 \\ \hline x \quad &= 14 \end{aligned}$
Addition Property of Inequality For real numbers a, b, and c, if $a < b$, then $a + c < b + c$. Also holds true for $>$, $\leq$, $\geq$, and $\neq$.	**Propiedad de desigualdad de la suma** Dados los números reales a, b y c, si $a < b$, entonces $a + c < b + c$. Es válido también para $>$, $\leq$, $\geq$ y $\neq$.	$\begin{aligned} x - 6 &< 8 \\ +6 \quad &+6 \\ \hline x \quad &< 14 \end{aligned}$
additive inverse The opposite of a number. Two numbers are additive inverses if their sum is zero.	**inverso aditivo** El opuesto de un número. Dos números son inversos aditivos si su suma es cero.	The additive inverse of 5 is -5. The additive inverse of -5 is 5.
algebraic expression An expression that contains at least one variable.	**expresión algebraica** Expresión que contiene por lo menos una variable.	

ENGLISH	SPANISH	EXAMPLES
AND A logical operator representing the intersection of two sets.	**Y** Operador lógico que representa la intersección de dos conjuntos.	$A = \{2, 3, 4, 5\}$ $B = \{1, 3, 5, 7\}$ The set of values that are in A AND B is $A \cap B = \{3, 5\}$.
angle A figure formed by two rays with a common endpoint.	**ángulo** Figura formada por dos rayos con un extremo común.	
area The number of nonoverlapping unit squares of a given size that will exactly cover the interior of a plane figure.	**área** Cantidad de cuadrados unitarios de un determinado tamaño no superpuestos que cubren exactamente el interior de una figura plana.	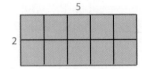 The area is 10 square units.
arithmetic sequence A sequence whose successive terms differ by the same nonzero number d, called the *common difference*.	**sucesión aritmética** Sucesión cuyos términos sucesivos difieren en el mismo número distinto de cero d, denominado *diferencia común*.	4, 7, 10, 13, 16, … $+3 +3 \ +3 \ +3$ $d = 3$
Associative Property of Addition For all numbers a, b, and c, $(a + b) + c = a + (b + c)$.	**Propiedad asociativa de la suma** Dados tres números cualesquiera a, b y c, $(a + b) + c = a + (b + c)$.	$(5 + 3) + 7 = 5 + (3 + 7)$
Associative Property of Multiplication For all numbers a, b, and c, $(a \cdot b) \cdot c = a \cdot (b \cdot c)$.	**Propiedad asociativa de la multiplicación** Dados tres números cualesquiera a, b y c, $(a \cdot b) \cdot c = a \cdot (b \cdot c)$.	$(5 \cdot 3) \cdot 7 = 5 \cdot (3 \cdot 7)$
asymptote A line that a graph gets closer to as the value of a variable becomes extremely large or small.	**asíntota** Línea recta a la cual se aproxima una gráfica a medida que el valor de una variable se hace sumamente grande o pequeño.	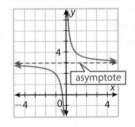
average *See* mean.	**promedio** *Ver* media.	
axis of a coordinate plane One of two perpendicular number lines, called the x-axis and the y-axis, used to define the location of a point in a coordinate plane.	**eje de un plano cartesiano** Una de las dos rectas numéricas perpendiculares, denominadas eje x y eje y, utilizadas para definir la ubicación de un punto en un plano cartesiano.	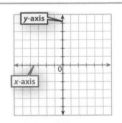
axis of symmetry A line that divides a plane figure or a graph into two congruent reflected halves.	**eje de simetría** Línea que divide una figura plana o una gráfica en dos mitades reflejadas congruentes.	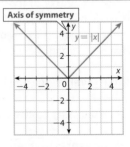

B

back-to-back stem-and-leaf plot (A graph used to organize and compare two sets of data so that the frequencies can be compared. *See also* stem-and-leaf plot.

diagrama doble de tallo y hojas Gráfica utilizada para organizar y comparar dos conjuntos de datos para poder comparar las frecuencias. *Ver también* diagrama de tallo y hojas.

Data set A: 9, 12, 14, 16, 23, 27
Data set B: 6, 8, 10, 13, 15, 16, 21

Set A		Set B
9	0	6 8
6 4 2	1	0 3 5 6
7 3	2	1

Key: |2| 1 means 21
7 |2| means 27

bar graph A graph that uses vertical or horizontal bars to display data.

gráfica de barras Gráfica con barras horizontales o verticales para mostrar datos.

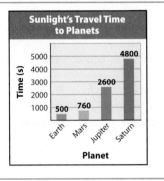

base of a power The number in a power that is used as a factor.

base de una potencia Número de una potencia que se utiliza como factor.

$3^4 = 3 \cdot 3 \cdot 3 \cdot 3 = 81$
3 is the base.

base of an exponential function The value of b in a function of the form $f(x) = ab^x$, where a and b are real numbers with $a \neq 0$, $b > 0$, and $b \neq 1$.

base de una función exponencial Valor de b en una función del tipo $f(x) = ab^x$, donde a y b son números reales con $a \neq 0$, $b > 0$ y $b \neq 1$.

In the function $f(x) = 5(2)^x$, the base is 2.

biased sample A sample that does not fairly represent the population.

muestra no representativa Muestra que no representa adecuadamente una población.

To find out about the exercise habits of average Americans, a fitness magazine surveyed its readers about how often they exercise. The population is all Americans and the sample is readers of the fitness magazine. This sample will likely be biased because readers of fitness magazines may exercise more often than other people do.

binomial A polynomial with two terms.

binomio Polinomio con dos términos.

$x + y$
$2a^2 + 3$
$4m^3n^2 + 6mn^4$

boundary line A line that divides a coordinate plane into two half-planes.

línea de límite Línea que divide un plano cartesiano en dos semiplanos.

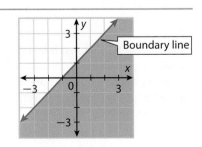

ENGLISH	SPANISH	EXAMPLES
box-and-whisker plot A method of showing how data are distributed by using the median, quartiles, and minimum and maximum values; also called a *box plot*.	**gráfica de mediana y rango** Método para mostrar la distribución de datos utilizando la mediana, los cuartiles y los valores mínimo y máximo; también llamado *gráfica de caja*.	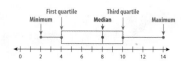

Cartesian coordinate system *See* coordinate plane.	**sistema de coordenadas cartesianas** *Ver* plano cartesiano.	
categorical data Data that are qualitative in nature, such as "liberal," "moderate," and "conservative."	**datos categóricos** Datos de índole cualitativa, como "liberal", "moderado" y "conservador".	
center of a circle The point inside a circle that is the same distance from every point on the circle.	**centro de un círculo** Punto dentro de un círculo que se encuentra a la misma distancia de todos los puntos del círculo.	
central angle of a circle An angle whose vertex is the center of a circle.	**ángulo central de un círculo** Ángulo cuyo vértice es el centro de un círculo.	
circle The set of points in a plane that are a fixed distance from a given point called the center of the circle.	**círculo** Conjunto de puntos en un plano que se encuentran a una distancia fija de un punto determinado denominado centro del círculo.	
circle graph A way to display data by using a circle divided into non-overlapping sectors.	**gráfica circular** Forma de mostrar datos mediante un círculo dividido en sectores no superpuestos.	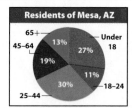
circumference The distance around a circle.	**circunferencia** Distancia alrededor de un círculo.	
closure A set of numbers is said to be closed, or to have closure, under a given operation if the result of the operation on any two numbers in the set is also in the set.	**cerradura** Se dice que un conjunto de números es cerrado, o tiene cerradura, respecto de una operación determinada, si el resultado de la operación entre dos números cualesquiera del conjunto también está en el conjunto.	The natural numbers are closed under addition because the sum of two natural numbers is always a natural number.

Glossary/Glosario

ENGLISH	SPANISH	EXAMPLES
coefficient A number that is multiplied by a variable.	**coeficiente** Número que se multiplica por una variable.	In the expression $2x + 3y$, 2 is the coefficient of x and 3 is the coefficient of y.
common difference In an arithmetic sequence, the nonzero constant difference of any term and the previous term.	**diferencia común** En una sucesión aritmética, diferencia constante distinta de cero entre cualquier término y el término anterior.	In the arithmetic sequence 3, 5, 7, 9, 11, …, the common difference is 2.
common factor A factor that is common to all terms of an expression or to two or more expressions.	**factor común** Factor que es común a todos los términos de una expresión o a dos o más expresiones.	Expression: $4x^2 + 16x^3 - 8x$ Common factor: $4x$ Expressions: 12 and 18 Common factors: 2, 3, and 6
common ratio In a geometric sequence, the constant ratio of any term and the previous term.	**razón común** En una sucesión geométrica, la razón constante entre cualquier término y el término anterior.	In the geometric sequence 32, 16, 8, 4, 2, …, the common ratio is $\frac{1}{2}$.
Commutative Property of Addition For any two numbers a and b, $a + b = b + a$.	**Propiedad conmutativa de la suma** Dados dos números cualesquiera a y b, $a + b = b + a$.	$3 + 4 = 4 + 3 = 7$
Commutative Property of Multiplication For any two numbers a and b, $a \cdot b = b \cdot a$.	**Propiedad conmutativa de la multiplicación** Dados dos números cualesquiera a y b, $a \cdot b = b \cdot a$.	$3 \cdot 4 = 4 \cdot 3 = 12$
complement of an event The set of all outcomes that are not the event.	**complemento de un suceso** Todos los resultados que no están en el suceso.	In the experiment of rolling a number cube, the complement of rolling a 3 is rolling a 1, 2, 4, 5, or 6.
complementary angles Two angles whose measures have a sum of 90°.	**ángulos complementarios** Dos ángulos cuyas medidas suman 90°.	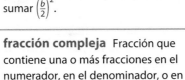
completing the square A process used to form a perfect-square trinomial. To complete the square of $x^2 + bx$, add $\left(\frac{b}{2}\right)^2$.	**completar el cuadrado** Proceso utilizado para formar un trinomio cuadrado perfecto. Para completar el cuadrado de $x^2 + bx$, hay que sumar $\left(\frac{b}{2}\right)^2$.	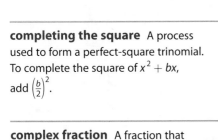 $x^2 + 6x + $ ▓ Add $\left(\frac{6}{2}\right)^2 = 9$. $x^2 + 6x + 9$
complex fraction A fraction that contains one or more fractions in the numerator, the denominator, or both.	**fracción compleja** Fracción que contiene una o más fracciones en el numerador, en el denominador, o en ambos.	$\dfrac{\frac{1}{2}}{1 + \frac{2}{3}}$
composite figure A plane figure made up of triangles, rectangles, trapezoids, circles, and other simple shapes, or a three-dimensional figure made up of prisms, cones, pyramids, cylinders, and other simple three-dimensional figures.	**figura compuesta** Figura plana compuesta por triángulos, rectángulos, trapecios, círculos y otras figuras simples, o figura tridimensional compuesta por prismas, conos, pirámides, cilindros y otras figuras tridimensionales simples.	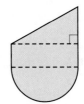

ENGLISH	SPANISH	EXAMPLES
compound event An event made up of two or more simple events.	**suceso compuesto** Suceso formado por dos o más sucesos simples.	In the experiment of tossing a coin and rolling a number cube, the event of the coin landing heads and the number cube landing on 3.
compound inequality Two inequalities that are combined into one statement by the word *and* or *or*.	**desigualdad compuesta** Dos desigualdades unidas en un enunciado por la palabra *y* u *o*.	$x \geq 2$ AND $x < 7$ (also written $2 \leq x < 7$) 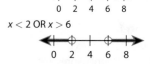 $x < 2$ OR $x > 6$
compound interest Interest earned or paid on both the principal and previously earned interest. The formula for compound interest is $A = P\left(1 + \frac{r}{n}\right)^{nt}$, where A is the final amount, P is the principal, r is the interest rate expressed as a decimal, n is the number of times interest is compounded, and t is the time.	**interés compuesto** Intereses ganados o pagados sobre el capital y los intereses ya devengados. La fórmula de interés compuesto es $A = P\left(1 + \frac{r}{n}\right)^{nt}$, donde A es la cantidad final, P es el capital, r es la tasa de interés expresada como un decimal, n es la cantidad de veces que se capitaliza el interés y t es el tiempo.	If \$100 is put into an account with an interest rate of 5% compounded monthly, then after 2 years, the account will have $100\left(1 + \frac{0.05}{12}\right)^{12 \cdot 2} = \$110.49$.
compound statement Two statements that are connected by the word *and* or *or*.	**enunciado compuesto** Dos enunciados unidos por la palabra *y* u *o*.	The sky is blue and the grass is green. I will drive to school or I will take the bus.
conditional relative frequency The ratio of a joint relative frequency to a related marginal relative frequency in a two-way table.	**frecuencia relativa condicional** Razón de una frecuencia relativa conjunta a una frecuencia relativa marginal en una tabla de doble entrada.	
cone A three-dimensional figure with a circular base and a curved surface that connects the base to a point called the vertex.	**cono** Figura tridimensional con una base circular y una superficie lateral curva que conecta la base con un punto denominado vértice.	
congruent Having the same size and shape, denoted by $\cong$.	**congruente** Que tiene el mismo tamaño y la misma forma, expresado por $\cong$.	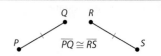
conjugate of an irrational number The conjugate of a number in the form $a + \sqrt{b}$ is $a - \sqrt{b}$.	**conjugado de un número irracional** El conjugado de un número en la forma $a + \sqrt{b}$ es $a - \sqrt{b}$.	The conjugate of $1 + \sqrt{2}$ is $1 - \sqrt{2}$.
consistent system A system of equations or inequalities that has at least one solution.	**sistema consistente** Sistema de ecuaciones o desigualdades que tiene por lo menos una solución.	$\begin{cases} x + y = 6 \\ x - y = 4 \end{cases}$ solution: $(5, 1)$
constant A value that does not change.	**constante** Valor que no cambia.	$3, 0, \pi$
constant of variation The constant k in direct and inverse variation equations.	**constante de variación** La constante k en ecuaciones de variación directa e inversa.	$y = 5x$ ↑ constant of variation

Glossary/Glosario

ENGLISH	SPANISH	EXAMPLES
continuous graph A graph made up of connected lines or curves.	**gráfica continua** Gráfica compuesta por líneas rectas o curvas conectadas.	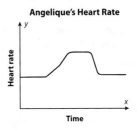
convenience sample A sample based on members of the population that are readily available.	**muestra de conveniencia** Una muestra basada en miembros de la población que están fácilmente disponibles.	A reporter surveys people he personally knows.
conversion factor The ratio of two equal quantities, each measured in different units.	**factor de conversión** Razón entre dos cantidades iguales, cada una medida en unidades diferentes.	$\dfrac{12 \text{ inches}}{1 \text{ foot}}$
coordinate plane A plane that is divided into four regions by a horizontal line called the *x*-axis and a vertical line called the *y*-axis.	**plano cartesiano** Plano dividido en cuatro regiones por una línea horizontal denominada eje *x* y una línea vertical denominada eje *y*.	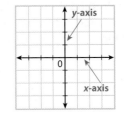
correlation A measure of the strength and direction of the relationship between two variables or data sets.	**correlación** Medida de la fuerza y dirección de la relación entre dos variables o conjuntos de datos.	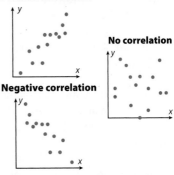
correlation coefficient A number *r*, where $-1 \le r \le 1$, that describes how closely the points in a scatter plot cluster around the least-squares line.	**coeficiente de correlación** Número *r*, donde $-1 \le r \le 1$, que describe a qué distancia de la recta de mínimos cuadrados se agrupan los puntos de un diagrama de dispersión.	An *r*-value close to 1 describes a strong positive correlation. An *r*-value close to 0 describes a weak correlation or no correlation. An *r*-value close to −1 describes a strong negative correlation.
corresponding angles of polygons Angles in the same relative position in polygons with an equal number of angles.	**ángulos correspondientes de los polígonos** Ángulos que se ubican en la misma posición relativa en polígonos que tienen el mismo número de ángulos.	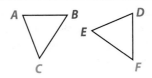 $\angle A$ and $\angle D$ are corresponding angles.

ENGLISH	SPANISH	EXAMPLES

corresponding sides of polygons Sides in the same relative position in polygons with an equal number of sides.

lados correspondientes de los polígonos Lados que se ubican en la misma posición relativa en polígonos que tienen el mismo número de lados.

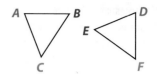

$\overline{AB}$ and $\overline{DE}$ are corresponding sides.

---

cosine In a right triangle, the cosine of angle A is the ratio of the length of the leg adjacent to angle A to the length of the hypotenuse.

coseno En un triángulo rectángulo, el coseno del ángulo A es la razón entre la longitud del cateto adyacente al ángulo A y la longitud de la hipotenusa.

$\cos A = \dfrac{\text{adjacent}}{\text{hypotenuse}}$

---

cross products In the statement $\frac{a}{b} = \frac{c}{d}$, bc and ad are the cross products.

productos cruzados En el enunciado $\frac{a}{b} = \frac{c}{d}$, bc y ad son productos cruzados.

$\frac{1}{2} = \frac{3}{6}$

Cross products: $2 \cdot 3 = 6$ and $1 \cdot 6 = 6$

Cross Product Property For any real numbers a, b, c, and d, where $b \neq 0$ and $d \neq 0$, if $\frac{a}{b} = \frac{c}{d}$, then $ad = bc$.

Propiedad de productos cruzados Dados los números reales a, b, c y d, donde $b \neq 0$ y $d \neq 0$, si $\frac{a}{b} = \frac{c}{d}$, entonces $ad = bc$.

If $\frac{4}{6} = \frac{10}{x}$, then $4x = 60$, so $x = 15$.

---

cube A prism with six square faces.

cubo Prisma con seis caras cuadradas.

---

cube in numeration The third power of a number.

cubo en numeración Tercera potencia de un número.

8 is the cube of 2.

---

cube root A number, written as $\sqrt[3]{x}$, whose cube is x.

raíz cúbica Número, expresado como $\sqrt[3]{x}$, cuyo cubo es x.

$\sqrt[3]{64} = 4$, because $4^3 = 64$; 4 is the cube root of 64.

---

cubic equation An equation that can be written in the form $ax^3 + bx^2 + cx + d = 0$, where a, b, c, and d are real numbers and $a \neq 0$.

ecuación cúbica Ecuación que se puede expresar como $ax^3 + bx^2 + cx + d = 0$, donde a, b, c, y d son números reales y $a \neq 0$.

$4x^3 + x^2 - 3x - 1 = 0$

---

cubic function A function that can be written in the form $f(x) = ax^3 + bx^2 + cx + d$, where a, b, c, and d are real numbers and $a \neq 0$.

función cúbica Función que se puede expresar como $f(x) = ax^3 + bx^2 + cx + d$, donde a, b, c, y d son números reales y $a \neq 0$.

$f(x) = x^3 + 2x^2 - 6x + 8$

---

cubic polynomial A polynomial of degree 3.

polinomio cúbico Polinomio de grado 3.

$x^3 + 4x^2 - 6x + 2$

---

cumulative frequency The frequency of all data values that are less than or equal to a given value.

frecuencia acumulativa Frecuencia de todos los valores de los datos que son menores que o iguales a un valor dado.

For the data set 2, 2, 3, 5, 5, 6, 7, 7, 8, 8, 8, 9, the cumulative frequency table is shown below.

Data	Frequency	Cumulative Frequency
2	2	2
3	1	3
5	2	5
6	1	6
7	2	8
8	3	11
9	1	12

Glossary/Glosario

ENGLISH	SPANISH	EXAMPLES

cylinder A three-dimensional figure with two parallel congruent circular bases and a curved surface that connects the bases.

cilindro Figura tridimensional con dos bases circulares congruentes paralelas y una superficie lateral curva que conecta las bases.

data Information gathered from a survey or experiment.

datos Información reunida en una encuesta o experimento.

---

degree measure of an angle A unit of angle measure; one degree is $\frac{1}{360}$ of a circle.

medida en grados de un ángulo Unidad de medida de los ángulos; un grado es $\frac{1}{360}$ de un círculo.

---

degree of a monomial The sum of the exponents of the variables in the monomial.

grado de un monomio Suma de los exponentes de las variables del monomio.

$4x^2y^5z^3$ Degree: $2 + 5 + 3 = 10$
$5 = 5x^0$ Degree: 0

---

degree of a polynomial The degree of the term of the polynomial with the greatest degree.

grado de un polinomio Grado del término del polinomio con el grado máximo.

$$3x^2y^2 \quad + \quad 4xy^5 \quad - \quad 12x^3y^2$$
Degree 4   Degree 6   Degree 5
Degree 6

---

dependent events Events for which the occurrence or nonoccurrence of one event affects the probability of the other event.

sucesos dependientes Dos sucesos son dependientes si el hecho de que uno de ellos ocurra o no afecta la probabilidad del otro suceso.

From a bag containing 3 red marbles and 2 blue marbles, draw a red marble, and then draw a blue marble without replacing the first marble.

---

dependent system A system of equations that has infinitely many solutions.

sistema dependiente Sistema de ecuaciones que tiene infinitamente muchas soluciones.

$$\begin{cases} x + y = 2 \\ 2x + 2y = 4 \end{cases}$$

---

dependent variable The output of a function; a variable whose value depends on the value of the input, or independent variable.

variable dependiente Salida de una función; variable cuyo valor depende del valor de la entrada, o variable independiente.

For $y = 2x + 1$, y is the dependent variable.
input: x output: y

---

diameter A segment that has endpoints on the circle and that passes through the center of the circle; also the length of that segment.

diámetro Segmento que atraviesa el centro de un círculo y cuyos extremos están sobre la circunferencia; longitud de dicho segmento.

---

difference of two cubes A polynomial of the form $a^3 - b^3$, which may be written as the product $(a - b)(a^2 + ab + b^2)$.

diferencia de dos cubos Polinomio del tipo $a^3 - b^3$, que se puede expresar como el producto $(a - b)(a^2 + ab + b^2)$.

$x^3 - 8 = (x - 2)(x^2 + 2x + 4)$

---

difference of two squares A polynomial of the form $a^2 - b^2$, which may be written as the product $(a + b)(a - b)$.

diferencia de dos cuadrados Polinomio del tipo $a^2 - b^2$, que se puede expresar como el producto $(a + b)(a - b)$.

$x^2 - 4 = (x + 2)(x - 2)$

ENGLISH	SPANISH	EXAMPLES
dimensional analysis A process that uses rates to convert measurements from one unit to another.	**análisis dimensional** Un proceso que utiliza tasas para convertir medidas de unidad a otra.	$12 \text{ pt} \cdot \frac{1 \text{ qt}}{2 \text{ pt}} = 6 \text{ qt}$
direct variation A linear relationship between two variables, x and y, that can be written in the form $y = kx$, where k is a nonzero constant.	**variación directa** Relación lineal entre dos variables, x e y, que puede expresarse en la forma $y = kx$, donde k es una constante distinta de cero.	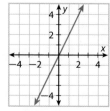 $y = 2x$
discontinuous function A function whose graph has one or more jumps, breaks, or holes.	**función discontinua** Función cuya gráfica tiene uno o más saltos, interrupciones u hoyos.	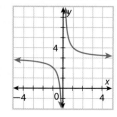
discount An amount by which an original price is reduced.	**descuento** Cantidad por la que se reduce un precio original.	
discrete graph A graph made up of unconnected points.	**gráfica discreta** Gráfica compuesta de puntos no conectados.	**Theme Park Attendance** 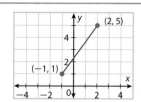
discriminant The discriminant of the quadratic equation $ax^2 + bx + c = 0$ is $b^2 - 4ac$.	**discriminante** El discriminante de la ecuación cuadrática $ax^2 + bx + c = 0$ es $b^2 - 4ac$.	The discriminant of $2x^2 - 5x - 3 = 0$ is $(-5)^2 - 4(2)(-3)$ or 49.
Distance Formula In a coordinate plane, the distance from (x_1, y_1) to (x_2, y_2) is $d = \sqrt{(x_2 - x_1)^2 + (y_2 - y_1)^2}$.	**Fórmula de distancia** En un plano cartesiano, la distancia desde (x_1, y_1) hasta (x_2, y_2) es $d = \sqrt{(x_2 - x_1)^2 + (y_2 - y_1)^2}$.	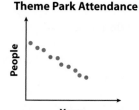 The distance from $(2, 5)$ to $(-1, 1)$ is $d = \sqrt{(-1 - 2)^2 + (1 - 5)^2}$ $= \sqrt{(-3)^2 + (-4)^2}$ $= \sqrt{9 + 16} = \sqrt{25} = 5.$
Distributive Property For all real numbers a, b, and c, $a(b + c) = ab + ac$, and $(b + c)a = ba + ca$.	**Propiedad distributiva** Dados los números reales a, b y c, $a(b + c) = ab + ac$, y $(b + c)a = ba + ca$.	$3(4 + 5) = 3 \cdot 4 + 3 \cdot 5$ $(4 + 5)3 = 4 \cdot 3 + 5 \cdot 3$
Division Property of Equality For real numbers a, b, and c, where $c \neq 0$, if $a = b$, then $\frac{a}{c} = \frac{b}{c}$.	**Propiedad de igualdad de la división** Dados los números reales a, b y c, donde $c \neq 0$, si $a = b$, entonces $\frac{a}{c} = \frac{b}{c}$.	$4x = 12$ $\frac{4x}{4} = \frac{12}{4}$ $x = 3$

Glossary/Glosario

ENGLISH	SPANISH	EXAMPLES
Division Property of Inequality If both sides of an inequality are divided by the same positive quantity, the new inequality will have the same solution set. If both sides of an inequality are divided by the same negative quantity, the new inequality will have the same solution set if the inequality symbol is reversed.	**Propiedad de desigualdad de la división** Cuando ambos lados de una desigualdad se dividen entre el mismo número positivo, la nueva desigualdad tiene el mismo conjunto solución. Cuando ambos lados de una desigualdad se dividen entra el mismo número negativo, la nueva desigualdad tiene el mismo conjunto solución si se invierte el símbolo de desigualdad.	$4x \geq 12$ $\dfrac{4x}{4} \geq \dfrac{12}{4}$ $x \geq 3$ $-4x \geq 12$ $\dfrac{-4x}{-4} \leq \dfrac{12}{-4}$ $x \leq -3$
domain The set of all first coordinates (or x-values) of a relation or function.	**dominio** Conjunto de todos los valores de la primera coordenada (o valores de x) de una función o relación.	The domain of the function $\{(-5, 3), (-3, -2), (-1, -1), (1, 0)\}$ is $\{-5, -3, -1, 1\}$.
dot plot See *line plot*.	**diagrama de puntos** Ver *diagrama de acumulación*.	

element Each member in a set or matrix. *See also* entry.	**elemento** Cada miembro en un conjunto o matriz. *Ver también* entrada.	
elimination method A method used to solve systems of equations in which one variable is eliminated by adding or subtracting two equations of the system.	**eliminación** Método utilizado para resolver sistemas de ecuaciones por el cual se elimina una variable sumando o restando dos ecuaciones del sistema.	
empty set A set with no elements.	**conjunto vacío** Conjunto sin elementos.	The solution set of $|x| < 0$ is the empty set, $\{ \}$, or $\varnothing$.
end behavior The trends in the y-values of a function as the x-values approach positive and negative infinity.	**comportamiento extremo** Tendencia de los valores de y de una función a medida que los valores de x se aproximan al infinito positivo y negativo.	
entry Each value in a matrix; also called an element.	**entrada** Cada valor de una matriz, también denominado elemento.	3 is the entry in the first row and second column of $A = \begin{bmatrix} 2 & 3 \\ 0 & 1 \end{bmatrix}$, denoted a_{12}.
equally likely outcomes Outcomes are equally likely if they have the same probability of occurring. If an experiment has n equally likely outcomes, then the probability of each outcome is $\frac{1}{n}$.	**resultados igualmente probables** Los resultados son igualmente probables si tienen la misma probabilidad de ocurrir. Si un experimento tiene n resultados igualmente probables, entonces la probabilidad de cada resultado es $\frac{1}{n}$.	If a fair coin is tossed, then $P(\text{heads}) = P(\text{tails}) = \frac{1}{2}$. So the outcome "heads" and the outcome "tails" are equally likely.
equation A mathematical statement that two expressions are equivalent.	**ecuación** Enunciado matemático que indica que dos expresiones son equivalentes.	$x + 4 = 7$ $2 + 3 = 6 - 1$ $(x - 1)^2 + (y + 2)^2 = 4$

ENGLISH	SPANISH	EXAMPLES
equilateral triangle A triangle with three congruent sides.	**triángulo equilátero** Triángulo con tres lados congruentes.	
equivalent ratios Ratios that name the same comparison.	**razones equivalentes** Razones que expresan la misma comparación.	$\frac{1}{2}$ and $\frac{2}{4}$ are equivalent ratios.
evaluate To find the value of an algebraic expression by substituting a number for each variable and simplifying by using the order of operations.	**evaluar** Calcular el valor de una expresión algebraica sustituyendo cada variable por un número y simplificando mediante el orden de las operaciones.	Evaluate $2x + 7$ for $x = 3$. $2x + 7$ $2(3) + 7$ $6 + 7$ 13
event An outcome or set of outcomes of an experiment.	**suceso** Resultado o conjunto de resultados en un experimento.	In the experiment of rolling a number cube, the event "an odd number" consists of the outcomes 1, 3, and 5.
excluded values Values of x for which a function or expression is not defined.	**valores excluidos** Valores de x para los cuales no está definida una función o expresión.	The excluded values of $\frac{(x+2)}{(x-1)(x+4)}$ are $x = 1$ and $x = -4$, which would make the denominator equal to 0.
experiment An operation, process, or activity in which outcomes can be used to estimate probability.	**experimento** Una operación, proceso o actividad en la que se usan los resultados para estimar una probabilidad.	Tossing a coin 10 times and noting the number of heads
experimental probability The ratio of the number of times an event occurs to the number of trials, or times, that an activity is performed.	**probabilidad experimental** Razón entre la cantidad de veces que ocurre un suceso y la cantidad de pruebas, o veces, que se realiza una actividad.	Kendra attempted 27 free throws and made 16 of them. The experimental probability that she will make her next free throw is $P(\text{free throw}) = \frac{\text{number made}}{\text{number attempted}} = \frac{16}{27} \approx 0.59$.
explicit rule for nth term of a sequence A rule that defines the nth term a_n, or a general term, of a sequence as a function of n.	**fórmula explícita** Fórmula que define el enésimo término a_n, o término general, de una sucesión como una función de n.	
exponent The number that indicates how many times the base in a power is used as a factor.	**exponente** Número que indica la cantidad de veces que la base de una potencia se utiliza como factor.	$3^4 = 3 \cdot 3 \cdot 3 \cdot 3 = 81$ 4 is the exponent.
exponential decay An exponential function of the form $f(x) = ab^x$ in which $0 < b < 1$. If r is the rate of decay, then the function can be written $y = a(1 - r)^t$, where a is the initial amount and t is the time.	**decremento exponencial** Función exponencial del tipo $f(x) = ab^x$ en la cual $0 < b < 1$. Si r es la tasa decremental, entonces la función se puede expresar como $y = a(1 - r)^t$, donde a es la cantidad inicial y t es el tiempo.	$f(x) = 3\left(\frac{1}{2}\right)^x$ 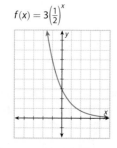
exponential expression An algebraic expression in which the variable is in an exponent with a fixed number as the base.	**expresión exponencial** Expresión algebraica en la que la variable está en un exponente y que tiene un número fijo como base.	2^{x+1}

ENGLISH	SPANISH	EXAMPLES

exponential function A function of the form $f(x) = ab^x$, where a and b are real numbers with $a \neq 0$, $b > 0$, and $b \neq 1$.

función exponencial Función del tipo $f(x) = ab^x$, donde a y b son números reales con $a \neq 0$, $b > 0$ y $b \neq 1$.

$f(x) = 3 \cdot 4^x$

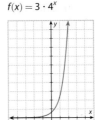

---

exponential growth An exponential function of the form $f(x) = ab^x$ in which $b > 1$. If r is the rate of growth, then the function can be written $y = a(1 + r)^t$, where a is the initial amount and t is the time.

crecimiento exponencial Función exponencial del tipo $f(x) = ab^x$ en la que $b > 1$. Si r es la tasa de crecimiento, entonces la función se puede expresar como $y = a(1 + r)^t$, donde a es la cantidad inicial y t es el tiempo.

$f(x) = 2^x$

---

expression A mathematical phrase that contains operations, numbers, and/or variables.

expresión Frase matemática que contiene operaciones, números y/o variables.

$6x + 1$

---

extraneous solution A solution of a derived equation that is not a solution of the original equation.

solución extraña Solución de una ecuación derivada que no es una solución de la ecuación original.

To solve $\sqrt{x} = -2$, square both sides; $x = 4$.
Check $\sqrt{4} = -2$ is false; so 4 is an extraneous solution.

---

factor A number or expression that is multiplied by another number or expression to get a product. *See also factoring.*

factor Número o expresión que se multiplica por otro número o expresión para obtener un producto. *Ver también factoreo.*

$12 = 3 \cdot 4$
3 and 4 are factors of 12.
$x^2 - 1 = (x - 1)(x + 1)$
$(x - 1)$ and $(x + 1)$ are factors of $x^2 - 1$.

---

factorial If n is a positive integer, then n factorial, written $n!$, is $n \cdot (n - 1) \cdot (n - 2) \cdot \ldots \cdot 2 \cdot 1$. The factorial of 0 is defined to be 1.

factorial Si n es un entero positivo, entonces el factorial de n, expresado como $n!$, es $n \cdot (n - 1) \cdot (n - 2) \cdot \ldots \cdot 2 \cdot 1$. Por definición, el factorial de 0 será 1.

$7! = 7 \cdot 6 \cdot 5 \cdot 4 \cdot 3 \cdot 2 \cdot 1 = 5040$

---

factoring The process of writing a number or algebraic expression as a product.

factorización Proceso por el que se expresa un número o expresión algebraica como un producto.

$x^2 - 4x - 21 = (x - 7)(x + 3)$

---

fair When all outcomes of an experiment are equally likely.

justo Cuando todos los resultados de un experimento son igualmente probables.

When tossing a fair coin, heads and tails are equally likely. Each has a probability of $\frac{1}{2}$.

---

family of functions A set of functions whose graphs have basic characteristics in common. Functions in the same family are transformations of their parent function.

familia de funciones Conjunto de funciones cuyas gráficas tienen características básicas en común. Las funciones de la misma familia son transformaciones de su función madre.

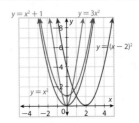

ENGLISH	SPANISH	EXAMPLES

first differences The differences between y-values of a function for evenly spaced x-values. | **primeras diferencias** Diferencias entre los valores de y de una función para valores de x espaciados uniformemente. |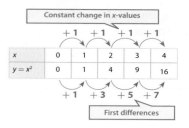

first quartile The median of the lower half of a data set, denoted Q_1. Also called *lower quartile*. | **primer cuartil** Mediana de la mitad inferior de un conjunto de datos, expresada como Q_1. También se llama *cuartil inferior*. | Lower half Upper half
18, (23), 28, 29, 36, 42
First quartile

FOIL A mnemonic (memory) device for a method of multiplying two binomials:
Multiply the **First** terms.
Multiply the **Outer** terms.
Multiply the **Inner** terms.
Multiply the **Last** terms. | **FOIL** Regla mnemotécnica para recordar el método de multiplicación de dos binomios:
Multiplicar los términos **Primeros** (*First*).
Multiplicar los términos **Externos** (*Outer*).
Multiplicar los términos **Internos** (*Inner*).
Multiplicar los términos **Últimos** (*Last*). |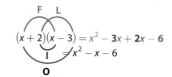

formula A literal equation that states a rule for a relationship among quantities. | **fórmula** Ecuación literal que establece una regla para una relación entre cantidades. | $A = \pi r^2$

fractional exponent *See* rational exponent. | **exponente fraccionario** *Ver* exponente racional. |

frequency The number of times the value appears in the data set. | **frecuencia** Cantidad de veces que aparece el valor en un conjunto de datos. | In the data set 5, 6, 6, 7, 8, 9, the data value 6 has a frequency of 2.

frequency table A table that lists the number of times, or frequency, that each data value occurs. | **tabla de frecuencia** Tabla que enumera la cantidad de veces que ocurre cada valor de datos, o la frecuencia. | Data set: 1, 1, 2, 2, 3, 4, 5, 5, 5, 6, 6, 6, 6
Frequency table:

| Data | Frequency |
|---|---|
| 1 | 2 |
| 2 | 2 |
| 3 | 1 |
| 4 | 1 |
| 5 | 3 |
| 6 | 4 |

function A relation in which every domain value is paired with exactly one range value. | **función** Relación en la que a cada valor de dominio corresponde exactamente un valor de rango. |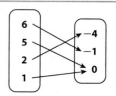

function notation If x is the independent variable and y is the dependent variable, then the function notation for y is $f(x)$, read "f of x," where f names the function. | **notación de función** Si x es la variable independiente e y es la variable dependiente, entonces la notación de función para y es $f(x)$, que se lee "f de x," donde f nombra la función. | equation: $y = 2x$
function notation: $f(x) = 2x$

ENGLISH	SPANISH	EXAMPLES
function rule An algebraic expression that defines a function.	**regla de función** Expresión algebraica que define una función.	$f(x) = 2x^2 + 3x - 7$ function rule
Fundamental Counting Principle If one event has *m* possible outcomes and a second event has *n* possible outcomes after the first event has occurred, then there are *mn* total possible outcomes for the two events.	**Principio fundamental de conteo** Si un suceso tiene *m* resultados posibles y otro suceso tiene *n* resultados posibles después de ocurrido el primer suceso, entonces hay *mn* resultados posibles en total para los dos sucesos.	If there are 4 colors of shirts, 3 colors of pants, and 2 colors of shoes, then there are $4 \cdot 3 \cdot 2 = 24$ possible outfits.

geometric sequence A sequence in which the ratio of successive terms is a constant *r*, called the common ratio, where $r \neq 0$ and $r \neq 1$.	**sucesión geométrica** Sucesión en la que la razón de los términos sucesivos es una constante *r*, denominada razón común, donde $r \neq 0$ y $r \neq 1$.	1, 2, 4, 8, 16, … $\cdot 2 \ \cdot 2 \ \cdot 2 \ \cdot 2 \quad r = 2$
graph of a function The set of points in a coordinate plane with coordinates (x, y), where *x* is in the domain of the function *f* and $y = fx)$.	**gráfica de una función** Conjunto de los puntos de un plano cartesiano con coordenadas (x, y), donde *x* está en el dominio de la función *f* e $y = f(x)$.	
graph of a system of linear inequalities The region in a coordinate plane consisting of points whose coordinates are solutions to all of the inequalities in the system.	**gráfica de un sistema de desigualdades lineales** Región de un plano cartesiano que consta de puntos cuyas coordenadas son soluciones de todas las desigualdades del sistema.	(2, 1) is in the overlapping shaded regions, so it is a solution.
graph of an inequality in one variable The set of points on a number line that are solutions of the inequality.	**gráfica de una desigualdad en una variable** Conjunto de los puntos de una recta numérica que representan soluciones de la desigualdad.	 $x \geq 2$
graph of an inequality in two variables The set of points in a coordinate plane whose coordinates (x, y) are solutions of the inequality.	**gráfica de una desigualdad en dos variables** Conjunto de los puntos de un plano cartesiano cuyas coordenadas (x, y) son soluciones de la desigualdad.	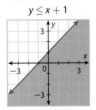 $y \leq x + 1$
graph of an ordered pair For the ordered pair (x, y), the point in a coordinate plane that is a horizontal distance of *x* units from the origin and a vertical distance of *y* units from the origin.	**gráfica de un par ordenado** Dado el par ordenado (x, y), punto en un plano cartesiano que está a una distancia horizontal de *x* unidades desde el origen y a una distancia vertical de *y* unidades desde el origen.	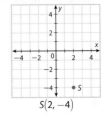 $S(2, -4)$

ENGLISH	SPANISH	EXAMPLES
greatest common factor (monomials) (GCF) The product of the greatest integer and the greatest power of each variable that divide evenly into each monomial.	**máximo común divisor (monomios) (MCD)** Producto del entero mayor y la potencia mayor de cada variable que divide exactamente cada monomio.	The GCF of $4x^3y$ and $6x^2y$ is $2x^2y$.
greatest common factor (numbers) (GCF) The largest common factor of two or more given numbers.	**máximo común divisor (números) (MCD)** El mayor de los factores comunes compartidos por dos o más números dados.	The GCF of 27 and 45 is 9.
greatest integer function A function denoted by $f(x) = [x]$ in which the number x is rounded down to the greatest integer that is less than or equal to x.	**función de entero mayor** Función expresada como $f(x) = [x]$ en la cual el número x se redondea hacia abajo hasta el entero mayor que sea menor o igual a x.	
grouping symbols Symbols such as parentheses ( ), brackets [ ], and braces { } that separate part of an expression. A fraction bar, absolute-value symbols, and radical symbols may also be used as grouping symbols.	**símbolos de agrupación** Símbolos tales como paréntesis ( ), corchetes [ ] y llaves { } que separan parte de una expresión. La barra de fracciones, los símbolos de valor absoluto y los símbolos de radical también se pueden utilizar como símbolos de agrupación.	$6 + \{3 - [(4 - 3) + 2] + 1\} - 5$ $6 + \{3 - [1 + 2] + 1\} - 5$ $6 + \{3 - 3 + 1\} - 5$ $6 + 1 - 5$ 2

H

ENGLISH	SPANISH	EXAMPLES
half-life The half-life of a substance is the time it takes for one-half of the substance to decay into another substance.	**vida media** La vida media de una sustancia es el tiempo que tarda la mitad de la sustancia en desintegrarse y transformarse en otra sustancia.	Carbon-14 has a half-life of 5730 years, so 5 g of an initial amount of 10 g will remain after 5730 years.
half-plane The part of the coordinate plane on one side of a line, which may include the line.	**semiplano** La parte del plano cartesiano de un lado de una línea, que puede incluir la línea.	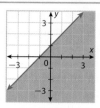
Heron's Formula A triangle with side lengths a, b, and c has area $A = \sqrt{s(s-a)(s-b)(s-c)}$, where s is one-half the perimeter, or $s = \frac{1}{2}(a+b+c)$.	**fórmula de Herón** Un triángulo con longitudes de lado a, b y c tiene un área $A = \sqrt{s(s-a)(s-b)(s-c)}$, donde s es la mitad del perímetro ó $s = \frac{1}{2}(a+b+c)$.	

Glossary/Glosario

ENGLISH	SPANISH	EXAMPLES
histogram A bar graph used to display data grouped in intervals.	**histograma** Gráfica de barras utilizada para mostrar datos agrupados en intervalos de clases.	
horizontal line A line described by the equation $y = b$, where b is the y-intercept.	**línea horizontal** Línea descrita por la ecuación $y = b$, donde b es la intersección con el eje y.	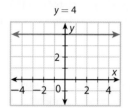
hypotenuse The side opposite the right angle in a right triangle.	**hipotenusa** Lado opuesto al ángulo recto de un triángulo rectángulo.	

identity An equation that is true for all values of the variables.	**identidad** Ecuación verdadera para todos los valores de las variables.	$3 = 3$ $2(x - 1) = 2x - 2$
inclusive events Events that have one or more outcomes in common.	**sucesos inclusivos** Sucesos que tienen uno o más resultados en común.	In the experiment of rolling a number cube, rolling an even number and rolling a number less than 3 are inclusive events because both contain the outcome 2.
inconsistent system A system of equations or inequalities that has no solution.	**sistema inconsistente** Sistema de ecuaciones o desigualdades que no tiene solución.	$\begin{cases} x + y = 0 \\ x + y = 1 \end{cases}$
independent events Events for which the occurrence or nonoccurrence of one event does not affect the probability of the other event.	**sucesos independientes** Dos sucesos son independientes si el hecho de que se produzca o no uno de ellos no afecta la probabilidad del otro suceso.	From a bag containing 3 red marbles and 2 blue marbles, draw a red marble, replace it, and then draw a blue marble.
independent system A system of equations that has exactly one solution.	**sistema independiente** Sistema de ecuaciones que tiene sólo una solución.	$\begin{cases} x + y = 7 \\ x - y = 1 \end{cases}$ Solution: $(4, 3)$
independent variable The input of a function; a variable whose value determines the value of the output, or dependent variable.	**variable independiente** Entrada de una función; variable cuyo valor determina el valor de la salida, o variable dependiente.	For $y = 2x + 1$, x is the independent variable.

Glossary/Glosario **G17**

ENGLISH	SPANISH	EXAMPLES
index In the radical $\sqrt[n]{x}$, which represents the nth root of x, n is the index. In the radical $\sqrt{x}$, the index is understood to be 2.	**índice** En el radical $\sqrt[n]{x}$, que representa la enésima raíz de x, n es el índice. En el radical $\sqrt{x}$, se da por sentado que el índice es 2.	The radical $\sqrt[3]{8}$ has an index of 3.
indirect measurement A method of measurement that uses formulas, similar figures, and/or proportions.	**medición indirecta** Método de medición en el que se usan fórmulas, figuras semejantes y/o proporciones.	
inequality A statement that compares two expressions by using one of the following signs: $<, >, \leq, \geq,$ or $\neq$.	**desigualdad** Enunciado que compara dos expresiones utilizando uno de los siguientes signos: $<, >, \leq, \geq,$ o $\neq$.	$x \geq 2$
input A value that is substituted for the independent variable in a relation or function.	**entrada** Valor que sustituye a la variable independiente en una relación o función.	For the function $f(x) = x + 5$, the input 3 produces an output of 8.
input-output table A table that displays input values of a function or expression together with the corresponding outputs.	**tabla de entrada y salida** Tabla que muestra los valores de entrada de una función o expresión junto con las correspondientes salidas.	Input, Output table: x: 1, 2, 3, 4; y: 4, 7, 10, 13
integer A member of the set of whole numbers and their opposites.	**entero** Miembro del conjunto de números cabales y sus opuestos.	$\ldots, -3, -2, -1, 0, 1, 2, 3, \ldots$
intercept See x-intercept and y-intercept.	**intersección** Ver intersección con el eje x e intersección con el eje y.	
interest The amount of money charged for borrowing money or the amount of money earned when saving or investing money. See also compound interest, simple interest.	**interés** Cantidad de dinero que se cobra por prestar dinero o cantidad de dinero que se gana cuando se ahorra o invierte dinero. Ver también interés compuesto, interés simple.	
interpolation Making a prediction using a value of the independent variable from within a model's domain.	**interpolación** Hacer una predicción con un valor de la variable independiente a partir del dominio de un modelo.	
interquartile range (IQR) The difference of the third (upper) and first (lower) quartiles in a data set, representing the middle half of the data.	**rango entre cuartiles** Diferencia entre el tercer cuartil (superior) y el primer cuartil (inferior) de un conjunto de datos, que representa la mitad central de los datos.	Lower half: 18, (23,) 28, Upper half: 29, (36,) 42. First quartile, Third quartile. Interquartile range: $36 - 23 = 13$
intersection The intersection of two sets is the set of all elements that are common to both sets, denoted by $\cap$.	**intersección de conjuntos** La intersección de dos conjuntos es el conjunto de todos los elementos que son comunes a ambos conjuntos, expresado por $\cap$.	$A = \{1, 2, 3, 4\}$ $B = \{1, 3, 5, 7, 9\}$ $A \cap B = \{1, 3\}$
inverse of a function The relation that results from exchanging the input and output values of a function.	**inverso de una función** La relación que se genera al intercambiar los valores de entrada y de salida de una función.	

ENGLISH	SPANISH	EXAMPLES
inverse operations Operations that undo each other.	**operaciones inversas** Operaciones que se anulan entre sí.	Addition and subtraction of the same quantity are inverse operations: $5 + 3 = 8, 8 - 3 = 5$ Multiplication and division by the same quantity are inverse operations: $2 \cdot 3 = 6, 6 \div 3 = 2$
inverse variation A relationship between two variables, x and y, that can be written in the form $y = \frac{k}{x}$, where k is a nonzero constant and $x \neq 0$.	**variación inversa** Relación entre dos variables, x e y, que puede expresarse en la forma $y = \frac{k}{x}$, donde k es una constante distinta de cero y $x \neq 0$.	$y = \frac{8}{x}$
irrational number A real number that cannot be expressed as the ratio of two integers.	**número irracional** Número real que no se puede expresar como una razón de enteros.	$\sqrt{2}, \pi, e$
isolate the variable To isolate a variable in an equation, use inverse operations on both sides until the variable appears by itself on one side of the equation and does not appear on the other side.	**despejar la variable** Para despejar la variable de una ecuación, utiliza operaciones inversas en ambos lados hasta que la variable aparezca sola en uno de los lados de la ecuación y no aparezca en el otro lado.	$10 = 6 - 2x$ $\underline{-6 \quad -6}$ $4 = \quad -2x$ $\frac{4}{-2} = \frac{-2x}{-2}$ $-2 = x$
isosceles triangle A triangle with at least two congruent sides.	**triángulo isósceles** Triángulo que tiene al menos dos lados congruentes.	

joint relative frequency The ratio of the frequency in a particular category divided by the total number of data values.	**frecuencia relativa conjunta** La línea de ajuste en que la suma de cuadrados de los residuos es la menor.	

leading coefficient The coefficient of the first term of a polynomial in standard form.	**coeficiente principal** Coeficiente del primer término de un polinomio en forma estándar.	$3x^2 + 7x - 2$ Leading coefficient: 3
least common denominator (LCD) The least common multiple of the denominators of two or more given fractions or rational expressions.	**mínimo común denominador (MCD)** Mínimo común múltiplo de los denominadores de dos o más fracciones dadas o expresionnes racionales.	The LCD of $\frac{3}{4}$ and $\frac{5}{6}$ is 12.
least common multiple (monomials) (LCM) The product of the smallest positive number and the lowest power of each variable that divide evenly into each monomial.	**mínimo común múltiplo (monomios) (MCM)** El producto del número positivo más pequeño y la menor potencia de cada variable que divide exactamente cada monomio.	The LCM of $6x^2$ and $4x$ is $12x^2$.

ENGLISH	SPANISH	EXAMPLES
least common multiple (numbers) (LCM) The smallest whole number, other than zero, that is a multiple of two or more given numbers.	**mínimo común múltiplo (números) (MCM)** El menor de los números cabales, distinto de cero, que es múltiplo de dos o más números dados.	The LCM of 10 and 18 is 90.
least-squares regression line The line of fit for which the sum of the squares of the residuals is as small as possible	**línea de regresión de mínimos cuadrados** La línea de ajuste en que la suma de cuadrados de los residuos es la menor.	
like terms Terms with the same variables raised to the same exponents.	**términos semejantes** Términos con las mismas variables elevadas a los mismos exponentes.	
line graph A graph that uses line segments to show how data changes.	**gráfica lineal** Gráfica que se vale de segmentos de recta para mostrar cambios en los datos.	
line of best fit The line that comes closest to all of the points in a data set.	**línea de mejor ajuste** Línea que más se acerca a todos los puntos de un conjunto de datos.	
line of fit *See trend line.*	**línea de ajuste** *Ver línea de tendencia.*	
linear equation in one variable An equation that can be written in the form $ax = b$ where a and b are constants and $a \neq 0$.	**ecuación lineal en una variable** Ecuación que puede expresarse en la forma $ax = b$ donde a y b son constantes y $a \neq 0$.	$x + 1 = 7$
linear equation in two variables An equation that can be written in the form $Ax + By = C$ where A, B, and C are constants and A and B are not both 0.	**ecuación lineal en dos variables** Ecuación que puede expresarse en la forma $Ax + By = C$ donde A, B y C son constantes y A y B no son ambas 0.	$2x + 3y = 6$
linear function A function that can be written in the form $y = mx + b$, where x is the independent variable and m and b are real numbers. Its graph is a line.	**función lineal** Función que puede expresarse en la forma $y = mx + b$, donde x es la variable independiente y m y b son números reales. Su gráfica es una línea.	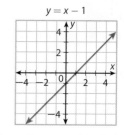
linear inequality in one variable An inequality that can be written in one of the following forms: $ax < b, ax > b, ax \leq b, ax \geq b$, or $ax \neq b$, where a and b are constants and $a \neq 0$.	**desigualdad lineal en una variable** Desigualdad que puede expresarse de una de las siguientes formas: $ax < b$, $ax > b, ax \leq b, ax \geq b$ o $ax \neq b$, donde a y b son constantes y $a \neq 0$.	$3x - 5 \leq 2(x + 4)$

ENGLISH	SPANISH	EXAMPLES

linear inequality in two variables An inequality that can be written in one of the following forms: $Ax + By < C$, $Ax + By > C$, $Ax + By \leq C$, $Ax + By \geq C$, or $Ax + By \neq C$, where A, B, and C are constants and A and B are not both 0.

desigualdad lineal en dos variables Desigualdad que puede expresarse de una de las siguientes formas: $Ax + By < C$, $Ax + By > C$, $Ax + By \leq C$, $Ax + By \geq C$ o $Ax + By \neq C$, donde A, B y C son constantes y A y B no son ambas 0.

$2x + 3y > 6$

---

linear regression A statistical method used to fit a linear model to a given data set.

regresión lineal Método estadístico utilizado para ajustar un modelo lineal a un conjunto de datos determinado.

---

literal equation An equation that contains two or more variables.

ecuación literal Ecuación que contiene dos o más variables.

$d = rt$
$A = \frac{1}{2}h(b_1 + b_2)$

---

lower quartile *See* first quartile.

cuartil inferior *Ver* primer cuartil.

mapping diagram A diagram that shows the relationship of elements in the domain to elements in the range of a relation or function.

diagrama de correspondencia Diagrama que muestra la relación entre los elementos del dominio y los elementos del rango de una función.

Mapping Diagram

---

marginal relative frequency The sum of the joint relative frequencies in a row or column of a two-way table.

frecuencia relativa marginal La suma de las frecuencias relativas conjuntas en una fila o columna de una tabla de doble entrada.

---

markup The amount by which a wholesale cost is increased.

margen de ganancia Cantidad que se agrega a un costo mayorista.

---

matrix A rectangular array of numbers.

matriz Arreglo rectangular de números.

$$\begin{bmatrix} 1 & 0 & 3 \\ -2 & 2 & -5 \\ 7 & -6 & 3 \end{bmatrix}$$

---

maximum value of a function The y-value of the highest point on the graph of the function.

máximo de una función Valor de y del punto más alto en la gráfica de la función.

$(0, 2)$

The maximum of the function is 2.

---

mean The sum of all the values in a data set divided by the number of data values. Also called the *average*.

media Suma de todos los valores de un conjunto de datos dividida entre el número de valores de datos. También llamada *promedio*.

Data set: 4, 6, 7, 8, 10
Mean: $\frac{4 + 6 + 7 + 8 + 10}{5}$
$= \frac{35}{5} = 7$

---

measure of an angle Angles are measured in degrees. A degree is $\frac{1}{360}$ of a complete circle.

medida de un ángulo Los ángulos se miden en grados. Un grado es $\frac{1}{360}$ de un círculo completo.

M $26.8°$

ENGLISH	SPANISH	EXAMPLES
measure of central tendency A measure that describes the center of a data set.	**medida de tendencia dominante** Medida que describe el centro de un conjunto de datos.	mean, median, or mode
median For an ordered data set with an odd number of values, the median is the middle value. For an ordered data set with an even number of values, the median is the average of the two middle values.	**mediana** Dado un conjunto de datos ordenado con un número impar de valores, la mediana es el valor medio. Dado un conjunto de datos con un número par de valores, la mediana es el promedio de los dos valores medios.	8, 9, ⑨, 12, 15 Median: 9 4, 6, ⑦, 10, 10, 12 Median: $\frac{7+10}{2}=8.5$
midpoint The point that divides a segment into two congruent segments.	**punto medio** Punto que divide un segmento en dos segmentos congruentes.	$A \quad\quad B \quad\quad C$ Point B is the midpoint of $\overline{AC}$.
minimum value of a function The y-value of the lowest point on the graph of the function.	**mínimo de una función** Valor de y del punto más bajo en la gráfica de la función.	$(0,-2)$ The minimum of the function is -2.
mode The value or values that occur most frequently in a data set; if all values occur with the same frequency, the data set is said to have no mode.	**moda** El valor o los valores que se presentan con mayor frecuencia en un conjunto de datos. Si todos los valores se presentan con la misma frecuencia, se dice que el conjunto de datos no tiene moda.	Data set: 3, 6, 8, 8, 10 Mode: 8 Data set: 2, 5, 5, 7, 7 Modes: 5 and 7 Data set: 2, 3, 6, 9, 11 No mode
monomial A number or a product of numbers and variables with whole-number exponents, or a polynomial with one term.	**monomio** Número o producto de números y variables con exponentes de números cabales, o polinomio con un término.	$3x^2y^4$
Multiplication Property of Equality If a, b, and c are real numbers and $a = b$, then $ac = bc$.	**Propiedad de igualdad de la multiplicación** Si a, b y c son números reales y $a = b$, entonces $ac = bc$.	$\frac{1}{3}x = 7$ $(3)\left(\frac{1}{3}x\right) = (3)(7)$ $x = 21$
Multiplication Property of Inequality If both sides of an inequality are multiplied by the same positive quantity, the new inequality will have the same solution set. If both sides of an inequality are multiplied by the same negative quantity, the new inequality will have the same solution set if the inequality symbol is reversed.	**Propiedad de desigualdad de la multiplicación** Si ambos lados de una desigualdad se multiplican por el mismo número positivo, la nueva desigualdad tendrá el mismo conjunto solución. Si ambos lados de una desigualdad se multiplican por el mismo número negativo, la nueva desigualdad tendrá el mismo conjunto solución si se invierte el símbolo de desigualdad.	$\frac{1}{3}x > 7$ $(3)\left(\frac{1}{3}x\right) > (3)(7)$ $x > 21$ $-x \leq 2$ $(-1)(-x) \geq (-1)(2)$ $x \geq -2$
multiplicative inverse The reciprocal of the number.	**inverso multiplicativo** Recíproco de un número.	The multiplicative inverse of 5 is $\frac{1}{5}$.

ENGLISH	SPANISH	EXAMPLES
mutually exclusive events Two events are mutually exclusive if they cannot both occur in the same trial of an experiment.	**sucesos mutuamente excluyentes** Dos sucesos son mutuamente excluyentes si ambos no pueden ocurrir en la misma prueba de un experimento.	In the experiment of rolling a number cube, rolling a 3 and rolling an even number are mutually exclusive events.

natural number A counting number.	**número natural** Número que se utiliza para contar.	1, 2, 3, 4, 5, 6, …
negative correlation Two data sets have a negative correlation if one set of data values increases as the other set decreases.	**correlación negativa** Dos conjuntos de datos tienen una correlación negativa si un conjunto de valores de datos aumenta a medida que el otro conjunto disminuye.	
negative exponent For any nonzero real number x and any integer n, $x^{-n} = \frac{1}{x^n}$.	**exponente negativo** Para cualquier número real distinto de cero x y cualquier entero n, $x^{-n} = \frac{1}{x^n}$.	$x^{-2} = \frac{1}{x^2}$; $3^{-2} = \frac{1}{3^2}$
negative number A number that is less than zero. Negative numbers lie to the left of zero on a number line.	**número negativo** Número menor que cero. Los números negativos se ubican a la izquierda del cero en una recta numérica.	−2 is a negative number. 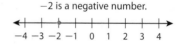
net A diagram of the faces of a three-dimensional figure arranged in such a way that the diagram can be folded to form the three-dimensional figure.	**plantilla** Diagrama de las caras de una figura tridimensional que se puede plegar para formar la figura tridimensional.	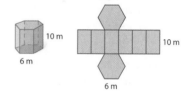
no correlation Two data sets have no correlation if there is no relationship between the sets of values.	**sin correlación** Dos conjuntos de datos no tienen correlación si no existe una relación entre los conjuntos de valores.	
nonlinear system of equations A system in which at least one of the equations is not linear.	**sistema no lineal de ecuaciones** Sistema en el cual por lo menos una de las ecuaciones no es lineal.	A system that contains one quadratic equation and one linear equation is a nonlinear system.
normal curve The graph of a probability density function that corresponds to a normal distribution; bell-shaped and symmetric about the mean, with the x-axis as a horizontal asymptote.	**curva normal** La gráfica de una función de densidad de probabilidad que corresponde a la distribución normal; con forma de campana y simétrica con relación a la media, el eje x es una asíntota horizontal.	

Glossary/Glosario

normal distribution A distribution of data that varies about the mean in such a way that the graph of its probability density function is a normal curve.

distribución normal Distribución de datos que varía respecto de la media de tal manera que la gráfica de su función de densidad de probabilidad es una curva normal.

nth root The nth root of a number a, written as $\sqrt[n]{a}$ or $a^{\frac{1}{n}}$, is a number that is equal to a when it is raised to the nth power.

enésima raíz La enésima raíz de un número a, que se escribe $\sqrt[n]{a}$ o $a^{\frac{1}{n}}$, es un número igual a a cuando se eleva a la enésima potencia.

$\sqrt[5]{32} = 2$, because $2^5 = 32$.

number line A line used to represent the real numbers.

recta numérica Línea utilizada para representar los números reales.

numerical expression An expression that contains only numbers and operations.

expresión numérica Expresión que contiene únicamente números y operaciones.

O

obtuse angle An angle that measures greater than 90° and less than 180°.

ángulo obtuso Ángulo que mide más de 90° y menos de 180°.

obtuse triangle A triangle with one obtuse angle.

triángulo obtusángulo Triángulo con un ángulo obtuso.

odds A comparison of favorable and unfavorable outcomes. The odds in favor of an event are the ratio of the number of favorable outcomes to the number of unfavorable outcomes. The odds against an event are the ratio of the number of unfavorable outcomes to the number of favorable outcomes.

probabilidades a favor y en contra Comparación de los resultados favorables y desfavorables. Las probabilidades a favor de un suceso son la razón entre la cantidad de resultados favorables y la cantidad de resultados desfavorables. Las probabilidades en contra de un suceso son la razón entre la cantidad de resultados desfavorables y la cantidad de resultados favorables.

The odds in favor of rolling a 3 on a number cube are 1:5.
The odds against rolling a 3 on a number cube are 5:1.

opposite The opposite of a number a, denoted $-a$, is the number that is the same distance from zero as a, on the opposite side of the number line. The sum of opposites is 0.

opuesto El opuesto de un número a, expresado $-a$, es el número que se encuentra a la misma distancia de cero que a, del lado opuesto de la recta numérica. La suma de los opuestos es 0.

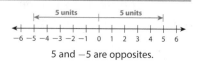
5 and -5 are opposites.

opposite reciprocal The opposite of the reciprocal of a number. The opposite reciprocal of any nonzero number a is $-\frac{1}{a}$.

recíproco opuesto Opuesto del recíproco de un número. El recíproco opuesto de a es $-\frac{1}{a}$.

The opposite reciprocal of $\frac{2}{3}$ is $-\frac{3}{2}$.

ENGLISH	SPANISH	EXAMPLES
OR A logical operator representing the union of two sets.	**O** Operador lógico que representa la unión de dos conjuntos.	$A = \{2, 3, 4, 5\}$ $B = \{1, 3, 5, 7\}$ The set of values that are in A OR B is $A \cup B = \{1, 2, 3, 4, 5, 7\}$.

order of operations A process for evaluating expressions:
First, perform operations in parentheses or other grouping symbols.
Second, simplify powers and roots.
Third, perform all multiplication and division from left to right.
Fourth, perform all addition and subtraction from left to right.

orden de las operaciones Regla para evaluar las expresiones:
Primero, realizar las operaciones entre paréntesis u otros símbolos de agrupación.
Segundo, simplificar las potencias y las raíces.
Tercero, realizar todas las multiplicaciones y divisiones de izquierda a derecha.
Cuarto, realizar todas las sumas y restas de izquierda a derecha.

$2 + 3^2 - (7 + 5) \div 4 \cdot 3$	
$2 + 3^2 - 12 \div 4 \cdot 3$	Add inside parentheses.
$2 + 9 - 12 \div 4 \cdot 3$	Simplify the power.
$2 + 9 - 3 \cdot 3$	Divide.
$2 + 9 - 9$	Multiply.
$11 - 9$	Add.
2	Subtract.

ordered pair A pair of numbers (x, y) that can be used to locate a point on a coordinate plane. The first number x indicates the distance to the left or right of the origin, and the second number y indicates the distance above or below the origin.

par ordenado Par de números (x, y) que se pueden utilizar para ubicar un punto en un plano cartesiano. El primer número, x, indica la distancia a la izquierda o derecha del origen y el segundo número, y, indica la distancia hacia arriba o hacia abajo del origen.

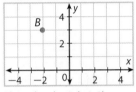

The ordered pair $(-2, 3)$ can be used to locate B.

origin The intersection of the x- and y-axes in a coordinate plane. The coordinates of the origin are $(0, 0)$.

origen Intersección de los ejes x e y en un plano cartesiano. Las coordenadas de origen son $(0, 0)$.

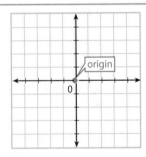

outcome A possible result of a probability experiment.

resultado Resultado posible de un experimento de probabilidad.

In the experiment of rolling a number cube, the possible outcomes are 1, 2, 3, 4, 5, and 6.

outlier A data value that is far removed from the rest of the data.

valor extremo Valor de datos que está muy alejado del resto de los datos.

Most of data   Mean   Outlier

output The result of substituting a value for a variable in a function.

salida Resultado de la sustitución de una variable por un valor en una función.

For the function $f(x) = x^2 + 1$, the input 3 produces an output of 10.

parabola The shape of the graph of a quadratic function.

parábola Forma de la gráfica de una función cuadrática.

ENGLISH	SPANISH	EXAMPLES
parallel lines Lines in the same plane that do not intersect.	**líneas paralelas** Líneas en el mismo plano que no se cruzan.	
parallelogram A quadrilateral with two pairs of parallel sides.	**paralelogramo** Cuadrilátero con dos pares de lados paralelos.	
parameter One of the constants in a function or equation that may be changed. Also the third variable in a set of parametric equations.	**parámetro** Una de las constantes en una función o ecuación que se puede cambiar. También es la tercera variable en un conjunto de ecuaciones paramétricas.	
parent function The simplest function with the defining characteristics of the family. Functions in the same family are transformations of their parent function.	**función madre** La función más básica que tiene las características distintivas de una familia. Las funciones de la misma familia son transformaciones de su función madre.	$f(x) = x^2$ is the parent function for $g(x) = x^2 + 4$ and $h(x) = (5x + 2)^2 - 3$.
Pascal's triangle A triangular arrangement of numbers in which every rowstarts and ends with 1 and each other number is the sum of the two numbers above it.	**triángulo de Pascal** Arreglo triangular de números en el cual cada fila comienza y termina con 1 y los demás números son la suma de los dos valores que están arriba de cada uno.	$$\begin{array}{c} 1 \\ 1\ \ 1 \\ 1\ \ 2\ \ 1 \\ 1\ \ 3\ \ 3\ \ 1 \\ 1\ \ 4\ \ 6\ \ 4\ \ 1 \end{array}$$
percent A ratio that compares a number to 100.	**porcentaje** Razón que compara un número con 100.	$\frac{17}{100} = 17\%$
percent change An increase or decrease given as a percent of the original amount. *See also* percent decrease, percent increase.	**porcentaje de cambio** Incremento o disminución dada como un porcentaje de la cantidad original. *Ver también* porcentaje de disminución, porcentaje de incremento.	
percent decrease A decrease given as a percent of the original amount.	**porcentaje de disminución** Disminución dada como un porcentaje de la cantidad original.	If an item that costs $8.00 is marked down to $6.00, the amount of the decrease is $2.00, so the percent decrease is $\frac{2.00}{8.00} = 0.25 = 25\%$.
percent increase An increase given as a percent of the original amount.	**porcentaje de incremento** Incremento dado como un porcentaje de la cantidad original.	If an item's wholesale cost of $8.00 is marked up to $12.00, the amount of the increase is $4.00, so the percent increase is $\frac{4.00}{8.00} = 0.5 = 50\%$.
perfect square A number whose positive square root is a whole number.	**cuadrado perfecto** Número cuya raíz cuadrada positiva es un número cabal.	36 is a perfect square because $\sqrt{36} = 6$.
perfect-square trinomial A trinomial whose factored form is the square of a binomial. A perfect-square trinomial has the form $a^2 - 2ab + b^2 = (a - b)^2$ or $a^2 + 2ab + b^2 = (a + b)^2$.	**trinomio cuadrado perfecto** Trinomio cuya forma factorizada es el cuadrado de un binomio. Un trinomio cuadrado perfecto tiene la forma $a^2 - 2ab + b^2 = (a - b)^2$ o $a^2 + 2ab + b^2 = (a + b)^2$.	$x^2 + 6x + 9$ is a perfect-square trinomial, because $x^2 + 6x + 9 = (x + 3)^2$.

Glossary/Glosario

ENGLISH	SPANISH	EXAMPLES
perimeter The sum of the side lengths of a closed plane figure.	**perímetro** Suma de las longitudes de los lados de una figura plana cerrada.	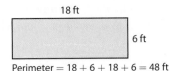 Perimeter = 18 + 6 + 18 + 6 = 48 ft
permutation An arrangement of a group of objects in which order is important.	**permutación** Arreglo de un grupo de objetos en el cual el orden es importante.	For objects A, B, C, and D, there are 12 different permutations of 2 objects. AB, AC, AD, BC, BD, CD BA, CA, DA, CB, DB, DC
perpendicular Intersecting to form 90° angles.	**perpendicular** Que se cruza para formar ángulos de 90°.	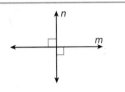
perpendicular lines Lines that intersect at 90° angles.	**líneas perpendiculares** Líneas que se cruzan en ángulos de 90°.	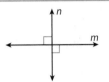
piecewise function A function that is a combination of one or more functions.	**función a trozos** Función que es una combinación de una o más funciones.	
plane A flat surface that has no thickness and extends forever.	**plano** Una superficie plana que no tiene grosor y se extiende infinitamente.	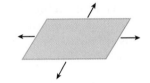
point A location that has no size.	**punto** Ubicación exacta que no tiene ningún tamaño.	$P \bullet$ point P
point-slope form The point-slope form of a linear equation is $y - y_1 = m(x - x_1)$, where m is the slope and (x_1, y_1) is a point on the line.	**forma de punto y pendiente** La forma de punto y pendiente de una ecuación lineal es $y - y_1 = m(x - x_1)$, donde m es la pendiente y (x_1, y_1) es un punto en la línea.	$y - 3 = 2(x - 3)$
polygon A closed plane figure formed by three or more segments such that each segment intersects exactly two other segments only at their endpoints and no two segments with a common endpoint are collinear.	**polígono** Figura plana cerrada formada por tres o más segmentos tal que cada segmento se cruza únicamente con otros dos segmentos sólo en sus extremos y ningún segmento con un extremo común a otro es colineal con éste.	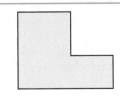
polynomial A monomial or a sum or difference of monomials.	**polinomio** Monomio o suma o diferencia de monomios.	$2x^2 + 3xy - 7y^2$

polynomial long division A method of dividing one polynomial by another.

división larga polinomial Método por el que se divide un polinomio entre otro.

$$x + 2 \overline{)\, x^2 + 3x + 5}$$
$$\underline{-(x^2 + 2x)}$$
$$x + 5$$
$$\underline{-(x + 2)}$$
$$3$$
$$\frac{x^2 + 3x + 5}{x + 2} = x + 1 + \frac{3}{x + 2}$$

---

population The entire group of objects or individuals considered for a survey.

población Grupo completo de objetos o individuos que se desea estudiar.

In a survey about the study habits of high school students, the population is all high school students.

---

positive correlation Two data sets have a positive correlation if both sets of data values increase.

correlación positiva Dos conjuntos de datos tienen correlación positiva si los valores de ambos conjuntos de datos aumentan.

---

positive number A number greater than zero.

número positivo Número mayor que cero.

2 is a positive number.

$$\xleftarrow{\quad} \underset{-4\ -3\ -2\ -1\quad 0\quad 1\quad 2\quad 3\quad 4}{+\!+\!+\!+\!+\!+\!+\!+\!+} \xrightarrow{\quad}$$

Power of a Power Property
If a is any nonzero real number and m and n are integers, then $\left(a^m\right)^n = a^{mn}$.

Propiedad de la potencia de una potencia Dado un número real a distinto de cero y los números enteros m y n, entonces $\left(a^m\right)^n = a^{mn}$.

$$(6^7)^4 = 6^{7 \cdot 4}$$
$$= 6^{28}$$

Power of a Product Property
If a and b are any nonzero real numbers and n is any integer, then $(ab)^n = a^n b^n$.

Propiedad de la potencia de un producto Dados los números reales a y b distintos de cero y un número entero n, entonces $(ab)^n = a^n b^n$.

$$(2 \cdot 4)^3 = 2^3 \cdot 4^3$$
$$= 8 \cdot 64$$
$$= 512$$

Power of a Quotient Property
If a and b are any nonzero real numbers and n is an integer, then $\left(\frac{a}{b}\right)^n = \frac{a^n}{b^n}$.

Propiedad de la potencia de un cociente Dados los números reales a y b distintos de cero y un número entero n, entonces $\left(\frac{a}{b}\right)^n = \frac{a^n}{b^n}$.

$$\left(\frac{3}{5}\right)^4 = \frac{3}{5} \cdot \frac{3}{5} \cdot \frac{3}{5} \cdot \frac{3}{5}$$
$$= \frac{3 \cdot 3 \cdot 3 \cdot 3}{5 \cdot 5 \cdot 5 \cdot 5}$$
$$= \frac{3^4}{5^4}$$

---

precision The level of detail of a measurement, determined by the unit of measure.

precisión Detalle de una medición, determinado por la unidad de medida.

A ruler marked in millimeters has a greater level of precision than a ruler marked in centimeters.

---

prediction An estimate or guess about something that has not yet happened.

predicción Estimación o suposición sobre algo que todavía no ha sucedido.

---

prime factorization A representation of a number or a polynomial as a product of primes.

factorización prima Representación de un número o de un polinomio como producto de números primos.

The prime factorization of 60 is $2 \cdot 2 \cdot 3 \cdot 5$.

---

prime number A whole number greater than 1 that has exactly two positive factors, itself and 1.

número primo Número cabal mayor que 1 que es divisible únicamente entre sí mismo y entre 1.

5 is prime because its only positive factors are 5 and 1.

Glossary/Glosario

ENGLISH	SPANISH	EXAMPLES
principal An amount of money borrowed or invested.	**capital** Cantidad de dinero que se pide prestado o se invierte.	
prism A polyhedron formed by two parallel congruent polygonal bases connected by faces that are parallelograms.	**prisma** Poliedro formado por dos bases poligonales congruentes y paralelas conectadas por caras laterales que son paralelogramos.	
probability A number from 0 to 1 (or 0% to 100%) that is the measure of how likely an event is to occur.	**probabilidad** Número entre 0 y 1 (o entre 0% y 100%) que describe cuán probable es que ocurra un suceso.	A bag contains 3 red marbles and 4 blue marbles. The probability of randomly choosing a red marble is $\frac{3}{7}$.
Product of Powers Property If a is any nonzero real number and m and n are integers, then $a^m \cdot a^n = a^{m+n}$.	**Propiedad del producto de potencias** Dado un número real a distinto de cero y los números enteros m y n, entonces $a^m \cdot a^n = a^{m+n}$.	$6^7 \cdot 6^4 = 6^{7+4}$ $= 6^{11}$
Product Property of Square Roots For $a \geq 0$ and $b \geq 0$, $\sqrt{ab} = \sqrt{a} \cdot \sqrt{b}$.	**Propiedad del producto de raíces cuadradas** Dados $a \geq 0$ y $b \geq 0$, $\sqrt{ab} = \sqrt{a} \cdot \sqrt{b}$.	$\sqrt{9 \cdot 25} = \sqrt{9} \cdot \sqrt{25}$ $= 3 \cdot 5 = 15$
proportion A statement that two ratios are equal; $\frac{a}{b} = \frac{c}{d}$.	**proporción** Ecuación que establece que dos razones son iguales; $\frac{a}{b} = \frac{c}{d}$.	$\frac{2}{3} = \frac{4}{6}$
pyramid A polyhedron formed by a polygonal base and triangular lateral faces that meet at a common vertex.	**pirámide** Poliedro formado por una base poligonal y caras laterales triangulares que se encuentran en un vértice común.	
Pythagorean Theorem If a right triangle has legs of lengths a and b and a hypotenuse of length c, then $a^2 + b^2 = c^2$.	**Teorema de Pitágoras** Dado un triángulo rectángulo con catetos de longitudes a y b y una hipotenusa de longitud c, entonces $a^2 + b^2 = c^2$.	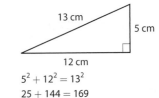 $5^2 + 12^2 = 13^2$ $25 + 144 = 169$
Pythagorean triple A set of three positive integers a, b, and c such that $a^2 + b^2 = c^2$.	**Tripleta de Pitágoras** Conjunto de tres enteros positivos a, b y c tal que $a^2 + b^2 = c^2$.	The numbers 3, 4, and 5 form a Pythagorean triple because $3^2 + 4^2 = 5^2$.

quadrant One of the four regions into which the x- and y-axes divide the coordinate plane.	**cuadrante** Una de las cuatro regiones en las que los ejes x e y dividen el plano cartesiano.	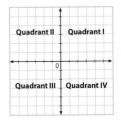

ENGLISH	SPANISH	EXAMPLES
quadratic equation An equation that can be written in the form $ax^2 + bx + c = 0$, where a, b, and c are real numbers and $a \neq 0$.	**ecuación cuadrática** Ecuación que se puede expresar como $ax^2 + bx + c = 0$, donde a, b y c son números reales y $a \neq 0$.	$x^2 + 3x - 4 = 0$ $x^2 - 9 = 0$
Quadratic Formula The formula $x = \frac{-b \pm \sqrt{b^2 - 4ac}}{2a}$, which gives solutions, or roots, of equations in the form $ax^2 + bx + c = 0$, where $a \neq 0$.	**fórmula cuadrática** La fórmula $x = \frac{-b \pm \sqrt{b^2 - 4ac}}{2a}$, que da soluciones, o raíces, para las ecuaciones del tipo $ax^2 + bx + c = 0$, donde $a \neq 0$.	The solutions of $2x^2 - 5x - 3 = 0$ are given by $x = \frac{-(-5) \pm \sqrt{-(5^2) - 4(2)(-3)}}{2(2)}$ $= \frac{5 \pm \sqrt{25 + 24}}{4} = \frac{5 \pm 7}{4}$ $x = 3$ or $x = -\frac{1}{2}$
quadratic function A function that can be written in the form $f(x) = a x^2 + bx + c$, where a, b, and c are real numbers and $a \neq 0$.	**función cuadrática** Función que se puede expresar como $f(x) = ax^2 + bx + c$, donde a, b y c son números reales y $a \neq 0$.	$f(x) = x^2 - 6x + 8$
quadratic polynomial A polynomial of degree 2.	**polinomio cuadrático** Polinomio de grado 2.	$x^2 - 6x + 8$
quantitative data Numerical data.	**datos cuantitativos** Datos numéricos.	
quartile The median of the upper or lower half of a data set. *See also* first quartile, third quartile.	**cuartil** La mediana de la mitad superior o inferior de un conjunto de datos. *Ver también* primer cuartil, tercer cuartil.	
Quotient of Powers Property If a is a nonzero real number and m and n are integers, then $\frac{a^m}{a^n} = a^{m-n}$.	**Propiedad del cociente de potencias** Dado un número real a distinto de cero y los números enteros m y n, entonces $\frac{a^m}{a^n} = a^{m-n}$.	$\frac{6^7}{6^4} = 6^{7-4} = 6^3$
Quotient Property of Square Roots For $a \geq 0$ and $b > 0$, $\sqrt{\frac{a}{b}} = \frac{\sqrt{a}}{\sqrt{b}}$.	**Propiedad del cociente de raíces cuadradas** Dados $a \geq 0$ y $b > 0$, $\sqrt{\frac{a}{b}} = \frac{\sqrt{a}}{\sqrt{b}}$.	$\sqrt{\frac{9}{25}} = \frac{\sqrt{9}}{\sqrt{25}} = \frac{3}{5}$

R

ENGLISH	SPANISH	EXAMPLES
radical equation An equation that contains a variable within a radical.	**ecuación radical** Ecuación que contiene una variable dentro de un radical.	$\sqrt{x + 3} + 4 = 7$
radical expression An expression that contains a radical sign.	**expresión radical** Expresión que contiene un signo de radical.	$\sqrt{x + 3} + 4$
radical symbol The symbol $\sqrt{}$ used to denote a root. The symbol is used alone to indicate a square root or with an index, $\sqrt[n]{}$, to indicate the nth root.	**símbolo de radical** Símbolo $\sqrt{}$ que se utiliza para expresar una raíz. Puede utilizarse solo para indicar una raíz cuadrada, o con un índice, $\sqrt[n]{}$, para indicar la enésima raíz.	$\sqrt{36} = 6$ $\sqrt[3]{27} = 3$

ENGLISH	SPANISH	EXAMPLES
radicand The expression under a radical sign.	**radicando** Número o expresión debajo del signo de radical.	Expression: $\sqrt{x+3}$ Radicand: $x+3$
radius A segment whose endpoints are the center of a circle and a point on the circle; the distance from the center of a circle to any point on the circle.	**radio** Segmento cuyos extremos son el centro de un círculo y un punto de la circunferencia; distancia desde el centro de un círculo hasta cualquier punto de la circunferencia.	
random sample A sample selected from a population so that each member of the population has an equal chance of being selected.	**muestra aleatoria** Muestra seleccionada de una población tal que cada miembro de ésta tenga igual probabilidad de ser seleccionada.	Mr. Hansen chose a random sample of the class by writing each student's name on a slip of paper, mixing up the slips, and drawing five slips without looking.
range of a data set The difference of the greatest and least values in the data set.	**rango de un conjunto de datos** La diferencia del mayor y menor valor en un conjunto de datos.	The data set {3, 3, 5, 7, 8, 10, 11, 11, 12} has a range of $12 - 3 = 9$.
range of a function or relation The set of all second coordinates (or y-values) of a function or relation.	**rango de una función o relación** Conjunto de todos los valores de la segunda coordenada (o valores de y) de una función o relación.	The range of the function $\{(-5, 3), (-3, -2), (-1, -1), (1, 0)\}$ is $\{-2, -1, 0, 3\}$.
rate A ratio that compares two quantities measured in different units.	**tasa** Razón que compara dos cantidades medidas en diferentes unidades.	$\frac{55 \text{ miles}}{1 \text{ hour}} = 55 \text{ mi/h}$
rate of change A ratio that compares the amount of change in a dependent variable to the amount of change in an independent variable.	**tasa de cambio** Razón que compara la cantidad de cambio de la variable dependiente con la cantidad de cambio de la variable independiente.	The cost of mailing a letter increased from 22 cents in 1985 to 25 cents in 1988. During this period, the rate of change was $\frac{\text{change in cost}}{\text{change in year}} = \frac{25 - 22}{1988 - 1985} = \frac{3}{3}$ $= 1$ cent per year.
ratio A comparison of two quantities by division.	**razón** Comparación de dos cantidades mediante una división.	$\frac{1}{2}$ or $1:2$
rational equation An equation that contains one or more rational expressions.	**ecuación racional** Ecuación que contiene una o más expresiones racionales.	$\frac{x+2}{x^2+3x-1} = 6$
rational exponent An exponent that can be expressed as $\frac{m}{n}$ such that if m and n are integers, then $b^{\frac{m}{n}} = \sqrt[n]{b^m} = (\sqrt[n]{b})^m$.	**exponente racional** Exponente que se puede expresar como $\frac{m}{n}$ tal que si m y n son números enteros, entonces $b^{\frac{m}{n}} = \sqrt[n]{b^m} = (\sqrt[n]{b})^m$.	$64^{\frac{1}{6}} = \sqrt[6]{64}$
rational expression An algebraic expression whose numerator and denominator are polynomials and whose denominator has a degree ≥ 1.	**expresión racional** Expresión algebraica cuyo numerador y denominador son polinomios y cuyo denominador tiene un grado ≥ 1.	$\frac{x+2}{x^2+3x-1}$
rational function A function whose rule can be written as a rational expression.	**función racional** Función cuya regla se puede expresar como una expresión racional.	$f(x) = \frac{x+2}{x^2+3x-1}$

ENGLISH	SPANISH	EXAMPLES
rational number A number that can be written in the form $\frac{a}{b}$, where a and b are integers and $b \neq 0$.	**número racional** Número que se puede expresar como $\frac{a}{b}$, donde a y b son números enteros y $b \neq 0$.	$3, 1.75, 0.\overline{3}, -\frac{2}{3}, 0$
rationalizing the denominator A method of rewriting a fraction by multiplying by another fraction that is equivalent to 1 in order to remove radical terms from the denominator.	**racionalizar el denominador** Método que consiste en escribir nuevamente una fracción multiplicándola por otra fracción equivalente a 1 a fin de eliminar los términos radicales del denominador.	$\frac{1}{\sqrt{2}} \cdot \frac{\sqrt{2}}{\sqrt{2}} = \frac{\sqrt{2}}{2}$
ray A part of a line that starts at an endpoint and extends forever in one direction.	**rayo** Parte de una recta que comienza en un extremo y se extiende infinitamente en una dirección.	D
real number A rational or irrational number. Every point on the number line represents a real number.	**número real** Número racional o irracional. Cada punto de la recta numérica representa un número real.	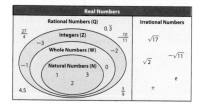
reciprocal For a real number $a \neq 0$, the reciprocal of a is $\frac{1}{a}$. The product of reciprocals is 1.	**recíproco** Dado el número real $a \neq 0$, el recíproco de a es $\frac{1}{a}$. El producto de los recíprocos es 1.	Number / Reciprocal: 2 → $\frac{1}{2}$; 1 → 1; -1 → -1; 0 → No reciprocal
rectangle A quadrilateral with four right angles.	**rectángulo** Cuadrilátero con cuatro ángulos rectos.	
rectangular prism A prism whose bases are rectangles.	**prisma rectangular** Prisma cuyas bases son rectángulos.	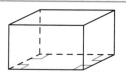
rectangular pyramid A pyramid whose base is a rectangle.	**pirámide rectangular** Pirámide cuya base es un rectángulo.	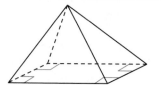
recursive rule for *n*th term of a sequence A rule for a sequence in which one or more previous terms are used to generate the next term.	**fórmula recurrente para hallar el enésimo término de una sucesión** Fórmula para una sucesión en la cual uno o más términos anteriores se usan para generar el término siguiente.	

ENGLISH	SPANISH	EXAMPLES
reflection A transformation that reflects, or "flips," a graph or figure across a line, called the line of reflection.	**reflexión** Transformación en la que una gráfica o figura se refleja o se invierte sobre una línea, denominada la línea de reflexión.	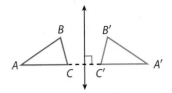
regular polygon A polygon that is both equilateral and equiangular.	**polígono regular** Polígono equilátero de ángulos iguales.	
relation A set of ordered pairs.	**relación** Conjunto de pares ordenados.	$\{(0, 5), (0, 4), (2, 3), (4, 0)\}$
repeating decimal A rational number in decimal form that has a nonzero block of one or more digits that repeat continuously.	**decimal periódico** Número racional en forma decimal que tiene un bloque de uno o más dígitos que se repite continuamente.	$1.\overline{3}, 0.\overline{6}, 2.\overline{14}, 6.77\overline{3}$
replacement set A set of numbers that can be substituted for a variable.	**conjunto de reemplazo** Conjunto de números que pueden sustituir una variable.	
residual The signed vertical distance between a data point and a line of fit.	**residuo** La diferencia vertical entre un dato y una línea de ajuste.	
residual plot A scatter plot of points whose x-coordinates are the values of the independent variable and whose y-coordinates are the corresponding residuals.	**diagrama de residuos** Diagrama de dispersión de puntos en el que la coordenada x representa los valores de la variable independiente y la coordenada y representa los residuos correspondientes.	
rhombus A quadrilateral with four congruent sides.	**rombo** Cuadrilátero con cuatro lados congruentes.	
right angle An angle that measures 90°.	**ángulo recto** Ángulo que mide 90°.	
rise The difference in the y-values of two points on a line.	**distancia vertical** Diferencia entre los valores de y de dos puntos de una línea.	For the points $(3, -1)$ and $(6, 5)$, the rise is $5 - (-1) = 6$.
rotation A transformation that rotates or turns a figure about a point called the center of rotation.	**rotación** Transformación que rota o gira una figura sobre un punto llamado centro de rotación.	

ENGLISH	SPANISH	EXAMPLES
run The difference in the *x*-values of two points on a line.	**distancia horizontal** Diferencia entre los valores de *x* de dos puntos de una línea.	For the points (3, −1) and (6, 5), the run is 6 − 3 = 3.

S

ENGLISH	SPANISH	EXAMPLES
sample A part of the population.	**muestra** Una parte de la población.	In a survey about the study habits of high school students, a sample is a survey of 100 students.
sample space The set of all possible outcomes of a probability experiment.	**espacio muestral** Conjunto de todos los resultados posibles de un experimento de probabilidad.	In the experiment of rolling a number cube, the sample space is {1, 2, 3, 4, 5, 6}.
scale The ratio between two corresponding measurements.	**escala** Razón entre dos medidas correspondientes.	1 cm : 5 mi
scale drawing A drawing that uses a scale to represent an object as smaller or larger than the actual object.	**dibujo a escala** Dibujo que utiliza una escala para representar un objeto como más pequeño o más grande que el objeto original.	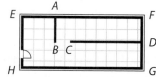 A blueprint is an example of a scale drawing.
scale factor The multiplier used on each dimension to change one figure into a similar figure.	**factor de escala** El multiplicador utilizado en cada dimensión para transformar una figura en una figura semejante.	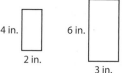 Scale factor: $\frac{3}{2} = 1.5$
scale model A three-dimensional model that uses a scale to represent an object as smaller or larger than the actual object.	**modelo a escala** Modelo tridimensional que utiliza una escala para representar un objeto como más pequeño o más grande que el objeto real.	
scalene triangle A triangle with no congruent sides.	**triángulo escaleno** Triángulo sin lados congruentes.	
scatter plot A graph with points plotted to show a possible relationship between two sets of data.	**diagrama de dispersión** Gráfica con puntos que se usa para demostrar una relación posible entre dos conjuntos de datos.	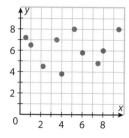

Glossary/Glosario

ENGLISH	SPANISH	EXAMPLES
second differences Differences between first differences of a function.	**segundas diferencias** Diferencias entre las primeras diferencias de una función.	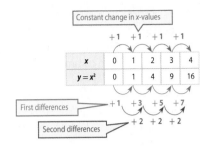

sequence A list of numbers that often form a pattern.	**sucesión** Lista de números que generalmente forman un patrón.	1, 2, 4, 8, 16, …
set A collection of items called elements.	**conjunto** Grupo de componentes denominados elementos.	{1, 2, 3}
set-builder notation A notation for a set that uses a rule to describe the properties of the elements of the set.	**notación de conjuntos** Notación para un conjunto que se vale de una regla para describir las propiedades de los elementos del conjunto.	$\{x \mid x > 3\}$ is read "The set of all x such that x is greater than 3."
significant digits The digits used to express the precision of a measurement.	**dígitos significativos** Dígitos usados para expresar la precisión de una medida.	
similar Two figures are similar if they have the same shape but not necessarily the same size.	**semejantes** Dos figuras con la misma forma pero no necesariamente del mismo tamaño.	
similarity statement A statement that indicates that two polygons are similar by listing the vertices in the order of correspondence.	**enunciado de semejanza** Enunciado que indica que dos polígonos son semejantes enumerando los vértices en orden de correspondencia.	quadrilateral $ABCD \sim$ quadrilateral $EFGH$
simple event An event consisting of only one outcome.	**suceso simple** Suceso que tiene sólo un resultado.	In the experiment of rolling a number cube, the event consisting of the outcome 3 is a simple event.
simple interest A fixed percent of the principal. For principal P, interest rate r, and time t in years, the simple interest is $I = Prt$.	**interés simple** Porcentaje fijo del capital. Dado el capital P, la tasa de interés r y el tiempo t expresado en años, el interés simple es $I = Prt$.	If $100 is put into an account with a simple interest rate of 5%, then after 2 years, the account will have earned $I = 100 \cdot 0.05 \cdot 2 = \$10$ in interest.

ENGLISH	SPANISH	EXAMPLES

simplest form of a rational expression A rational expression is in simplest form if the numerator and denominator have no common factors.

forma simplificada de una expresión racional Una expresión racional está en forma simplificada cuando el numerador y el denominador no tienen factores comunes.

$$\frac{x^2 - 1}{x^2 + x - 2} = \frac{(x-1)(x+1)}{(x-1)(x+2)}$$

$$= \frac{x+1}{x+2}$$

Simplest form

---

simplest form of a square root expression A square root expression is in simplest form if it meets the following criteria:
1. No perfect squares are in the radicand.
2. No fractions are in the radicand.
3. No square roots appear in the denominator of a fraction.

See also rationalizing the denominator.

forma simplificada de una expresión de raíz cuadrada Una expresión de raíz cuadrada está en forma simplificada si reúne los siguientes requisitos:
1. No hay cuadrados perfectos en el radicando.
2. No hay fracciones en el radicando.
3. No aparecen raíces cuadradas en el denominador de una fracción.

Ver también racionalizar el denominador.

Not Simplest Form	Simplest Form
$\sqrt{180}$	$6\sqrt{5}$
$\sqrt{216a^2b^2}$	$6ab\sqrt{6}$
$\frac{\sqrt{7}}{\sqrt{2}}$	$\frac{\sqrt{14}}{2}$

---

simplest form of an exponential expression An exponential expression is in simplest form if it meets the following criteria:
1. There are no negative exponents.
2. The same base does not appear more than once in a product or quotient.
3. No powers, products, or quotients are raised to powers.
4. Numerical coefficients in a quotient do not have any common factor other than 1.

forma simplificada de una expresión exponencial Una expresión exponencial está en forma simplificada si reúne los siguientes requisitos:
1. No hay exponentes negativos.
2. La misma base no aparece más de una vez en un producto o cociente.
3. No se elevan a potencias productos, cocientes ni potencias.
4. Los coeficientes numéricos en un cociente no tienen ningún factor común que no sea 1.

Not Simplest Form	Simplest Form
$7^8 \cdot 7^4$	7^{12}
$(x^2)^{-4} \cdot x^5$	$\frac{1}{x^3}$
$\frac{a^5 b^9}{(ab)^4}$	ab^5

---

simplify To perform all indicated operations.

simplificar Realizar todas las operaciones indicadas.

$$13 - 20 + 8$$
$$-7 + 8$$
$$1$$

---

simulation A model of an experiment, often one that would be too difficult or time-consuming to actually perform.

simulación Modelo de un experimento; generalmente se recurre a la simulación cuando realizar dicho experimento sería demasiado difícil o llevaría mucho tiempo.

---

sine In a right triangle, the ratio of the length of the leg opposite $\angle A$ to the length of the hypotenuse.

seno En un triángulo rectángulo, razón entre la longitud del cateto opuesto a $\angle A$ y la longitud de la hipotenusa.

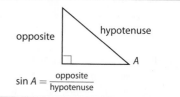

$$\sin A = \frac{\text{opposite}}{\text{hypotenuse}}$$

---

skewed distribution A type of distribution in which the right or left side of its display indicates frequencies that are much greater than those of the other side.

distribución sesgada Tipo de distribución en la que el lado derecho o izquierdo muestra frecuencias mucho mayores que las del otro lado.

ENGLISH	SPANISH	EXAMPLES
slope A measure of the steepness of a line. If (x_1, y_1) and (x_2, y_2) are any two points on the line, the slope of the line, known as m, is represented by the equation $m = \frac{y_2 - y_1}{x_2 - x_1}$.	**pendiente** Medida de la inclinación de una línea. Dados dos puntos (x_1, y_1) y (x_2, y_2) en una línea, la pendiente de la línea, denominada m, se representa con la ecuación $m = \frac{y_2 - y_1}{x_2 - x_1}$.	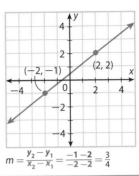 $m = \frac{y_2 - y_1}{x_2 - x_1} = \frac{-1-2}{-2-2} = \frac{3}{4}$
slope-intercept form The slope-intercept form of a linear equation is $y = mx + b$, where m is the slope and b is the y-intercept.	**forma de pendiente-intersección** La forma de pendiente-intersección de una ecuación lineal es $y = mx + b$, donde m es la pendiente y b es la intersección con el eje y.	$y = -2x + 4$ The slope is -2. The y-intercept is 4.
solution of a system of equations Any ordered pair that satisfies all the equations in a system.	**solución de un sistema de ecuaciones** Cualquier par ordenado que resuelva todas las ecuaciones de un sistema.	$\begin{cases} x + y = -1 \\ -x + y = -3 \end{cases}$ Solution: $(1, -2)$
solution of a system of inequalities Any ordered pair that satisfies all the inequalities in a system.	**solución de un sistema de desigualdades** Cualquier par ordenado que resuelva todas las desigualdades de un sistema.	$\begin{cases} y \leq x + 1 \\ y < -x + 4 \end{cases}$ (2, 1) is in the overlapping shaded regions, so it is a solution. 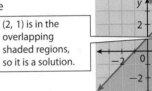
solution of an equation in one variable A value or values that make the equation true.	**solución de una ecuación en una variable** Valor o valores que hacen que la ecuación sea verdadera.	Equation: $x + 2 = 6$ Solution: $x = 4$
solution of an inequality in one variable A value or values that make the inequality true.	**solución de una desigualdad en una variable** Valor o valores que hacen que la desigualdad sea verdadera.	Inequality: $x + 2 < 6$ Solution: $x < 4$
solution of an equation in two variables An ordered pair or ordered pairs that make the equation true.	**solución de una ecuación en dos variables** Un par ordenado o pares ordenados que hacen que la ecuación sea verdadera.	(4, 2) is a solution of $x + y = 6$.
solution of an inequality in two variables An ordered pair or ordered pairs that make the inequality true.	**solución de una desigualdad en dos variables** Un par ordenado o pares ordenados que hacen que la desigualdad sea verdadera.	(3, 1) is a solution of $x + y < 6$.
solution set The set of values that make a statement true.	**conjunto solución** Conjunto de valores que hacen verdadero un enunciado.	Inequality: $x + 3 \geq 5$ Solution set: $\{x \mid x \geq 2\}$

square A quadrilateral with four congruent sides and four right angles.

cuadrado Cuadrilátero con cuatro lados congruentes y cuatro ángulos rectos.

---

square in numeration The second power of a number.

cuadrado en numeración La segunda potencia de un número.

16 is the square of 4.

---

square root function A function whose rule contains a variable under a square root sign.

función de raíz cuadrada Función cuya regla contiene una variable bajo un signo de raíz cuadrada.

---

standard form of a linear equation $Ax + By = C$, where A, B, and C are real numbers and A and B are not both 0.

forma estándar de una ecuación lineal $Ax + By = C$, donde A, B y C son números reales y A y B no son ambos cero.

$2x + 3y = 6$

---

standard form of a polynomial A polynomial in one variable is written in standard form when the terms are in order from greatest degree to least degree.

forma estándar de un polinomio Un polinomio de una variable se expresa en forma estándar cuando los términos se ordenan de mayor a menor grado.

$4x^5 - 2x^4 + x^2 - x + 1$

---

standard form of a quadratic equation $ax^2 + bx + c = 0$, where a, b, and c are real numbers and $a \neq 0$.

forma estándar de una ecuación cuadrática $ax^2 + bx + c = 0$, donde a, b y c son números reales y $a \neq 0$.

$2x^2 + 3x - 1 = 0$

---

statistics Numbers that describe a sample or samples.

estadísticas Números que describen una o varias muestras.

---

stem-and-leaf plot A graph used to organize and display data by dividing each data value into two parts, a stem and a leaf.

diagrama de tallo y hojas Gráfica utilizada para organizar y mostrar datos dividiendo cada valor de datos en dos partes, un tallo y una hoja.

Stem	Leaves
3	2 3 4 4 7 9
4	0 1 5 7 7 7 8
5	1 2 2 3

Key: 3|2 means 3.2

---

step function A piecewise function that is constant over each interval in its domain.

función escalón Función a trozos que es constante en cada intervalo en su dominio.

---

stratified random sample A sample in which a population is divided into distinct groups and members are selected at random from each group.

muestra aleatoria estratificada Muestra en la que la población está dividida en grupos diferenciados y los miembros de cada grupo se seleccionan al azar.

Ms. Carter chose a stratified random sample of her school's student population by randomly selecting 30 students from each grade level.

---

subset A set that is contained entirely within another set. Set B is a subset of set A if every element of B is contained in A, denoted $B \subset A$.

subconjunto Conjunto que se encuentra dentro de otro conjunto. El conjunto B es un subconjunto del conjunto A si todos los elementos de B son elementos de A; se expresa $B \subset A$.

The set of integers is a subset of the set of rational numbers.

ENGLISH	SPANISH	EXAMPLES

substitution method A method used to solve systems of equations by solving an equation for one variable and substituting the resulting expression into the other equation(s). | **sustitución** Método utilizado para resolver sistemas de ecuaciones resolviendo una ecuación para una variable y sustituyendo la expresión resultante en las demás ecuaciones. |

Subtraction Property of Equality If a, b, and c are real numbers and $a = b$, then $a - c = b - c$.

Propiedad de igualdad de la resta Si a, b y c son números reales y $a = b$, entonces $a - c = b - c$.

$$\begin{array}{r} x + 6 = 8 \\ \underline{-6 \quad -6} \\ x \quad = 2 \end{array}$$

Subtraction Property of Inequality For real numbers a, b, and c, if $a < b$, then $a - c < b - c$. Also holds true for $>$, $\leq$, $\geq$, and $\neq$.

Propiedad de desigualdad de la resta Dados los números reales a, b y c, si $a < b$, entonces $a - c < b - c$. Es válido también para $>$, $\leq$, $\geq$ y $\neq$.

$$\begin{array}{r} x + 6 < 8 \\ \underline{-6 \quad -6} \\ x \quad < 2 \end{array}$$

---

supplementary angles Two angles whose measures have a sum of 180°.

ángulos suplementarios Dos ángulos cuyas medidas suman 180°.

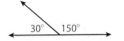

---

surface area The total area of all faces and curved surfaces of a three-dimensional figure.

área total Área total de todas las caras y superficies curvas de una figura tridimensional.

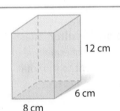

Surface area
$$= 2(8)(12) + 2(8)(6) + 2(12)(6)$$
$$= 432 \text{ cm}^2$$

---

symmetric distribution A type of distribution in which the right and left sides of its display indicate frequencies that are mirror images of each other.

distribución simétrica Tipo de distribución en la que los lados derecho e izquierdo muestran frecuencias que son idénticas.

---

system of linear equations A system of equations in which all of the equations are linear.

sistema de ecuaciones lineales Sistema de ecuaciones en el que todas las ecuaciones son lineales.

$$\begin{cases} 2x + 3y = -1 \\ x - 3y = 4 \end{cases}$$

---

system of linear inequalities A system of inequalities in which all of the inequalities are linear.

sistema de desigualdades lineales Sistema de desigualdades en el que todas las desigualdades son lineales.

$$\begin{cases} 2x + 3y > -1 \\ x - 3y \leq 4 \end{cases}$$

---

systematic random sample A sample based on selecting one member of the population at random and then selecting other members by using a pattern.

muestra sistemática Muestra en la que se elige a un miembro de la población al azar y luego se elige a otros miembros mediante un patrón.

Mr. Martin chose a systematic random sample of customers visiting a store by selecting one customer at random and then selecting every tenth customer after that.

Glossary/Glosario

ENGLISH	SPANISH	EXAMPLES
tangent In a right triangle, the ratio of the length of the leg opposite ∠A to the length of the leg adjacent to ∠A.	**tangente** En un triángulo rectángulo, razón entre la longitud del cateto opuesto a ∠A y la longitud del cateto adyacente a ∠A.	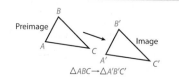 $\tan A = \dfrac{\text{opposite}}{\text{adjacent}}$
term of a sequence An element or number in the sequence.	**término de una sucesión** Elemento o número de una sucesión.	5 is the third term in the sequence 1, 3, 5, 7, …
term of an expression The parts of the expression that are added or subtracted.	**término de una expresión** Parte de una expresión que debe sumarse o restarse.	$3x^2 + 6x - 8$ ↑ ↑ ↑ Term Term Term
terminating decimal A decimal that ends, or terminates.	**decimal finito** Decimal con un número determinados de posiciones decimales.	1.5, 2.75, 4.0
theoretical probability The ratio of the number of equally likely outcomes in an event to the total number of possible outcomes.	**probabilidad teórica** Razón entre el número de resultados igualmente probables de un suceso y el número total de resultados posibles.	In the experiment of rolling a number cube, the theoretical probability of rolling an odd number is $\frac{3}{6} = \frac{1}{2}$.
third quartile The median of the upper half of a data set. Also called *upper quartile*.	**tercer cuartil** La mediana de la mitad superior de un conjunto de datos. También se llama *cuartil superior*.	Lower half Upper half 18, 23, 28, 29, (36,) 42 Third quartile
tolerance The amount by which a measurement is permitted to vary from a specified value.	**tolerancia** La cantidad por que una medida se permite variar de un valor especificado.	
transformation A change in the position, size, or shape of a figure or graph.	**transformación** Cambio en la posición, tamaño o forma de una figura o gráfica.	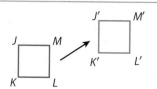 $\triangle ABC \rightarrow \triangle A'B'C'$
translation A transformation that shifts or slides every point of a figure or graph the same distance in the same direction.	**traslación** Transformación en la que todos los puntos de una figura o gráfica se mueven la misma distancia en la misma dirección.	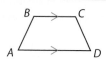
trapezoid A quadrilateral with exactly one pair of parallel sides.	**trapecio** Cuadrilátero con sólo un par de lados paralelos.	

ENGLISH	SPANISH	EXAMPLES
tree diagram A branching diagram that shows all possible combinations or outcomes of an experiment.	**diagrama de árbol** Diagrama con ramificaciones que muestra todas las combinaciones o resultados posibles de un experimento.	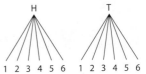 The tree diagram shows the possible outcomes when tossing a coin and rolling a number cube.
trend line A line on a scatter plot that helps show the correlation between data sets more clearly.	**línea de tendencia** Línea en un diagrama de dispersión que sirve para mostrar la correlación entre conjuntos de datos más claramente.	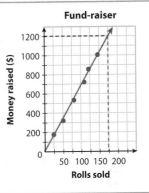
trial Each repetition or observation of an experiment.	**prueba** Una sola repetición u observación de un experimento.	In the experiment of rolling a number cube, each roll is one trial.
triangle A three-sided polygon.	**triángulo** Polígono de tres lados.	
triangular prism A prism whose bases are triangles.	**prisma triangular** Prisma cuyas bases son triángulos.	Bases
triangular pyramid A pyramid whose base is a triangle.	**pirámide triangular** Pirámide cuya base es un triángulo.	
trigonometric ratio Ratio of the lengths of two sides of a right triangle.	**razón trigonométrica** Razón entre dos lados de un triángulo rectángulo.	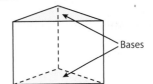 $\sin A = \frac{a}{c}$, $\cos A = \frac{b}{c}$, $\tan A = \frac{a}{b}$
trinomial A polynomial with three terms.	**trinomio** Polinomio con tres términos.	$4x^2 + 3xy - 5y^2$
two-way frequency table A frequency table that displays two-variable data in rows and columns.	**table de frecuencia de doble entrada** Una tabla de frecuencia que muestra los datos de dos variables organizados en filas y columnas.	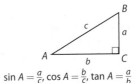

For the two-way frequency table example:

	Preference		
Pet	inside	Outside	Total
Cats	35	15	50
Dogs	20	30	50
Total	55	45	100

union The union of two sets is the set of all elements that are in either set, denoted by ∪.

unión La unión de dos conjuntos es el conjunto de todos los elementos que se encuentran en ambos conjuntos, expresado por ∪.

$A = \{1, 2, 3, 4\}$
$B = \{1, 3, 5, 7, 9\}$
$A \cup B = \{1, 2, 3, 4, 5, 7, 9\}$

---

unit rate A rate in which the second quantity in the comparison is one unit.

tasa unitaria Tasa en la que la segunda cantidad de la comparación es una unidad.

$\frac{30\text{ mi}}{1\text{ h}} = 30$ mi/h

---

unlike radicals Radicals with a different quantity under the radical.

radicales distintos Radicales con cantidades diferentes debajo del signo de radical.

$2\sqrt{2}$ and $2\sqrt{3}$

---

unlike terms Terms with different variables or the same variables raised to different powers.

términos distintos Términos con variables diferentes o las mismas variables elevadas a potencias diferentes.

$4xy^2$ and $6x^2y$

---

upper quartile *See* third quartile.

cuartil superior *Ver* tercer cuartil.

---

value of a function The result of replacing the independent variable with a number and simplifying.

valor de una función Resultado de reemplazar la variable independiente por un número y luego simplificar.

The value of the function $f(x) = x + 1$ for $x = 3$ is 4.

---

value of a variable A number used to replace a variable to make an equation true.

valor de una variable Número utilizado para reemplazar una variable y hacer que una ecuación sea verdadera.

In the equation $x + 1 = 4$, the value of x is 3.

---

value of an expression The result of replacing the variables in an expression with numbers and simplifying.

valor de una expresión Resultado de reemplazar las variables de una expresión por un número y luego simplificar.

The value of the expression $x + 1$ for $x = 3$ is 4.

---

variable A symbol used to represent a quantity that can change.

variable Símbolo utilizado para representar una cantidad que puede cambiar.

In the expression $2x + 3$, x is the variable.

Venn diagram A diagram used to show relationships between sets.

diagrama de Venn Diagrama utilizado para mostrar la relación entre conjuntos.

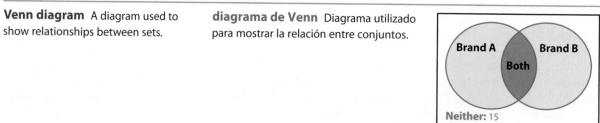

ENGLISH	SPANISH	EXAMPLES
vertex of a parabola The highest or lowest point on the parabola.	**vértice de una parábola** Punto más alto o más bajo de una parábola.	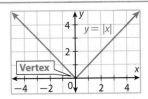 The vertex is $(0, -2)$.
vertex of an absolute-value graph The point on the axis of symmetry of the graph.	**vértice de una gráfica de valor absoluto** Punto en el eje de simetría de la gráfica.	
vertical angles The nonadjacent angles formed by two intersecting lines.	**ángulos opuestos por el vértice** Ángulos no adyacentes formados por dos líneas que se cruzan.	$\angle$**1** and $\angle$**3** are vertical angles. $\angle$**2** and $\angle$**4** are vertical angles.
vertical line A line whose equation is $x = a$, where a is the x-intercept.	**línea vertical** Línea cuya ecuación es $x = a$, donde a es la intersección con el eje x.	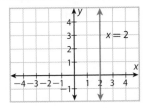
vertical-line test A test used to determine whether a relation is a function. If any vertical line crosses the graph of a relation more than once, the relation is not a function.	**prueba de la línea vertical** Prueba utilizada para determinar si una relación es una función. Si una línea vertical corta la gráfica de una relación más de una vez, la relación no es una función.	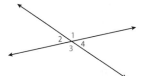 Function Not a function
volume The number of nonoverlapping unit cubes of a given size that will exactly fill the interior of a three-dimensional figure.	**volumen** Cantidad de cubos unitarios no superpuestos de un determinado tamaño que llenan exactamente el interior de una figura tridimensional.	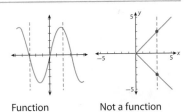 Volume $= (3)(4)(12) = 144 \text{ ft}^3$
voluntary response sample A sample in which members choose to be in the sample.	**muestra de respuesta voluntaria** Una muestra en la que los miembros eligen participar.	A store provides survey cards for customers who wish to fill them out.

whole number A member of the set of natural numbers and zero.

número cabal Miembro del conjunto de los números naturales y cero.

0, 1, 2, 3, 4, 5, …

x-axis The horizontal axis in a coordinate plane.

eje x Eje horizontal en un plano cartesiano.

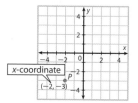

x-coordinate The first number in an ordered pair, which indicates the horizontal distance of a point from the origin on the coordinate plane.

coordenada x Primer número de un par ordenado, que indica la distancia horizontal de un punto desde el origen en un plano cartesiano.

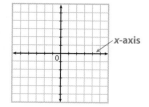

x-intercept The x-coordinate(s) of the point(s) where a graph intersects the x-axis.

intersección con el eje x Coordenada(s) x de uno o más puntos donde una gráfica corta el eje x.

The x-intercept is 2.

y-axis The vertical axis in a coordinate plane.

eje y Eje vertical en un plano cartesiano.

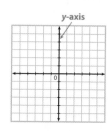

y-coordinate The second number in an ordered pair, which indicates the vertical distance of a point from the origin on the coordinate plane.

coordenada y Segundo número de un par ordenado, que indica la distancia vertical de un punto desde el origen en un plano cartesiano.

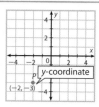

ENGLISH	SPANISH	EXAMPLES

y-intercept The *y*-coordinate(s) of the point(s) where a graph intersects the *y*-axis.

intersección con el eje *y* Coordenada(s) *y* de uno o más puntos donde una gráfica corta el eje *y*.

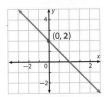

The *y*-intercept is 2.

Z

zero exponent For any nonzero real number *x*, $x^0 = 1$.

exponente cero Dado un número real distinto de cero *x*, $x^0 = 1$.

$5^0 = 1$

---

zero of a function For the function *f*, any number *x* such that $f(x) = 0$.

cero de una función Dada la función *f*, todo número *x* tal que $f(x) = 0$.

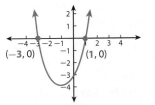

The zeros are −3 and 1.

Zero Product Property For real numbers *p* and *q*, if $pq = 0$, then $p = 0$ or $q = 0$.

Propiedad del producto cero Dados los números reales *p* y *q*, si $pq = 0$, entonces $p = 0$ o $q = 0$.

If $(x - 1)(x + 2) = 0$, then $x - 1 = 0$ or $x + 2 = 0$, so $x = 1$ or $x = -2$.

Glossary/Glosario

Index

Index

N

O

P

Q

R

Index

W

weather, 189, 250, 266, 434

X

x-intercept, 164, 663

Y

y-intercept, 164

Z

zero
  as exponent, 337
  finding axis of symmetry using, 664
  of a function, 663
  significant digits and, 9
zero product property, 571–574, 580

TABLE OF MEASURES

LENGTH

1 inch = 2.54 centimeters

1 meter = 39.37 inches

1 mile = 5,280 feet

1 mile = 1760 yards

1 mile = 1.609 kilometers

1 kilometer = 0.62 mile

MASS/WEIGHT

1 pound = 16 ounces

1 pound = 0.454 kilograms

1 kilogram = 2.2 pounds

1 ton = 2000 pounds

CAPACITY

1 cup = 8 fluid ounces

1 pint = 2 cups

1 quart = 2 pints

1 gallon = 4 quarts

1 gallon = 3.785 liters

1 liter = 0.264 gallons

1 liter = 1000 cubic centimeters

SYMBOLS

$\neq$	is not equal to		π	pi: (about 3.14)
$\approx$	is approximately equal to		$\perp$	is perpendicular to
10^2	ten squared; ten to the second power		$\parallel$	is parallel to
			$\overleftrightarrow{AB}$	line AB
$2.\overline{6}$	repeating decimal 2.66666...		$\overrightarrow{AB}$	ray AB
$\lvert-4\rvert$	the absolute value of negative 4		$\overline{AB}$	line segment AB
$\sqrt{}$	square root		m$\angle A$	measure of $\angle A$

FORMULAS

Triangle	$A = \frac{1}{2}bh$	Cone	$V = \frac{1}{3}\pi r^2 h$
Parallelogram	$A = bh$	Pyramid	$V = \frac{1}{3}Bh$
Circle	$A = \pi r^2$	Pythagorean Theorem	$a^2 + b^2 = c^2$
Circle	$C = \pi d$ or $C = 2\pi r$	Quadratic Formula	$x = \dfrac{-b \pm \sqrt{b^2 - 4ac}}{2a}$
General Prisms	$V = Bh$	Arithmetic Sequence	$a_n = a_1 + (n-1)d$
Cylinder	$V = \pi r^2 h$	Geometric Sequence	$a_n = a_1 r^{n-1}$
Sphere	$V = \frac{4}{3}\pi r^3$